D0021306

DICTIONARY OF WINES AND SPIRITS

Dictionary of Wines and Spirits

Pamela Vandyke Price

First published in Great Britain in 1980 by
Northwood Publications Ltd

This edition published in 1986 by
Peerage Books
59 Grosvenor Street
London W1
by arrangement with B. T. Batsford Ltd

© Northwood Publications Ltd and Pamela Vandyke Price, 1980

ISBN 1 85052 053 4

Printed in Czechoslovakia
50614

This book is dedicated to the memory of

Ronald Avery
(1899-1976)

a great personality, an outstanding wine merchant,
a beloved friend.

ACKNOWLEDGEMENTS

This book represents the work of at least a hundred people in addition to the author. There are the government bodies who have supplied information and checked references, and who, by helping me to know more about the wines and spirits of their countries, have broadened the scope of many entries. There are the trade and professional associations, whose members have been generous with advice and the sharing of their own experiences. There are members of numerous firms who, from the chairmen to the telephonists, have patiently and unselfishly assisted my researches. My colleagues among the wine writers have benevolently allowed me to draw upon their own writings, the magazines they edit and the books they have compiled.

To cite a few names would risk discourtesy to many and to cite all would require more space than even my indulgent publishers can provide. May those who use this be aware that it is very much a corporate effort, although the personal opinions – and any mistakes – should be ascribed to me alone.

Yet there are some who have, throughout this considerable work, made it possible for me to finish. Douglas Westland, my publisher for several years, has by his interest and encouragement made me hope that this is one of my best books. Diana Briscoe, who has patiently untangled a mammoth web of text, has brought to her task intelligence and most conscientious editing. Finally Mrs Margaret Bird, my friend for many years, has surpassed herself in deciphering my handwriting, sorting out my typed drafts, and checking many references that I could not verify. My especial thanks and gratitude to you all.

LIST OF MAPS AND DIAGRAMS

It should be noted that these are sketch maps, intended to give the approximate positions of the various vineyards both in relation to each other and to such easy-to-find landmarks   towns, major roads, river – which would feature on a detailed regional map. Space limitations make it impossible to include every winery, village, vineyard site or estate; the more so as in many countries, the boundaries are continually being extended or revised and new wineries are being opened. For comprehensive information, consult a book specialising in the area concerned (see Bibliography).

PREFACE

This book provides a variety of guidelines for all who want to know a little more about the wines and spirits they drink than is given by the names or by what is on the label of the particular bottle. It gives definitions of the principal wines and spirits, plus advice on serving them; provides some background to the drinks and famous vineyards of the world; and relates some anecdotes which may be useful to remember certain names, brands and estates.

It should be stressed that this is a book for the amateur in the original sense of the word, meaning 'lover': there are technical books for the scientists and members of the wine trade; volumes of history for the person seeking more detailed backgrounds; and records of tastings for anyone curious about what this personal experience has meant to somebody else. Here you will find the references with which to start learning, because no single book could ever contain everything about wines and spirits. Explanations have been kept as simple as possible – only the arrogant and insensitive try to impress by using elaborate technicalities and obscure references. They are unlikely to be any good at tasting, or indeed good company, so they can be ignored.

Drinks are intended for enjoyment, which is why I have never been able to understand the solemnity and pretentiousness with which some supposed 'authorities' share a bottle with others, or even attempt to teach. If one cannot find stimulation, delight and laughter in things that matter a great deal, from God to the grape, then I think there is something amiss – either with the would-be student or, more often, with the self-appointed 'expert'.

What I have tried to do throughout is to convey my own enthusiasm for the wines that I myself enjoy, also to draw attention to those that have either not yet achieved popularity or that are somehow 'unfashionable', maybe because people cannot pronounce their names, or think them other than they are. This happened for many years with the admirable sherry-style wines made in countries other than Spain: they were not simply indifferent imitations of sherry, but wines deserving respect in their own right. Of course I do not, as an individual, like certain wines – and this includes some very great names indeed – but I can admire them and see why they have won their reputations.

In my opinion, it is essential to separate personal preferences from overall assessments of quality when one is writing about wine; but it takes some experience and a willingness to be always truthful to be able to do so. Many writers seem unable to differentiate between what they like and what they find 'good' or 'bad'. If one cares to submit oneself to some instruction and, eventually, to go through some 'blind' tastings, it is salutary to discover how considerations of price, the reputation of a great label and the circumstances in which one may be drinking, as opposed to tasting, influence one's judgement, often too favourably.

However the approach to wines and spirits must always be personal and it is for each person to work out his or her own methods. It may be some encouragement for beginners – although we are all beginners with every glass we pick up – to know that I, born in the English Midlands between the wars, had absolutely no experience of winedrinking in my own home – the occasional 'drink', no more – there was the Great Depression, then there was World War II. It was only when I was turned thirty that the sudden death of my doctor husband attracted the sensitive and thoughtful kindness of many members of the wine trade. Although I am proud of my teachers, including the very great late Allan Sichel, it is always possible for anybody to pursue a subject for which they care passionately. In recent years, I have seen with great satisfaction the way many young people, in and outside the wine trade, have achieved academic triumphs in examinations in wines and spirits. They can taste, with assurance and authority, wines that had hardly been heard of thirty years ago!

This, then, is a book that contains much information that I would have found useful as a beginner, in which I have voiced some of the views my own friends and students have found helpful, and that incorporates much material that I have abbreviated from many reference works compiled by numerous respected authors from this, and other, countries. All are acknowledged – but few will be as portable as this dictionary which, I hope, may send readers to consult weightier tomes.

The assembly of the information is entirely my own work: many editors and compilers of reference books rely far too much, in my view, on the sense, knowledge and truthfulness of their assistants, who may be fallible, ignorant of some subjects and, possibly without knowing it, prejudiced in many ways. Here I am the only one who can have made the mistakes, which gives the book some consistency. May those who find errors deal gently with me – and let me know, so that future editions can be corrected.

PAMELA VANDYKE PRICE
LONDON, 1980

INTRODUCTION

No portable volume could contain the name of every wine and spirit registered for sale – or recorded in history. The list of brand names in any trade directory is long, even in close print, and with the names of estates, wineries, alternative names for grapes, sites within a vineyard, companies dealing in wines and spirits, the terms used in various languages – it would require an encyclopaedia of many volumes if all these were included. Even then, it would be out of date before one single section had been completed.

The extensive Bibliography at the back of the book suggests where the person interested in pursuing the study of any particular wine or spirit can look. In this book therefore, I have concentrated on recording *basic information* to serve and inform the potential buyer of a bottle, someone looking at a wine list, visiting a wine region, or talking about wines and spirits. This arbitrary decision means that, for example, only a few brand names are included – because they are either interesting or unique of their kind. However it includes many wineries (which may or may not mean the name of the owning firm), when the wines may be fairly widely-known; the major distilleries; the most famous estates in the classic wine regions; and those in the New World whose wines are often featured on export lists; plus technical terms. These may be either those used in general conversation about wine, or simply the better-known forms of the trade's 'in talk' or even jargon.

The book aims to give some form of reference for what may be seen on the label of a wine or spirit in most regions and to show how this information may be interpreted. It also gives some indication as to the specialised significance of words approved for labels: what they imply as well as what they mean, in the dictionary senses of the words. (Compilers of dictionaries often err over legal definitions of wine and the implications of terms in this particular sphere.) The classed growth clarets are all given, but not all the 'climats' of Burgundy – though I think I have included the most important and best known. The great German shippers and owners can seldom be cited – there are just too many – but I have included some. Where an estate belongs to a particular firm, I have indicated this, otherwise concentrating on such label names that may be of interest.

With the huge liquor corporations, I have restricted mentions to the main estates, properties, distilleries and installations they own, as this is not a book for the person concerned with business. Indications are given as to who owns what, but to give an adequate entry under 'Seagram', for example, would mean greatly increasing the size of the book. There cannot, for reasons of space, be references to even the main cocktails of the world, but some of the most famous are mentioned when a little background knowledge can be of interest.

There are no vintage reports. If you are interested in the year by year variations of a particular wine, you will probably already receive vintage notes from your supplier, read the magazines that publish such reports and, maybe, form your own opinions from your own experiences (always the most valuable thing to do). Nothing dates a book faster than statements about dates and prices, so these are not included here; although I have indicated which wines are likely always to be expensive, if genuine, even when they are not in very short supply.

Nor do I make any judgements about wines that are 'good' or 'bad'. This has always seemed risky to me, because taste is such a personal matter and one person may sincerely be unable to like, say, a particular first growth claret, but thoroughly enjoy a much humbler wine. To pronounce about 'the best' in this way seems to me as useless as to 'expose' malpractices, something I have often been urged to do, but for which I have never had enough space or time in print! To say that something is, overall, 'best' risks giving the person who just cannot enjoy it a feeling of inferiority – and, perhaps, they may decide that 'all this wine talk is so much poppycock and I'm going to stick to beer in future'.

To 'expose' a wine in print (that, if the producer asks me about it, will get my spoken criticism if I think it distorted or badly made) risks destroying the confidence of the drinker in the wine trade in general. There are far more good wines than bad and far more honest growers, shippers and merchants than rascals. Indeed, if anyone should be 'exposed', it is the silly sort of customer who insists on paying an uneconomic price for a famous name – somebody, somewhere, will be tempted to print the labels for that buyer! Every trade and profession has its unscrupulous members, but the wise buyer knows that it is impossible to accept a bargain as genuine when it simply cannot be that cheap. If the buyer has not taken the trouble to know what may be costly and what might be cheap then frankly he deserves what he may get – and I might be even more critical of the type of woman who 'leaves it to the men'.

In addition, I have felt free to express my personal opinions about a number of matters – terms such as 'wine snob', 'expert', 'taste', 'vintage' – some of these are used casually and sometimes incorrectly; some expressions have specific implications within the world of wine, so I have explained these. Other subjects are the centre of much discussion, so I have indicated this, providing sufficient information for the intelligent to hold their own in any conversation relating to these matters. In numerous instances I have included words that have been queried by some of the many students I have been privileged to teach, whose liveliness of mind has greatly broadened my own experience of drinks and drinkers. Many of the things they have queried have been what I should have liked to know when I was beginning to learn about wines and spirits, but was often too hesitant to ask. Expressions such as 'ullage' or 'full long cork', when heard or seen for the first time can be baffling – the ordinary dictionary can seldom help. Yet they are common in wine talk, so it is necessary to understand what they mean if the user is to make adequate contact with those with greater experience and knowledge.

I have also tried to indicate some words that mean something in New World countries but which are scarcely known in the United Kingdom or to English-speaking Europeans. It is useless trying to continue a conversation if you are uncertain as to the meaning of 'Balling', 'varietal', 'crush': of course the wine trade will know, but I am an outsider, writing for other outsiders.

Finally, people – other dictionaries do not, as far as I know, include the names of those who, by their past work, have made it possible for wine writers today to do theirs. Obviously the names of great winemakers would greatly increase the entries and I have omitted these, except where their names are perpetuated in their firms, their estates or their wineries: some of these wrote about wine better than any professional writers. Among those I must cite my own teacher, the late Allan Sichel: yet I have not given him an entry, simply because he only wrote one book and therefore is not a point of reference for those who neither knew him nor read his book or articles before they dated. Ronald Avery, to whom this book is dedicated, was not a writer – yet his influence on the wines of his family firm will always be considerable.

The people named in this book are those writers to whom the reader may wish to refer, but all are now deceased. It would be difficult to give an appraisal of one's contemporaries and colleagues; although their many excellent writings are listed in the Bibliography. But it can be of use to know who certain people were and when they were writing, what their influence was, how accurate or otherwise they were in their time, and whether they are worth consulting by present winelovers. This I have tried to do.

How to use the Dictionary
If you want to look up something you read or hear, there are several possible places to look: try under the most obvious name, either of country, region, name of property or winery, sometimes of a very well-known brand; but go on looking if you do not immediately find the word you initially seek. For example, you will find the reference to the Robert Mondavi winery and wines under 'M' as all names of people are placed under their surname. However in some American reference books, it will come under 'R'. If you look up 'Moscato', you will find a cross reference to 'Muscat', because this is the main 'family name' of the grape variety, which may be called Moscato, Muscatel, Muscadelle according to the language of the country in which it is grown. All entries beginning 'Le' or 'La', such as 'La Mancha', will be found under the following word's initial: so 'La Mancha' is found under 'M'. All cross-references to other entries are printed in **bold type**.

Capital letters and spellings

A few explanations are necessary about the way in which I have written the entries. Proper names have capital letters. This, in my understanding of the term, means all place and grape names. I differ from many colleagues in this, but to write 'I have been in Champagne studying champagne' looks odd and inconsistent. Words such as claret, hock, sherry, port, do not get capitals however: they are, as I see them, styles of wines that can be defined, but which do not reproduce in their spelling the exact names of the places from which they derive.

It should also be realised that there are many variations in the way place and wine names are spelled, even in the country of their origin. My editors and I have attempted to be consistent in a way that may make the names easier to register for readers. Spellings are perplexing anyway: when the New World wineries use the name 'chateau', they do *not* put the accent on the first 'a' (as in the French *château*). It may bewilder them if I suddenly pop it on; yet the circumflex gives the French speaker a notion as to how the word should be pronounced, in French. For this reason too I have put accents of French names and words on the relevant letter, even when this is a capital. I note that the French are beginning to do this on signposts – the accent indicates the pronounciation, so it may as well go on. Yet there appears to be no general ruling as to the use of hyphens in France: some wine names are hyphenated, others are not; so the editors and I have again attempted to do what may make the name easiest to understand.

Pronunciation

The pronunciation guide is something my editors have requested and I have done my best to supply. I have not used the phonetic alphabet, simply because I doubt that the ordinary hesitant reader might know how to sound some of it; phonetics is a specialised study. The sounds I have tried to indicate are those of the ordinary 'southern English' as spoken by people in England: i.e. by me! One has to be definite at some stage. Just because I know that many friends in the United States differentiate only very slightly between a 'd' and a 't' (so that *château* from their lips sounds more like 'shadow'), and because the estate names of many South African friends include such gutterals (as in 'loch') that my efforts to pronounce the names make them laugh; that is, in my opinion, no reason for not attempting to give some guide to pronunciation that may be intelligible to a wine waiter, someone in a shop, or anybody in a wine region.

A

A.O.C., A.C.   See *Appellation d'Origine Contrôlée*.

A.P.   See **German Wine Law**.

Aberfeldy   Perthshire **whisky distillery**, built in 1896 by 'Whisky Tom' Dewar.

Aberlour-Glenlivet   James Grant built this distillery at Aberlour, Banffshire, in 1826, but it was enlarged in 1973. Most of the **whisky** made there goes for **blending**.

Abbocato   This Italian term implies that the wine (it often refers especially to the wines of **Orvieto**) is semi-sweet. The term *amabile* is also used. See *muffa nobile*.

Abocado   Spanish term for a slightly sweet wine.

Abricotine   See **apricot liqueurs**.

Abruzzi   See **Italy**.

Absinthe   A very dry, highly alcoholic herbal spirit, containing, among other flavourings, anise and wormwood (*Artemisia absinthium*), evolved in the 18th century by a Dr Pierre Ordinaire, a Frenchman then living in in **Switzerland**, whose formula passed to Henry Louis **Pernod**, of Pontarlier, in 1797. Because of the narcotics in the original recipe, absinthe was banned in **France** in 1915, and it is still forbidden to sell it there, in the **U.S.**, and in Switzerland; but Pernod still make a liqueur flavoured with **aniseed** bearing the house name. In the south of France a similar sort of drink is called **pastis**, the most famous manufacturers being the houses of **Ricard** and Berger.

   All these drinks are served accompanied by a glass of water which is added to the spirit, in the proportions of five to one, turning it cloudy. For a sweeter drink, a lump of sugar is placed on a perforated spoon and the water dripped through. A brand of pastis called Casanis is also made in **Corsica**. A '*Perroquet*' is **crème de menthe** and pastis, topped up with water, a '*Tomate*' is **grenadine** plus pastis and water.

Abteilikoer   Literally 'Abbot's liqueur', this is a herb-based **liqueur**, of aromatic style, made in Germany, and popular as a **digestive**.

1

Acetic Term used to describe a wine that has virtually become **vinegar** – which is acetic acid.

Acetobacter Type of bacteria, which is a potential danger to wine, because the **enzymes** it contains work in the ethyl **alcohol** of a wine and change it into **vinegar** – **acetic** acid.

Acidity This is something that can be either good or bad in a wine. Good acidity produces freshness, crispness and vivacity; bad acidity can produce sour wine (**vinegar**). There are different types of acid found in wine or found at different times, and this is a matter for the laboratory to deal with. But in general, somebody who is talking using a wine vocabulary will always mean praise by commenting 'acidity good', which implies balance – not too little, not too much. It is essential for a certain type of acidity to be present in any good wine which would otherwise be sloppy and flat. It is this type of good acidity that gives white wines their fresh, crisp character. But as this acidity is pronounced in most young wines, it can be tiring for the taster who has to try a number of them and who generally notices the acidity afterwards.

Adega Portuguese word, signifying the **winery** up country – in reference to **port** – where the wine is first made.

Advocaat Made from egg yolks and either spirits or wine, this is a type of drink that is served both before and after meals. The best-known brands are made in Holland, but there are versions made in the U.K., although their right to the name has been legally forbidden. It is only very slightly higher in alcohol than table wine. Sometimes flavoured versions are produced, and it is also used in certain mixes, especially the 'Snowball' combined with fizzy lemonade.

Aerated wines See **carbonated wines**.

Aglianico Red wine **grape** used in southern **Italy**. It is said to have come from **Greece** (like the white grape, **Greco**). In **Campania**, the main regions of production appear to be around Formia, **Irpinia**, **Vesuvius** and the islands of **Capri** and **Ischia**.

Agrafe The clamp that fits over the top of the **cork** and fastens below the lip of **bottles** of **sparkling wine** to hold on the cork in wines made by the **Champagne method** before they receive their second cork, if a **crown cork** is not used. It may remain as the only fastening of the cork in certain other sparkling wines that are sold without being twice corked.

Aguardiente Spanish for 'spirit'.

Ahr Wine region in the north-west of **Germany**, where both red and white wines are made, rather more of red. They do not, however, attain more than pleasant everyday quality and, as they are seldom available outside Germany, they are interesting wines to try on their home ground.

Aiguebelle French liqueur, supposed to be made from 50 different herbs, available in both green and yellow. Made by Trappist monks, it was first sold in the 19th century.

Aix-en-Provence The vineyards in this southern part of **France** make red, white and pink wines, some of pleasant quality, often sold as Coteaux d'Aix-en-Provence.

Albano White wine of the **Emilia-Romagna** region of **Italy**. It is made from the **grape** of the same name and is usually slightly luscious and full in character, although its actual sweetness can vary. There are dry Albanos which are perfectly acceptable with meat and fish, as well as sweeter ones which are more in the nature of **dessert wines**.

Alcohol Although there are various different kinds of alcohol, it is only ethyl alcohol that is involved with drinks that can be taken with safety for the drinker. It is not known which was the first alcoholic drink to be evolved – wine, **mead** or beer – but such records as exist from 10,000 years ago in Sumeria and ancient Egypt include references to **fermented** liquids. There is some alcohol – 0.003% approximately – in the bloodstream of even a lifelong and complete 'teetotaller', and there was even a very little alcohol in a drink as apparently 'non-alcoholic' as stone ginger beer. But, for the person who drinks for civilised enjoyment, the alcohol in a drink serves two purposes: it has an effect on the drinker, providing a 'lift' and acting as a food, and it keeps the drink itself free from infection and in good condition.

Alcohol, in one form or another, is the second oldest disinfectant in the world (the oldest is the urine of a healthy, clean-living human), and its addition to water, when the supply of this might be questionable, was sound sense, as was its use in cleaning wounds, as in the parable of the Good Samaritan. This is why spirit is used so much in medicine today. This is why those who use each other's **glasses** at **tastings** (provided, of course, that they do not suffer from any sort of nose or mouth infection) do so without hesitation – fermented liquor usually kills off potentially harmful bacteria which flourish in drinks such as milk, for example. Alcohol can be used to assist the treatment of many physical conditions, although of course it can be abused as well as used. A doctor has said: 'Alcohol is not the direct cause of any known disease and there is none that it will cure.' Its presence in whatever liquid is in the glass of the drinker should be something that never obtrudes in what should be an enjoyable and civilised exercise – drinking.

Alcoholic strength See **strength**.

Alcool blanc Literally 'white alcohol', so-called because the **liqueurs** made are kept in glass, not **wood**, and therefore gain no colour during the process of maturation. They are usually simply **distilled** from fruit and not sweetened or otherwise flavoured, so that the flavour of the fruit is pronounced. In Alsace and some of the other regions where they are made, it is traditional to serve them in a medium-sized **glass**, previously filled with lumps of ice, which are swirled round to chill it; then, when the ice is tipped out, the fruit brandy is poured in, and the **bouquet** is released from the chilled glass – exactly the reverse of what happens in the service of **Cognac** or **Armagnac**. A fruit brandy is, in fact, only a 'liqueur' in a general sense – it is really a brandy. It is usually a good **digestive**.

Some of the best known are: kirsch (from cherries), framboise (raspberries), fraise (strawberries), myrtille (bilberries), mirabelle (small golden plums), quetsch (Switzen plum), prunelle sauvage (sloe), poire

3

Williams (William pear), houx (holly berry), coing (quince), alisier (rowanberry), cumin (cummin), and tutti frutti (a mixture of fruits). There are, of course, different names for the same liqueurs in different countries: slivovitz is a Yugoslavian or Romanian plum brandy, himbeergeist is a German or Swiss raspberry brandy. The method by which these are made varies slightly, some being made by distillation of the fruit mash, others by **maceration** of the fruit in alcohol and the distillation of the result.

Aldehyde Alexis Lichine defines the aldehydes as 'a halfway step between alcohols and acids and are formed by the oxidation of alcohols'. I cannot improve on this except to say that, for the lay drinker, it is really only important to know that aldehydes are one of the important components of wine – unless you are a chemist who will understand the technicalities anyway.

Aleatico di Portoferraio Sweetish, deep coloured wine from **Elba** made from a type of **Muscat grape**, here having the same name as the wine. It is reputed to be high in iron and therefore a type of tonic.

Alella Region in the Catalonian area of **Spain**, producing white and red wines.

Alexander Valley Region in Sonoma, **California**, U.S., where there are a number of **wineries**.

Algeria Wines were planted along what is now the Algerian coast in classical times, but the Algerian vineyards as they exist today were started by the French colonists in the early part of the 19th century. The provinces where **vines** are grown are those of Oran, Alger and Constantine, and although some white wines are made, the greater part of the quality production is of red wines.

Algerian wines received a bad and not altogether deserved reputation when they were shipped to a wine-starved U.K. during the war, although even some of these were of passable quality. At their best, they can give pleasurable drinking in the medium price ranges and, before Algeria became independent in 1962, were sent in increasing quantities to France. Here they were often used for **blending**, but in fact the wines of certain producers were sold and enjoyed by themselves. After 1962 the majority of the French who had owned the vineyards had to leave, and the problem of maintaining the quality they had achieved was inevitably great.

Up to this time it is probably true to say that Algerian wines were, overall, the best of those produced in North Africa, but now stricter controls in France prevent the use of Algerian wines for blending. The absence of skilled winemakers in Algeria these days, plus the circumstance of Algeria being an Islamic country, make it difficult to know what may be the future of these wines. Algerians may prefer to cultivate vines for table grapes and to plant other fruit.

Alicante (1) **Spanish** red wine.

Alicante (2) See **grenache.**

Alicante-Bouschet A **grape** developed for high yield, making rather undistinguished red wines in the French Midi and some parts of **California**.

Aligoté (Pronounced 'al-ly-got-ty') White **grape**, used in **Burgundy** for the less expensive white wines, to which it gives its name. It makes pleasant, slightly tough, dryish wines, but nothing of fine quality. It is a very good 'casual' wine and, from a good producer, can these days achieve moderate to good quality. Traditionally it is the white wine base of the Burgundian drink **kir**. See *Vin blanc cassis*.

Alisier See *alcool blanc*.

All Saints An **Australian** vineyard, near Rutherglen, between New South Wales and Victoria, concentrating on the production of **dessert** and **fortified wines**. It is owned by a religious community.

Allasch, alasch Type of **kümmel**, taking its name from Allasch, near Riga in the **U.S.S.R.**, which was known for caraway seeds.

Allen, H. Warner C.B.E. (1881-1968) An important wine writer whose work seems now to be almost ignored, but who does not deserve this neglect. He was a classical scholar at Oxford and gained an extensive knowledge of wine while he was for ten years Paris correspondent of *The Morning Post*. He spent some years working with the historic wine merchants in St James's, Berry Bros & Rudd, and wrote an account of the firm. His numerous books on the main wines of Europe and his historical accounts of the evolution of certain wines and their place in the writings of the ancients are all extremely readable, although he was of a time when graceful, sometimes ornate prose was in fashion, so that he has gained a somewhat undeserved reputation for 'purple passages'. In fact he is very easy to read. In person, he was a wholly delightful and approachable man, with great sensitiveness – he was a mystic and wrote about this as well, collaborated with E.C. Bentley in a detective story and to the end of his life remained alert and interested in everything around him.

Allesverloren One of the fine wine estates in the Malmesbury region at the Cape, in **South Africa**. It gets its name because, in the late 18th century, the owners regularly drove to church in Stellenbosch, many hours away and, during one such absence, the local bushmen raided and destroyed the house and outbuildings. The returning family could only say 'All is lost' (*All es verloren*). In the present century, the future Prime Minister, Dr D.F. Malan, was born there. Among the range currently made is a fine port style wine.

Allt a'Bhainne (Pronounced 'Alter-vane' stressing 'vane') The new Dufftown **whisky** distillery, built by Chivas Bros.

Almadén California wine producer on a large scale. The first plantings were made in 1852 at Los Gatos in the **Santa Clara Valley**, but Almadén's holdings are now extensive and about half of them are in the Gavilan Mountains in San Benito. A very wide range of wines, red, white, rosé, **dessert wines** and **sparkling wines** is made, the latter undergoing **fermentation** in **bottle**. There are also a number of **jug wines**. For the table wines, many classic wine **grapes** are used, plus the **Zinfandel**. Some wines are **estate-bottled** and dated for their **vintage**. Almadén have two tasting rooms open to the public: at San Juan Bautista, in the Plaza; and on Highway 152, Pacheco Pass Road. Almadén has had various owners but today belongs to National Distillers. Some of the wines are available in the U.K.

Aloxe-Corton (Pronounced 'Al-oss') Parish in the **Côte de Beaune** in

ALSACE, FRANCE

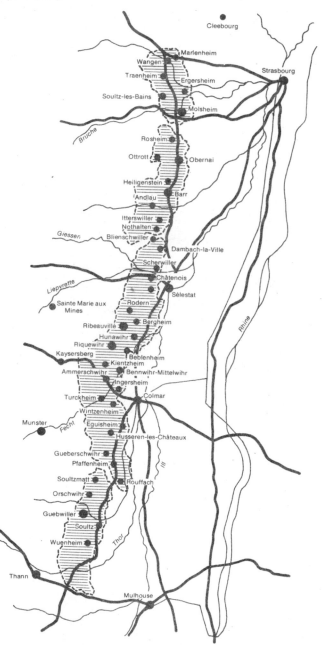

Burgundy, making mostly red wines, but including part of the great Corton-Charlemagne white wine vineyard. See **Côte d'Or**.

Alpenkraeuterlikoer German **liqueur**, based on alpine herbs and roots, also incorporating wormwood. Brownish or yellow-green in colour and fairly high in **strength**.

Alsace Important wine region in the north-east of **France**. Wines have been made here for centuries – Queen Elizabeth I drank 'Elsasser' – but, during the period in the 19th century when Alsace belonged to Germany until the end of World War I, the wines and vineyards suffered a serious decline. Today the wines are of excellent quality and admirable value, although for some curious reason, they are difficult to introduce to the general public: yet I have never found any Alsace wine ('Alsatian is the dog', the late André **Simon** would growl) that is even slightly defective and many people would do better to buy good Alsace than mediocre German wines.

The most important wines are white. The **Riesling, Gewurztraminer, Tokay** (Pinot Gris), **Muscat, Sylvaner, Pinot Blanc grapes** are the most important. A blend of grapes will make a wine called *Zwicker* or, if what are considered to be 'noble' grapes only are used, it will be called *Edelzwicker*. The Riesling is certainly the noblest of all the grapes, making distinguished, dry wines; the spicey Gewurztraminer is the grape that usually appeals most immediately to the beginner in wine, with its full, aromatic style. Tokay is said by some to have been brought back from the medieval wars in **Hungary** by the mercenary, Baron Schwendi, but some Hungarians think that the grape was actually brought to Hungary by the Alsaciens; although today's Hungarian **Tokay** has nothing to do with this particular grape. Tokay makes a dry, full wine; the Pinot Blanc a full, slightly minerally dry wine. The Muscat is extremely 'grapey' as to **bouquet** and full in character – people either like it very much or not at all. The Sylvaner makes a light, fresh wine. The Pinot Noir is used to make deep pinky-red wines. Some **sparkling wine** is made. See *crémant*.

The wines vary, both from year to year and from **winery** to winery, the name of the grape and the producer being given on **labels** and each establishment making a range of wines of individual style. In general, most Alsace wines are at their best up to about 5 years from their making, but exceptional **vintages** can make long-lived wines and the special wines of great years can live for 20 or more. There are few specific vineyards, but some that do feature on labels include: Sporen, Kaefferkopf, Mamberg, Zahnacker, Rangen, Kanzlerberg, Wannen and Brand. It should be appreciated that different grapes may be planted in these, according to the aim of the owner of a particular plot within the overall site. Sometimes a proud grower will make a 'late picked' wine or even one made from specially selected individual grapes, but these are rare and, of course, expensive.

The wines are bottled in the *flûte d'Alsace*, the tall, tapered green **bottle** that is either 24 fl. oz (72 cl), containing 23 fl. oz (70 cl), or a slightly larger size, containing 26 fl. oz (75 cl) of wine, produced because of a recent law for the **U.S.** and certain other markets.

The whole Alsace wine region is beautiful: the *route du vin* is literally garlanded with flowers, the picturesque houses and ancient buildings complementing the solid cellars and wine houses. The local food is rich and superb.

Altar wine   Used for Holy Communion, this must be pure and unadulterated natural (table) wine, but both the Roman and Anglican churches sanction the use of either red or white. See **Communion wine**.

Alto   Estate in the Stellenbosch area of the Cape, **South Africa**, originally part of a larger property. Its situation, on the slopes of the Helderberg, caused its owner to name it Alto, after the mountains. Although the overall vineyard had been cultivated since the 17th century, serious wine production was only started with the division of the estate in the 1920s. Alto became well known for its red wines, started by the first owner, Hennie **Malan**. The Alto Rouge of today is made in virtually the same way and with the same proportions of **grape varieties** as at the outset, so adroit was Malan's skill. Interesting experiments with other grapes and with straight grape varieties have been started and the estate maintains its high reputation.

Alto Adige   (Pronounced 'Ahl-to Ad-di-jee' stress the initial syllables) Vineyard region of northern **Italy**, usually combined with that of the adjacent **Trentino**. The Alto Adige is sometimes referred to as the South Tyrol and in fact its white wines do bear some resemblance to certain of the light, fragrant, moderately fruity **Austrian** whites. Some of the best known come from **Terlano**, north of Bolzano. Terlano wine itself is traditionally a mixture of **Pinot** Blanc, two forms of **Riesling**, **Sauvignon** and **Sylvaner**. Some wines are marketed under the names of the particular **grapes** making them – e.g. Terlano Riesling Italico. A local red wine is the Grauvernatsch.

Alvarelhão   **Grape** of Portuguese origin, used for some **U.S. dessert wines**.

Amabile   See *abboccato*.

Amaretto di Saronno   Very popular fruit **liqueur** – at one time top in Italy and third in popularity in the U.S. – this is made at Saronno, near Lake Como, by the Reina family. Its origin is supposed to be in 1525, when the painter, Bernardino Luini, was commissioned to paint frescoes on the local shrine of Our Lady of the Miracles. Luini took as his model for the Madonna the young widow running the local inn and she was so delighted with her picture that she made the artist a Christmas Eve gift of a drink using the almonds and apricots from her garden with **brandy**.

Amarone   The full name of this **Italian** red wine is properly **Valpolicella** Recioto Amarone and it comes from the **Verona** region. Amarone is a very big, full wine, of a colour that some writers describe as 'garnet red'.

Ambonnay   One of the villages of the Montagne de Reims in **Champagne**, where still red **Coteaux Champenois** wine is made.

Amer Picon   Bitters, invented by a distiller in the French army in **Algeria** in 1835. Pinkish-red, slightly orange-flavoured, drunk as an **apéritif** or **digestive**.

Americano   Originally a mixed **apéritif**. consisting of about one-third **Campari** bitters to two-thirds sweet **vermouth**, diluted with soda if liked. It must always be well stirred, so that the Campari mixes with the vermouth. The garnish should be a slice of orange, not the usual lemon. Nowadays several firms market ready-mixed Americano, but I have never found any except that of Gaudin (based on Chambéry vermouth) to be satisfactory, as they tend to be sweetish and sticky. A good Americano, properly made, is an excellent and refreshing drink.

Amontillado See **sherry**.

Amoroso A type of sweet *oloroso* **sherry**, taking its name from that of a well-known vineyard. As a term, *amoroso* tends to be less used nowadays, as this type of wine is generally categorised as a cream sherry.

Ampelography 'The scientific description of the vine', according to *The Shorter Oxford Dictionary*. But the term is sometimes used today to refer specifically to the study of **grapes**.

Añada Young **sherry** of one **vintage**, kept separately and not yet **blended** with other sherries. It seldom remains like this for more than a couple of years.

Anghelu Ruju Red **Sardinian** wine, which appears to be sweetish in style and above table wine **strength**, so that it is often drunk as an **apéritif** or after meals. The name means 'red angel'.

Angelica **Liqueur** flavoured with angelica, made in various places. The East German version is called krambambuli; there is also one made in France, called Liqueur d'Angelique, based on **Cognac**. The herb gets its name – in Latin *Angelica archangelica* – because it is said to flower on 8 May, St Michael's Day.

Angelikalikoer German **liqueur**, based on angelica, a plant which gets its name because it was supposed to be 'of the archangel', and helpful as a preventative against the plague. There are several types made in different parts of the world including Spain and California, but the German type is slightly bitter and is mostly used as an ingredient in mixed drinks.

Angludet, Château d' Estate in **Cantenac**, in the **Médoc** region of **Bordeaux**, with an old-established reputation. The property was run down at the time of the 1855 **classification** and so does not appear in this list, but it now ranks as a *cru bourgeois exceptionnel*. It belongs to Peter Sichel, who was the first person from outside France to be Président of the Bordeaux Growers' Syndicat. The **clarets** possess both charm and quality.

Angostura **Bitters**, invented by Dr Johann Gottlieb Benjamin Siegert who, after serving against Napoleon, went to Venezuela, where he was in charge of a hospital at Angostura (later renamed Cuidad Bolívar). In 1824 he invented an *Amaro Aromático* for digestive disorders. Some confusion has arisen about the name, but in fact the bark of the Venezuelan Angostura tree has nothing to do with the formula: this is still a secret in the possession of the Siegert family. Mark Twain refers to Angostura Bitters in a letter to his wife from London in 1874. Angostura sales boomed in the U.S. under **Prohibition**, because the bitters were classed as 'medicinal' and could be sold. It can be used to improve the flavour of certain sauces, salad dressings and gravies, as well as for 'pink gin' and in **Champagne cocktails**.

9

Angove   One of the wine families of **Australia** and a firm still in the wine trade. Angoves make a wide range of wines of all types, but are also well reputed for their St Agnes **brandy**.

Anise del Mono   Spanish **aniseed liqueur**, which may be dry or sweet, made in Barcelona.

Aniseed   This herb (*Pimpinella anisum;* in French, *anis*) originally came from Asia Minor and is found throughout the Mediterranean countries. It is used in the making of a range of **liqueurs** in many countries. A 16th century writer recommends it as 'good against belchings and upbraidings of the stomacke'.

Anisette   The most famous **aniseed**-flavoured **liqueur** is that of the founder of the French liqueur business, the 18th century lady from Bordeaux, Marie Brizard. She nursed the poor and sick and was given a recipe for a semi-medical drink by a grateful West African patient. On this she established her business, in partnership with Jean-Baptiste Roger: the name of the firm – Marie Brizard et Roger – still indicates their association. The establishment today makes a wide range of liqueurs, but their anisette is possibly the best known. Other aniseed-flavoured liqueurs include **Anise del Mono** from Spain; Anisetta Stellata from Italy; Escarchardo from Portugal; La Tintaine from France; **Mastika** from Greece and the Balkans; Oxygenée, which is made in both France and the U.S.; Tres Castillos from Puerto Rico; **ouzo** from Cyprus and Greece; and **pastis**.

Anjou   Wine region around Angers on the River **Loire** in **France**, making red, white, rosé and **sparkling wines**. The region was the ancient comté of the Plantagenet family which St Bernard called 'the devil's brood'. Henry Plantagenet, Count of Anjou, married Eleanor of Aquitaine in 1152, before he became Henry II of England in 1154. This is why there are many links between this part of France and England.

The wines are becoming of increasing importance and can be both charming and delicately aristocratic. The pink wines are very popular, both in the U.K. and France, and those made from the **Cabernet Franc grape** are usually superior in quality – they will be labelled 'Rosé du Cabernet'. Nowadays the pink wines are by no means as dry as they used to be, catering to popular taste. Sweetish white wines, made by the action of *Botrytis cinerea*, are produced south of Angers at **Bonnezeaux**, **Coteaux du Layon**, **Quart de Chaume** and the **Coteaux de l'Aubance**, as well as some dry wines, made from the **Chenin Blanc** grape. Savennières, on the **Coteaux de la Loire**, makes very good whites, both dry and slightly sweet. Around **Saumur**, dry white still, *pétillant* and sparkling wines are made; there are also the reds of Saumur-Champigny from the Cabernet Franc.

Annaberg   Estate in the **Palatinate** region of **Germany**, making fine wines. The first successful plantings of the **Scheurebe grape** were made there.

Apéritifs   The word comes from the Latin *aperire* – to open, hence it has been associated with the drink at the opening of a meal. A good apéritif should stimulate the appetite and prepare the palate for what is to be served. Obviously a wide variety of drinks can be served as apéritifs, including

sparkling wines, dry white or **rosé** wines, spirits, **cocktails** and certain **liqueurs** that are not too sweet, such as those containing **aniseed**. More specifically, commercial apéritifs are usually wine-based drinks, with particular flavourings, such as **Dubonnet, St Raphael, Lillet** and all the **vermouths**.

Apetlon   **Austrian** town near the Neusiedler See, famous for the work there of the great winemaker, Dr Lenz **Moser**, who, by his method of 'high cultivation' (*hochkultur*) which is now usually known by his name, radically altered the training of vines so that mechanical methods can be used in many vineyards. Estimates indicate that about 75% of Austrian vineyards now follow this.

Apfelsinenlikoer   Not, as might be assumed, anything to do with apples, but a German liqueur, based on oranges. See **orange liqueurs**.

Aphrodisiacs   Throughout history a search has been made for the love potion or creator of sexual desire and guarantee of satisfactory performance – and some revolting concoctions have been evolved. But, scientifically, there is no such thing. As a wise physician commented, what a fairly high protein diet, convenient circumstances and the presence of an attractive person of the required sex cannot accomplish, will not be achieved by anything out of any bottle.

Appellation Contrôlée, Appellation d'Origine Contrôlée   The latter is more correct: but is often abbreviated as A.O.C., as well as A.C. It is a system of control applied to wines in **France**. The local syndicates in each wine region determine the conditions according to which the A.O.C. is awarded and the overall supervision is in the hands of the Institut National des Appellations d'Origine, usually referred to by its initials as **I.N.A.O.** The laws, varied according to region, determine: the **vines** planted and their method of cultivation and **pruning**; the exact location of the vineyard; the permitted yield at the **vintage**; the minimum **alcoholic** content of the wines; and the method by which the wines are made. There are gradations of *appellation*, some fitting inside each other: for example, A.O.C. **Bordeaux**, then Bordeaux Supérieur, then perhaps **Médoc**, then one of the Médoc *communes*, such as **Pauillac** or **Margaux**. The higher the *appellation*, the potentially higher the price of the wine.

However it is important to realise that the A.O.C. is exactly what its name implies – an award of a certificate of supervised origin. It is thus a pedigree of the better wines of France. It is not – except by implication – a guarantee of quality. This, as always, is a matter for the individual producer to see to and it is perfectly possible for an A.O.C. wine to be unworthy of its pedigree or, indeed, be downright poor as a wine. This is one of the reasons why the possession of the A.O.C. is not going to ensure that the buyer of a **bottle** of wine gets a good wine – although he stands a good chance of doing so. Wines sold in Britain are now subject to the laws accepted by the European community and the A.O.C. applies here – it did not for wines bought before 1973.

Another point to remember is that a wine with a great name should bear the *appellation* appropriate to itself – for example, one of the great red

Burgundies, publicised just as A.O.C. 'Bourgogne', could certainly be a risk to the drinker, because these wines should have a superior *appellation*. Conscientious producers, in unsuccessful years or because for some reason they are not satisfied with the wines they have made, will 'declassify' them to a lower *appellation* – they may still be good wines but not worthy of the top A.O.C. even if the authorities permitted it to be awarded. The essential is to remember that the A.O.C. is a controlled system of production, only indirectly an indication of quality. But all the finer French wines should possess an A.O.C. The I.N.A.O. also controls the production of spirits. The one exception is **Champagne** – legally it is only necessary for labels of this wine to bear the description *Vin de Champagne*. See **V.D.Q.S.,** *vin de pays*.

Applejack   The American name for apple brandy, somewhat equivalent to **Calvados**. Since early times the New England region has made this spirit, usually by a double **distillation** in a **pot still**. The distillate is broken down with water and matured in oak.

Appleton   Jamaican estate famous for its Appleton white **rum**, founded in the 17th century by the Yorkshireman, John Appleton. It is made today according to an 1825 formula.

Apricot liqueurs   These are made in many countries and strictly they should be made by **distilling** fermented apricots and the kernels when the result will be pure white. In fact many good types are produced by **macerating** the fruit in **brandy** and possibly adding the extract of the kernels, when the liquid will be orange-coloured. Well-known brands are Marie Brizard's **Apry**, Garnier's Abricotine, but most **liqueur** establishments make an apricot liqueur. The white type, often found in eastern Europe, is exemplified by the Hungarian Barack Palinka.

Apry   **Apricot liqueur** made by the firm of Marie Brizard, Bordeaux.

Apulia   The most prolific wine region of **Italy**, in the south, supplying many of the wines for making into **vermouth** and used in wine-based **apéritifs**. The wines, together with those of the **Basilicata** and **Calabria**, are interesting to the traveller, but seldom seen outside their own region. A number of full, sweet wines are made, as well as the usual reds and whites. They can provide pleasant drinking and are worth investigation by holiday-makers.

Aqua vitae   Latin for 'water of life', the term was used in medieval and even later times to signify spirits. It is possible that it originated as *aqua vine* (water of wine) when **distillation** was still a novelty, or even *aqua vite* (water of the vine). In some historic writings, *aqua vitae* may actually mean **brandy**, the spirit of wine, rather than a spirit such as **gin** or **rum**. It is a term not used nowadays except in the words that derive from it, such as **aquavit**.

Aquavit   There are various ways of spelling this: aqvavit in Danish, aquavit in Swedish, and both spirits are also referred to as **schnapps**: also spelt in various ways according to the country. In Germany this term signifies virtually any strong drink. Danish aqvavit has always been made mostly from grain – 'the Danish grape' – but rye and, increasingly, potatoes are also used. It is usually flavoured with caraway and is one of the great national drinks of the

Scandinavian countries. Danish aqvavit, especially the Aalborg brands of Danish Distilleries, is famous and there are various types, most of them stronger than the Swedish brands, some being flavoured with spices, **aniseed** and dill. Linie of Trondheim in Norway make a tea-coloured aquavit that, the label relates, has been sent to Australia and back, the label giving the ship and dates of the trip, something that makes customers very choosy about selecting a particular vessel travelling at a particular time. Aquavit is made in Germany and the Low Countries as well and there are various slightly flavoured versions.

Aquavit is always served iced and is an admirable accompaniment to the open sandwiches and piquant snacks served in the northern countries. Conventionally, aquavit or schnapps is drunk in a gulp – hence the small glasses – but because of its strength the drinker first takes a bite of some food, preferably something with herring. If a succession of glassfuls are to be served, it is permitted to 'bite' the second drink in half, the third in three; in other words, to spread out the tot.

A ritual is attached to the saying of 'skol' with schnapps: drinkers raise glasses, look into each other's eyes and sometimes link arms. The procedure varies according to the country but although, at a dinner, the hostess may 'skol' all the guests or a guest in particular, the guests must never 'skol' her – as otherwise she would have to drink separately with each of them! The traditional chaser for schnapps is lager, but it is such a clean spirit that it may be served before a meal when wine is to follow.

Aramon   Black **grape**, grown extensively in the south of **France** and a little in **California**. It has never been used for fine wines, but it can be useful as it is very prolific in yield. It tends to lack colour, so that growers find it necessary to use some other grape that will serve to tint the **must**. Other names for the Aramon include Ugni Noir and Pisse-vin.

Arbois   There is a saying about Arbois wines that 'The more you drink, the more upright you stand'. But there's another one to the effect that 'One only drinks a glass at a time of the good wine of Arbois'. See **Jura**.

Ardbeg   Independently owned **distillery** on the isle of Islay (pronounced 'Eye-ler', stress the first syllable). Most of the **whisky** it makes goes into various **blends** of Scotch.

Ardèche   Region in the **Rhône** area of **France**, where increasing quantities of good and still inexpensive wine are being made, notably from the **Gamay grape**. The **Coteaux du Tricastin** and Côtes du Vivarais are in the south of the region.

Ardmore   **Distillery** built at Kennethmont, west Aberdeenshire, in 1898 by William Teacher. The **whisky** it makes is still used in the famous and popular blend of Highland Cream.

Argentina   It may surprise many to learn that this country is the fourth largest producer of wine in the world, and the largest in South America, because only a small proportion of the wine is exported, and only recently have any Argentine wines been available in the U.K. But vineyards have been cultivated since the 16th century, although it is only in the past 100 years that wine has been produced on a large scale for commercial purposes. Most of the wine is produced in the north, and the prime region is Mendoza province, with the neighbouring region of San Juan. Rio Negro, La Rioja and Catamarca also make wine in quantity. Various classic wine **grapes** are cultivated and a wide variety of wines – **fortified** as well as table and **sparkling** – are made. Recently legislation has been brought in to protect the quality of the wines and the way in which they should be named. Although it seems unlikely that, to date, any wines of more than medium to good quality have been made in the Argentine, it appears definite that those in the everyday category are both varied and of sound character, so that, with production increasing yearly, plus improved means of transport, they may become widely known in export markets within the near future.

Arinto   See **Bucelas**.

Armagnac   One of the world's great **brandies**, made in the Gers (pronounced 'Jair') département in the south-west of **France**. This was formerly the province of Gascony, homeland of D'Artagnan. The region is now strictly delimited into the regions of Tenarèze, Haut-Armagnac and Bas-Armagnac, (the latter usually considered the best) and production is rigidly controlled. A mixture of **grapes** are used, some of them the same as those used for **Cognac**, other peculiar to the Pyrenees. A special type of still is used, many of these travelling about the region. A single **distillation** is made and this must be done by the April following the wines' **vintage**. The period of maturation takes place in **casks** of local oak.

The different firms – none of them as large as the Cognac concerns – use their own system of grading their Armagnacs according to age and quality but a XXX or **three star** Armagnac will be 3 years old, a **V.O.** from 5 to 10, a **V.S.O.P.** from 10 to 15. *Hors d'age* means that the brandy is at least 25 years old but, after about 30 years in **wood**, the Armagnac tends to get too 'spirity'. The **bottle** often used is the flattish, squat, flagon type, known as a *basquaise*, but other shapes are also used.

Some people mistakenly suppose that Armagnac is 'weaker' than Cognac, but this is not so – it is a brandy, and may be made according to the strength required. What is usually true is that Armagnac tends to be gentler in character than most Cognac, and some people consider it 'feminine' as a brandy, whereas Cognac is 'masculine'. It has a pronounced but delicate **aroma**, quite different from any Cognac. It is drunk all over the world, but in the U.K., where appreciation of fine Cognac possibly affects the market for Armagnac it is not very widely known, although those who do, like it very much. As with all fine brandy, Armagnac should be served in **glasses** that are of a size to be cupped in the hand and these should never be artificially heated over a flame. A newish drink, called the *Pousse Rapière* (sword thrust) consists of a measure of Armagnac, topped up with the very dry local **sparkling wine** of the Gers and garnished with a slice of orange, the peel twisted over the brandy to give added zest.

Aroma Some people suppose this to be same as the **bouquet** but the distinguished writer Alexis Lichine differentiates it by saying it is the impression a young wine makes on the **nose**. I prefer the definition of my own teacher, the late Allan Sichel: 'The aroma is roughly speaking the smell of the taste, whilst the bouquet is the impersonal collection of smells given off by the wine, mostly the product of the maturing process and recognised by the nose alone. The one is projection (aroma), the other (bouquet) the very substance itself'. A wine can, in my view, be aromatic without having much bouquet, the different smells that make up the aroma can be pronounced, even strident – but they can only indicate what is there, in the wine. Whereas almost any wine has, or should have, an aroma, only the better possess a bouquet.

Arquebuse Cusenier's white **digestive**, found by some to be slightly easier to swallow than **Fernet Branca**.

Arrack (Many variant spellings) The word comes from the Arabic, meaning 'sweat' or 'juice'. This is a spirit, usually of coarse type, which may be **distilled** from a variety of things – dates, palm sap, rice, milk, sugar-cane, etc. – in the Middle and Far Eastern countries. Variations on its name include raki.

Artisan growth See *cru*, **bourgeois growth**.

Arvèze See **gentian**.

Ashton Wine estate in the Robertson region at the Cape in **South Africa**.

Aspect This word risks being misunderstood in wine talk because it more correctly means the 'outlook' of a vineyard, not what the vineyard looks like. The aspect includes the angle at which the vineyard is sited; its relation to the sunlight, especially the way and time at which the sun will strike the **vines** (whether slantingly or from on high); and whether the greatest heat will fall on the vineyard in the morning or afternoon. The rows of vines are planted to achieve the best aspect. Anyone who is able to view steeply terraced vineyards on slopes such as those alongside the winding **Mosel** will see how the aspect of one small patch of vines is quite different from that of one almost alongside.
· Ideally, in many instances, vineyards of the northern hemisphere face in a southerly direction, because this way they enjoy some protection from the cold winds coming from the north; they also benefit by getting the sun's rays in the morning or at least by midday, because this is when night dews can be dissipated and the greatest heat is bestowed on the vines. (Anyone who sunbathes knowns that tan is best acquired in the morning sun.)

Assmannshausen Vineyard in the Rheingau (see **Rhine**) in **Germany** where red wines are produced, of a pleasant character when good, although never to be compared in quality with the great red wines of France. White wine is also made there. The **grape** for the red wines is the **Spätburgunder**, which is a type of **Pinot Noir**.

Asti Small town in **Piedmont**, north **Italy**, where a wide range of quality wines is made, not just the well-known **Asti Spumante**. Others include the sparkling **Moscato d'Asti**, a sweet **Malvasia**, and red wines such as **Grignolino**, **Freisa** and **Barbera**, all with the suffix 'd'Asti'.

Asti Spumante The best-known **sparkling wine** of **Italy**, produced in **Piedmont**, mostly around Canelli and **Asti**. It is made from the Moscato or **Muscat grape**, mostly by means of a combination of the **Charmat** and **transfer methods** plus individual variations, due largely to Carlo Gancia. It is ready to drink when the **bottles** are offered for sale which is why it does not bear a **vintage** date. It is fairly definitely scented and 'grapey' in flavour. It should be served like any quality sparkling wine, chilled, and in a goblet or tulip **glass**.

Asti Spumante may be drunk at any time, but is especially enjoyable with ices, any Italian type of cake, and fresh fruit or fruit salad. It may also be served with first courses, especially those rich in mayonnaise, as the fruitiness of the wine 'cuts' the richness of the sauce. A number of widely reputed establishments make good Asti. The bottles carry a seal showing the patron saint, San Secundo, and the name of the local *consorzio*.

Atholl Brose A mixture of **whisky**, oatmeal, honey and cream, combined – for the commercial product – according to a secret formula. There are many recipes for the making of Atholl Brose, and that of the ducal family of Atholl does not include cream. The legends associated with its making are at least as old as the 15th century and it is traditional as a New Year drink, being piped into the mess of the Argyll and Sutherland Highlanders at that time, with every officer and man having a **quaich** of it.

Auchentoshan (Pronounced 'Och-'n'-toshn' stressing 'Och') This is a **whisky** distillery at Old Kilpatrick, Strathclyde, which carries out a triple **distillation**. It markets its Scotch as a single malt.

Auchroisk **Whisky distillery** near Mulben, Banffshire, owned by **I.D.V.**

Audacia Wine estate near Stellenbosch, **South Africa**.

Aude Extensive wine region in the south of **France**, on the Mediterranean and hinterland. Red, white and pink wines are made. Although they were formerly used for **blending** and **vermouth** production, today's improved technology makes it possible for some to be pleasant drinks that feature on export lists. See **Gard, Hérault, Languedoc**.

Auldana Vineyard and **winery** near Adelaide, **Australia**.

Aultmore **Distillery** at Keith, Banffshire, owned by a subsidiary of **D.C.L.** Most of the **whisky** goes for **blending**.

Aum See **casks**.

Aurum See **orange liqueurs**.

Auslese See **Germany, German Wine Law**.

Ausone (Pronounced 'O-zone') A *premier grand cru classé* of St Émilion in the **Gironde** region of **France** and possibly the best-known wine of this area, together with **Cheval Blanc**. Opinions tend to vary about its precise degree of greatness, but it is always at least a very fine wine. The cellar is unusual in that it is in the rock of the hillside down which the vines grow. The name is supposed to derive from a villa belonging to the classic poet, Ausonius, imperial tutor and consul and a great lover of wine and food according to his verse. But there are several sites claiming to be the original villa he owned in the Gironde and in fact he may have lived in several.

Australia   The first **vines** were planted in Australia by the first settlers in 1788, and although production on a commercial scale took some time to develop, the Australian wine industry today is very important and expanding. Unfortunately the very finest of its wines are seldom seen outside Australia. The U.K. and **U.S.**, however, import some. Both English-speaking countries are coming to appreciate Australian wines in their own right, not merely as the dark red 'tonic' wines that first made their mark in export markets. A large proportion of the crop is **distilled**, much of it for use in **fortified wines** and **brandy**, but a wide range of fortified and table wines is also produced in the wine regions. These because of the size of the country, are extensive. There are many firms which are family concerns, and wines sold under family names and bearing the names of estates on their **labels** are representative of Australia's best in many instances. Examples are **Angove**, **Hardy**, **Lindeman**, **McWilliams**, **Penfold**, **Seppelt** and **Wynn** among others.

A further point of interest is that in some regions, such as the **Hunter River**, the *Phylloxera* did not invade, so that the wines are made from vines of ungrafted stock. For the most part, classic **grape varieties** are used, but Australian **oenologists** have contributed to the improvement of wine throughout the winemaking world. **Roseworthy College** is famous among oenological institutions, so that certain grapes not common in European vineyards are used to make first-rate table wines, such as the **Schiraz**.

It should be remembered, when appraising wines bearing a **vintage** on their labels, that the vintage in the southern hemisphere occurs in the spring of the year of its date, so that such wines will be approximately 6 months in advance of European wines of the same age. But in fact, although many Australian wines improve greatly with age, there are not usually great climatic variations between one year and another, so that the vintage date is useful for indicating maturity rather than the individuality of a particular year. Also, the great **wineries** usually make a whole range of wines, still wines of all types, **sparkling** and, often, **dessert** and fortified wines, each indicative of the style of the establishment, so that the name of the producer is of prime importance. Although the descriptive names supposed to relate to European vineyards – Chablis, Burgundy, Sauternes – are still sometimes used, nowadays Australian wines are beginning to drop these names, and assert themselves in their own right, as well as using some estate names.

The main areas of Australian wine production, together with some of the great estates and wineries, are: Western Australia, with the **Sandalford**, Valencia and **Houghton** vineyards, the last two belonging to the **Emu Wine Company**; South Australia, with the great **Barossa Valley** wineries, including Seppelt, **Gramp** (Orlando), Penfold, **Smith** (**Yalumba**), **Saltram** (Angaston), the **Kaiserstuhl** Co-operative, and **Buring** (**Chateau Leonay**); in the Southern Vales region a famous name is **Reynella**, founded in 1838, and others are **Seaview**, and **Hardy's Tintara**. Near Adelaide is the Magill region, also **McLaren Vale**, and there are also the important vineyards of **Coonawarra**, **Clare**, **Watervale**, Modbury, Hope Valley and Highcombe, and the **Murray**

AUSTRALIA (SOUTH-EAST)

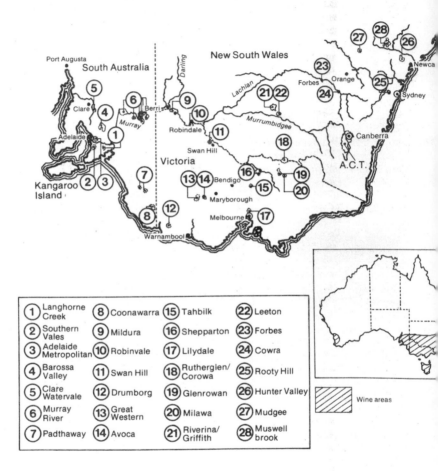

① Langhorne Creek	⑧ Coonawarra	⑮ Tahbilk	㉒ Leeton
② Southern Vales	⑨ Mildura	⑯ Shepparton	㉓ Forbes
③ Adelaide Metropolitan	⑩ Robinvale	⑰ Lilydale	㉔ Cowra
④ Barossa Valley	⑪ Swan Hill	⑱ Rutherglen/ Corowa	㉕ Rooty Hill
⑤ Clare Watervale	⑫ Drumborg	⑲ Glenrowan	㉖ Hunter Valley
⑥ Murray River	⑬ Great Western	⑳ Milawa	㉗ Mudgee
⑦ Padthaway	⑭ Avoca	㉑ Riverina/ Griffith	㉘ Muswell brook

▨ Wine areas

—————— Rivers
– – – – – State boundary
················ Wine areas

River Irrigation Area, where Angove and the Lyrup Co. are proprietary firms, and **co-operatives** include **Waikerie**, **Renmark**, **Berri** and **Loxton**.

In Victoria possibly the most important prestige name is **Tahbilk**, and the significant name for sparkling wines is **Great Western**; this, it should be noted, is nothing to do with the American sparkling wine (see **Finger Lakes**). It is a vineyard, owned by two firms, one of them Best, but the larger holding being that of Seppelt, who make the sparkling wine Great Western. This is considered as the best or certainly one of the best in Australia, where it is quite legally referred to as 'Champagne'. Rutherglen, Glenrowan, **Wahgunyah**, Wangaratta and **Mildura** are other important vineyards – wines made by the **Chaffey Brothers** at Mildura are marketed under the name **Mildara**, which should not be confused with the vineyard name.

New South Wales is where winegrowing on a commercial scale was first started in Australia, and many of the estates and wineries are still in the hands of the families who founded them. The region may be roughly divided into three: the Hunter River, **Corowa** and the **Murrumbidgee** irrigation area. Penfolds, Lindeman and McWilliam are the important producers of quality wines; some of the estates are Cawarra, **Ben Ean**, **Dalwood**, Glen Elgin, **Mount Pleasant**, Rosehill, Happy Valley, Bellevue, Tyrrell's HVD and **Lake's Folly**.

In addition to sparkling wines, Australia also produces **pearl wines**, which are slightly more sparkling than *pétillant* wines but not fully *mousseux*. These are not usually seen outside their homeland, nor are Australian brandies; but one **liqueur**, Marnique, is occasionally found on export lists.

Austria   Both red and white wines are made in the east of Austria, although it is possibly the white that achieves most quality. There are several regions: the Burgenland, near the **Hungarian** border; the Danube area, including Krems and **Wachau**; the Weinviertel, north of Vienna, with the Vienna Woods vineyards and Gumpoldskirchen, and Styria, by the **Yugoslav** frontier. The Grüner Veltliner **grape** makes some of the best whites. The **Riesling**, **Rheinriesling**, **Muscat-Ottonel**, **Furmint** and **Gewürztraminer** are also used for good white wines, some of which have a touch of *pétillance* while young. The red wines are usually made from the Burgunder grape and, although they can be pleasant, they are not in the same class as the best whites. Around Vienna, numerous small country inns specialise in the *heurige* wines, made from local grape **varieties** such as Nussberger, Grinzinger, **Neuburger** and Sieveringer, which are offered for sale while they are very young by green boughs being hung outside the establishment.

One important event in wine history has been the work of Dr Lenz **Moser**, an Austrian, who evolved a method of training vines high, spaced out so that a **tractor** could cultivate them, and arranged up even steep slopes so that, without terracing, vines could be cultivated. His methods were much suspected when first put into practice but in fact the Lenz Moser method of **high cultivation** is now followed in many vineyards making white wines in other countries.

Austrian wine **labels** often bear descriptive terms, indicating that the grapes have been late vintaged or specially picked over. Personally, I feel that the character of such Austrian wines as I have tried is so dissimilar from the character of German wines that I rather deplore the tendency to imitate the German classics. The delicacy of Austrian wines is one of their charms and does not need to be masked by contrived sweetness. The young wines are delicious fragrant drinks, the well-known brand 'Schluck' (gulp) being popular, but the individuality of both reds and whites according to area and **winery** deserves developing. For travellers, the Austrian wine towns and village are wholly charming.

Auxerrois   See **Pinot.**

Auxey-Duresses   Village in the **Côte de Beaune**, **Burgundy**, making red and some white wines that can be very good. They certainly deserve serious attention when coming from a reputable source.

Avelsbach   Ruwer vineyard, of which the Altenberg, Herrenberg and Vogelsang sites are possibly the best known. The **Hohe Domkirche** of Trier, which owns certain portions of sites, puts the prefix 'Dom' on to their names. The **State Domain** owns the Hammerstein site.

Ay   (Pronounced 'Eye') See *blanc de noirs*, **Champagne**.

Ayl   (Pronounced 'Eyel') Wine village on the **Saar** of which the best-known site is Kupp.

B

B. and B.   This is **Bénédictine** and **brandy**, ready-mixed in the commercial version, or you can make up your own.

B.O.B.   The initials stand for 'Buyer's own brand' – the wine or spirit put out by a firm (**shipper** or merchant) under its own **label**, instead of bearing that of the establishment supplying it in the country of production. The term is most usually applied to house **Champagnes**.

B.V.   Short for **Beaulieu** vineyard in **California**, **U.S.**   The pronunciation of the first word, even in the American manner (Bowl-you) proved a deterrent to many potential customers, so these days the labels of this fine wine bear the initials B.V.

Bacardi   This is a brand name, and not just a type of white **rum**, but it is one of the most important in the world. Originally made in Cuba, it is now made in a number of countries, including Spain; but all the Bacardi drunk in the U.K. is imported from Nassau in the Bahamas.

Bacharach   One of the vineyards of the **Mittelrhein** situated on the left bank of the river, making wines which, although they seldom attain to even approximately the quality of the greatest of the Rheingau wines from the right bank further up the **Rhine**, can be very pleasant.

Backsberg   Wine estate at the foot of the Simonsberg, at the Cape in **South Africa**, making fine table wines.

Badacsóny   **Hungarian** district making fine white wines, with a long history of winemaking.

Baden   Region in the south-west of **Germany**, producing large quantities of red and white wines, which are not often seen on export lists. They have not, until recently, produced wines which achieve more than everyday quality on any significant scale, but improvements in winemaking and viticulture make it possible that this will not always be so. Up until the *Phylloxera*, Baden was the largest wine-producing region in Germany. There are some great estates and a variety of **grapes** is cultivated, although not a high proportion of **Riesling**. The main vineyards in the region are the Bodensee, Markgräflerland, Kaiserstuhl (nothing to do with the **Australian** vineyard of the same name), Ortenau,

Bergstrasse and Krachgau. In this region, as in **Württemberg**, *Weissherbst* is also made, a type of rosé.

Baden-Württemberg   This region in south **Germany** makes an enormous amount of wine, including large quantities of red and some rosé. As the inhabitants are the largest wine consumers in Germany, it is not surprising that comparatively little is exported, and in fact the bulk comes into the category of 'open wine' or **carafe** wine. A variety of **vines** are used: Trollinger and **Spätburgunder** (the **Pinot Noir**), for the better red wines; **Riesling**, **Traminer**, **Ruländer** (the Pinot Gris) and **Sylvaner** for the whites. The Spätburgunder makes a wine called *Weissherbst*, which is rather like a pale rosé. The best **Baden** wines come from the Ortenau, a region which extends north-east upwards from Offenburg to Baden-Baden, where there are some individual estates, probably the most famous being that of Schloss Stauffenburg. In **Württemberg** a pinkish wine, made from red and white **grapes**, is an easy carafe drink, but its name – *Schillerwein* – is supposed to refer to its flickering pinkish-gold colour and has nothing to do with the poet Schiller, whose name is also confusingly associated with Stuttgart.

Baerenfang   Literally 'the **liqueur** to catch bears' – because this golden-yellow liqueur, from East Prussia, is based on **honey**.

Bagaceiro   Portuguese version of **Marc**.

Balatón   The region of Lake Balatón, in **Hungary**, has a long tradition of winemaking. Wines made around here usually bear its name on the **labels**.

Balblair   Whisky distillery at Edderton, Tain, Ross-shire, in what has been called 'the parish of peats' – hence the flavour of this particular malt.

Balling   South African method of measuring the sugar content or ripeness of the **grapes**. It is measured with a **saccharometer**, calibrated so as to show the density of the liquid – the saccharometer floats in the **must** and the level of the liquid is read against the degree on the instrument. One degree Balling equals 1% total extract, this consisting of sugar, acid and other non-sugar extracts. See **Baumé**, **Gay Lussac**, **Oechsle**, **proof**, **strength**.

Balmenach-Glenlivet   Distillery at Cromdale, Grantown-on-Spey. It is recorded that it made **whisky** which used to be bottled for the Gairloch Hotel, for the use of Queen Victoria and her entourage.

Balthazar   See **bottle**.

Balvenie   (Pronounced 'Bal-vee-ny' stressing 'vee') **Whisky distillery** at Dufftown, Banffshire, built by William Grant from the stones of the former castle of Balvenie. The twin distillery is **Glenfiddich**. Although the two distilleries are fed by the same spring, the two malts are markedly different in character. Derek Cooper, in his book, suggests that this is possibly due to the different design of the stills in the respective distilleries. But the difference is still one of the 'mysteries' that make great spirits, as well as great wines, fascinating.

Banana   See **crème de banane**.

Bandol   Wine region in **Languedoc**, in the south of **France**, producing red, white and rosé wines. Up until recently these have been considered purely 'holiday' wines, but great strides have been made in improving their quality and the wines from individual estates are of interest: many attain true quality, especially the reds. See **Provence**.

Banff   At Mill of Banff, this **distillery** contributes to the **whisky** blends of the **D.C.L.**

Banyuls   This is, strictly, a sweetish wine from the western Mediterranean **French** coast; but it can also be used as a generic name for sweetish wine-based **apéritifs** and *vins doux naturels*.

Barack Palinka   See **apricot liqueurs**.

Barbaresco   Piedmont red wine, made near the town of the same name in **Italy** from the **Nebbiolo grape**. Full, slightly soft (when mature) and generally pleasant.

Barbera   A black **grape**, much cultivated in **Italy**, where it is used in many blends and also for the wines that bear its name. It is especially successful in **Piedmont**, where the Barberas of **Asti**, Monferrato and Alba are well known. Barbera makes good red wines, though sometimes they need age to shed their astringency. Some *pétillant* and slightly sweet Barberas may also be found locally.

Bardolino   Wine from the **Veneto** region of **Italy** from vineyards extending along Lake Garda, made from the Corvina and Negrara grapes, plus Molinara and **Rondinella**, it is a bright red in colour, with great charm because of its fresh, supple character. Its crisp, appealing fragrance is particularly delightful if it is not served tepid. It was a favourite of the early 20th century caricaturist and writer, Max Beerbohm.

Barolo   One of the greatest red wines of **Italy** made in the *commune* of Barolo in southern **Piedmont**, and entirely from the **Nebbiolo grape**. It is capable of great improvement with age, and some people liken it to a red **Burgundy.** But, although it has the same sort of gentle, expansive style, it is quite different, slightly tougher and more initially assertive, with a curious fragrance that has been known to remind commentators of tar and violets. Its alcoholic **strength** can reach the upper limits for table wines.

Barossa Valley   Important South **Australian** vineyard area, north of Adelaide. It was named after a village called Barrosa *(sic)* near Cadiz, where the English forces defeated the French in the Peninsular campaign against Napoleon. A wide range of table wines and **brandy** is made.

Barsac   Region south of **Bordeaux**, adjoining that of **Sauternes**, where the great sweet wines are made. But the Barsacs have a curious and individual flavour, with a 'lift' which finishes virtually dry. The two great properties are **Coutet** and **Climens**.

Basilicata   Sometimes also known as **Lucania**, this is the region of the instep on **Italy**'s 'boot', producing a range of wines, most of which go up to the north for blending. The red **Aglianico** del Vulture (the wine is named for the local mountain) is, however, well reputed.

Basquaise   The flattish, flagon-like **bottle** that is used for many of the **Armagnacs**.

Batailley   Classed 5th growth of **Pauillac** making very firm, full wine. See **Bordeaux, classification**.

Bâtard-Montrachet   See **Puligny-Montrachet**.

Baumé   (Pronounced 'Bow-may') Measurement of sugar in wine: 1° Baumé is approximately equal to 0.6oz (18g) of sugar to each 1.76 pt (litre) of wine. A luscious table wine may have 3-5° Baumé, a fairly dry wine about 1° Baumé. With **fortified** or certain specially made **dessert wines**, the degrees Baumé may be very much higher, but they are subject to controls, so as not to risk distorting the essential character of the wine. This is why the term 'dry', whether relating to **sherry** in the *fino* range, or in a flowery-smelling table wine, is both variable and a matter of personal preference. One firm's 'dry' may be somebody else's 'medium'.

Béarn   This is the old French name for the region in the south-west of **France**, adjoining Gascony and abutting on the Pyrenees. Red, white and pink wines have been made there for centuries; the best known is probably the sweet white **Jurançon**, although nowadays there is more dry white made. One is often told about fine wines, of proud traditions and historic associations, being produced in minute quantities, but I have never found these and it is possible that there was never anything of outstanding quality made in the region – had there been, it would probably have survived.

The reds tend to be rather harsh and 'peasanty' in character; the pink wines pleasant holiday drinks; both dry and sweet white are agreeable. I would hazard a guess that, if you want a superior wine made in this part of the world, you would find better quality over the border in **Spain** – the French wines of further north (Bordeaux) will be what the locals often drink today.

Beaujolais   The region lying south of **Mâcon** along the west bank of the River Saône just to the north of Villefranche, in **France**, which produces red wine specially celebrated for its quaffability. 'Empty the casks!' is the motto of the Beaujolais **wine fraternity**. Most of the wine is red and is from the **Gamay grape**, although nowadays a little white is made. See **St Véran**. It has a beautiful bright red colour, with a fresh **bouquet** and fruity flavour. It is seldom a wine to benefit by age, although there are occasional exceptional years when it can be kept if from an outstanding region or vineyard; 10 years is certainly a long life for a Beaujolais, and most of it should be drunk young. But by 'young' several different things can be meant: 2 or 3 years is acceptable for good Beaujolais, certainly for an ordinary district wine, as compared to a 'growth' or *commune* Beaujolais or one from a single estate.

The fact that the season's new wine can be delicious drunk straight from the **cask** has resulted in a vogue for this very thing and, to cater for the restaurant taste in first Lyons, then Paris (where the arrival of the new wine would be announced by posters), and nowadays Britain, some of the wine is made specifically to be drunk very young indeed – the vinification is special. Beaujolais, Beaujolais Supérieur and Beaujolais-Villages may be sold as *Nouveau*, usually from 15 November. The wines of the specific growths or *crus* may not be sold until 15 December. In recent years much publicity has been

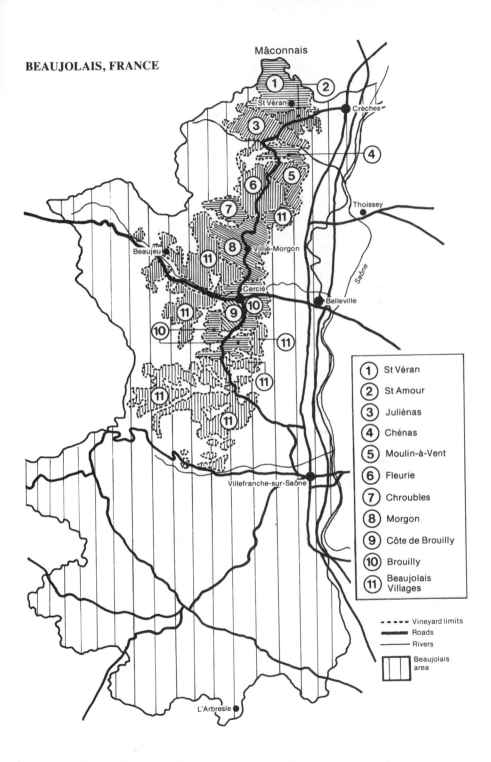

BEAUJOLAIS, FRANCE

Mâconnais

St Véran

Crèches

Thoissey

Saône

Beaujeu

Villié-Morgon

Cercié

Belleville

Villefranche-sur-Saône

L'Arbresle

1 St Véran
2 St Amour
3 Juliénas
4 Chénas
5 Moulin-à-Vent
6 Fleurie
7 Chroubles
8 Morgon
9 Côte de Brouilly
10 Brouilly
11 Beaujolais Villages

- - - - - Vineyard limits
━━━━━ Roads
───── Rivers
Beaujolais area

given to the 'race' of shippers to get their wine to the various outlets in time, but in fact this activity is quite unnecessary – the wine can be moved in the normal way, it is only that it cannot be sold prior to the agreed date (which is sometimes altered). My own view is that, on its home ground, very young Beaujolais can be delicious, but by Christmas it may be tired and without charm – and even fizzing or bitter in the New Year! In many years when really good Beaujolais can be made, shippers may prefer to keep their wines for this 'real thing'. In indifferent years, the *Nouveau* wines appear in abundance and are at least drinkable for a few months.

Made in the normal way, an ordinary young Beaujolais is delicious when a year old and it and a *Beaujolais de l'année*, a wine offered for drinking within a year of its **vintage**, may be served chilled; this imitates the temperature at which it would be if brought straight from the cellar and polishes up the freshness of the wine.

CATEGORIES OF BEAUJOLAIS: In ascending order of quality they are: Beaujolais, Beaujolais Supérieur, Beaujolais-Villages (the wines from 30 *communes*, which may join their names with that of Beaujolais), and the 'growths' or '*crus*': **St Amour**, Juliénas, **Chénas** (final 's' pronounced in both these names), **Moulin-à-Vent**, Fleurie, **Chiroubles**, Morgon, **Brouilly**, and Côte de Brouilly. Each of these has characteristics of its own, but it is worth remembering that the wines of Morgon are usually the toughest and can last longer than most Beaujolais; those of Juliénas are very fruity; those of Fleurie both flowery and fruity; those of Moulin-à-Vent are full but possess a certain elegance; those of Brouilly and Côte de Brouilly have a full but slightly 'steely' style; those of Chiroubles have great fruit and lightness.

Beaujolais is always worth a separate categorisation on the wine list. It is very much an enjoyable everyday wine and can be a fine wine, but the real thing cannot be cheap – certainly not nowadays. True Beaujolais has the fruity smell of the **Gamay** and the refreshing flavour of this **grape** and no stickiness, heaviness or coarse fat flavour belongs in this excellent wine.

Beaujolais blanc A small quantity of white wine is made in the Beaujolais, from the **Chardonnay grape**. It enjoys much popularity, doubtless because of its scarcity, but I admit to finding it a dull drink, never more than adequate in quality. See **St Véran**.

Beaulieu (Pronounced 'Bowl-you') As the word is supposedly difficult for the American public, a range of brand names, usually incorporating the prefix 'Beau' are in use, or just initials. See **B.V.** It is a famous **California** vineyard in the **Napa Valley**, founded at the beginning of the 20th century by Georges de Latour, and still run by his family. Table wines, **sparkling wine** and a type of **sherry** are made, and the quality of all is very high indeed. Beaulieu wines are available in the U.K., having been selected as outstanding by Averys of Bristol.

N.B. The two **English vineyards** established at Beaulieu (pronounced 'Bew-ley') in Hampshire, producing good white and rosé wines in recent years, should not be confused with the Californian Beaulieu.

Beaumes de Venise   Town in the Vaucluse in the south-eastern region of the **Rhône** in **France**, famous for its wines made from the **Muscat grape**. They are sweet in a concentrated but not cloying way and, chilled, are very pleasant **dessert wines**. See *Vin doux naturel.*

Beaune   Centre of the **Burgundy** vineyards, notable for the firm red wines bearing its name, the fine whites and also for the **Hospices de Beaune**. Some of the site names of Beaune that are well known are: Les Marconnets, Les Fèves, Les Bressandes, Les Grèves, Les Teurons, Les Perrières, Les Épenots, Clos des Mouches, Les Vignes Franches, but the list is long. Beaune Fèves and Beaune Grèves are usually considered very good, a well-known plot in the latter being the Vigne de l'Enfant Jésus. Beaune Clos de la Mousse is part of the Marconnets vineyard. It is important not to confuse the **A.O.C.** Beaune with that of **Côte de Beaune Villages**, which is completely different and includes a number of other well-known names.

Beaunois   Local name used in **Chablis** for the **Chardonnay grape**.

Beauséjour   This property, in the *Côtes* region of the *Premiers Grands Crus Classés* of **St Émilion**, was partitioned between Messrs. Duffau and Fagouet when it was divided. Its wines are usually pleasing and of engaging, often fine quality. The Fagouet section is the largest.

Beerenauslese   This term is usually only associated with **German** wines but is sometimes applied to others. It means 'selected berries', and implies that the **grapes** have been picked out individually, not by bunches, for their quality and maturity and that the wine made from them will be full and sweet, but of delicacy and charm – and may be expensive.

Beeswing   Curious form of **deposit** occasionally found in **port**. It does look exactly like a section of insect's wing, but in fact it is the tissues of the grape flesh. Some writers say it can occur in red table wines, but I only know of it in connection with port and am informed that, with the scientific and hygienic methods of winemaking today, it is now very rare.

Belair   One of the *Premiers Grands Crus* of **St Émilion**, in the *Côtes* region. The estate is of ancient foundation and, according to tradition, one of its owners (then the English Governor of the region) received the surrender of the great French warrior, Bertrand du Guesclin, who remained his prisoner on parole at Libourne. In the 19th century its wines became famous and, for some while, Belair disputed with its neighbour, Château **Ausone**, the right to be the great wine of the area. Today its wines, not widely seen on export lists, are nevertheless esteemed for their quality plus a certain refinement they can achieve in some **vintages**.

Belgrave   Classed 5th growth of St Laurent which, as this parish has no **A.O.C.**, bears the A.O.C. Haut-Médoc. As it adjoins the **St Julien** boundary, it was at one time considered to be a St Julien. Some people like to think that the name – common, however, to several other properties – was the origin of the name of Belgrave Square in London. See **Bordeaux, classification**.

Bellarmine   Fat-bellied glazed jug, used for serving drinks. Its name derives from that of Cardinal Bellarmine (1542-1621), a famous lover of the good

27

things of life. It appears to have been in use in Britain from about the beginning of the 18th century. It would now be something of a rarity, but the word does occasionally feature in the world of antiques.

Bellet   Wine region in **Provence** in the south of **France**, producing red, white and rosé wines. These are seldom seen on export lists, but they can make very agreeable drinking for those on holiday in the region.

Bellingham   **South African** wine estate near Wellington, making fine table wines. The property is particularly beautiful.

Ben Ean   The **winery** of this name in the **Pokolbin** region of **Australia** was established by John Mcdonald in 1870. It was bought by Frederick **Lindeman** in 1912 and is now one of the most important centres for Lindeman's in the **Hunter Valley**. The name is used in conjunction with their **Mosel**.

Ben Nevis   This **distillery**, at Lochy Bridge, Fort William, makes both malt and grain **whisky**. The former owner, Long John Macdonald, who built it in 1825, has his name commemorated in the concern of Long John Distilleries.

Ben Wyvis   Invergordon Distillers opened both a malt and grain **distillery** at Invergordon in 1965, some of the **whisky** going into fine quality **blends**.

Bénédictine   This **liqueur** was evolved in 1510 by the Benedictine monk, Dom Bernardo Vincelli, at Fécamp in Normandy. It became famous as a medicine against malaria, then prevalent around the monastery in the swampy countryside. Although the Abbey at Fécamp was destroyed in the French Revolution, the recipe was preserved and the liqueur is still made in the rebuilt establishment. It is a type of **digestive**. The initials D.O.M., on every bottle, stand for *Deo Optimo Maximo* (To God most good, most great). See **B. and B.**

Benicarlo   Full, robust red wine from Valencia, in **Spain**, formerly often used to augment even fine **clarets** and give them the sort of taste liked by the undiscriminating public.

Benmarl   Small estate in **New York State**'s **Hudson River Valley**, making a variety of wines that seem well reputed.

Benriach-Glenlivet   **Distillery** at Longmorn, Elgin, Morayshire, producing **whisky** used in several well-known **blends**.

Benrinnes   **Whisky** distillery on the slopes of Ben Rinnes at Aberlour.

Benromach-Glenlivet   **Whisky** distillery belonging to the **D.C.L.** at Forres, Morayshire.

Bereich   See **German Wine Law**.

Bergamottelikoer   German **liqueur** based on bergamot, an aromatic herb often used in drinks. It is yellowish-green in colour and slightly citrus-flavoured.

Bergerac   Region in the south-west of **France** about 80 miles (128 km) east of **Bordeaux**, making both red and white wines and some **sparkling wine** (Pécharmant). The best known is probably **Monbazillac**, a golden, sweetish wine, formerly very popular before the prevailing fashion for dry drinks. The chalky **soil** of most of the region is conducive to the making of pleasant, lightish wines, very acceptable at moderate prices on export markets nowadays.

Beringer   **Winery** in the north of the **Napa Valley** in **California**, in production since 1879. As it made **communion wine**, it was able to keep going during **Prohibition**.

Berlinerweiss   Lightly alcoholic drink, of a fizzy type, based on raspberries, and usually served in a glass rather like a gigantic **Champagne** saucer.

Bernkastel   This is a picturesque town, linked by a bridge with its twin, Kues (Cues) across the **Mosel**. The wines are justly renowned, possessing both immediate charm and freshness and nobility. Some of the better-known sites are: Badstube, Braunes, Rosenberg, Schlossberg, and Graben; but the most famous is the great Doktor, which rises directly behind Bernkastel. Its name is supposed to derive from the time when one of the Prince Bishops of Trier was cured of an illness by the wine. The Bernkasteler Doktor site is owned principally by Deinhard of Coblenz, other portions belonging to Wwe. Thanisch and F. Lauerberg. The wines usually command very high prices. The spelling 'Doktor' is traditional and the Nazis enforced its use, so today most owners have retained it, although the Thanisch establishment uses 'Doctor'.

Bernkastel-Kues   See **Bernkastel**. The wines of the **Cusanusstift**, or St Nikolaus Hospital, come from some of the fine wine vineyards. Other famous sites are Johannisbrünchen, Cardinalsberg, Lay, Rosenberg and Paulinshofberg.

Berri   **Co-operative winery** and **distillery** in the Berri-Parmera region on the **Murray River** in **Australia**. A huge range of wines is made, many of them much praised. The outsider must comment that it seems a pity to continue using classic wine names, such as 'port', 'sherry', 'Moselle', 'sparkling Burgundy' and so on, when the **grapes** are often totally unrelated to those that make the European originals. One must reasonably assume that the character of the wines is different as well. But those who enjoy the Berri wines may think this an ungracious comment.

Beychevelle   Classed 4th growth of **St Julien** and one of the well-known **clarets**, additionally reputed by reason of the size of the property and its beautiful gardens. The name comes supposedly from the expression *Baissez les voiles* ('Strike sails'), the salute exacted from ships passing up or down the **Gironde** from the time when the Grand Admiral of France, the Duc d'Épernon, lived there and required the gesture to be made. This is why there is a ship on the label. See **Bordeaux, classification**.

Bianco   This Italian word means 'white' and is often used to differentiate Italian wines that otherwise have the same name as those that are red or pink. Its most celebrated use, however, must certainly be in connection with **vermouth**. A vermouth that is *bianco* is supposed by large numbers of people to be dry – I suppose because of its light colour   but in fact the majority of all *biancos* of this type are definitely sweet. Of course, each vermouth house makes its own individual style of vermouth and the character of each *bianco* varies. But the *biancos* are usually much sweeter than the ordinary dry white type of vermouth.

Bin   **Rack**, shelf or holder for the storage of **bottles** on their sides. A 'bin end' is an odd lot of wine that may feature on a list as a sale bargain. 'To bin' means to store wine in tiers. Nowadays, metal racks make this easy but until recently odd spaces in cellars had to be filled with wines ranged on top of each other, only with the aid of lathes. Binning of this kind requires great skill — for it should be possible to walk on the top of a properly 'set' bin, even if this is 4-5 ft (1.2-1.5m) high. Also it should be possible to withdraw a single bottle from far down the tiers without any subsidence. Good binning is a cellar form of architecture.

Bingen Important wine region in the **Nahe** valley, in **Germany**.

Birnengeist German pear **liqueur**. See *alcool blanc*.

Bischöfliches Konvikt Usually shortened to 'Konvikt' (or 'hostel'), this is one of the three religious establishments at Trier, on the **Mosel**. It owns six major estates in the Mosel, as well as possessing many interests in the wine trade and enjoying a high reputation for its wines. See **Hohe Domkirche**.

Bischöfliches Priesterseminar The seminary (training college) for priests at Trier, in the **Mosel**. It owns seven estates: three in the Mosel, three in the **Saar** and one in the **Ruwer**. Originally these were bought with a gift from the Elector Clemens Wenzeslaus in 1773. See **Hohe Domkirche**.

Bishop This is a hot drink, consisting of **port**, simmered with an orange stuck with cloves and slightly sweetened. Lemon, ginger, cinnamon and allspice can also be added to taste. For Cardinal, **claret** is substituted for the port; for Pope, **Champagne** is used.

Bitters As the name implies, bitter tasting drinks which are usually assumed to have tonic or slightly medicinal properties. The most famous are possibly **Angostura, Campari, Underberg, Ferro China** and **Fernet Branca**. Bitters are well known as pick-me-ups but, in Italy, the huge range of them available is not only due to their **digestive** properties but because many Italians believe them to have **aphrodisiac** properties. Bitters are sometimes merely used as additives to other drinks. The older word for bitters is **elixir** which is why **Martini & Rossi**'s brand name for their bitters is 'Elixir Martini'. See **Amer Picon, orange bitters, peach bitters, Toni Kola**.

Bittertropfen Literally 'bitter drops', this German herb **liqueur** is used to season mixed drinks.

Blaauwklippen **Stellenbosch** wine estate in **South Africa**, under **vines** since 1692; the handsome house was built at the end of the 18th century. As well as making wines, it produces cheeses and also contains a museum.

Black Malvoisie See **Cinsaut**.

Black Velvet Half-and-half **Champagne** and Guinness. Scorned by some, it is nevertheless a nourishing and comforting sort of drink. It is also sometimes known as a 'Bismarck'. Cyril Ray says it was first made at Brook's Club in London.

Black wines See **Cahors**.

Bladnoch The most southern **whisky distillery** for malt in Scotland, at Bladnoch, Wigtownshire.

Blagny A red wine made in the **Côte de Beaune**. Not to be confused with **Meursault-Blagny**, which is a white wine from the same region.

Blair Athol **Distillery** at Pitlochry, founded in 1826 but certainly a place where distilling had been in progress for years before that. It now belongs to Arthur Bell (whose Scotch is the top selling **whisky** in Scotland).

Blanc de blancs Literally 'white from whites', that is, a white wine made only from white **grapes**. The term is mainly associated with such **Champagnes** as are made solely from the **Chardonnay** or **Pinot Blanc** grapes and are very light and elegant; what might be categorised as 'morning Champagnes'. Unfortunately the fictional character James Bond made this type of Champagne very fashionable – although he knew little about wine – and it is by no means invariably 'the best'. As a result, many other wines make more use of the term nowadays; sometimes absurdly, as with a straight **Sauvignon** labelled *blanc de blancs*. How could a white wine, made from one white grape, be anything else?

Blanc de noirs A white wine made from black **grapes**. As most grape juice is vaguely grapefruit-juice colour (the only exceptions being certain types of grapes known as *teinturiers* and not widely used), it is quite possible to make a white wine from black grapes if the skins of the grapes are not allowed to tint the **must**. In the **Champagne** region, such a wine may sometimes be found, the most notable being some of the wines of Ay. Whereas many Champagnes made solely from black grapes can be heavy and too assertive to be charming, the Ay wines possess great finesse and delicacy.

Blanc fumé The local name used in the upper **Loire** for the **Sauvignon grape** that is used for the quality wines. The most famous of these is **Pouilly** Blanc Fumé, but white **Sancerre** is also made from the Sauvignon.

Blanco Spanish for 'white'.

Blanquette See **Mauzac**.

Blanquette de Limoux The region making wines of this name is near Carcassonne, in the south-west of **France**. There is a still white wine made, but the most famous wine is the **sparkling** white, made by the **Champagne method**. The **grape** used is the **Mauzac** which, because of the white underside of its leaves, gives the curious name of *blanquette* to the wines. The winemakers have registered the sparkling wine as *le plus vieux brut du monde* and they claim that, because of their proximity to the Catalan and Iberian **cork** oak forests, they were able to seal the sparkle in their vivacious wines even before Dom Pérignon did this in the 17th century in **Champagne**.

Blauer Portugieser Although other names are Oporto in **Hungary**, and Oporto Rebe in **Germany**, this black **grape** is of Austrian origin. It appears to be cultivated in various regions, including the **Tarn**. It can also be used as a table grape.

Blauer Spätburgunder This black **grape**, possibly originating in **Burgundy**, is a late ripener as its name implies. It was first planted in **Germany** in the 14th century. See **Pinot Noir**.

Blaye Wine region of **Bordeaux**, producing both white and red wines, usually of no more than good everyday quality.

Blaxland, Gregory One of the pioneers of the **Australian** wine business. Sometime between 1816-18 he planted **vines** in the Parramatta Valley, that he had brought from the Cape of Good Hope. In 1822 he shipped a pipe of red wine, **fortified** with **brandy**, to London: this was awarded a Silver Medal by the Society for the Encouragement of the Arts in 1823. In 1828 he was given the gold 'Ceres Medal'. His work on **grape varieties** was of the greatest importance in these early days.

Bleasdale   South **Australian** vineyard, near Langhorne Creek.

Blend   This word has come to mean something that is condemned as wrong in the minds of those who know little or nothing about wine – because of the occasional 'exposures' in the newspapers of wines **cut** with wines other than those of the name on the label. But, unless a wine is made from one single vinestock (see **vine**), it will be obvious to the sensible that every single wine is a blended **wine** in one way or another. A wine may be made from a blend of **grapes**, the different *cuvées* or vattings may be blended together when a quantity of wine is made on the same property; the wine of one **vintage** may be blended with that of another to the improvement of both – as occurs with most **Champagne** and many **sparkling wines**, also with the good branded wines or *vins de marque* for everyday drinking; and the wine of several small plots may be blended together to improve the whole, sold under the name of the overall vineyard (see **Burgundy**). All **sherry** is a blend, all **port** except for vintage port, all **Madeira** except for the very occasional vintage wines. To sneer at a wine as 'a blended wine' is to reveal that one knows nothing about the way wine is made.

What, occasionally, people can fairly complain of, is the blending in of wines from regions outside that of the region named on the **label**. But as this 'stretching' enables passable wine to be made in some years or in some vineyards where otherwise this could not happen, and as the public taste can bring pressure on growers as well as shippers to alter the character of their wines, the whole question is complex and debatable. The strict control of what may be stated on the label is, in theory, admirable. But what about the customers who will not pay a fair price for a genuine wine, such as **Chablis**, or who would not like the real thing at all if they got it? Ideally, nobody should 'drink the label' or, equally, the name. But people do and, at least as far as public companies in the wine trade are concerned, they must attempt to make a profit by satisfying public demand. The blending of wine, such as making the *cuvée* in Champagne, is a skilled and delicate business; the blending of **Cognac** likewise. It is right to speak of the art of the blender and it is paying tribute to him to pay a fair price for wines and spirits and obtain them from a reputable source, whether from a large concern or a small one.

Blind   To 'taste blind' is to **taste** without having any prior knowledge — or possibly only an indication — as to what is being tasted. This means that whatever is in the **glass** must be appraised without regard to its reputation, price or anything except what the wine (or spirit) can actually 'say' to the taster. It is illuminating to do this, because, however much a taster thinks he is uninfluenced by a wine's **label**, personal preferences or the sort of prejudices that may have been formed about certain wines, it is impossible to clear one's mind of all these things. The wine as seen 'naked' can be a disappointment or a revelation of delight.

However, there is a tendency, among the enthusiastic, to indulge too much in blind tasting, in my opinion. It can be discouraging if a taster lacks wide experience, so as to have an inkling, for example, as to whether a wine is of an 'off' vintage, or whether an estate may have recently been replanted, or whether the method of vinification may have been radically altered. All these things can affect the verdict of the blind taster, but may be intelligent 'mistakes' even if the taster does not divine what the wine is. If you do not know why you have gone wrong, or cannot interpret what the wine has 'told' you, it is easy to think that you cannot taste well.

What is of importance is for serious winelovers to taste blind wines that they think they can recognise: between brand and brand, detecting **vintages**, working out specific **grapes** or classic areas. Indeed, this type of exercise is stimulating when the tasters know what the wines are and taste them first being aware what each one is. Later the bottles are masked and changed in order, so that the second part of the tasting is blind. It can enable people to register certain smells and taste sensations, regardless of anything else. But wines selected for this purpose should be straightforward – it is always possible to catch even the experienced with a wine not quite typical, or some novelty. Or, if you taste only from the list or from the establishment of one single merchant or maker, you may rely too much on his house style, which may not be as typical as you suppose; so other wines, within the same price range, should be put alongside those that the taster supposes he already knows.

It must be emphasized that an ability to taste blind does not constitute an overall great knowledge of an authority in wine – it is a great skill and can be a great pleasure. What is perhaps the most surprising thing about tasting blind, is the revelation that some **wine experts** are almost lost without knowing what a wine is: whereas beginners, lacking even the words to express their impressions, can be far more interesting and intelligent about expressing what they experience.

Boal   See **Bual, Madeira**.

Boca   Red **Italian** wine from the Novara Hills in **Piedmont**, made with a high proportion of the **Nebbiolo grape** (called Spanna in this area). The wine benefits greatly from maturation in **bottle**, when it achieves considerable quality.

Bocksbeutel   The dumpy green flagon-like **bottle** used for the finer wines of **Franconia** in **Germany**, the Maerwein of Neuweier in **Baden**, and for some Chilean white wines. The name is supposed to derive from the wineskin in which wines were once carried; other associations include the carrier-bag used by German housewives, and the scrotum of a goat. Modified versions of the *bocksbeutel* are used for other wines from various regions.

Bodega   Store for wine in the **sherry** district of **Spain**.

Bomfim, Quinta do   This belongs to the great **port** house of **Warre**, and is at Pinhão, on the River Douro.

Bommes District within the great white wine region of **Sauternes** in the **Bordeaux** area. The most famous vineyards, making sweet white wines, are Châteaux **Lafaurie-Peyraguey**, La Tour Blanche, Rayne-Vigneau, **Rabaud-Promis**, and Rabaud-Sigalas.

Bonarda The full name of this red wine is Bonarda dell'**Oltrepò Pavese** and it comes from **Lombardy** in **Italy**.

Bonesio Winery in the **Santa Clara Valley**, in **California**, **U.S.**

Bonfoi **South African** wine estate in the **Stellenbosch** region.

Bonnezeaux (Pronounced 'Bon-zo') Region within the **Côteaux du Layon** vineyard area in the **Loire**, in **France**, making wines of a fullness and lusciousness that can be very attractive. They are mostly famous for their sweet wines but some are made which, although full, are essentially dry.

Bontemps The small wooden bowl in which eggwhites were whisked for **fining** the wines in former times in the f3Gironde region. Today it gives its name to the **Bordeaux wine order**, the Commanderie du Bontemps du Médoc et des Graves, whose officers wear a toque-like hat with a crown of white fabric – to represent the eggwhites.

Boonekamp A general German name for bitter **liqueurs**, mostly of a **digestive** nature. Some are supposed to have aperient qualities as well.

Boordy Vineyard **Winery** in Maryland, **U.S.**, of fairly recent foundation.

Bordeaux This is the region around the town of this name in the west of **France**, sometimes also known as the **Gironde**, according to French département traditions, whereby the area is named for its principal river. The Bordeaux region is responsible for more fine wine than any other of the French wine areas. It produces red, dry white and sweet white wines and a little **sparkling wine**. Those who especially love the wines of Bordeaux will affirm that there is at least one among them to suit every occasion and partner any food. The area is extensive and the range of wines considerable – it is this variety that accounts for the endless discussions about the table wines of Bordeaux.

The main regions – which should be referred to under their separate headings – are: **Médoc**, **Graves**, **St Émilion**, **Pomerol**, **Entre-Deux-Mers**, **Premières Côtes de Bordeaux**, **Bourg**, **Blaye**, **Sauternes**, **Barsac**, Graves de Vayres, **Fronsac**, **Loupiac**, **Cérons**, **Sainte Croix du Mont**, **St Foy Bordeaux** and a few others, such as the St Émilion vineyards that preface this name with Lussac, Graves, Sables, **St Georges** and Montagne. There are also the parishs or *communes* of the Médoc: **Moulis**, Listrac, **Margaux**, **St Julien**, **Pauillac** and **St Estèphe** being the most important, into which this area is subdivided. The **Sauternes** region is also divided like this: important names being **Bommes**, Fargues, Preignac, also Illats and Podensac.

The word 'claret', used only in the U.K. for the red wines of Bordeaux, comes from *clairet*, a medieval word for a iight coloured (*clair*) wine. This phrase was originally used to differentiate the true red Bordeaux wines from those of the hinterland, often deep in tone, which were shipped through the port of Bordeaux. Recently there was a problem when the EEC attempted to

BORDEAUX AND BERGERAC, FRANCE

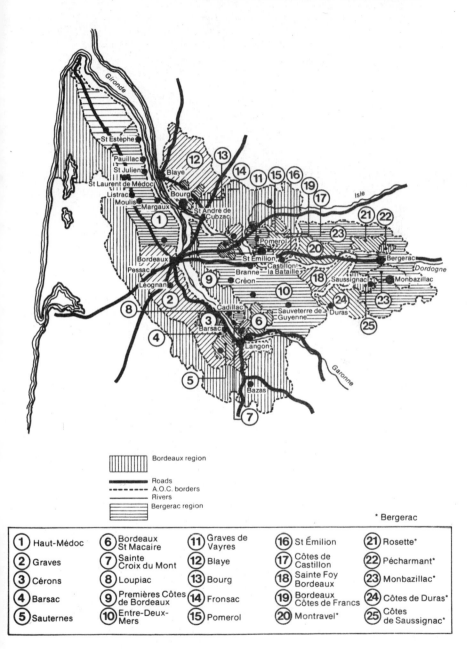

Bordeaux region

Roads
A.O.C. borders
Rivers
Bergerac region

* Bergerac

1 Haut-Médoc
2 Graves
3 Cérons
4 Barsac
5 Sauternes

6 Bordeaux St Macaire
7 Sainte Croix du Mont
8 Loupiac
9 Premières Côtes de Bordeaux
10 Entre-Deux-Mers

11 Graves de Vayres
12 Blaye
13 Bourg
14 Fronsac
15 Pomerol

16 St Émilion
17 Côtes de Castillon
18 Sainte Foy Bordeaux
19 Bordeaux Côtes de Francs
20 Montravel*

21 Rosette*
22 Pécharmant*
23 Monbazillac*
24 Côtes de Duras*
25 Côtes de Saussignac*

ban the use of the word claret, but the British were able to prove its traditional usage on their wine **labels**, although all other countries use the term 'red Bordeaux'. **Clairette** is a different sort of wine.

In 1152 the heiress of Aquitaine, Eleanor, formerly wife of the King of France, married Henry Plantagenet who became Henry II of England in 1154. For 299 years the English crown held the Gironde, plus other properties that extended from the Loire to the Pyrenees and over to the edge of Burgundy. The English drank claret from that time and, even when they lost their holdings in France, they remained loyal to the red wines of Bordeaux. The Scots were also traditional claret drinkers. At one time, to drink red Bordeaux was a sign of adherence to the Stuart cause – those who accepted 'Dutch William' as King, chose other tipples from Dutch **gin** to **port**.

There always has been a debate among twentieth century drinkers as to whether claret or **Burgundy** is the world's greatest red wine and it is said with some truth that, whereas anyone with an adequate purse can drink a great claret every week or month, no one is likely to drink a great red Burgundy more than a few times in a decade. The larger area and enormous variety of Bordeaux wines put them within the reach of many buyers; although in recent times the demands of export markets – often for the sheer status symbol of the 'great names' on **labels** – plus the artificial exaggeration of prices, because of people buying 'for investment' (i.e. resale), have made the better clarets into extremely expensive wines. Even the great sweet wines, so long neglected, have also become sought after. This would not be a matter for regret, were one sure that the drinkers of these wines were buying them for enjoyment; but it is to be feared that the majority drink them to show off or put them away until the price they can command at auction will be very high.

The principal grapes used for red Bordeaux are: **Cabernet Sauvignon, Cabernet Franc**, **Merlot**, and **Petit Verdot**. For the white wines, the main grapes are the **Sauvignon, Sémillon** and **Muscadelle**. In the ordinary way, the wine is made by allowing the freshly-pressed **must** to become wine by the process of **fermentation**, then the wine is matured in **wood** until it is ready to be bottled. But this natural process is nowadays rendered more complex by certain techniques which do make it possible to produce drinkable wine in years that might previously have been complete losses, or yield sour wines that might be disagreeable. Subject to strict controls, some **chaptalisation** is permitted. The wine does not always mature in wood but often spends its pre-bottle life in a **vat** or tank of either stainless steel or a special type of concrete. Fermentation is controlled, so that the temperature of the fermentation vat does not rise dangerously high; the white wines are often subjected to the process of *débourbage* (cleansing) in their initial stages. The **hat** (mass of grape debris) is now only allowed to remain in the fermentation vat for a shortish time – if left several weeks, as in the past, the wines would be hard and take 20 or more years to 'come round', something wholly uneconomic nowadays. But modern **filtration** and surveillance enables much cleaner and more reliable wines to be made, so that winemaking is not a chancy business and wines can travel to climates through greater extremes of heat or cold than would previously have been possible.

It is the finest wines that have made the reputation of Bordeaux and it is they that get most publicity – both red and white. But, thanks to modern knowledge, there are now hundreds, possibly thousands, of smaller-scale Bordeaux wines that can give pleasure on export markets, as well as locally. The *commune* wines are also well made today. It must never be forgotten that, although certain of the greatest red Bordeaux, in outstanding years, can live as long if not longer than any other table wine and remain truly 'living', these are the exceptions. Age alone does not improve all wines. Curiously, the great years for the sweet whites of Bordeaux do not often coincide with the great **vintages** for the reds. Nor should it be assumed that, merely because some drinkers find claret the greatest red wine of all, the beginner will inevitably like or be impressed by it. Claret is not a wine to be casually chosen and, because it can made demands on the mind as well as the senses of the drinker, it is not the 'when-in-doubt' choice from the list. But the wines of Bordeaux merit exploration, both because of their interest and because they have been those that have established the standards of integrity and excellence for many of the most respected authorities on wine.

Borgoña   Term loosely used in the Iberian Peninsula to indicate a red wine of fairly robust and heavy character. It should not be assumed that there is any other resemblance to **Burgundy**.

Boschendal   Wine estate in the Groot-Drakenstein area of the Cape, **South Africa**. It has been under **vines** since the 17th century, when French Huguenots, among them some of the now famous de Villiers (prominent in Cape wine history), settled there. Today the house not only produces a range of wines but has an excellent restaurant. Visitors are also allowed to see the beautiful old house.

Botrytis cinerea   The Latin name for the fungus or mould that, given certain conditions, attacks certain **grapes** in certain regions. In France it is called *pourriture noble*, in Germany *edelfäule*, in Italy *muffa nobile*. In England it is usually referred to as 'noble rot', to differentiate it from the more usual type of grey rot that also attacks grapes to their detriment. *Botrytis* attacks grapes when outside conditions tend to be both warm and somewhat foggy, as can occur late in a vintage season. The grapes shrink, the skin contracting and resembling old, shrivelled suède, the juice inside each grape is concentrated, becoming intensely sweet, while the outside of each grape developes a fuzzy mould as on withered raisins quite dried up. If you taste a grape like this, it will, literally, melt in the mouth! Because the noble rot has to be allowed time to develop and affect the grapes, considerable risks are involved by leaving them on the vines. Sometimes, vineyard owners prefer to pick the grapes while the weather remains good and simply put all of them into the **vat** for fermentation.

If the noble rot grapes are to be picked, they have to be selected, usually one by one, in good years by small bunches, very seldom by the whole bunch, as *Botrytis* does not attack all the grapes in a bunch at the same time and at the same rate. This means that pickers have to be experienced in knowing exactly when a particular grape should be picked and, also, that the teams of workers often have to pass through a vineyard many times, picking a few grapes from each bunch at a time. All this makes for an expensive wine at the end. However, the greatest sweet wines are made in this way, in the **Quart de Chaume** region of the **Loire**, some in **Monbazillac**, as well as in **Germany** (the *trockenbeeren* and *beerenauslesen* wines) and some late harvested wines of **South Africa**, in addition to the **Sauternes**.

Some interesting experiments have been made in certain **U.S.** vineyards, where the *Botrytis* has been artificially induced, so as to act on fully ripe grapes; but it seems that, to date, this is still not wholly satisfactory. As in South Africa, many of the U.S. vineyards have climates that are dry rather than humid; unlike those of the **Gironde**, **Rhine**, **Mosel** and **Loire**, where early autumn mists encourage the action of the fungus.

Botticino   Red wine from the Brescia region in **Lombardy**, **Italy**, between the lakes of Iseo and Garda. Philip Dallas reports that it can contain up to 15% of wine from other regions and also several different **grapes** from **Piedmont**, the **Alto Adige** and **Tuscany**.

Bottles   Although up to the present time the choice of a bottle for a particular drink has enabled a huge variety of shapes and colours to be put on the market, the situation tends to be towards standardisation, both because of regulations governing the size and type of bottle for certain drinks, when there are any traditions associated with these, and because variations in bottles are increasingly difficult to obtain. The big manufacturers of bottles – and the small glass firms are nowadays fewer in number than before the war – devote most of their production to bottles for chemical purposes and, above all, for beer. There is a wish to make all bottles of standard contenance, (about 26 fl.oz (75cl) at the time of writing) no matter what shape, but this presents great problems. Winegrowers, **shippers** and spirit manufacturers who, for a century or more, have always been associated with certain types of bottles, rightly resent a move to do away with an individuality that makes it easy for the public to recognise their products at first glance. Also certain sizes have become accepted as suitable for certain liquids.

In addition, with wine it is virtually impossible to state that, because a bottle is a certain size, the contents will also be a certain exact amount: in bottling tiny variations inevitably occur, and while wines are being matured, some bottles may become **ullaged**. The amount of this can be negligible as far as the informed drinker of fine wine is concerned, but it would obviously be ridiculous for an **estate-bottled** wine, carefully matured for some years, to be rejected by the ignorant or even subjected to prosecution because it contained ½ fl. oz (15ml) less than its stated contents. If everything were bottled in one size of bottle, it might be possible to make an absolute ruling as regards permitted ullage, but clearly this state of affairs can never easily come to pass, although strenuous attempts at standardisation are being made within the EEC and elsewhere at the time of writing. Finally – which is often

COMPARISON OF BOTTLE CAPACITIES

The 'standard' wine bottle is frequently assumed to have a capacity of 75 centilitres (0.75 litre): nowadays, it may be 72 cl or even 70 cl. This contenance should be stated on the label. Traditionally, the Burgundy bottle has a capacity of 75-78 cl; Champagne has 78-80 cl (a magnum being two 'bottles' of Champagne, but a magnum of table wine would be slightly smaller). Rhine, Mosel and Alsace wines are between 70-72 cl. This simplified 'bottle scale' shows the approximate liquid contents in both metric (centilitres and litres) and Imperial (fluid ounces) measurements. The bottle size mostly used for wine bottled in the U.K. will be the 26²/₃ fl.oz. (75 cl) type. The litre size (35 fl.oz.) is increasing in popularity for inexpensive wines and often the larger size bottle is used in 'Duty Free' shops for both wines and spirits.

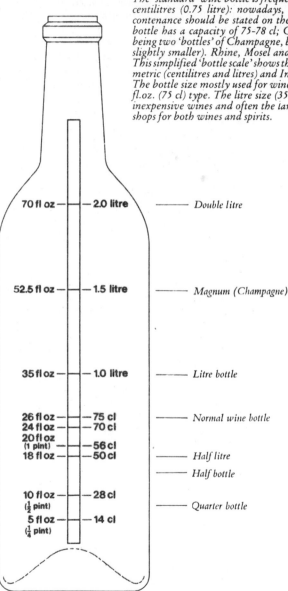

70 fl oz	2.0 litre	Double litre
52.5 fl oz	1.5 litre	Magnum (Champagne)
35 fl oz	1.0 litre	Litre bottle
26 fl oz	75 cl	Normal wine bottle
24 fl oz	70 cl	
20 fl oz (1 pint)	56 cl	
18 fl oz	50 cl	Half litre
		Half bottle
10 fl oz (½ pint)	28 cl	Quarter bottle
5 fl oz (¼ pint)	14 cl	

forgotten – the length of the **cork**, which also varies, takes up a varying amount of space, so when is a 'full' bottle full? Although until recently 26 fl. oz (75cl) was generally assumed to be the size of a 'standard' bottle, nowadays many table and **fortified wines** are put into 25 fl. oz (70cl) bottles.

As the following list of certain bottle sizes show, there are variations, often because of the shape of the bottle or, as with **sparkling wines** (which must have thicker bottles to resist the pressure inside), its thickness. Certain wines – such as **Tokay** and **Chianti** in a **flask** – are bottled in 17.5 fl. oz (50cl) and 35 fl. oz (1 litre) sizes respectively.

Type of traditional bottle	Fluid ounces	Approximate capacity Centilitres
Bordeaux	26	74/75
Burgundy	27	75/78
Champagne	28	80/81
Alsace	25½	72/73
Rhine	25	70/72

In the U.K. the standard **Bordeaux** and **Burgundy** bottles, filled to the cork, are accepted as 'reputed quarts'. This means that a case of 12 bottles of wine is equal to 2 gals (9 litres), which affects the calculated duty.

Colours of bottles are also, in the wine regions, controlled; but there are variations of tone of glass. In general, the type of colour has a purpose – wines that need shielding from the light, either because they are delicate or because they are to be laid down for some time, are usually bottled in dark-coloured glass, whether green or brown. Inexpensive wines or those that are to be drunk while young and fresh, tend to be bottled in pale or clear glass. Regional traditions are strong; for example, all **Rhine** wines are bottled in brown glass, all **Mosel** in green. The more usual regional bottles, with their special names, will be found under their separate entries.

It is worth stressing that it is always difficult to identify a bottle exactly, simply by looking at it. For example, the type of bottle used for quality **Chianti** that can improve in bottle is the square-shouldered sort, like that used for Bordeaux red wines; the shoulders of the bottle made the shape a good one for **binning** in the days when bottles supported themselves like the arches of a cathedral, instead of being binned in **racks**, and the angle of the shoulder would hold back any **deposit** before it could rush into the **glass** or **decanter**. But anyone just looking at a Chianti bottle of this type – or that of a fine red **Rioja** – would find it virtually impossible to distinguish the exact variations in measurements (though these exist) that differentiate it from a Bordeaux bottle. The sloping-shouldered bottle of the **Loire** also looks similar to that of Burgundy, although it isn't quite the same. This shape, and the elongated bottle used for German and some other wines, is one that has evolved for wines not usually long maturing in bottle or not throwing a very heavy deposit. They are more difficult to bin well in the traditional manner and, in general,

STANDARD BOTTLE SHAPES

Bordeaux (red & white)

Burgundy (red & white)

Rhine and Mosel

Champagne and sparkling wines

Alsace

Côtes de Provence

Chianti flask (½ or 1 litre)

Traditional port bottle

Bocksbeutel, for Franconian steinwein

sloping-shouldered bottles are for wines that seldom require long maturation or decanting. Large bottles, especially for cheap wines, are increasingly popular nowadays and the 35 fl. oz (1 litre) and 70 fl. oz (2 litre) are much used.

Large bottles		*bottles*
Champagne bottle sizes:	magnum	2
	jeroboam	4
	rehoboam	6
	methuselah	8
	salmanazar	12
	balthazar	16
	nebuchadnezzar	20
A *Bordeaux jeroboam* is		5
An *impériale* (sometimes used for fine claret) is		8
A *chiantigianna* (for Chianti)		3pt/1.75 litres

Gallon (4.5 litre) jars or even larger sizes, in the form of **demijohns** or carboys, are also much used.

Bottle age   This term means the period a wine has spent in **bottle**, during which it undergoes certain changes and can develop to advantage. Few wines are at their best when first bottled, although some regain their original freshness within a matter of weeks or even days. However the finer wines usually benefit by maturation in bottle and many, such as the great **clarets** and vintage **port**, can live in bottle for a lifetime, should their **vintage** and the way they have been made be propitious. In general most wines benefit from some bottle age: even non-vintage **Champagnes** improve with 6 months' additional maturation after the insertion of the second **cork**. Some small-scale wines improve likewise, but care should be taken not to leave them for long periods – most are made to be drunk while fairly young. Only experience and the advice of a wine merchant can provide reliable information about bottle age, but with any fine wine – white as well as red – the chance to gain some age in bottle can be a definite advantage and improve the ultimate quality. See **wood**.

Bottle stink   Term used to describe the rather stale, flat smell that sometimes comes off a wine immediately after the **bottle** has been opened – and that may, occasionally, give the impression that the wine is in some way 'off'. It is, in fact, the smell of the small amount of air that has been imprisoned in the bottle, maybe for a long time. **Decanting** will dissipate this or, if the wine is not to be decanted, leaving the cork drawn for a few minutes will allow the air from outside to get to the inside of the bottle and disperse the stale air. The **cork** can then be lightly replaced. It is advisable to do this with white wine as well – 5 or 10 minutes with the cork drawn, then replaced, can make a great difference to the initial impression made by some fine wines. Otherwise they may, at first pouring, seem dumb and dull. Many wines have been rejected as **'corked'** because of the drinker being confused by a disappointing first sip.

If a wine has to be tasted and either accepted or rejected immediately after the cork has been drawn – as can happen in a restaurant – then the **taster** should shake it around well in the glass, actually shaking it up as well as swinging it round, so as to air it as much as possible to get rid of any bottle stink before tasting. Ideally, after the **wine waiter** has presented the bottle, ask for the cork to be drawn at once and then, a few minutes later, request that the wine should be poured for appraisal.

Bouchet   Local name in the **St Émilion** region of Bordeaux for the **Cabernet grape**. The Cabernet Sauvignon is the Petit Bouchet, the Cabernet Franc the Gros Bouchet. Do not confuse this name with Bouschet, the surname of a man who evolved a number of hybrid vines, used for bulk cropping.

Bouchonné   French for 'corked'.

Boukha   This is an *eau-de-vie* made from figs, served as either an **apéritif** or **liqueur** in **Tunisia** and other north African countries. It is sometimes referred to as Mahia.

Bouquet   For this, I can do no better than quote the late Allan Sichel: 'The **aroma** is roughly speaking the smell of the taste, while the bouquet is the impersonal collection of smells given off by the wine, mostly the product of the maturing process and recognised by the **nose** alone. The one is a projection, the other the very substance itself.'

It is, however, a term used rather loosely by many, when what they often mean is just 'smell' – not the same thing. After some thought, the **taster** can work out the exact definition preferred, but in general the word refers to the 'collection of smells'. These may not always be pleasant, although certainly when the word 'bouquet' is used, the implication will be that it is a pleasant one. See **tasting terms.**

Bourbon   See **whiskey.**

Bourg; Côtes de Bourg   Regions in the **Bordeaux** area, on the east bank of the Garonne. Both red and white wines are produced, but it is the reds that now often feature on export lists. They can be well made and, by their sturdy robust style, appeal very much to **claret** lovers who enjoy a 'little' red Bordeaux for everyday drinking.

Bourgeois growth   See *cru*. The **classification** of the fine wines of **Bordeaux** is always being discussed, but alterations are often bitterly resented by owners. But many 'classed growths' are nowadays often only a very little superior in quality to the finest bourgeois growths, thanks to the care and skill devoted to cultivation and winemaking. There need be nothing to hesitate about in choosing a good bourgeois or, even, an artisan growth. Indeed it can be of the greatest interest to see how bourgeois growths mature, because, as they usually come on a little more rapidly than the classed growths, their performance can indicate what their more expensive neighbours may possibly do later as regards progress. A serious winelover would certainly prefer to drink a good bourgeois, possessing a growing reputation for quality, than a classed growth of an inferior vintage and the quality of which may, through mismanagement, have declined. The growths have been categorised, some being rated as 'exceptional', such as Chateau d'**Angludet**.

Bourgueil (Pronounced 'Bor-guy') Part of the **Touraine** region in **France**, producing red and some rosé wines made from the **Cabernet Franc grape**. Some people find a flavour of raspberries or violets in the wines. The fresh fruitiness of these wines is brought out by serving them cool – as is traditional in the region. See **St Nicolas de Bourgueil**.

Bouscaut Estate in the parish of Cadaujac in the **Graves**, south of **Bordeaux**, making good red and white wines. It now belongs to an American syndicate.

Bouschet See **Merlot**.

Bouzy Rouge The best-known still red wine of the **Champagne** region, for obvious reasons. But Bouzy makes still whites as well as reds, now both categorised as **Coteaux Champenois**.

Bowmore This **whisky distillery** was established in 1779, the oldest on the isle of Islay (pronounced 'Eye-ler').

Boyd-Cantenac Classed 3rd growth of **Margaux**, the wine itself being made at **Ch. Pouget**. See **Bordeaux, classification**.

Braes of Glenlivet Banffshire **whisky distillery**, built in 1973 and belonging to the mighty **Seagram** organisation. It contributes to various well-known blends nowadays: such as 'Passport' and '100 Pipers'.

Branaire-Ducru Classed 4th growth of **St Julien**, now owned by M. Tapie, formerly in the wine business in **Algeria**. See **Bordeaux, classification**.

Brand, Eric See **Redman**.

Branded cork See **corks**.

Brandewijn, **Brandywine** This latter term came into the English language in the 17th century. It was assumed by many who then used it to mean 'burnt wine', hence **brandy**, the distillate of wine. But, although in Holland the term *brandewijn* means a **distillate**, the base of this need not be a spirit resulting from the distillation of wine at all. See **Maltwine**. The old use of 'brandywine' was probably a general imprecise term, meaning any sort of spirit that was not **gin** (which would have been referred to as 'Hollands').

Brandy This is a **distillate** of wine which, in French-speaking countries, is more specifically referred to as a *fine* to distinguish it from fruit brandies, or *alcools blancs*, which are distilled from fruits. Brandy can be made wherever wine is made but, as it can also be made from other things than the fermented juice of the **grape**, a reputable wine merchant will usually label it according to whether it is 'grape brandy', or has the prefix of a country's name. In every country making grape brandy there will be a difference in the spirit, and also the different brandy establishments will have their own styles, as well as a range of different qualities. The supreme brandy of the world, however, is indisputably **Cognac**, which can only come from the delimited area in the Charente region of France, although versions of its name, sounding similar, even if spelled differently, are made in many countries. The other great brandy is **Armagnac**. There are different sorts of regional brandies in France, including a vast range of fruit brandies. See **marc, grappa**. The New World brandies are of enormous importance too. The establishments that make quality brandies distilled from wine usually make at least one type that is

COGNAC AND ARMAGNAC, FRANCE

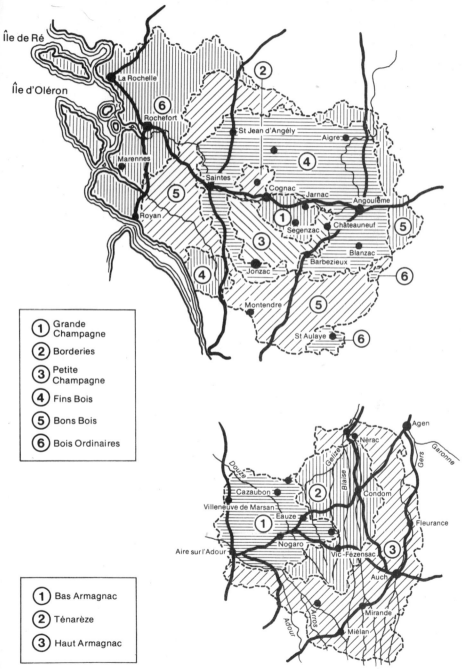

Île de Ré

Île d'Oléron

La Rochelle

⑥ Rochefort

St Jean d'Angély

Aigre

④

Marennes

Saintes

⑤ Cognac Jarnac

Angoulême

Royan

① Segenzac Châteauneuf ⑤

③ Blanzac

Barbezieux ⑥

④ Jonzac

Montendre ⑤

St Aulaye ⑥

① Grande Champagne

② Borderies

③ Petite Champagne

④ Fins Bois

⑤ Bons Bois

⑥ Bois Ordinaires

Agen

Douze Gélize Nérac Garonne

Blaise Gers

② Condom

Cazaubon

Villeneuve de Marsan

① Eauze Fleurance

Aire sur l'Adour

Nogaro Vic-Fézensac ③

Auch

Adour Arros Mirande

Miélan

① Bas Armagnac

② Ténarèze

③ Haut Armagnac

intended as an ingredient in a mixed drink, and another of superior quality, intended for drinking by itself. The latter type is usually drunk as a **digestive**.

It is worth noting that the use of the huge balloon **glass** and the heating of the glass over a flame are practices deplored by all who make the good brandies of the world and everyone who knows anything about the way they should be served. A brandy glass should not be larger than the hands can hold easily and the heat of the cupped palms alone should gently warm the spirit in the glass. If the glass is heated, the **aroma** is thrown off before the drinker can begin to enjoy it, and only a spirity smell and taste remain. The drinker may scorch his hands into the bargain! If a very large glass is used, the delicacy of the **bouquet** can be appreciated only with difficulty and may indeed be prevented from giving pleasure because of being dissipated in the goldfish-bowl receptacle.

The colour of brandy is not usually a sure guide to its quality, but the smell and the way the spirit slides down the glass are: if you want to know what a brandy is really like, put a little on your palm (if you haven't used scented soap or hand lotion) and sniff it when the spirit has evaporated. After the brandy has been drunk, sniff the empty glass – and note whether there is any trace of it on the sides of the glass. In this way, it is possible to detect any additional sweetening or flavouring, as of caramel; and to see, from the glass, if the spirit clings or simply slides off.

Brane-Cantenac (Pronounced 'Bran') Classed 2nd growth of **Cantenac-Margaux**, which was bought and developed by Baron de Brane at the beginning of the 19th century. It has the **A.O.C. Margaux**. See **Bordeaux, classification**.

Brauneberg (Pronounced 'Browny-berg') **Mosel** vineyard usually making outstanding wines of nobility as well as charm. The best-known sites are Falkenberg, Hasenläufer and Juffer.

Brazil A wide range of table, **sparkling** and **apéritif** wines are made in Brazil, but they are seldom seen on export lists, although some are now finding outlets in the **U.S.** Many of the classic wine **grapes** are used in the production of wine, and the influence of Italian settlers is noted.

La Brède This beautiful, moated estate in the **Graves**, south of **Bordeaux**, was the home of the great thinker, Montesquiou (1689-1755). Now owned by the Comtesse de Chabannes, it produces a pleasant white wine.

Breganze Region in the **Veneto**, in northern **Italy**, making both white and red wines. Some of them are produced from classic **grape varieties**, including **Tocai**, the two **Cabernets**, **Trebbiano**, **Malvasia** and **Pinot Noir**.

Breton Name given to the **Cabernet Franc grape** in **Touraine**, supposedly because in the 17th century Cardinal Richelieu's intendant in the region was the Abbé Breton, who had **vine** cuttings sent up from **Bordeaux** to improve the vineyards.

Brimmer See **Humpen glass**.

Brolio (Pronounced 'Broh-lyo') Castle of great magnificence in the **Chianti** region of **Italy**. It is the property of the **Ricasoli** family and, in the 19th century, one of them evolved what is today the basic method of making Chianti.

Although Brolio makes wines of notable quality, the present Baron, together with a few other important growers, decided to leave the Chianti Classico *consorzio*. That is why the Brolio wines do not now bear the black cockerel label of the Classico association. They are usually excellent Chianti Classico wines.

Brombeerlikoer   A German **liqueur** made from the juice of ripe blackberries.

Brontë   Honey and herb **liqueur**, made in Yorkshire.

Brora   See **Clynelish**.

Brouilly, Côtes de Brouilly   (Pronounced 'Brew-yee') Regions of the **Beaujolais**, producing red wines of a certain style of body and, almost, toughness, capable of being very fine.

Bruichladdich   (Pronounced 'Brew-ich-lad-die' stressing 'lad') **Whisky distillery** on Islay (pronounced 'Eye-ler'), and the most westerly of all distilleries. It is owned by Invergordon Distillers. Derek Cooper, an authority on the subject, says that its malt has 'notable mildness as compared with the massive peaty assault of **Laphroaig**'.

Brunello   **Tuscan** red wine, the full name of which is Brunello di Montalcino. It is made from the Brunello **grape**, a type of **Sangiovese**, and is very full-bodied and ample in character, capable of maturing for a long time both in **wood** and **bottle** and developing much quality. Some people consider a good Brunello to be one of Italy's greatest wines.

Brut   (Pronounced 'Brute') This French term is usually associated with **Champagne**, although it can be applied to any wine when it is wished to indicate that the wine is absolutely dry, with no added sweetening.

Bual, *Boal*   (Pronounced 'Bwahl') The second version of the name is the Portuguese spelling. This is one of the **Madeira grapes**, making a full, opulent wine, usually deep brown in tone, with a luscious style.

Bucelas   North of Lisbon in **Portugal**, this region makes white wines that today are dry or dryish; although in the past they tended to be quite sweet and many received **fortification** with **brandy**. Charneca and Bucelas are the main wine villages; the principal **grape** appears to be the Arinto, a form of **Riesling**. There are plenty of references to Bucelas in English history, as Wellington's army acquired a taste for it when they were encamped at **Torres Vedras**.

Buchu   A **brandy** is made from, and even with, this herb, something of a speciality of the **Paarl** region of the Cape, **South Africa**. It is extremely pungent and is recommended as a **digestive**, a lotion for wounds, bruises and apparently almost any ill.

Buck   A long mixed drink, of lemon juice, a spirit and carbonated water.

Buck's fizz   Invented at Buck's Club, London in 1921 by Pat McGarry, the barman. It consists of one-third freshly-squeezed orange juice, two-thirds non-vintage **Champagne**, and a teaspoonful of **grenadine**. It is a delicious mid-morning or late-night drink. In France it is known as a 'Champagne-orange', in Italy as a 'Mimosa'. It can, in fact, be an enjoyable drink if made with any good **sparkling wine** – but the orange juice *must* be fresh. The original drink was made with Bollinger.

Budafok   Headquarters of the **Hungarian** State wine cellars, which were founded in the 18th century.

Buena Vista   Notable **California** vineyard at Sonoma, north of San Francisco. It was established in 1857, by Count Agoston **Harászthy**. Although it went through a depressed period at the beginning of the 20th century, it now makes a range of table wines that are praised by many authorities.

Bukettraube   **Grape** grown for wine in **South Africa**, where it makes an unusually scented white wine.

Bulgaria   Wine is produced throughout Bulgaria and, in recent years, the quantity has been enormously increased. The achievement is remarkable in view of the fact that, until less than a century ago, the country that is now Bulgaria was under Turkish rule and winedrinking forbidden. The whole wine trade is controlled by a monopoly, Vinimpex. There are some important local vine **varieties**, including **Dimiat**, which makes white wines; **Gamza**, which makes red; and Mavrud, also making red. Other vines from Balkan countries and the classic wine regions of the world are also cultivated, and the wines are usually named after the vine making them. Trakia – meaning Thrace – is an exception, and this is a pleasant dryish white wine. It is generally considered that the Bulgarian whites are better than the reds; but the latter, such as Gamza and **Kadarka**, can be very pleasant and achieve good quality at what are still quite low prices.

Bull's Blood   See **Egri Bikavér**.

Bully Hill   Winery in **New York State, U.S.**

Bumper   The dictionary definition of this is 'a glass filled to the brim' (which does not imply the drink is a fine wine or the drinker is of any discrimination) or, in consequence, a large helping. The term originates in the 17th century when it was a common custom to drink heavily when the **toast** or the occasion was important.

Bundarra   Old-established **Australian** vineyard, in north-east Victoria.

Bunnahabhain   (Pronounced 'Bun-ner-harv-n' stressing 'harv') **Whisky distillery** on the isle of Islay (pronounced 'Eye-ler'), which makes a malt used in the well-known bl‿nd 'Famous Grouse', of Highland Distilleries.

Burgenland   See **Austria**.

Bürgerspital zum Heiligen Geist   The Citizens' Holy Ghost Hospice was founded in the early 14th century in **Franconia** and endowed with vineyards which still support it. The establishment's wines are of high quality.

Buring   One of the most respected names in **Australian** winemaking. One branch, through T.C. Hermann Buring, in partnership with Carl Sobels, established the 'Quelltaler' establishment, south of Clare, in the South Australian **Clare-Watervale** region. The word 'Quelltaler' may be roughly translated as 'Springvale'. The company make respected white wines and are proud, according to the authority, Len Evans, that it was one of their wines that was the first Australian wine to be served at the Lord Mayor's Banquet, at London's Guildhall.

A cousin of this branch, Leo Buring, started a distinguished career in wine at Australia's **Roseworthy College**, going on to **Geisenheim** in Germany and Montpeller in France. His first commercial success was with a rather sweet white wine, 'Ringolde', made near Sydney. In 1945, he bought and rehabilitated a vineyard and winery in the **Barossa Valley**, which was to become known as **Chateau Leonay** *(sic)*, although Leo Buring died in 1961 before the work was finished. The **winery** is now a large-scale producer, owned by **Lindeman**'s Wines since 1962.

Burgundy   Region in the east of **France** where wine has been made since at least 600 B.C. It includes **Chablis**, the **Côte d'Or** and southern Burgundy – the **Côte Chalonnaise** and the **Mâconnais**. Some wine lists put **Beaujolais** in with Burgundy, but as the **grape** is different and as the different wines of the Beaujolais deserve separate appraisal in their own right, the trend now is to keep Burgundy and Beaujolais apart. The English-speaking countries tended to be late in getting to know the wines of Burgundy, both because the Dukes of Burgundy were the allies of the Kings of France and because for three centuries the English crown had domination over the **Bordeaux** region. But nowadays Burgundy is enormously popular, the drawbacks to its world-wide fame being that there is never enough to satisfy demand (the area is small compared to Bordeaux), so prices are very high.

The majority of the public have a totally erroneous idea of what fine Burgundy, red or white, is really like when genuine. The whites are dry – Chablis very much dryer than the average drinker sincerely enjoys – with great delicacy and, often, fullness of body. The reds should be elegantly fragrant, with a velvety, balanced flavour. Too often the public get the impression that white Burgundy is just 'light and dry', the reds 'big and full'. There are commercial Burgundies of this type but even if, nowadays, their souped-up style owes nothing to their being 'stretched' with fatter southern wines; they are poor, untypical and commercialised examples of one of the world's greatest red wines. The naming of the wines also presents some difficulty to those who know little and care less about the subject.

The **Pinot Noir** is the only grape used for the finest red wines. The **Chardonnay** and the Pinot Blanc are used for the finest whites, and the **Aligoté** for white wines of everyday character. **Bourgogne-Passe-Tout-Grains** is the name that must be used for wines in which the Pinot Noir and the **Gamay** (the grape of the Beaujolais) are mixed, at least one-third being Pinot Noir. Because of its northerly situation, the wines of the Burgundy vineyard are helped in their **fermentation** by the addition of some sugar to the **must**, according to the **chaptalisation** process. The sugaring is strictly controlled but, as sugar can mask imperfections in a wine, a possibly indifferent red Burgundy can be made almost too 'rich and velvety'. True red Burgundy should be a fragrant but fresh supple wine, never assertive or treacly. However the 'real thing' can never be cheap, because of the demand and because the vineyards are small.

Burgundy vineyards are not like other big wine estates. They are much

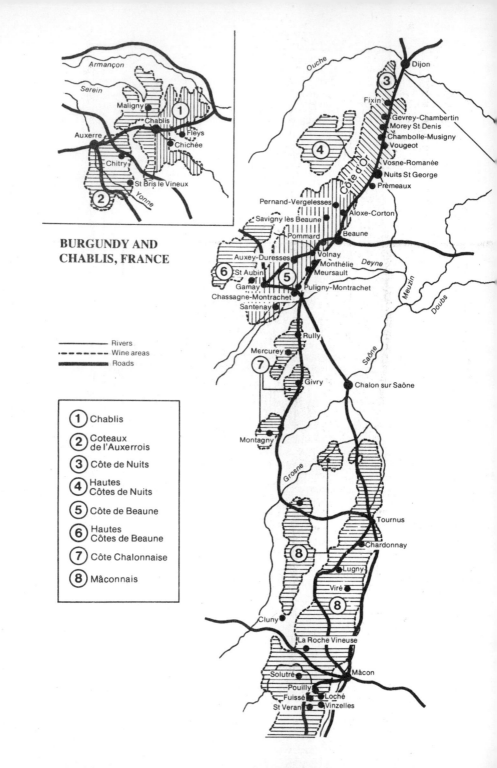

Armançon

Serein

Maligny

Chablis

Auxerre

Fleys

Chichée

Chitry

St Bris le Vineux

Yonne

BURGUNDY AND
CHABLIS, FRANCE

Ouche

Dijon

Fixin

Gevrey-Chambertin

Morey St Denis

Chambolle-Musigny

Vougeot

Vosne-Romanée

Nuits St George

Prémeaux

Pernand-Vergelesses

Aloxe-Corton

Savigny lès Beaune

Pommard

Beaune

Auxey-Duresses

Volnay

Monthélie

Meursault

Deyne

St Aubin

Gamay

Puligny-Montrachet

Chassagne-Montrachet

Santenay

Côte d'Or

Meuzin

Doubs

Rully

Mercurey

Givry

Saône

Montagny

Chalon sur Saône

Grosne

Tournus

Chardonnay

Lugny

Viré

Cluny

La Roche Vineuse

Solutré

Pouilly

Fuissé

Loché

St Veran

Vinzelles

Mâcon

	Rivers
	Wine areas
	Roads

1 Chablis

2 Coteaux
de l'Auxerrois

3 Côte de Nuits

4 Hautes
Côtes de Nuits

5 Côte de Beaune

6 Hautes
Côtes de Beaune

7 Côte Chalonnaise

8 Mâconnais

smaller and each vineyard within its named parish may be divided up into different sites or *climats* each with its own name. The situation is complicated still further by the fact that each site may have several different owners and there will certainly be many different owners in each vineyard. As each of these owners will gather the grapes and make the wine from their particular 'patch' (for the areas concerned are really more like market gardens or even allotments in size), there will be a corresponding variation between the products of all those who are concerned with making the wine, even though it bears the one name, even in the same **vintage**. Even when someone does own the whole site, unless the owner bottles all his own wine, variations will occur (as with wines made in other parts of Burgundy) when the various **shippers** buy and handle the wine. If the wine is not bottled on the spot, then even more variations may occur when it is bottled by those who buy and bottle it in export marketing. This need not essentially affect the quality of the wine, although it does explain why it is of the greatest importance to know the name of the shipper, and also the source of supply if this is not the same. The wine of company A will be different, however slightly, from that of company B; even when the wine name is the same and the vintage the same. Both wines can be good, but they will be different. This is why those who are interested in wine like to see the name of the shippers in the Burgundy section of a wine list – they will, in the course of gaining experience, have come to form personal preferences about the style of wine made by Company X as against that made by Company Y. It also explains why prices can vary so much, because one establishment may have very high standards about the way they handle their wines, another be not so conscientious. Because of the smallness of the vineyards, too, buyers of the wines usually pick **cask** by cask when selecting their purchases and their agents make sure that only those particular casks go to the cellars of the shippers.

NAMES: The way in which Burgundies are named is rather complex, but in general the fine wines, named alone, are superior to those which add on the name of the village to the name of the fine vineyards. For example, Le Musigny and Le Corton are great vineyards, and wines simply bearing their names will be superior to those labelled **Chambolle-Musigny** and **Aloxe-Corton**. There are also vineyards which are allowed to add their names on to the name of the great vineyard of the area. For example, Charmes-Chambertin and **Vosne-Romanée**; and among the white wines, **Puligny-Montrachet** and Aloxe-Corton. But, just to complicate the issue still further, the white **Corton-Charlemagne** is superior to the white Corton. (The whole question of Burgundy site names, place names and A.O.C.s is one that can only adequately be dealt with at length: see Bibliography.) All this will have shown why the person who says 'I don't know anything about wine, but I like Nuits-St-Georges', has given himself away as definitely knowing nothing at all about wine!

In addition to the vineyards with their own *Appellations Contrôlées*, which are shown in detailed maps of the Burgundy region, there are also many fine vineyards which merely use the words *Premier cru*, plus the name of the relevant village, on their **labels**. This is for the very good reason that to have a more detailed nomenclature would increase their tax rating.

REGIONS: The **Côte d'Or**, which runs from Dijon to just south of **Beaune**, is divided into the **Côte de Nuits**, and the **Côte de Beaune**. The Côte de Nuits, so called because of **Nuits-St-Georges** being the chief town, is famous for its red wines which are among the greatest in the world. A very little white is also made there. The **rosé** wine of **Marsannay-la-Côte**, made solely from the Pinot Noir, is an outstanding example of a pink wine. The Côte de Beaune makes some very fine red wines and the finest white Burgundies of all, with the sole exception of **Chablis**, which is north-west of the main Burgundy region, and which makes white wines only. The **Côte Chalonnaise** and the **Mâconnais** produce both red and white wines, of which the Mâconnais makes slightly more white than red, and Côte Chalonnaise about three-quarters red.

SERVING BURGUNDY: Red and white Burgundies tend to mature more quickly than the great red Bordeaux, although there are also notable exceptions. It is not usual in France to **decant the great red Burgundies, although drinkers elsewhere can do as they wish if the wine has thrown a deposit**. The use of *coupes monstres* (gigantic **glasses** holding a bottle or more each) for fine Burgundy is also something often encountered in France, and in the type of chi-chi restaurant elsewhere that caters for the sort of customers who 'drink the labels'. But this is disliked by most serious lovers of wine, as the exaggerated aeration of the wine can distort its whole character. The use of such enormous glasses is, ultimately, a matter of personal preference, but the stressing of the smell of the wine at the possible expense of the enjoyment of its flavour – after it has crawled across an infinite area of glass before it can reach the drinker's mouth – has often tended to cause some makers of red Burgundy deliberately to produce wines that are heavily scented and therefore vulgarly unbalanced. Red Burgundy that is balanced, with the elegance that this fine wine should possess, is at its best in a thin, clear, tulip or goblet-shaped glass of fair size – as is any good wine.

Some people believe that red Burgundy is 'stronger' than other red wines. Because of the way it is made, it may certainly be a degree or a degree and a half higher in alcoholic **strength** than, say, some **clarets**, but I should be surprised to hear that this affects the drinker to any marked extent. What most critics mean by 'stronger' is that the beautiful smell of Burgundy gives an impression of importance (a souped-up commercial Burgundy will caricature this) and they therefore assume that this wine, 'big' in character, is going to make demands on the consumer. Of course it does – a great wine is obviously going to make more of an impression and possibly exercise the senses and mind more than a commonplace wine. But this doesn't mean the wine is 'stronger'.

As for the arguments about the merits of red Burgundy against **claret**, these are likely to go on until the end of time – praise be! I would merely suggest that, in my opinion, the appeal of most fine claret is cerebral, that of the fine red Burgundies to the senses. Red Burgundy needs to be enjoyed in the context of a meal; claret can be magnificent with only bread, butter and cheese (of the best quality, of course). It is perhaps fairer to say that most drinkers begin by loving red Burgundy – which makes an immediate appeal and, as has been said, to the senses – and possibly come later to the appreciation of claret when experience has been gained and they are prepared to use their minds on a wine. But there can be little argument about the magnificence of white Burgundy – it is, to many, the world's most all-purpose wine, because certain examples are of sufficient weight and body to accompany meat, even game, as well as all types of fish, shellfish and crustacea and, as far as the subtler wines are concerned, to be as much of a delight to explore as the red wines of Burgundy and Bordeaux put together! but the great white Burgundies from the Côte de Beaune and Chablis are rare and wonderful experiences to drink – and one has to pay for them. Care should always be taken never to overchill such wines and lose the beautiful, complex **bouquet** that many reveal. They are, additionally, difficult to know and, at least for me, almost the most taxing wines of all to taste, because of their delicacy and complexity. The white wines from the southern part of the region are more straightforward and possibly easier to appraise.

Busby, James (1801-71) Possibly the best-known name in the history of Australian winemaking. Born in Edinburgh, he came to **Australia** in 1824 with his father, an engineer and surveyor. He had already made up his mind that the country was ripe for development as regards **vines**: he had actually studied vines and winemaking in France so as to fit himself for what he felt was his life work. An area on the **Hunter River**, later known as **Kirkton**, was made available to Busby, where good wine was made from the vines cultivated there. Busby then began to publish, as well as teaching viticulture and his books exerted great influence. The most famous of them, published in 1830, contains the famous quotation 'The man who could sit under the shade of his own vine, with his wife and children about him, and the ripe clusters hanging within their reach, in such a climate as this (New South Wales) and not feel the highest enjoyment, is incapable of happiness and does not know what the word means.'

Subsequently, Busby travelled in the French and Spanish vineyards, writing about the vines he studied there, and which he tried to import to Australia. He only had a moderate success, because many of them were lost due to lack of care. Later, Busby became British Resident in **New Zealand** and finally returned to England, apparently dissatisfied with his achievements. These, however, were great in his time and have resulted in the establishment of many of the traditions of Australian winegrowing.

Butt See **casks, sherry.**

Buzbag See **Turkey.**

Buzz To 'buzz the bottle' is interpreted by many people as meaning 'to send the bottle round (the table)'. But the expression has quite another meaning – certainly in the U.K. The word was originally spelt 'buz' and is quoted in Thomas Love Peacock's novel, *Gryll Grange* (1860). A 'buzz' occurs when the wine in the **decanter** is poured into the glass of the drinker before whom it arrives, during its circulation around the table, and the amount remaining in the decanter at that stage empties the decanter completely and exactly fills the glass of the drinker – who will probably have previously guessed that it might do so, and who therefore pours it out to fill his glass to the brim – or even slightly bulging over the brim, without spilling. Originally, as the late H. Warner **Allen** states, a wager was involved as to whether the bottle would be 'buzzed' or not and the person who judged correctly, picked up the decanter and proved the point, was given a bottle by everyone around the table. Today, in a more moderate fashion, the person who achieves a buzz merely gets a helping of the next bottle, in addition to the buzzed wine in his glass. I am told that the custom still prevails at some colleges, but it is definitely an old-fashioned one. The expression appears to refer mainly to **port**.

Byrrh   A French **apéritif**, rather sweetly-bitter, evolved in the **Roussillon** region of France by a shepherd of the Pyrenees, Simon Violet, in 1866. It is claimed that it was the first apéritif in which quinine was added to the wine. The owners of the firm making Byrrh at Thuir claim that they possess the biggest **cask** in the world – it is certainly gigantic.

C

C.I.V.C. Stands for Comité Interprofessionel du Vin de Champagne. See **Champagne,** *Grandes Marques.*

C.L.O.C. A Danish caraway **liqueur**, the initials standing for *Cumin liquidum optimum castelli* (The best caraway in the castles). The name is also that of a **gin** put out by the Danish house responsible for most of the Danish liqueurs and other spirits in general.

Cabernet The Cabernet Sauvignon and the Cabernet Franc are two of the great red wine **grapes** of the world, being used in the **Bordeaux** region. The Cabernet Franc is used for the finer red wines of the **Loire**. They are cultivated in many other parts of the world, including the **U.S., South Africa** and **Australia**, as well as in other European countries. If the term 'Cabernet' is used on an eastern European wine **label**, this usually means the Cabernet Franc. The two grapes make quite different styles of wine. The Cabernet Sauvignon, which gives the backbone and nobility to claret, makes firm, sinewy, lengthy wines; the Cabernet Franc makes very fresh, lightly fruity, crisp wines with pronounced colour.

Cabinet, Kabinett See **German Wine Law.**

Cacao mit Nuss See **chocolate liqueurs.**

Cadillac **Bordeaux** wine region on the right bank of the Garonne, specialising in white wines, which often attain reasonable quality nowadays.

Cahors Vineyard in the Lot region of **France**, where both white and red wines are produced; the latter, made from the **Malbec grape**, are the most famous. Known in early medieval times as 'black wines' because of their dark colour, they were often used to 'help' the lighter wines of the **Bordeaux** region. They have recently been awarded an **A.O.C.** The true 'black wines' are comparatively rare. They remain in **cask** for many years, apparently without deterioration, and they are said to possess revitalising properties. Wines made in the same region can be pleasant, but are not quite in the same category as the real 'black wine'.

Cairanne Vineyard region at the bottom of the **Rhône**, producing pleasant white, red and pink wines.

Calabria The foot region of the 'boot' of **Italy**, where a quantity of red and white wine is produced, virtually none of it seen on export lists. See **Cirò**, **Greco** di Gerace, **Montonico**.

Caldaro, Kalterer The Italian and German name of the wines made around the Lago di Caldaro in the **Alto Adige** region of **Italy**. The wines are red and highly reputed.

Caledon One of the official wine regions of **South Africa**.

California The most important wineproducing region in the **U.S.**, making by far the largest proportion of all wines – still, **sparkling** and **fortified** – of that country. The vines are the *Vitis vinifera* type and, in many instances, the winemakers produce a whole range of different types of wine from each **winery**, although there are also some specialist makers.

Vines were introduced to California by the Jesuits, who brought cuttings from their settlements in Mexico, including the variety known as **Mission**, of European origin. The Franciscan, Father Junipero **Serra**, planted the Mission grape at Mission San Diego de Alcalá soon after it was established in 1769, but the Jesuit Father Juan Uguarte made the first plantations of wine vines in Baja, California, at the end of the 17th century. From the beginning of the 19th century, the lay holdings of vineyards increased, some of the owners being of European families already familiar with winegrowing. In the middle of the century, the Hungarian, Ágoston **Harászthy**, 'Father of California wine-growing', introduced a wide variety of different grapes from Europe. The wine industry became large-scale and prosperous, even after the ravages of *Phylloxera*. The establishment of the Wine Board and, later, the specialised department for the study of vines, winemaking and the science of viticulture and viniculture at the University of California, achieved world fame and influence. Familiarly known as **Davis**, this department's **oenologists** have introduced some of the techniques, now taken for granted, to vineyards all over the world; the work done here is of inestimable significance.

California wines – the word is used by the producers without the final 'n' – enjoy much respect in the world of wine today, although it seems rather foolish to conduct tastings at which wines from California are pitted against those from European classic vineyards, by way of establishing that the California wines are 'as good and often better'. The quality standards of the best wines of California are certainly very high indeed; but of course the wines are *different*, because they come from vineyards that are different as regards **soils**, climates and are made according to methods that are often quite different from wines made elsewhere. California wines are indeed often admirable, but must fairly be considered in their own right.

It is worth noting, too, that quality standards of the different wineries can differ greatly and, in addition, a wine labelled with the name of a grape – the U.S. term being **'varietal'** – need not legally be made with that grape only. At the time of writing, the percentage required is being raised from 51 to 85%, and certain of the most respected producers always use only 100% of the one grape variety, but nevertheless such variations in proportions can affect

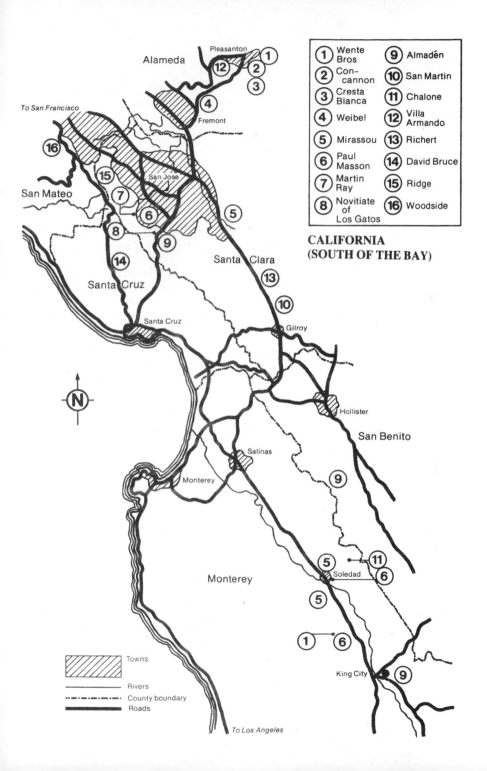

**CALIFORNIA
(SOUTH OF THE BAY)**

① Wente Bros	⑨ Almadén
② Con-cannon	⑩ San Martin
③ Cresta Blanca	⑪ Chalone
④ Weibel	⑫ Villa Armando
⑤ Mirassou	⑬ Richert
⑥ Paul Masson	⑭ David Bruce
⑦ Martin Ray	⑮ Ridge
⑧ Novitiate of Los Gatos	⑯ Woodside

Towns
Rivers
County boundary
Roads

CALIFORNIA (CENTRAL VALLEY)

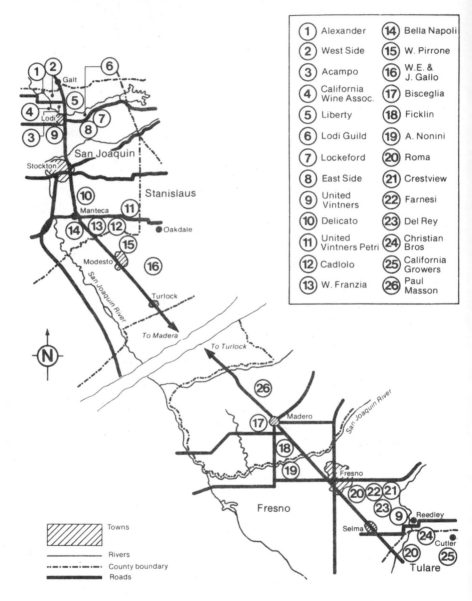

①	Alexander	⑭	Bella Napoli
②	West Side	⑮	W. Pirrone
③	Acampo	⑯	W.E. & J. Gallo
④	California Wine Assoc.	⑰	Bisceglia
⑤	Liberty	⑱	Ficklin
⑥	Lodi Guild	⑲	A. Nonini
⑦	Lockeford	⑳	Roma
⑧	East Side	㉑	Crestview
⑨	United Vintners	㉒	Farnesi
⑩	Delicato	㉓	Del Rey
⑪	United Vintners Petri	㉔	Christian Bros
⑫	Cadlolo	㉕	California Growers
⑬	W. Franzia	㉖	Paul Masson

Towns
Rivers
County boundary
Roads

overall styles to a considerable extent.

Much use is made of the **Zinfandel** grape, possibly of European origin but now definitely a North American variety, from which red wines are made. Well-known wine grapes that are widely cultivated include the whites: **Sémillon, Chardonnay, Chenin Blanc, Sauvignon, Riesling, Traminer** and **Sylvaner**. There are, however, many others in cultivation. The most important black grapes include: **Pinot Noir, Cabernet Sauvignon, Gamay, Grenache, Petite Sirah, Carignan**, and the Italian grapes **Barbera** and **Grignolino**. Many varieties of these classics have been developed and some of the produce obtained by crossings of basic types have yielded interesting results: the **Emerald Riesling** (a cross of the White or **Rheinriesling** and a local **Muscadelle**) and the **Ruby Cabernet** (a cross of the Cabernet Sauvignon and the Carignan) are of particular interest.

The main styles of table and fortified, as well as sparkling wines, are made in California, although methods of production vary a great deal. It is unfortunate that the names of European wines are still used in many instances, because these 'ports', 'sherries' and the sparkling wines allowed to be termed 'Champagne' in the U.S., very seldom resemble European wines, likewise the wines labelled as 'Sauterne' (the final 's' is often omitted). The sparkling wines will state on their **labels** whether they are 'fermented in *this* bottle', which means that they are produced according to the **Champagne method**, or 'fermented in bottle', which implies that they are made by the *cuve close* or **transfer method**. Wines made sparkling by pumping in **carbon dioxide** must state on their labels that they are **'carbonated'**.

There are several main regions devoted to wine production in California, the size of which should be borne in mind by anyone thinking of a 'vineyard' in terms of the small-scale European estates or general vineyard areas. The south coast makes rather light wines, plus many still and sparkling table wines. The San Joaquin Valley produces table wines and **dessert wines** of various types. The central region produces large quantities of table wines, including many of the **'jug'** wines (the term means bulk branded wines for everyday consumption). The Sacramento Valley produces many **apéritif** and dessert wines. The north coast region, the most important of all for quality wines, is extensive and is subdivided into Sonoma-Mendicono, **Napa Valley**-Solano, **Livermore**-Contra Costa, **Santa Clara** – San Benito – Santa Cruz. (For reference to specific wineries, see the different entries under their names as well as regions.)

Increasing numbers of California wines are being exported, but European drinkers should be aware that, because production of the very finest is always unequal to demand, it is not fair to appraise these wines solely by the examples available on export markets. The very best are rare, expensive and able to stand comparison with some of the best of European wines – but, even in their homeland, they are not always easily available.

California Wine Association This firm, at Lodi, in **California**, was established in the 19th century. It now produces a range of table wines and **brandy**.

Calisay   Sweetish, herby Spanish **digestive liqueur**.

Calon-Ségur   Classed 3rd growth of **St Estèphe** and one of the larger properties. Its name comes from *calon* or *calonne*, the medieval French term for a skiff used as a ferry across the **Gironde**, and from the Président de Ségur, its owner in the 18th century. Although he owned **Lafite** and **Latour** as well, he always said his heart belonged to Calon – which is why there is a heart on the label. The wine is always a big one and you either like it very much or find it too assertive. See **Bordeaux, classification**.

Caluso   Region in **Piedmont, Italy**, making white wines, some of which are sweet and made by the *passito* process of drying before pressing. The **Erbaluce vine** is used exclusively.

Calvados   Apple **brandy**, distilled from a mash of apples, fermented with **yeast**, subjected to two **distillations** and thereafter matured in oak for 6 to 10 years, according to the regulations that control its production in Normandy. The Calvados of the Vallée d'Auge has its own **A.O.C.** It has been made from about the 16th century in the region. Its use is either as a **digestive** at the end of a meal or, in Normandy, to make the *trou* (hole) *normande*.

In the U.S. the spirit is referred to as **'applejack'**. A type of apple spirit can be made wherever apples are extensively cultivated. Calvados should not be confused with *eau-de-vie-de-cidre*, which is a spirit actually distilled from **cider**, something rarely met with nowadays.

Camensac   Classed 5th growth of the Médoc. Being in the *commune* of St Laurent, which has no separate **A.O.C.**, it bears the A.O.C. Haut-Médoc. It is a wine seldom seen nowadays. See **Bordeaux, classification**.

Campania   This is the **Italian** wine region around the Bay of Naples, including the islands of **Capri** and **Ischia**, the **Vesuvius** area, and that of **Irpinia**. Well-known wines include **Lacrima Christi** and **Falerno**.

Campari   Evolved by Gaspare Campari in Milan in 1867, used in many mixtures, but also widely drunk with soda. A drink including Campari should always be stirred, as even the addition of soda is not enough to mix it in the glass. The garnish of an **Americano** should ideally be a slice of orange, not lemon. See **bitters**.

Campbell   One of the old-established **Australian** wine families, first in wine in the 1880s, now owners of the Bobbie Burns and Silverburn **wineries**, near Rutherglen, Victoria.

Campbeltown   Region in the Mull of Kintyre, Scotland, at one time famous for the **distilleries** making the **whisky** typical of the region. Today there are only those of **Glen Scotia** and **Springbank**: the latter is the only one available as a bottled Scotch of the region, the other is used for **blending**.

Canada   Wines have been made by missionaries in Canada since the 17th century, chiefly in southern Ontario. Recently, serious experiments have been made and plantings increased to further the wine industry as a commercial project, and a variety of wines, table, **fortified** and **sparkling**, are now being produced. As in **England**, **hybrids** are cultivated for the purpose of winemaking. It must be admitted that, as Canadian wines are seldom available outside their homeland, pronouncements about them are difficult to make. My impression is that, as yet, in spite of conscientious attempts to make wine in a climate that is more suitable to **vines** than might be supposed, the quality of the wines is not yet marked. The adoption of modern winemaking and viticultural techniques may have a beneficial effect on Canadian wines of the future.

Canadian whiskey   See **whisky**.

Canaiolo   One of the black **grapes** used for **Chianti**.

Canandaigua Wine Company   Important **winery** in **New York State**, also owning wineries in Virginia and the San Joaquin Valley.

Cannellino   See **Frascati**.

Cannonau   **Sardinian** wine named after the **grape** from which it is made. There is a white wine of this name, but the red and rosé, which may be either dry or slightly sweet, are possibly better known.

Canon (1)   This is a *Premier Grand Cru Classé* of **St Émilion**, situated in the *Côtes* area. It is an old-established property, its vineyards being in a single group, on top of the old quarries where the Girondin refugees unsuccessfully attempted to hide from the Terror in the French Revolution. The wines are usually full, firm and can attain fine quality.

Canon (2)   Well-known château in the *Côtes* Canon Fronsac region of the **Bordeaux** vineyards.

Canon-La-Gaffelière   Estate in the *Côtes* of **St Émilion**, making good wines. See **Bordeaux, classification**.

Cantemerle   A 5th classed growth of the **Médoc** in the parish of Macau which, not having a specific **A.O.C.**, necessitates the wine having the A.O.C. Haut-Médoc. The wine is very fine indeed, with all the fascination, charm and distinction of great **claret**, plus an elegance and subtlety typical of the vineyard. Under **vines** since the Middle Ages, the estate was run for over 60 years in this century by the late M. Pierre Dubos. He was famous in Bordeaux for his dedication and the way in which he kept a detailed record of each day's temperatures, every procedure relating to the vines and wine. The property is one of the most liked and respected in the Médoc. It is now run by M. Henri Binaud, head of the firm of Beyerman. The property of La Tour de Mons, at Soussans in **Margaux**, also belongs to the estate and makes fine wines. See **Bordeaux, classification**.

Cantenac-Brown   Classed 3rd growth of **Cantenac-Margaux**. The imposing château has nowadays no connection with the vineyard. See **Bordeaux, classification**.

Cantenac-Margaux   The district in the **Médoc** adjoining **Margaux**, which is the *commune* to give its name to the **A.O.C.** Sometimes people are confused because properties such as **Brane-Cantenac, Palmer, Kirwan,** and **Le Prieuré** are referred to as being 'Cantenac' although they bear the A.O.C. 'Margaux'. This is because these vineyards have been permitted to use the *commune* name Margaux since 1954. See **Bordeaux**.

Canzem   See **Kanzem**.

Caol Ila   (Pronounced 'C'l Ee-ler') **Whisky distillery** on the Isle of Islay, making fine malt Scotch.

Cap Corse   A wine-based **apéritif**, dark reddish-brown, with a slight smell and taste of vanilla. Medium fruity, medium sweet in taste. It is made near Bastia, in **Corsica**.

Cap-de-Mourlin   Very ancient estate in the *Côtes* of **St Émilion**, belonging to the family who have given it their name for five centuries. See **Bordeaux**.

Capataz   Spanish word for 'cellarman', who exercises considerable authority in the *bodegas*. See **Sherry**.

Caperdonich   **Whisky distillery** in Rothes, Morayshire, the name of which means 'The Secret Well'. In fact, it uses the waters of the same burn as **Glen Grant**.

Capo Ferrato   Red wine from **Sardinia**.

Capri   Red, white and pink wines are labelled with the name of this Italian island, but a lot comes from **Ischia**, Procida and the mainland of **Italy**. The white wine, slightly minerally in flavour with quite a fresh smell, is possibly the best known and most highly esteemed.

Capricornia   Australian **liqueur** made from tropical fruits.

Capsule   The cap, often of metal foil or of plastic, which goes over the top of the **bottle**, protecting the **cork** and also provides additional sealing if the wine should seep through the cork at all (see **weeper**). Sometimes, with plastic capsules, there is a perforated strip to tear off when the capsule is to be removed. Otherwise, with the metal type, the correct thing to do is to cut the capsule so that the whole piece covering the top of the bottle may be taken off. It is important to expose the entire lip of the bottle because, if the wine is poured over the capsule or any ragged edges, the metallic contact may affect the taste.

   Very skilful people will cut round the top of the capsule so that a small portion remains attached, and then simply bend back the top of this like a lid. Some wine waiters even cut this 'lid' so that it makes a loop to hold the cork – a very pretty presentation. As the part of the capsule that covers the upper section of the neck of the bottle can be decorative, especially with some German wines, this enables the 'dressing' of the bottle to be largely preserved; but the whole capsule may be removed if there is any doubt as to what to do. Indeed, if the wine is to be **decanted**, it is probably better to do so, because then its passage right through the neck of the bottle to the lip may be observed.

Carafe   Container for open wine, served at the table. A carafe may, in fact, do double duty as a **decanter** in the home (the wine cork usually fits into the neck should it be necessary to seal it, or else a wedge of clean tissue may be used). However it may also be a jug. See *pichet*. The (U.K.) Weights and Measures Order, 1976, requires all premises selling wine by the carafe to state the amount the carafe contains – 9 fl. oz (25cl), 17.5 fl. oz (50cl), 26 fl. oz (75cl) and 35 fl. oz (1 litre) – and to display a notice about this.

   The expression 'a carafe wine' is sometimes used to imply something inferior but it should not do so; the carafe wine of a restuarant should be the manager's standby, and of a quality, however cheap, that encourages the hesitant drinker to take more than a **glass** at a time. If you are buying a carafe, check the size, as it is difficult to judge by looking. If you plan to use it for bottles of wine, it is annoying to find that it will only take 17.5 fl. oz (50cl).

Carbon dioxide CO_2 is produced during the process of **fermentation** and, in most still wines, it is simply given off into the atmosphere while the **must** is being worked on by the **yeasts**. This is why anyone going round a **winery** is usually warned, if they climb up to look into a fermentation **vat**, not to breathe in – inhaling carbon dioxide at this stage can make one ill. But in the making of **sparkling wines**, the carbon dioxide that would be given off in the second stage of fermentation, subsequent to the first tumultuous fermentation, is trapped in the wine whether in a sealed vat or in **bottle**. It therefore remains in the wine as a sparkle – perfectly harmless and a delight to the drinker. Its action accelerates the effect of **alcohol** on the human system, which is why a convalescent may be given a sparkling wine, to buck up the patient and stimulate appetite; also why a sparkling wine 'gets the party going' faster than a still one.

The slight 'prickle' or *spritzig* sometimes noted in a quality wine is usually carbon dioxide. As it has been found that this indication of the wine being still 'working' also has the effect of retarding any loss of freshness or even **oxidisation** it is fairly common practice nowadays for many dry white wines bottled in hot places to be given a shot of CO_2 to keep them in condition.

Carbonated wines   Wines made sparkling by pumping **carbon dioxide** (CO_2) into them. In past times, they were rightly considered of poor quality, the bubbles being large, rising slowly and not for long and, because the base wine was usually poor, they were generally unattractive. Nowadays improvements in winemaking have resulted in many wines that are lightly carbonated – the result being a *pétillance* rather than a sparkle – and that are attractive and sound. Some from **Luxemburg**, very slightly fizzy, have already won a public in various export markets, including the U.K. It is now realised that a very slight addition of carbon dioxide to a wine gives it an attractive *'spritzig'* that it might not otherwise possess once past its extreme youth. Because the CO_2 prevents **maderisation**, the wine's freshness can be preserved, so the judicious use of the gas can be advantageous with many wines. The finer wines, of course, are not treated in this way; but some inexpensive wines can be both made more attractive and kept in condition for longer as a result. They are known as *vins gazéifiés* in **France**. See **Champagne method, Charmat method, cuve close, transfer method**.

Carbonnieux   Property in the parish of Léognan in the **Graves**, south of **Bordeaux**. It produces both red and white wines, though more white than red, the latter being rare outside the region. The best-known story associated with Château Carbonnieux relates to the time when it belonged to the Abbey of Sainte Croix in Bordeaux. The Benedictines of the establishment, seeking to extend their export markets, sent quantities of wine successfully to teetotal Turkey, having labelled it *Eau Minérale de Carbonnieux*. Another version of this tale explains that a beautiful Bordelaise, captured by a Turkish pirate and sent to the Sultan's harem, persuaded him that she must have supplies of the 'mineral water' of her home to preserve her charms. Both the red and white wines are of fine quality.

Cardow   **Whisky distillery** in Knockando, Morayshire, which now belongs to the firm of John Walker. They make a single malt Scotch called Cardhu.

Carema   **Piedmont** red wine from a *commune* of the same name north of **Turin**, in **Italy**, which appears to be good when it has attained sufficient maturity in bottle. It is recommended that it should be opened several hours in advance of being drunk.

Carignan, Carignane, Cariñena   This black **grape** is apparently of **Spanish** origin, coming from Aragón. But it is much cultivated in the south of **France** today, in the French Mediterranean regions, and also in northern regions of Spain. It is of enormous importance in **California**. It was said to be the most planted grape in France in 1968 and the second most important in California. It is much used in **blends** of grapes and appears to yield well, providing a slight toughness to the ultimate wine; personally, I often detect a slightly 'tarry' aftertaste from this grape. It does not make wines of finesse and quality, except in certain blends, but can provide sturdiness and a defined, well-coloured style in medium priced wines.

Cariñena (1)   See **Carignan**.

Cariñena (2)   Defined wine region in Aragón, in **Spain**, making chiefly red wines of a bright, deep tone, plus a little white and some sweet white.

Carlsberg   Czech **digestive liqueur**, not to be confused with the Danish beer establishment of the same name.

Carmeline   Green-yellow herby **liqueur**, formerly produced in **Bordeaux** by Sécrestat, not now made.

Carmenère   Black **grape** at one time planted in significant proportions in many of the finer vineyards in **Bordeaux**, but nowadays seldom included there.

Carneros Creek   Vineyard and **winery** region in the **Napa Valley, California**, where a number of producers own plots.

Carpano   Oldest of all the **vermouth** establishments. It was set up by Antonio Benedetto Carpano in Turin in the late 18th century. In 1786, the first 'commercial' drink, which Carpano called 'vermouth' – using the German term *wermut* for **absinthe** (wormwood) – was offered for sale. The Carpano bar became so popular that it had to remain open for 24 hours a day! It was frequented by many celebrities and, in 1876, the latest 'Carpano mix' was evolved – **Punt e Mes**. Today Carpano vermouths are still widely appreciated.

Carricante   White wine **grape** used in **Sicily**.

Carruades de Château Lafite   Wine made at Château **Lafite**, but from vines that have not yet reached complete maturity. It is always a good wine, but by no means cheap. But it should never be confused with the *grand vin* that is Lafite. See **Moulin des Carruades**.

Cartizze   Town in the **Veneto** region of **Italy**, around which vineyards make white wines of quality, varying from still to **sparkling**, dry to sweet.

Casel See **Kasel**.

Casks Most of the main wine and spirit regions have their own individual types of cask, although the size and proportions of these are now usually controlled by legislation. Sometimes, however, these names vary and local names for casks of different sizes are found everywhere. The German name for a cask is *fass*. The following table gives the approximate capacity of the better-known casks for the classic wines and spirits:

	Contents	Gallons	Litres
Pipe	Port, Tarragona	115	522.48
	Madeira	92	418.00
	Marsala	93	422.54
Butt	Sherry	108	490.98
	Whisky	108	490.98
Hogshead	Bordeaux or Burgundy*	49	221.00
	Australia	63	286.40
	Whisky	55	249.20
	Brandy	60	272.60
Puncheon	Brandy	120	545.20
	Rum (this can vary greatly)	93	422.50
Aum	Hock	30	135.40
Halbstück	Rhine wine	134	610.00
Halbfuder	Mosel	128	580.00

<table>
<tr><td></td><td>(The half casks are more often used for actually selling or quoting prices of Rhine and Mosel wines.)</td></tr>
<tr><td>Container</td><td>This measure, used for shipping bulk wines, may be either 535 gallons (2,432.16 litres) or, in the form of stainless steel porter casks, 585 gallons (2,659.47 litres).</td></tr>
<tr><td>A quarter</td><td>is a quarter of the standard-sized cask used for the wine or spirit.</td></tr>
<tr><td>An octave</td><td>is an eighth of the standard-sized cask used for the wine or spirit.</td></tr>
</table>

*There can be a slight difference between the hogshead as used in Bordeaux and Burgundy. For the *barrique de Bordeaux*, capacity is about 47-49 gallons (214-223 litres); for the *pièce de Bourgogne*, capacity is about 48-51 gallons (218-232 litres) when these are used for storing and maturing the wine. The 48 gallon (218 litre) size is the approximate measure of a *barrique de transport*.

Cassis (1) Literally 'blackcurrant'. A **liqueur** made from blackcurrants is a **Burgundy** speciality, particularly around Dijon. It is very sweet and fruity and is used for flavouring sweets and ices. In other countries a similar type of liqueur may be made (see *vin blanc cassis*, **kir**, **Aligoté**). Strict controls are exercised in the production of cassis. Most firms make a range, at different strengths: 14° for the more usual and kitchen purposes, 15° or more for crème de cassis, 20° for what may be termed 'supercassis' or '*double crème*', and at least one firm makes one of 25°. Because of the **duty** levied, this last is not often seen outside its homeland. Higher strength does not simply mean that higher strength **alcohol** is used, but that the blackcurrants have to steep longer in the molasses spirits, so that the juice is of higher strength when it is **distilled**.

Good cassis should be red-purple, rather thick in texture, with the **alcohol** and the fruit balancing each other. One firm famous for its cassis – Trénel – date their cassis, because they state that, after about a year, the spirit 'eats' the fruit and although the drink may be perfectly palatable, it will decline in the enjoyment of the fruity richness. Those who are tempted by a 'special bargain price' for a bottle of cassis should be careful to study the label – noting the alcoholic **strength** and the exact description. A blackcurrant-flavoured spirit is not at all the same as cassis.

Cassis (2)   Wine produced in the vineyards of the hinterland of the small town, Cassis, in **Provence**. Pleasant red, white and pink wines are made, though they are seldom more than good 'holiday' drinks.

Casteggio   See **Clastidio**.

Castel Chiuro   Red wine made in the **Valtelline**, by the Nino Negri winery and highly praised by Philip Dallas in his book on Italian wines.

Castelli Romani   Delimited wine region of **Italy** in **Lazio**, being an area in the Alban hills near Rome. Most of the wines made here are white, ranging through dry, semi-sweet and sweet, but there are some red wines as well. The best known is **Frascati**.

Cataratto   Sicilian **grape**, used in the blends of **Marsala** as well as for some **Sicilian** table wines.

Catawba   This **grape** is native to the **U.S.** where, about 1823, it was discovered on the banks of the Catawba River, in North Carolina. It is a light pink in colour and the wines it makes – white, red, pink and **sparkling** – have a full, almost musky scent. Catawba wines became widely known in the 19th century and, although authorities seem hesitant to grade the grape and its wines as more than averagely pleasant, it yields wines that have been and are popular.

Cava   Term used by **Spanish** producers of *sparkling wine*, meaning that the wine has been made by the **Champagne method** and so is of superior quality.

Caymus Vineyards   **Winery** at Rutherford, **Napa Valley, California.**

Cayo Verde   U.S. **liqueur**, based on limes.

Cédratine   Citrus **liqueur** made in **Corsica**.

Cellatica   Red wine from around the town of the same name, near Brescia in **Lombardy, Italy**. Large quantities appear to be made and Philip Dallas says that it is slightly similar to **Botticino**. Originally only made from the **Schiava grape**, other **varieties** are now permitted.

Centerbe   See **Mentuccia**.

Centrifuge   This appliance is part of the basic equipment in many **wineries** today. Essentially, the wine is spun in it so that any 'solids' may be removed and thereby any risk of certain undesirable conditions arising is minimised.

Cerasella   **Liqueur** made in Italy from cherries and some mountain herbs to make it a **digestive**, red in colour. Supposed to have been popular with the Italian poet and thinker, d'Annunzio.

Cerasuolo di Vittoria **Sicilian** red wine, that becomes markedly pale with age.

Ceres See **South Africa**.

Cérons White wine region south of **Bordeaux** in the **Gironde** region of **France**. The wines are flinty and fragrant, varying from fairly dry to lightly luscious, and can be very pleasant.

Chablais Nothing to do with **Chablis** in France, this is a region in the **Vaud** district of **Switzerland**, where white wines are produced, possibly the best known being those of Aigle.

Chablis Although quite apart from the **Burgundy** vineyard region, Chablis is a Burgundy; but not the only white one, as is sometimes erroneously supposed. It is in the département of the Yonne and, before the *Phylloxera*, was responsible for one-third of all Burgundy produced, most of the wine going to Paris. Today, the vineyard area is much smaller (which is why cynics say that it would be impossible for the region to supply all the 'Chablis' drunk in Paris alone), and only wines of quality are produced, all of them white.

True Chablis, however, is not yellow in tone at all, but lemony with a curious greenish tinge at the edge of the wine; it is rather pale and definitely not the more golden colour of other white Burgundies. Also, unlike them and most white wines, it does not usually darken with age. It is a very dry wine, far too dry for many people really to like. It is also, so far as the great growths are concerned, a very big, imposing wine, able to complement rich fish dishes with unctuous sauces. Real Chablis is almost minerally dry, and this extreme dryness, especially at the end of the wine (the taste that lingers in the mouth), plus the odd, shimmering pale colour, are the clues to 'the real thing'. There is nothing wrong in people not liking it – probably very few beginners or the inexperienced in wine would do so, and would be far more pleased with a **Muscadet** or white wine from the **Loire** (which is quite close to the Chablis vineyard in its **Sancerre** and **Pouilly** regions). As real Chablis cannot possibly be cheap, it must be stressed that no open or **carafe** wine offered as 'Chablis' is likely to be 100% genuine Chablis, simply because there is just not enough to go round at a low price. The wine so referred to may be perfectly good and even have some Chablis in it; but it is actually more likely to be a white **Mâcon** or something similar.

THE GRAND CRUS: These are Blanchots, Les Clos, Valmur, Grenouilles, Vaudésir, Les Preuses and Bougrots. Moutonne is a growth that is considered by many to be a *Grand Cru*, but which is not officially acknowledged as such.

THE PREMIERS CRUS: These are Chapelot, Côte de Fontenay, Vaupulent, Fourchaume, Mont de Milieu, Montée de Tonnerre, Pied d'Aloup, Vaucourin, Vaulorent, Beauroy, Beugnons, Butteaux, Châtains, Côte de Léchet, Les Forêts, Les Lys, Mélinots, Montmain, Séché, Troesme, Vaillons, Côte de Vaillons, Vosgros.

Chablis by itself on a **label** means that the wine will come from one of the individual vineyards of the district, although it can only be a named plot if from one of those authorised by **I.N.A.O.** Petit Chablis comes from plots behind the main Chablis vineyard, and is not necessarily an inferior wine to ordinary

Chablis, although it will be a smaller-scale wine than one of the great growths.
Chacolí **Spanish** wine from the Vascongadas region in the north-east. Travellers have reported on it, but apparently did not think much of it. Jan Read says that it is a slightly *pétillant vino verde*, made in both red and white.
Chaffey The Chaffey brothers founded the town of **Mildura** in Victoria, in 1887, bringing water to what was virtually a desert from the **Murray River**. They first made wine in 1891, near Mildura at a **winery** eventually named **Mildara**. This is a huge concern nowadays, buying **grapes** from local vineyards and making wine at an outstandingly modern winery, the only large concern in the vicinity. Chaffey are especially reputed for their **brandies** and sherry style wines, although table wines of many types are also made. See **Australia, irrigation**.
Chai The term used in the **Bordeaux** region for the store place in which wines are kept in **cask** while at the property where they have been made. The nature of the **soil** makes it impossible for true cellars to be made below ground in most of the **Gironde**. The *maître de chai* is a very important person, in charge of the wine throughout its life at the estate (his title may be translated as 'cellarmaster').
Chalone Winery in **California** above the Salinas Valley, especially well known for its classic white wines.
Chambers **Australian** family wine firm, established in the 19th century near Rutherglen, Victoria. The name of the **winery** is Rosewood.
Chambertin One of the world's most famous vineyards, in the **Côte de Nuits** of **Burgundy**. Chambertin Clos de Bèze is the other great name in the overall **Gevrey-Chambertin** region. Other sites that may put their names before that of Chambertin are: Charmes, Latricières, Griotte, Mazy, Chapelle and Ruchottes. All are usually fine. Chambertin is an old site, supposedly owing its name to the sagacity of a peasant named Bertin who, seeing the success of the Clos de Bèze vineyard belonging to the monks established at the Abbey of Bèze, bought the adjacent plot, henceforth known as the *Champ de Bertin*. Chambertin appears always to have been highly regarded; Napoleon I, associated with many fine drinks and dishes for no possible reason that I can understand, is known to have loved the wine and took supplies of it to Russia – bottles supposedly coming from his commissariat fetched huge prices subsequently! Chambertin and Chambertin Clos de Bèze have 25 owners, so, as may be deduced, the styles of the wines bearing the two names can vary very much. Usually expensive, they are capable of great nobility and breed when at their best.
Chambéry See **vermouth**.
Chambéryzette See **strawberry vermouth**.
Chambolle-Musigny Parish in the **Côte de Nuits** in **Burgundy**, famous for many wines which mostly tend to a particular charm and delicacy of style that is appealing. The **A.O.C.**s are Le Musigny (a very little white wine is made as well as red) and Bonnes-Mares. In conjunction with the parish name, there are such sites as Les Amoureuses, Les Charmes and Les Bonnes-Mares.

Champagne The wine that comes from a defined area in the north of **France**, around the valley of the River Marne and Reims, Épernay and Ay. It has a proud history, and it was the wine offered to the Kings of France at their Coronation. But, although the wines of the Champagne region were known since at least Roman times (the Romans built many of the great galleries cut out of the chalky limestone, where the cellars are now), they were not fully sparkling until the 18th century. The then cellarmaster at Hautvillers, Dom Pérignon, discovered both how to make up the **blend** of wines from different vineyards to preserve their quality and how, helped by the rediscovery of **cork**, it was possible to seal wine in **bottles** and thus to preserve the natural vivacity for which the region's wines were already famous. The evolution of the **Champagne method** has produced the wine as we know it today, but it is now made within a smaller area than that used in the last century, and quality control is very strict. Even on a **B.O.B.**, a code number enables the source of the wine to be quickly traced should there be any query about it.

There are many styles of Champagne and most of the great houses, including the *grandes marques*, have several. Until comparatively recently it was only the British who liked a really dry wine, but now various types are usually made: *brut* or 'nature' means that the wine contains little or no added sweetening; extra *sec*, extra dry, *très sec* mean that it is slightly sweetened; dry or *sec* will be sweetish; *demi-sec* is sweet; and *doux* very sweet. The latter is seldom seen today – it used to be popular in Imperial Russia – but some of the great houses make a 'rich' Champagne which can be a delectable wine. It is admirable for dessert or for times, such as late afternoon or if somebody is tired, when a bone-dry drink is not as enjoyable.

VINTAGE CHAMPAGNE: The wine made from one year, although it is permitted to add up to 20% of the wine from another year to assist the quality.

NON-VINTAGE CHAMPAGNE: The greater part of all Champagne made. By judicious blending of wines from different years, quality is maintained, although it should be remembered that often a Champagne establishment will make several qualities of wine, even of non-vintage.

PINK CHAMPAGNE: Made either by allowing the skins of the black **grapes** in the **vat** to remain until they have just tinted the wine slightly, or else by blending in some of the red wine of the Champagne region (see **Bouzy rouge**). Champagne rosé is usually non-vintage, but some houses do make a vintage pink.

Blanc de blancs literally means 'white from whites'.

Most Champagne is a blend of the **Pinot Noir** (black) and **Chardonnay** (white) grapes. The white grapes give the wine finesse and delicacy, the black grapes give body and fragrance. But sometimes a Champagne will be made from white grapes only – this is usually very delicate and light. In spite of James Bond, it is by no means 'the best' Champagne: only a type which, in some circumstances, can be delicious (see below). There is also a *blanc de noirs*, from black grapes only, which is rarely seen outside the region.

LUXURY CHAMPAGNE: Many of the great Champagne houses select an

CHAMPAGNE, FRANCE

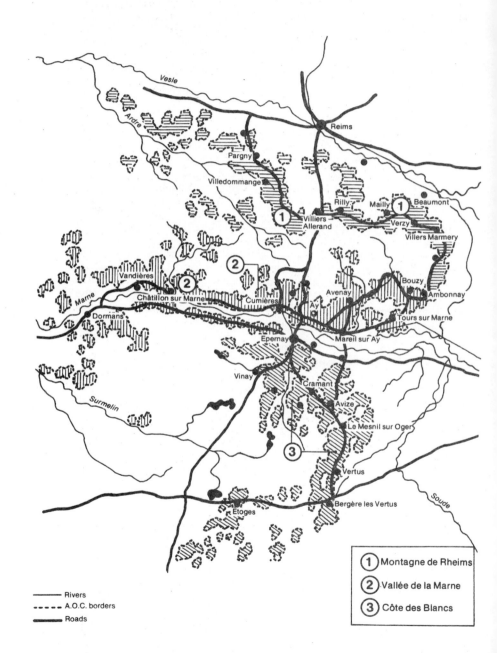

especially fine *cuvée* (vatting) to be kept apart when the wine is made. This is later presented as a supreme wine. It is, of course, more expensive than ordinary Champagnes, and may be put into a special, decorative **bottle** – there are even some matured in elegant **decanters**. Such wines are very fine and definitely in the 'special occasion' category. They are meant to be appreciated and it would be foolish, and indeed ostentatious, to serve them when a generally acceptable 'party' sort of wine is what is required. Among the better-known luxury wines are: Dom Pérignon, Dom Ruinart, Diamant Bleu, Roederer Cristal, Mercier Réserve de l'Empéreur, Taittinger Comtes de Champagne, and Chasteau de Irroy. Although some of these are *blanc de blancs*, not all luxury Champagnes are; but most are labelled with a vintage. An additional explanation is required for Bollinger R.D.: the initials stand for 'recently disgorged', the wine being matured on its first cork for longer than usual, and the date of the disgorging being stated.

AGE: Champagne without a **vintage** date is ready to be enjoyed as soon as it is offered for sale. With vintage Champagne, it is generally true that the wine begins to be at its best from 7 to 12 years from its vintage, once it has been disgorged and is on its second cork. Wine left on its first cork can remain in good condition – in the cellars where it was made – for much longer than this. But once it is on its second cork, the wine begins to change and, eventually, decline so that, once it has been moved from its original cellars, its age must be observed because age alone is not necessarily a good thing in any wine. Old Champagne tends to darken in colour and lose its sparkle; it can still be a very good drink for those who like it but this is a personal preference.

STILL CHAMPAGNE: They are the still wines of the region. These were known as *vins nature de la Champagne*; but the correct name now is **Coteaux Champenois**.

SERVING: Champagne should be served at a refreshingly cool temperature, but not so chilled that it is impossible to enjoy the **bouquet**. Many authorities agree that the temperature of a cool cellar – about 37-46°F (5-8°C) – is ideal, except on a very hot day, when a slightly lower temperature may be more acceptable or on occasions when a sweetish wine may call for an even lower temperature. The wine should be chilled in either an ice-bucket, containing a mixture of ice and water (never ice alone, which will have little effect), or in a refrigerator. The former will chill the bottle faster as a rule. Do not keep wine long-term 'on ice' or in the refrigerator, as after some time it deteriorates and will taste and smell strange if left indefinitely.

GLASSES: The most important thing about Champagne or sparkling wine **glasses** is that they should be either goblet, tulip or *flûte* shaped, and of reasonable size. The 'saucer' glass is always bad, with the possible exception of the type that is fairly deep with a hollow stem, within which the bubbles can rise.

Champagne cocktail There are many variations on this, but basically it is usually made by rubbing a lump of sugar on the skin of an orange, to take on the 'zest', then adding a couple of drops of **Angostura bitters** to this. Put the sugar in a glass with a tablespoonful of **brandy**, and top up with **Champagne**. Variations include **frosting the glass**, using orange **Curaçao** or strawberry **vermouth** instead of brandy. A surprising difference – and improvement – is achieved by allowing the sugar-Angostura-brandy mixture to stand for an hour before topping up with the **sparkling wine**.

Champagne method   This is the means whereby the greatest **sparkling wine** in the world – **Champagne** – is made, and is also the process used to make fine sparkling wines in other regions. If the Champagne method is used for sparkling wines in **France** – and in many other countries too – the fact will be stated on the **label**. Such wines cannot be cheap and, even though they may not all be of outstanding quality, none will be less than very good; it is not otherwise worth subjecting them to the Champagne method.

Each of the great Champagne houses and establishments making sparkling wines by this method will have its own individual procedures but in general the process is essentially as follows. The base wine should be one with a fairly high degree of acidity (which is why most quality sparkling wines are white, and from northern vineyards), and be at least of moderate, but preferably of high, quality. The wine is made in the usual way, the various types of **grapes** being selected and **blended** according to the skill and experience of the maker. Then, in the spring, the various wines are made into the different *cuvées* and the wine is bottled before the second **fermentation** can take place, and the *prise de mousse* (taking on of the sparkle) occurs when this fermentation begins in the **bottle**. The **carbon dioxide** cannot be given off and so is retained in the bottled wine.

In former times, the first **cork**, made of cork, was fastened on to the bottle and held there by a metal clip, called an *agrafe*. But the rising price of cork has resulted in the increasing use of a **crown cork** for the first cork, which is clipped on to the top of the bottle; it contains a sliver of cork, plus a small plastic cup, into which the **deposit** drains. Use of the crown cork, originally much frowned on by many Champagne establishments, seems perfectly satisfactory, since a neutral plastic (lining the metal cap) has been perfected and the majority of Champagnes receive a crown cork as their first stopper today. It has been pertinently commented that there are far fewer **corked** bottles recently, because it is possible to achieve a more thorough sterilisation with a crown cork than an ordinary cork. Some houses, however, continue to use cork for the first corks of their luxury and **vintage** Champagnes. It is possible to see which type of cork has been used by looking at the neck of the bottle: if the *agrafe* has been put on, the neck will have a squared-off flange on to which the clip can be attached. If a crown cork has been used, the neck will have only a rounded flange.

Any sediment left in the wine is then made to adhere to this first cork by turning the bottle almost upside down with its neck in a **rack** (called a *pupitre*). A band of men go round, shaking each bottle regularly by the base and giving it a slight turn, both to one side and so that it is progressively turned upside down. It can then be **binned**, still upside down, with the neck of one bottle resting in the **punt** of another; and can remain like this, with the wine still on its first cork, for years without deterioration. When required for selling the bottles are 'disgorged': that is, the *agrafe* and the first cork are removed – taking with them the sediment adhering to the cork – and the second cork is put in, together with any **dosage**, or sweetening, according to the type of wine it is wished to make (see *brut*). In former times, this was done by hand, very quickly, so as to lose as little as possible of the wine. Nowadays the process is simplified in most establishments by freezing the necks of the bottles. Thus the little lump of ice that comes out with the cork contains the sediment, and the bottle can then receive its dosage and any necessary topping-up. The second cork is topped by a metal cap, which prevents the wire muzzle that holds it down from biting into the cork. Then the bottle is 'dressed' with a foil **capsule** covering the cork, with its **label**, any neck label and/or back label. Finally, covered in tissue, it goes to be packed in a wooden case or strong carton. With the finer Champagnes, a further period of maturation in the cellars then takes place to 'marry' the wine with the dosage after the operation of *dégorgement*, as previously described.

It is the skill of man and the amount of time involved that make the Champagne method lengthy and costly, and why it is not worth while applying it to a wine of inferior quality. Essentially, it is because wine made in this way spends most of its life in bottle that it must be expensive. As well as the huge corks used and the elaborate 'dressing' of the bottles, the bottles themselves have to be extra thick to resist the internal pressure, and the packing and carriage adds to the expense involved. See *Grandes Marques*, **Charmat method**, *cuve close*, **carbonated wines, transfer method**.

Champigny A red wine, crisp and high in acidity, light in character, from a small vineyard near **Saumur** in the **Loire** valley.

Chapellet **Winery** in the **Napa Valley, California**, making red and white table wines which are gaining favourable comments from those who know them. All come from the **grapes** of the winery's own vineyards.

Chaptal The Minister of Agriculture of Napoleon I who, although he did not invent the system of adding sugar to the **must** of wine in cool vineyards where **fermentation** might be difficult in all but exceptional years, gave his name to the first decree whereby musts in such vineyards were authorised to receive sugar. See **Chaptalisation**.

Chaptalisation The process of adding sugar to the **must**, so as to assist the **fermentation**, especially in northern vineyards where there may not be sufficient natural sugar in the **grapes** to enable an acceptable wine to be made. Chaptalisation is permitted, although strictly controlled, in the making of **Burgundy** and, in certain circumstances, in making other classic wines.

Chardonnay Sometimes incorrectly referred to as the Pinot Chardonnay, this is the great white **grape** of the fine white **Burgundies**, and of **Champagne**. It is also grown in many other parts of the world.

Charmat method Monsieur Charmat, at the beginning of the 20th century, perfected and commercialised the system whereby a quality **sparkling wine**

may be made in a sealed vat (*cuve close*); thereby saving time, money and labour. The best known wine made by this process is Veuve du Vernay, produced by Charmat's own firm. Many good sparkling wines are made by this method, including those that would not improve with the longish maturation involved with the **Champagne method**. See **carbonated wines, transfer method**.

Charneco   Parish in the **Bucelas** region of **Portugal**, which some authorities think may be the 'Charneco' mentioned by Shakespeare. The wines are also referred to in Dickens' *Sketches by Boz*; and it is known that the officers in Wellington's army enjoyed the wines during the Peninsular Campaign, 1808-14.

Chartreuse   Liqueur and **digestive** named after the Charterhouse (Chartreuse) founded by St Bruno near Grenoble in France in 1084. The present building, after many were destroyed by fire, is at Voiron, and the liqueur became famous when, in 1848, a group of French army officers were billeted there. Subsequently, as a result of increased demand, a **distillery** was built nearby at Fourvoirie. When the Carthusians were expelled from France in 1903, they took the recipes for both the green and yellow liqueur with them to **Tarragona** in Spain, but production was resumed when they returned to France in 1931. The liqueur is alcoholically strong, but the green is stronger than the yellow. Both are slightly 'herby'. Elixir Végétale, also made at the distillery, is very strong indeed, and is traditionally taken by putting a few drops on a lump of sugar.

Chassagne-Montrachet   Parish in the **Côte de Beaune** in **Burgundy**, making both white and red wines. Part of the great **Montrachet** vineyard is also in this parish. Although it is the white wine that is most usually seen on lists, the red Chassagne-Montrachet, Clos St Jean, is also famous and, because of its delicacy and suppleness, the wine is thought by some to resemble those of the **Côte de Nuits**.

Chasselas   (Pronounced 'Shas-lah') There are a number of different members of the Chasselas family, but essentially it is a white **grape**, possibly brought to Europe by the Romans. The Chasselas Doré is the most popular French table grape. Quantities of wine are made from it, but generally nothing very fine; however, improved methods may alter this. In the **U.S.**, it is known as the Golden Chasselas. Perhaps the most significant region in which it is cultivated is that of the upper **Loire**: the **Sauvignon** is used for **Sancerre** and **Pouilly Fumé**; but the Chasselas for ordinary Pouilly-sur-Loire. It is also used in **Alsace**, where there are various local names, including **Knipperlé**.

Château   This term, used in a French wine context, means some kind of specific estate producing wine. See *Clos*, *Domaine*. It is not allowed to be used for a wine that does not come from the property named. In many New World **wineries**, however, where **grapes** and wine may be bought in from regions outside the particular estate, the term *Château* is sometimes used both for the installations and for the wines put out under their **label**, so that here the word need not indicate that there is any sort of *château* responsible.

The word is capable of wide interpretations in **France**, however: the *château* may be some form of country house, even the remains of a castle, it may be a modest building – or not even a building at all. There is, for example, no *château* at **Léoville-Barton**; the vineyard is separate from the vineyard of **Langoa-Barton**, but only the latter exists as a *château* in the form of a building. Some French wine *châteaux* are beautiful and historic buildings but an imposing mansion does not necessarily mean that a correspondingly fine wine will be made at the estate. The expression 'a *château* wine' may be translated as 'an estate wine' – that is, wholly produced on the property. *Petits châteaux* is a term for small-scale estate wines, often referring to the **bourgeois growths** of **Bordeaux**, because the term *château* is so widely (but not exclusively) used in this region. There are *Châteaux* in the wine regions of the **Loire**, in the south of France, in **Alsace** and in **Burgundy**.

Château-bottling (This section also covers estate-bottling and domaine-bottling.) At one time bottling by a reputable and experienced wine merchant was accepted as satisfactory for even the greatest wines. Today, modern technological advances have made it difficult for small firms to enjoy the resources enabling the finest and most delicate wines to be handled so as to be in prime condition in even the most remote export markets. Therefore – and because of increased demand and improvements in communications – there is an overall tendency for all fine wines to be bottled either at the estate where they are made, or at least in the country where they are made.

It is usual for château-bottled wines to be slightly slower to come to their prime than those bottled where they are sold; and the general opinion is that, if a comparison is made, the château-bottled wine will be slightly, but definitely, superior in quality and clarity of character than the wine bottled elsewhere. But there can be, of course, indifferent château-bottlings! The assumption that a château-bottled wine is absolutely genuine is fair to make – but if someone is going to be unscrupulous, they are capable of tampering with wine at any stage. It is also true to say that the best bottlings of firms with reputations as high as those of the great properties are in no way inferior to the château-bottlings. The infinitesimal difference appears to come from the fact that the wine is moved, in **cask**, away from its home, and subjected to travel and variations of temperature before finally going into **bottle**.

In recent years some of the great estates of **Bordeaux** experimented with producing non-vintage château-bottled wines, so as to provide fine wines of standard quality which will not vary, even if a succession of **vintages** are not good. There is much to be said on both sides of this question, but the traditional lover of **claret** usually thinks that it is precisely the variations from year to year that make this wine so fascinating. Most great properties have, or can have, their brand name on a non-vintage wine label, under which a wine not quite worthy of the *château* label can be sold. Improvements in winemaking have made it possible to produce wine of moderate quality in years which, formerly, would have been complete disasters. The person who wants to 'drink the label' of a wine, but who will not risk the variations of a vintage, is often depriving himself of seeing the wine at its best. The non-vintage château-bottling was not successful in Boreaux and was mostly discontinued.

Château-Chalon   Not an estate, but a general name for the finest **vins jaunes** of the **Jura** region of **France,** coming from a particular group of vineyards.

Chateau Chevalier (*sic*)   **Winery** in the **Napa Valley, California.**

Chateau Leonay (*sic*)   This property is on the North Para River in **Australia**'s **Barossa Valley.** It was first planned and established by Leo **Buring,** an outstanding wine man, who died in 1961 before he could see the property finished. The following year it was bought by **Lindeman**'s and is now an enormous concern, producing **fortified** as well as table wines. As with many **wineries** of the New World, the bulk of the **grapes** used comes from outside growers, but the estate owns vineyards in several regions.

Chateau Montelena (*sic*)   **Napa Valley winery** near **Calistoga, California.**

Chateau Souverain (*sic*)   Newish **winery** of the **Napa Valley** in **California** which, in spite of its name indicating an estate, buys in **grapes** to make its wines. They can attain good quality.

Chateau Yaldara (*sic*)   A **winery** in the **Barossa Valley** region of **Australia,** making a variety of wines but especially known for its **sparkling wines.** The aboriginal word *yaldara* in fact means 'sparkling'. It was established after World War II by a German, Hermann Thumm, who came from a **Rhine** wine family. He was in business in Iran, involving winemaking, when he was interned in 1941. As an internee, Herr Thumm was sent to Australia and in 1946, he decided to remain. He eventually rehabilitated a ruined 19th century winery in the style of a European wine estate. This is Chateau Yaldara.

Châteauneuf du Pape   The vineyards at the southern end of the **Rhône** in **France** produce what is possibly the most famous of Rhône wines. They are mostly red, although a little white is also made, produced both by large establishments and on a few big estates. Thirteen different types of **grape** are permitted to be used, including the principal grapes of the **Côtes du Rhône.** The wines tend to be a little suppler and rounder than the young **Côtes du Rhône** wines and many people who like a full, robust wine would be far better pleased with these, which are still reasonable in price, than with a genuine but expensive red **Burgundy** or a distorted 'commercial' version.

Châtillon-en-Diois   The wines of an area in the Drôme, within the **Rhône Valley,** making red, white and pink wines.

Chénas   Beaujolais vineyard area, producing full, fruity red wines.

Chenin Blanc   One of the great white wine **grapes** of the world, this is best known in **France** for the wines it makes along the **Loire,** varying from dry to very sweet, still to **sparkling.** Its local name there is Pineau de la Loire. It is also widely cultivated in many New World vineyards, where it seems to be used mostly for making dry or medium dry wines, although some sweet examples are also to be found. For me, the Chenin Blanc has an individual fragrance that I describe as 'honey and flowers'. The fresh, flowery initial smell has an underlying soft, honeyed note, even with the dry wines, rather evocative of the clover florets that children suck.

Cheri-Suisse   See **chocolate liqueurs**.

Cherry brandy   There are a number of these, varying in character. That made in Denmark by the House of Heering is widely known, its name now being Heering's Cherry Brandy. Grant's Morella Cherry Brandy has been made in England for over a century; Lamb and Watt of Liverpool make one; and there is another English one sold under the name 'Trotosky'. Cherry brandy is produced in many countries, but it is worth remembering that it is not the same as an *alcool blanc*, such as **kirsch**, which is **distilled** from cherries, or the same as **maraschino**. Guignolet, the French name for a type of cherry, is made at Angers in France. In the 19th and early 20th centuries, it was often traditional to drink cherry brandy from a flask taken out while hunting or shooting, as its warming, refreshingly fruity character seemed appropriate at such times.

Cheval Blanc   A *premier grand cru classé* of **St Émilion** in the **Gironde** region of **France**. It never makes less than a fine wine and some people would rate it as equal with the finest red wines of the **Médoc**. Its vineyards touch those of **Pomerol** so that, unlike the other great St Émilion vineyard, Château **Ausone**, which is in the heart of the St Émilion vineyard, Cheval Blanc wines possess a touch of the stony character that gives elegance as well as body. Because of the name, it has sometimes erroneously been supposed to be a white wine; but it has never made anything except red.   See **Bordeaux, classification**.

Chevaliers du Tastevin   Well-known French **wine order**, of which there are now many, established (or revived) in the Depression between the world wars to create interest in the wines of **Burgundy**. In 1944 the order bought the Château du **Clos de Vougeot**, where their principal ceremonies are held. Membership is an honour – but it can be arranged and should not be automatically assumed to be a privilege reserved only for those truly knowledgeable about Burgundy.

Chianti   (Pronounced 'Key-an-ty') Strictly delimited area in **Tuscany**, in **Italy**, producing what is possibly the best-known of all Italian red wines. It is important, however, to realise that it is only since comparatively recent legislation and the **D.O.C.** that the region has been strictly delimited and that there are some good red **Tuscan wines** that cannot use the name because they are produced outside the Chianti area or have not chosen to join the Chianti Classico *consorzio*, or the other Chianti regional associations. The great producers **Brolio** and Antinori recently withdrew from the Chianti Classico association. Nor can the white wine of the region now be called 'white Chianti', the term 'Tuscan wine' or a regional name must be used. The **grapes** mainly used for Chianti are **Sangiovese** (which predominates), **Canaiolo, Trebbiano** and **Malvasia**, although different producers may vary the proportions.

Chianti which is meant to be drunk while it is young and fresh is, when intended for sale in Italian markets, made with the *governo all'uso toscano*. This gives it a slight 'prickle' on the tongue, almost as if it were a *pétillant* wine. Some people like this, others do not – but it is wrong to reject an 'Italian style' Chianti because it is 'working', as some Anglo-Saxon drinkers do. Chianti of the finer qualities, that is intended to gain from slow maturation in **bottle**, is never subjected to the *governo*. A *Riserva* is matured in **wood** for 3 or more years. The wicker-covered globular Chianti **flask** is likewise only used for wines meant to be drunk while they are young; the finer wines are laid down in bottles which are like the square-shouldered Bordeaux **bottle** in shape, although in fact they have a very slightly shorter neck. Chianti of this quality can have a long life and develop great charm and subtlety. See *chiantigianna*.

CHIANTI CLASSICO : Wine from an area defined within the Chianti region bearing a **label** showing a black cock on a gold ground. Other areas bear the names of the regions within the Chianti district, each one bearing a special label. The other regions, in addition to the Classico area, are: Putto, Montalbano, **Rufinà**, Colli Senesi (Sienese Hills), Colli Aretini (Arezzo Hills), Colli Fiorentini (Florentine Hills), and Colline Pisane (the smaller-scale hills around Pisa. It should be stressed that the wines, although individual, should be appraised according to the personal taste of the drinker. By the term 'Chiati Classico' no degree of superior quality is intended. In one recent judging, a Chianti from outside the Classico region was put first.

Chianti Rufinà has confused some drinkers, but this region is nothing to do with the great establishment of **Ruffino**; its label carries a device of cherubs. Possibly the most famous of quality Chiantis is that of Brolio, and the estate of the Barone **Ricasoli**, whose family have been influential in the Italian wine world for many generations, is impressive. The Ricasoli family own other estates as well. Some other famous producers are Melini, Antinori and Frescobaldi, who make the Nipozzano wine. It is always important to be precise about the house that produces a Chianti, as each has its own style and will, therefore, vary.

Chiantigianna   The 60 fl.oz (1.75 litre) **bottle** now becoming popular for ready-to-drink **Chianti**.

Chiaretto del Garda   Red and rosé **Italian** wines from **Lombardy**. Some of them are made from the **Merlot grape**, others from a combination of Italian wine grapes. They are light in style and are often served cool.

Chiavannasca   Local name in the **Valtelline** region of **Italy** for the **Nebbiolo grape**.

Chicha   **Peruvian** drink made of corn and molasses.

Chig-Ge   Mongolian alcoholic drink of fermented mares' milk, like **koumiss**.

Chile   Both red and white wines are made in Chile, but it is the reds that have become best known on export markets. The **grapes** used to make the wines are European classics. Although as yet the wines available in the U.K. have been of no more than very good everyday quality, it may well be that some will achieve even higher standards in the future. The significant thing about all the Chilean wines, which include sweet and **sparkling wines**, is that, as the *Phylloxera* has never attacked the vines in this country, they are not grafted and, therefore, can give an idea of what wine produced from *nacional* vinestocks is like. Some of the estate wines display good quality and it may well be that this country will provide some most interesting wines for all drinkers, now that transport is easier.

China Marco Polo wrote in 1275 that the inhabitants of Peking enjoyed a very light-coloured, scented **rice wine**. A type of beer, **cider** and various **liqueurs** are also made in China, but few are known outside the country. *Mao tai* is a distillate. *Shao hsing* is a rice wine; traditionally made at the birth of a daughter, then kept until her wedding: *Kuei hua chen chiew* is a type of rice beer, formerly prepared only for the Imperial Family: *Mei kuei lu chiew* is a **digestive liqueur** from Tientsin: *Mui guy lu* is a type of rice **gin**.

Chinon Wine region on the River Vienne, tributary of the **Loire** in **France**, making red wines from the **Cabernet Franc grape**. They can, in the right kind of year, achieve a fruity charm and delicate flavour that is extremely pleasant. Rabelais praised them, and although they do not always bear **vintage** dates, they can age very pleasantly. They should never be served warm – indeed, on their home ground they may be served at cellar temperature (cool) to show off their character.

Chiroubles **Beaujolais** vineyard area producing red wines with great fruit and, usually, a very alluring **bouquet**. .

Chocolate liqueurs Chocolate is the base for a number of popular **liqueurs: crème de cacao**, put out by many firms, is possibly the best known. Originally the beans for the finest **liqueurs** of this type came from Chouao, a suburb of Caracas in Venezuela, but the term 'chouao' is now used generically for Venezuelan cacao beans. Chocolate liqueurs may be brownish or white, as with the German Cacao mit Nuss, or the Royal Mint-Chocolate, evolved by Dr Peter Hallgarten. He subsequently produced Royal Orange-Chocolate Liqueur, and others involving chocolate plus ginger, cherry, brandy, raspberry, lemon and coffee flavourings. Vandermint is a Dutch chocolate mint liqueur; Sabra is an Israeli chocolate and bitter orange liqueur; Cheri-Suisse is a Swiss chocolate and cherry liqueur.

Choum A **digestive liqueur** made from fermented rice in Vietnam. The matured type is known as *tchoung-tchoung*. See **gingseng pu chiew**.

Christian Brothers This concern is the largest church property producing wine in the world. It also makes **brandy**, **altar** and **communion** wines, and produces table grapes. The Christian Brothers are a Roman Catholic monastic teaching order, founded in Rome in the 17th century. Although they take vows and wear habits, they are not priests. The correct name for the concern is Mont La Salle Vineyards. The Brothers have three **wineries** in the **Napa Valley** and two in San Joaquin, **California**, which support the Brothers' schools and novitiate. The table wines are sold without **vintage** dates, as they are often blended so as to achieve continuity of style. The table wines are pleasant; although those I have tasted have achieved no more than medium quality. **Fortified wines** are also made. The Brothers own vineyards as well as their wineries, and all are attractively arranged for tourists to visit.

Cider Alcoholic beverage made from apples. It is big business in the drinks trade in the U.K., where cider has been made and appreciated for centuries. The cider press was basic equipment in many country houses and some private makers are recorded as having played tricks on visiting foreigners by serving

'**English wine**' of an impressive quality, which was actually cider. Many beautiful cider glasses were made at this time. Today, there are a number of British firms producing a range of ciders and many of these have premises open to visitors, where old cider-making equipment and historical objects associated with cider may be seen.

Cider is also made in Normandy, where there have been vast apple orchards from very early times; it is traditional in some places to serve it in a *bol* (a shallow pottery cup). Cider is also made in the Channel Islands. See **Applejack, Calvados**.

Cinqueterre   Italian white wine, made both dry and sweet, from **Liguria**. It gets its name from the five 'lands' that make up the vineyard region. Some of the vineyards are so inaccessible that they have to be cultivated by workers let down on ropes from the tops of cliffs, others can only be reached by boat. The **Vernaccia grape** is the predominating **variety**.

Cinsaut   Black **grape**, used extensively in the **Rhône** Valley, also planted in **California**, where its name is the Black Malvoisie. In **South Africa**, it is called Hermitage and is of considerable importance, also **Australia**.

Cinzano   One of the great **vermouth** firms, still a family business. The Cinzanos have family records going back to 1568 and they have been making cordials and **distilling** since 1705. They lived near Turin, amid orchards and ample supplies of fruits of all kinds. In the 18th century they became established in Turin, where they succeeded so well with their shop that business connections were formed in Nice, **Savoie** and South America by the middle of the 19th century. Eventually they took over a previously royal establishment at Santa Vittoria d'Alba, which became widely known when the film, *The Secret of Santa Vittoria* related how huge supplies of wine, concealed from the occupying Germans during World War II, remained hidden in spite of threats and atrocities. The Cinzano establishment now owns many other interests, including the huge **Florio** establishment at **Marsala**. The name will be most familiar, however, because of Cinzano's *'Bianco'* – the world's best known white **vermouth** – which pioneered the sales of this type of vermouth and which still dominates the market.

Cirò   Italian wine region in **Calabria**, where what appears to be a good red and some pink and white wines are made.

Cissac   Region in the **Médoc**, making pleasant wines, of which the best known is certainly that of Château Cissac. Its dedicated owner, Louis Vialard, has augmented the advantages it enjoys from its proximity to Château **Lafite**, through his care and adroit publicity.

Clairet   See **claret**.

Clairette (1)   Name used in **Australia** for the **Mauzac** grape.

Clairette (2)   This is a white **grape** grown for centuries in many Mediterranean countries, where it makes a variety of wines, sweet and dry, and at one time was much used for **vermouth**. The full name is apparently Clairette Pointue or Clairette Verte. Should not be confused with the **Australian** name.

Clairette **(3)**   Not the same as **claret**, this term means a light, pinkish wine from the **Bordeaux** region. Its production is governed by regulations. It can be a pleasant picnic or light meal wine, but no more. It is rarely exported.

Clairette de Die　Wine from the vineyards around Die, in the Drôme region of **France** – the Drôme is a tributary of the **Rhône**. The **Clairette** and **Muscat grapes** are used for rosé and white wines, some of them **sparkling**. These last are made either by the **Champagne method** or else by keeping the wine in a . sealed cask and allowing the **carbon dioxide** in it to be retained, thereafter bottling while the sparkle is still in the wine. They are dry and crisp.

Clare　Sometimes known in books as 'Clare-Watervale' for its 2 main towns, this is the most northern of the vineyard areas of South **Australia**. A wide variety of wines are made and some of the **wineries** date from the middle of the 19th century. The red wines are especially reputed; but many others, including **fortified wines**, are also made.

Clarendon　Vineyard region in **South Australia**.

Claret　The word orginally derived from *clairette*, signifiying a light coloured wine, typical of the reds of **Bordeaux**, and used to differentiate these from the darker up-country wines often used for blending with them in years when they lacked colour and body. In time the term became used by the English and, subsequently, the British, for all the red wines of Bordeaux; although rather oddly no other country even seems to have made use of the word. In recent times, there was much trouble among the members of the EEC, when it was wished to suppress the use of the word 'claret' on wine labels – the British won that battle, because of the precedents established by using that name. However, the U.K. is still the only country where its use is accepted and understood.

Clarete　Term often used in the Iberian Peninsula to signify red wines that are light in style, as compared with the weightier reds or *borgoñas*. It should in no way be associated with **claret**, which it does not resemble at all.

Classico　See **Chianti,** *consorzio.*

Classification　This term, used generally in connection with wine, usually means the ranging in five *crus* (growths) of the wines of the **Médoc** (and one red **Graves**) in 1855. The outstanding red wines of the **Bordeaux** region had, in fact, been 'classified' since the early part of the 18th century, but in 1855 the syndicate of Bordeaux brokers carried out the classification of the red wines of the **Gironde** and of the **Sauternes** and **Barsacs** for the Universal Exhibition in Paris. It should be stressed that this arrangement was essentially for the purpose of sorting out the wines according to the price they might be counted on fetching.

　The 1855 classification of the Médoc (except for **Haut Brion**, then classed among the 1st growths, no red wines from any other region were included) still stands; although there is now considerable argument about a reclassification. Some estates have been rearranged, a few have disappeared, properties have changed hands and quality has varied. **Mouton-Rothschild**, classified as a 2nd growth in 1855, now often fetches a price as high as any of the other 1sts and objected strongly to being described as 'second', adapting the motto of the

Rohan family as: *'Premier ne puis, deuxième ne daigne, Mouton suis'* (First I can't be, second I won't be, I'm just Mouton). Due to the assiduous campaigning of its owner, Baron Philippe de Rothschild, it was reclassified as a 1st growth in 1973. But, understandably, other owners whose properties might be classed down on any rearrangement, object violently to any change, and so do those who, often with reason, think they might possibly go up much higher than the suggested alterations indicate – and that their prices imply.

It is probably fair to say that all the classed growths of the Médoc are fine wines, and that the majority of them still set a standard – for quality as well as a for price. But the categorisation into five sections is often misleading today, because some 5ths, 4ths and 3rds often rate higher, as regards quality, than some 2nds. There is even one 1st growth that went through a period during which it did not, in the opinion of many, deserve its high position.

The Sauternes and Barsacs were classified, as has been stated, in 1855. The white wines of Graves were classified in 1959. The red wines of **St Émilion** were classified in 1955, and the red Graves in 1953. It will be noted that, in the lists of these classified wines, the subdivisions vary slightly. It should also be remembered that it is not obligatory for the property to indicate its classification on its **label**: for example, **Latour** does, but **Lafite** does not. The **bourgeois growths** of the Médoc were classified in 1932 and 1966. They are not listed here for reasons of space, but the fact of their having been classified may be given on their labels and the complete list is given in Cocks and Feret, *Bordeaux et ses Vins*, or other detailed reference works. See Bibliography.

1855 Classification of Red Wines (as originally given)

PREMIERS CRUS/1st GROWTHS

Ch. Lafite	Pauillac
Ch. Margaux	Margaux
Ch. Latour	Pauillac
Ch. Haut Brion	Pessac (Graves)
(Ch. Mouton-Rothschild	Pauillac (since 1973))

In 1973 a decree of the French Ministry of Agriculture was issued, whereby the first five wines of the 1st growths were stated to be of equal worth and it was said that their names should henceforth be given in alphabetical order – that is:

Château Lafite Rothschild
Château Latour
Château Margaux
Château Mouton Rothschild

and 'by assimilation' (because it is in the Graves and not the Médoc),

Château Haut Brion

Why anyone bothered to issue this decree and why anybody should attach the slightest importance to it, is something that will doubtless baffle British drinkers, as it does me. The quality of the wines is not affected at all and the discriminating will continue to believe that certain of these fine wines are better than certain others, which of course they are entitled to do; as they are entitled to their personal preferences as to which they like best – not always the same thing. However, I am citing the decree as something that has become law in France, apparently considered of importance by some French people.

DEUXIÈMES CRUS/2nd GROWTHS

Ch. Rausan-Ségla	Margaux
Ch. Rauzan-Gassies	Margaux
Ch. Léoville-Lascases	St Julien
Ch. Léoville-Poyferré	St Julien
Ch. Léoville-Barton	St Julien
Ch. Durfort-Vivens	Margaux
Ch. Lascombes	Margaux
Ch. Gruaud-Larose	St Julien
Ch. Brane-Cantenac	Cantenac
Ch. Pichon-Longueville	Pauillac
Ch. Pichon-Longueville-Lalande	Pauillac
Ch. Ducru-Beaucaillou	St Julien
Ch. Cos d'Estournel	St Estèphe
Ch. Montrose	St Estèphe

TROISIÈMES CRUS/3rd GROWTHS

Ch. Kirwan	Cantenac
Ch. d'Issan	Cantenac
Ch. Lagrange	St Julien
Ch. Langoa	St Julien
Ch. Giscours	Labarde
Ch. Malescot-St-Exupéry	Margaux
Ch. Cantenac-Brown	Cantenac
Ch. Palmer	Cantenac
Ch. Grand La Lagune	Ludon
Ch. Desmirail	Margaux
Ch. Calon-Ségur	St Estèphe
Ch. Ferrière	Margaux
Ch. Marquis d'Alesme-Becker	Margaux
Ch. Boyd-Cantenac	Margaux

QUATRIÈMES CRUS/4th GROWTHS

Ch. St-Pierre-Sevaistre	St Julien
Ch. St-Pierre-Bontemps	St Julien
Ch. Branaire-Ducru	St Julien
Ch. Talbot	St Julien
Ch. Duhart-Milon	Pauillac
Ch. Pouget	Cantenac
Ch. La Tour-Carnet	St Laurent
Ch. Lafon-Rochet	St Estèphe
Ch. Beychevelle	St Julien
Ch. Le Prieuré-Lichine	Cantenac
Ch. Marquis-de-Terme	Margaux

CINQUÈMES CRUS/5th GROWTHS

Ch. Pontet-Canet	Pauillac
Ch. Batailley	Pauillac
Ch. Haut Batailley	Pauillac
Ch. Grand-Puy-Lacoste	Pauillac
Ch. Grand-Puy-Ducasse	Pauillac
Ch. Lynch-Bages	Pauillac
Ch. Lynch-Moussas	Pauillac
Ch. Dauzac	Labarde
Ch. Mouton d'Armailhacq (*now* Mouton Baronne Philippe)	Pauillac
Ch. du Tertre	Arsac
Ch. Haut-Bages-Liberal	Pauillac
Ch. Pédesclaux	Pauillac
Ch. Belgrave	St Laurent
Ch. Camensac	St Laurent
Ch. Cos-Labory	St Estèphe
Ch. Clerc-Milon-Mondon	Pauillac
Ch. Croizet-Bages	Pauillac
Ch. Cantemerle	Macau

1855 Classification of White Wines

GRAND PREMIER CRU

Ch. Yquem	Sauternes

PREMIERS CRUS/1st GROWTHS

Ch. La Tour-Blanche	Bommes
Ch. Peyraguey (Clos Haut-Peyraguey)	Bommes
(Lafaurie-Peyraguey)	Bommes
Ch. Rayne-Vigneau	Bommes
Ch. Suduiraut	Preignac
Ch. Coutet	Barsac
Ch. Climens	Barsac
Ch. Guiraud	Fargues
Ch. Rabaud (Rabaud-Promis)	Bommes
(Sigalas-Rabaud)	Bommes
Ch. Rieussec	Barsac

DEUXIEMES CRUS/2nd GROWTHS

Ch. Myrat	Barsac
Ch. Doisy (Doisy-Daëne)	Barsac
(Doisy-Védrines)	Barsac
(Doisy-Dubroca)	Barsac
Ch. Peixotto (part of Rabaut-Promis)	Bommes
Ch. d'Arche	Sauternes
Ch. Filhot	Sauternes
Ch. Broustet	Barsac
Ch. Nairac	Barsac
Ch. Caillou	Barsac
Ch. Suau	Barsac
Ch. de Malle	Preignac
Ch. Romer (2 proprietors)	Fargues
Ch. Lamothe	Sauternes
Ch. Lamothe-Berguey	Sauternes

1959 Classification of White Graves*

Ch. Bouscaut	Cadaujac
Ch. Carbonnieux	Léognan
Ch. Olivier	Léognan
Domaine de Chevalier	Léognan
Ch. Malartic-Lagravière	Léognan
Ch. La Tour Martillac	Martillac
Ch. Laville Haut Brion	Talence
Ch. Couhins	Villenave-d'Ornon

*__Haut Brion Blanc__ was not included in this classification at the request of the proprietor.

1953 Classification of Red Graves

Ch. Bouscaut	Cadaujac
Ch. Haut Bailly	Léognan
Ch. Carbonnieux	Léognan
Domaine de Chevalier	Léognan
Ch. de Fieuzal	Léognan
Ch. Olivier	Léognan
Ch. Malartic-Lagravière	Léognan
Ch. La Tour Martillac	Martillac
Ch. Smith-Haut-Lafitte	Martillac
Ch. Haut Brion	Pessac
Ch. Pape Clément	Pessac
Ch. La Mission Haut Brion	Talence
Ch. La Tour Haut Brion	Talence

1954 Classification of St Émilion

PREMIER GRAND CRU CLASSÉ

Ch. Ausone	Ch. Cheval Blanc
Ch. Beauséjour-Duffau	Ch. Beauséjour-Fagouet
Ch. Belair	Ch. Canon
Clos Fourtet	Ch. Figeac
Ch. La Gaffelière	Ch. Magdelaine
Ch. Pavie	Ch. Trottevieille

GRAND CRU CLASSÉ

Ch. L'Angélus	Ch. L'Arrosée
Ch. Balestard-La-Tonnelle	Ch. Bellevue
Ch. Bergat	Ch. Cadet-Bon
Ch. Cadet-Piola	Ch. Canon-La-Gaffelière
Ch. Cap-de-Mourlin	Ch. Chapelle-Madelaine
Ch. Chauvin	Ch. Corbin-Giroaud
Ch. Corbin-Michotte	Ch. Coutet
Ch. Croque-Michotte	Ch. Curé-Bon
Ch. Fonplegade	Ch. Fonroque
Ch. Franc-Mayne	Ch. Grand-Barrail-Lamarzelle
Ch. Grand-Corbin-Despagne	Ch. Grand-Corbin-Pécresse
Ch. Grand-Mayne	Ch. Grand-Pontet
Ch. Grandes Murailles	Ch. Guadet-St-Julien
Ch. Jean Faure	Ch. La Carte
Ch. La Clotte	Ch. La Clusière
Ch. La Cousparde	Ch. La Dominique

Ch. Larcis-Ducasse
Ch. Larmande
Ch. Lasserre
Ch. La-Tour-du-Pin-Figeac-Moueix
Ch. Le Châtelet
Ch. Le Prieuré
Ch. Moulin-du-Cadet
Ch. Pavie-Macquin
Ch. Petit-Faurie-de-Souchard
Ch. Ripeau
Ch. St-Georges-Côte-Pavie
Ch. Tertre-Daugay
Ch. Trois-Moulins
Ch. Villemaurine
Clos des Jacobins
Clos St Martin

Ch. Lamarzelle
Ch. Laroze
Ch. La-Tour-du-Pin-Figeac-Bélivier
Ch. La-Tour-Figeac
Ch. Le Couvent
Ch. Mauvezin
Ch. Pavie-Décesse
Ch. Pavillon-Cadet
Ch. Petit-Faurie-de-Soutard
Ch. Sansonnet
Ch. Soutard
Ch. Trimoulet
Ch. Troplong-Mondot
Ch. Yon-Figeac
Clos La Madeleine

Clastidio, Casteggio Lombardy region around the town of Casteggio (*Clastidium* in ancient Roman times) making a variety of wines.

Clavelin A bottle used in the Jura for *vins jaunes*, such as **Château-Chalon**. It is dumpy, with squarish shoulders, and holds about 22 fl.oz (63 cl).

Clerc-Milon-Mondon Classed 5th growth of **Pauillac**, recently acquired by **Mouton-Rothschild**. See **Bordeaux, classification**.

Climat A specific plot within a vineyard; an expression used in **Burgundy**. The name of the *climat* can be of great importance in assessing the quality – and the price – of a wine.

Climens One of the great **Barsac** estates, which some rate as the greatest of this region; although other people would put **Coutet** higher.

Clinet Estate in the **Pomerol** region, which makes pleasant red wines. See **Bordeaux**.

Clone This term, increasingly heard used by those discussing **vine varieties**, means a specific strain, deriving from one particular vine.

Clos The word means 'enclosure' and is often used to indicate a vineyard surrounded by a wall. Although the prefix is most associated with **Burgundy**, it may be found in other French wine regions.

Clos de Bèze See **Chambertin**.

Clos de Tart One of the great growths of **Morey-St-Denis** in the **Côte de Nuits** in **Burgundy**. It has been under **vines** at least since the 12th century, when it belonged to a religious order associated with a Cistercian sisterhood, who made the wines from their vineyard famous. During the French Revolution, the property was seized by the state. Today it belongs to the large firm of Mommessin and is unusual in that it is wholly under their sole ownership. The wine enjoys a great reputation.

87

Clos de Vougeot   One of the most famous vineyards of the **Côte de Nuits** in **Burgundy**: a single estate (owned by about 100 different proprietors), in the parish of Vougeot. The château was built in the 16th century by the Cistercians, and now belongs to the **Chevaliers de Tastevin**, the Burgundy wine order. It is so highly regarded that regiments of the French army, passing the property, traditionally salute it. The red wines are generous, robust and easy to like although perhaps lacking a little in subtlety. A little white, made in the parish of Vougeot, is sold as Clos Blanc de Vougeot.

Clos du Roi   One of the most famous vineyards of **Aloxe-Corton** in **Burgundy**.

Clos Fourtet   *Premier Grand Cru Classé* of **St Émilion**, known for its full, rather soft fine wines. The prefix '**Clos**' is unusual in the region but its use does not necessarily mean – as is sometimes affirmed – that the wine is a **Burgundy**. See **Bordeaux, Classification**.

Clynelish   (Pronounced 'Clyne-leash' stressing 'leash') **Whisky distillery** in Brora, Sutherland, Scotland, now belonging to a subsidiary of the **D.C.L.** In fact, this is a new distillery, as the name has been changed and the old Clynelish must now be called Brora.

Cochylis   Vine disease.

Cockburn   (Pronounced 'Coh-burn' stressing 'Coh') The full name of this **port shipper** is Cockburn Smithes and as they are now associated with Martinez Gassiot and Mackenzie, overall they are often refered to as Cockburn, Martinez, Mackenzie. Founded in 1815, Cockburn is a highly respected establishment; their ports sell throughout the world. Their **vintage** wines enjoy great fame, notably the vintages of the early part of the century. I once ventured to describe the style to one of the directors as 'steel under velvet' – the vintage ports usually have great charm plus firmness

Cocktail   The origins of this word are obscure, some people claiming that it is an Indian, Mexican or Aztec word. It seems definitely to have been first used in the **U.S.**, possibly from the very beginning of the 19th century, and implies a mixed drink based on spirit or spirits, including **bitters** and served in a small glass.

Coda di Volpe   Literally 'fox tail', the name of a **vine** cultivated in **Campania**, south **Italy**, which is reported to yield good wines.

Coffee liqueurs   Coffee is the main flavouring in a number of popular **liqueurs**, which are generally dark brown. The best known is probably Tia Maria, which is Jamaica **rum** and coffee extracts. Kahlúa, a Mexican coffee liqueur, made for European markets by the House of Heering in Denmark, and Gallweys Irish Coffee Liqueur are also well known, but most countries produce such liqueurs.

Coffey, Aeneas   An Irishman, an excise officer in Dublin, who patented a type of still, in 1831, that bears his name. This is the Coffey, **patent** or continuous still, whereby the process of **distillation**, formerly only possible in the **pot still**, was able to be carried on quickly, on a large scale and at a fairly reasonable cost.

Cognac   A spirit **distilled** from wine in the Charente region in the west of

France, acknowledged to be the world's supreme **brandy**. **Brandywine** or *'brantwijn'* – literally 'burnt wine' – is supposed to have been first made around Cognac and Jarnac in the 17th century, when there was a glut of wine and the current wars made trade with the Low Countries difficult. The distillate disposed of the excess wine, was easier to transport (in smaller quantities than wine), and proved very popular.

The Cognac region today is divided into areas, strictly controlled by law. They are, in ascending order of quality: Bois Communs, Bois Ordinaires, Bons Bois, Fins Bois, Borderies, Petite Champagne, Grande Champagne. The names refer to the type of countryside from which the brandies come. The word 'Champagne' is nothing to do with the sparkling wine, although the soil of these regions is actually similar to that of **Champagne**, meaning 'level open countryside'.

Cognac is made by a double distillation and then matured in **wood** – ideally, **casks** of oak. It only matures in wood – and not indefinitely. After a certain point, depending on the Cognac, it will begin to decline; from the moment it is **bottled**, its age is arrested. The skills of the **blender** in each Cognac establishment enables different brandies to marry so as to preserve the quality of the different styles of Cognac particular to each house: from the everyday type to the fine **liqueur** Cognacs. Cognac may be sold under the name of the region from which the components of the blend come, but any labelled 'Fine Champagne' must contain not less than 50% of Grande Champagne. In the finer Cognacs there will be a high proportion of old brandies, but French law does not now permit any Cognac to bear a **vintage label**, even if it is made only from the brandies of a single year. This means that there is no such thing as 'vintage Cognac' in France, unless in the personal reserves of a member of a Cognac establishment.

Before the U.K. joined the EEC, British merchants could ship a vintage Cognac and mature it in the U.K. The important thing about this was that Cognac matured in the wet bonds of Britain was quite different from an identical Cognac kept and matured in France because of the difference in the atmosphere. The French Cognac tended to be more advanced, a little sharper and more assertive; the British version, slower to mature, was very delicate and possibly more subtle. This kind of Cognac, often referred to as 'old London landed' or 'old landed', is a great rarity and a precious – and expensive – commodity. Nowadays anyone who does ship a spirit of this kind cannot put a specific vintage date on it, even if he does know its age. But the essential thing to remember is that the spirit will not mature any more when it is bottled, so that, if it is only a young brandy then, it will not get any better or smoother. The kind of specialist wine merchant in whose cellars old landed Cognac with a vintage date may still be found, will usually label it with the date of bottling, so that the buyer can see its true age. Any picturesque dressing-up of a **bottle** to imply age is pointless chi-chi.

Each of the Cognac houses has its own system of grading its brandies and there is no legislation establishing or controlling the use of descriptions such as

V.S.O.P. (supposed to stand for 'very special old pale'), or the number of stars on the label. The 'everyday' brandies are intended for drinking with water or soda or as ingredients in mixed drinks. The luxury Cognacs are for drinking alone, usually at the end of a good meal. But the use of huge **glasses**, warmed over a flame, is incorrect for any brandy, whether Cognac or otherwise. Similarly, the popular belief that a Cognac is 'better' if it is either dark or pale – according to the fashion of the moment – is erroneous. It is true that brandy can lighten in colour as it ages, but it takes colour from its cask and may also be coloured by the addition of caramel to satisfy the customers who prefer a particular tone of Cognac. The only thing that should guide someone choosing Cognac is the style preferred as the result of experience – each house has its own individuality – and the occasion when the brandy is to be drunk. See **three star**.

Coing See *alcool blanc*.

Cointreau See **Curaçao**.

Colares Region near Lisbon in **Portugal**, making both white and red wines, although the reds are better known, able to mature and demonstrate great quality. The vines are curiously and haphazardly cultivated in sand dunes; because of this, they have never needed to be grafted because the *Phylloxera* aphis has not attacked them. They are seldom seen outside their region and therefore deserve attention by visitors.

Coleburn-Glenlivet A **whisky distillery** owned by the **D.C.L.** at Elgin on Speyside. Its products are used for **blending**.

Colli Albani Literally, the wines of the Alban Hills in **Lazio, Italy**. They are all white, including some rather sweetish aromatic wines. Much liked, especially at the papal summer resort in the hills, Castel Gandolfo.

Colli Piacentini The Piacenza hills region in **Emilia-Romagna, Italy**, making red and white wines of medium and good quality, of which the red **Gutturnio** is pleasant.

Collins A long drink, containing lemonade, carbonated water and some spirit. The Tom Collins, possibly the best-known version, got its name because of being made with Old Tom **gin**; the John Collins was made with Hollands gin.

Collio Goriziano The wines of the Gorizia Hills, in **Friuli-Venezia Giulia**, which may also sometimes be simply called Collio. Many of these wines, made on the border between **Italy** and **Yugoslavia**, are white; but some reds are also made. They usually seem to be called after the **grapes** that produce them.

Colorino **Grape** that may be used for **Chianti**.

Colour The colour of a wine is of great importance – but sometimes can be misleading. It should always give pleasure to the eye and possess a 'living' tone. But having said this, there are many exceptions to such generalisations as are usually made. The charts that are becoming fashionable accompaniments to **wine tasting** amaze me by the range of words refering to colours they sometimes provide for the taster – but, as some people have an acute sense of colour and others rather a limited one, it seems more practical to evolve one's own set of terms relating to colour. Gold, lemon-gold, light straw, greenish-lime for white wines; purple, plum, tawny red, crimson, rhododendron, azalea for red and pink wines: these are a few of the words I use myself.

White wines tend to deepen in colour as they age and sweet white wines usually begin by being more definitely golden than dry wines. A notable exception is **Chablis**, with its odd, pale tone that possesses a shimmer of green – something no imitation of this wine ever reproduces. Red wines, however, tend to lighten as they get older and this also applies to **port**; some young red wines are almost black-purple in their youth. (The 'purple stainéd mouth' of Keats' poem certainly might refer to anyone tasting young reds, when one acquires a black tongue, like a chow.) Naturally, the type of **grape** used wields an influence on the colour of the wine; both because of the varying tones of its juice (although most freshly-pressed grape juice is pale green, like grapefruit juice) and because of the difference in the pigmentation of the skins of the black grapes. In hot vineyards the sun develops this, so that the wines are darker red than those in northern vineyards. This is why a Mediterranean **rosé** can be almost the colour of a light red wine, and a rosé from some cold, northern vineyard will be very pale. If the **must** is slightly heated, more colour can be given to northern red wines.

However in some years certain wines are simply lighter than usual, in others darker. Various respectable methods of treating them can remedy a defect of colour. Before anyone thinks this unnecessary, may I advise the doubter to get a friend to add a little dark red colouring to a red wine without letting the taster see – and then try it. You will almost invariably comment that the darker wine has more 'body', even if it is exactly the same wine! This is why professionals often taste samples in a 'black' or dark coloured **glass**; so that they cannot be influenced, however slightly, by their eye telling them what the wine tastes like. There is also the problem of colours being altered in different lights. The light up in the dry atmosphere of the Douro Valley, where a **shipper** may be looking at samples of young port, is quite different even from the light in the **lodges** in **Vila Nova de Gaia**; and the light by which a Swedish buyer will appraise a wine will be different from that in the tasting room of a merchant in Bristol, even though all are looking at the wine by the light of the same sun. This is why it is of great importance to match up samples of wines and spirits sold under brand names; there must be continuity. There are also fashions in, say, pale coloured Scotch, or dark coloured **rum**, as well as in certain wines; so that people who buy what they have seen advertised or tried in tastings want the colour to be the same, even if this does not, truly, affect the taste of the drink. A little experience will acquaint anyone with some knowledge of the main colours of the principal wines and spirits and, it should not be forgotten, in looking at these colours, some account should also be taken of the viscosity of the liquid – the actual texture it shows in the glass and how it falls down the sides of the bowl (see **legs**). It is extremely difficult, even with the best colour reproduction systems, to give exact pictures of the colours of wines, so that books are not always helpful.

There are two ways of looking at colour: the most usual is to tilt the tasting sample in the glass away from the taster, over something white, and note the gradations of colour from the **miniscus** down to the central point, which I refer to as the 'eye'. One thus sees a range of tones. It is worth knowing that, in comparing wines, the wine in which a number of tones can be seen, even while it is still young, tends to be a wine with more to give the drinker and it will probably be the more expensive sample. Of course with a very dark red wine, such as a young port of a certain type of **vintage**, the colour will be so dark that shades of tones can hardly be noted, and with very pale white wines the lightness makes this type of appraisal equally difficult. People do occasionally hold a glass up to the light, but not as often as many suppose. As for the appraisal of a wine's colour by candlelight, this is a pretty piece of chi-chi today. It is sometimes necessary in a cellar where there is no other form of lighting; it is 'atmospheric' (whatever that means) at certain types of wine parties. But serious tasting is done either by daylight or strong artificial light, in lab-like surroundings of white paint, white tiles or white plastic on the tasting bench, a north light and possibly a white wall outside the window.

Some tasters also find it interesting to stain a piece of white cloth with a drop of the wine being tasted, as this, spreading out into rings of shading, can also indicate something of the wine's character. But this can become complicated and more for the laboratory to investigate. The simple explanations of colour can be overlooked when people are trying to be clever: a very pale red wine may simply be so because, either just before or during the vintage, there was a lot of rain! A very dark-toned **sherry** may be neither sweet nor particularly old; it could be one taken from a bottle that has been opened for weeks and standing in a strong light or the artificial light of a bar, when the wine has become **maderised**!

One of the most significant things about colour in wine was said by my own great teacher, Allan **Sichel**: 'The colour can tell you something as to how far a wine is from its beginning – it cannot tell you how near it is to its end.' Colour should be observed and enjoyed: you should then go on to smell and taste.

Columbard, Columbar This white **grape** was first planted in the Charente region of **France**. The authority on grapes, Lucie Morton, says that its wines appealed to the Dutch, who were trading with the area, more than the wines made from the established **Folle Blanche.** It is still used for **Cognac** and, in the **Bordeaux** area, is planted in the white wine regions of **Entre-Deux-Mers** and **Blaye**. It is also used in **California**.

Columella, Lucius Junius Moderatus His dates are uncertain, but he flourished about the middle of the 1st century A.D. Born in southern **Spain,** possibly in Cadiz, it is not known when he went to **Italy**, but he died in Tarentum. He is known today for his works *De Arboribus* (On Trees) and *Re Rustica* (Of Country Things). The latter includes an important section on the cultivation of the **vine, pruning, grafting** and general care. His possible knowledge of Spanish viticulture and viniculture makes this of great interest, as what he wrote had a subsequent effect on vines and wines in Italy.

Commandaria The great **dessert wine** of **Cyprus**, known from medieval times. In the country it is produced in huge jars from cultures; but in the modern **wineries** it is made like any sweet wine. It is capable of ageing for a very long time. Dark brown, luscious and capable of great quality, Commandaria is one of the classic wines of the world. It gets its name from the 'commanderies' into which Cyprus was at one time divided. The Order of the Knights of St John of Jerusalem owned the section that yielded the best wine.

Commune French for 'parish'. The word, used in a wine context, implies a parish wine, such as **St Émilion** or **Margaux**, which may or may not bear a **vintage** date. The wine should be typical of the area but, even though it may in fact contain wine from individual properties (which for various reasons may have been declassified), it will be a general representative of its region, no more. See **A.O.C.**

Communion wine There are no absolute rules about this, except that the wine should be a natural one: that is, a **table**, not a **fortified**, wine. It can be red or white and, simply because it is easier to drink a sweetish wine when one is fasting (hence the cup of sweet wine with which the Passover fast is broken), they are usually on the sweet side. These are the rulings that apply to both the Church of England and the Church of Rome. Certain establishments specialise in providing wine that has been approved by the religious authorities for use in the sacraments.

However, in times of shortage or emergency, it appears from historical records that occasionally fortified wine has had to be used or, as occurred on the battlefield of Culloden in 1745, the dying Lord Strathallan was given communion by an Episcopal minister in 'whisky and oatcake, the requisite elements not being obtainable'. Churches who do not accept the use of a fermented beverage for the administration of the sacraments, appear to use grape juice for the purpose.

Concannon Vineyard and **winery** in the **Livermore Valley, California**. The founder originally made wines for religious purposes – so, during **Prohibition**, business was able to continue. It is still a family concern, making a range of table wines and reports speak highly of the winery's **Sauvignon Blanc**.

Concongella Vineyard in **Australia's Great Western** region.

Concord This grape belongs to the *Vitis labrusca* strain. It is deep red and the majority of **New York State** vineyards are planted with it. The wines it makes are soft, both red and white, and very perfumed. It is used a great deal in the kitchen for making sweet dishes and as a flavouring, and it has become popular because of its use in making **kosher wines**.

Condrieu A white wine, made from the **Viognier grape**, in the **Rhône** Valley in **France**. It is full in character and very distinctive in flavour. As it is made in very limited quantities it is not often seen outside the region; but at the Restaurant de la Pyramide at Vienne, made world-famous by the late Fernand Point (his widow and chef still maintain the establishment), it is Condrieu that is the usual 'house wine'.

Cònero Red wine from the **Marche** region of **Italy**.

Conestoga Vineyards   Pennsylvania **winery** in the U.S.

Congenerics   Without describing these in chemical terms, it is roughly true to say that they are the 'extras' in spirits, apart from the **alcohol** – the elements that remain in the **distillate** that give spirits such as **brandy** and malt **whisky** their charm and individuality. They are not relevant to the quality of the spirit, but it is thought by many medical authorities that it is the congenerics that make some spirits more conducive to producing hangovers than others. For example, **vodka** is low in congenerics, and so is beer, whereas Bourbon, malt whisky, brandy and **rum** are fairly high. The research is still continuing.

Conigliano   Region in the **Veneto, Italy**, making good quality white, red and **sparkling wines**.

Conseja Regulador   The controlling body of a **Spanish** wine region.

Consorzio   **Italian** wine producers grouped themselves together into *consorzii* so as to supervise and control winegrowing and making. The different groups were each known separately as a *consorzio*, a term that might be translated almost by the old term 'guild'. Today the trade associations have either assimilated or bypassed the *consorzii* in many instances, but their work is of great significance and members are highly influential in establishing standards and maintaining quality traditions. The *consorzii* of the various wine regions have done valuable work in establishing traditions and maintaining the quality of their wines. In some instances, however, certain large-scale producers have decided to withdraw from the local *consorzio*, because they feel they can sell wines more effectively if they act independently.

Constantia   Birthplace of the Cape vineyards in **South Africa**. The first vintage was made here, near Cape Town, in 1659. See **Groot Constantia**.

Consumo   Portuguese term for everyday red or white table wine – the type made at the estate for current consumption.

Container   See **casks**.

Continuous still   See **Coffey still, patent still**.

Convalmore   Whisky distillery at **Dufftown**, Banffshire, now owned by the **D.C.L.**

Co-operative   This term is capable of a number of interpretations but, in general, a 'co-op' is an association of winegrowers who need one **winery** to process and, at need, keep and market their wines. Small-scale growers can obviously not install machinery on a large scale, for using only once a year at **vintage** time. The work of the co-operatives has made it possible for many growers to remain in business and, within certain organisations, to continue making individual wines. Some co-ops are highly reputed: there is, for example, one in south **Burgundy** where the most respected foreign buyers purchase wines, each one of these individual to the particular **vatting**. This type of co-op can make a range of different quality wines, as well as handling the **grapes** for small proprietors who otherwise might not have been able to remain in business. The co-ops also often enjoy the services of famous **oeonologists** as consultants.

Although sometimes somewhat slighting references may be made, in a region abounding in fine estate wines, to a 'wine from the co-op'; it is very often the co-op wines whose steady production has enabled peasant growers to remain in business and therefore to attract a market for the comparatively inexpensive wines – which, later, may attract buyers to buy the finer products.

Cook **New Zealand** wine company of considerable influence and importance, in winemaking as well as in the large scale of their business.

Coolalta **Australian** vineyard, in the **Hunter River Valley**, owned by **Lindeman**.

Coonawarra Important **Australian** wine region, near the border of South Australia and Victoria, it is famous for its wines. The climate, rather cool and changeable, means that the character of each **vintage** will vary. Typical **soil** of one part is the *terra rossa*, which is unusual in the production of fine wines; but the subsoil, of chalk and limestone, and the presence of fossils in the dark, clay-like soil in other parts all contribute to wines of individuality and stylishness. The red wines have probably made the reputation of the region in export markets, but plantings of **grapes** for white wines are also considerable. The main **wineries** are run by **Wynn, Mildara, Lindeman, Penfold** and Hungerford Hill. The most famous individual range of wines is possibly that produced by Wynn at their huge winery, under the name 'Coonawarra Estate'. The name 'Coonawarra' is an aboriginal word, meaning 'wild honeysuckle'.

The comparison of some of the reds with **claret** is often made but, in spite of the use of the **Cabernet Sauvignon** grape, I think there is merely a likeness, not a direct similarity. The interest of these wines is considerable however.

Copita Literally 'little mouthful'. The term used for an elongated tulip-shaped **glass** with a short stem, as used for **sherry**.

Corban **New Zealand** vineyard and **winery**, established at the beginning of the 20th century. A wide range of table, **fortified** and **sparkling wines** is made.

Corbières Wine region in the south of **Languedoc** between Narbonne and the Spanish frontier. The wines are mostly red, made chiefly from the **Grenache, Carignan**, Terret Noir and **Picpoul grapes**, with a full-bodied character and clean fragrance.

Cordial This word originates in the Latin *cor*, signifying 'belonging to the heart'. Therefore, from the Middle Ages, a cordial usually meant a stimulant or reviver. It became used mainly for sweetish spirit drinks. The small 18th century 'cordial **glasses**', still found in antique shops, were made to serve the strong, warming drinks which were offered as revivers at the end of an evening when, after the men had finished the serious drinking around the dining table and the ladies had taken tea in the withdrawing room, all needed a strong, slightly **digestive** type of drink when they met again before ending the party.

Cordial Médoc Sweetish, red **liqueur**, made by Jourde of **Bordeaux**.

Corks The cork oak, *Quercus suber*, source of the best cork for sealing **bottles**, has flourished in parts of Europe for thousands of years, and in fact the use of cork for stoppering bottles or wine containers was known to the Assyrians, ancient Egyptians, Greeks and Romans. Pitch was often used by the latter two peoples to seal the cork firmly. However the use of cork in the world of wine then declined, although it still survived in certain Mediterranean regions, notably in Catalonia, where there are still vast cork forests. It appears to have been known in England before the 17th century – perhaps introduced by traders. It is possible, though one cannot be sure, that monks from the Benedictine monastery at Barcelona may have visited their brothers at Hautvillers in **Champagne** where, at the end of the 17th century, the cellarmaster Dom Pérignon achieved the triumphs of making up the *cuvée* and, by the use of cork, sealing the bottle so as to retain the natural sparkle in the wine. Previously the only way wine was sealed was by a type of wooden bung, often wrapped in an oily cloth. This made it impossible for wine to remain long in bottle; such bottles as existed were more in the nature of **carafes** from which the wine was served after being drawn from the **cask**.

The cork oak must be at least 20 years old before its bark can first be stripped, then 8 to 9 years must elapse before subsequent strippings. The stripped cork is cut into sections, then boiled and, if first-class cork is involved, left to mature outdoors. Corks are cut either by hand from blocks of solid cork, or else by machine. Hand-cut corks are basically straight sided, with rounded edges, and are superior for sealing. All corks, after cutting, must be trimmed and cleaned so that grain markings are removed. In former times, they were washed before being inserted, but nowadays they are sterilised and may also be subjected to hot or cold waxing, for easier corking.

SIZES: A 'full long' cork, used now only for vintage **port** and occasionally for the finest red wines, is a 2 inch (5 cm) cork, nearly always hand cut. It will be appreciated that the slight bulge in the neck of the bottle used for vintage port is to accommodate the cork and enable it to swell and grip the bottle. The fine **clarets** and red **Burgundies** are nowadays usually corked with the Bordeaux cork, measuring 1⅞ in (4.75 cm). Wines which are not intended for long-term laying down are usually corked with a 'short long' cork, of 1¾ in (4.5 cm). Half bottles may be corked with the same length of cork as bottles; this is usual in the U.K., but varies throughout Europe, where shorter corks may be used, and also where different bottles and 35 fl.oz (1 litre) bottles are widely used.

OTHER STOPPERS: A '**stopper** cork' is the type often used for non-vintage **fortified wines** – a metal or plastic top of greater diameter being attached to a cork. A 'crown cork' is a layer of cork within a metal cap which has to be levered off – the kind of top used on many soda or fizzy drink bottles. An 'alka type seal' is a metal cap that comes over the top of the bottle, within which there is a plastic stopper. This is the sort of closure much in use in wines for everyday consumption in Europe. A plastic stopper may be used for a variety of fine wines nowadays, including **sherry** and certain sparkling wines. Because these are not intended to be kept for long periods before being drunk, the use of plastic is an economy and has not apparently had any effect on the wines.

CHAMPAGNE CORKS: Cork is still used for the finer **Champagnes**, although experiments have been made with plastic for the less expensive wines. The Champagne cork can be both costly and difficult to make. The very finest type of second cork is made of several pieces of fine quality cork stuck together so that, rather like the butcher's chopping block, they take the strain of the wine's pressure and expand within the bottle neck. The top of the 'mushroom' of the Champagne cork obviously need not be of the same quality as that part of the cork which is in contact with the wine, although it must be strong. The metal **capsule** on the top was evolved to prevent the wire or string holding the cork in from biting through the cork. Many Champagne corks are made with a layer or more of cork fragments bonded together – or 'agglomerated' – except for the part in contact with the wine and on the top. The use of a wholly *non-agglomé* cork today is both expensive and, some would say, not necessary because of improvements in the making of the wine. But one great Champagne house still refuses to use fragmented corks.

BRANDED CORKS: The wines of many of the great estates have corks on which the name of the property and the **vintage** of the wine are branded. The presence of such a cork should indicate the genuineness of the wine. But in certain years of war or crisis in the past, when corks were difficult to get, many estates were obliged to use ordinary corks, so that the fact that a cork of, say, a 1943 classed growth **claret** is not branded, is not a fair reason for suspecting that the wine is not what it purports to be on the **label**. Merchants often use branded corks, but the detail on these is usually confined to their name or initials. A Champagne cork is usually branded on its base – the part in contact with the wine – when it is branded at all, although there may also be an additional brand on the side of the cork.

STAINING: Obviously a red wine will, after a while, stain the cork with which it has been in contact. It is unlikely that a wine bearing a vintage date of 10 years earlier will have a dead-white cork. However there are certain circumstances when it might and, as the staining of a cork varies according to the precise intensity of the colour of the wine, the type of cork, and whether this is waxed or not, instantaneous condemnation and rejection of a wine because its cork is not as stained as the purchaser expects, is unwise without a lot of experience. For example, sometimes wines are rebottled, both to suit the requirements of a market – bottles into halves, or, indeed, to bottle off **deposit** – or because the supplier has reason to believe that the cork may not be holding up as well as it should. There may be a trace of seepage (the bottle is then described as a **'weeper'**), or the wine may be very old, or may have had originally to be bottled when corks were in short supply. Recorking in such conditions can do no harm at all: indeed, it may preserve the wine. See **corked**.

Corked, corky It is probably true that far more bottles are returned to their source of supply as being 'corked' than actually are so. Drinkers often just do not like a wine, mistake a touch of **'bottle stink'**, or a defect such as the use of a dirty bottle, a touch of woodiness (from a faulty stave in the **cask**), or simply bits of **cork** in the wine, for 'corkiness'. It is also sometimes difficult to tell when a wine is first poured whether or not it is corked – the corkiness may only develop to a pronounced extent after a few minutes or even half an hour. But there are several things to bear in mind: drinking a corked wine may be unpleasant – depending on the degree to which it is corked – but will not harm the drinker. The smelling of the cork (see **decanting**) will not inevitably indicate whether or not it is corked, and the actual smell of corkiness is not, to everyone, a smell of clean cork – to some people it is evocative of chlorine, to others of drains.

In general, a wine that smells of little at the outset, that then has a smell unlike that of a wine at all, and that develops a type of flat, chemical sort of flavour will probably be a wine that can be described as 'corked'. If one is in doubt, a comparison of the questionable bottle with that of another one usually clears up any hesitation – although there have been instances when three bottles in succession have all been corked! This is also why it is essential always to taste each bottle *separately*, in a clean **glass**, so as to avoid the risk of pouring corked wine on top of sound wine.

The cause of corkiness is not necessarily a faulty cork, or the action of the cork weevil, or a seepage of wine through the cork; although it can sometimes be related to one or more of these. But if the drinker can distinguish, with a faulty wine, between one that is corky, one that is musty, and one that is casky, the three main faults that may be found in a wine in bottle will be recognised. In each instance, the bottle, sealed up again, should be returned to the source of supply as soon as possible, and the supplier should be notified as to the comments passed when the bottle was opened.

However, in restaurants, many bottles in perfect condition are returned, simply because drinkers chose something they didn't like, or couldn't taste after drinking quantities of spirits. The wise *sommelier* will simply agree that the customer is always right, replace the bottle or advise another wine, and drink the rejected wine for his supper, if not returning it to the supplier.

Corkscrew   Because of the comparatively recent use of **cork** to stopper the wine **bottle**, the corkscrew (or bottlescrew as it was first called) did not come into being until the beginning of the 18th century. It is surprising that, with the great variety on the market at the present time, very few sold to the general public are of the slightest use in getting a cork out of a bottle. Whatever type is selected, there are a few things that every efficient corkscrew should have: it should be long enough to go to the bottom of a full long cork; it should not have sharp edges on the sides of the spiral, which will cut up the cork and possibly make the whole thing crumble; and, most important of all, the spiral should be a true spiral, and continue in its curve right to the tip. The type of corkscrew that ends in a sharp point, like a gimlet, will merely pierce through the cork and not grip it, so that, as it is pulled, it may simply be drawn straight back through the now-disintegrating cork. A good corkscrew, of whatever type, should have a long screw, of rounded material, and, whether a single or double spiral, one should be able to look up through it, like looking up a spiral staircase.

Corn whiskey   See **whisky**.

Cornas   See **Hermitage**.

TYPES OF CORKSCREWS

Double screw cork extractor. The top lever inserts the screw then the lower lever is turned to raise the cork.

A modern type of cork remover for use **only** on still wines in standard-shaped (cylindrical full bottles. The needle is inserted into the centre of the cork, the black button pressed once to inject CO_2 gas from a Sparklet bulb (type used to make soda water). Pressure of the compressed gas then raises the cork. Another type of remover forces air through the needle by means of a pumping action to raise the cork.

A butterfly cork extractor. The screw is inserted then the side levers are lowered to pull it out. The top of the extractor is a lever for 'crown' corks.

Two-pronged extractor. Particularly useful for corks that may crumble. The longer prong is inserted first then the other. The prongs grip the cork and a slight turn of the handle enables the cork to be extracted. (Sometimes called 'The bad butler's friend'.)

The right and wrong types of screw

The left-hand one is virtually a gimlet which merely pierces the cork. The right-hand one has sharp edges which will cut into the cork and risk breaking it. The central example is rounded, a complete spiral to go through the cork, hold it, and, without breaking, enable it to be pulled out without damage.

Waiter's corkscrew with penknife (for cutting metal or plastic capsules). Corkscrew with lever in the body of the device plus prong that incorporates a 'crown' cork remover.

Corowa **Australian** vineyard region in New South Wales, known because of **McWilliams** quality wines.

Corsica This island has proud traditions of winemaking, but not until recently were its wines seen outside their homeland. However the development of the island for tourist trade, and the settlement there by many **Algerian** winemakers forced to leave North Africa, has given a great impetus to wine and it is likely that many Corsican wines will be featured on export lists in the near future. The whites are especially reputed – Napoleon I was supposed to like them – but rosés, reds and a sweet wine are also made. The improvement of their quality means that tourists should try as many as possible on the spot. As yet, the wines are of no more than pleasant everyday quality, but there seems no reason why they should not achieve more. Possibly the best-known Corsican wines are those from the Patrimonio region, making red, white and rosé; this area has an **A.O.C.** Other areas are Sartène, La Balagne and the Ajaccio hills, and the table wines and sweet wines of the Cap Corse peninsula: these last are often made from the **Muscat grape**.

Cortaillod (1) **Swiss** red wine from **Neuchâtel**.

Cortaillod (2) Swiss name for the **Pinot Noir**.

Cortese (1) **Italian grape**, used to make the dry, white **Gavi Cortese** in **Piedmont**.

Cortese (2) Wine made in the **Oltrepò Pavese** region of **Italy**.

Corton-Charlemagne One of the greatest of all white **Burgundies** in the **Côte de Beaune**, in the parish of **Aloxe-Corton**. The name derives from a belief that this part of the vineyard once belonged to the Emperor Charlemagne. Two of the main owners of Corton-Charlemagne are the well-known shippers Louis Jadot and Louis Latour. The wine is big, 'bloomy', very impressive and usually very expensive.

Corvina See **Valpollicella**.

Corvo Red and white wines, made at Casteldaccia, near Palermo in **Sicily**, but not, as some writers describe, from 'vineyards surrounding the **winery**'. In fact, there are no vineyards in the immediate vicinity! The aim of the producers is to make wines generally typical of Sicily, and **grapes** come from all over the island to make non-vintage wines. The same winery makes excellent **sparkling wines**.

Cos d'Estournel (Sound the 's', as in 'cos lettuce') Classed 2nd growth of **St Estèphe**, making very fine wines. (The staff at **Lafite** often say that, if they can't drink Lafite, they prefer Cos, which is as unlike Lafite as can be!) The property is remarkable for the 'Chinese' architecture of its château. See **Bordeaux, classification**.

Cos Labory (Sound the 's', as in 'cos lettuce') Classed 5th growth of **St Estèphe**, next to **Cos d'Estournel**, making wines of excellent quality today. See **Bordeaux, classification**.

Cosecha This Spanish word means 'harvest' and implies a **vintage**, which will appear on the **label**.

Costières du Gard Vineyard region in the **Hérault**, just west of the **Rhône**

Valley and south of Nîmes. It makes red, white and pink wines, which can be very pleasant and definitely better than what are merely categorised as 'holiday drinks'. The red is the one best known to export markets and Château Roubaud possibly the most familiar estate name: it first appeared on British wine lists in the 1950s. The surprisingly good dry whites should be sampled by visitors however, and the pink, a robust southern rosé, is also pleasing.

Costozza   Region near Vicenza, in **Italy**, making white, red and rosé wines in small quantities.

Cot   Oo-fashioned French name for the **Malbec grape variety**, a term seldom used nowadays.

Côte   French word for 'slope', implying the side of a hill. Wine from a slope is usually better than wine from flat land, and the sites half or two-thirds up the slope are usually superior to those at the top or bottom, because they are both slightly sheltered and better drained.

La Côte   The vineyard of **Vaud**, in **Switzerland**, which is situated on the sloping north shore of the Lake of Geneva, between Geneva and Lausanne. The wines are mostly white. Not to be confused with *Côte*.

Côte Blonde   See **Côte Rôtie**.

Côte Brune   See **Côte Rôtie**.

Côte Chalonnaise   This region is in south **Burgundy**, and produces red and white wines. The **Pinot Noir** is used for the reds; the Pinot Blanc and **Chardonnay** are used for the whites. The **grapes** must be grown from sites in the parishes of **Givry, Mercurey, Montagny** and **Rully**. Some **sparkling** white wines are also made. The wines can be particularly charming by reason of their freshness, scent and elegance; but they seldom have long lives.

Côte de Beaune   Section of the **Côte d'Or** in **Burgundy**, around the town of **Beaune**. Notable for fine red wines, which are very pleasing though at their greatest perhaps not quite as fine as those of the **Côte de Nuits**; and also for the very greatest white Burgundies, apart from those of **Chablis**. Villages associated with wines include: **Pernand-Vergelesses**, Ladoix-Serrigny, **Savigny**-lès-Beaune, **Aloxe-Corton, Pommard, Volnay, Monthélie, Auxey-Duresses, St Romain, Meursault Blagny, Gamay,** St Aubin, **Puligny-Montrachet, Chassagne-Monrachet, Santenay,** Chagny, **Dezize-lès-Maranges** and Chorey-lès-Beaune.

Côte de Beaune Villages   According to this particular **A.O.C.**, these wines are red, and the blends of at least two wines from those possessing various different A.O.C.s.

Côte de Bourg   See **Bourg**.

Côte de Brouilly   See **Brouilly, Beaujolais**.

Côte de Nuits   Section of the **Côte d'Or** in **Burgundy** running from just south of Dijon almost to **Beaune**. The principal villages associated with wines are: Chenôve, **Marsannay-la-Côte, Fixin**, Brochon, **Gevrey-Chambertin, Morey-St-Denis, Chambolle-Musigny, Vougeot,** Flagey-Echézeaux, **Nuits-St-Georges**, Prémeaux, and Prissey. This is the area that makes the finest red Burgundies of all, though a very little white wine is also made. See **Clos de**

Vougeot. The Côte de Nuits wines are distinguished by their delicacy and profundity.

Côte des Blancs   Region near Épernay in **Champagne**.

Côte d'Or   The part of **Burgundy** where the most famous vineyards for red and white wine are situated. Literally 'golden slope', it is a ridge of vineyards, running from just south-west of Dijon to south of **Beaune**. It is made up of the **Côte de Nuits**, where the very finest red wines come from, from Dijon to **Nuits-St-Georges**; and the **Côte de Beaune**, around the town of Beaune, which region produces many fine red wines and the finest whites.

Vineyards featured on labels:

FIXIN: Clos de la Perrière.

GEVREY-CHAMBERTIN: Chambertin and Chambertin Clos de Bèze (ranking equally), Ruchottes-Chambertin, Chapelle-Chambertin, Mazoyères-Chambertin, Griotte-Chambertin, Mazis-Chambertin, Latricière-Chambertin, Charmes-Chambertin, Clos St Jacques, Véroilles, Fouchère, Estournelles, Gazetiers.

MOREY-ST-DENIS: Clos St Denis, Les Bonnes Mares (part), Clos de la Roche, Clos des Lambrays.

CHAMBOLLE-MUSIGNY: Le Musigny, Les Bonnes Mares (part).

VOUGEOT: Clos de Vougeot.

FLAGEY-ECHÉZEAUX: Les Grands-Echézeaux, Les Echézeaux du Dessus.

VOSNE-ROMANÉE: La Romanée, Romanée-Conti, Le Richebourg, La Tâche, Les Verroilles.

NUITS-ST-GEORGES: Les St-Georges, Les Boudots, Les Cailles, Les Cras, Les Murgers, Les Porrets, Les Pruliers, Les Thorey, Les Vaucrains.

ALOXE-CORTON: Le Corton, Le Clos du Roi, Les Renardes, Les Chaumes, Le Charlemagne.

PERNAND-VERGELESSES: Île de Vergelesses.

SAVIGNY: Les Vergelesses, Les Marconnets, Les Jarrons.

BEAUNE: Les Fèves, Les Grèves, Les Cras, Les Champimonts, Les Marconnets, Les Bressandes, Clos de la Mousse, Clos des Mouches.

POMMARD: Les Épenots, Les Rugiens-Bas, Le Clos Blanc.

VOLNAY: Les Caillerets, Les Champans, Les Freimiets, Les Angles.

MEURSAULT: Les Santenots-du-Milieu, Les Perrières (white).

PULIGNY-MONTRACHET: Le Montrachet (part).

CHASSAGNE-MONTRACHET: Le Montrachet (part).

SANTENAY: Les Gravières.

See also under the specific names of the more famous wines and the **Hospices de Beaune**.

Côte Rôtie   Red wine region on the west bank of the **Rhône** in France; the centre is Ampuis. The **grapes** used are the black, called Serine or **Syrah**, and the white **Viognier**. The Côte is divided into the Côte Brune and the Côte Blonde: a picturesque legend relates that these got their names from being the dowries of the two daughters of a medieval lord – a blonde and a brunette. A more logical explanation is that the **soil** is differently coloured: light and dark. The wines are full-bodied and 'gutsy', capable of much improvement if allowed to mature for some time.

Coteaux French for 'hillsides', as in **Coteaux du Layon**, the hillsides along the River Layon. Wines from such slopes are usually of better quality than those of vineyards on flat land.

Coteaux Champenois The still wines of the **Champagne** region which, since 1974, have received their own **A.O.C.** Subject to strict controls, they cannot simply be made from any **grapes** or wines left over after Champagne is made. The proportion allowed to be made into Coteaux Champenois from the various vineyard regions is decreed by the C.I.V.C. Most are white, made from the **Chardonnay**, but there are some red wines, notably those of **Bouzy**, Cumières, Ambonnay, Ay, Dizy, Rilly, Verzenay and Villedommange. Sometimes the Coteaux Champenois are put into bottles sealed with an ordinary **cork**; some use a crown cork; a few even have the *agrafe* still clipping down the first cork, because the wine always tends to have an innate liveliness.

In style, both white and red are rather big, assertive and, perhaps, somewhat lacking in subtlety. They are never cheap. As obviously the Champagne winemakers can, in good years, earn more from their wines if these are the **sparkling** type, the quantity of still wine is seldom great, but it enjoys a novelty value. In years when the **vintage** is sparse, most of the wine is needed for Champagne and little Coteaux Champenois will be made.

Coteaux de la Loire A subdivision of the **Anjou** vineyards, the best-known wine being the white Savennières. See **Loire**.

Coteaux d'Aix-en-Provence See **Aix-en-Provence**.

Coteaux de l'Aubance The white wine region of the Aubance Valley, in **Anjou** on the **Loire**. The wines can be dryish, but the best known are sweet or definitely sweet, often as the result of the action of *Botrytis cinerea*. Some pink wine is also made.

Coteaux du Languedoc Wines from different regions in the **Hérault**, mostly red and rosé, but with some whites. They are now often sold under their own names and provide pleasant, comparatively inexpensive drinking. Formerly such wines were either only drunk locally or, if produced on a large scale, were often used for making **vermouth** or other **apéritif** wines. The emergence of these and vast number of *petits vins* shows the seriousness of French producers in attempting to improve vine cultivation and winemaking in what were previously merely bulk wine regions. However, even the most lavish publicity cannot make a small-scale wine into a fine one. With prices of the French classic wines very high, some misguided attempts have been made to try and convince buyers of these little wines that they are almost as good as the great **Burgundies** and **Bordeaux**. They are not and never can be. As quality is inevitably related to price, the public cannot expect great drinking experiences from these otherwise pleasant little wines: they should forget the snobbery of the French **label** and, if they can afford a little more, look for lesser-known wines from other countries. See **wine snob, Languedoc**.

103

Coteaux du Layon   The vineyards of the Layon, a tributary of the **Loire** in **France**, which produce dry white and rosé wines and some very fine white **dessert wines**, of which **Quart de Chaume** is possibly the most famous. The sweet wines of **Bonnezeaux** are also of high quality.

Coteaux du Loir   Vineyards on the Loir, a tributary of the **Loire**, producing red, white and rosé wines.

Coteaux du Tricastin   **Côtes du Rhône** vineyard in the Drôme region, mostly producing red wines which have recently become very popular on export markets because of their low price and pleasant, robust character.

Côtes de   There are a number of other wine regions in **France** entitled to called themselves *Côtes de* . . . They include: Côtes d'Agly, Côtes de **Bergerac**, Côtes de **Blaye**, Côtes de Bordeaux St Macaire, Côtes de Buzet, Côtes Canon Fronsac, Côtes de **Duras**, Côtes de Haut-Roussillon, Côtes du **Jura**, Côtes du Marmandais, Côtes de **Montravel**, Côtes de **Toul**, to cite the list given in the latest edition of Lichine's *Encyclopedia*.

Many of these are seldom seen on export markets; others, thanks to modern improvements in winemaking and freight facilities, do provide pleasant drinking outside their homeland. The Buzet, Canon Fronsac, Marmandais and Provence wines are among the latter. But for details about any of them, more comprehensive works of reference on French wines, notable those of **V.D.Q.S.** status, should be consulted.

Côtes de Castillon   These wines, from the eastern part of the **Gironde** in **France** near **Bordeaux**, are both red and white. With improvements in vinification, they are becoming of wider commercial interest and of good quality.

Côtes de Provence   Region in the south-west of **France** on the Mediterranean, where large amounts of pink, white and red wine are made. Today these wines are featured on export lists and the waisted, curvaceous **bottles** of many of them make them pleasant novelties. The pink and the red wines appear to have appealed most to markets outside the region. The wines of **Bandol, Cassis** and those properties where large concerns are now making pleasant wines that do not cost a great deal, are of interest.

Côtes de Ventoux   The foothills of Mont Ventoux at the bottom of the **Rhône** valley, in **France**, where pleasant red and rosé wines are made.

Côtes du Forez   Region in **France** at the top of the **Loire**, where wines of pleasant style are now being made, especially from the **Gamay**.

Côtes du Lubéron   Region of the **Rhône** Valley in **France**, making red and white wines that, in recent years, have achieved some quality.

Côtes du Rhône   Vineyards in the south of **France**, stretching along the **Rhône** valley from just south of Lyon to north of Avignon. Red, white and rosé wines are made. The finer quality wines are sold under the names of their *communes*, the lesser ones may just be termed 'Côtes du Rhône', sometimes with the addition of a site name. A variety of different **grapes** may be used, according to region, but those in fairly wide use include the **Syrah, Grenache, Mourvèdre**, Terret Noir, **Picpoul** (for red wines); Marsanne, Roussanne and **Viognier** for the whites. See entries under specific wines, including **Cairanne, Châteauneuf**

du Pape, Condrieu, Gigondas, Hermitage, Lirac, Tavel.

Cotnari Wine from Moldavia in **Romania**, considered to be that country's greatest white wine. It is slightly sweet and full, and is made from a blend of the native vines – Grasa, **Feteasca**, Frincuça, in equal proportions of 30% and 10% of Tamiloasa.

Couhins, Château (Pronounced 'Coo-ahns') An attractive estate in the **Graves** region of **Bordeaux**, making very pleasant dry white wines.

Coulure Vine disease, when the **grapes** fail to plump out and eventually drop off.

Country wines This term has come into use in the U.K. for alcoholic beverages of approximately **table wine strength**, made from fruits, flowers and vegetables (elderflowers, apples, cherries, parsnips, damsons and so on). They therefore do not conform to the definition of **wine**. There is an enormous interest in the making of these country wines and large numbers of people produce their own, belong to societies concerned with such drinks and compete in annual fairs and competitions. It is a foolish ntion to suppose that such drinks are, even at their best, 'better' than fine wines, but a good country wine can be extremely enjoyable. A knowledge of how wine is made, gained by making such drinks oneself, can enhance the appreciation of wines and spirits enormously.

Courtier This term is the French word for a broker (in wine).

Coutet (Pronounced 'Koo-tay') One of the great estates in **Barsac** which, being within the **Sauternes** region, can call itself either Sauternes or Barsac. The wine is especially fine, sharing with the other great Barsacs the characteristic of a slightly dry finish, or lift, at the last moment of savouring the taste. The name is supposed to derive from *couteau* (knife). Although most of the wine is **estate-bottled**, at one time some was bottled in England, the proprietor giving the privilege of using château **labels** to the firm shipping and bottling.

Cradle This term, more or less interchangeable with that of 'wine basket', refers to the device that holds a **bottle** of wine in a recumbent position, so that it may be drawn from the wine **bin** or **rack** without altering its position from the horizontal to the vertical. The purpose, of course, is to avoid any serious disturbance of such **deposit** as may be in the bottle, by standing the wine up and then being obliged to serve it without enough time for the deposit to slide from the side of the bottle to the base. If a bottle that has thrown a heavy deposit is drawn from the bin and brought to table in a cradle or basket, then whoever is handling it should draw the **cork** and pour while the bottle remains horizontal, either into a **decanter** or, at need, into six or seven **glasses**. The bottle should be gradually tilted but the wine should never be allowed to slop back and churn up the deposit. See **service of wine**. This operation should, in a restaurant that cares for the niceties of service, be conducted either on a table placed alongside that of the diners or, if this is awkward, then it can be carried out on a sideboard after the bottle has been presented. What, unfortunately, often happens, however, is that the bottle is pulled out of the bin and held upright while someone rushes it to the dining-room, where it is then fitted into a cradle or basket before being shown to the diner – the deposit being thoroughly shaken up in the meantime!

It is to be utterly regretted that it is the love of chi-chi by the public and ignorance on the part of many restaurateurs that results in bottles in cradles or baskets being put on to otherwise impeccably-set dining-tables. In my opinion, they have no more place there than has the chamber-pot underneath the table. If a cradle or basket has been used for decanting, then the empty bottle, (standing upright on a coaster or mat) plus its cork, is what should go on the table for the interested to examine. If there is no deposit in the wine, why put it in a cradle at all? Yet I have seen bottles of all sorts put in baskets because the public are supposed to like this pointless form of presentation. Apart from anything else, unless the pourer wedges the bottle firmly into the basket or is sure that the cradle will hold it firmly, it is extremely difficult to pour from a cradle or basket except for those with enormous hands and experience in serving wine. The cradle or basket also takes up far more room on any table than an upright bottle.

Cragganmore   **Distillery** at Ballindalloch, Banffshire, making **whiskies** used for **blending**.

Craigellachie   **Distillery** at the town of the same name, Banffshire, whose **whiskies** go for **blending**. They contribute to the famous blend, White Horse.

Craigmoor   Vineyard and **winery** established in 1858 in the **Mudgee** region of New South Wales, **Australia**. A range of red and white table wines and certain **fortified** and **dessert wines** are produced.

Cream sherry   See **Sherry**.

Crémant   Term used to describe a wine not as fully sparkling as **Champagne** or one fully *mousseux*. The pressure inside the bottle is not as great, being about 4 atmospheres, whereas a fully **sparkling wine** will have 5-5.5 atmospheres. In **Alsace**, however, the very strictly controlled fully sparkling wines made by the **Champagne method** are referred to today as *'crémants'*.

Crème   Prefatory term for a wide range of drinks that can be loosely categorised as **liqueurs**. They have been made for centuries: old recipe books of the American colonies contain a number of instructions for making 'creams', including the rather unusual ones with mint, laurel, jasmine, absinthe and roses. (The product of the dairy never seems to have been involved.) The *crèmes* are not necessarily sweet and today's regulations mean that the word following the term *'crème'* is that of the main flavouring – such as Crème de genièvre, the Dordogne Valley liqueur made from juniper berries.

The words *'double crème'* have also been assumed by some to imply that the liqueur is doubly sweet or doubly **strong** alcoholically, but this is not so; in general, the *'double'* means that the drink contains double quantities of whatever flavours it. However, as the concentration of ingredients will more than double if double quantities are used, sometimes only about half as much again will be used, so as to maintain the balance of the liqueur.

Crème d'ananas   Pale yellow, sweet, pineapple **liqueur** made in several parts of the world, including Hawaii.

Crème de banane   Very sweet banana **liqueur**, sometimes yellow, sometimes white. It is made in various countries, including **Greece, Cyprus** and **Australia**. 'Mus' is a Turkish brand.

Crème de cacao   See **chocolate liqueurs**.

Crème de menthe   One of the best-known **digestive liqueurs**, flavoured, as might be deduced from the name, with mint. It can be white as well as the dark, bright green that is most familiar. Cusenier's Freezomint is well known, also the Pippermint of Get Frères, but virtually every liqueur house produces some type of mint spirit.

Crème de noisette   See **nut liqueurs**.

Crème de noix   See **nut liqueurs**.

Crème de Noyau   See **Noyau, nut liqueurs**.

Crème de roses   **Liqueur** made from the oils of rose petals.

Crème de violettes   **Liqueur** made from the petals of violets, very scented and sweet. Crème Yvette, an American brand, was named for the French diseuse, Yvette Gilbert.

Crème mitt Nuss   See **nut liqueurs**.

Crépy   White wine from **Savoie**, in the east of **France**, to the south of the Lake of Geneva. Some of the wines are slightly *pétillant*.

Cresta Blanca   Established in the **Livermore Valley** in **California** in 1882, this winery achieved fame for certain of its white wines made from the **Sémillon grape**, which received a hand-applied infection of *Botrytis cinerea*, thereby enabling them to produce concentratedly sweet wines. The dry climate prevents the natural formation of the *Botrytis*. Today this winery belongs to a company called Guild.

Croattina   **Vine** used to make some of the red and pink wines of **Lombardy, Italy**, notably **Frecciarossa**.

Croft   **Port** firm (also now important in the **sherry** world), founded in 1678. It is the property of **I.D.V.** The wines have great grace and easy charm.

Croizet-Bages   Classed 5th growth of **Pauillac**, owned by the proprietor of **Rauzan-Gassies**. See **Bordeaux, classification**.

Crozes Hermitage   See **Hermitage**.

Cru   This French word means 'growth'; but it is a noun and not the past participle of the verb *croître* (to grow), which would be *crû*. It is usually employed in referring to a vineyard of quality and hence to the wine produced there. Frequently one of the classed growths (*crus classés*) of **Bordeaux** are cited in association with this word. See **classification,** *grand cru*.

Crush   Noun used in many of the English-speaking New World wine regions to signify the amount of **grapes** crushed: e.g. 'The crush last year was less than average.'   See *Fouloir égrappoir*.

Crusta   A mixed drink, for which there are many recipes. The distinguishing factor is that the **glass** is lined completely with orange or lemon peel.

Crust   A type of **deposit** particularly associated with vintage **port**, but other wines can throw a crust. It has never been defined, but I consider it to be a heavier, bulkier deposit, holding more firmly to the inside of the **bottle**, than the ordinary sediment. Obviously wines that have thrown a crust must be **decanted** off this, so that they are bright in the drinker's **glass**. The presence of a crust, however, is certainly indicative of a quality wine and also one that has a long life – during which it will 'feed' on its crust. Very old wines have sometimes completely consumed and dissolved the crust that was originally in the bottle.

It should be remembered, if one has to handle these old wines, that a hand-blown bottle may be rougher inside – the crust will cling more tightly to it than to a machine-made bottle; also that certain wines, notably port, were at one time put into 'shot' bottles (the inside of which was previously pitted with shot) so that there should be a roughness for the deposit to adhere to.

The most important thing with a crust is that it should be allowed to form and hold in the early stages of the wine's bottle life: sometimes early bottling or another event, or simply the type of **vintage**, will cause the wine to throw a heavy deposit. The port trade are definite that, if a vintage port is allowed to form its crust tranquilly for the first five years of its life, it can thereafter be moved, even violently shaken up, and the wine will thereafter settle and reform the crust perfectly satisfactorily. But if it is disturbed during the first years, then somehow the crust never seems to form satisfactorily. When the wine is later decanted, it may be found that minute particules of what should have been a firm crust are in suspension in the wine. Nothing can be done about this – even the finest filter will not remove them.

Crystals These are found in both red and white wines. They may appear as tiny shining splinter-like attachments to the **cork**, or else be seen in the **bottle**. They are **tartrates**, precipitated at some stage by the wine and it is no use trying to tell people that their presence is indicative of quality – the ignorant resent them being there and tend to send the wine back. Careful **decanting** can, of course, prevent them getting into anyone's **glass** and, as even the greediest is not likely to suck the cork, their being on it does not matter. They cause trouble to wine merchants, most of whose customers like their wines 'star bright'. They do not realise that, every time a wine is put through a filter, something of its quality and delicacy, as well as the actual 'bits' is removed. However the presence of tartrates is both a sign of quality and a harmless indication that the wine in which they appear has not been filtered, treated and generally rendered insipid so as to satisfy those who are offended by the slight **deposit** – just as our squeamish ancestors used tinted glasses to shield from their eyes the presence of **flyers** in white wines.

Cuaranta-y-tres A yellow, herby Spanish **liqueur** made, as its name implies, from 43 different herbs.

Cues or **Kues** Vineyards facing **Bernkastel**, on the **Mosel**. See **Cusanusstift**.

Cuisine This word is accepted by the latest edition of *The Small Oxford Dictionary*, so I suppose I have to accept it as well. But I find it a silly and affected term (see *vigneron*). Its definition is 'style of cooking', but in so many instances the words 'cookery', 'recipes' or 'gastronomy' might be used instead. If, as is possible, the word *cuisine* is intended to indicate the difference between ordinary home cooking and (often supposedly) French chef cookery, then I can understand. But far too often the word carries the implication *haute cuisine* which, to me, is something totally different from the attempts to reproduce certain classic French recipes in the limitations of a family kitchen, often with substitute ingredients. As always, the use of a word that is unpretentious is to be preferred to one that suggests any form of superiority on the part of the speaker or writer.

In talking about wine, however, the word *cuisine* has a somewhat sinister implication. '*Ce n'est que la cuisine*' means 'It's just a cooked-up thing' meaning that the wine has been 'made' by some undesirable technical adjustment. Examples of this occur when public demand for something 'full-bodied' or 'big' causes some producers to distort a wine's character so as to please a particular market. Souped-up red **Burgundies**, red **Rhônes** that are described as 'big and blackstrap' are typical wines resulting from a little 'cooking'. There was also one well-known classed growth (see **classification**) that achieved enormous popularity among people who like aggressive **clarets** – they usually add 'with bite' – because the makers used to concentrate some of the **must**. The result was a very full, coarse, assertive sort of wine not liked by many lovers of claret; but it made a great deal of money for the owner and certainly provided a type of enjoyment for certain sorts of drinker.

Cultivar Term used in **South Africa** to signify a particular **variety** of **vine**.

Cumin See *alcool blanc*.

Cup A mixed drink, which is usually assumed to be cold nowadays, although in fact it can be hot. There is no dividing line between cups, **punches** and other mixtures prepared for a number of people. The most famous cup of all is probably **Pimm's**, although this is described by the makers as a **sling**.

Curaçao (Pronounced 'Cure-ass-saow') The bitter oranges from the island of Curaçao off the coast of Venezuela first gave the name to this orange-flavoured **liqueur**, but nowadays oranges from other sources are also used. Only the peel is employed in the making. Many firms make Curaçao throughout the world but chiefly it comes from both France and Holland. In the latter country blue, green, brown varieties of Curaçao are made, as well as the white and orange-coloured types. The flavour of good orange Curaçao is fruity but refreshingly slightly bitter. The name 'Triple Sec' is given by many liqueur houses to the product. The house of Cointreau in Angers, which was founded in 1849, gave their liqueur their own family name in order to distinguish it. Cointreau is now one of the biggest-selling liqueurs in the world and the drink is often served 'on the rocks', both as a **digestive** and even as an **apéritif**. See **orange liqueurs**.

Curé-Bon-La-Madeleine This château is in the *Côtes* of **St Émilion**, between the properties of **Belair**, **Ausone** and **Canon**. It was owned by a real Curé, whose name was Bon, at the beginning of the 19th century. He left it to his nephew who, wishing to perpetuate the name and to differentiate the property from others, added the word 'Madeleine' to their names, but the curé's own name as the prefix. It has since been known as Château Curé-Bon-La-Madeleine. The estate is a classed growth of St Émilion and its wines, when they are seen on lists, are usually very good, although the yield is small, so that they tend to be rare. See **Bordeaux, classification**.

Cusanusstift, Cusanushaus The charitiable foundation established by Cardinal Nikolaus von Cues, the great mystic, mathematician and thinker of the 15th century, at the town opposite **Bernkastel** on the **Mosel**, which depends on the produce of the vineyards with which it is endowed, in a similar way to the **Hospices de Beaune**. The Hospital cares for 33 old men; the number must be maintained.

Customs The U.K. Customs levy duty on goods being brought into the country; whereas the **Excise** levy duty on liable goods which are produced in the U.K.

Custoza White wine from the **Veneto** region of **Italy**. It appears to be only made in small quantities and the authority Philip Dallas has been unable to find it, although he has traced references to it.

Custozza Region in the Berici Hills, south of Vicenza, **Italy**, making white, red and pink wines.

Cut This verb is not often used nowadays, but it signifies 'to **blend**'. For example, in the 19th century, **claret** might be 'cut' with the darker, weightier wines of **Spain**, giving it a false 'body' and obvious crude appeal.

Cuva Large **cask** of the **Rioja** region in **Spain**, containing 5,499 gallons (25,000 litres).

Cuvaison Recently established **winery** in the **Napa Valley, California**.

Cuve La *cuve* is the vat; *la cuvée* is the vat's contents, hence a particular lot or portion of wine. The word *cuvée* is also sometimes used rather loosely to indicate a **blend** in relation to certain wines blended at the time they are first made. For example, in **Champagne** it may be said that a certain blend of wine is a successful *cuvée*. In Champagne, too, the first 440 gallons (2,000 litres) of juice extracted from the regional type of press are known as the *vin de cuvée*. *Tête de cuvée* is an expression sometimes seen on **labels** and refers to the wine selected as being the best from a particular lot of a specific property.

Cuve close The method of making **sparkling wines** by putting them into a sealed vat (*cuve close*), so that the **carbon dioxide** gas cannot be given off at the time of the second **fementation**, but is retained in the wine. It saves time, money and labour. See **Champagne method, Charmat method, transfer method, carbonated wines.**

Cynar (Prononced 'Chi-nar') Italian **apéritif**, made from artichokes. It is very bitter and although some people find it refreshing, others definitely cannot like it. It is served like **Campari**, with ice and a splash of soda.

Cyprus Cyprus has a long association with wine and is particularly interesting to winelovers because the *Phylloxera* has never infected the vineyards, so that the vines are ungrafted. There are several native **grapes**, of which the

Opthalmo and Mavron (black) and **Xynisteri** (white) are the most notable. Recently the rehabilitation of the vineyards has resulted in certain classic wine grapes being tried, though it is as yet too early to pronounce on the effects they may have on the wines. Although the most famous traditional Cyprus wine is **Commandaria**, it is for the **fortified** sherry-style wines that Cyprus has become the third most important source of supply for wine to the U.K. The bulk of these wines are sweet **sherry**, but medium and dry wines are also made, the latter even including some made from native **flor**.

The principal **wineries** are in or near Limassol, on the south coast, and are huge, very modern concerns. There are three large companies and some smaller ones, each of them making a range of table wines. Most make **brandy**, some **liqueurs** and **ouzo** as well. Red, white and rosé table wines of various qualities are made, and recently some *pétillant* wine. In general, the reds are full, rather soft and fairly fragrant, and seem often to taste at their best in a colder climate, such as that of the U.K.; the rosés are very much fuller in style than might be expected, also deep in colour. The dry whites can achieve crisp, slightly aromatic quality, a tribute to the skill of those who make them; the sweeter wines are full and fairly scented, not necessarily cloying. Although the wines are good with Mediterranean dishes, they can also be served satisfactorily with stews, meat and fish dishes typical of northern countries. The main wineries are KEO, SODAP, ETKO, LOEL and Haggipavlu for **brandy**.

Czechoslovakia   Wine is made in several parts of this country where, in fact, there is an ancient tradition of winemaking. But as yet the Czech wines are seldom seen on export markets. The Slovakian region is generally considered the most important, and the best wines are white. Throughout the country, both red and white wines are made, but the whites would appear to achieve the higher quality.

D

D.C.L. These initials stand for The Distillers' Company Limited, which should in no way be confused with The Worshipful Company of **Distillers**. The D.C.L. was registered in 1877, when six lowland Scottish grain distillers merged, being joined by three others over subsequent years. The prime purpose of the original merger was so that the malt distillers, who were making **gin** spirit, could deliver this to the rectifiers who made the finished product. The concerns were thus able to supply first London and, subsequently, many other markets with their products, not limiting themselves to grain **whisky** or gin.

Each firm within the D.C.L. sells its brands in competition with the others, acting quite independently and maintaining individual house styles. They do not own shops and, within the U.K., sell mostly to wholesalers. In export markets, they are of enormous importance, generally selling to specific distributors appointed for particular territories. They are one of the largest commercial concerns in the U.K., wielding great power. Their headquarters in London is in a very fine 18th century mansion in St James's Square.

D.O.C. Stands for *Denominazione di Origine Controllata*, a law established in **Italy** in 1963 affecting Italian-bottled wines only. It determines the area within which certain wines may be produced, the **soil** and arrangements of the vineyards, the **grapes** and **blends** of grapes, method of cultivation, yield of the vineyard and method of vinification, and such details as length of maturation and whether wines of different **vintages** can be blended. **Bottles** and **labels** similarly come under control, as well as the names of both wines and firms. Penalties for infringement can be the closing of an offending establishment for a year and a heavy fine on each gallon (4·5 litres) of wine to which a false description was applied.

Although the D.O.C. is often likened to the French *Appellation d'Origine Contrôlée*, it does not really work in the same way. The administration is centralised, and does not depend, as does the A.O.C., largely on the local syndicates. The local *consorzii* have been responsible for much of the pioneer work that has resulted in the D.O.C., but it comes under the Ministry of

Agriculture in Rome. Some famous wines have not as yet been awarded the D.O.C., although more are receiving it.

A superior classification, that of *Denominazione di Origine Controllata e Guarantita* (D.O.C.G.), is intended for the finest wines, sold in specific bottles, with a government warranty. Possession of the D.O.C. – indicated by the label bearing its name – ensures the pedigree of the wine, where it comes from, how it is made, and how it should be labelled and presented. But although it would be unlikely that a wine possessing the D.O.C. would be bad, the quality of a wine still remains the responsibility of the producer alone. In conversation, D.O.C. wines are often referred to as 'Dock' wines – the abbreviation sounds a little odd to anyone not expecting this form of it.

Dailuaine-Glenlivet (Pronounced 'Dell-you-in.' stressing 'you') **Whisky distillery** in Carron, Morayshire, making Scotch used in the blends of the **D.C.L.**

Daiquiri Drink evolved by the servant of the manager at the Daiquiri tin mine in Cuba, in the 1890s. It is a mixture of white **rum** and lime juice, and was liked by the late President Kennedy.

Dallas Dhu (Pronounced 'Dul-les Doo', stressing 'Doo') **Whisky distillery** in Forres, Morayshire.

Dalmatia See **Yugoslavia**.

Dalmore **Whisky distillery** at Alness, Ross-shire.

Dalwhinnie **Whisky distillery** at the place of the same name, licensed to James Buchanan, a subsidiary of the **D.C.L.**

Dalwood **Australian winery**, established in 1831 (by convict labour) in the **Hunter River Valley**. In 1908 it was bought by **Penfolds** and today specialises in quality table wines.

Danzig Goldwasser The firm of Der Lachs first made this **liqueur** in 1598. Their name means 'salmon'; this symbol was originally moulded on the **bottle**. Since very early times the tonic and revivifying properties of gold dust in drink have been widely credited, but the original Goldwasser was simply pure white, flavoured with **aniseed** and caraway. **Danzig Silverwasser** is a similar drink. Both are now made in West Berlin.

Daō (Pronounced 'Daowng' – through the nose) One of the best-known **Portuguese** wine regions, in the middle of the country, around the River Mondego. Red and white wines are made, the larger firms having made an enormous impression on export, as well as local, markets by the improvement in quality effected by their use of modern equipment and technology. Red Daō is an assertive, gutsy wine, often capable of great improvement in **bottle** and therefore usually benefitting by some aeration before drinking. The white wines are full, slightly aromatic and fat; good partners to robust fish dishes and rather oily recipes.

Dauzac Classed 5th growth of Labarde-**Margaux**, which therefore (because this parish has no **A.O.C.**) bears the A.O.C. Haut-Médoc. It belongs to Alain Miailhe, owner of **Pichon-Longueville** Comtesse de Lalande. See **Bordeaux, classification**.

Davis   World-famous department of **oenology** at the University of **California**.
Dealul Mare   Romanian wine region north of Bucharest.
Deanston   Whisky distillery at Doune, in Scotland. Originally a cotton mill
   designed by the famous Richard Arkwright, of 'Spinning Jenny' fame, it was
   converted to distilling in 1965, the water of the River Teith being just as useful
   for this as for cotton.
Débourbage   This French word has come into wine talk in recent times
   because, especially for the dry whites of **Bordeaux**, the process of *débourbage*
   (meaning 'cleansing') is often involved. The fresh **must** goes into a
   tank – usually stainless steel – together with **sulphur dioxide**, and stays there
   for 24 hours. The solid matter in the liquid is thereby removed and the wine is
   protected from too much exposure to the air and consequent darkening of
   colour.
Decanting, decanter   The process by which certain wines are poured out of the
   bottle into a container (decanter) from which they are to be served. It is often
   assumed that a wine that does not throw a **deposit** does not therefore have to be
   decanted. This is not so. The wine should, of course, be poured off any deposit,
   because its brightness in the glass is one of its charms and any deposit floating in
   it will mask the beautiful colour. Also, deposit – 'bits' – will affect the taste,
   because it will affect the way the wine feels in the mouth. A wine should also be
   decanted if it is desired to 'air' it by exposing it to the atmosphere, both to
   accustom it to the temperature of that atmosphere and subsequently to aerate
   the wine itself by releasing it to the air. This is so that it can either spread itself
   and develop its beautiful smell and fullness of flavour to the utmost, or it can be
   smoothed out and 'brought on' if it is a wine that must be opened before the
   time when it will be at its peak for enjoyable drinking, such as may occur with
   great **clarets** of a long-lasting **vintage**.
   Red wines are those most usually associated with decanting; but certain fine
   old white wines, especially those that have thrown a slight deposit – such as
   the great **Sauternes** – can also be decanted to great advantage. It should be
   remembered that, in this instance, the decanter should be chilled as well as the
   bottle of wine. Vintage **port** should always be decanted, because of its heavy
   deposit and **crust**. Any fine **claret** also deserves decanting: 'an old wine
   deserves it, a young wine needs it', has been pertinently said. Red **Burgundy** is
   seldom decanted in **France**, but it too can benefit by the process.
   However the real criterion of whether to decant or not is personal – if you
   like your wine decanted, have it decanted. The way to find out is to take two
   bottles of the same wine, decant one before drinking time, according to
   whatever is advised or at least an hour in advance, and compare the wine from
   the decanted bottle with that from the bottle not decanted. Some authorities in
   the wine trade do not decant even their finest red wines (except possibly
   vintage port), but merely stand up the bottles and draw the corks ahead of
   time. But it is fair comment to say that they are in the minority. However the
   decanter is not often used in France or in the New World and when it is, it is

114

often merely used as a receptacle for the wine, into which deposit and all is poured without care. This is mere chi-chi. But the British, who have some reputation for knowing about fine classic wines, do tend to prefer their wines decanted. Therefore it is worthwhile seeing whether an individual likes wines served in this way before dismissing it as a mere piece of *garniture*.

In fact, there is often a simple explanation for the use – or absence – of the decanter in various wine regions and countries. Today's winelover may not have realised that, when a decanter was not easy to obtain, even the wealthiest person in a wine region might not have had one to use! Recently I was asked why decanters are seldom used in **Australia** and I replied that I did not suppose the 19th century settlers regarded glassware as essential equipment when planning what baggage they could stow in the holds of the sailing ships. They could not count on cheap local labour in Australia and, by this time, needed to bring with them such mechanised agricultural and, even, industrial equipment as was available when they left Europe. In **South Africa**, on the other hand, the first settlers and winemakers arrived in the 17th century. They could call on slave workers and they were already familiar with the table glass and similar luxuries that had become routine domestic utensils in wealthy Holland because of the rise of the great glassworks, especially in England and Ireland, at this time. The Dutch also used glass – **flasks** as well as drinking vessels – for spirits as well as wine. New arrivals in the 'colonies' that are now the **U.S.** also either brought their upper class European traditions with them or, later, often came from parts of Europe where glass manufacturing was already an important business – such as Bohemia (Czechoslovakia), Poland, Scandinavia and parts of France. They were accustomed to some extent to the existence of the decanter and the use of different glasses for different drinks.

The major influence, however, is that of the British glassworks which perfected a way of making glass in the 17th century that caused *verre anglais* to be in great demand for wine bottles. English and Irish glass was a great status symbol on the tables of the nobility and the 'new rich' at a time of great expansion of trade. The decanter became associated with certain drinks virtually created for the British market – port, **Madeira** and **sherry** – all of them arriving in quantity at British ports. Madeira was also very popular in North America. Then, when the evolution of the bottle enabled certain table and **fortified wines** to be laid down, the heavy deposit thrown by these wines made the use of the decanter pertinent so that the fine crystal wine glasses were not clouded with 'bits'.

I have been told by the late Allan Sichel that it was only in the late 1940s that he managed to convince what was then the top hotel and restaurant in Bordeaux that he, and people like him, wanted their great wines decanted. In Burgundy in the mid-1950s I remember an otherwise fine restaurant where, when the *sommelier* was asked to decant a very old wine, he simply tipped it, deposit and all, into a **carafe**! Only with the influx of tourists and potential wine buyers into many wine regions did many local hoteliers become aware of the correct use of the decanter – and many remain ignorant of it to this day. But,

DECANTING FINE WINES AND PORT

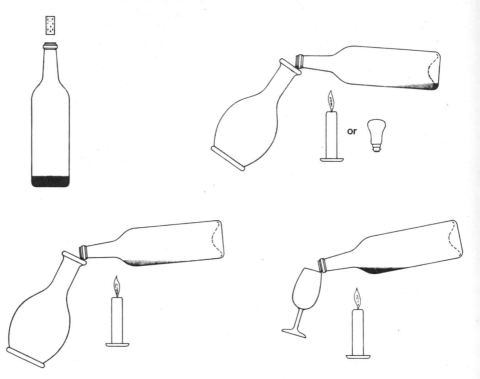

1.   Bottle has been standing up, so that deposit has settled in base of the punt. Note quantity and type of deposit by lifting bottle to the light. Open in usual way, taking great care that the deposit is not shaken in the process.

2.   Put some form of light – candle, battery torch, or light bulb – on the table below the shoulder of the bottle. Pour wine slowly into the decanter, directing flow down the side without splashing. At start of the operation, the decanter will be tilted more towards the bottle. As the bottle is progressively gradually tilted, the decanter will be held more upright.

3.   Watch as the deposit moves from, the base of the bottle and slides up until it is momentarily retained by the bottle's shoulder. Do not tilt the bottle backwards, keep it inclined, set decanter down.

4.   Pour the remainder of the wine into a glass, stopping pouring as soon as any deposit comes into the neck of the bottle or is about to pass into the glass. Set bottle down. The bright wine in the glass may be used as a tasting sample or added to the wine in the decanter.

as the customer ought to get what he pays for, so he should get his wine decanted if he wishes, whether or not the locals bother to decant. They are not necessarily 'right', any more than those of us who prefer our wines decanted are 'wrong'.

TYPES OF DECANTER: These vary greatly. Squat, rectangular or oddly-shaped ones are associated with spirits; rather bulbous, short-necked and heavily-cut ones with vintage port and, possibly, sherry or Madeira; and the pot-bellied, long-necked type with table wines. Lipped decanters or jugs are often called 'claret jugs' but can be used for any table wine; if they have silver or plated lips or lids, take care the polish does not impart any flavour. Triangular decanters are known as 'ship' decanters, so called because their shape made them particularly stable when used on board a sailing vessel. Although decanters may be coloured, the beauty of a wine's colour can be appreciated in the decanter as well as in the glass and therefore transparent glass or crystal is ideal.

THE METHOD OF DECANTING: This is straightforward – for the really hesitant layman, a wine can, on request, be decanted into a clean bottle by the merchant. The bottle should, in advance, have been stood upright so that any deposit may sink down to the base. If a bottle must be drawn straight from its recumbent position in the bin, then a **cradle** should be used to hold it in the same position, while the cork is drawn and the wine poured. The **capsule** should either be wholly removed or a cut made round under the flange of the bottle neck, so that the piece of capsule over the cork can be lifted. It is important that the capsule is removed sufficiently to enable the wine to be poured without running over any of the capsule. Should this remain high up around the neck, the capsule may give the wine an unpleasant metallic taste. Then the wine is poured into the decanter, carafe or clean bottle with a steady, unhurried flow; ideally the wine should slide down the side of the decanter, instead of splashing into it.

There should be a light, either underneath the neck of the bottle or behind the wine as it is poured; this will show when any deposit comes up from the base of the bottle into the out-going wine, so that pouring may cease. A candle, electric light bulb or torch will serve for this purpose. At no time should the bottle be tilted down towards the decanter and then raised again, as this will churn up any deposit in the wine and all poured after that will be cloudy. This is why the use of the wine cradle for serving wine around a table is pointless, because the wine is merely stirred up by the tilting up and down of the bottle in the cradle. When the wine has been decanted, the bottle with the dregs is stood upright, either on the sideboard or a table apart, depending on whether diners will wish to inspect it (sometimes it is put on the table for people to see). The decanter is either stoppered or the stopper is left out, according to whether it is wished to 'air' the wine a little more.

The bottle should be handled throughout with the aid of a perfectly clean cloth or napkin which is used, first, to wipe the neck and top of the bottle before the capsule is cut, then to wipe the top of the cork after the capsule is removed, finally to wipe the neck after the cork has been drawn. This sort of cloth should never be washed in detergent or used for anything except handling glasses and decanters.

CLEANING: Decanters should be cleaned by rinsing thoroughly in fresh hot water. If they are seriously stained, then anything that will clean false teeth (or even bleach) may be used to remove any marks inside, but then the vessels must be very thoroughly rinsed. Ideally they should then be dried, which may be achieved, even with the long-necked type, by poking a cloth down into them with the aid of a skewer or long-handled wooden spoon. (For display purposes decanters are often cleaned inside with twisted spills of newspapers but this imparts a smell). Otherwise they can be drained upside down. Any trace of liquid inside should be dried out before they are put away, as stale water can create a stale smell inside, and it is undesirable to have to rinse (and attempt to dry) a decanter immediately before it is to be used. Stoppers can either be left out or only lightly inserted, to avoid any stale air being trapped inside.

Dégorgement, Disgorging See **Champagne Method**.

Deidesheim See **Palatinate**.

Delaforce **Port** firm, founded in 1868, with members of the family still active in it. It is also influential in the production of good quality **Portuguese** table wines, which are put out under the **label** of the firm directly responsible. The ports have very fine construction and are markedly aristocratic.

Delheim **Winery** near Stellenbosch, **South Africa**, now making a name for its table wines. The estate was originally known as Driesprong.

Demi-sec The term literally means 'half dry' but, as applied to most wines and certainly to **Champagne**, it will mean that the **dosage** has been sufficient to make the wine definitely sweet to most tastes.

Demijohn This word derives from the French term *Dame Jeanne*, a large glass container, usually protected by exterior wickerwork. This is used for small quantities of fine wines and for spirits. There is no official size, although it usually is a gallon (4·5 litres) or more. See **bottles**.

Deposit Many wines, both white and red, which are capable of a fairly long period of maturation in **bottle**, tend to throw a deposit in certain years. Vintage **port**, which throws a **crust**, is the supreme example of this. The wine will live on this deposit and its presence can be a great asset, as an indication both of quality and potential long life. The absence of sufficient skilled **wine waiters**, whose art in **decanting** will secure a star-bright wine poured off its deposit, and the belief by the ignorant that 'bits' in wine are bad, has led to many wines being rebottled off their deposit before they are sold to certain markets more concerned with what they suppose to be 'hygiene' rather than appreciation of wine. If any wine has thrown a deposit and if, once the wine (white or red) has been carefully poured off this (so that the deposit does not get into the wine in decanter or **glass**), the wine itself both smells and tastes good, there is nothing to worry about in the presence of a deposit – rather the contrary. The wine lives on its deposit and the presence of this is usually indicative of a quality product.

The type of deposit varies considerably, from the hard crust of a well-kept vintage port, to a very fine dust-like deposit (difficult to remove except by the aid of filter paper or a very fine-meshed decanting funnel). There can also be a sludge-like greasy deposit that fortunately clings to the **punt** by means of its own stickiness. No study of deposits appears to have been made, but different wines do throw different types of deposit. Red **Burgundys**', for example, is finer and more dust-like than most of the **clarets**. This circumstance may also have influenced local practices as to whether or not to decant.

Before you start decanting, carefully examine the bottle with a strong light behind it, so as to try and see the type of deposit inside. If, when you draw the bottle from the bin, you examine it before you stand it upright, the deposit may begin to move and indicate something about its consistency.

Desmirail   Classed 3rd growth of **Margaux** which has now been incorporated into the **Palmer** property; hence the name is seldom seen, although Palmer has the right to use it. See **Bordeaux, classification**.

Dessert wine   As *The Oxford Dictionary* definition of 'dessert' is the fruit or sweetmeats served after the meal, the term 'dessert wine' means a wine that can accompany the last food on the table – not, as is often supposed, the wine to partner the sweet course. The term 'dessert' is used loosely these days and in the **U.S.**, it signifies puddings, pastries, ice-cream, sweet soufflés and sorbets. None of these are 'dessert' in the English sense of the term. The **fortified** wines, such as **port**, dessert **sherry**, dessert **Madeira** are the most famous dessert wines, but the great **Sauternes** and some other sweet **table wines** are equally suitable for serving with dessert – though fine fruit plus nuts, rather than sweetmeats, are the ideal choice. Old **claret** can also be served. A dessert wine need not necessarily be very sweet but, coming after other wines, it should have more 'weight' and importance than those that precede it. There is every argument for the revival of dessert wines at more everyday meals than formal dinners; especially as a pudding or sweet is often refused by many people, who prefer cheese and then fruit.

Devonvale   Estate near Stellenbosch, **South Africa**, owned by Bertrams, producing fine table wines.

Dézaley   Famous **Swiss** vineyard in the **Lavaux** region, producing a fairly deep gold white wine, highly esteemed.

Dezize-les-Maranges   The best-known name of three **Côte de Beaune** villages (the others are Cheilly and Sampigny), making both red and white wines.

Dhron   (Pronounced 'Drohn') **Mosel** vineyard making fine wines, the Dhronhofberger being the best-known site. These wines are assertive, though elegant, with great distinction.

Diamond Creek   Vineyard on the side of Diamond Mountain in the **Napa Valley, California**.

Dienheim   (Pronounced 'Deen-hime') Wine parish in the Rheinhessen (see **Rhine**) region of **Germany**. Goldberg, Krötenbrunnen and Kandelweg are possibly the best-known sites.

Digestives   Drinks taken to promote the digesting of food, therefore usually but not invariably served at the end of a meal. **Bitters** and certain dry or very herby **apéritifs** taken before food could also be considered as aids to digestion; a **liqueur** that might be supposed to round off a good meal could, in general, also be referred to as a digestive. Obvious digestives are **Kümmel, Izarra, La Vieille Cure, Galliano**. The **aniseed**-flavoured liqueurs, such as **anis**, could also easily be served as a preface to a meal.

Dimiat   **Bulgarian** white **grape**, grown for wine and the table.

Dingac   **Yugoslav** white wine, made from **grapes** that are late picked and then dried in the sun before being pressed, thereby imparting some sweetness.

Distillation   The process whereby most spirits are made. In very general lay terms, it takes place when a liquid is vaporised, so that the vapours given off are caught and condensed, to make another liquid. When, in the first instance, an alcoholic beverage is distilled, the alcohol in it will vaporise at a lower temperature. The vapours given off can be kept and used to make a liquid with a stronger alcoholic content, because the water will not be given off so soon. This is done either in a **pot still**, or a continuous, **patent** or **Coffey still**. The spirits made in pot stills (such as **Cognac** and malt **whisky**) tend to be more individual – which does not necessarily mean either better or inferior – than those made in a patent still. Distilling is a strictly controlled process in most countries and also a source of considerable revenue due to **Customs & Excise** duties levied on spirits.

Distillers, The Worshipful Company of   Not to be confused in any way with The Distillers Company Limited (**D.C.L.**). It received its charter in 1638, being founded by two eminent physicians, one of whom was the well-known Sir Theodore de **Mayerne**, who attended King Charles I and Queen Henrietta Maria. They attempted to control the quality of 'Artificial and Strong Waters' and, at the outset, were primarily concerned with seeing that **vinegar**, beer and ale were wholesomely made and ensuring that those who were distilling for medical or cosmetic purposes did not pervert their craft. The Distillers still restrict membership of their company to those who are in some way definitely connected with the craft of distilling. They are unusual as a City company in that they do not and never have possessed a hall of their own. They originally shared the premises of The Cooks' Company: nowadays they often hold their ceremonies at **Vintners'** Hall.

Dizy   Parish near Ay in **Champagne**.

Dock glass   A **glass** shaped like an elongated tulip, or a largish sherry *copita*, used for sampling or critically tasting wines.

'Dock' wines   See **D.O.C.**

Dolceacqua   Red wine from the **Ligurian** region of **Italy**, full in character and reputedly once liked by Napoleon I.

Dolcetto   **Piedmont** red wine, made from the **Nebbiolo grape** in **Italy**.

Dôle   Not to be confused with the town in France, this is possibly the best-known **Swiss** red wine. From the **Valais** region, it is made from the **Gamay grape**. There is also another red wine made from the **Pinot Noir**, called Petite Dôle.

Domaine de Chevalier   Property in the parish of Léognan in the **Graves**, south of **Bordeaux**, slightly unusual in this area for being a *domaine* instead of a *château*. It makes both red and white wines but only about one-third of the production is white. Both red and white, however, are usually very fine, sensitive, delicate but fruity wines, much appreciated by those experienced in **claret**.

Domitian   Roman Emperor (A.D. 81-96) who issued a decree prohibiting the extension of Italian vineyards and requiring vineyards in the provinces of the Roman Empire to be uprooted so that only half their area was still cultivated. He is supposed to have done this to encourage the cultivation of grain, more important for the preservation of civic satisfaction than wine, but it may be doubted as to whether the wily peasants of the time complied wholeheartedly with this decree. It was rescinded by the Emperor Probus two centuries later.

Donnaz   Red **Italian** wine from the Aosta Valley in **Piedmont**. It is mainly made from the **Nebbiolo grape** and Philip Dallas says that, in the French-speaking part of the region, it is known as the Picoutener. The wine seems capable of attaining quality and is apparently supposed to have **aphrodisiac** properties.

Doppelkorn   See *Kornbranntwein*.

Dordogne   See **Bergerac**, **Monbazillac**, **Pécharmant**.

Dosage   The sweetening (usually cane sugar dissolved in wine) which is given to a **sparkling wine** before the second **cork** is inserted. This makes the wine reach a degree of slight to definite sweetness, according to the type of wine it is wished to make. Known as *liqueur d'expédition* in **France**. See **Champagne method**.

Doux   French word meaning 'sweet', which usually implies that the wine is very sweet. See **Champagne**.

Dow   **Port** firm, making very well-constructed wines, with what I usually note as a markedly aromatic **bouquet**.

Drambuie   A **whisky**-based **liqueur** (which can be drunk at any time), with a romantic history. Prince Charles Edward Stuart, 'Bonnie Prince Charlie', flying for his life after the defeat at Culloden in 1745, was befriended by Mackinnon of Strathaird, to whom he gave the recipe for his personal drink. The Mackinnon family, although now marketing the liqueur, still keep the formula a secret. The late Mrs Gina Mackinnon, head of the clan, mixed the base herself before sending it to the production plant. The word means 'the drink that satisfies' in Gaelic: *an dram buidheach*.

Drayton   **Australian** wine dynasty, established in the **Hunter Valley**, New South Wales. The founder of the firm was born in England in 1820, setting up in the **Pokolbin** region in 1850. The family name is the only one of those shown on the map of the original land grants of the area, that is still in business on the spot.

Drumborg   **Winery** in the **Great Western** region of **Australia**, currently being developed by **Seppelts**.

Dry Creek   **California winery**.

Dry martini   This, certainly the most famous **cocktail** in the world, is not required to have capital letters, since a court judgement decreed that it was so well-known internationally that it was a commodity in its own right. Essentially it consists of **gin** and dry **vermouth** but, as whole books have been written about it, the subject is complex.

In the 19th century, a 'Martinez' cocktail was made in the **U.S.** with gin (the sweet type) and vermouth. In the 1860s, it has been established, **Martini & Rossi** were not exporting their dry vermouth to the U.S., although **Noilly Prat** was. However, as John Doxat relates, the barman in the Knickerbocker Hotel in New York in the pre-1914 period, was a man called Martini de Arma de Taggia. He made a popular drink with Martini dry vermouth; Doxat thinks that the drink was named for the man, not for the vermouth. What is certain is that the original mixture seems to have been either half and half or at least only a little more gin than vermouth. Between the wars, the drink became 'dryer' – in other words, the proportion of gin was increased. After World War II, very little vermouth began to be used and there has since grown up a 'mystique' of spraying the glass with a little vermouth or rinsing it with some and tipping it out. It is also claimed that certain vermouths – even if they are eventually tipped out of the mixing jug – have a profound effect on the ultimate mix.

This seems reasonable, but it still perplexes me that the ability to make a dry martini appears to be something of a status symbol in certain groups of society: if people want a drink that is virtually straight gin (one would have thought more attention might be paid to this), with a hint of other flavouring, then why are they not able to make their own mix and leave it to others to concoct their version of something refreshing and able to tone up the palate? As for those who stand around drinking such a basic mixture for an hour or more, I admit that I cannot understand why they do – other drinks would either be more immediately stunning or more interesting. It is also worth noting, for those who do enjoy one or two drinks of this kind before a meal, that the palate will have been dulled for anything delicate as regards wine. A robust and fairly middle-grade wine is the only thing to follow, unless you have a 'blotting-paper' course at the beginning to revive the palate (and sober up the drinker). However, it is useless to deny that the dry martini is made – and endlessly discussed – all over the world, so it must have some charm that has so far eluded me.

Dubonnet   A well-known French **aperitif**, wine-based and flavoured with herbs. It was evolved by Joseph Dubonnet, a Paris wine merchant, in 1846. Today it is made at Thuir, in the south-west of **France**. The best-known type is pinkish red, but there is another, known as Dry Dubonnet, which is pale gold and dryer. Can be drunk neat, in mixes, or with soda.

Ducru-Beaucaillou   Classed 2nd growth of **St Julien**, adjoining **Beychevelle**, whose wines it can slightly resemble. See **Bordeaux, classification**.

Dufftown-Glenlivet, The   **Whisky distillery** at Dufftown, Banffshire, bought by Bell's in 1933. It is said of Dufftown that 'Rome was built on seven hills, Dufftown stands on seven stills', which it does.

Duhart-Milon (Pronounced 'Doo-ah Mee-on') Classed 4th growth of **Pauillac**, which was recently acquired by **Lafite**, who have planted the vineyard in the same proportions of **grape varieties** as that of Lafite. See **Bordeaux, classification**.

Duras Region to the south-east of **Bordeaux**, in which both red and white wines are made. Some of them, especially the whites, are of pleasant character.

Durfort-Vivens Classed 2nd growth of **Margaux**, which now belongs to the proprietor of **Brane-Cantenac**. See **Bordeaux, classification**.

Durif This black **grape** may be the **California Petite Sirah**. It gets its name because it was propagated by a Dr Durif around 1880. It appears to make wines of only ordinary quality.

Dürkheim See **Palatinate**.

Dürnstein **Austrian** village in the **Wachau** region, making good wines.

Dutch gin See **gin**.

E

E.V.A. See **English wines**.

East India This is a term now seldom used, but it was formerly applied to a certain type of brown **sherry** given additional ageing by being used as freight in vessels sailing to and from the East Indies. See *Retour de Indes*.

East-Side Winery Co-operative in Lodi, **California**.

Eau-de-noix See **nut liqueurs, Mesclou**.

Eau-de-vie Literally water of life. This French term signifies **brandy**, either **grape** brandy or some other kind, such as a fruit brandy. See *alcool blanc*.

Eau-de-vie-de-cidre See **Calvados**.

Ebereschenbranntwein **German fruit brandy** made from rowanbérries (the fruit of the mountain ash), red in colour with a very fresh, almost bitter fruit flavour. See *alcool blanc*.

Edel (Pronounced 'Eh-dell') German term used to describe spirits which are made solely from the fruit named on the **label**. *Edel-branntwein* is a collective term for **arrack**, **brandy**, fruit brandies, **gentian**, **gin**, **rum**, and **whisky**, no aromatics or sweetening being allowed in the mash used. *Edel-obstbranntweins* are fruit brandies (*alcool blanc*) in the true sense – white distillates of whatever fruit is named on the label – kirsch, mirabelle and so on. Large quantities are made in **Baden**.

Edelfäule (Pronounced 'Eh-deli-foyle') See *Botrytis cinerea*.

Edelperl See **Luxembourg**.

Edelzwicker Term used to describe an **Alsace** wine made from a mixture of **grapes** defined as 'noble'.

Edmeades Vineyards Recently established **winery** in Mendreino, **California**.

Edradour Scotland's smallest **distillery** at Pitlochry, Perthshire. The **whisky** it produces goes into some of the most famous **blends**, including 'House of Lords' and 'King's Ransom'. The staff number three!

Eger See **Hungary**.

Egg flip See **advocaat**.

Égrappage Process whereby the **grapes** are removed from their stalks before being put into the **vat**. There are various ways in which this is done: by rubbing the bunches of grapes by hand through a wooden sieve, by passing them through a mechanical stripper, and so on. Much depends on the type of wine that it is wished to make. The presence of the stalks in the '**must**' could make the wine tough, woody and literally stalky. Obviously a fine, delicate wine deserves detailed, often costly attention; whereas an everyday robust wine does not need it to the same extent. The matter is primarily one to concern the winemaker rather than the drinker; but any visitor to a wine region will note the different methods employed when watching the grapes brought to the presshouse or **winery**, and processed on arrival. See *fouloir égrappage*.

Egri Bikavér   Red **Hungarian** wine. The term means 'Bull's Blood of Eger', the Eger district being traditionally well known for wines. Bull's Blood is made from a blend of **Kadarka, Pinot Noir** and **Merlot grapes**. Its name dates from the siege of the fortress of Eger by the Turks in 1552, when the Hungarian women, fighting alongside their countrymen, are said to have served copious quantities to the defending garrison to strengthen them. Anyway the fortress did not yield and the Turks withdrew. Both **vintage** and non-vintage wines are produced today; the former are capable of marked improvement and refinement in **bottle** with ageing.

Egypt   Wine has been made in Egypt since ancient times, but the modern wine industry was only started in this century. The wines have been praised by travellers, but as yet production does not enable them to be featured on export lists.

Eierlikoer   German egg-flip (see **advocaat**). 'Eiweinbrand' is the brand name of the best-known type, in which the only alcohol is **brandy**.

Einzellagen   A single vineyard in German terminology.

Eiswein   (Pronounced 'Ice-vine') A phenomenon among **German** wines which, originally made through force of circumstances and more or less by chance, is now a sought-after rarity, often commanding very high prices when it can be found. Essentially, to make an *eiswein*, there must be a severe night frost, when the fully ripe or even overripe **grapes** are actually frozen hard. When gathered early in the morning, they are rushed to the presshouse and go into the press still frozen. The juice inside the grapes is naturally concentrated, and the pressing goes on for as long as this concentrate flows. Subsequent **fermentation** at a low temperature presents special problems.

The wines are worthy of consideration anyway, because they are usually made in years not otherwise outstanding for quality, when grapes may have been left on the vines in the hope of their ripening still more. The *eiswein* usually rank well above the normal run of wines. They are curious in style, delicate in character and are never cheap. They can only be made in the classic regions of the **Rhine** and the **Mosel** and it is worth noting that some reputable authorities deplore the growing frequency with which they are being made. Some equally reputable growers refuse to make them at all. My own description of them is that they are 'ghost wines' – shadows of what the fully ripe wines of high quality might be; but they do possess an individual delicate style. See **German Wine Law**.

Eitelsbach (Pronounced 'Eye-tels-bark') **Ruwer** vineyard, the Karthäuser Hof wines being possibly the best known, but the Marienholz and Sonnenberg sites also produce fine, very definite wines.

Elba The most famous of wines made on this island is **Aleatico di Portoferraio**, a rather luscious and sweetish wine, from a type of **Moscato grape**. There are red and white wines made on Elba, but as yet they are not featured on many export lists. The **Sangiovese** grape is used for some of the better reds.

Elgin This oddly-shaped and ill-proportioned **glass** is named for the 7th Lord Elgin (1766-1841) who removed the collection of marbles that now bear his name from the Parthenon in Athens. This was at the turn of the 18th to 19th centuries, when he was envoy extraordinary at the Porte (Constantinople). It is fair to say that, although the Earl paid over £50,000 for these, the price given by the British nation when they were bought for the British Museum was only £30,000. However this lord, Thomas Bruce, who was also 11th Earl of Kincardine, was apparently otherwise a parsimonious man. He therefore had a particular type of glass designed for his use that gives the impression of holding more than it does. It has a short stem, with a tallish bowl having inward curving sides, turning out at the rims, and somewhat thick.

This type of glass – the larger size is named the **schooner** for no reason that I can understand – is totally unsuitable for presenting any drink except a pick-me-up to the lips of any lover of wine. The glass is too small anyway; it is on too short a stem to enable it to remain away from the heat of the hand, yet it is of a shape that does not permit the wine in it to be swirled around to release its **bouquet** as its outward-curving rim throws the smell away from the nose of the drinker. The mean measure usually also involves the glass being filled to the brim; which is why large numbers of people are astonished to be told that sherry has a smell – as served in an Elgin, it is impossible to be aware of this! One is told that catering establishments continue to buy this horrible glass because 'the public like it'. It is doubtful if any intelligent drinker could like such a thing and the wise will request an ordinary Paris goblet in which to drink the wine – or spirit – for which they are paying, should a restaurant or pub put any drink into the Elgin glass. It has nothing whatever to recommend it and is not even vaguely attractive in appearance.

Elixir The origin of this word is the Arabic 'El ikser', which is the expression for the philosopher's stone, possession of which enabled the owner to turn base metals into gold. It became associated with drinks of medicinal and revivifying character. See **Angostura**, **bitters**, **Campari**.

Elixir d'Anvers Yellowish-green and bitter-sweet **liqueur**, made by De Beukelaer of Antwerp in Belgium.

Elixir d'Armorique Herb **liqueur** made in Normandy.

Elixir de Mondorf A sweetish tonic **liqueur**, made in **Luxembourg**.

Elixir de Spa A sweetish tonic **liqueur**, made at Spa in Belgium since the 17th century, when the original formula was evolved by the Capuchin Friars.

Elixir Martini See **bitters**.

Elixir Végétale See **Chartreuse**.

Elliott   **Australian** wine family, whose founder settled in the **Hunter Valley** region in the 1890s. He named his property Oakvale, and the family's red wine is now given this name. The Elliotts also make white wines and have acquired the Belford and Tallawanta vineyards.

Eltville   Town in the centre of some of the most famous of the Rheingau vineyards (see **Rhine**), which is also the headquarters of the **State Domain**. This was, at one time, the residence of the Archbishops of Mainz, the Prince Electors. The wines are both delicate and slightly austere, very distinguished. Graf zu Eltz owns Schloss Eltz and the Burg Eltz, and Freiherr Langwerth von Simmern a huge 17th century mansion, both of which are associated with fine wine production.

Elvira   Grape of the U.S., not much grown, but reported to be useful for making wines with *Botrytis cinerea*.

Emerald Riesling   A white **grape**, evolved in **California** from a cross of white **Riesling** and **Muscadelle**. Wines made from it seem to me to have a pleasant freshness but little of the nobility of the Riesling Europeans know. They usually seem rather soft and sweetish.

Emilia-Romagna   Wine region of **Italy**, which is especially famous for its food and cooking. Both red and white wines are made; the most famous are probably the sparkling red **Lambrusco** and the white **Albano**.

Emu   This well-known name was registered in 1883 by the manager of The Australian Wine Company. By 1925 the Emu Company was by far the most important supplier of **Australian** wines to the U.K. and also to Canada. The Company now owns vineyards and also put out wines and **brandy** they have bought in. They appear to concentrate on bulk wines for the mass market. Before controls on **labelling** and advertising became strict, their wines were sold in the U.K. before 1939 with claims for 'tonic' properties. In the sense that all wine is in one form a tonic, they almost certainly were.

Enemies to wine   There are many foolish notions current about dishes with which certain wines will not 'go'. It is equally to the point to state that there are certain people – heavily scented, both male and female, with cigarettes alight throughout a meal, drinkers of several double measures of spirits prior to any fine wines, and those who, if they see a fancy **label**, hear a wine name mentioned in some gossip column and know that a certain **bottle** has attained a high price in a well-publicised sale – with whom not even a modest wine will 'go' either. Circumstances are equally harmful: a crowded, smoky, noisy atmosphere, or any form of distraction such as an argument, (not, be it noted, a discussion), some sort of 'show' as in a night club, or simply the sort of company who admit honestly, that what they eat and drink is not of the slightest interest to them. For such, the choice of wine is easy: something cheap (**decanted**, if they are likely to be impressed) but good as the host has got to drink it too. There may also be just the 'one righteous man' who will appreciate a drink that may not come his way as routine. There are reports of rich people who give guests cheap wine, themselves drinking something special; this would seem to me the negation of what is understood by the word 'hospitality'.

There are, however, some foods that will not be good partners to good wines. The obvious example is anything with **vinegar**, which naturally will change the taste of any wine in the mouth if it is assertive in any dish. There are, though, two points to bear in mind: the first is that a salad, as such, is not the type of dish with which one would anyway serve a fine, much less a delicate wine. At the sort of formal meals still affected by what is the conventional type of menu, salad if served will not appear until the table wine is finished or nearly so. Also – for one should never be bound by convention – it depends on the salad and even more on the dressing as to what damage this may do to the wine.

If a 'French dressing' consists of two or three parts of oil to one of vinegar – and malt vinegar at that, (Raymond **Postgate** admitted it was useful in the making of certain pickles but otherwise said it served only to remove the varnish from furniture) – then of course the vinegar will 'turn' any wine being drunk alongside the salad. Some people use lemon juice – I admit I find this insipid in most salads – others a little of the wine, which to me seems peculiar. But I have known some of the greatest authorities on wine make no adverse comment (which they were quite capable of doing) when they had salad at my table. This was because the dressing would always have been five or six parts of whatever oil I had thought appropriate, plus a very small 'one' of my own wine vinegar. This has never seemed to do any harm to the wine – and, in case the reader begins to be apprehensive about 'all that oil', it should be noted that the oil is used to coat the salad first, the vinegar acting as a very light final condiment immediately prior to serving.

Then there are the very strongly-flavoured foods, such as curry or anything with a pronounced spice dominating the flavours. It is possible to take wine with these – but how easy will it be for you to taste anything except the food? If wine is to be served, then something fairly robust, of no special style is all that is required. The same applies to Chinese, Japanese and Indonesian dishes – they are not intended to be partnered by a wine. If very strong spirit-based drinks have been served before a meal, then any delicate wine will make only a feeble impression on the palate – serve a good but assertive wine and, ideally, have a first course to refresh the palate.

Eggs, because of their usually unctuous and palate-coating character, are also not ideal with fine wines. For eggy dishes and egg sauces, something faintly assertive in the medium range is preferable. Some people get a taste of metal if they drink red wine with eggs or white fish, but this is personal (I don't). Ham is sometimes cited as the 'problem' dish – but again, how is it cooked? If in wine, then serve the same sort of wine. If in cider, why not cider? Anything with a very fruity addition, such as pineapple, oranges or apricots will, because of the fruit's **acidity**, assert itself against the wine, so choose something slightly sweet and suave to counteract this.

Sweets do mask the taste of a wine, because of the sugar – the easiest way to conceal the defects in a wine is to sweeten it! So a sweet dish will prevent any delicate flavours being noted from the wine, just as a strongly-smelling dish will counteract any delicate **bouquet**. The odd way in which many French will serve a bone dry **Champagne** at the end of a meal, accompanying a creamy, fruity pudding or ice is strange: something sweeter and more luscious will usually seem better. Anything enriched with **liqueurs** will also have too pronounced a flavour to enable the wine to make its effect. With savoury things, or anything very salt or piquant, no wine can compete. Lemons, citrus fruits in general, anything with a really strong flavour, such as mint, caraway, treacle and toffee will defeat most wines. If you want to serve dishes involving them, finish the wine beforehand.

The service of after-dinner mints before or even with the **port** is an incomprehensible notion to the winelover – and really will not enhance the flavour of the mint any more than the wine! The really palate-stunner, however, is chocolate. Even coffee is not quite as definite in making it impossible to taste anything else afterwards – which is why, at a dinner when the wines are of any importance, there should be a pause before the coffee. But for an hour or more after chocolate, the mouth really does not seem able to register anything. Although most of those who have taught me share my love of chocolate, the only thing to drink with or immediately after it is a spirit in some form.

Enfer d'Arviers   Red wine from the Aosta Valley in **Piedmont, Italy**, made from the Petit Rouge **grape** and reported as scented and full. Appears to improve greatly with maturation in **bottle**.

English wine   Wine has been made in many parts of the British Isles for a very long time – **vines** were first introduced by the Romans. The *Domesday Book* survey of 1086 records 83 established vineyards and, until the 14th century, vineyards increased in number. Religious establishments usually maintained them and the great private houses often planted them as well. A probable climatic change, making England a cooler country, and the association of the **Bordeaux** region with the English crown for three centuries, plus England's alliance with **Portugal** in the 14th century, contributed to a decline in English viticulture. However, even after the dissolution of the monasteries in the 1530s, some vineyards were still producing for the owners of great properties up to 1914. Most of these vineyards were, naturally, in the south of the country but they were quite extensive.

In 1965 some enthusiasts started what became the English Vineyards Association (E.V.A.), which today has several hundred members. Many of these grow vines and make wine on a small scale, primarily for their own consumption, but there are also a number of large vineyards which make their wines commercially, and which are sold as good wines in their own right, not mere curiosities. The E.V.A. has drawn on the experience of European winemakers and its wines are seriously made. The most successful of them so far have been white, although a certain amount of rosé and even occasional red wines are produced. The Merrydown Wine Co. at Horam, Sussex, acted as winemaker to E.V.A. members operating on a small scale and, in addition to making wine itself, has an experimental vineyard. The English vineyards are not only in the south now, thanks to modern techniques which enable wine to be made in what previously would have been almost impossible conditions; a well-known vineyard in Lincolnshire makes good white wine commercially, and there are others planted even further north. Most of the vineyards are along the south coast especially in Kent and Hampshire; but there are several producing commercially in Suffolk and Norfolk. Some of the best are in Somerset.

Some of the classic wine **grapes** are used, notably the **Riesling** and **Sylvaner**, the **Müller-Thurgau**, **Chardonnay** and certain **hybrids**. It is probably fair to say that, while it seems unlikely that any English wine will attain the heights of greatness compared with the classics, there are good prospects in England for pleasant crisp, dryish wines of a wide variety. It has even been possible to make an *eiswein* in one English vineyard! Another grower diverted part of his crop into a **Champagne method** wine.

Enkirch   **Mosel** vineyard.

Entre-Deux-Mers   The region in the **Bordeaux** wine area 'between the two seas' – that is, between the rivers Garonne and Dordogne. It is chiefly known for its light, dryish white wines, although red wines are also made there. These whites can achieve good everyday quality and sometimes more, although they have suffered from the inferior and anaemic wines formerly sold under the name.

Enzian   Term used to signify **gentian liqueurs** in certain countries.

Enzyme   A chemical substance excreted by **yeast**, responsible for **fermentation**.

Épernay   See **Champagne**.

Episcopal   Because of the colours involved, this mixture takes its name from the church. Usually it is a half and half mixture of yellow and green **Izarra**, poured over crushed ice and served in a goblet with straws, either as a **digestive** or a drink between meals.

Erbach   Parish in the Rheingau, on the **Rhine** in **Germany**, especially famous for the **Marcobrunn** vineyard.

Erbaluce   **Italian vine** making white wines, cultivated north of **Turin** in **Piedmont**.

Erden   A parish on the middle **Mosel** in **Germany** of which one of the best-known wines comes from the Treppchen site.

Ermitage   See **Switzerland**.

Erzeugerabfüllung   Expression which, according to the new **German Wine Law**, replaces other terms denoting **estate-bottling** for wines in the *Qualitätswein bestimmer Anbaugebiete* (QbA), or *Qualitätswein mit Prädikat* (QmP) categories.

Escarchardo   See **anisette**.

Escorial   Brand name for a German yellow or green **liqueur**, slightly similar to Chartreuse. See *klosterlikoer*.

Espumoso   Correct descriptive term for **Spanish sparkling wine**. By a 1973 agreement between France and Spain, the term *Champaña* was banned. See **Perelada**.

Est! Est!! Est!!!   A white wine, which can be dry, or slightly sweet, and sometimes very slightly **sparkling**, from Montefiascone in **Lazio** in **Italy**. The wine gets its name because, in the 12th century, Bishop Johann Fugger, travelling from Augsburg to Rome for the Coronation of Emperor Henry V, sent his steward ahead of him to sample the quality of the wines at the various inns. If he approved of the wine, he was to chalk 'Est!' on the door. At Montefiascone he chalked the word three times. Both the steward and the Bishop stayed on at Montefiascone and the Bishop actually died there, stipulating that a **cask** of wine should be poured over his grave on the anniversary of his death. This bequest was countermanded by the local Bishop some years after, who ruled that it should go to the seminary of Montefiascone to be drunk by the inmates.

Esters   The reaction of the **acids** and **alcohol** in a wine, resulting in the smell or **bouquet**.

Estremadura   See **Portugal**.

Estufa   (Pronounced 'Esh-schtou-fa') The place where **Madeira** wines are heated to achieve their unique flavour and curious character.

Étampé   The French term for 'stamped' or 'branded', used generally in association with **corks** – e.g. a branded cork marked with the name and date of the wine.

Etiquette   This French word means 'bottle label', that is, the main body **label**.

Etna   Both red and white wines are produced in the **Sicilian** vineyards around Etna. Because of the volcanic nature of the soil, they have a distinctive flavour; some people describe it as 'minerally'.

Étoile   One of the good white wines from the **Jura** region of **France**.

Etruscan wines   So called because the region in Grosseto in **Tuscany** now making them was a known Etruscan settlement. The La **Parrina** establishment makes good reds and whites, deserving wider appreciation.

Ettaler   German herb **liqueurs**, made at Kloster Ettal near Oberammergau, in green and yellow.

L'Évangile   Estate in **Pomerol** in the **Bordeaux** vineyard, usually making refined wines.

Ewell   **Australian** vineyard near Adelaide, founded in 1841.

Excelsior   Vineyard in the Goulburn Valley of Victoria, **Australia**. It was originally planted by an Austrian, Trojano Darveniza, who had bought it in 1871 and was cultivating wheat, until fear of a surplus caused him to turn over part of it to wine. The family still run the firm and make a variety of table and **fortified wines**.

Excise   The establishment responsible for the tax and also the tax levied on produce of the home country – i.e. Britain – as compared with **Customs** duty, which is levied on imported produce.

Extract   The ordinary winedrinker may not hear this term much, but it signifies something so important that it is included here. Extract is the whole of the elements that get into the **grapes** from the subsoil through the **vine**'s roots. These go deep (the taproot of a mature vine is at least 12 ft (3.65m) in length) and can spread out into a variety of different subsoils as well as drawing on different supplies of moisture. As R. E. H. Gunyon explains: 'Depending on how the vine is **pruned**, these elements are distributed to a greater or lesser degree among the fruit that the vine has been pruned to bear.' Generally, the higher the extract, the longer the wine will take to come to maturity. Extract is assessed in the laboratory and should not be confused in any way with **tannin, acidity** or any of the things that can be noticed in **tasting**.

Although in certain years – such as 1961 in **Bordeaux** – extract is high, the wines are not necessarily a boon to the producers because, as they have to wait for a long time until the wine is mature or sometimes even vaguely drinkable, capital is tied up. Even if they sell such wines to their own satisfaction, merchants and **shippers** are also faced with the problem of keeping stocks for many years: each case of wine costs them money for every day that it occupies space in their cellars. This is why great wines are not money-spinners, however high their prices when they come up for sale: they simply cost too much to produce and keep until their prime. In many instances, therefore, a vine will be pruned to bear rather more fruit so that the extract can be distributed among the grapes, and a wine lower in extract but coming to its peak fairly soon will result. This pleases those engaged in the business, including the taxman.

Extremadura   Wine region in south-west **Spain**, making a variety of table wines and, apparently, both a white and a red wine produced by the action of **flor**. Although these wines can, according to Jan Read, be found sometimes in Madrid, they are rare outside their region, even in Spain.

Ezerjó   **Hungarian vine** now considered native to that country, but possibly originally coming from **India**. It makes a white wine which is possibly at its best when dry, but a sweet version is also made. It is cultivated in the Mór district.

F

Factory House   The original headquarters of the British 'factors' or merchants dealing in various commodities in Oporto. It is a fine establishment, famous for its dining-rooms: one is used solely for the drinking of vintage **port**. The regular weekly Wednesday luncheons are for men only. The British port houses now comprise the members. When Wellington's staff were entertained here at the end of the Peninsular War, they signed the visitors' book, which may still be seen.

Fairview   Estate in **Paarl, South Africa**, which launched its wines as single property wines in 1974, sold under individual **labels**. Before then, they were bought for blending by the **K.V.W.** The vineyard is fairly recently established, but since the beginning of the century it has been producing red wine of quality, although now a little white is also made. Today it belongs to Cyril Back, brother of the owner of **Backsberg** and its wines, notably the **Pinotage**, are greatly respected.

Falerno   Wine from the **Campania** region of **Italy**, which derives its name from Falernum, the Volscian capital (which in fact was near Rome, whereas the wine region referred to is near Naples), and which is vaguely related to the Falernian wine of classical times. Red and white wines, and a sweet red are made, but are seldom seen outside the region.

Falkenstein   Vineyard at **Konz**, in the **Saar** Valley, belonging to the **Freidrich-Wilhelm Gymnasium** at Trier. Its *commune* of origin is not mentioned when it is listed.

Fara   **Italian** red wine from the Novara Hills, **Piedmont**, the foundation of which is the **Nebbiolo grape**.

Faro   **Sicilian** red wine, made near Messina. It is rather light in character and, although not often seen on export lists, is well reputed and deserves drinking by travellers.

Fass   See **casks**.

Feints   Name for the last runnings of the first still in making Scotch **whisky**.

Fendant   **Swiss** wine **grape**, which in fact is related to the **Chasselas**, making pleasant white wines with a distinctive **bouquet**, especially in the **Valais**.

Fermentation   This process, whereby **grape** juice – or other juices containing certain **yeasts** – are converted into an alcoholic beverage, is both complex and simple. Those who are able to understand a little chemistry are advised to refer to one of the specialised studies of the subject. But for those who cannot, the following gives a basic guide to what goes on.

It was Louis Pasteur who was mainly responsible for the first exact studies of fermentation. Grape juice, left alone, ferments naturally, up to the stage that it reaches about 14% of **alcohol**, when it stops. Extremes of heat and cold can, throughout, stop the wine yeasts working, just as yeasts in breadmaking will be stopped if the temperature of the kitchen is suddenly raised or lowered. Yeast varies according to different places, and there are different types of yeast. Certain wines, such as **port**, have their fermentation arrested by the addition of alcohol at a precise point – this also stops the yeasts working. But yeasts cannot work if they are weak or if there is insufficient sugar in the **must** on which they, or rather the **enzymes** they excrete, can act. This is why a certain amount of sun and warmth is important in regions where wine is to be made, as sun will make grapes fairly high in sugar whereas cold will make them too acid. Rain will also simply wash the bloom – which holds the yeast – off the grapes, so that fermentation in a wet year will be difficult. If fermentation is interrupted by some sudden climatic change, then it has to be started again and the result, in terms of wine, is seldom fine quality; more yeast may be added if the conditions are very difficult, or if existing strains are too weak.

Most wines have two fermentations or, one might say, their fermentation takes place in two stages. The first, usually tumultuous and rapid, takes place immediately the yeasts begin to work in the fresh must at vintage time. The fermentation slows down and then may cease as the weather gets cooler. The secondary fermentation may take place soon after the first – in some instances this is desirable, so that the wine may be completely 'made' as soon as reasonably possible – or else there may be a pause during the cool weather, and the secondary fermentation takes place in the spring of the year after the **vintage**. With certain **sparkling wines**, such as **Champagne**, the second fermentation in the spring is deliberately brought on so that the carbonic acid gas, which is the gas that creates the bubbles, may be controlled and contained within the bottle. In the ordinary way this gas is given off; which is why one is advised not to lean over a **vat** where wine is fermenting because of the danger of being overwhelmed by this happening. Breathing in the **carbon dioxide** can, at best, make one ill.

The exact type of fermentation will vary according to each type of wine and the year in which it is made. But while wines are in full fermentation, or are 'working', they cannot be tasted accurately and should not be drunk – as they then continue to ferment inside the drinker. If in doubt, a wine that tastes vaguely 'beery' or lacks its usual smell, and is vaguely fizzy in the mouth, should be rejected as fermenting; although on occasions people at tastings have been known to pour lavish praise on a wine in this condition! A very little *pétillance* or a *spritzig* trait, however, can be a pleasant asset, indicating that a wine is young, vigorous and vivacious. Many great white wines are charming in this state, once they have been fully made, and there are some wines which are specifically made to accentuate and retain this type of secondary fermentation, such as the *vin fou* of the **Jura**, and *vinho verde* of north **Portugal**.

A wine may also suddenly show signs of fermenting again long after it should normally have ceased to do so. This is a matter for the specialist to deal with, and can be attributed to a number of causes. Anyone sure that this is what an otherwise matured wine is doing should ask advice and, if possible, return the wine as soon as may be, in its sealed **bottle**, to the source of supply. But one should not confuse the curious way in which many fine wines tend to go slightly out of condition at two periods of the year, with fermentation. In the spring at the **flowering** of the vine, and in the autumn at the **vintage**, the wine in the **bottle** may show that it is still, mysteriously, linked to its source of life, the vine; and for a little while it may lose its **bouquet** and much of its taste and be at less than its best. This is not a type of fermentation. See **malo-lactic fermentation, pasteurisation**.

Fernet Branca Italian **bitters**, admirable as a pre-**digestive**, after-dinner drink or pick-me-up. They may be taken straight or with soda. Evolved in 1845 by Fratelli Branca of Milan. They, like **Ferro China**, are believed by many Italians to have **aphrodisiac** properties. See **elixir**.

Ferreira Important name in the history of wine in **Portugal**, both for table wines and for **port**. In the early 19th century, one of the most remarkable **women** in wine, Doña Antonia de Ferreira, married her cousin of the same name and, when he died, she continued to run his wine business. Respected by the entire port trade even during this most conservative period, she was also much loved by her family. On one occasion she took one of her daughters out of the country so that the girl should not be forced into an unwelcome marriage with an influential man (and later was able to marry the one of her own preference). Doña Antonia escaped drowning in the accident on the Douro when Baron **Forrester** disappeared when their shallow-bottomed boat capsized, because she and her companion floated to safety on a sandbank, borne up by their crinolines.

Her name is still remembered vividly in the port world, for once, when I took a taxi and was trying to make the driver grasp my rudimentary Portuguese to the effect that I wished to go to the Ferreira establishment, he suddenly understood: 'Ah, the House of the Ferreira lady!' Ferreira ports demonstrate 'Portuguese style' ports superbly – finely-knit, sensitive wines, their great **vintages** are remarkable and worth the serious attention of port lovers. Their table wines, privileged by a tradition of great winemakers in the firm, are very good.

Ferrière Classed 3rd growth **Margaux**, at present run by the owners of **Lascombes**. See **Bordeaux, classification**.

Ferro China Italian aromatic **bitters**, in style resembling **Fernet Branca**. See **digestives, elixir**.

Feteasca alba, neagra White and black **Romanian** grapes, cultivated in the

Odobesti region.

Fettercairn This 18th century **whisky distillery** in Kincardineshire was established in 1824 in commercial production. Its single malt is Old Fettercairn.

Fetzer Vineyards and **winery** near Mendocino, **California**, established since World War II, reported as making sound wines.

Feuerheerd Wearne (Pronounced 'Foyer-haird') **Port** firm, founded in 1815. Unfortunately I have never been able to try their port.

Fiana Dry white wine made in small quantities in **Campania**, **Italy**.

Fiasco Italian word for 'flask'. It is used to mean the partly straw-covered bulbous **bottles**, which were given the protective jacket of straw so as to prevent them breaking when hung up or several bottles carried together. The *fiasco* is used for wines intended for immediate consumption, as it cannot be laid on its side. It is chiefly associated with **Chianti** and its capacity, when used for this wine, is 17·5 fl. oz (50cl), 1·75 pt (1 litre) or larger. The **Orvieto** flask, however, contains 26 fl. oz (75cl) only.

Ficklin Vineyard and **winery** in the San Joaquin Valley, **California**, established in 1946 and very well reputed for the **port** type wine on which they concentrate. The business is run by the Ficklin family, who also make a small quantity of grapes into table wines. The use of certain Portuguese port **grapes**, careful vinification and intelligent observation of advice from **Davis** make the Ficklin **fortified wine** of great interest, as the region is very hot. The prestige of the winery is high.

Fieuzal Situated in the parish of Léognan in the **Graves**, it makes red wines, plus a small amount of white. It is not often seen on lists but those who have been able to taste it, report its quality in both red and white.

Figeac A *château* in St Émilion, but close to the **Pomerol** region, which has long been famous for fine, noble wines, made by a respected owner. See **Bordeaux, classification**.

Filfar See **orange liqueurs**.

Filhot (Pronounced 'Fee-yoh') A **Sauternes** *château*, classified as a 2nd growth in 1855. It produces fine Sauternes and, in recent years, a dry wine of quality as well. See **Bordeaux, classification**.

Filtration The process whereby wines are filtered, so that **deposit** and particles remaining in them are removed and the wine can be 'star bright' as it goes into the glass. Unfortunately the prevalent taste is for star bright wines at all costs, even when fine wines, which live to a certain extent on their deposits, are involved. Correct **service** will ensure that no healthy wine is in a cloudy state when it is poured; but although the brilliant colour – red or white – of a fine wine is one of its charms, to be set off by a good **glass**, it is important to remember that the smell and flavour of a wine are important assets as well. A certain amount of filtration is, of course, essential for wines to be in good condition, but excessive filtering can take something from the wine each time it takes place, so that brightness is not a quality to be achieved regardless. The insistence of certain markets on wines without a deposit at all has resulted in many of the finest being rebottled before they are sold. Consequently there is a risk of deterioration or, at best, the guts are partially removed from the wine.   See **château-bottling**, **crystals**, **fining**.

Filzen   Mosel vineyard.

Fine   (Pronounced 'feen') *Une fine* is **brandy** distilled from wine. *Une fine à l'eau* is brandy (which in a good restaurant should be **Cognac**) with water. Sometimes regional brandies of this type bear the name of the region – e.g. Fine Marne. *Une fine* is not the same as **marc**; it usually matures more quickly and is smoother, more delicate, and lighter in colour – and generally more expensive.

Finger Lakes   Region in upper **New York State** in the U.S., so called because the lakes spread out, looking on the map rather like the fingers of an open hand. The area has produced a variety of wines since the 1830s. Many are made from the American native **vines**, of which the best known is probably *Vitis labrusca* **Concord**. Some people find a curious taste and smell about these which is generally described as 'foxy' – it has a pronounced scent – and many accustomed to wines made only from *Vitis vinifera* cannot appreciate the different character. It is something that should be approached with an unbiased mind if possible: well-made wines from wineries where skill and care have built the reputation of their products can be enjoyed by most unprejudiced people. Use of the more usual types of *Vitis vinifera* is under experiment – formerly it was considered that the region is too far north, with too severe a climate to allow this vine to thrive, but modern viticulture may change this view.

Possibly the best-known type of wine from the Finger Lakes is the **sparkling wine**, which U.S. legislation allows to be called 'Champagne', although this would be contrary to British and French law. Critics affirm that the sparkling process subdues the 'foxiness' but this is something to be decided by the individual drinker. It is worth bearing in mind that the **Great Western** sparkling wine of the Finger Lakes is not connected with the Great Western vineyard in **Australia**. Great Western in this American context is made by the **Pleasant Valley** Wine Co. founded in 1860. Other important wineries are: **Taylor** Wine Co., Urbana Wine Co., **Bully Hill**, **Gold Seal**, Vinifera, Boordy, **Widmer's** Wine Cellars. In the **Hudson River Valley**, there are the Hudson Valley Wine Co. and the **High Tor** estate.

Fining   This term is sometimes confused with **filtration**, but is quite different. A fining agent attracts to itself certain particles floating in the wine, which might be adversely affected by their action (this is different from removing the wine from its **deposit**). Various substances are used for fining, including egg whites, blood, fish finings and even water, but this is a technical matter and should not concern the ordinary drinker. The lay person may, however, sometimes encounter a wine at the property where it is made which is 'on finings' – in other words, it is undergoing fining, or else it may have recently been fined. In such instances it cannot fairly be tasted until it has fully recovered. The French verb is *coller*. See ***Bontemps***.

Fino   See **sherry**.

Fior d'Alpi   Italian **liqueur** made by several firms, usually put in tall bottles, with a twig inside each, with lumps of crystallised sugar on it. The liqueur is fairly pungent and refreshing.

Fitou   Wine region on the Mediterranean **French** coast, in the south-west, near **Corbières**. A rather soft, pleasant red wine and some white are made, and esteemed locally. These wines are likely to become more widely known.

Fixin   (Pronounced 'Fis-sin') This parish, in the **Côte de Nuits** in **Burgundy**, is one of several that may sell some of their wines with the **A.O.C.** Vins Fins de la Côte de Nuits, or as Côte de Nuits Villages. However the quality of Fixin has attracted the attention of reputable British **shippers** and therefore it is often now seen on lists under its own name. Its character is usually elegant and charming, with a certain marked fruitiness. See **Côte d'Or**.

Flagey-Echézeaux   See **Burgundy, Côte d'Or**.

Flaschengärung   German term indicating that it is a **sparkling wine** made by the **transfer method**.

Fleurie   See **Beaujolais**.

Floc de Gascogne   Somewhat similar to **Pineau des Charentes**, this **apéritif** is unfermented **grape** juice, plus **Armagnac**.

Flor   The curious covering of **yeast** that 'flowers' on the surface of certain wines, notably **sherry**, changing their style. Louis Pasteur, born in **Arbois** in the **Jura**, discovered the action of bacteria by his researches into the local wines, some of which grow a flor or, as it is known in French, a *voile* (veil). Different yeasts can make a great difference to the wines on which they work, but sherry yeast is particularly strong: in some countries, sherry yeasts are imported to make the wine of sherry style. Native flor, however, is also used for many of the quality **Cyprus** and **South African** sherries. The whole action of yeast is rather uncanny for the non-chemically minded, but there are many yeasts involved with winemaking as well as flor, and they are, in a sense, the spark that gives life to any alcoholic beverage. Anyone who notes a covering of something vaguely woolly or furry on a wine that has been left open for some time will probably be seeing a type of flor − it will not make the wine harmful, although it will not necessarily enhance its taste.

Florio   One of the big names in **Marsala**. The Florio establishment, which itself belongs to **Cinzano**, has absorbed the old British **wineries** of Ingham, Whitaker and Woodhouse, although retaining their historic names.

Flowering   The flowering of the **vine** in the spring, the French is *fleuraison*. The **vintage** usually occurs 100 days after the flowering which, ideally, should take place quickly, leaving the newly formed **grapes** in good condition.

Flûte   A type of **glass**, like an inverted isosceles triangle, as used for **Champagne** (pictured in many still-life studies) and certain **sparkling** and still wines. The wine's vivacity is prolonged by contact with the glass.

Flûte d'Alsace   The sloping-shouldered green **bottle**, used for the wines of **Alsace**. It is very slightly longer than the bottles of similar shape used for German and similar wines, and its use is protected by French legislation. At present, 2 sizes of bottle are in use, but the 26 fl.oz (75cl) bottle will probably eventually become universal.

Flyer   Term for a particle floating in wine. This need not be in any way harmful to it, although the Victorians developed a squeamishness about seeing flyers. That is why white wines, in which these were most easily noticed, were served in coloured **glasses** to spare the sensibilities of the drinkers. Today modern methods of winemaking – and more sense about winedrinking – have done away with complaints about flyers, although it must be stated that they can and do exist, particularly in certain very fine wines, of which they can be an integral part. Those who return fine white wines because they have thrown a **deposit** or have 'bits floating in them' – except, of course, if the wine itself is out of condition or bad – are being snobbish rather than wise. Correct **service** will obviate a wine being made cloudy from deposit, and the presence of a flyer in the glass will not affect the taste. See **crystals**, **decanting**, **filtration**.

Fojaneghe   The full name of this red wine is Bossi Fedrugotti Fojaneghe, and it is made in the **Trentino-Alto Adige** region of **Italy**, from the three black **grapes** that are the foundation of **claret** (**Cabernet Sauvignon**, Cabernet Franc and **Merlot**), given age in **cask** and **bottle**. Only a small quantity is produced. It is a pleasant, full, fragrant wine, worthy of interest.

Folle Blanche   The white **grape** formerly much used for **Cognac**, but now being superseded there by other **varieties**. What many travellers to Brittany do not realise is that the Folle Blanche is in fact the **Gros Plant du Pays Nantais** which makes a very sharp, acid white wine. As the Picpoul, this is also one of the grapes cultivated in the **Rhône** and the south. Its **acidity** can contribute zest and crispness to wines that might otherwise be flabby.

Fonseca   One of the great family names in the history of **Portugal's** wine industry, associated with an important production of table wines as well as Fonseca **port**. Fonseca ports are, of course, 'Portuguese' ports, but very finely constructed wines – the British port **shippers** respect them.

Foppiano   Winery in **California**.

Forbidden Fruit   American **liqueur**, made of citrus fruits and honey.

Foreshots   First part of the running of the first still in making Scotch **whisky**.

Forrester, James (1809-61)   One of the great names in the history of **port**. He went to **Portugal** to join his uncle's firm of Offley, Webber and Forrester in 1831 and became widely liked and respected. In particular, he was a superb mapmaker and his hand-drawn maps, some of remote regions never previously detailed, are masterpieces of delicacy and accuracy. His overall interests included fruits, vegetables, olives, pests and diseases of the vine, about which he wrote in detail. He also made an unparalleled collection of figures wearing the regional costumes of Portugal. His influence on the port trade was great and he appears to have been a friend of the peasants who worked for him as well as of the nobility, royalty and the British and Portuguese in the wine trade alike. His life ended when the boat on which he was travelling on the Douro, in the company of Doña Antonia **Ferreira**, capsized after hitting a rock; the women floated to safety, but the Baron, who was wearing a money belt holding wages for his workers, disappeared and his body was never found. Unfortunately I have never been able to try Offley Forrester ports.

Forst See **Palatinate**.

Forster Jesuitengarten One of the best-known wines of the **Palatinate** in **Germany**.

Fortified wine This term, as used in the U.K., means a wine literally made stronger – that is 'fortified' – by the addition of **brandy** at some stage in its production. **Sherry**, **port**, **Málaga** and **Marsala** are the best-known examples. Recently a definition of the term for EEC countries encountered problems because the French, who do not make wines that are fortified in this way (*vins doux naturels* are slightly different), wished the term to be *vin de liqueur*. This was opposed by Britain, because of the obvious confusion that would be risked by the use of the term '**liqueur**' in relation to a wine. In EEC documents, however, this is now adopted except in the U.K.

In the **U.S.**, however, it seems that the term is still under discussion. In the early part of the 20th century, it was the practice there to categorise as 'dry' any wines under 14% of alcohol by volume, and as 'sweet' those wines over 14%. Obviously, this was wholly unsatisfactory – a great **Sauternes** or *trockenbeerenauslese* can hardly be associated with the term 'dry', and how can a superb *fino* be categorised as 'sweet'? In the 1930s, the North Americans altered the nomenclature to '**light**' and 'fortified', but this still did not satisfy them: for some reason that I do not understand, the term 'fortified' appeared to risk abuse. It is, however, stupid to denounce the word, as does one contemporary authority, as 'misleading' and to say that it 'was originally coined by the British who still stubbornly cling to it despite our (the U.S.) appeals to change'. (Why the logical use of an English word should be misleading and why those who speak the English language as it is generally understood in the British Isles should, for any reason, be prevented from using it? Just one more argument in favour of distinguishing between 'American' and 'English' English!)

Some Americans apparently would have liked to substitute the terms 'appetizer and dessert wines' for 'fortified', although this was not permitted. The advertising controls in the U.S. are tight. The English speaker can only be thankful that such a clumsy and misleading phrase was avoided. The Americans are now not allowed to use the term 'fortified' on **labels** or even in **wineries**: instead of 'fortifying room', the sign on the door must read 'brandy addition room'.

The U.S. have had further problems because, in stating the alcoholic **strength** on labels, some firms were stressing this – thereby implying that strength was equivalent to quality. Regulations now limit the type size in which strength is stated and it appears that there is now a more general use of the term 'table wine' for what the U.K. would refer to as **light wines**. There are some states in the U.S. that still require labels to give the alcoholic strength, whereas in the majority this is optional.

A term in increasing use, however, is that of 'soft' or 'extra light table wines' – both equally baffling to the outsider. Although the situation is changing all the time, it appears that, in **California**, table wines have been required to reach a minimum of 10% of alcohol by volume; certain highly-respected winemakers, specialising in fine wines, have queried this because, as with many European wines, some delicate wines may be as low as 7%. (High alcoholic strength is not, in itself, any quality asset, unless you are the type of peasant drinker who simply wants a wine with a kick.) Permission has had to be applied for in order to produce such wines which will, by their nature, be lower in alcohol than the required 10% and yet which can still be labelled as 'table wine'. These 'soft' or 'extra light' wines are now available all over the U.S. and therefore these descriptions must come into common parlance. See **heavy wines**.

Fortino   **Winery** in the **Santa Clara** Valley, **California**.

Fouloir égrappoir   The use of this French term seems inevitable, because, although the English translation might be rendered as 'crusher de-stalker', this is both clumsy and tends to complicate the understanding of the process. The most usual form of the *fouloir égrappoir* gets the **grapes** off their stems in various ways, such as by being spun over a spiked drum. They then go into a receptacle like a large truckle, which has a screw running across the bottom; as the grapes fall on to this, the action of the turning screw breaks up the fruit and carries it out of the receptacle, eventually to the **fermentation vat**. The process is quite simple but sometimes people who are expecting to see the sort of **press** that comes down on the grapes and squeezes them by pressure, cannot understand the action of the screw.

If the screw is speeded up, the grapes are crushed more roughly; if it is slowed down, the action is gentler. Sometimes the grapes – stems, stalks and all – are tipped straight down into the *fouloir*, sometimes they pass via the *égrappoir* and then just the fruit falls on to the screw; it depends on the type of wine to be made and the technique of the winemaker. In some wine regions, visitors may be informed that the harvested grapes are *foulés mais pas égrappés*, signifying that the stalks and stems all go straight into the vat. It is these stalks and stems that give astringency and contribute **tannin**. Sometimes this is required, at other times not. See **hat**.

Fraise   See *alcool blanc*.

Framboise   See *alcool blanc*.

France   In some years France produces more wine than **Italy**, in others Italy more: but no other country surpasses these two in quantity and wine is a very important part of the French economy. Sometimes people express the view that too much attention is paid to French wines, but there are several reasons why they must always be considered by the winelover, the serious drinker and the compiler of any wine list. Firstly, the tradition of winegrowing in France is very old and the wide range of both red and white wines made in the country has given experience and authority to French winemakers. Secondly, wines often described as 'classic' tend to be predominantly French, simply because they are the wines on which drinkers have formed their standards. Finally the detailed pleasure and fascination provided by the finest of the quality wines has been a source of discussion among serious winelovers for generations.

The bulk of wine produced in France is wine for everyday consumption, not the sort of wine that will improve by maturation in bottle. This is known as *vin de consommation courante*. The branded wines are known as *vins de marque*. The regional wines are often in the **V.D.Q.S.** category, the finer wines are **A.O.C.** and, in more recent times, the categories of *vins de pays* and **V.Q.P.R.D.** have been added. Unless a drinker is a prejudiced and chauvinistic person, he will admit that the two finest red **table wines** in the world are **claret** and **Burgundy**, and that the finest **sparkling wine** is **Champagne**. Anyone pro-French will assert further that the dry white wines of Burgundy and the **Loire** are supreme examples of this type of table wine and that the **Sauternes** are great among any of the sweet wines of the world. The latter claim could admittedly be argued, especially by a German! But not only are such French wines at least among the finest of their kind, but their world fame has enabled many to form judgments about wines from even a slight knowledge of them.

Just as many of the finest table wines are French, so are the two great **brandies** of the world – **Cognac** and **Armagnac**. France also produces a huge variety of **liqueurs**. The range of drinks available within nearly all the provinces of France is therefore great and it would be possible, from France alone, to pick wines and spirits appropriate for virtually any occasion and to be served with any dish, even exotic, and unlike any French dishes as could be imagined. This is why, in restaurants of more than strictly regional scope and in wine merchants of any pretensions to a comprehensive list, French wines and spirits will be prominently featured. Huge books have been written on even the smaller wine regions of France. References to the main wine regions should be made – see **Alsace**, **Bordeaux**, **Burgundy**, **Champagne**, **Languedoc**, **Loire**, **Rhône**, – and the numerous subdivisions within them, etc. The most famous of the classic wines have separate entries under their names, and those who wish to know more details should consult the Bibliography for further reading.

Recent improvements in both vinegrowing and winemaking, as well as the care of wines that have to travel, have made it possible to market wines from many regions that previously could, at best, only be thought of as holiday wines and for local consumption. At the same time, no amount of money will make a great wine in an unsuitable vineyard – although it can make a pleasant one in many vineyards. Nor is the respect in which the great French classic wines are rightly held something that can justify anybody considering any French wine to be 'better' than any other in the medium and inexpensive price ranges. This is where the **wine snob** does harm to himself and his guests on many occasions, such as when a 'great' or demandingly interesting wine is not required – as on a picnic, or with wholly casual food – and when something that is not French may offer better value and provide more enjoyment.

FRANCE (GENERAL)

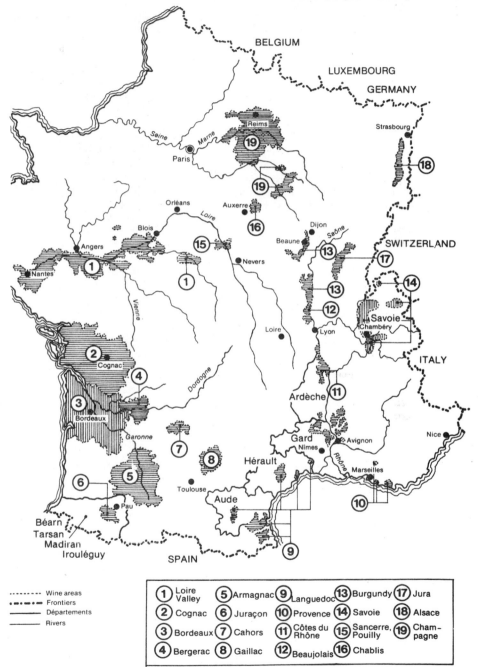

① Loire Valley	⑤ Armagnac	⑨ Languedoc	⑬ Burgundy	⑰ Jura
② Cognac	⑥ Juraçon	⑩ Provence	⑭ Savoie	⑱ Alsace
③ Bordeaux	⑦ Cahors	⑪ Côtes du Rhône	⑮ Sancerre, Pouilly	⑲ Champagne
④ Bergerac	⑧ Gaillac	⑫ Beaujolais	⑯ Chablis	

------- Wine areas
·—·—·— Frontiers
——— Départements
——— Rivers

It is often very difficult to persuade hesitant winebuyers that, in spite of the wonders provided by French wines, the mere fact of a wine's being French cannot guarantee that its drinking qualities will be superior to all others! The south of France wines, for example, can be very good small-scale drinks these days but, when the international currency situation puts them into the high medium or expensive price range, the British drinker cannot expect them to taste better than their own potential allows – however much they may cost. At the same time, within France itself there can be remarkable value – often bypassed when people 'drink the label': for example, many people will often buy even a very ordinary **German** wine rather than an Alsace – which Germans themselves buy simply because it is such good value and high quality – or they will opt for a white Burgundy of a doubtful year and possibly dubious provenance rather than choose a good white Loire.

Franciacorta   These wines come from a small region between Brescia and Lago d'Iseo, in **Lombardy, Italy**. It is thought that the name may originate from that of the town of Cortefranca – or possibly the wine gave its name to the town. The red, from a blend of **grapes** that include the **Cabernet Franc**, **Barbera**, **Nebbiolo** and **Merlot**, is said to age well. The white, from a **Pinot**, seems to be best when drunk young.

Franciscan Vineyards   **Winery** in the **Napa Valley, California**.

Franconia   **German** wine region, east of Mainz and centred on Würzburg, which is a beautiful town, rich in art treasures and fine buildings, gardens and churches. The Staatsweingut Hoffkellerei (Court Cellar), the **Juliusspital**, the Residenz (a great baroque palace belonging to the von Schönborn family), the Bayerrische Landesanalt für Wein und Gartenbau (Bavarian Institute for Viticulture and Horticulture), and the **Bürgerspital zum Heiligen Geist** are essential places to see.

Most Franconian wines are white, although a few reds are made, of which that of **Iphofen** is possibly the best known. Otherwise the **Müller-Thurgau** accounts for about half of the **vines** planted; the **Silvaner** – which here gives of its best – for a third. The Franconian wines, famous since the Middle Ages, are dry. The adjective 'steely' is often used to describe them and today they tend to lack the immediate appeal that is useful to publicise wines outside their own areas. The term '*Steinwein*' (stone wine) is generally used for Franconian wines, but, strictly, it should only be used for those produced from the actual Stein site, at Würzburg. The 'stone' or dry style typifies most of them, although in some exceptional years wines of more concentration and even sweetness are made. The *bocksbeutel* is distinctive and limited to these wines.

Frandsdruift   See **Palomino, South Africa**.

Franken   See **Franconia**.

Franzia   **Winery, in California**, making a range of inexpensive wines. Now owned by Coca Cola.

Frascati   Wine region within that of the **Castelli Romani** in **Lazio** in **Italy**, making dry, semi-sweet and sweet white wines, and a little red wine. The finest is considered to be the sweet Frascati, often referred to as Cannellino. It is very fragrant and the colour, of all the white wines, is assertively golden. This type of Frascati is said to be made with the action of the ***Botrytis cinerea***, which is produced because of the humid climate. However there appears to be considerable differences of opinion about this wine, some makers apparently trying to get rid of the *Botrytis* if it is present; others stating that it was the presence of the *Botrytis* that earned a poor reputation for Frascati wines as 'bad travellers'.

Some form of **pasteurisation** seems often to be employed in order to keep control of the evolution of the wine from the arrival of the freshly-picked **grapes**. This prevention of the *Botrytis* is apparently what makes the dry wines; but they, made like the other from the **Trebbiano** grape of **Tuscany** and the Yellow Trebbiano, locally called 'Greco', do usually produce a fairly soft, slightly perfumed wine anyway. My tasting notes often use the term 'Everton toffee' for anything made from the Trebbiano.

Frecciarossa   **Italian** wines made by a single family, Odero, who produce red, white, rosé, and a slightly sweet white wine. The village that gives the wines their name is in the **Oltrepò Pavese** in **Lombardy**. The **labels** bear French descriptive terms. The wines enjoy a high reputation.

Freemark Abbey   **Winery** in **Napa Valley**, **California**; producing table wines made from single **grape varieties** that have won considerable acclaim for quality.

Freezomint   See **crème de menthe**.

Freisa   Several wines of this name are made in the various regions of the hills outside **Turin**, in **Piedmont**. They are made from the Freisa **grape**, which produces red wines, pleasantly crisp in some examples, others tending towards a soft style. Some people mistake Freisa wines for sweet wines rather easily, because they confound the Italian word with the French for strawberry (*fraise*). I myself used to think that the Italian word meant a strawberry **liqueur**.

Friedrich-Wilhelm Gymnasium   One of the great schools in Trier, at the heart of the **Mosel**, which, together with the Bischöfliches Weingüter, **Vereinigte Hospitien** and the Staatsweingut, sells part of the wines with which it is endowed at auction – the Grosse Ring and Kleine Ring – which of course attract much publicity. See **Hohe Domkirche**.

Friuli-Venezia Giulia   Wine region in the north-east of **Italy**, making both red and white wines. Many are named after classic wine **grapes** from which they are made, such as **Tocai**, **Sauvignon**, **Cabernet**, **Pinot Bianco** and Grigio, **Merlot** and so on. The most famous of all is **Picolit**, which is a deep straw-coloured sweetish wine.

Frizzante   This Italian term implies that the wine is slightly sparkling or rather definitely *pétillant*. It is not the same as *spumante*, which indicates a fully **sparkling wine**. See *crémant*.

Fronsac   Region in the **Bordeaux** area, lying west of **Pomerol**, producing mainly red wines, which can attain a certain elegance and charm. The region includes Côtes Canon Fronsac, of which there are two properties called

Canon, and eight other vineyards using the word in their names (the great Ch. Canon, however, is in **St Émilion**.   See *Côtes*.

Frontignac   **Grape** being cultivated in the Cape vineyards, **South Africa**, mostly for experimental purposes at present. Formerly used in parts of Southern **France**.

Frontignan   Region in the **Hérault**, **France**, south-west of **Montpellier**, well known for its **Muscat** wines.

Frosting glasses   This always looks very impressive, but is easy to do. Damp the edge of the **glass** and then dip it in caster sugar. If you rub the edge with a slice of orange, people wonder why the drink has a subtle difference. For a very fresh drink, use a slice of lemon.

Füder   **Mosel cask**, containing about 211 gallons (960 litres).

Furmint   A white **grape,** introduced to **Hungary** about the Tartar invasion in 1241, by the King who invited Walloon winegrowers to settle in the country. They brought with them this grape, called *froment*, possibly because the wine it produces is the colour of ripe wheat. It is also grown in **Italy** and in **Germany** as well as throughout central and south-eastern Europe.

Fût   French word meaning a **cask** of any size. Sometimes particularly used to signify 'an empty cask'.

G

Gaeiras White and red wines from around the picturesque town of Óbidos in **Portugal**. The reds are very pleasant, mouth-filling drinks.

La Gaffelière One of the *Premiers Grands Crus Classés* of **St Émilion**, situated in the *Côtes* region of the vineyard. It is sometimes referred to as La Gaffelière Naudes, but the latter part of the name has been dropped in recent years. The wines have a full, agreeable style in general. See **Canon-La-Gaffelière**.

Gaillac Region near **Bordeaux** in the south-west of **France**, making a wide range of still wines, some red, but mostly white and rosé, and some **sparkling** and *pétillant* wines. They are not often seen outside the area and should certainly be tried by the traveller on the spot. They are not, as some writers have stated, mostly sweet, although some sweet wines are made.

Galicia Region in north-west **Spain**, making quantities of white and red wines. The slightly fizzy whites are somewhat akin to the *vinhos verdes* of neighbouring **Portugal**. But there seem to be plenty of others and those of **Valdeorras** are beginning to be seen on export lists. Pink wines appear also to be made there. Travellers to Santiago de Compostella should profit by any opportunity to try the regional wines.

Galliano Yellow Italian **liqueur** in a tall **bottle**, based on herbs, and named after Major Guiseppe Galliano, who succeeded in halting the Ethiopian forces at Enda Jesus in the war of 1895-6. Popular in the **U.S.**

Gallo The biggest **winery** in the world, established in 1933 in **California**. They possess their own **bottle** factory and buy **grapes** from many growers. The brothers Gallo are the sole owners. They have become well known for their jug **wines**, as well as making fruit-flavoured 'wines'. They also have some wines named for the grape that makes them.

Gallweys Irish Coffee Liqueur See **coffee liqueurs**.

Gamay The full name of this **Beaujolais** black **grape** is Gamay Noir à Jus Blanc. It was banned in 1395 by Philippe le Hardi (Bold), Duke of Burgundy, possibly because it was encroaching on the plantations of **Pinot Noir** in **Burgundy**, but is extensively cultivated today. It yields a fruity, delicious, brilliant red wine. Plantations elsewhere in **France** have increased and the

Gamay is found in the **Loire**, the **Ardèche**, the **Côtes du Forez**, and in many *vins du pays*. It is also planted in other countries, but it is worth noting that, in some **California** Gamays, the term 'Gamay Beaujolais' is often used. This is not, however, the true Beaujolais grape; it is now thought to be a type of Pinot Noir. If the Gamay Noir à Jus Blanc is used for quality California wines, the grape name is often given as 'Napa Gamay'. There are other Gamays, some of them recommended for use in France.

Gambellara   Region in the **Veneto** area of **Italy**, making a wide range of wines, still and **sparkling**, also *vin santo*. The greater proportion of these seem to be white.

Gamza   Bulgarian black **grape**.

Gard   Picturesque region in the south of **France**, which, until recently, produced large quantities of wine, much of which went for **blending**, or for sale as the purely 'local' wine. Today this is one of the regions making wines that are popular far outside their region, as **V.D.Q.S.** and *vins du pays*. They usually have a pleasant 'warm' character; both white and red, when well made, can give pleasure as small-scale drinks anywhere. See **Aude**, **Hérault**, **Languedoc**.

Garda   See **Italy**.

Garganega   Italian white **grape**, used in the **Veneto**.

Garnacho   See **Grenache**.

Garrafeira   Portuguese wine term, implying that the wine so **labelled** has been matured in **bottle**.

Gattinara   Italian red wine made near the town of the same name in **Piedmont**. It is highly esteemed and can benefit greatly from maturation in **bottle**.

Gauloise   A very old French **apéritif**, seldom seen nowadays, but formerly made in three styles, dry, medium and sweet. The makers claimed that it was this that gave the famous French cigarette its name.

Gavi Cortese   Philip Dallas calls this 'the most distinguished dry white table wine of **Piedmont**'. It is made from the **Cortese grape** and can apparently benefit by moderate **bottle age.**

Gay Lussac   Joseph Gay-Lussac (1778-1850) was a French chemist who is now best known for the system, which bears his name, of measuring the **strength** of alcoholic beverages. This is the simple one of expressing the strength in terms of percentage of **alcohol** by volume. Most people find it easier to understand than the British system of **proof**. See **Balling**, **Baumé**, **Oechsle**.

Gebirgsbitter   German bran**dy** with additional aromatic and **bitter** ingredients. It may be brown or green in colour.

Geisenheim   Rheingau vineyard region (see **Rhine**) which is also famous for the great German Wine Institute, consulted by winemakers all over the world.

Geist   Term used in German to describe certain types of fruit **liqueur**, distilled from unfermented berries, apricots or peaches, plus the addition of **alcohol**. See *alcool blanc*, *eau-de-vie*, *wasser*.

Genever   See **gin**.

Gentian   An ingredient in a number of **apéritifs** and **liqueurs**, bitter in flavour, but possessing **digestive** properties. Suze, which is bright yellow, is one of the

148

best-known French apéritifs, light in alcohol. Arvèze is another from the Auvergne. *Enzian* liqueurs from Bavaria also include this ingredient.

German Wine Law This latest attempt to protect quality and simplify regulations came into force in 1971. Unfortunately, as often happens when laws and regulations have to be written down, many problems subsequently arose: there are numerous alterations, modifications and discussions as to the interpretation of the Law. Essentially, the potential customer should know that certain controls are exercised and that the **label** of any German wine indicates what the bottle contains. Lowest of all, there is *Tafelwein*, which can be a **blend** of wines from other EEC countries with some from Germany; then there is *Deutscher Tafelwein*, which must be wine from Germany only, and from one of five authorised regions: Mosel, Rhein, Main, Neckar and Oberrhein. Above these two lowest categories, each bottle will bear what is called the A.P. number. The initials stand for *Amtliche Prüfingsnummer*, signifying that the wine has passed both laboratory and tasting tests, in which it must achieve its category's minimum mark to qualify.

Above the category of *Deutscher Tafelwein*, comes the category *Qualitätswein bestimmer Anbaugebiete*, a term usually shortened to 'QbA'. These wines have also to satisfy various tests, must be typical of their region and **grape** and, if they bear any site or vineyard name, at least 75% of the wine in the **bottle** must actually be from that site. The 11 wine regions are: **Ahr, Baden, Franconia, Hessische Bergstrasse, Mittelrhein, Mosel-Saar-Ruwer, Nahe**, Rheingau, Rheinhessen, Rheinpfalz (**Palatinate**) and **Württemberg** (see **Rhine**). **Liebfraumilch** comes into this category. Wines above the *tafelwein* and QbA wines cannot be sugared in any way and the use of the term *Natur*, sometimes formerly seen, is no longer permitted.

The top quality wines are in the category *Qualitätswein mit Prädikat*, or 'QmP'. According to the region from which the wine comes, it must achieve the requisite qualities, the right level of sugar in the **must**, and the right level of **alcohol**. The first section in this category is that of *Kabinett*, a term that implies something special, set apart. Then there are the *spätlese* or late harvested wines; then the *auslese* wines, made from bunches of grapes specially selected for ripeness among those that are late picked. The *beerenauslesen* and *trockenbeerenauslesen* wines are late picked, and made from individually selected grapes, not just bunches. The last category is made from grapes left to dry (*trocken* is German for 'dry') on the vine so that the small amount of juice each grape contains is of concentrated sweetness. An *eiswein* is a wine made from grapes actually frozen when put into the press – it usually is made in a year that may otherwise have not been remarkable but when some grapes are left on the vines until the winter frosts; some wine of this type is even occasionally made in January following the vintage.

Germany Although Germany produces some of the finest white wines in the world, the quantity of wine produced is comparatively small beside the yield of **France, Italy, Spain** and the **Argentine**. The vineyards of Germany are the most northern in the world and nearly all the wines – and certainly all the

GERMANY

FRANCE

LUXEMBOURG

Bonn
Remagen
Königswinter
Bad Neuenahr
Ahrweiler
Altenahr
Linz
Rolandsbogen
Koblenz
Bad Ems
Boppard
Kochem
Oberwesel
Schloss Vollrads
Lorch
Rauenthal
Ostrich
Hoch
Alf
Zell
Bacharach
Rüdesheim
Mainz
Assmanshausen
Bingen
Piesport
Bernkastel-Kues
Rüdesheim
Nierstein
Neumagen-Dhron
Bad Kreuznach
Trier
Eitelsbach
Niederhausen
Gunters-blum
Igel
Kasel
Schloss Böckelheim
Bad Munster am Stein
Alzey
Waldrach
Oberemmel
Saarburg

Ahr · Mosel · Lahn · Ruwer · Nahe · Glan · Saar

(1) Ahr	(5) Rheingau	(9) Hessiche Bergstrasse
(2) Mosel-Saar-Ruwer	(6) Rhein hessen	(10) Württemberg
(3) Mittelrhein	(7) Rheinpfalz (Palatinate)	(11) Baden
(4) Nahe	(8) Franken (Franconia)	

●—●—●—● Frontiers
––––––– Wine areas
───────── Rivers
·─··─··─·· River frontier

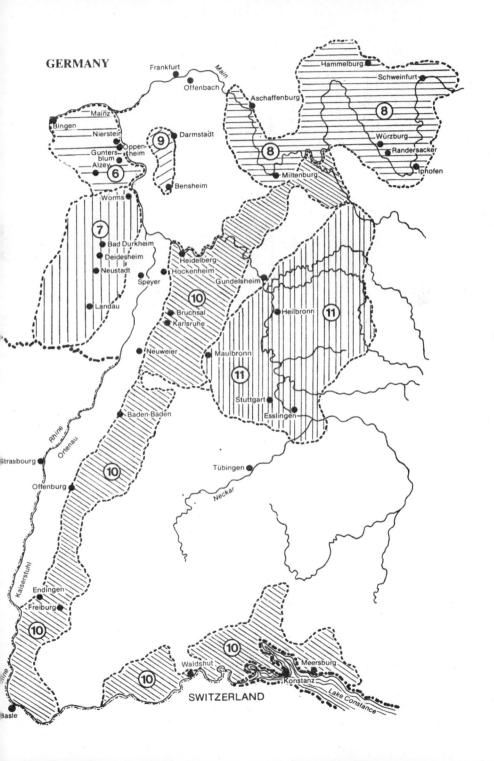

finest wines – are white. The main areas are: the **Rhine**, the **Mosel**, the **Palatinate** (or Pfalz), **Nahe**, **Franconia**, and **Baden-Württemberg**. In the last region a large amount of red wine is made; but few of this region's wines are exported. Many of the German vineyards have been cultivated since Roman times, and the finest wines command record prices. This last kind of wine is possibly most enjoyable when served by itself, outside the context of a meal, because the delicacy of a *beerenauslese*, *trockenbeerenauslese* and *eiswein* is best appreciated without the distraction of any other flavour or smell. There is, of course, a vast amount of German wine intended for everyday drinking as well and among drinkers outside Germany, **Liebfraumilch** is possibly the best-known name.

In 1971, the new **German Wine Law** began to operate and this changed the **labelling** of wines, although of course wines bottled before this date will bear descriptions in use at the time they were made. The complexities of the new law are still being sorted out, but in general the German wines are now put into three categories:

tafelwein or table wine;

qualitätswein or quality wine;

qualitätswein mit prädikat, a quality wine with qualifications. Only wines that come into the last category may bear the descriptions previously recognised:

spätlese – late picked

auslese – selected bunches of grapes

beerenauslese – selected grapes

trockenbeerenauslese – selected overripe grapes

All these wines contain only their natural sugar, varying according to the degree of ripeness attained when the **grapes** were picked, and may not be sweetened in any other way.

With the finest wines, grape **varieties** may be specified; but if they are not, it is assumed, on the Mosel, that the **Riesling** alone is used. As these wines are made in fairly small quantities, the actual **cask** number may also be given: each cask differing slightly. The name of the owner, or the establishment owning the vineyard, is also usually given on labels of the finest wines. The length of such names can be confusing to the non-German speaker, but it should be remembered that the precision with which German wines are named is essentially a safeguard to ensure the consumer getting exactly what is required. The difficulties attending production of German wines – climate, steepness of many of the vineyards, sensitive nature of the **vines** – throws added responsibility on the growers and **shippers**. It is said that, nowadays, it is more important to know the different styles of different shippers than to know **vintages**, and certainly the great vintage years are rarer in Germany than, usually, in France; the skill of modern winemaking enables passable and even good wine to be made in years that might, in former times, have been disastrous. It is the individual firm who can keep the wine true to the style of its region and its vintage (even when it has to be assisted by the laboratory in a poor year), and who can enable it to show itself to advantage in a good year.

An increasing quantity of **sparkling wine** is made in Germany and this is known generally as *sekt*. Some of it is made according to the **Champagne method**, but most is made by the *cuve close* or **Charmat method**. Many fruit and other **liqueurs** are made in Germany, including **bitters**; but although these are exported, they tend not to be so well known outside their own country. Abbreviations often used on wine lists indicating the areas from which German wines come are:

M. – Mosel.

N. or Na. – Nahe.

P. – Pfalz.

Rg. – Rheingau.

Rh. – Rheinhessen.

R. – Ruwer.

S. – Saàr.

Gevrey-Chambertin   Parish in the **Côte de Nuits** in **Burgundy**, where wines of a special sort of nobility and masculine style are made. The **A.O.C.**s are **Chambertin**, Chambertin Clos de Bèze, and six others which have the names of the site as prefix to the word Chambertin. The best-known sites of Gevrey-Chambertin, which are connected with the A.O.C. Gevrey-Chambertin, include Les Clos St Jacques, Les Véroilles, Bel-Air, Aux Combottes, Cazetiers, Combe-aux-Moines, and Estournelles; but there are a number of others. See **Côte d'Or**.

Gewürztraminer   (Pronounced 'Ger-vertz-tra-mee-ner' stressing 'vertz') This is an important white **grape**, which seems to have originated in the **Palatinate** and been introduced to **Alsace** after 1870. The word itself means 'spicey Traminer' and the true **Traminer**, also sometimes called the **Savagnin Blanc**, is no longer used in Alsace. The Gewürztraminer is a very aromatic wine (the 'beginner's wine' in Alsace), appealing and capable of achieving great subtlety and finesse when well made. It appears to be grown in some **California** regions, where it is known as the Red Traminer. In **Germany**, the word is either spelt 'ü' or 'ue' without the umlaut. In **France**, it is always spelt 'u' without the umlaut.

Geyser Peak   Sonoma **winery** in **California**, now owned by the Schlitz Brewery.

Ghemme   **Italian** red wine from the Novara Hills region of **Piedmont**. It is made using about 60% of **Nebbiolo**.

Gigondas   Wine town at the bottom of the **Rhône** Valley in **France**, where good red wine is produced from a mixture of **grapes**. Formerly often sold as **Châteauneuf-du-Pape**, these wines are now gaining fame and popularity in their own right.

Gin   A spirit that can be made in various ways, but the well-known London dry gin is produced by **distilling** a fairly pure grain or cane spirit (already distilled) together with certain flavourings, such as juniper, coriander, orris and so on. (Gin gets its name from *genièvre*, the French for juniper, a common

153

ingredient.) The gin is carefully controlled, so that the best of the distillation only is reserved to bear the name of the product, quality and continuity of style being scrupulously preserved. Gin has a long history and although at one time it was drunk much by the 'wretched poor' trying to warm and cheer themselves, it is nowadays a truly classless drink. Good gin is a very 'clean' drink and the foundation of many of the classic **cocktails**. Although many countries now make their own, London dry gin is still admitted to be the supreme type.

Flavoured gins, such as orange and lemon gins, are not now as popular as they were some years ago, but **sloe gin** is still made and drunk quite a lot. Plymouth gin is rather more definitely flavoured than London gin. Dutch gin, also known as Hollands, Genever, and Schiedam, has a rather full flavour compared with London gin. Steinhaeger is German gin. Old Tom is a sweetened London gin, once very popular and now mostly drunk in the northern export markets. It was this gin that gave the name to the long drink, Tom **Collins**; while the original John Collins was made with London dry gin.

Ginger liqueurs A good example of this kind of thing is a Dutch version, known as 'The King's Ginger Liqueur' which, according to tradition, was a favourite drink of Edward VII as a warming draught after driving in his 'horseless carriage'. It was evolved by the St James's wine firm of Berry Bros. See **liqueurs**.

Gingseng piu chiew This is a type of **choum**, infused with a root native to north Vietnam. There are various kinds: *ruou seu* is scented with lotus flowers, *ruou cuc* with chrysanthemum, *ruou tam* is slightly **sparkling**, *ruou tiêt dê* is a mixture of **alcohol** and goats' blood.

Girò di Cagliari Red wine from **Sardinia** which is mostly sweet, but some dry and a *liquoroso* is also made.

Gironde The Rivers Dordogne and Garonne flow into the estuary of the Gironde. The Gironde is the département of **France** in which the wine region of **Bordeaux** is situated.

Giscours Classed 3rd growth from the parish of Labarde-**Margaux**, in the **Médoc**, formerly highly reputed for fine wines. It was in decline until its acquisition in 1954 by Monsieur Tari, a winemaker from **Algeria**, who is restoring its quality. See **Bordeaux, classification**.

Givry A region in the **Côte Chalonnaise** in south **Burgundy**, producing both white and red wines, though mostly the latter. They can be very pleasant and usually offer good value when they are shipped outside **France**.

Glasses Although there are many different types, the ideal glass is simply one that shows off its contents for the maximum enjoyment of the drinker. For all wines and for most spirits this means that this is: a glass that is clear and colourless, so that the colour of the drink may be appreciated; a glass that stands on a stem, so that the temperature of the hand need not heat up a chilled wine in the bowl of the glass; a glass of reasonable size — the smell of the contents cannot be enjoyed if the glass is filled by more than two-thirds, and ideally it should only be half filled; a glass the sides of which either go straight

SHAPES OF GLASSES

Paris goblet }

Correct for all still, sparkling, and fortified wines

{ *Tulip glasses*

*Sherry copita
'a 'dock' or tasting glass
is of similar shape)*

Brandy balloon

*Conventional glass for German
and Alsatian wines*

Brandy glass (French)

Anjou regional glass

Champagne flûte

up, or else curve slightly outwards and then inwards, so that the **bouquet** of the contents is not thrown out when the wine is moved round in the glass.

Either the elongated tulip shape, or the squatter onion shape (Paris goblet) are ideal for all still and **sparkling wines** and also for the **fortified wines**. A very thin glass, or one made of crystal, is ideal for the **service** of fine drinks, but it is better to have a cheap glass of the right shape and size than something expensive that is otherwise all wrong for the display of the drink. A 10 oz (280 ml) glass is virtually all-purpose for all table and sparkling wines. An 8 oz (225 ml) size is also acceptable, or a 6 oz (170 ml) for **apéritif** wines. Anything smaller is not only a mean measure but, half or two-thirds filled, looks insignificant.

For **brandy** (see **Cognac** and **Armagnac**): glasses should always be of sufficient size to show off the fragrance of the spirit, but not too big to be cupped in the palm of one hand – two hands for a woman. They should always have incurving rims, although some excellent glasses have an upright section up to the rim, after the inward curve of the glass from the bulbous bowl.

For **digestives, schnapps, vodka**: as these drinks are meant to be swallowed without the appreciation of their bouquet, they can be served in small glasses, of any shape, filled to the brim. Pick-me-ups can also be served in such glasses.

For **fruit brandies**, *alcools blancs* and similar drinks: the glass should be of sufficient size to enable the liquid to be swirled around – and to hold the ice cubes that chill the glass in preparation.

For **sherry**: if the tulip or goblet is not used, then the traditional Spanish *copita*, an elongated tulip on a short stem, is ideal. Its stem is usually slightly shorter than that of an ordinary wine glass.

For **port**: it is essential that the glass is not too small, especially for **vintage** port. A 5½ oz (155 ml) is the smallest acceptable and a larger size is often better. Traditionally, the Paris goblet is the basic shape, but any glass with an incurving rim is acceptable.

For **sparkling wines**, including **Champagne**: in addition to the ideal glasses cited above, a very elongated tulip may be used or, as is sometimes seen in France, the tall narrow *flûte* glass may be used (this glass allows less 'spread' of the wine, which takes longer to go flat). Otherwise there is the very old type of glass, a deep saucer with a hollow stem. These are seldom seen except as antiques as they are very difficult to keep clean: but because they only expose the wine to a little air and a lot of glass surface, they prolong the time during which the bubbles rise. The shallow Champagne 'saucer' is a glass with nothing to recommend it: it gives a mean measure, it flattens the wine quickly and it overturns easily. If a saucer-shaped glass must be used, then it should be a deepish saucer.

CUT GLASS: Although this can be beautiful as glass and look elegant on the table, the use of cutting on the bowl of a glass inevitably requires that the glass should be thick. Therefore the supreme enjoyment of wine, experienced by the skin-thinness of uncut crystal in the hand, is denied the drinker. It must be admitted that crystal is not an economic proposition for anyone who does not, personally, wash up by hand! But heavy cutting is best left to be bestowed on the feet or stems of glasses and for **decanters**, as far as the service of very fine wines is concerned.

REGIONAL GLASSES: Many wine regions have specially shaped glasses. Although these are interesting and often beautiful, it is not necessary to use any other than the glasses recommended for the service of any wine.

Glayva A herb and spice **liqueur, whisky**-based.

Glen Elgin This **whisky distillery** at Longmorn, Elgin, was founded in 1898 by the famous 'Restless Peter' Mackie, of White Horse fame. It is on sale as a single malt.

Glen Grant In full, the name of this **whisky distillery** in Rothes, Morayshire, is Glen Grant-Glenlivet. It was established in 1840 by Major James Grant. Its malt is world-famous and various types, of different **proofs** and ages, are made. In 1978 it was bought by **Seagrams**. It is one of the Speyside malts known to be used in the **blended** Scotch, Queen Anne.

Glen Mist Scotch **whisky liqueur**, in which herbs, spices and honey are used. It is matured in whisky **casks**, and is wholly produced and bottled in Scotland.

Glen Mhor This Inverness **distillery** was founded in 1892. It is named after 'the Great Glen' and is reported as a full, big **whisky**.

Glen Moray-Glenlivet **Whisky distillery** at Elgin, owned by Macdonald & Muir.

Glen Rothes-Glenlivet The **distillery** was built in 1878; the **whisky** is described as 'peaty. . . full of character'. The new stills are exact copies of the old ones. The first spirit flowed from the stills in 1879, on the night when the bridge over the River Tay collapsed in a storm while a train was passing over it.

Glen Scotia This Campbeltown **whisky distillery** was built in 1832 and is described as 'full, rich, robust and peaty'.

Glen Spey Rothes **whisky distillery**, built in 1885.

Glenallachie **Whisky distillery** built in 1967 at Aberlour, Banffshire.

Glenburgie-Glenlivet **Whisky distillery** founded in 1810 – therefore possibly the longest working distillery still in business – at Forres. Owned by Hiram Walker, who use the whisky in their 'Glencraig' vatted malt and the 'Old Smuggler' blended Scotch.

Glendronach This **whisky distillery** at Huntly, Aberdeenshire, was built in 1826. William Teacher have owned it since 1960 and the modernising process has apparently left the floor maltings as they were. Glendronach malt is sold as aged for 8 and 12 years and has a rather fluid but assertive style.

Glendullan Dufftown **whisky distillery**, owned by the **D.C.L.**

Glenfarclas-Glenlivet **Whisky distillery** built at Ballindalloch in 1836. Controlled by the Grant family, it produces a single malt that is highly regarded.

Glenfiddich This is the only Speyside **distillery** that bottles its own Scotch and it is still owned by the family of Grant. The first **whisky** ran from its stills on Christmas Day, 1887. The Grant blend is 'Standfast', named for the battle-cry of the Grant clan. Adjacent, the other Grant whisky, **Balvenie**, is quite different, although both are close together in **Dufftown** and both draw their water from the same spring.

The former malt barn has been converted into a reception area for visitors, tours are well organised and about 50,000 drams of Scotch are given away annually – no wonder that Glenfiddich is known through the world and is probably the top selling malt. The firm have received the Queen's Award for Industry.

Glengarioch This **whisky distillery** at Old Meldrum, Aberdeenshire, was founded in 1797. It was closed in the 1960s because of lack of water. Since 1972 a single malt bearing its name has been on sale.

Glenlivet, The This, sometimes referred to as 'Smith's Glenlivet', gets its name from George Smith. He started making – and smuggling – **whisky** in 1817, but craftily realised that **distilling** under licence might, long-term, be a more profitable venture. He took out a licence in 1824; this was the origin of The Glenlivet Distillery. This whisky became so popular that others began to use its name and local distilleries sold their produce as the only one until, in 1880, legal action established George Smith's Glenlivet as the only one. Some other whiskies can add the name 'Glenlivet' to their own if they wish. In 1978 The Glenlivet was bought from the family who owned it by the House of **Seagram** (an offer from the Japanese Suntory having been refused). The whisky is described by Derek Cooper as 'delicate and full flavoured': it is certainly a distinguished and aristocratic spirit, whether or not the drinker finds it the outstanding Scotch of the world.

Glenmorangie (Stress 'mor') This **whisky distillery** at Tain, Ross-shire, has been producing Scotch since 1842. The word *morangie* means low level ground. The establishment is run by Macdonald & Muir, who bought it in 1918, and whose descendants still work there. It is described as 'gentle and delicate' – certainly a flowing, supple Scotch.

Glenturret **Whisky distillery** at Crieff, Perthshire, built in 1775.

Glenugie Owned by Long John International, this Peterhead **whisky distillery** was built in 1875.

Glenury-Royal This Stonehaven **whisky distillery**, in Kincardineshire, was set up in 1836. The spirit it produces is now mainly used for **blending**.

Glenvale Vineyard and **winery** established at **Hawkes Bay, New Zealand**, in 1933.

Goede Hoop **Stellenbosch** estate, **South Africa**, under **vines** since the 17th century, now producing table wines of which the reds are especially well reported.

Gold Seal **New York State winery**, founded in 1865. Thanks to the work of European authorities, it pioneered *Vitis vinifera* wines in this region.

Gönc See **Tokay**.

Gorny Doubnyak A bitter **liqueur** from the **U.S.S.R.**

Governo In full, *governo all'uso toscano*. The procedure which gives certain types of **Chianti**, and sometimes other Italian wines, a type of secondary **fermentation**, with the result that the wine has a liveliness that is almost *pétillance*. It is induced by the addition of a rich **must** when the first fermentation is over. This is a style of wine that Italians like, but wines on export markets may or may not be made with the *governo* according to the taste of the buyers. A wine that gives the impression of 'working' or fermenting, however, when it is made in this way should not be rejected as faulty. The clean, fragrant smell should indicate that it is not undergoing any true fermentation.

Graach   **Mosel** vineyard making wines of a slightly austere but usually noble style, much liked by the experienced. The most famous site is Himmelreich. Josephshöfer is wine from Graach which up to now has been sold without the village's name; it gets its name from Joseph Hain, who bought it at the beginning of the 19th century, and later sold it to Kesselstadtt to whom it still belongs in entirety.

Grafting   Since the ravages of the *Phylloxera* in most of the vineyards of the world in the 19th century, the majority of wine **vines** have been grafted on to American stock, which is resistant to the *Phylloxera* aphid. There are a few vineyards, however, which have never become infected with the *Phylloxera*, so that grafting of vines within them is not necessary and the national stock is grown. It is a continual source of debate to winelovers whether wine made from grafted stock is better than, inferior to, or simply different from that of ungrafted vines, given exactly similar conditions. But in general it may be assumed that all the wines in the inexpensive and medium price ranges and most in the fine wine ranges are made from grafted vines. See *nacional*.

Graham   **Port** firm, founded in 1814. I usually find their wines graceful and elegant.

Gramp   One of the great names in **Australian** wine history. Johann Gramp arrived from Bavaria in the first half of the 19th century and, in 1847, planted a small vineyard at Jacob's Creek, the very first in the **Barossa Valley**. His first **vintage** – made from this vineyard about 1 mile (1.6 km) from the present Orlando installation – was in 1850; it filled an 'octave' or one-eighth of a **cask**, and was a light white wine. In 1887 Gustav Gramp, Johann's son, took over the firm and moved the **winery** to Rowland Flat, its present site. The firm became part of the Reckitt & Colman organisation in 1970, but there are still members of the Gramp family on the board. A huge range of wines is produced today: still table wines of all types, **fortified wines**, **sparkling** and **pearl wines**. Some of them attain quality recognised throughout the world.

Gran spumante   **Italian** white **sparkling wine**, made by the **Champagne method** in **Lombardy** from **Pinot Nero** and Pinot Grogio **grapes**; not necessarily within the region producing **Asti Spumante**. Several reputable houses make it and it should be served like any quality sparkling wine. The wine can be dry or varying in degrees of sweetness.

Grand cru   According to a law passed in 1964, this expression, meaning 'great growth', can only be used if in conjunction with an **A.O.C.** of which it is part. For example, there are *grand crus* of **Chablis** and St **Émilion** in the A.O.C.s of those regions. See *cru*.

159

Grand Marnier   This is one of the great orange-flavoured liqueurs, made on a basis of **Cognac** (not just **brandy**). The other is Curaçao. The company that makes it is Marnier-Lapostolle and the formula was evolved in 1880. There are two types, Cordon Rouge and Cordon Jaune, the latter being slightly lower in alcoholic **strength**. See **orange liqueurs**.

Grand-Puy-Ducasse   Classed 5th growth of **Pauillac**, portions of which have now been joined to other estates. The *château* in Pauillac itself, facing the river, is the headquarters of the **Médoc** wine fraternity and houses a small museum. See **Bordeaux, classification**.

Grand-Puy-Lacoste   Classed 5th growth of **Pauillac**, which is unusual in that it has remained completely intact ever since the 1855 **classification**. The word *puy* is Old French for 'a high point', and the estate stands high above Pauillac. The wine is well reputed, of a definite, almost assertive style. See **Bordeaux**.

Grande Champagne   See **Cognac**.

Grandes Marques   This term is used for an organisation in **Champagne**. The Syndicat du Commerce des Vins de Champagne was formed in 1822, then made into a professional syndicate in 1884. The organisation was for some time the only official body that was able to defend the interests of Champagne and the Champagne houses. The formation of the C.I.V.C. in 1945 then established an effective body to combat abuses. The Syndicat since has made itself (in 1964) into the Syndicat de Grandes Marques de Champagne (the use of the word *de* and not *des* indicates that the list is not exclusive). At present the list of houses belonging to this syndicate is: Ayala, Billecart Salmon, Bollinger, Canard Duchêne, Clicquot Ponsardin, Deutz & Geldermann, Heidsieck Monopole, Charles Heidsieck/Henriot, Krug, Lanson, Laurent Perrier, Masse, Mercier, Moët & Chandon, Montebello, Mumm, Perrier Jouët, Joseph Perrier, Piper Heidsieck, Pol Roger, Pommery & Greno, Ch. & A. Prieur, Louis Roederer, Ruinart, Salon, and Taittinger/Irroy. It would appear – for information is not easy to get – that the original dozen establishments of the group are those who organise the 'Champagne Academy'. This scheme allows selected students of the wine trade to spend a period annually as guests of the Champagne houses; they are trained in all the details of the **Champagne method**, working in the cellars, tasting and studying seriously as well as being entertained.

Grapes   It is the fruit of *Vitis vinifera* that provides the raw material for winemaking. Throughout the world a huge variety of grapes is grown to be used for wine, and each part of the grape contributes something to the end-product: the skin, the pips, the pulp with its content of sugar and **acidity**. Some wines are made from a single grape: for example, the great red **Burgundies** are made solely from the **Pinot** Noir. Alternatively they may be made from a specific combination of grapes, such as the great red **Bordeaux**, which are made from the **Cabernet Sauvignon** and Cabernet Franc, **Petit Verdot**, **Merlot** and sometimes the **Malbec**. Sometimes both black and white grapes are used, as in **Champagne**, where the Pinot Noir and **Chardonnay** are used for most of the wine.

Grapes, like any other crop, do well or not so well according to where they are grown. Certain of those that make the great wines are vulnerable to climatic and other hazards, although the quality of the wine they can produce makes the winegrowers take the risk of their being able to withstand any damage. Some grapes can make a quality wine in one region, but not so fine a wine in another; the **Riesling** being an outstanding example all over the world. In addition, certain grapes are particularly suited to certain winemaking processes; for instance, the high sugar content in the **Muscat** grape makes it difficult to use in producing a quality **sparkling wine** by the **Champagne method**, although it can be satisfactorily used in the *cuve close* process.

One of the most complicated subjects is the naming of grapes, because some have completely different names according to where they are grown, even though they may be of one type. Others, inevitably, adapt themselves to local conditions and almost change their style into something different from that of their origin. The local, or national, name for a grape may be different from the generally accepted international name, and even the greatest experts argue about whether certain grapes really are the same as others, or completely different varieties. The **Riesling**, for example, has many different names: in **Baden** it is known as the Klingelberger. The terms **Rheinriesling** and Johannisberger are other versions of its name, the latter being used sometimes in the **U.S.** The Welsch- or Wälschriesling, however, cultivated all over the world, has many different names – Grey, **Emerald**, Missouri are a few used in the U.S. and it is the Olaschriesling in **Hungary**. Other countries often just label the wine 'Riesling' without specifying the exact name, just as some wines are labelled 'Cabernet' without any indication as to whether they are made from the Cabernet Sauvignon or Cabernet Franc.

One generalisation about grapes that can be made is that red grapes are usually referred to as 'black'. A vew varieties have pinkish juice and are known as *teinturiers* or 'dyers' because of this, but usually all grape juice is white, and only gains colour from being left, during **fermentation**, in contact with the skins of black grapes. Therefore white wine is usually made from white grapes, red wine from black. Then, many wine grapes are not pleasant to eat – table grapes are not often able to be used for winemaking as they tend to be sweeter, larger, and thin skinned, containing a higher proportion of water than the grapes from a wine **vine**. Pickers who eat while working choose the sweeter types. The pale greenish grapes are referred to as 'white', although sometimes white grapes are actually yellowish, or even tinged with pink on their skins. Some grapes in certain regions are susceptible to a particular type of fungoid infection, known as *Botrytis cinerea*, which shrivels them and results in a very sweet, concentrated wine being made. In general, grapes are picked by bunches, as they ripen, but for these specially overripe grapes it is necessary to pick cluster by cluster and also grape by grape, passing through a vineyard several times. See also **Germany, Sauternes**.

Grape names are often used for the names of the wines made, and this practice, known in the U.S. as naming according to **varietals**, is helpful if no specific place name can be associated with the wine. But a wine made from exactly the same grape variety will vary enormously according to where the grapes are grown and the way the wine is made; so that some caution should be exercised in assuming that, say, a wine labelled **Muscat** is inclined to be sweet – it could be extremely dry, as well as very sweet indeed.

The study of grapes is highly specialised, and the use of grapes is subject to strict legislation in the winegrowing regions. The following list, however, includes some of the classic wine grapes used in European vineyards, which are also found in other winegrowing regions. Anyone able to compare the shapes of bunches, size and depth of **colour** of grapes, and formation of leaves when visiting vineyards, will register what certain grapes actually look like. But very few fine wines actually 'taste of the grape' in the sense that they resemble, either in smell or flavour, the sort of grape taste that the public associate with this fruit in its dessert form. A wine that is actually 'grapey' by description is inclined to be the exception rather than the rule, as the process of fermentation changes the grape juice in a radical way. The Muscat is an exception.

Some classic wine grapes (under the names by which they are best known)

Black grapes	*White grapes*
Cabernet Sauvignon	Riesling
Cabernet Franc	Sauvignon Blanc
Petit Verdot	Sémillon
Merlot	Chardonnay
Cinsaut	Chénin Blanc
Gamay	Gewürztraminer/Traminer
Pinot Noir	Muscat
Grenache	Palomino
Syrah	Pedro Ximenez (P.X.)
Muscat	Sylvaner
Nebbiolo	Chasselas
Sangiovese	Müller-Thurgau
Spätburgunder	Vernaccia
Lambrusco	Viognier
Cannonau	Terlaner
Grignolino	Savagnin
Poulsard	Muscadet
Trousseau	Furmint
Nerello Mascalese	Inzolia
Frappato	Grecanico
Pignatello	Cataratto
Mourisco	Trebbiano

In some wine regions, grape varieties exist which are thought by some to be

native to those regions. The California **Zinfandel** is a notable example of this.
See **vines, hybrids,** *Vitis vinifera,* **varieties** and specific grape names.

Grappa   Spirit distilled from the residue of grapes left after the final pressings
for wine. This is the name by which **Marc** is known in Italy.

Grasparossa   This is a **Lambrusco** from the Castelvetro region of **Emilia-
Romagna** and is apparently made as both a dry and a slightly sweet red wine.
The vine used for it is apparently so named because the *graspa* (stalks) of the
grapes are red (*rosso*).

Grauburgender   See **Pinot, Rülander.**

Grauvernatsch   See **Alto Adige.**

Grave del Friuli, Grave del Piave   (Pronounced 'Grah-vay') Wine regions in
the **Veneto** and **Friuli-Venezia.**

Graves   The region south of **Bordeaux** making both red and white wines which,
as its name implies, is predominantly gravelly. The red Graves are very
fascinating to lovers of fine **claret,** slightly spicy, delicate and subtle. The
whites should be fresh, dry, but gently fruity.

Graves de Vayres   See **Bordeaux.**

Great Western (1)   In 1860 a firm was founded near Hammondsport, **New York
State,** where its 'champagne' proved so good that it was referred to as 'the great
champagne of the west'. Henceforth the wines were called 'Great Western'.
Pleasant Valley, the main company, now produces a number of wines, some of
which are well liked. The **sparkling wine** is made by the **transfer method.**

Great Western (2)   A region in Victoria, **Australia,** where **sparkling** and **pearl**
wines are made. Originally it got its name from the steamship *Great Eastern*
and from the name – Western – of one of the mine wardens, for the area was
mining country. Some of the early settlers came from France and other
European wine regions and explored the vinegrowing possibilities, with such
success that the area became famous for its sparkling wines and the old mining
galleries were used for wine storage. **Seppelt's** Great Western Winery includes
over 5 miles (8 km) of these galleries or 'drives'.

Greco   **Italian** white **grape,** actually the Yellow Trebbiano, which is used in the
Campania region to make Greco di Tufo, also for the white **Cirò** wines of
Calabria. Greco di Gerace is well reputed and appears to be high in alcoholic
strength.

Greece   Red, white and rosé wines are made in many parts of Greece, but at the
present time comparatively few are exported, and those that are come from a
few large concerns, making ranges of wines, mostly of the everyday type.
Much Greek wine is resinated (see **retsina**), but not all. There is also some
luscious sweet wine, of which **Mavrodaphne** and the **Samos Muscat** (a dry
version is also made) are probably the best known. Otherwise Greek wines are
sold under their brand names and do not usually bear a **vintage** date. Some of
the reds benefit greatly by a little **bottle age.** The dry whites tend to be rather
strong in flavour, without much delicacy. Greek wines are probably best
enjoyed with Greek food or at least dishes of a Mediterranean type and it is not
necessary to drink only white with fish, red with meat. The rosés, like those of

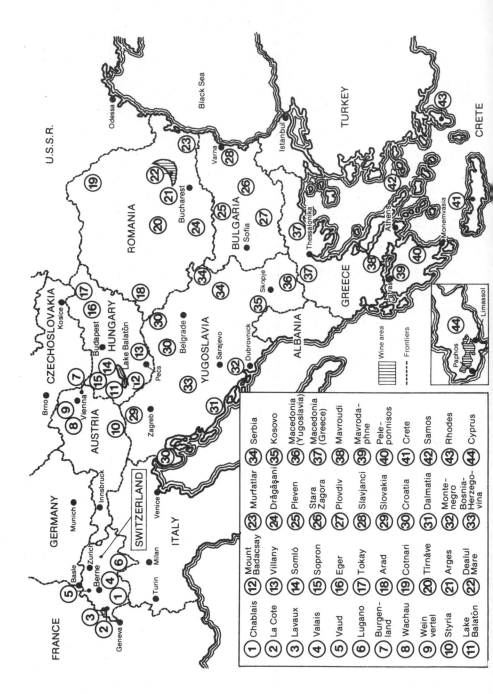

many southern countries, tend to be darker in colour and fuller in style than is often expected of a pink wine.

Green wine   See *vinho verde*.

Grenache   This black **grape** originated in **Spain** where its name is Granache, Garnacho, or Alicante. It is used for a number of wines, including **Châteauneuf-du-Pape** and **Tavel**. Some is planted in **California**.

Grenadine   Sweetish, pinkish-red in colour and originally a syrup from pomegranates, used to flavour drinks. Sometimes it can have a slight alcoholic content. Generally used as a sweetening agent.

Grignolino   Name of an **Italian** wine **grape**. The Grignolino is cultivated in **California** and other vineyards.

Grignolino d'Asti   A red wine made in **Piedmont**. There are both still and **sparkling** versions of this wine.

Grillet   (Pronounced 'Gree-yay') This vineyard, which is just under 4 acres (1.6 ha) in size, is on the west bank of the River **Rhône**, near **Condrieu** in **France**. The wine it makes, from the **Viognier grape**, is described as white, but in fact it is of a curious tone. In former times in some years it was almost pinkish-gold; but now it is essentially a straw-yellow of medium to deepish tone as a result of more up-to-date vinification methods, the flavour being very definite and assertive. Château Grillet has been very much praised, and it can certainly be a fine wine, but whether it really is one of the great wines of the world, in addition to being one of the strangest and rarest, could be debated. The scarceness is due to the fact that only about 2,500 bottles are made yearly, all bottled at the tiny property. Although the famous Restaurant de la Pyramide at Vienne usually has several on its list, outside the region Château Grillet is difficult to find. The estate, which has its own **A.O.C.**, is the smallest region in France to possess this.

Grinzinger   See **Austria**.

Grog   Generally today this signifies a hot drink, usually **rum** and hot water, taken for slightly medicinally warming purposes. The name comes from Admiral Vernon, who always wore a grogram cloak, and who ordered the watering of the daily ration of rum issued to the Royal Navy in 1740. The word 'groggy' coming from the noun, originally signified being drunk; later unsteady or unwell.

Groot Constantia   **Constantia** is one of the defined wine regions of the Cape in **South Africa**, but Groot Constantia is the beautiful house dominating a particular wine estate above Cape Town. In 1679, Simon van der Stel, Commander of the Cape Colony, arrived and achieved astonishing results in founding towns, settlements and arranging for agriculture and business to make the Cape more than just a place of call for ships. He was granted the property on Table Mountain in 1685 and built the house in 1692; previously, he had planted the first **vines** at the Cape.

After Simon van der Stel's death, the property was divided, but the wines gradually became famous and, in the 18th and 19th centuries, were exported to all who could afford them, thanks to the efforts of Hendrik Cloete, who bought

Groot Constantia in 1778. Both white and red wines were made and sent to many European courts – Napoleon insisted on drinking Constantia during his last days at St Helena. In 1885, the Government bought the estate and today it is run by its own board, under the Ministry of Agriculture.

Several wines are made now, red and white, and quality appears to be progressively improving. Although Groot Constantia wines cannot be usually found in shops, visitors to the estate are able to buy them and thousands from all over the world arrive annually, to see the superb house and impeccably cared-for property, which is undoubtedly one of the most famous wine estates in the world.

Gros Plant See **Folle Blanche**.

Gros Plant du Pays Nantais A white, rather acid wine, from the sea end of the **Loire**. Some is now exported. It goes well with crustacea and shellfish with mayonnaise. See **enemies of wine**.

Grosslage A vineyard grouping in German terminology.

Gruaud-Larose Classed 2nd growth of **St Julien**, very popular because of its delicacy and charming **bouquet**. Before 1934, **labels** differentiated between Gruaud-Larose-Sarget and Gruaud-Larose-Faure. The vineyard was divided over a century ago and not joined up again until Monsieur Cordier, owner of Ch. **Talbot**, achieved its unification. See **Bordeaux, classification**.

Grumello Red wine made in **Lombardy, Italy**, which must have not less than 95% of **Nebbiolo** in it.

Gruner Veltliner A grape. See **Austria**.

Grünhaus This **Ruwer** estate belongs today to the von Schubert family (no relation to the composer), but the wines are known as Maximin Grünhauser because the vineyard was formerly the property of the St Maximin Abbey in Trier. The wines produced from the Herrenberg and Abtsberg sites are generally considered outstanding.

Guignolet See **cherry brandy**.

Guild One of the largest concerns making wine in the **U.S.**, with numerous **wineries** in **California**.

Guimaraens **Port** firm, founded in 1832, with members of the family still active in the wine trade. This firm, together with that of Wiese & Krohn, at one time had a woman as their chief **taster**. This – together with the work of Doña Antonia **Ferreira** – must give the lie to anyone silly enough to suppose that wine is a 'man's world' and that women are in any way handicapped in tasting. If a woman can handle the complexities of port, in what is a highly conservative and sometimes prejudiced masculine world even to this day, then women in general are potentially capable of tasting at any level: as the wiser members of the wine trade have always known them to be. See **women**.

Guiraud See **Sauternes**.

Gutturnio Red **Italian** wine, made in the region of the Piacenza Hills in **Emilia-Romagna**. It is made from about 60% **Barbera** and 40% Bonarda **grapes**. Although it does not often feature on export lists, it possesses a pleasing style and fair standard of quality.

H

Hagebuttenlikoer   German **liqueur** made from rosehips, yellowish in colour.
Halb-und-Halb, **Half and Half**   See **orange liqueurs**.
Halbfüder   See **casks**.
Halbstück   The **cask** size used in the **Palatinate** and Rheinhessen regions of Germany, holding about 132 gallons (600 litres).
Hallcrest   Vineyard in the Santa Cruz Mountains, **California**, which specialises in white wines.
Hallgarten   Not to be confused with the well-known British **shipper** of German wines, this region on the Rheingau (see **Rhine**) is the highest of the vineyards of the district. The most notable sites are Deutelsberg and Rosengarten.
Hamilton, Richard   Born in Scotland in 1792, he settled in Adelaide Metropolitain, **Australia**, in 1837 – one of the very first winemakers to be established in that continent. The original estate was called Ewell, after a previous Hamilton home in Surrey, England. The estate has kept some of the original **vines** planted by Richard Hamilton in a property that is now in a busy suburb, but the Hamiltons, who still run the business, own vineyards elsewhere, including the **Barossa Valley**, Springton, and at Nildottie on the **Murray River**. In addition to table wines, the firm also produces **brandy**.
Hanap   Ceremonial cup used in **wine order** rituals. See **loving cup**.
Hanepoot   **South African** name for a **grape** that seems to be the **Muscat** d'Alexandrie. It is used for making both dry and sweet wines, as well as being sold as a table grape.
Hanzell   **Winery** and vineyards just north of Sonoma, **California**, built on the model of **Clos de Vougeot** by James D. Zellerbach in 1951. He had been **U.S.** Ambassador to **Italy** and particularly enjoyed **Burgundy** among European wines. His property was given the name Hanzell after his wife (Ilana) and himself. The top authorities at **Davis** were consulted about equipment and procedures, although the owner insisted on using French oak **casks** for maturation. But innovations, such as cold **fermentation**, were also introduced, and the first wines met with great praise, in Europe as well as in California. Zellerbach died in 1963, but the winery was subsequently bought by Mrs Mary

167

Schaw Day, although much of the equipment had been sold. Hanzell wines, never produced in large quantities, are today in great demand among serious winelovers and they appear to be of fine quality.

Harászthy, Ágoston May or may not have been a genuine 'Count', a title he always used, but is famous as the 'father of **California** viticulture'. He left **Hungary** as a political refugee in the 1840s and first settled in Wisconsin, where he tried to grow **vines** unsuccessfully, but he did grow hops and engaged in many enterprises. He moved to the west and in 1849 became the first sheriff of San Diego, where he also planted vines, before moving on to San Francisco, where he again set up in business. His sons married the two daughters of General Vellejo, owner of a wine estate called Lachryma Montis, whose products were apparently well regarded.

Harászthy established the **Buena Vista winery** and its vineyards in 1857 and in the following year published a *Report on Grapes and Wines of California*, in which he stated his belief that the region could make wines as fine as any. Following this, he toured the European vineyards, returning with many cuttings, some of which he planted in his own property, selling others, for by this time his activities had attracted the attention of other winemakers who began to make quality wines. Buena Vista was at this time thought to be the largest vineyard and winery in the world; its products were sold through offices throughout the U.S. and even exported to London. Unfortunately, the vines were attacked by the *Phylloxera* and the winery itself was almost destroyed by a fire. Unable to carry on for lack of funds, Harászthy left California and went to Nicaragua, where he started a **distilling** operation, using sugar cane, having a government contract granted to him. However, in 1869 he disappeared – it is thought he fell into an alligator-infested river.

Harászthy's son, Arrad, who had been sent to study with Moët et Chandon at Épernay, was unable to make fine **sparkling wine** in California and eventually became a wine merchant in San Francisco, although he later bought another vineyard, the Orleans. The Buena Vista winery was virtually shaken apart by the San Francisco earthquake of 1906; but, as the site was not built on, it was found possible to revive the estate in 1943. Harászthy's influence may not have been as great as was, at one time, supposed. Undoubtedly others contributed substantially to the establishment of the first wineries and vineyards on a commercial scale in California. But he was an effective pioneer figure; and it was not only his picturesque ways that drew the attention of many people to California and its potential in wine – he was also a remarkably able wine man.

Hardy One of the important names in **Australian** wine history. Thomas Hardy, of Honiton in Devon, arrived in Australia in 1850, first working for John **Reynell** and then in various ventures. He married his cousin, Joanna Hardy, and bought a property near Adelaide, which he called Bankside, making his first **vintage** in 1857. In 1859 Hardy shipped two **hogsheads** back to England – this may have been the first bulk shipment of Australian wine to the home country. In 1876, Hardy bought Tintara, a vineyard near **McLaren Vale**.

This had been previously developed by Dr Kelly, an important writer on vines and winegrowing and an excellent winemaker, who had unfortunately gone bankrupt. From the first purchase of Tintara, Hardy extended his business, buying more vineyards and extending his **winery** and storage cellars. Hardy died in 1912 and, during his lifetime, he had made a giant contribution to winemaking, as well as exerting influence in many other spheres. McLaren Vale honoured him with a monument which, authority Len Evans relates, is possibly the only memorial to a winemaker in Australia.

The Hardy family continued the expansion of the already great wine business, buying **Waikerie** on the **Murray River** and Dorrien in the **Barossa Valley**. The original Tintara ceased to operate in 1926, but the activities were moved to another of the first Thomas Hardy installations – the Mill Cellars, converted from an old flour mill. Further extensions of Hardy holdings are going on all the time. At first, Hardy used to sell their wines under the Tintara **label**, but today the name Hardy is featured more. A wide range of wines is made and the **McLaren Vale** red table wines appear to enjoy a particular reputation for quality. The Hardy family are still active in the business.

Iárslevelü **Hungarian** white **grape**, meaning 'lime flower', because of the shape of the leaf.

Iat The 'hat' or *chapeau* is the thick mass of grapeskins, pips, stems and stalks that settles on the top of the **fermentation vat**. It is virtually all the debris of the **grapes** that has been allowed to pass into the vat along with the juice. The length of time that this is allowed to remain on the top of the **must** while it becomes wine, has a marked effect on the ultimate wine; because the astringency and **tannin** of the vegetable matter, plus the colouring in the skins of black and red grapes, will be absorbed. Sometimes the hat is regularly broken up with paddles, and pushed down into the must, to ensure that it has maximum contact with the future wine. In the past, the hat would remain on some wines for three or more weeks – as in **Bordeaux** – resulting in wines that took a long time to become drinkable. Today it is usually only in contact with the must for a matter of days.

Hattenheim In the centre of the Rheingau (see **Rhine**), this is the centre of many vineyards producing very popular fine wines. It is also one of the residences of Graf von Schönborn, one of the most famous proprietors.

Haut Bages Libéral Classed 5th growth of **Pauillac**, the final word of its name referring to one of the early owners of the property. See **Bordeaux, classification**.

Haut Bailly Property in the parish of Léognan in the **Graves** making red wines only, which can achieve great quality.

Haut Batailley A 5th classed growth of **Pauillac**, which was part of Châte... **Batailley** until 1942. See **Bordeaux, classification**.

Haut Brion The great red wine from the parish of **Pessac**, in the **Graves** region, just south of **Bordeaux**. It has a long history and at one time was known in Britain as '**Pontac**' because it was owned by the Pontac family. Pepys mentions 'Ho Bryen that hath a good and most particular taste'. Haut Brion was the only wine from outside the **Médoc** to be included in the 1855 **classification**, when it was placed among the other 1st growths of **Lafite**, **Latour** and **Margaux**. With the classification of the Graves in 1953 and 1959, it was also rated a 1st growth of that region. The estate was bought in 1935 by the American banker, Clarence Dillon, and it is very renowned in the **U.S.**, although in recent years prices for it in Europe - and the opinions of several who should know - do not always rate it equal with the other 1st growth **clarets**.

It is always a big wine, sometimes having a special taste that reminds people of a roasted, almost scorched, flavour. The vineyard is planted with 55% **Cabernet Sauvignon**, 22% Cabernet Franc, and 23% **Merlot**. In 1958 a new **bottle** was designed for the wine, slightly more squat than the most traditional Bordeaux bottles and with a slim neck. The estate also produces an important white Graves, **Haut Brion Blanc**.

Haut Brion Blanc   The fine white wine produced by Château **Haut Brion** in the **Graves** region south of **Bordeaux**. Comparatively small quantities are made and it is much in demand in the **U.S.**

Hawkes Bay   One of the most important vineyard areas in **New Zealand**, where a religious mission first planted a vineyard in 1851.

Hazendal   Estate at **Stellenbosch**, **South Africa**, built towards the end of the 18th century. In recent years it has been thoroughly re-equipped and is making table wines of fine quality.

Healy, Maurice (1887-1943)   This Irish K.C., who wrote an amusing account of his experience in *The Old Munster Circuit*, is known in the world of wine for his book *Stay Me with Flagons*, first published in 1940. It was subsequently edited with notes by Ian Maxwell Campbell, who really did know something about wine and was a respected author himself (*Wayward Tendrils of the Vine*, 1947). Healy's book is discursive, opinionated and, like many of the wine books by those who are merely winedrinkers, it is not always factually sound. But it has a great following, although I myself put this kind of book into the 'meringue and millefeuille' category of wine literature – a little goes a long way – yet many people find this sort of stuff appealing. Healy writes an entire section on **Burgundy** without ever having been there or, indeed, apparently having read much about it! He certainly could have done both!

Heather ale   Scottish traditional drink, which was supposed to have been made to a recipe that perished centuries ago with the last of the family to whom it was entrusted. However, references to heather ale occur in the 18th and 19th centuries, and F. Marian McNeill gives a recipe for it in *The Scots Cellar*.

Heavy wines   The term relates to wines that are higher in alcoholic **strength** than 14% of **alcohol** by volume (see **Gay Lussac**), and which therefore pay a higher rate of duty to the **Customs** and **Excise** in the U.K. than **light** or **table wines**. See **fortified wines**.

Heck   The Heck brothers were the children of a Strasbourg winemaker, who managed the **sparkling wine** concern of Cook, in St. Louis, **U.S.** They have been influential in the world of wine all their lives and, after World War II, bought the **Korbel winery** and cellars, dating from 1886, on the Russian River in **California**. Visitors are proudly told that the sparkling wine is all 'fermented in *this* bottle' – exactly following the **Champagne method**.

Hectare   Metric measure of area equalling 10,000 square metres. One hectare equals 2·471 acres; abbreviated to 'ha.'.

Hectolitre   Metre liquid measure equalling 100 litres. One hectolitre is 21·9976 gallons. Abbreviated in writing to 'hl.', and in speech to 'hecto'.

Heeltap   This curious word derives from the 'lift' or wedge of leather used to increase the height of a shoe heel. In the 18th century it began to be used for the draining of wine or spirits at the bottom of a **glass** – possibly because, seen through the glass, this small amount of drink could have resembled the layer of leather. If there happened to be any **deposit** in these dregs, as must often have been evident in the days before much **filtration** before bottling, the resemblance would have been even more marked. Consequently the exhortation 'No heeltaps!' came to mean that the contents of the glass were to be drained completely, so that nothing was left. A heeltap glass is one that has no foot. See **stirrup cup**.

Heidelbeergeist   German **liqueur** made from bilberries, either by **distilling** the fermented fruit juice, or else by mixing the berries with **alcohol**. See *alcool blanc*.

Heitz, Joe   Bought his first **winery** in **California** as recently as 1961. Prior to that, during his period in the U.S. army, he had worked part-time in a winery. He studied **oenology** seriously after World War II, subsequently working at **Davis**, also for **Gallo** and other wineries, including **Beaulieu**. He is greatly admired for his wines made from classic wine **grapes** and his reputation throughout California is very high. A European can immediately make contact with a Heitz wine, although each retains its California individuality.

Henderson   This region near Auckland, **New Zealand**, is the biggest area under vines in that country. Vines were first planted there at the beginning of the 20th century, but serious large-scale wine production was started after World War II.

Hennessy, Richard   Born in County Cork, he joined the Irish Brigade to fight for the Stuart cause against 'Dutch William'. After being wounded, he spent part of his convalescence in **Cognac** and shipped back some **casks** of the **brandy** to friends in Ireland. The Cognac proved so popular that the Hennessy firm was founded in 1765. Today it is an enormous concern, and still a family business. The Hennessys, French and English, are also influential in the racing world.

Henschke   Important wine family in **Australia**'s **Barossa Valley**. The first of the name arrived in 1842 and soon afterwards began farming near Keyneton, although his son was the first to start planting **vines** and made his first **vintage** in 1868. The family expanded their business but, although the firm is still a family concern, its production is limited. Quality is the prime aim as regards the range of table wines made – they make no **fortified wines** and their red table wines are reported as of special quality.

Hérault   (Pronounced 'Eh-row') This area, with the départements of **Gard**

and **Aude**, forms the largest wineproducing region in **France**. Much of the production of wine has been for the branded *vins de marque*, for making into **vermouth** or wines of very ordinary quality, but recently some of them have begun to achieve an independent standing as *vins de pays*. Thanks to the improvements in winemaking and because of the tremendous increase in the prices of fine wines, there is a move to introduce some of these previously unknown local wines as good, though modest, drinks in their own right and under their own names. Some of the wines of **Languedoc**, such as the **Clairette**, those of the **Costières du Gard** and the sweet *vins doux naturels*, make very interesting drinking for those on holiday in the region and they may appear on wine lists in export markets in the future. Red, white and rosé are all to be found.

Hermitage (1) (Pronounced 'Erm-it-age') Vineyard of the **Rhône** Valley, making fine red and white wines. The spectacular terraced vineyards are dominated by a tiny chapel which, some believe, was where St Patrick planted the first **vines**. It is also the hermitage of Gaspard de Stérimberg who, in the 13th century, retreated from the world after the Albigensian Crusade, horrified at man's cruelty to man. He is said to have offered wine from the vineyards he cultivated to those who came to him for advice. Tain l'Hermitage, with its twin town, Tournon, across the Rhône, is the centre of the northern section of the **Côtes du Rhône**. The vineyards are steeply terraced above the river: those of Hermitage and Crozes Hermitage are on the east bank; those of St Joseph, Cornas and St Péray are on the west bank. Both red and white wines are produced, the reds of the Hermitage vineyards usually being considered the finest. In the St Péray vineyard, the white **sparkling wines** are made.

Hermitage (2) See **Cinsaut**.

Hessische Bergstrasse In German, this means 'Hesse mountain road' and, although the region is the smallest of German wineproducing areas, it is very picturesque. It is on the east bank of the **Rhine**, from south of Darmstadt nearly to Heidelberg. The Staatsweingut owns an important vineyard here.

Het Pint New Year drink traditional in Scotland, made of ale, **whisky** and eggs. Sir Walter Scott always drank it at Hogmanay.

Heurige (Pronounced 'Hoy-rig-ger') The 'new' or latest **vintage** of the **Austrian** wine made in the Vienna Woods region, of which Grinzing is the best-known village. It is usually drawn from the **cask** and can be sold from 11 November onwards. By 31 December of the next year, it cannot be called *Heurige* any more. The inns that display a wreath or garland as a sign that the sell this, are only allowed to if the wine comes from their **winery**.

High cultivation See **Austria**, Dr **Moser**, **trellising**.

High Tor Vineyard in **New York State**'s **Hudson Valley**, established in 1954.

Highball A long drink, essentially **whisky** (of any kind the drinker pleases), poured over ice-cubes and with added carbonated water.

Highland Park Kirkwall **whisky distillery** on Orkney, sited where the smuggler, Magnus Eunson, operated. (As a preacher, he was able to keep his illicit Scotch under the pulpit!) It is described as 'malty', but I particularly like it and find it delicately distinctive and fragrant.

Hillside Whisky distillery originally established in Montrose, Angus in 1897. It now belongs to the **D.C.L.**

Himbergeist See *alcool blanc*.

Hine, Thomas Born in Dorset, he went to Jarnac at the end of the 18th century, his family having been disadvantaged because they had been Protestant supporters of the Monmouth rebellion. He worked for the house of Delamain and married one of the daughters, starting his own firm in 1817. He never became French and nor did his son, who was actually Mayor of Jarnac. Today the Hines are still a family firm and have kept up with their English relations in the wine trade. Their trademark – a hind – is a play on the name, which remains a great problem in pronunciation to most French.

Hochheim This town, actually on the River Main, which runs into the **Rhine**, produces fine wine from its vineyards but is possibly most famous for having given the word '**hock**' to the English language. This is supposed to have originated with Queen Victoria, after whom the Viktoriaberg site is named; but in fact the name seems to have been in use earlier than her accession in 1837. The name 'hock' appears to have been an abbreviation of 'hockamore', the anglicised form of *hochheimer*, for which *The Oxford Dictionary* gives the earliest usage as 1625.

Hock The word used in Britain and on many British wine lists to denote the wines of the **Rhine**. The name is supposedly derived from **Hochheim**; but the use of 'hock' instead of 'Rhenish' appears to have been current at least in the early part of the 19th century and even much earlier.

Hoffmann Australian wine dynasty, whose founder, Samuel Hoffmann, arrived in 1848 and began to cultivate **vines** on the North Para River, in the **Barossa Valley**. The vineyards and **winery** have passed directly from father to son and today the Hoffmanns concentrate on making quality red wines and **fortified wines** at the North Para Wines installations.

Hogsheads See **casks**.

Hohe Domkirche This **German** establishment – meaning the 'cathedral' – is one of the vineyard-owning properties now swallowed by the Bischöfliche Weingüter at Trier. See **Preisterseminar** and **Bischöfliches Konvikt**.

Hollands See **gin**.

Holunderbeerlikoer German **liqueur** made from ripe elderberries.

Honiglikoer German **liqueurs** based on honey, of which the most famous is **Baerenfang**.

Hopfenbitter German **brandy** made slightly bitter by adding hop buds.

Hospices de Beaune The organisation comprises the actual hospital and the old peoples' home in **Beaune**, which was founded by the then Chancellor of the Duchy of Burgundy, Nicolas Rolin and his wife, Guigone de Salins in 1443. They endowed the foundation with vineyards and these were added to by benefactors throughout the centuries. It is the sale of the wines of these vineyards that supports the Hospices.

Since 1859, the sale has been a public one, held on the third Sunday in November – unless, as in certain years, the **vintage** has been poor, when the wines are sold privately. Originally the sale was held in the cellars of the Hospices; nowadays it takes place in the marketplace, covered in for the occasion. The function is made the excuse for great celebrations in **Burgundy**, notably the '*Trois Glorieuses*'. These three feasts are given over the weekend of the sale: Saturday and Sunday nights at the cellars of the Bastion in Beaune and at **Clos de Vougeot** respectively; the Monday lunch of La Paulée is at **Meursault**, with ceremonies, installations of new members in the local wine order, songs and speeches by local and widely known personalities. The commercial aspect of the sale is important, because this is the first public showing of the wines of the current vintage, and the prices reached – even though these are sometimes extra-high for the occasion – indicate the level of the prices of other wines as well. The *cuvées* bear the names of the donors and are all in the **Côte de Beaune**; sometimes the white wines make the record price but all the wines may be regarded as good. **Marc** is also sold.

Anyone can buy at the Hospices, the sale is attended by wine merchants, **shippers**, buyers of huge retail chains, and restaurateurs from all over the world. Bidding takes place *à la chandelle*: the autioneer takes bids while a taper burns down, then a second taper is lit and bidding is open only while this burns. Some reference books mention a single taper or even three, but there are invariably two.

Hot bottling Topic that occurs in many wine discussions, especially in relation to **German** and other delicate wines. Cold sterile bottling, evolved in the period between the wars, is effective but somewhat time-consuming. For hot bottling – of inexpensive wines – the wine is quickly heated to 120-130°F (49-55°C), via a heat exchanger, and this kills off any undesired **yeast**, etc. If hot bottling is done well, the wine should not be affected although, because the process inevitably involves some loss of **bouquet**, the very finest wines are never hot bottled. Hot bottled wines can usually be recognised because, when they cool, the wine shrinks and there will be more **ullage** in the bottle than usual.

Houghton Vineyard in the middle **Swan Valley**, Western Australia, first planted by the ex-Indian Army Colonel Houghton in 1833, with vine cuttings brought from **South Africa**. The property now belongs to the **Emu Wine Co**. A wide range of table and **fortified wines** are produced.

Houx See *alcool blanc*.

Hudson Valley Region in **New York State** where a number of **wineries** have been established.

Huelva **Spanish** wine region in the south-west of the country, abutting on the **Portuguese** frontier. It makes a large quantity of wine, red and white of ordinary quality, some good white. There is also some white that, being high in **strength** and able to grow **flor**, is handled somewhat like a *solera*-produced **sherry**. It is difficult to know much about these wines, but some would appear to be bought and used for **blending** by large concerns elsewhere in Spain.

Humpen glass **German** wine **glass**, especially traditional in Bavaria and Saxony. It is rather like a concave barrel, without a stem and for ceremonial purposes was often cut, engraved and coloured. The English term for this type of glass is a 'brimmer'.

Hungary It is considered by those who should know that the finest wines of south-eastern Europe are made in Hungary, in addition to **Tokay**, which is one of the great wines of the world. There is a very long and proud tradition of winemaking, and the wine institutes today carry these on. A high proportion of the country is under **vines** and some of these are, as might be expected, classic **varieties**, such as **Riesling, Sylvaner**, **Pinot Blanc**, Pinot Noir, **Cabernet Franc** and Cabernet Sauvignon. Native **grapes** include the white **Hárslevelü**, Mézesfehér, Kéknyelü, and Szlankememkå and the black **Kadarka**, which is found throughout this part of Europe, but seems to produce at its best in Hungary.

All types of table wine are made, but possibly the best known on export markets are those made around Lake **Balatón** and in the Mount **Badacsony** district, and from the vineyards around the beautiful town of Eger, which are responsible for white and red table wines respectively as far as the English-speaking drinker knows them. Villány, Somló and Sopron are also extremely important regions: **Pecs**-Villány wines, white and fragrant, and Villányi Burgundi are very easy to like. The best Somló wines are white and made from the **Furmint** grape; those of Sopron most likely to be met with on export markets are red, made from a grape that seems to be a type of **Gamay**, excellent drunk while it is young and fresh. Pleasant white wines are also made in Sopron.

It is significant that it was a Hungarian, Ágoston **Harászthy**, who, quite justifiably, has been called the father of **California** viticulture. In the middle of the 19th century he went to the U.S. and planted vineyards, of which the most famous is probably **Buena Vista** in Sonoma County. In 1861 he visited Europe at the request of the Governor of California and returned with cuttings of 300 grape **varieties**, thereby establishing many of these in the California vineyards. See **Egri Bikavér, Zinfandel**.

Hunter River One of the earliest founded and most important wine regions in New South Wales, **Australia**. James **Busby**, who arrived in Sydney in 1824, pioneered the planting of classic European wine **grapes** here and the region is one of the few where *Phylloxera* did not infect all the vineyards. **Fortified** as well as table wines are made and individual estates, making quality wines, are beginning to gain reputations in overseas markets. The very finest wines, however, are seldom exported, as home demand for them always exceeds the supply. Travellers should take every opportunity to try the best products of what is, by now, a historic and, in many ways, classic New World vineyard area. Climatic variations here make **vintage** dates of importance for some wines.

Hybrids Each country produces wine experiments with the use of hybrids but the fine wines of the world come only from *Vitis vinifera*. The hybrids have, however, contributed to wine production in areas where *Vitis vinifera* will not thrive, and their use has resulted in wines of everyday quality being made. Hybrids are usually named after the people who have evolved them. Their use, especially in classic wine regions, is very strictly controlled, indeed often forbidden, and they may not be associated in any way with wines made from permitted wine **grapes** of *Vitis vinifera*. Obviously, though, the position regarding their use must be constantly subject to review and revised legislation. See **cultivar, grapes, varieties, English wines**.

Hydrometer   Device for measuring the sugar content of **must** and thus, by implication, the **alcoholic** content of the finished wine. See **saccharometer**.

I

I.N.A.O. The Institut National des Appellations d'Origine Contrôlées is generally referred to by its initials – I.N.A.O. This body administers the *Code du Vin* in **France**. See **A.O.C.**

I.V.P. The Instituto do Vinho do Porto (Port Wine Institute) is the governing body that controls both the Casa do Douro (the association of farmers and growers) and the Gremio dos Exportadoros do Vinho do Porto (the association of port **shippers**). Its controls are strict and it issues a seal to be attached to each **bottle** of **port** before this is shipped. It establishes the prices of **grapes**, **must** and **brandy**.

Ice Saints See **Saints**.

Idaho This **U.S.** state is now trying to produce commercial wines from locally-grown grapes.

Imotski Region in Dalmatia, **Yugoslavia**, producing red and white table wines.

Imperial **Whisky distillery** at Carron, Strathspey, built in 1897.

Impériale A large **bottle** sometimes used in the **Bordeaux** region, especially for very fine wines. Its contents equal about 8 ordinary bottles of 26 fl. oz (75 c) capacity (1.32 gallons or 6 litres).

Inchgower This **whisky distillery** was first established in 1822, at Tochienial. It was removed to Inchgower in 1871. It now belongs to Arthur Bell.

India **Vines** have been grown and wine made from them in India for many centuries, but for many reasons – including the religious ban on **alcohol** for adherents to Islam – there is no substantial local demand for wine. Spirits, however, are made in fair quantities. It is nevertheless difficult to gain any idea of the quality of these products.

Inferno Red wine from the **Valtelline** region of **Lombardy**, in **Italy**, which must have at least 95% of the **Nebbiolo** grape in it. The name has (fortunately) nothing to do with the character of the wine and also should not be confused with any similar brand name.

Infusion This process, whereby many **apéritif** wines and **vermouths** are made,

177

requires the additives to be put into the liquid – rather as a tea-bag is added to water.

Ingelheim   Wine region in the Rheinhessen (see **Rhine**) region of **Germany**, where red wines are produced.

Inglenook   **Winery** and vineyard in **California**'s **Napa Valley**, founded in 1879, now the property of the vast firm Heublein. The winery has been reputed for the quality of its wines since its beginning. Today, although its range has been extended, reports indicate that the top wines maintain their quality.

Ingwerlikoer   German **ginger liqueur**.

Inverleven   This Dumarton **distillery** is situated on the 'Highland line', and was built in 1938. The **whisky**, however, is classed as a Lowland malt. Unusually, the making of both grain and malt whisky may be seen here.

Iphofen   Wine town in **Franconia** noted for its quality wines. See *bocksbeutel*.

Irancy   A village near **Chablis** in northern **Burgundy**, **France**, where red and rosé wines are made, often of pleasant quality.

Irish coffee   A **jigger** of Irish **whiskey** plus strong black coffee, with sugar if liked, poured into a glass and drunk through thick cream poured on the top. Variations are Swiss coffee (kirsch), French coffee (**Cognac**), Caribbean coffee (**rum**), and Gaelic coffee (Scotch); but nothing seems quite as agreeable as the original combination.

Irish Mist   **Liqueur** produced by the Tullamore **Distillery**, according to an Austrian's recipe (said to be of Irish origin) based on heather honey and **whiskey** – a type of drink the Distillery had been trying to create as a revival of 'heather wine'. It is very popular in the **U.S.**

Irish whiskey   See **whisky**.

Irouléguy   White and red wines of the Basses Pyrénées region of **France**; some rosé is also made bearing this name. These wines can be pleasant, but hardly more, and are usually 'holiday wines'.

Irpinia   This is a region in **Campania**, **Italy**, which Philip Dallas divides into the **Taurasi**, making reds, and Greco di Tufo, making whites, near the town of Benevento. Both wines are said to have been made since ancient times. The Taurasi red is made from about 70% **Aglianico grapes**, the white from the **Greco** and **Coda di Volpe**. Both sound to be worth trying for anyone visiting the region.

Irrigation   Wine made from vineyards that have been irrigated tends to be different from that from vineyards wholly dependent on the natural rainfall of the region. This is obvious: the water plumps out the **grapes** just as they need sufficient moisture – whether taken in from the foliage or via the roots – in order to fill out. Too much water may affect their content and result in a lack of certain elements essential to making good wine. The matter is complex and need not concern the ordinary drinker very much, especially as regards European wines, because the majority of these are made in vineyards where irrigation is not only unnecessary, but forbidden; and where the rainfall in nearly all years is adequate. Irrigation is now allowed in some German vineyards.

In many of the vineyards of the New World, however, irrigation is not only permitted but essential: in some of these vineyards, the **micro-climates** are such that parts of one vineyard might be unable to produce grapes in good condition without irrigation, both because of the dryness of the atmosphere and because of the absence of water in the subsoil. In addition, the irrigation of some patches of vineyard is necessitated by the circumstance of sections of subsoil being thick clay, which would either retain any naturally falling water too much – so that the vine roots would risk rotting – or being so porous that the water falling on the vineyard would drain away too rapidly to be absorbed by the vine roots. So many large New World vineyards make wines which are the produce of a vineyard wherein parts may be irrigated and parts not. It has been pertinently remarked that some classic wine grapes, in New World vineyards that are irrigated, actually get less water than they would do naturally in some better-known European vineyards!

The intricacy of the matter is great, because water falling on to a vineyard will come from a different source from that draining through the subsoil. Therefore water used for irrigation must be suitable for the purpose – not just wet. There are also different methods of irrigating: the spray method, whereby a fine mist of water is directed over the whole vine or row of vines; and the drip method, whereby a pipe laid alongside the vine roots slowly drips moisture into the **soil**. The particular portion of vineyard, the grapes and the exigencies of the climate all affect the way in which irrigation is used and the extent to which a wise winemaker will adapt it to his needs, without risking a fall in the quality of the eventual wine. The hazards of winemaking seem to indicate that judicious irrigation can be as beneficial as judicious **chaptalisation**.

Irrymple Wine region in Victoria, **Australia**.

Irsch Wine village on the **Saar** in **Germany**, of which the best-known site is the Hubertusberg. See **Mosel**.

Ischia As well as producing wines that may be labelled **Capri**, there are red and white wines made on Ischia. These deserve investigation by travellers, although the quantity produced is not likely to make them seen on export markets. See **Italy**.

Israel Wines have, of course, been made in Israel since wine was first made in the world. As a modern industry, winemaking was virtually started by Baron Edmond de Rothschild at the end of the 19th century and today wines are still made essentially along the lines of **French** production. There is some tradition for the making of sweetish white wines, as these are associated with religious usage, both to break a fast – when a sweetish wine is obviously more suitable – and for formal feasts, but some dry whites are also made. Exports to both the U.K. and **U.S.** are being expanded, both of these whites and the fullish, rather soft reds. Israel is not, as yet, a very wine-minded country and consumption per head is low: but there is no reason why the wines should not attain recognition and appreciation for their straightforwardness and agreeable quality. See **kosher wines**.

Issan, Château d' A classed 3rd growth of **Cantenac-Margaux, Bordeaux**. It is the property of the Cruse family, who bottle it nowadays in their Bordeaux *chais*, so that there is none available as **château-bottled**. It was a favourite wine of the Court of the Austro-Hungarian Empire in its last days. Its beautiful *château*, rather unusually for the **Médoc**, is really old, dating from the 17th century. See **classification**.

Italian Riesling See **Wälschriesling**.

Italian-Swiss Colony Winery at Asti in Sonoma County, **California**, established in 1881 to assist Italian and Swiss immigrants. Now owned by the firm of Heublein and producing popular wines.

Italy In some years, Italy produces more wine than any other country in the world. The **vine** is cultivated almost everywhere, and a very wide variety of table wines, **sparkling wines**, **liqueurs** and **vermouths** are made, plus **Marsala** in **Sicily**. In the past, Italian wines have not been widely known on export markets, except in countries where the Italian emigrant communities are large, because production formerly tended to be by small growers. Their methods were sometimes haphazard and therefore they seldom achieved notable quality on a large scale; so they were not able to follow up successful wines when they did produce them. Today the situation is changing. The large concerns, hitherto often primarily concerned with vermouth or liqueur production, have recently started influencing these peasant proprietors and government controls have been instituted to ensure that the different regions make their wines in ways that are both traditional and sound. Their work is best known for the system of **D.O.C.** Producers who previously could sell all they made to local outlets, or at least within Italy, are now looking seriously at export markets.

With wine consumption rising throughout the world and technical improvements enabling good wine to be made in a larger scale, Italian wines are becoming increasingly important everywhere. The very finest Italian wines are definitely among the great wines of the world, but these naturally do not often feature on wine lists. Although some of the best-known Italian wines are best when consumed while they are young and fresh, some of the reds are capable of great improvement with maturity, and the makers are proud of their quality as well as their charm. There are so many names – of **grapes** as well as of wines – that detailed reference to Italian wines in general is difficult. They vary according to the region and, as has been indicated, according to the type of producer. See Bibliography.

Starting with the islands: Sicily makes Marsala and a wide range of red and white table wines; **Sardinia** has a number of sweet **dessert wines** and table wines, also an odd wine of higher than table wine strength, called **Vernaccia**. The regions of **Calabria**, **Basilicata** and **Puglia** produce quantities of rather everyday wine, seldom seen outside its homeland and much used for **blending** and making into vermouth. In the **Campania** there are the wines from volcanic soil around the Bay of Naples, of which **Lacrima Christi** is the most famous; from around Rome the **Lazio** wines include **Frascati**; from the Abruzzi region there is **Montepulciano** among others; from **Umbria**, there are **Orvieto** and **Torgiano**; and from the **Marche**, **Verdicchio**, with many others. In the north, the **Friuli-Venezia Giulia** region makes plenty of pleasant light wines; the **Veneto** has the well-known **Soave** and **Valpolicella**, plus a number of red and white wines; and there is a big range from the **Alto Adige**, where the whites are likely to be those least known in export markets. Regions of major importance are **Tuscany** (**Chianti**, **Brunello** and many others), **Emilia-Romagna** (**Lambrusco**, **Albano** and others), **Lombardy** (the Garda wines, including **Bardolino** and those of the **Oltrepò Pavese**), and **Piedmont** which, in addition to the great reds **Barolo** and **Barbera**, produces the sparkling wines of **Asti** and, in and around **Turin**, the most important **vermouths**.

Well-known Italian liqueurs include **Strega**, **Amaretto di Saronno**, **Galliano**, **Sambucca** and literally hundreds of others. There are **bitters** in great abundance and many types of **apéritif**, **digestive** and sweet alcoholic drinks.

As might be expected, Italian wines are mostly good partners to the regional dishes and there are no hard and fast rules about red wine with meat, white with fish – an Italian will simply drink whatever is preferred – although the sweet wines, such as *vin santo* and those made from *passito* grapes, are more commonly drunk with fruit or a light sponge cake type of sweet course. The majority of the table wines are either non-vintage or else at their best when drunk young and fresh, although some of the finer reds are capable of great improvement by leaving in **bottle** for some time, and these will have a **vintage** on their **labels**. One quite interesting thing is that, although most vintages in Italy are such that good wines are widely made, some of the exceptional years – notably for the great reds – are often those years when other European vineyards have a bad time: for example, 1968. So such years can be useful choices if the wines feature on restaurant lists. Each one of the major wineproducers will put out a range that is individual in style; so that drinkers must try several from each well-known named region, in order to get an idea as to which firm's wines they prefer. The few great estates, such as those in Chianti, make wines as individual as any other private properties.

In general, the Italians accept and enjoy their long tradition of winedrinking with lighthearted appreciation; wine is seldom revered, made a status symbol or even regarded as the focal point of a meal – the food as well as the wine is always considered. This is pleasant, although it may astonish drinkers from other countries to see the casual way in which even fine wines are handled – **corks** drawn through **capsules**, bottle necks unwiped, **decanting** very seldom done and, unfortunately for the majority of winelovers accustomed to showing some respect to wine (and food), cigarettes and even pipes smoked during the course of meals, often by the producers themselves! It is partly this happy-go-lucky attitude that sometimes puts Italian wines at a disadvantage, compared to those made in countries where less obviously favourable conditions have obliged the makers to take more detailed trouble over cultivation and production and to adopt more care about the preparation and service of bottles. But those producers who are alert to what export

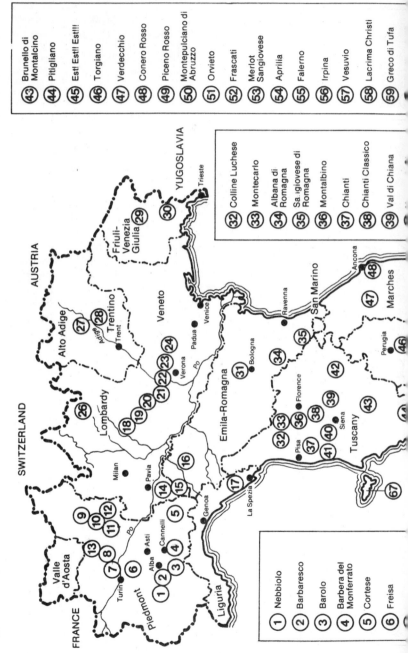

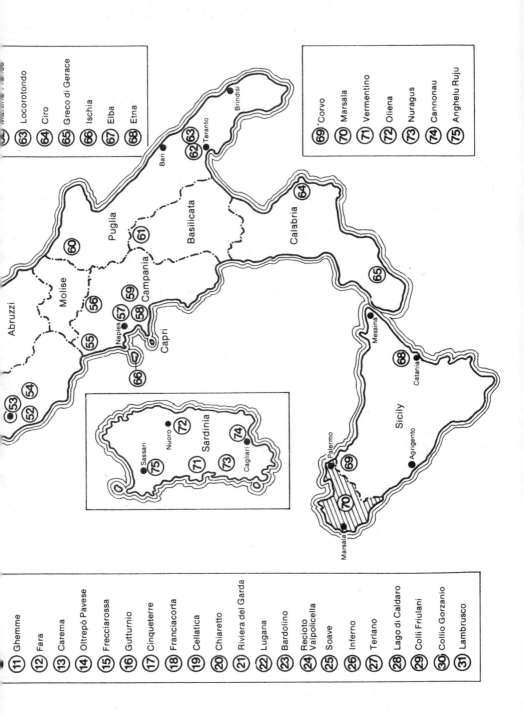

63 Locorotondo
64 Ciro
65 Greco di Gerace
66 Ischia
67 Elba
68 Etna

69 Corvo
70 Marsala
71 Vermentino
72 Oliena
73 Nuragus
74 Cannonau
75 Anghelu Ruju

Brindisi

Taranto

Bari

62 63

Puglia

60

61

Basilicata

64

Molise

Campania

56

59

Abruzzi

57

58

55

Naples

Capri

66

53 54

52

Calabria

65

Messina

Catania

68

Sicily

Palermo

69

Agrigento

70

Marsala

Sardinia

Nuoro

72

74

Sassari

75

71

73

Cagliari

11 Ghemme
12 Fara
13 Carema
14 Oltrepò Pavese
15 Frecciarossa
16 Gutturnio
17 Cinqueterre
18 Franciacorta
19 Cellatica
20 Chiaretto
21 Riviera del Garda
22 Lugana
23 Bardolino
24 Recioto Valpolicella
25 Soave
26 Inferno
27 Terlano
28 Lago di Caldaro
29 Colli Friulani
30 Collio Gorzanio
31 Lambrusco

markets require, and who realise that at least a number of Italian wines are capable of attaining high levels of quality and of being valued outside the informal type of restaurant trade, are attempting to raise standards. Equally the official controls are serious about maintaining traditional characteristics while encouraging up-to-date methods.

Ivancie **Winery** in Denver, Colorado, **U.S.,** now producing wines from locally-grown **grapes**.

Izarra **Liqueur** of the Basque country in the south-west of **France**. The word is Basque for 'star'. It is made from Pyrenean herbs, honey, flowers and **Armagnac,** being aged in **wood**. There are two kinds, yellow and green; the latter being slightly stronger. Izarra was first made in 1835.

J

Jacobsdal Estate near False Bay in the **Stellenbosch** region of **South Africa**, near the sea and virtually without water except for the slight rainfall. It specialises in red wines.

Jägermeister Dark red **German** liqueur, of **digestive** and tonic character.

Jasnières A dryish white wine, from the **Touraine** region of the **Loire**, made from the **Chenin Blanc grape**.

Jenever See **gin**.

Jerez See **sherry**.

Jeroboam See **bottles**.

Jerzu Region in **Sardinia**, known for its pink and red wines, of both dry and sweet type, made from the **Cannonau grape**. Philip Dallas reports them as having a most unusual **bouquet** and a dry, oddly elegant flavour.

Jigger Bar measure of 1¼ fl. oz (40ml).

Johannisbeerlikoer Nothing to do with any of the wine properties, this is a German blackcurrant **liqueur**. See **cassis**.

Johannisberg (1) Wine region of the Rheingau (see **Rhine**) in **Germany** producing some of the finest and best-known wines.

Johannisberg (2) A **Swiss** white wine made in the **Valais** region, from the **Müller-Thurgau grape**. It is crisp, lightly scented and very much a wine to sip on a sunlit terrace with mountains in the background.

Johannisberger See **Riesling**.

Johanniswein German word used to signify the finest wine of a producer. At Deidesheim it is blessed on 27 December, the feast of St John, 'the beloved disciple'. Sometimes offered to honoured guests or on very special occasions.

John Collins See **Collins**.

Josephshöfer See **Graach**.

Jug wines This term is used in the **U.S.** to signify wines for casual, everyday consumption – i.e. cheap. **Australia** and, progressively, **South Africa** use the expression for this type of wine but it does not seem to have become known as yet in the U.K. The British might call them '**carafe** wines' or *ordinaires* – for them, the word 'jug' is associated with the 'little brown jug' of the song, which originally held beer.

Jugoslavia See **Yugoslavia**.

Julep This word is of Persian origin according to some authorities: doctors in Iran use a similar term to describe pleasant-tasting additives to curative mixtures. The drink is traditional in the southern parts of the U.S., and the Bourbon Institute's recipe for mint julep is: 2 oz (55 ml) Bourbon, 1 tablespoonful water, lump of sugar, 4 sprigs of mint, and crushed ice. All ingredients except the Bourbon are put into a tall **glass**. The Bourbon is then added and the drink must not be stirred – I have never been able to understand why not.

Juliénas See **Beaujolais**.

Juliusspital The 'Julius Hospice' founded and endowed with vineyards in the 16th century by Julius Echter von Mespelbrunn, at **Würzburg** in **Franconia**. The wines are bottled in the flat green *bocksbeutel* and are dry, rather steely in character, of fine quality.

Jura (1) Region east of **Burgundy** in **France**, making some of the most unusual of French wines. Until recently, these were seldom seen outside the region, but they have begun to be exported now and are always of interest. The area is historically important, as far as wine is concerned, because **Arbois** (with Poligny one of the main wine centres) was the birthplace of Louis Pasteur, who also worked in the region. His discovery of the existence of bacteria was due to his research on the action of the **flor** (*voile* in French), which is unique to Jura wines among all those of France. Ordinary red, white and rosé wines of different qualities are made, also the sparkling *vin fou*, **Étoile**, *vin de paille* and *vin jaune*, the most famous of which is that of **Château-Chalon** in its dumpy *clavelin* **bottle**.

Jura (2) The Campbells of Jura built this **whisky distillery** in the middle of the 19th century and the first bottling of Isle of Jura malt was in 1974. George Orwell wrote his novel *Animal Farm* while staying nearby.

Jurançon Wines from the south-west of **France**, the vineyards being on the foothills of the Pyrenees. Both red and white wines are made but the white is often superior. It was formerly all sweet or comparatively so, but nowadays a dry wine is made as well, though it is fairly full in character. The wine of Jurançon is supposed to have been that used to moisten the lips of the newly-born future Henry IV of France: he also had his mouth rubbed with garlic.

K

K.W.V. Short for Ko-öperative Wijnbouwers Vereniging. See **South Africa**.

Kabinett See **Germany, German Wine Law**.

Kadarka A red wine **grape** important through the whole of central and south-eastern Europe, and making excellent wines in **Hungary** and **Yugoslavia**. It gets its name from the Albanian town of Shkodër, which we know as Scutari.

Kaefferkopf The well-known vineyard of Ammerschwihr, in **Alsace**.

Kahlúa See **coffee liqueurs**.

Kaiserstuhl (1) See **Baden**.

Kaiserstuhl (2) See **Australia**.

Kallstadt See **Palatinate**.

Kalterer (1) Red wine of the southern part of the **Austrian** Tyrol.

Kalterer (2) See **Caldaro**.

Kanonkop Estate near **Stellenbosch, South Africa**, making good **table wines**.

Kanzem, Canzem **Saar** vineyard, of which the Sonnenberg, Altenberg and Berg are well-known sites.

Kapuzinerlikoer German 'Capuchin' **liqueur**, based on oils of celeriac, cinnamon, sweet oranges, cumin, fennel and mace, with **brandy**. Brown in colour.

Karmeliterlikoer German **liqueur**, based on herbs, yellow-green in colour.

Karpi **Liqueur** made in Finland from cranberries and other fruits. See *alcool blanc*.

Kartaeuserlikoer German **liqueur**, similar in style to **Chartreuse**.

Karthäuser Hof An estate on the Karthäuser Berg in the **Ruwer**, once the property of Dominicans and later Carthusians, from whom it gets its name. After being secularised, it was sold in 1802 to the Rautenstrauch family, who still own it. The wines' names are prefaced by that of **Eitelsbach** in which parish it lies, and there are various site names also.

Kasel, Casel One of the regions producing fine wines in the **Ruwer** valley, a tributary of the **Mosel**.

Kay Bros In 1890, Herbert and Frederick Kay established their Amery vineyards in the Southern Vales region of **Australia**. A wide range of wines is made. The firm belongs to the **McLaren Vale** Wines' association.

Kéknyelü   See **Hungary**.

Kenwood   Sonoma Valley **winery** in **California**.

Keppoch   Region near **Coonawarra**, **Australia**, now being developed for **vines**.

Kerner   White **grape** evolved from a cross of the Trollinger and the **Riesling** by the Wine Institute in Weinsberg, who named it for Justinus Kerner, a poet and official of the town in the late 18th and early 19th century.

Kernobstbranntwein   Collective term for **German** fruit brandies based on apples or pears. See *alcool blanc*.

Kesten   **Mosel** vineyard.

Kiedrich   Region in the Rheingau (see **Rhine**), producing wines that can achieve outstanding charm and elegance as well as quality. The Gräfenberg and Sandgrube sites are possibly the finest; part of the latter is in **Eltville**, but some consider the Kiedrich section to produce the better wines.

Kina Lilet   See **Lillet**.

Kinclaith   This Glasgow **whisky distillery** was built by Long John Distillers in 1957.

Kir   Originally '*vin blanc cassis*' and made in **Burgundy** from the dry white **Aligoté** plus a little **cassis liqueur**, it is now generally known by this shorter name and is made up in many regions and countries. It is named for the late Canon Félix Kir, Mayor of Dijon and a great Résistance hero, who loved all the good things of life.

Kirkton   **Australian** vineyard on the **Hunter River**, planted in 1830 by the great James **Busby**, founder of Australian viniculture. Uprooted in 1924, although the name is still in use as a brand.

Kirsch   See *alcool blanc*.

Kirsch-Gewuerzlikoer   **German liqueur** made from cherries and herbal essences. See *alcool blanc*.

Kirwan   Classed 3rd growth of **Cantenac** with the **A.O.C. Margaux**. It gets its name from British owners in the 15th century. It is now owned by Schröder & Schÿler, and the wines are never bottled at the property, but at the firm's **Bordeaux** cellars. See **classification**.

Klevner   See **Pinot**.

Klingelburger   See **Riesling**.

Kloster Eberbach   (Pronounced 'Eh-ber-bach') A Cistercian monastery on the **Steinberg**, adjoining the **Erbach** vineyard, north of **Hattenheim** on the **Rhine**. Established in the 12th century, after which it was active in cultivating and extending its vineyards. It was secularised in 1803 by Napoleon and given to the Duchy of Nassau, but in 1866 the Dukes yielded their property to Prussia and the estates became part of the now famous and respected **State Domain**. Visitors may see round the monastery. Kloster Eberbach is now the place where many of the sessions of the German Wine Academy are held, attracting students from all over the world.

Klosterbitter, klosterlikoer The first is a German **bitter digestive liqueur**; the second is rather sweeter. The first part of the name implies their origin in a religious house – but in fact most religious establishments made up their own medicinal drinks in the Middle Ages.

Knickebein A mixed drink, composed of **liqueurs** and fruit syrups, with an unbroken egg yolk in the glass. Many different types are listed in **cocktail** recipe books.

Knipperlé **Alsace** name for the **Chasselas grape**.

Knockando This I.D.V. **whisky distillery** in Morayshire was built in 1898.

Knockdu This **whisky distillery** at Knock, Banffshire, was the first malt distillery to be built by the **D.C.L.** in 1893.

Kohlensäure, mitgesetzter German term indicating that it is a **carbonated wine**.

Konz **Saar** vineyard, of which the **Falkenstein** estate, belonging to the **Freidrich-Wilhelm Gymnasium** at Trier, is probably best known.

Kopke, C. N. Founded by a German in 1638, this is the oldest of the firms established to make and market **port**. At one time it belonged to the English but it is now owned by the Portuguese. I cannot pronounce on the style because I have never had a Kopke port.

Korbel (1) Vineyard and **winery** in Sonoma, **California**, especially famous for its **sparkling wines**.

Korbel (2) **Winery** on the **Russian River** in **California**, making **sparkling wines** by the **Champagne method** since 1896, plus table and **dessert wines** and **brandy**.

Kornbranntwein Literally, German for 'corn **brandy**', this is a **distillate** made from rye, oats, barley or buckwheat. *Korngenever* is corn **gin**: *Doppelkorn* is slightly higher in strength than *Kornbranntwein* (38° percentage of **alcohol** by volume as compared with 32°).

Kornell, Hans He grew up in **Germany**, where his father was a winemaker. He studied at **Geisenheim** and in France, Italy and England, and arrived in **California** in 1939. Literally penniless, he started his career as a labourer. In 1942 he made the first Kentucky 'Champagne', using California wine. He now makes **sparkling wine** by the **Champagne method** at his **winery** in Sonoma. (This name should not be confused with **Korbel**.)

Kosher wine This is the wine used for Jewish religious observances and, in particular, for Passover, in addition to the cup served at Friday evening meals and on the evening before any special festival or on days of particular significance. The wine must be a natural wine, made according to specifications of the Jewish authorities and with the supervision of a minister. It tends to be sweet – very sweet when it is the wine used to break the fast before Passover. For obvious reasons, a very dry wine would not be acceptable at such a time when the body needs reviving with what, in ancient times, would have been a wine rich in sugar. Today, kosher wine is made in the **U.S.** almost entirely from the **Concord grape**. According to Lichine, the centres are **New York State** and Chicago; during **Prohibition**, some **wineries** were able to keep in production because they supplied kosher wine. See **Communion wine**.

Koumiss Fermented milk, the source being the cow, the mare or the camel. Sometimes available in the countries where these animals are plentiful and other liquor is not.

Krambambuli See **angelica**.

Kreuznach Winegrowing region of the River **Nahe** in **Germany**.

Kroatzbeerlikoer German blackberry **brandy**. See *alcool blanc*.

Krug, Charles This is a **winery** in **Napa Valley, California**, founded by Charles Krug in 1861. Krug was a Prussian, a colourful character, who achieved much from his friendship with Ágoston **Harázthy** and other pioneers of wine-making. He was actually known as 'the King of Napa Valley', teaching many who subsequently became famous. In 1943 the **Mondavi** family acquired the Charles Krug winery, and **label** their best wines 'Charles Krug'. A range of table wines is produced and the winery was the first in California to make wines from the **Chenin Blanc grape**.

Krupnick Polish **honey liqueur**.

Kümmel (Pronounced 'Kim-mel' stressing 'kim') A **liqueur** flavoured with caraway seeds. There are various kinds, the earliest probably being that made by Lucas Bols in Amsterdam in 1575.

Kvass A type of Russian beer, flavoured with mint or cranberries.

L

Labels The paper label, adhering to the **bottle**, is a comparatively recent introduction to the world of drink. Except for the most famous wines of all, which are usually labelled at the estates making them, the bulk of wines shipped before 1914 to the U.K. would probably be bottled either by the merchant selling them, or by the **shipper**, who would put on his own labels only when the customer required the wine from stock. But frequently a consignment of wine would simply be bottled and remain unlabelled, the bin label of the supplier and the purchaser being the only means of identification. Again, except for the most famous estates, wines tended to be sold far more by the generic names, or simply the names of their regions. This is why **decanter** labels made prior to the present day so seldom bear names of specific wines but only types of wine.

Labels are subject to control and it is generally true to say that the more famous the wine, the stricter the regulations governing its label. What is allowed to be stated on the label and what must be stated are both subject to the various local and national (and, now, international) codes governing such matters. For example, with wines bottled in **France**, no implication may be made *via* the name that a wine comes from an individual estate if it does not, and for certain export markets the fluid content of the bottle must be stated. The size of lettering, as well as wording, is also in some instances subject to regulations and, if the actual source of supply of a wine is not stated plainly, there is usually a reference number by which it can be identified. U.K. regulations governing wines bottled in Britain are not yet as strict but are becoming more rigid. The size and positioning of labels is also, in many instances, controlled.

Generally, the label of an **estate-bottled** wine and that of one bottled by a shipper somewhere other than at the estate, are markedly different; the use of different colours and possibly different designs makes the distinction plain. But sometimes, as a mark of confidence in the shipper, an estate or a big **winery** will allow the use of their own labels by the shipper, although the words 'estate-bottled' or a similar phrase obviously cannot be used, and there will

MOSEL-SAAR-RUWER

1975er

•*Wiltinger Scharzberg*

Erzeugerabfüllung

•Staatsminister a. D. Van Volxem

Oberemmel/Saar

Riesling

Qualitätswein mit Prädikat Kabinett

Amtl. Prüf. 3 525 856 3 76

Grade of wine	Control number
Grape variety	Manner of harvesting
Name of producer	Producer's cellars
Vineyard area (Grosslagen)	Bottled by the producer
Defined region (Gebeit)	Single vineyard (Einzellagen)

usually be the shipper's name somewhere, either on the bottom of the label or on a separate label, such as a strip label. The size and content of all these separate labels is also usually subject to local or national regulations, such as the strip seal of paper that goes over the top of the capsule of a *vinho verde*; but tags, attached to the neck of a bottle and falling free, tend to be more in the nature of trimmings to enhance the sales appeal of the bottle, and they are not so rigidly controlled.

The design of a label, obviously, is something for the individual firm or estate to decide, and there are many theories about this. **Mouton Rothschild**, in recent years, has employed a succession of famous artists to design its labels; Château **Lafite** has never changed its original design at all. Some properties have tried to update their labels, occasionally with disastrously vulgar results, in attempts to appeal to the varied winedrinking public and especially the North American market. Others have attempted to be archaic rather than historic in their presentations of bottles. But in general terms it may be stated that the finer wines, in all price ranges, high and low, tend to be labelled and their bottles presented with the good taste and discretion, plus practicability, that usually indicate a quality product. Sometimes when a property changes hands, the new owners have the label redesigned; although as a design the new version may be more attractive and conspicuous, it is not necessarily more successful in attracting sales or appealing to discriminating winelovers. The redesigned **Léoville-Barton** label (done at the wish of the **U.S.** firm of **Seagram**) is an example of this. The very lavish label, elaborate dressing of the bottle (and outlandish bottle shapes as well) very often indicate that the wine inside may not be its own best advocate. As it is obvious that the cost of all the strident presentations has to come from somewhere, it is usually the quality of the wine that suffers.

The terms 'strip label', 'back label' and 'neck label' are self-explanatory; but sometimes there is confusion between the neck label and the **capsule**, although these are two separate things. The **vintage** of a wine may be on the body label, or the neck label, or on a separate 'vintage label'.

Lachlan Valley   Family **winery** in New South Wales, **Australia**, making a variety of red, white and **fortified wines**.

Lacrima (Lachryma) Christi   Red and white wines – though the white is the better known – from the volcanic slopes of Mount Vesuvius, near Naples, in **Italy**. The white wine is traditionally served at room temperature and not chilled. It is made from the **Greca** della Torre **grape**. The red is made from two varieties of the **Aglianico** grape. Pink and **sparkling wines**, of varying types, are also made. Local producers will tell visitors that, in 1892, it was a Lacrima Christi from the Vesuvius vineyards that won the title at a Vienna wine congress of 'best wine in the world'. The wine gets its name because of a legend that Christ, looking down on the beautiful Bay of Naples, wept at the sins of the inhabitants. See **Vesuvio**.

Lafaurie-Peyraguey   (Pronounced 'Pay-rah-gay') Property making fine sweet white wine at **Bommes**, in the **Sauternes** region.

Lafite, Lafite-Rothschild Château Lafite, in the parish of **Pauillac**, in the **Médoc** in **France**, is one of the five 1st growths (see **classification**) and is considered by many to be the greatest red wine in the world. Early spellings of the name include 'Laffite', 'Lafitte' and 'Laffitte' but, as some of these are names of lesser properties elsewhere, only the spelling as first given is now used. However, 'Lafitte' is still the name of the street in Paris where the headquarters of the Rothschild bank is established. The vineyard is planted with **Cabernet Sauvignon**, Cabernet Franc, **Petit Verdot** and **Merlot**, the fairly high proportion of the latter giving Lafite its extraordinary **bouquet** and special appeal. The great 'library' in the cellars is the store for wines going back to the 18th century.

The property has a long history, but it was sold to Baron James de Rothschild in 1868 and remains the property of his descendants. The exquisite château **label**, a 19th century engraving, shows the house almost exactly as it still is, but one thing not visible on the label is the famous 'pepperpot' shaped tower, with a crest of five arrows crossed and fanning out on the top. This is a Rothschild symbol, signifying the five Rothschild brothers from Frankfurt who founded the international banking dynasty at the turn of the 18th and 19th centuries. The *château* itself is still frequently used by the family.

Lafite, always a fine Pauillac, has a peculiar charm and fascination, especially in years when the Merlot ripens fully and the wine is able to develop its graceful subtlety; the light or 'off' years can also be a delight. The French Rothschilds are much involved with the great estate and it is significant that, even though Lafite's wine has always commanded a high price and demand perennially exceeds supply, it was not until 1948 – 80 years after the Baron James bought the property (which he never lived to visit) – that a profit was made! The vineyard and *cuverie* have received the benefit of this constant ploughing-back of money made. See **Bordeaux, Carruades, Moulin des Carruades**.

Lafon-Rochet Classed 4th growth of **St Estèphe**. It belongs to the Cruse family and has recently been much modernised, so that its wine may be seen more frequently. See **Bordeaux, classification**.

Lagar The place where the **grapes** are trodden, in the **port** region – literally 'the treading tank'. A *lagar* of the traditional type – now being replaced by more modern pressing methods – is a deepish walled receptacle, usually rectangular, mostly made out of granite, although the authority George Robertson says that slate is sometimes used. To 'cut a *lagar*', a number of men line up, after having had their legs inspected by the supervisor for cleanliness – they wash before work – and then two lines, facing each other, march across the tank, in military precision, forcing down the grapes with their feet and legs. It is a strenuous activity, even when, as the juice flows and rises in the *lagar*, the treaders break free from each other and dance – but always continue treading. As well as the sergeant-major-like commands of the supervisor, a band plays, the workers sing and are frequently refreshed by tots of **bagaceira** and cigarettes.

The scriptural statement that someone has 'trodden the wine press all alone' is to be borne in mind here. It would be a very great ordeal, requiring much strength and endurance, for a single person to tread out the equivalent of even a small *lagar*.

Lagavulin Distillery at Port Ellen, on the Isle of Islay (pronounced 'Eye-la'). It was established in the 18th century, and produced quantities of illicitly distilled **whisky**, before being bought by the firm of J.L. Mackie, for legal purposes in 1835. This firm later evolved the great brand, 'White Horse', to which Lagavulin still contributes.

Lage (Pronounced 'Lah-ger') German word for a plot or specific site in a vineyard – rather like the **Burgundian** *climat*. See **German Wine Law**.

Lagrange Classed 3rd growth of **St Julien**, which underwent a decline from which it may now be emerging. See **Bordeaux, classification**.

Lagrein A wine that is made from the **grape** of the same name in the **Trentino-Alto Adige** region of north **Italy**. Most of it is pink.

Lágrima Spanish word meaning 'tear' (the kind you weep), and the name of a sweet white wine from **Málaga**. The name refers to the circumstance that, according to the traditional methods, only the drops, free-flowing from the grapes like tears, were used for the juice to go to the **fermentation vats**.

La Lagune Classed 3rd growth of the **Médoc** from the *commune* of **Ludon**, which has no **A.O.C.**, so that the **label** bears the A.O.C. Haut-Médoc. Early in this century, it was called Grand La Lagune, to distinguish it from other properties of the same name. Its wines are of a special charm and enticing finesse and, although the vineyard has undergone certain vicissitudes – including major replanting in the mid-1950s – its reputation has been maintained for quality.

Lake's Folly Dr Max Lake is one of the best-known names in **Australian** winemaking at the present, as well as being a respected wine writer. His own vineyard is in the **Hunter Valley** and is called Lake's Folly. He makes red wines, using **Cabernet Sauvignon** and also **Hermitage**.

Lalande de Pomerol A subdistrict of **Pomerol** producing red wines.

Lambrusco An unusual **Italian** wine from **Emilia-Romagna**, made from the **grape** of the same name. Most of it is dry, although some sweet is made, but the curious thing is that it is both red and **sparkling** – not, however, in the way that the *vins mousseux* are. In spite of having a lot of froth when first poured, it is more like a *pétillant* wine to taste. Its freshness can be very pleasing with certain rather rich dishes, especially pork (after all, the British cut the fatness with apple sauce). In its own region, it is recommended as the perfect wine for *zampone* (stuffed pig's trotter) which can be served hot or cold, as the fruitiness and slight fizz balance the succulence of the *zampone*. Because of the silly supposition that it is somehow 'better' to 'drink dry', many people have avoided trying Lambrusco, hearing that it is sweet; but it is usually no more so than ripe fruit is sweet. It makes a good partner to cold cuts, even when served with potato salad and any form of mayonnaise, and it can be a delightful between-times refreshment as well.

Landskroon   Wine estate on the slopes of the **Paarl** mountain range, in **South, Africa**, under vines since 1692 and today run by one of the great names among many wine families at the Cape – de Villiers. It is especially reputed for its red wines.

Langhorne Creek   This region near Adelaide, **Australia**, was named after Alfred Langhorne, who settled there with his cattle in 1841. The **soil** is rich and the rainfall low, so that **irrigation** of the vineyards by means of the Bremer River is essential. A wide range of table and **fortified wines** are made.

Langoa Barton   Classed 3rd growth of **St Julien** and a particularly charming *château*, currently the home of the Anglo-Irish Ronald Barton, whose family have been in the **Bordeaux** wine business for three centuries. Langoa and **Léoville-Barton** are made in the same presshouse and kept in the same cellars, but there is usually a slight additional quality to the wines of Léoville-Barton. Langoa is never **château-bottled**. See **classification**.

Languedoc   Strictly speaking, this region, more fully termed 'Languedoc-**Roussillon**', is an overall name for the area that includes the wines of the **Hérault** and adjoining regions in the south of **France**, in the hinterland and along the coast. Huge quantities of wine are produced, nowadays many of them becoming known as individual drinks among the *vins de pays*.

Laphroaig   (Pronounced 'Laff-royg' stressing 'royg') **Whisky distillery** at Port Ellen on the Isle of Islay (pronounced 'Eye-la'), founded in 1820. It still malts its own barley and, until very recently, the head of the distillery was a woman – the only female distiller in Scotland. Laphroaig is now owned by the firm of Long John and it is one of the ingredients in the blended Scotch, 'Islay Mist'. By itself, it is an outstanding whisky, too assertive in flavour and aroma for many. Some people liken the taste to that of iodine, others to cough mixture! It is very 'big' with many conjoined fragrances and tastes, slightly evocative of pine and tar to my mind, with a long accelerating flavour. Laphroaig is definitely the type of straight malt Scotch that created the belief that this sort of whisky was too 'strong' for people leading rather sedentary, urban lives, but it is an aristocrat of its kind.

Lascombes   (Pronounced 'Lass-komb') Classed 2nd growth of **Margaux**, with a world-wide reputation for its rather velvety, attractively-smelling **bouquet** and flavour. It belonged to Alexis Lichine, with some of his various associates; but it is now the property of Charrington Vintners who have greatly improved the estate and the house, with resultant improvements in the wine as well. See **Bordeaux, classification**.

Latin America   See **Argentina, Brazil, Chile, Uruguay**.

Latour   Château Latour, in the parish of **Pauillac**, in the **Médoc** in **France**, is one of the five 1st growths and also one of the world's greatest red wines. It has been famous for many centuries. In 1842 it became a company, to which only members of the family owning it could belong. In 1962 the de Beaumont family, descendants of the Ségurs, who had acquired it through marriage in the 17th century, sold their interest to Lord Cowdray. He took 51%, the firm of John Harvey of Bristol bought 25%, the remaining 24% stayed French. The

LATIN AMERICA

①	Valle de Tulum
②	Aconcagua Prov.
③	Valparaiso Prov.
④	Santiago Prov.
⑤	Maipo Valley
⑥	O'Higgins Prov.
⑦	Colchagua Prov.
⑧	Curicó Prov.
⑨	Talca Prov.
⑩	Maule Prov.
⑪	Linares Prov.
⑫	Nuble Prov.
⑬	Conception Prov.
⑭	Bio-Bio Prov.
⑮	Malleco Prov.
⑯	Cautin Prov.

●━●━●━●	Frontiers
────	Provinces
────	Rivers
▬●▬●▬●	River frontiers
══════	River and province

property gets its name from the squat, rounded tower that stands in the vineyard; this once formed part of a fortification against pirates. The stony vineyard of Latour is particularly rich in quartz: the Marquis de Ségur, a former owner who was also the proprietor of **Lafite** and **Calon-Ségur**, once wore some of these stones, polished like diamonds, on his coat. Asked by the King about these splendid buttons, he replied 'They are the diamonds of my estate'.

In recent years the property has been much modernised. The installation of stainless-steel **fermentation vats** on a large scale and the complete rehabilitation of the vineyard and the house has made a great overall improvement even to this magnificent wine. The wine is always of a very noble style. It usually takes a considerable time to mature in good and great years, but the 'off years' of Latour are remarkable and can last far beyond what would be supposed. The proportion of **Cabernet Sauvignon** in the vineyard is about 80%. See **Bordeaux, classification**.

Latricières-Chambertin Red **Burgundy** from the parish of **Gevrey-Chambertin**, making fine wines.

Lavaux Region between Montreux and Lausanne in **Switzerland**, making good white wines. The best known is probably **Dézaley**.

Laville Haut Brion One of the great white wines of the **Graves** region, just south of **Bordeaux**. It is owned by the proprietor of **La Mission Haut Brion**, and the wine is considered as fine as any of the white Graves, with a great style, fruitiness and crisp, dry finish.

Lazio (Pronounced 'Lat-see-oh') **Italian** wine region around Rome, producing the wines of the **Castelli Romani**, Apulia, the wines of Cesanese, and **Est! Est!! Est!!!** To English readers, it may be more familiar as *Latium* (the Latin name).

Leasingham See **Stanley**.

Lebanon Wines have been made in Lebanon and Syria for many centuries, but the modern wine industry was only really established during and after the last war, first of all to satisfy the demands of French troops stationed in the country. Table wines are made of various types, and can be pleasant and interesting. As they are seldom seen on export lists, they merit the attention of travellers in this part of the world.

Lees The residue or **deposit** left in the **cask** after the wine has been drawn off (see **rack**). Wine bottled directly off the lees, without being subjected to any treatment, can produce a slightly different style with certain wines (see *sur lie*). When a merchant does his own bottling, he may sell off the wine that is beginning to run directly off the lees as cooking wine, not because it is bad, but because the public tend to be suspicious of a wine that is not star bright. See **filtration, ullage**.

Legana Tasmanian vineyard, in the Tamar Valley, labelling its products 'Chateau Legana' (*sic*). See **Australia**.

Legs Term which refers to the trails that flow down the side of a wine **glass** after the wine has been swirled around. They indicate the viscosity of the wine and are best known as present in great sweet wines. However their presence is usually a sign of quality in any wine. Other terms for this include 'tears' (in French *larmes*); in Germany the expression 'Gothic windows' is occasionally used.

Leiwen (Pronounced 'Lie-ven') Vineyard on the **Mosel** making fine wines typical of the region; the most famous sites are Klostergarten and Laurentiuslay.

Lemon gin See **gin**.

Léognan (Pronounced 'Lay-oh-nyong') See **Graves**.

Léoville Formerly one of the largest estates in the **Médoc**, created by a **Bordeaux** merchant in 1638 and named for a Président of the Parlement of Bordeaux in the middle of the 18th century. The property was divided during the revolution. See **Léoville-Barton, Léoville-Lascases, Léoville-Poyferré**.

Léoville-Barton Classed 2nd growth of **St Julien**, its suffix deriving from its purchase at the beginning of the 19th century by Hugh Barton and the firm of Barton and Guestier (pronounced 'Gay-tee-ay'). At one time the vineyard was considered the least of the three **Léovilles**, but since 1945 its consistently high quality and charm have made it one of the most popular of all **Médocs**. A very good wine to begin one's acquaintance with **claret**. See **Bordeaux, classification**.

Léoville-Lascases (Pronounced 'Lass-kass') Classed 2nd growth of **St Julien** and the largest of the three **Léovilles**. The *château's* imposing gateway, shown on its **labels**, is on the side of the road running through the main wine estates of the **Médoc** and the boundary of the vineyard is also the limit of St Julien – **Latour** is alongside Lascases. This accounts for the wine being somewhat more assertive and **Pauillac** in character than a typical St Julien. Lascases went through a phase when its wines were infrequently seen and often of only passable quality, but in recent years they have improved enormously and nowadays achieve nobility as well as charm. See **Bordeaux, classification**.

Léoville-Poyferré (Pronounced 'Pwah-fer-ray') Classed 2nd growth of **St Julien**, which made exceptionally fine wines in the 1920s, but which in recent years has sometimes rather disappointed, although it is now beginning to show a definite revival of quality. See **Bordeaux, classification**.

Lessona Red wine from the Novara Hills in **Piedmont, Italy**, made from the **Nebbiolo grape** and capable of achieving considerable quality after maturation in **bottle**.

Levante Region in **Spain**, near Valencia, where rather ordinary wines are made today. Because of their robust, assertive character, they are used for **blending** and also some sweet white wine is made. In the past, the wines of this area were often used to **cut** with those of **France**. **Benicarlo** was the best-known wine of this type.

Liebfraumilch This is probably the best known of all **German** wines – yet it is a type of wine and not one specific wine. Originally the name was used to describe the wine of the Liebfrauenstift (Church of Our Lady) at **Worms** but later legislation specifically prevented the use of the term in association with the wine of this vineyard. Today, according to the **German wine law**, Liebfraumilch is classed as a **QbA**. It must be a white quality wine from the regions of Rheinhessen, **Nahe**, **Pfalz** and Rheingau, made from the **Riesling**, **Silvaner** or **Müller-Thurgau** grapes, and possessing a 'mild' taste. It has to pass the required examinations for quality and receives a number (the A.P.) when it does so. In fact, most Liebfraumilch comes from the Rheinhessen, as the fullish wines of this region made good popular drinks. See **Rhine**.

Liebfraumilch is a wine unknown in Germany – to the astonishment of many visitors – because it was created as a style of German wine specifically for the export trade, so as to introduce the non-German public to a German wine. The outstandingly successful 'Blue Nun' Liebfraumilch, of H. Sichel & Son of Mainz, was first evolved in the 1920s: a courageous venture at a time when Germany was recovering from World War I and the great depression was obviously on the horizon. Today Blue Nun is possibly the biggest-selling branded white wine in the world! Nearly all the important **shippers** make a Liebfraumilch according to their own standards of what is good and what their customers want: some make a non-vintage wine, **blending** for consistent quality always; others use a blend of wines from a single year and put on a **vintage**. The style may vary considerably, so may the price. The eye-catching **labels** and unusual names often seen on bottles of Liebfraumilch are the shippers' means of attracting the attention of the public to what is, essentially, a generic German wine, aimed at pleasing the non-German consumer outside Germany (see **Corvo**, blended to represent a 'typical' **Sicilian** wine).

The Liebfraumilch question is often much debated: some very respected authorities, including shippers, believe that it is virtually a brand name, with no advantage to the drinker who might be more interested and learn something from wine bearing the name of its region. Other equally respected people believe that the consistency of quality has the enormous advantage of being able to please world markets – very delicate German wines are obviously difficult to ship to many countries – and that it is important for people to know a wine that will please them easily, with a name they can pronounce, subject to strict quality controls imposed by legislation as well as the standards of the makers. It is probably fair to say that many people have become interested in German wines – and possibly wines in general – by drinking someone's Liebfraumilch and enjoying it. However, if they confine their drinking entirely to Liebfraumilch, they may miss many pleasurable experiences and are limiting their knowledge.

Liebich Family firm in the **Barossa Valley** of **Australia**, established in 1918 by the late Benno Paul Liebich. The **winery**, whose products are sold under the name 'Rovalley', deals mainly with the catering trade, supplying it with bulk wines.

Lieser (Pronounced 'Lie-zur' stressing 'Lie') Vineyard on the **Mosel**. The Niederberg is the best-known site, though there are others producing wines that are usually fine.

Light wines   Nothing to do with the character of the wines, this term in the U.K. indicates wines of **table wine strength** – that is, not more than 14% of **alcohol** by volume. **Heavy wine** duty does not therefore have to be paid. See **Gay Lussac, proof**.

Liguria   **Italian** wine producing region, extending from the hinterland of La Spezia to Ventimiglia, formerly making a wide variety and large quantity of wines. Today the red and white wines are in smaller supply, the best-known being the red of **Dolceacqua** and the white of **Cinqueterre**.

Lillet   A type of **vermouth** made in **Bordeaux**. There are two types, red and white, but it is the dry white that is known outside **France**. It can be drunk neat or in mixes. The use of the name in the form 'Kina Lilet' is sometimes seen in the southern regions of France.

Limoux   Town in south-west **France**, where the vineyards make the well-known **Blanquette de Limoux**, and also a still white wine of good quality.

Lindeman   One of the most respected names in **Australian** winemaking. Henry John Lindeman, son of a doctor, who himself qualified at St Bartholomew's Hospital in London, arrived in Australia in 1840. His first vineyard was on the Paterson River, a tributary of the famous **Hunter River**, which he called Cawarra. He extended his properties, buying a vineyard at **Corowa** in 1872 and, subsequently, vineyards called Felton and Southern Cross. He was a lifelong advocate of winedrinking as an asset to health – and a deterrent to the abuse of spirits. The Lindeman family continued to expand, buying the properties called Porphyry and Sunshine at the beginning of the 20th century. In 1912, the old-established vineyard **Ben Ean** and that called **Coolalta** were purchased by a member of the family, which also acquired **Kirkton** through marriage – a Lindeman girl married the nephew of the great James **Busby**.

Lindemans became a public company in 1953 and bought **Chateau Leonay** (*sic*) and a **winery** at **Coonawarra** in 1965. Today the Lindeman concern produces a very wide range of wines, including **fortified wines, sparkling wines** of various sorts, including some made by the **Champagne method**, and red and white table wines, from a variety of different classic **grapes**. They often attain extremely high quality and the successive winemakers of the firm have contributed a great deal to the traditions of Australian wines.

Lindisfarne   **Whisky**-based British **honey liqueur**.

Linkwood   **Whisky distillery** in Elgin, Morayshire, making a rather light type of straight malt. It was built in 1821.

Lipari   The Lipari Islands, also known as the Aeolian Isles, off the coast of **Sicily**, produce a respected **Malvasia** sweetish white wine.

Liqueur d'Angelique   See **angelica**.

Liqueur d'expédition   See **dosage**.

Liqueur d'or   A type of **liqueur** with flakes of gold in it, the most famous being made by the French firm of Garnier since 1890. See **Danzig Goldwasser**.

Liqueur des Moines   French **liqueur** made from aromatic plants and **Cognac**, yellow in colour.

Liqueur wines See *vin de liqueur*.

Liqueurs Drinks which have an alcoholic base, varying in **strength**, and of great variety in flavour. They are not internationally defined, although the producing countries control the different types by legislation. Terms such as 'liqueur **brandy**', 'liqueur **whisky**' are not precise; although they do imply the special and high quality of the spirit. However, in French law, a *liqueur* is actually a sweetened spirit: *'fine'*, *'demi-fine'* and *'surfine'* are terms referring to the strength and sweetness. *Surfine* is the highest in strength and sweetest; the *demi-fine* is the least sweet.

The use of the word *double* as, for example, in 'double **crème** de **cassis**' usually means that the liqueur contains twice the quantities of the flavouring agents, but when this might unbalance the overall proportions of the drink, the *'double'* may only be 50% more. Some people confuse the *'double'* term with something to do with alcoholic **strength**, or sweetness, but this is not so – a *'double'* liqueur is about as high in strength as a *surfine*, and its sweetness naturally depends on the sweetness of the product making the drink and how much of this is actually 'doubled'.

The liqueur market seemed to undergo a decline after World War II, both because liqueurs cannot be cheap – on account of the duty paid on their strength – and also because they seemed to belong to a more leisured way of life. Many of them today, however, are drunk at any time, even as **apéritifs** – as witness the popularity of **Cointreau** 'on the rocks' – although most English-speaking people would generally assume them to be drinks taken after the end of a meal.

There are many different basic types, and although there are few hard and fast definitions, it is important to note the difference between a liqueur flavoured with a fruit, flower or berry (such as **crème de menthe** or crème de cacao) and one made from a actual distillate of the fruit or berry, such as framboise, poire Williams, kirsch. See **distillation**. These latter are more properly *eaux-de-vie* than just liqueurs. As they should be served differently from the flavoured liqueurs and are sweet only because of the sweetness of the fruit, they form a separate group. See *alcool blanc*.

Liquoroso Italian term for a type of wine that is definitely sweet and of rather high **strength**, though not necessarily over **table wine** strength, and not necessarily **fortified**.

Lirac Wine town at the bottom of the **Rhône** Valley in **France**, where good white, red and rosé wines are produced.

Listan See **Palomino, sherry**.

Listrac See **Bordeaux**.

Littlemill This **distillery** at Bowling, Dumbarton is very old – **whisky** was possibly made there in the 14th century. Most of its produce today goes for **blending**, but there is a single malt sometimes available.

Live Oaks **Winery** in **Santa Clara Valley, California**.

Livermore Valley This area in **California** is the home of some of the most important **wineries** of this region.

Loch Lomond **Whisky distillery** built in 1966, at Alexandria, Dumbarton-shire, Scotland. Owned by Barton Distilling.

Lochside This **whisky distillery** at Montrose, Angus in Scotland, was built in 1957. In 1973, it became the property of a Madrid firm.

Lodge Meaning winestore, from the Portuguese word *loja*. The word refers in particular to the stores of the **port shippers** in **Vila Nova de Gaia** in north **Portugal**, or to any winestore in this region that is above ground – differentiating it from a cellar which is below ground. The term is also used for the winestores of **Madeira**.

Lodi Region in the north of the San Joaquin Valley in **California**, including many **wineries**.

Logroño (Pronounced 'Log-rohn-yo' stressing 'rohn') Centre of the **Rioja** wine region on the River Ebro in **Spain**.

Loire (Pronounced 'Lwah') This is the longest river in **France** and there are many vineyards along its banks and those of its tributaries: the Vienne, Cher, Loir, Layon, Indre and Sarthe. Red, white and rosé wines and **sparkling wines** are made, and have been for many centuries from a variety of **grapes** (see **Anjou, Jasnières, Muscadet, Pouilly-sur-Loire, Quincy, Reuilly, Sancerre, Saumur, Touraine, Vouvray**). In general, the Loire wines are light and elegantly charming in character, most of them being at their pleasantest when drunk young and fresh but a few, including some of the sweet wines of the **Coteaux du Layon** and the reds of **Chinon, Bourgueil** and **St Nicolas de Bourgueil**, are capable of achieving great quality if made so that their maturation in **bottle** will bring out subtleties of style. It is, however, difficult to achieve this nowadays, when wines cannot, for economic reasons, be kept for long maturation.

Although most Loire wines were considered 'bad travellers' until comparatively recently, it was not the wines themselves that were inadequate in this way. Local demand often took all the wine made and haphazard methods of transportation could damage even the most robust wine. Nowadays a greater area is under **vines**, the winemakers have more knowledge of the technical resources on which they can draw, and rapid transport makes it possible for Loire wines to go all over the world. They are not, however, as well known as I think they deserve, except possibly for **Muscadet** and the pink wines of **Anjou**. Northern export markets do not find it easy to like the crispness of many of the whites and reds, so that even Muscadet and many of the **rosé** wines have been deliberately softened to please palates that prefer a touch of roundness, even sweetness. The really sweet wines are much neglected because of the preference for wines that are supposedly 'dry'; however softened these may be.

Until recently, Loire wines were definite bargains, but there have been several small **vintages** lately and this, combined with a greater popularity for them in their own country, has sent prices up. It is strange that they have been so neglected in England – seat of the Plantagenets – and a pity that many of the public do not accept that a fine Loire, from a reputable producer, is worth

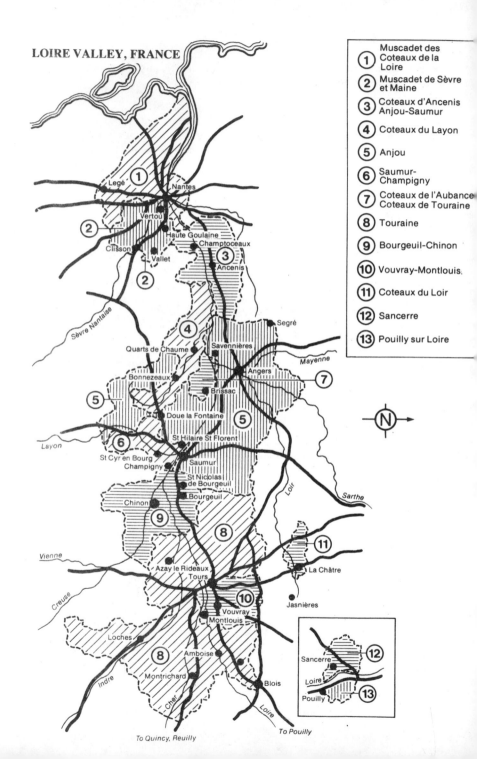

LOIRE VALLEY, FRANCE

1　Muscadet des Coteaux de la Loire

2　Muscadet de Sèvre et Maine

3　Coteaux d'Ancenis Anjou-Saumur

4　Coteaux du Layon

5　Anjou

6　Saumur-Champigny

7　Coteaux de l'Aubance Coteaux de Touraine

8　Touraine

9　Bourgeuil-Chinon

10　Vouvray-Montlouis.

11　Coteaux du Loir

12　Sancerre

13　Pouilly sur Loire

at least as much as, say, an indifferent white **Burgundy** or a rather dull 'little' **claret**. For those who do not 'drink the label' (see **wine snob**), there is great delight and interest in Loire wines.

Lombardy   Important wine region in north **Italy**, including the wines around Lake Garda such as **Lugana**, also the **Valtelline** and **Franciacorta** wines.

Lomond   This **whisky distillery**, at Montrose in Scotland, is owned by the mighty Hiram Walker establishment.

London gin   See **gin**.

Longmorn-Glenlivet   This **distillery** at Longmorn, Elgin, Morayshire, in Scotland was built in 1894. Its **whisky** is highly reputed.

Longworth   In the early part of the 19th century, Nicholas Longworth founded a wine industry at Cincinnati, in the **U.S.** This was so successful that the state of **Ohio** produced twice as much wine as **California** until the **vines** were virtually totally destroyed by various diseases in the 1860s. Today attempts are being made, with some success, to revive the wine business in this area.

Lorraine   Wines have been made in the region of eastern **France** since early times, but today they are seldom seen outside their own area. The best known are possibly the *vin gris* made around **Toul**.

Loupiac   Region on the north bank of the River Garonne, in the **Gironde** region, which makes sweetish white wines, which in some people's opinion, are rather like small-scale **Barsacs**.

Loving-cup   The tradition of the loving-cup is very old. Essentially, it is the sharing of a drink as part of a ceremony of welcome and expression of friendship: in ancient times, an elaborate drinking vessel would be preferred to a guest and both he and the host would drink from it. The sharing of a cup, a practise common to other religions as well as Christianity, indicated fellowship, the drinkers being bound by this experience to respect each other. There was also the custom of the host or someone of his household – such as the daughter of the establishment – first drinking from the cup and then offering it to the honoured guest, as a sign that the wine was wholesome.

Today the loving-cup is still passed at many City of London and other ceremonial feasts and banquets. The cups used often have two handles, so that their considerable weight may be easily held and passed around. What happens can vary according to the occasion, but frequently the procedure is that the cup is offered, with a bow, by someone who takes off the cover (if there is one) and then stands facing the drinker in an attitude of respect; the drinker, having bowed and received the cup, drinks from it, meanwhile facing the one who has proffered it. At the same time, the person on the other side of the drinker also stands up and faces away from them – so that the back of the drinker is guarded against any enemy. The drinker then puts down the cup and bows to the offerer – on his or her right. Then he passes it to the left, where the person who had been standing to guard the back of the drinker, turns to them, bows, receives it and drinks in their turn, the person on their left meanwhile rising to guard them. The procedure generally takes place at the end of formal banquets and is accompanied by music.

The loving-cup – or, sometimes, cups – pass round the whole company of diners, are then returned to the original cup-bearer, and the covers (if any) are put on and the cups returned to their place. The sort of wine used varies, but is usually the type of **dessert** or **fortified wine** that might be served at the end of this sort of meal. Except for the three persons who stand while involved with the passing of the cup, the company remain seated.

Low wines   Expression used for the first **distillation** of Scotch (see **whisky**) and nothing to do with wine.

Loxton   In the **Murray River** valley, **Australia**, this **co-operative** was set up in 1949. It produces both wines and **brandy**.

Lucania   See **Basilicata**.

Ludon   Parish in the **Médoc** of which the famous **classed growth** is **La Lagune**. See **Bordeaux, classification**.

Lugana   These white wines come from a region in **Lombardy, Italy**, just south of the picturesque town of Sirmione. The Lugana wines are white, made from the **Trebbiano grape**, and possess an agreeable fragrance and smooth, flowing style, with sufficient weight to serve as accompaniments to many dishes.

Lunel   Region near Montpellier, in the south of **France**, where **Muscat** wines are made of various types.

Lutomer, Ljutomer   White wine from the Lutomer-Ormuz district of **Yugoslavia**. Different **grapes** may be used, but the wines made from the varieties of **Riesling** grapes usually have this added to their names on the **label** for export markets.

Luxembourg   These wines are pleasant and several export markets have learned to appreciate them but, although the vineyards often border the **Mosel**, they have little in common with the **German** wines or any others from **France**. All are white, light in style and **grapes** such as the **Riesling**, **Traminer**, **Sylvaner** and others are used. The Luxembourg *pétillant* wine, Edelperl, has achieved a modest success in the U.K. It is slightly gasified by the addition of carbon dioxide. Compared with the wines of Germany or **Alsace**, these wines seem lightweight and even thin; but they can be pleasant drinks on the spot.

Lynch-Bages   (Pronounced 'Lainch-Baahj') Classed 5th growth of **Pauillac**, this property gets its name from having once belonged to an Irishman called Lynch, who was Mayor of **Bordeaux**. Today it belongs to the Cazes family. The wines are usually very big and of a most definite, almost rich, character. They are so individual that they are either liked very much or not at all. Lovers of predominantly elegant, delicate **clarets** tend to find Lynch-Bages not to their taste, as it is extremely assertive. See **classification**.

Lynch-Moussas   Classed 5th growth of **Pauillac**, getting its name from an Irishman (see **Lynch-Bages**). The wine is sold today mainly in Belgium and Holland. See **Bordeaux, classification**.

Lyncrest   **Winery** recently established in the **Napa Valley, California**.

M

Macallan Sometimes called Macallan-Glenlivet, from Craigallachie, this malt is one of the great Speyside whiskies, noble and much respected. Its licence was taken out in 1824 and it was bought by the Robert Kemp family in 1892 – they still run the establishment.

MacArthur, John Arrived in **Australia** in 1790. He is famous for being the first person to import merino sheep as well as one of the pioneer winemakers. With his sons, he toured various French and Swiss wine districts at the beginning of the 19th century and made the first plantations of **vines** in 1820 – the very first commercial vineyard and winemaking installation in that continent. The MacArthur sons continued their father's remarkable work, and MacArthur wines won awards in London in the early 1840s. William MacArthur's book on vine culture was of enormous influence; he also founded the New South Wales Vineyard Association in the 1850s.

Macduff This Banff **whisky distillery** was built in 1966 and makes the malt called Glendeveron.

Maceration This process means the softening of something by steeping it in a liquid, as with the various things that contribute to the making of **vermouth**.

Macération carbonique This term refers to a process that some winemakers disdain, saying that much wine made in the normal way is made using the process anyway (rather like certain chefs who say that they have always used *Cuisine minceur* or *Nouvelle cuisine*). There are also those who make it sound so difficult to grasp – obviously details of processes vary from region to region – that the ordinary drinker is thoroughly confused. So no attempt at entering into details on what is a fairly complicated technique of winemaking will be attempted here. In essence what *macération carbonique* achieves is the production of a fruity, slightly soft-bodied wine from **grapes** that might be hard, **tannic**, stalky while young, and which might take a long time to become reasonably drinkable. This has obvious advantages in certain regions, where the small-scale wines (formerly made only for local and domestic use) simply cannot complete in the more important outside markets with the quality of more famous wines, even with long-term maturation and careful making. Nor

207

can these regions satisfy the demand for easy, everyday wines that are quickly ready and possess qualities that appeal to a wide public.

In very general terms, the process requires that the grapes be left to press themselves, and not be whipped off the stems by the *fouloir-égrappoir*. While they are all piled up in their bunches, not only does juice begin to run from them because of their own weight, but also a type of **fermentation** starts taking place within each grape. After a set time, the grapes are then processed in the usual way – whatever it is in that region. High standards of cleanliness and supervision are essential, as otherwise the grapes would simply rot. But the resulting wine will be soft, fruity and usually very fragrant – almost from the first weeks after it has been made. This means that it can be bottled early and need not spend time in **cask** or **vat**, and that it is ready to drink immediately it is in **bottle** – all obvious economic advantages. The process seems to have been first used significantly in the **Rhône** Valley, in the middle of this century; but it is now involved with many other wines in different parts of the world. Sometimes only a proportion of a wine will be made utilising the *macération carbonique* process; at others the wine will be wholly made according to this method.

The essential character of the wine does not alter, except that it is ready to drink after months, instead of years. Even with long keeping (a costly procedure) some *petits vins* would simply never achieve the quality level of the great ones but, made ready to enjoy while they are young, their essential attributes are maintained. Only the elements that would otherwise have to be smoothed out by time are removed. For example, the **Cabernet Sauvignon** – backbone of the sort of red wines that, at their finest, have the longest lives of any table wine – can be grown on what were formerly unregarded plots owned by peasant farmers. It can be used to make a wine that has the **colour**, **bouquet** and basic flavour of a good red with a touch of class bestowed by the great grape; but it can be sold at a fraction of the price of the great **clarets** or Cabernet Sauvignons of the New World. The **Carignan**, a grape that tends to make wines with a harsh, almost bitter, aggressive style if processed in the usual way, can be used to yield wines which possess the warmth and sturdiness of the south without any of the characteristics that could usually only be softened by time. The numerous good *vins du pays* could never have attracted buyers from regions outside their own without making wines by the *macération carbonique* method.

The ordinary drinker should not bother about trying to notice this – it is part of winemaking technique, like the use of certain things for **fining** or a particular bottling procedure. If, however, you are interested in the backstage routines of the wine world, it is worth bearing in mind that if you try a new wine and are impressed by its fruit – although it is comparatively inexpensive and comes from a region either previously little-known or from a grape not associated in your mind with the sort of agreeably-smelling, mouth-filling, clean, fresh wine of this kind – then it is very likely that at least some of this will be the result of the *macération carbonique* process.

Mackenzie   Firm well known for its **ports** and **sherries**. See **Cockburn**.

Mâcon, Mâconnais   (Pronounced 'Mac-kon', stressing 'Mac') This region is in south **Burgundy**, between the bottom of the **Côte de Beaune** and the **Beaujolais**. Red, white and pink wines are made there and, in fact, before controls became strict around 15 years ago, a great deal of 'Chablis' was possibly Mâcon Blanc. The red wines were also sometimes sold under labels bearing far more illustrious names. The region has been making wines for many centuries, however, and today they deserve appraisal in their own right. The Benedictine monks of Cluny, established in the region in the 10th century, exerted enormous influence – oddly enough Cluny was founded in 910 by the Duke of Aquitaine, whose lands extended right across France into Burgundy! The Cluny monks were termed 'the American Express of the Middle Ages' by historian Sir Stephen Runciman and throughout Europe they wielded immense power, as regards learning, cultivation and research. They also specialised in viniculture.

In the 17th century, a Mâcon winemaker, Claude Brosse, who was disappointed at being unable to sell his wine locally, loaded an ox cart and travelled to Versailles, the court of Louis XIV, the 'Sun King'. Brosse was a giant of a man and, when he attended Mass in the royal chapel, he attracted attention because it was thought he was standing up – risking a rebuke from the guards – when he was actually kneeling down. The King then called for him and eventually placed an order for his wine, so making Brosse's fortune.

Best-known of all Mâcon wines is probably the white **Pouilly Fuissé**. This is light, dry, fairly full and pleasant, made from the **Chardonnay grape**. Wines of similar style are made in the parishes of Pouilly Loché, Pouilly Vinzelles; even single vineyards from the parishes of Vergisson, Solutré and Chaintré as well as Pouilly itself are sometimes seen on labels nowadays. Unfortunately, Pouilly Fuissé recently became tremendously popular in the U.S., which sent prices rocketing above European purse limits. It is odd that a wine that can never be more than a fairly good drink should have enjoyed such a vogue, but it is possible that both British and American drinkers acquire a taste for it when they feel that they can with assurance pronounce its name!

Another well-known white wine from this region is **St Véran**, which also enjoys a fashionable popularity. It got its **A.O.C.** as recently as 1971 and many people considered it as a somewhat superior wine to white Beaujolais – another wine enjoying a run from the smart drinking public. Personally, I have never found either of these two wines more than adequate, fullish, dry whites: they do not seem to have subtlety or finesse, although they can be possible alternatives to the expensive white Burgundies. Other whites, however, have achieved high quality and seem more interesting: these include Mâcon Lugny, Mâcon Viré and Mâcon Clessé. Part of the Lugny vineyard also makes the truly fine Clos du Chapître, a wine with intensity and breeding.

The red Mâcons are mostly made from the **Gamay** grape, but some **Pinot Noir** is also used. Personally, I find that these Gamay wines lack the fleshy, lip-smacking style of the Beaujolais reds, although they can be agreeably fresh and crisp. The Pinot Noir Mâcons and the rosé wines are pleasant, but perhaps not more as yet. Today this type of Burgundy can represent both quality and pleasant drinking: a good Mâcon, white or red, is certainly a more interesting drink, with definite character, than an indifferent 'commercial' Burgundy from a vineyard further to the north.

Macvin   Regional speciality of the **Jura** region of France, which is sweetish and pungent, spiced with cinnamon, coriander and other ingredients. The name derives from *marc-vin*, because the local red wine has its fermentation checked by the addition of *eau-de-vie-de-marc*.

Madeira   This is one of the great **fortified wines**, made on the island of the same name. The word means 'wood' and originated because, when it was first explored by the Portuguese in 1418, it was covered with trees, which the discoverers burnt down (the fire lasted 7 years). This greatly enriched the **soil**. The wine was first exported unfortified, but they began to add **brandy** to it about the middle of the 18th century.

Because Maderia came under the English crown for a while as part of the dowry of Catherine of Braganza, Charles II's queen, links with Britain were formed early and many of the wine firms are still British. It became very popular in America in the late 18th century because of a legal technicality, which permitted Madeira to be imported by any ship. Even though it might come via Britain, it was not subject to the controls on wine from Europe, which could only go to the New World in British ships, because technically Madeira was in Africa. This appealed to those who, before the War of Independence, wished to defy the British authorities. Madeira became popular everywhere during the Napoleonic wars, when **French** wines were obviously difficult to get. The sea voyages to the **U.S.** (as they now were) and the Far East, with the wine slowly heating up during the trip, enormously improved the wines, often taken on as ballast. This resulted in the system of gradually heating them, known as *estufagem*, which now substitutes for the sea voyages.

Madeira is made as all wine is made, the **fermentation** being subsequently either arrested (as far as the very sweet wines are concerned), or slowed down (for the drier wines) by the addition of **brandy**. The wine is then subjected to the gradual heating and cooling that gives it a special character and is then put into a *solera* and matured like **sherry**. Madeira disputes with sherry the distinction of being the longest lived wine in the world, and 18th century wines still survive. Sir Winston Churchill, visiting the island, once remarked in wonder 'Do you realise that when this wine was made, Marie Antoinette was still alive!' But **vintage** wines are very seldom made today, the dates shown on some **bottles** being those of the establishment of the *solera*. However some very old wine will be in each fine Madeira.

The main types are all called after the **grapes** from which they are made: **Sercial**, which is the dryest; **Verdelho**, which sometimes recalls a nutty flavour to people; **Bual** or *Boal* (the latter is the Portuguese spelling), golden-brown and fairly sweet; and **Malmsey** or Malvasia, dark brown and lusciously sweet, though never cloying. Each of the great Madeira wine houses makes a slightly different style of wine. Some also make **blends**, to which they attach a brand name, such as the well-known **Rainwater**.

Madeira should be served in tulip-shaped **glasses** or medium size goblets, like **port**. The dry type may be slightly chilled if it is wished, but in fact Madeira is a robust sort of wine and this is not essential, although pleasanter for **apéritifs**. The **decanting** of great old **dessert** Madeiras, however, is advisable; simply because a handsome decanter shows off the **colour** of the wine. Madeira was, in former times, the traditional refreshment for a bank manager or lawyer to offer favoured customers. It was also known in the Far East as 'S.S.S.' – for subalterns' soothing syrup – because it was considered a less taxing drink for the younger men in the mess, who had not become accustomed to the heat of India so as to be able to drink much port with impunity. In the 19th century household it was often taken with a piece of Madeira cake when the master of the house returned in the evening (this was before the days of apéritifs before meals) and ladies would drink it as well, with perfect respectability. Sercial and Verdelho are sometimes served with a clear soup, but can also accompany certain first courses of fish. Bual and Malmsey are for dessert – either with something sweet or with fruit. Although many of the firms making Madeira belong to the Madeira Wine Association, not all do.

Maderisation   A term sometimes applied to white wines which, either because of age or bad keeping, have developed a brown hue, due to exposure – however slight – to the air. The taste need not necessarily be unpleasant, so as to prevent the wine being drunk – but it will change what should have been the essential flavour. A wine that should be crisp, fresh and rather delicate will lose by being maderised; a wine that is fuller, softer and, in certain instances, aged for unusual periods in **cask**, may actually gain from this maderisation. Maderisation, unless excessive, should not be sufficient reason for rejecting a **bottle** in a restaurant: although it should be commented on if it occurs in a fine white **Burgundy**, or similar wine, where it can affect the enjoyment of the wine. See **Madeira**.

Madiran   Red wine from the Pyrenees region of **France**, very pronounced in character, partly and sometimes substantially made from the **Tannat grape**. A little white Madiran is also made. Neither are often seen outside the region.

Magdelaine   Château Magdelaine is a classed 1st growth of **St Émilion**. See **Bordeaux, classification**.

Magnifico   The slightly bulbous-shaped **bottle** used for **Chianti Ruffino** of a quality capable of improving by maturing. The name appears to have originated in the U.S., where this Chianti is the best-selling variety.

Magnum   See **bottles**.

Mahia   See **Boukha**.

Mailly   One of the wine villages in the **Champagne** region.

Maître de chai   See **chai**.

Majorca   Both Majorca and Minorca make wines, interesting to visitors but not much exported. The chief regions are those of Benisalem, Palma, Felanitx and Manacor, making mostly red wines and some pink ones, a little white being made at Buñols. There are also several **distilleries**: **gin** has been made on Minorca since the beginning of the 19th century, when Lord Nelson used the place as a harbour, because the local people realised that the fleet would be a good market for a spirit.

Málaga   Wine from Andalucia in the south of **Spain**. It is not actually made from the Málaga **grape**, but its production is strictly controlled. The most famous is probably **Lágrima**, which is white and rather sweet; another is Negro. Traditionally Málaga is sweetish or very sweet and was enormously popular in the days when the scarceness and cost of sugar caused people to consume vast amounts of all sweet wines when they could be got. Today some dry Malaga is also made, but the popularity of the wine in general has declined. It is not fortified with **brandy** but, at its best, is made in a type of *solera* system (see **sherry**). Old wine **labels** bearing the name 'Mountain' refer to Málaga. See **Tent**. It may be served by itself between meals, or with dessert fruit.

Malan   One of the great names in **South African** wine history. Malans have made wine at a number of estates and have influenced the technical progress of many wines. Today, the best-known estate owned by a Malan is **Allesverloren**.

Malartic-Lagravière   Estate in the **Graves** region of **Bordeaux**, making red and white wines, both of some quality. See **classification**.

Malbec   Black **grape** cultivated on the **Gironde** and the **Loire**, which imparts a type of softness to the wines in which it is used. Sometimes it plays an important part in pink wines. Another name is the Cot and, occasionally, the **Cahors**.

Malescot-St-Exupéry   Classed 3rd growth of **Margaux**, which gets its name from the same family as that of the famous airman and writer. It now belongs to Paul Zuger, who is doing much to revive its quality, which had declined. See **Bordeaux, classification**.

Malmesbury   Wine region of **South Africa**, of which the best-known estate is probably **Allesverloren**.

Malmsey   One of the main types of **Madeira**, very luscious and dark brownish in colour. It is served as a **dessert wine** or on its own. The name comes from the **grape**, and this originated in the Mediterranean where its Greek name is Monemvasia, which became Malvoisie or Malvasia. The grape is in fact one of the classic wine grapes of the world, the **Pinot**.

Although the unfortunate Duke of Clarence, brother of King Edward IV, is popularly supposed to have been drowned in a butt of Malmsey while imprisoned in the Tower of London, there seems to be no historical basis for this story. Malmsey is mentioned on several occasions in Shakespeare, but it is possible that the term was used generally for any sweetish, rather rich wine – a popular drink at a time when sugar was expensive and a rarity.

Malo-lactic fermentation   This is part of the **fermentation** process, in which the malic acid in the wine is converted into lactic acid and **carbon dioxide**. A wine undergoing this change will have an odd, flattish smell that can definitely evoke the smell of milk and will certainly not be presenting itself adequately for **tasting**. While the wine is in a large **vat** or in a **cask**, the malo-lactic fermentation can be observed and it passes quickly. It can, however, present many problems if it takes place once the wine has been bottled, for then the sealed container – the **bottle** – may be unable to contain the fizziness of the wine and the **corks** may blow or, at best, the wine may be strange and unsatisfactory to taste.

Certain wines seem to progress without difficulty through the various stages of fermentation, especially today, when the skill of the winemaker enables their evolution to be observed and controlled. Other wines are definitely difficult as regards their malo-lactic fermentation, chiefly because, unless the process takes place actually during the first fermentation or follows it within a fairly short time, it appears difficult to know when it may occur. There is no reason for the ordinary winedrinker to be much concerned with this aspect of winemaking, although the chemist will probably be interested. But, when young wines are being tasted from vat or cask, the possible presence of the malo-lactic fermentation should be remembered. Ideally, most winemakers prefer always to get the malo-lactic fermentation over early in a wine's life. In some cases, they suppress it so as to achieve a greater – i.e. more definite – **acidity** in the ultimate wine.

Malt   See **whisky**.

Malta   A little red and white wine is made on Malta and Gozo, but the quantity, as well as the quality, make it virtually solely for local consumption.

Maltwine   Nothing to do with wine as such, this is a spirit, made by three **pot still** distillations of a mixture of rye, barley and maize. In its original form, Hollands or Dutch **gin** was made by **distilling** maltwine with juniper and other herbs but, due to the expense of maltwine, grain spirit was subsequently used. In contemporary Dutch gin, there will probably only be a very small proportion of maltwine; although 'old' Geneva may contain up to 30% maltwine.

Malvasia, Malvoisie   See **Malmsey, Pinot**.

Malvoisie, Black   See **Cinsaut**.

La Mancha   Adjacent to **Valdepeñas** and almost in mid-**Spain**, this area, associated with Don Quixote, makes a vast quantity of red, white and pink table wine. The Valdepeñas wines appear to have attracted more attention but visitors to Spain should certainly try the La Mancha local wines, for which the curious *tinajas* are used.

Mandarin   Orange flavoured and coloured **apéritif**.

Mandarine   See **orange liqueurs**.

Mandement   Wine region on the west side of Lake Geneva, in **Switzerland**, producing both red and white wines. The latter are supposed to have a taste associated with hazelnuts.

Mandrolisai   Red wine from the mountainous regions of **Sardinia**, which Philip Dallas considers is a type of **Cannonau**.

Mantonico   Wine from **Calabria, Italy**, which Philip Dallas reports as being about 16° of alcohol by volume and virtually a **dessert wine**; although apparently it becomes progressively dry after spending as long as 4 years in **wood**.

Mantua Hills   The Italian name for these wines is Colli Morenici Mantovani del Garda, in the **Lombardy** region of **Italy**. A variety of wines are made but as yet little seems to be known about them.

Manzanilla   See **sherry**.

Maraschino   This is a **liqueur** made from the **distillate** of **fermented** Maraschino cherries. It was originally made in Dalmatia, now part of **Yugoslavia**. It is white in colour and its flavour is especially useful in making many sweet dishes, although it is served as a liqueur as well. A famous brand is that of Drioli, evolved first over two centuries ago in Venice, and still sold in the four-sided straw-cased **bottle**. Another is Luxardo.

Marc   (Pronounced 'Mar') This is the spirit **distilled** from the mass of compressed **grapes** left after the final pressing for wine. It can be a quality product, with distinct regional characteristics. One of the most famous is Marc de Bourgogne, made in **Burgundy**. Marc is always high in **strength** and, unless properly matured, it can be rather raw and fiery. In other words, it is a drink to treat with caution and, possibly, respect.

Marche   Wine region of **Italy**, of which the most famous wine is the dry white **Verdicchio** dei Castelli di Jesi.

Marchese Santeramo   Red wine made in **Puglia**, south of Bari in **Italy**, which Philip Dallas considers 'exceptional' by any standards. Obviously tourists in the area should make an attempt to try it. Simply that it has not got the **D.O.C.** – something that appears to worry some who have reported on this wine – need not concern winelovers who care about wine more than about pieces of paper and sets of regulations.

Marcobrunn, Markobrunn   Vineyard at **Erbach** in the Rheingau (see **Rhine**), which gets its name from the landmark marking the border of the two parishes, **Hattenheim** and **Erbach**, which is a fountain (German being *brunnen*). The wines of Marcobrunn are world-famous. Graf von Schönborn and Freiherr Langwerth von Simmern own important sites within the vineyard, the other owners of significance are the **State Domain** and **Schloss Reinhartshausen**.

Margaux, Château   In the parish of **Margaux** in the Médoc in **France**, this is one of the five classed 1st growths (see **classification**). It has made wine at least since the 15th century. The present elegant house and the beautiful *chai* were designed by Combes, pupil of the great Victor Louis, at the beginning of the 19th century. M. Pierre Ginestet, who formerly owned Ch. Margaux, acquired sole control of it in 1949, and made many modernisations and improvements; in the opinion of many the quality of the wine declined over a certain period because, it was considered, the vineyard was not properly treated after being replanted subsequent to the *Phylloxera*. The vineyard is planted with about 50% **Cabernet Sauvignon** and 35% **Merlot**. The wine, at its best, is very charming with a beautiful **bouquet**, elegant balance and the nobility of great **claret**.

In 1966 the owner decided to market some **château-bottled** non-vintage wine, from both Margaux and his then other estate, **Cos d'Estournel**, but this practice seems to have been dropped. It was a means of appealing to the

American market in particular and, of course, enabled a wine of a certain quality to be ordered anywhere with confidence – at a fairly high price. But lovers of classic **claret**, for whom the variation provided by **vintages** is one of the great fascinations, deplored the idea; although the example was followed by some other proprietors. A little white wine was made at Ch. Margaux also. See **Pavillon Blanc**. The property recently changed hands, and lovers of claret hope that the numerous improvements being made will result in an improvement in the wines as well.

Margaux *Commune* of the **Médoc** famous for the 1st growth, Château **Margaux**. Châteaux **Palmer, Rausan-Ségla, Rauzan-Gassies, Lascombes** and **Le Prieuré** are also well-known names. The wines have great charm and a special type of generous fragrance, plus much fruit, and they are easy to enjoy. In outstanding years they can possess a nobility and firmness of character that enables them to be as great as all but the finest **Pauillacs** – and even then some would dispute this qualification!

Marie Jeanne A **bottle** sometimes used in the **Coteaux du Layon** region of the **Loire**. It looks in shape like a magnum of **Champagne**, but in fact holds only about 1¾ bottles, instead of a full 2 bottles. The shape is the same as a **Burgundy** bottle.

Marillenbrand German **apricot brandy**, made in the south of the country.

Marino Nothing to do with **San Marino**, this is one of the wines of the **Castelli Romani**, from **Lazio** in **Italy**. The white wine is considered the most definite in style, but a pink and a red wine are also made.

Mark A **shipper's** 'mark' is the particular style of a wine that must be followed or copied from year to year, so as ensure continuity of the wine's quality and character. For example, a **sherry** or **port** will be made up to follow an established mark.

Marnique See **orange liqueurs, Australia**.

Marquis d'Alesme-Becker Classed 3rd growth of **Margaux**, and run by the owner of Malescot-St-Exupéry. See **Bordeaux, classification**.

Marquis de Terme Classed 4th growth of **Margaux**, of which the wines are not often seen in the U.K., though they should be of interest because they are made somewhat unusually, being left in the **vat** for a year and then for 2 more years in **wood**. See **Bordeaux, classification**.

Marsala This is one of the major **fortified wines** of the world, although it has fallen slightly out of fashion in recent times. It is made in and around Marsala, in the south of **Sicily**, and was evolved, in its present form, by John Woodhouse of Liverpool, who began exporting it from Marsala in 1773. Further refinements were introduced in its production by Sir Benhamin Ingham, a little after Woodhouse, and by Whitaker, his descendant. There are several large establishments making this wine in Marsala, as well as the three with the English-sounding names: all of the last today are under the control of **Florio**, founded in 1833, which belongs to **Cinzano**.

Marsala is rather a complex wine. It is first made as all wine is made, then small amounts of sweet concentrated *sifone* (see *mistelle*) with **brandy** are added and *vino cotto*, so called because it is heated concentrate. These are **blended** and matured in a *solera* system (the Marsala pipe is 93 gallons or 423 litres), like **sherry**. All fine Marsala is matured for some time; the type described as *vergine* must be at least 5 years old. Although all Marsala is full in character, some exceptional wines are actually quite dry, but of course it is the sweet type that is used for the making of zabaglione.

Dry Marsala can be served like dry **Madeira** or white **port**, as an **apéritif**, or with certain first courses such as antipasto. The sweeter wines are for serving with **dessert** or for enjoying by themselves. Marsala all'uovo is enriched with egg yolk; there are also Marsalas flavoured with almonds, coffee, chocolate, banana, strawberry or mandarin, although these are usually only found in Italian communities.

Marsala is associated with Garibaldi, because he landed at this port before the great march on Rome, and also with Nelson, who ordered 500 pipes of the wine in 1800 for his fleet. The letter of contract with John Woodhouse, showing Nelson's signature with his left hand, is still in existence.

Marsannay-la-Côte One of the villages in the **Côte de Nuits** in **Burgundy**, notable for a very fine rosé wine.

Marsanne See **Rhône**.

Martell One of the greatest of **Cognac** establishments, whose **brandy** dominates the U.K. market. It was founded in 1715 by Jean Martell of Jersey and is still a family business.

Martin One of the big names in **Australian** winemaking. Henry Martin came from England in 1851 and eventually married one of the Clarks, the family who owned **Stonyfell** until adverse economic conditions obliged the sale of the property. Henry Martin worked for the then owner, who was not interested in wine, and achieved great success, the Stonyfell wines winning prizes abroad. The estate is now associated with **Saltram**, but Stonyfell wines continue to enjoy a considerable reputation.

Martina Franca Wines from a region in **Puglia**, **Italy**, where quantities are made – including a **sparkling wine**. Few seem to be exported and many will be used for **blending** and selling to the big **vermouth** concerns.

Martinez Gassiot See **Cockburn**.

Martini, Louis A family-owned **winery** in the **Napa Valley**, **California**. Louis Martini came to the **U.S.** from **Italy** and, after studying in several wineries, founded his own in 1906. The range of wines concentrates on quality lines; the reds in particular are popular for their straightforward ample style. The original Louis Martini did much to pioneer the sale of California wines under American, rather than European style, names. (Nothing to do with **Martini & Rossi**).

Martini & Rossi One of the mighty firms primarily making **vermouth**. It was founded in 1840, in succession to a very old-established house, Martini & Sola. The firm is still a family concern, with world-wide interests in wines as well as vermouth. The headquarters, at Pessione near **Turin**, produces quantities of **sparkling wine**. Pessione is also the site of the Martini Museum, which is one of the most important wine museums of the world.

Marzemino   Red wine from the **Trentino** region of **Italy**, made from the **grape** of that name, and referred to in Mozart's opera *Don Giovanni* as 'excellent'.

Masson, Paul   (Americans stress second syllable, Britons the first). This huge concern belongs to the **Seagram** organisation and has several large installations in Pinnacles, **Monterey**, Saratoga, Soledad and the **Santa Clara Valley**. The wines today are widely known and have even made some impact on the U.K. market. A wide range is produced, including fully **sparkling wines** and a **port** style, which is well reputed. One of their best-known wines is the white Emerald Dry, made from the **Emerald Riesling grape**.

The original Paul Masson, a Burgundian, married a daughter of Charles LeFranc. The latter was already established in the Monterey region, as well as owning **Almadén**. Masson formed his own company in 1892: he survived **Prohibition** because of his permit to make 'medicinal **Champagne**'. Eventually he sold out to Martin **Ray**; Seagrams took over in 1942.

Master of Wine   The Wine and Spirit Association of Great Britain and the **Vintners' Company** instituted the study sessions and examinations which qualify successful candidates for membership of the Institute of Masters of Wine and to use the initials M.W. after their names. The Institute has now detached itself from the Vintners. There are only just over a hundred members, as the written papers and tasting examinations are extremely difficult. They deal with the theory and technicalities of the wines and spirits of the world, plus trade history and practice.

Mastika   Derived from a resinous shrub, this sweetish **Greek** drink is sometimes also used to flavour **ouzo**.

Mataro   See **Mourvèdre**.

Mathius, J.   Winery in **Napa Valley, California**.

Matino   See **Salento**.

Mauzac   See **Blanquette de Limoux**.

Mavrodaphne   Rather a luscious dark brown wine of **Greece**. The name means 'dark Daphne' and is picturesquely supposed to refer to a black-haired girl called Daphne.

Mavron   See **Cyprus**.

de Mayerne, Sir Theodore (1573-1655)   He was one of the two founders of The Worshipful Company of **Distillers**. He was a remarkable man, born in **Switzerland** and studying and working in **Germany** and **France**. He then became Royal Physician to James I, Charles I and Charles II, and was much loved as a doctor, experimenting with numerous things that are taken for granted today, such as calomel. He also investigated enamelwork, devised cosmetics for Queen Henrietta Maria and wrote up his cases with authority and sense. His association with the Distillers was obviously based on his interest in improving the quality of 'strong waters', and 'the making of beeregar and alegar in the Cities of London and Westminster'. A cookery book written by him appeared after his death as well.

Mazer   A drinking vessel, usually of wood bound and mounted with silver or metal, dating from about the 13th to 16th centuries, and found throughout Europe. The Scottish type is usually mounted on a stem as well. See **mead**.

McLaren Vale   Region near Adelaide, in **Australia**, an **old-established** area making fine wines. See **Hardy, Reynell, Southern Vales**.

McWilliam   Important name in **Australian** and **New Zealand** wine history. The firm was founded in 1877, at **Corowa** in the **Murray River** region; but in the early 20th century the McWilliam organisation increased enormously in size, building new **wineries** and establishing vineyards. They have installations in several parts of New South Wales, at Robinvale in Victoria and in New Zealand. In 1932, they became associated with the owner of the **Mount Pleasant** vineyard in the **Hunter Valley**, and later acquired the whole property. The area under vines at all their properties, which include those of Lovedale and Rosehill in the Hunter, is being extended and their installations are apparently very up-to-date. A variety of table wines is made, those from the specific estates achieving considerable quality.

Mead   A very ancient drink, made by fermenting honey. It was made in pre-Roman times in Britain, when – as for many years – honey was the only means of sweetening. It survived as a drink until fairly recently, being made in country houses, but at the present time it is rather a curiosity and not much of a commercial drink, although it is commercially made. The traditional vessel in which it was drunk was called a **mazer**. Metheglin was a type of mead, flavoured and enriched with herbs and spices, which was a speciality of the west of England and particularly of Wales.

Mechanical harvesting   Among the numerous changes in vineyard routines today, the use of the mechanical harvester must be considered as one of the most important, after the **tractor**. The machines – which naturally vary in type and detailed operation – straddle the rows of **vines** and, as they pass over them, paddle-like arms agitate the vegetation so that the bunches of **grapes** are detached and drop into a container. Peas are picked in a similar way in many countries. From reports of results, it would seem that the grapes thus 'vintaged' can be in prime condition and the vines do not appear to suffer from the buffeting they receive. It is true that the mechanical harvesters so far appear to have been used for vineyards on fairly flat surfaces, and they need careful direction by skilled drivers, but it is certain that the use of such machines must increase – if only because of the difficulty of obtaining labour at economic rates in many vineyards. If it can be established that the use of these harvesters does not in any way affect the vines, then the potential of the harvester would appear considerable. It is considered likely that a mechanical **pruning** device may soon be evolved.

Médoc   Region within the **Bordeaux** area, extending from just north of the city of Bordeaux, up the west side of the Garonne estuary. Some of the finest of all **clarets** are produced within it. In the subsection Haut-Médoc, the parishes of **St Estèphe, Pauillac, St Julien, Moulis, Margaux, Cantenac** and Macau all make great and very good wines.

Meerendal   Durbanville wine estate in **South Africa** – the only one of the region. Not under **vines** until this century, known for red and **port** style wines.

Meerlust   Estate on the edge of the **Stellenbosch** region, **South Africa**, granted to its first owner in 1693 and the property of the Myburgh family since 1756. Although some white wine is made, the stress is on reds. The present owner is making interesting experiments with **grape varieties**, as well as having achieved great quality with the different blends of red wines he produces.

Meier   This is the name of a large **winery** in **Ohio, U.S.**, making a range of wines from native **grapes**.

Melon de Bourgogne   See **Muscadet**.

Menthe   See **Crème de menthe**.

Mentuccia   This Italian **liqueur**'s name means 'little bit of mint'. It is sometimes known as *Centerbe*, because it is said to contain 100 herbs from the Abruzzi Mountains. It is also sometimes known by the name of its inventor, (Fr) San Silvestro.

Mercurey   A region in the **Côte Chalonnaise** in southern **Burgundy**, producing mostly red wines of charm and distinction.

Merlot   The full name of this black **grape** is Merlot Noir. It is grown in many parts of the world, in some areas in southern **France**; but its greatest importance is possibly in the **Bordeaux** region, where it is one of the **claret** grapes, being known in the **St Émilion** area as the Bouschet. The Merlot contributes a gracious softness and fragrance to many clarets. **Lafite** is one of the great estates where the charm of wines of a typical year owe much to the plantings of Merlot – the velvety charm can be pronounced. The grape is, however, susceptible to many wine diseases and therefore vulnerable in years that are less than ideal. The Merlot is a grape that is often eaten by vintagers, because it is sweetish and thirst-quenching – whereas most wine grapes are sour and unattractive when raw.

Merrydown   This **winery** and estate of Horam Manor in Sussex is of importance as the headquarters of the English Vineyards Association. See **English wines**. Its directors started by producing **cider**, but extended operations to include **country wines**, made from fruits other than **grapes**. They acted as a **winery** for members of the E.V.A. who did not possess suitable equipment for processing their own grapes. They have an experimental vineyard of considerable importance, sell wines made by E.V.A. members, and issue news about English vineyards. Their own wines are invariably pleasant and well made.

Mersin   A type of **curaçao** made in Turkey, called after the port of that name.

Mertesdorf   Village in the **Ruwer** valley.

Mesclou   A local speciality of the Dordogne Valley in **France**, this is a combination of *eau-de-vie-de-prune*, the 'prune' in this instance being a type of greengage, and *eau-de-noix*, which is made from walnuts. It is an odd drink but well worth trying by the traveller.

Mesimarja   Finnish **liqueur** made from Arctic brambleberries.

Metala   Vineyard established in 1890, near the Bremer River, **Australia**. Its wines are now made at **Stonyfell** and they enjoy considerable repute.

Metheglin   See **mead**.

Methuen Treaty   This treaty, which is frequently referred to in any discussion of **Portuguese** wines, was made between Britain and Portugal in 1703 and, because it provided preferential treatment for Portuguese wines, was a heavy blow to the **French** wine trade in what had been a traditional market. The long-term significance of the treaty, however, was the stimulus it provided for the **port** trade. In 1866, Gladstone terminated the treaty. This is why French wines once again dominated the British winedrinking scene in the latter part of the 19th century.

Methuselah   See **bottles**.

Meunier   Black **grape** belonging to the **Pinot** family, hence its fuller name: Pinot Meunier. It is used in **Champagne** and is apparently sturdy in regions where frost is a menace. It gets its name from being dusty-white like the coat of a miller, the French word for which is *meunier*.

Meursault   Centre of the white wine region in the **Côte de Beaune** in **Burgundy**. A very little red wine is made also. The fine Meursaults are a beautiful golden colour, with marked fragrance and charm and, in certain years, they can last a surprising time as far as white wines are concerned, retaining their qualities. The best-known site names are Les Perrières, Les Charmes, Les Caillerets, Les Genevrières, Les Poruzots and La Goutte d'Or. Admirers of these wines have some justification for considering them the finest white wines in the world.

Mezcal   Sometimes confused both with **pulque** and **tequila**, this is a spirit (*aguardiente*) made in Mexico by **distilling** the liquid produced from the cooked 'pines' of the *Agave* or Maguey plant. It is always drunk straight.

Mézesféher   See **Hungary**.

Micro-climate   This term, which wine enthusiasts may encounter, means exactly what it implies – a particular climate prevailing in a small region. It is the micro-climates of some wine regions which account for the diversity of the wines made therein: for example, the 'draught' that comes through one small opening in a range of hills may freshen a small area, while neighbouring plots suffer from excessive heat and dryness. The rain that waters one allotment-sized patch often tends to stop, as if cut off like a curtain, within a particular range, so that while a vineyard on one side of a small road enjoys adequate rainfall, that on the other side tends to be too wet or too dry. Mists and fogs form more over one plot than another, the angle of the morning sunlight strikes a segment of one vineyard especially favourably, the **aspect** of another catches the maximum amount of warmth during the day. In another, the heat of certain hours of sunshine are captured because of the protection of a rock or slope of land; in yet another the clouds sailing over a nearby ridge tend to break and water one piece of an area, while adjacent sites are mostly dry.

These all contribute to micro-climates, as do the reflections from any water or patch of light-coloured earth, the adjoining plantation of trees or clearances of vegetation and any rise or fall in rivers or levelling of ground. The **vine** is sensitive and, often, the factors that make one quite small plot different as regards climate from its neighbours cannot be easily noted. Perhaps the first recorded instance of anyone perceiving such a thing is the old story of the Emperor Charlemagne noticing that the snows melted soonest around the keep he had built at Ingelheim, which gave him the idea that these slopes might be favourable to vine cultivation, as indeed was so.

Middelvlei   Estate near **Stellenbosch, South Africa**, making both red and white wines, of which the reds have achieved considerable repute.

Midi   Loosely-used term, because the region is not defined. It implies the area to the west of the mouth of the River **Rhône** in **France**, extending through the **Hérault** and **Languedoc**, where a vast quantity and variety of wines of generally ordinary quality are produced. Many of them are intended for **blends** or for making into **vermouth**.

Milawa   Vineyard near Wangaratta, in north-west Victoria, **Australia**. It was established as a farm in 1857 and made its first wine in 1889. The Brown family run it; one of their ancestors married the daughter of the original farmer. Red and white table wines of quality are made, as well as some **fortified wines**.

Mildara   **Winery** established near **Mildura**, in **Australia's Murray River** Valley by the **Chaffey** brothers. Today the establishment has built up a great reputation for its **sherries** and **brandies**, but they now make other red and white table wines the **grapes** for which are drawn from the huge number of small-scale local growers.

Mildew   The most notorious form of this **vine** disease is *Oidium Tuckerii*, so called because it was a Mr Tucker, gardener to a gentleman at Margate, who discovered it in the vine house in 1845. The disease, usually referred to as 'Powdery Mildew', probably came to Europe from the **U.S**. It could have been carried with imported ornamental plants, such as Virginia creeper or vines, as it is found on these plants in the U.S. and Japan, although native American **grapes** appear to have some resistance to it. The mildew attacks leaves, stems and fruit, which fail to grow and eventually die and fall off. By 1852 all the vineyards of Europe and North Africa were trying to deal with this apparently mortal threat to the wine business, although the mildew did not actually kill the vine. However its spores were dispersed by wind and rain, so that it was extremely difficult to combat. Fortunately, it was found that dusting with **sulphur** would check the mildew and protect the vines, because, by increasing the **soil** acidity, the sulphur somewhat disinfected the vineyard as well as the plants. Today this treatment is routine in virtually all vineyards and winegrowers who cannot get sulphur – as occurred during World War II in many instances – have serious difficulties.

The great authority on vine diseases, George Ordish, calls the *Oidium* plague a rehearsal for the subsequent appalling disaster of the ***Phylloxera***. He also makes the interesting point that many of the domestic vines which were trained on trellises and over porches and walls in the country houses of

Britain – either for table grapes or, even at that stage of the 19th century, for winemaking – would have survived if they had ben treated with sulphur. He thinks that it was the failure of such vines, due to mildew, that created the notion that vines cannot be grown even in the south of England – as they are now.

Mildura   Town on the **Murray River**, **Australia**, which became very important in winemaking in the latter part of the 19th century, especially as the result of the achievements of the Canadian-born **Chaffey** brothers. It was W. B. Chaffey who founded the company here which is rather confusing named **Mildara**.

Millburn   This Inverness **whisky distillery** was first established in 1807.

Miltonduff-Glenlivet   Elgin **whisky distillery**, built in 1824.

Minho   (Pronounced 'Meen-yoh') Region in north **Portugal**, where *vinho verde* is made.

Miniscus   This word is not found in the usual dictionaries, but it means the edge or slight bulge of liquid where, within a **glass**, the wine contacts the rim of the vessel. The **colour** of the miniscus can be indicative of many things – according to the original tone and colour of the wine, the rim will usually lighten as the wine ages and, in certain instances, it can show the rate of maturation. The tawny to a pale gold aureole of old **claret** is one example. With some lightish-toned red wines, the miniscus can seem very pale, even bluish. Certain red **Rhône** wines appear almost solidly black-red until they have acquired some **bottle age**. In white wines, the miniscus can also be so light that it is virtually colourless. This point may be the easiest to see some of the delicate lights in the wine: for example, the odd greenish glint in true **Chablis**, unique as far as I know, can be seen at the rim.

Another thing to look for in the miniscus is the way in which the wine clings to the glass – or does not. Some poeple assume that a wine appearing to be thick, almost semi-oleaginous at the rim, leaving long trails down the sides of the glass if swirled around, is inclined to be a sweet sticky kind of wine, but this is not so. The suggestion of a firm texture and an almost glutinous character is usually indicative – in a table wine – of definite character and quality. (See **legs**.) In a sweet wine, of course, the rim will be thicker and more 'oily', and naturally also in many **fortified wines**, but a young claret or red **Burgundy** may indicate its future promise of greatness by this definite, apparently thick miniscus in addition to any indications provided by the colour.

Minorca   See **Majorca**.

Mirabelle   See *alcool blanc*.

Mirassou   **California winery** in San José which owns a number of vineyards in different regions. The first wines were made as long ago as 1858 by a Frenchman, Pierre Pellier, and the original Pierre Mirassou married one of Pellier's daughters. The wines were bulk products until recently, but now the firm is selling under its own **labels**.

Mis en bouteille   *La mise* is the process of putting the wine into **bottle**, as expressed in the French language. The phrases *Mise en bouteille au château,*

Mise du domaine, Mise en bouteille au domaine, Mis en bouteille à la propriété all mean that the wine has been bottled at the estate where it was **vintaged**. But there are other phrases which are sometimes taken to imply estate-bottling, which do not, in fact, mean this. *Mis en bouteille à Bordeaux* (or **Beaune**), for example, which is often seen on the **labels** of fine wines shipped by most reputable firms, simply means that the wine will have been bottled by them in **Bordeaux**. By bottling there, for wines of the region, they simply ensure that the wines do not have to travel far before being bottled.

Mis en bouteille en France on the label of a reputable **shipper**, the address of the French establishment also being given, or phrased as *Mis en bouteille dans nos chais à Beaune*, is equally definite: the wine has not moved far from where it was made, or at least it has not been moved out of the country in which it was made. However the phrase *Mis en bouteille dans nos chais* by itself, with an unknown or fancy-sounding name, is merely pretentious, if nothing worse; as is *Mis en bouteille dans les caves du propriétaire* – for where are those cellars, and who is the owner?

Bottling in the country of origin, if not the actual region, is increasing. But it should be stressed that a British-bottled wine, from a reputable shipper, can also be a wine of quality and, indeed, of interest: it may have matured a little faster than that bottled at the property – to whose progress it therefore will serve as a guide. The very finest wines are always bottled where they are made, simply because there are too many risks attendant on their being transported. See **Château-bottling**.

Mission   **Grape** so called because it appears to have been the first vine brought to **California** for winemaking by the Franciscan, Junipero **Serra**. It is still much grown but does not appear to have produced any wines of special quality.

La Mission Haut Brion   Great estate in **Pessac** (actually some of it is in Pessac and some in Talence) in the **Graves**, just outside **Bordeaux**. The red wine it produces is always fine, with the balance admirably preserved between definiteness of character and discreet nobility. Many people rate the fine wines of La Mission as equal to and often superior to those of **Haut Brion**. The estate, now owned by M. Henri Woltner and his brother, got its name because the vineyard was founded by the priests of the Mission of St Vincent de Paul in the 17th century: they also built the chapel. M. Woltner evolved a system of vinification that was, at the outset, much suspected by his colleagues and competitors, but which seems to have pioneered the controlled system of vinification now seen on many other estates. The wine is not actually bottled at the property, but at the firm's Bordeaux cellars, a special authorisation allowing the *château* label to be used. M. Woltner owns the red wine property of **La Tour Haut Brion**, and also the white wine estate **Laville Haut Brion**.

Mistelle   Grape juice and spirit, used a great deal in the making of certain types of **apéritifs** and **liqueurs**, and sometimes for **vermouth**.

Mittelheim   This Rheingau vineyard (see **Rhine**) gets its name because the village and vineyards are halfway between **Östrich** and Winkel. The best-known site is probably Edelmann.

Mittelmosel   As its name implies, the middle section of the **Mosel**, within which the most important vineyards are situated, extending from Trier down to Alf-Bullay.

Mittelrhein   Region along the **Rhine** from where the River **Nahe** flows into it, to Bonn. The vineyards, on both sides of the river, are not among the most distinguished of the Rhine, but they are certainly extremely picturesque, and the wines they produce can be of better than ordinary quality. Boppard, Oberwesel, **Bacharach**, Steeg and Oberdiebach are names of villages at the centre of vineyards.

Modena   **Italian** region in **Emilia-Romagna**, making various **Lambrusco** wines.

Moelleux   **French** word meaning 'like bone marrow' – that is, soft, concentrated. The word is sometimes seen on the **labels** of French wines and denotes a sweet wine.

Moffat   Inverhouse Distillers, a U.S. firm, took over this firm in 1964 and it now makes a malt **whisky**, Glen Flagler, at its Airdrie **distillery**.

Mogen David Wine Corporation   This **winery**, in Chicago, is possibly the largest in the midwest region of the **U.S.** Known, as its name implies, for **kosher wines**.

Monbazillac   Wine from the **Bergerac** region in the south-west of **France**. It is white and sweet, produced by the action of *Botrytis cinerea* like **Sauternes**. At one time it was widely known and highly esteemed, but nowadays is seldom seen outside the region.

Mondavi   One of the great names in contemporary **California** winemaking. The Mondavi family bought the **winery** that bears their name in 1966. They also own and run Charles **Krug**, and some vineyards as well. **Robert Mondavi** has had a great effect on winemaking and is influential in the **Napa Valley** for his work on the control of quality and his educational efforts among wine appreciation groups. Mondavi wines are restricted in range, but the stress of the production is on quality and in demonstrating the character of single **grape varieties** as grown in the Napa Valley.

Mondavi, Robert   Winery founded in 1966 in **California**'s **Napa Valley** by the widely respected winemaker of that name. He previously worked at Charles **Krug** which the **Mondavi** family bought in 1943.

Monica   A vine that makes several of the **Sardinian** red wines. That of Cagliari is reputed as being of special quality.

Monimpex   The state agency for exporting wines and spirits from **Hungary**.

Monopole   Used as a name alone, this imples 'an exclusivity'. More specifically the term is used for the brand wines of some owners, who thus maintain continuity of quality and who can use their *monopoles* for wines they do not wish to sell as estate wines. Examples of this are Barton & Guestier's Prince Noir, or Calvet's Tauzia Monopole.

Montagne   Estate near **Stellenbosch**, **South Africa**, one part of a larger property cultivated since the beginning of the 18th century. It has only been specifically a wine estate since recent times. There are considerable innovations and improvements being carried out; and the wines, both white and red, achieve progressive quality.

Montagny A *commune* in the Côte Chalonnaise in south **Burgundy**, producing good white wines. Some of these, thanks to modern methods of vinification, deserve to be better known. There are a number of specific vineyard site names which may sometimes be given on **labels**.

Montalbana See **Chianti**.

Montalcino This region in the Siena Hills in **Tuscany**, **Italy**, makes the **Brunello** de Montalcino from a type of **Sangiovese grape**. As produced by the family of Biondi Santi, it is a remarkable red wine, capable of very long maturation in **bottle** and a life of 50 years or more in a good **vintage**. It is not, however, a wine to order casually in a restaurant, because it needs a considerable amount of airing before it is served. People are agreed that it should be opened (it is up to the individual whether or not to **decant**) at the latest early in the morning for serving at dinner and, preferably, 24 hours in advance of drinking: only in this way can the wine show its quality. Drinkers should also be warned that it tends to be in the higher reaches of **strength** as far as table wines are concerned.

Montana Important **winery** in **New Zealand**, established in 1944.

Montánchez Wine village in the **Extremadura** region of **Spain**, which is reputed for its hams and also for a red wine that grows a **flor**. Jan Read relates that it and a white wine that also grows a flor are made in the most simple way here, often in the earthenware *tinajas*. Obviously, both should be sampled by anyone in the vicinity or in such eating-places in Madrid where the wines are on sale.

Monte Aguila Spicy **digestive** Jamaican **liqueur**.

Montecarlo Nothing to do with the town in the south of France, this is in **Tuscany**, **Italy**, near Lucca. Red and white wines are made, the red being apparently similar to **Chianti**, and made from the same **grapes**; the white is mostly **Trebbiano**.

Montefiascone See **Est! Est!! Est!!!**

Montepulciano The full name of this is Vino Nobile di Montepulciano. It comes from **Tuscany** in **Italy**, and is similar to **Chianti**. It is a red wine that benefits by ageing in **bottle**. Its name is supposed to derive from the fact that it used to be the drink of the nobility of the region: it is referred to in the 14th century.

Monterey Important vineyard region in **California**. Many of today's vineyards were established in the mid-19th century. The Salinas Valley is noted as likely to produce first-rate wines in the near future and some of the plantations are of ungrafted classic **vines**. See **Masson**, **Almadén**, **Mirassou**.

Monterrey Region in **Galicia**, **Spain**, making red wines. Jan Read says that they make the strongest wines of Galicia.

Monthélie (Pronounced 'Mon-tay-ly') Village in the **Côte de Beaune** producing red wines and a little white. See **Burgundy**.

Montilla Until the definition of the sherry region in 1933, the Montilla wines were regarded as a type of **sherry**. But in fact they are different, being produced further inland and, although mostly the vineyards are on *albariza* soil, the principal **grape** here is the **Pedro Ximenez**. The wines are fermented in *tinajas* before passing into the *solera* system. They tend in general to be naturally higher in **alcohol** than the wines of Jerez, so that they may not be **fortified** at all, or only slightly. Some are bottled in tapering **bottles**, rather like those used for **hock**.

Montlouis　White wine from the **Loire**, which can be still, *pétillant* or **sparkling**. It has sometimes been likened to **Vouvray**, which is on the north bank of the river, whereas the Montlouis vineyards are on the south. It can be pleasant but is not usually very distinguished. Up to now, it has seldom been seen outside its region, but improved methods of making have permitted some exports.

Montpellier　Estate at Tulbagh in **South Africa**, dating from the early 18th century and carefully restored after the 1969 earthquake, which damaged this house and that of **Twee Jongezellen**. The first owner, Jean Joubert, named the property after his French home town. It now belongs to Mr and Mrs De Wet Theron, a name especially famous in the Tulbagh area; Mr De Wet Theron is also an authority on **brandy**. Montpellier's white wines are well known, their **Gewürztraminer** making a great initial success.

Montrachet　(Pronounced 'Mon-rash-ey') The name derives either from the Latin *Mons rachicensis* or French *Mont arraché* meaning 'the hill from which the trees have been pulled up'. Small vineyard in the **Côte de Beaune** producing very fine dry white wines, and lying partly in both the **Puligny-Montrachet** and **Chassagne-Montrachet** *communes*, which also produce fine white wines. Other vineyards are Bâtard-Montrachet, Chevalier-Montrachet, Bienvenue-Bâtard-Montrachet and Criots-Bâtard-Montrachet. There are certain internal site names (see **Burgundy**) attached to some of these which may be given on the **labels** of the finest wines, but Le Montrachet is the supreme vineyard.

Montravel　(The 't' is silent) See **Bergerac**.

Montrose　(The 't' is not sounded in French, but in English it is optional) The *château* wines of a classified 2nd growth in the *commune* of St Estèphe in the **Médoc**. The name may come from the pinky heather which covers the site, hence 'the pink hill'. See **Bordeaux, classification**.

Mooiplas　**Stellenbosch** wine estate in **South Africa**, farmed since the early 18th century but concentrating on **vines** since the early 1960s. White and red wines are made.

Moonshine　Term used in the 18th century and sometimes since to imply a smuggled spirit, or one home made but escaping paying duty. It has tended to be applied to the various types of **whisky** and whiskey. See **Excise**.

Moorilla　Estate in **Tasmania** near Hobart, first planted in 1964 in a variety of **vines**.

Mor　A region to the north-east of Lake **Balatón** in **Hungary**, producing dry white wines.

Morey-St-Denis　*Commune* in the **Côte de Nuits** in **Burgundy**, famous for outstanding red wines, including those with the **A.O.C.** Clos de la Roche, Bonnes-Mares, Clos-St-Denis and, possibly most famous, **Clos de Tart**. The wines usually combine a charm and easy appeal with a certain elegance and firmness. See **Côte d'Or**.

Morgon See **Beaujolais**.

Moriles Part of the **Montilla** vineyard region.

Morio-Muskat A **hybrid** of the **Sylvaner** and **Pinot Blanc grapes**.

Morocco Wines were made in Morocco in classical times, but it was only when the **French** took control of the country in 1912 that **grapes** for winemaking were cultivated on a large scale. Most types of table wine are made, including a *vin gris* particular to Morocco, but in general it is the reds that are the most successful and popular in export markets. Unfortunately with the tightening of French legislation about wine, it has now been made impossible for Moroccan wines even to pass through France for re-export, something that has seriously affected the wine business. It may well be that the vineyards will have to be abandoned in favour of some other fruit crop. At their best, Moroccan reds can be full-bodied, well balanced and pleasing in the middle ranges of wines, especially when they have had a little **bottle age**.

Morris, George Francis Planted the Mia Mia estate, near Rutherglen in **Australia**, in 1859 after his arrival from Bristol. His family still continue at the property, which is now owned by Reckitt & Colman. A variety of **vines** are grown, but possibly the best known is a **dessert Muscat**.

Mortlach This **Dufftown distillery** dates from 1823 and its **whisky** is described as 'full and fruity'. The church of Mortlach is both beautiful and famous as being where, in 1010A.D., Malcolm II defeated an invading force of Danes.

Moscatel, Moscato See **Muscat**.

Moscatel de Setúbal Defined region near Lisbon in **Portugal** for a particular sweet white wine which is made from Moscatel **vines**, both black and white **grapes** being used. The **fermentation** is checked by the addition of **alcohol**. There is also a red wine of this type, of which little appears to be known. The firm of J. M. da Fonseca at Azeitão have a virtual monopoly of production. The wines have very long lives and are all very sweet with a definite smell and flavour of **Muscat**, according to authority Jan Read.

Moscato d'Asti A wine similar in general style to **Asti Spumante** but lower in alcoholic **strength**. Very seldom seen in the U.K.

Mosel (French: Moselle) This river runs almost directly south to north in central **Germany**, joining the **Rhine** at Coblenz, although the intricacies of its detailed winding make it extraordinary to follow. That explains why the wines from adjoining vineyards may be so different from each other – their outlook can be opposite. The slate topsoil of the best vineyards and the preponderance of the **Riesling grape** account for the quality and delicacy of the finest wines, which can achieve greatness in certain years, and which invariably give pleasure. It is probably true that the Mosel wines are the easiest German wines for the beginner to like, because of their freshness and elegant fruitiness; they also appeal to the knowledgeable because of their naturalness and the way in which they can vary, and they also succeed in producing the great *auslese* and *beerenauslese* wines from the greatest estates. The river is beautiful throughout and the towns and villages very picturesque.

Some of the outstanding vineyards to the north are: **Zell, Leiwen, Neumagen, Trittenheim, Dhron, Erden, Piesport, Brauneberg, Bernkastel, Graach, Wehlen, Zeltingen, Uerzig, Traben-Trarbach** and Enkirch. There are many site names within the vineyards, of which probably the most famous is the Doktor vineyard, above Bernkastel. Other great sites are Wehlener Sonnenuhr, Piesporter Goldtröpchen and Graacher Himmelreich. Some of the most renowned owners in the region are: the **Bischöfliches Konvikt, Vereinigte Hospitien, Bischöfliches Priesterseminar**, all in Trier; J. J. Prüm of Wehlen, Berres of Uerzig, Freiherr von Schorlemer of Lieser; Thanisch, Kesselstadt, and the **State Domain**. The finest wines come from the Middle Mosel (**Mittelmosel**), although those from vineyards above Trier (Upper Mosel) and those below Alf-Bullay (Lower Mosel) can be very pleasant drinks.

Mosel wines, and the wines of the **Saar** and **Ruwer**, which are tributaries of the Mosel, are all presented in elongated green **bottles**. If tradition is being followed, the **glasses** in which they are served may have green stems. The very finest wines, served in their homeland, may be offered in Treviris glasses; these, made in Trier, have rather shallow bowls, with a particular pattern of cutting on them. It is also traditional to offer the finer of two great wines in a smaller glass. Although the lesser Mosels can be served most agreeably with certain foods, the very fine wines are possibly at their most enjoyable when served quite by themselves, or, when the sweeter wines are offered, with a few slightly sweet biscuits or dessert fruit. Then their delicate flavour and beautiful **bouquet** can be fully appreciated.

Moser, Dr Lenz The late Dr Moser, an **Austrian** winemaker, evolved a system generally referred to as that of 'high cultivation', whereby **vines** were allowed to grow high, to escape ground frosts, and mechanical means were worked out so that machines could do much of the hard vineyard work.

Moulin à Vent One of the finer growths of **Beaujolais**, capable of achieving elegance and, in certain years, of maturing for a longish period.

Moulin des Carruades Wine made in certain good years of the second pressings from the **Lafite** vineyards, and entitled to the **A.O.C. Pauillac** if it reaches the requirements of that *appellation*. It is always **château-bottled** and is the monopoly of the huge firm of Nicolas (the largest wine-buying concern in the world) on the condition that it is not sold outside France. See **Carruades de Château Lafite**.

Moulis Vineyard region in the **Médoc** area of **Bordeaux**, making wines capable of achieving subtlety and finesse. They are undeservedly little known.

Mount Eden **Winery** and vineyards in the **Santa Clara Valley, California**, which became worthy of notice when Martin **Ray**, having sold his previous holdings in Santa Cruz, moved to the next slopes. His reputation for making firm, assertive wines had made him famous.

Mount Pleasant (1)   Well-known wine estate in the **Hunter Valley, Australia**, first put under vines in 1880. It was given its name in 1925 by the then owner, Maurice O'Shea, who had studied **vines** and wines in Europe and who henceforth made wines of great quality and exerted tremendous influence on Australian winemaking in general. The property became associated with the **McWilliam** family and business in 1932 and the McWilliams eventually bought it, retaining Maurice O'Shea as manager and director for the rest of his life. He continued to make remarkable wines.

Mount Pleasant (2)   **Winery** and vineyards in Augusta, Missouri, **U.S.**; an old-established enterprise still producing wines from both classic vinestocks and **hybrids**.

Mourisco   One of the black **grapes** used for **port**.

Mourvèdre   Black **grape**, of **Spanish** origin but grown in **France** since the 16th century. It is not a prolific yielder and tends to make hard wines that require a longish period of maturation. It is being planted in certain regions of **Bandol** and the **Côtes de Provence**. Another name used for this grape is the Mataro.

Mousseux   (Pronounced 'moos-ser' stressing 'ser') Term used in **France** and, generally, elsewhere to signify a fully **sparkling wine**. **Champagne** is a *vin mousseux* – but all *mousseux* wines are not Champagne. See *crémant*.

Mouton d'Armailhacq   See **Mouton Baron Philippe**.

Mouton Baron Philippe   This property, previously joined with **Mouton** (**Rothschild**) in the 18th century, was owned by the d'Armailhacq family subsequently, until it was sold back to Baron Philippe de Rothschild in 1933. The Baron gave it his own name in 1956, quite in accordance with the tradition that the estate takes the name of its owner, and also because it was thought that d'Armailhacq was a difficult name to use in commerce. The wine is typical of **Pauillac** and although it is not as *grand* as Mouton Rothschild, it can be very fine. In 1977 Baron Philippe changed the name to **Mouton Baronne Philippe**, in memory of his wife Pauline, who had died in 1976. The wine, of course, has not been altered.

Mouton Baronne Philippe   The renamed **Mouton Baron Philippe**, in memory of Baron Philippe's second wife, the former Pauline Potter. She was an American whose interest and enthusiasm inspired the remarkable wine museum at **Mouton Rothschild**.

Mouton Cadet   This wine, possibly the biggest selling **claret** in the world, was evolved in the slump of 1933. At this time, and with some of the older **vintages**, some of the wine from the great vineyard of **Mouton Rothschild** itself went into the **blend**, but nowadays, although it is claimed that there is always some **Mouton** and some **Mouton Baronne Philippe** in Mouton Cadet, it is essentially a branded wine, bearing only the **A.O.C.** 'Bordeaux'.

It is made at Mouton, but can come from anywhere in the **Bordeaux** region; it always bears a vintage and, for the British market, has had 2 years in **bottle** before being sold. The confusion that sometimes arises about Mouton Cadet is that people often believe it to be the second growth of Mouton itself, like the **Carruades de Château Lafite**, but it is nothing of the kind.

Mouton Rothschild Château Mouton Rothschild, in the parish of **Pauillac** in the **Médoc**, is one of the greatest red wines of the **Bordeaux** region. In 1855, it was classed as 1st of the 2nd growths (see **classification**), but this always seemed unfair to the owners, who have adopted and adapted the famous motto of the great Rohan family (also associated with Bordeaux); '*Roi ne puis, prince ne daigne, Rohan suis*' (I can't be king, I won't be prince, I'm Rohan) as '*Premier ne puis, deuxième ne daigne, Mouton suis*'. Indeed, Mouton has long commanded the same sort of prices and has been assessed on the same level of quality as the other 1st growths. After much campaigning on the part of Baron Philippe de Rothschild, Mouton was categorised as a 1st growth in 1973 and a decree ordains that these wines must be given in alphabetical order.

The name is variously attributed to a hillock (*mothon*); to the Lord of Mouton who was the owner before the Rothschilds acquired it (which seems most likely); and also that it was the little undulations in the vineyard that suggest the woolly backs of a flock of sheep (*moutons*). Mouton always makes a very assertive wine and the proportion of **Cabernet Sauvignon** in the vineyard is high.

Since 1922 the property has been run by Baron Philippe de Rothschild (then 21), who has made it both remarkable and beautiful. It was he who had the idea of commissioning different artists of world fame to design the **labels** for each year since 1945. He and the Baroness also collected and directed the wonderful wine museum in the *château*. Both because of its exhibits – all objets d'art to do with wine – and because of the beauty and ingenuity of the way in which they are arranged, this should be visited by any winelover if possible, although, as the museum is not open, application to see round has to be made in advance.

Mudgee Region in New South Wales, **Australia**, where vineyards were first planted in the middle of the 19th century. The most important single estates appear to be Craigmoor (established in 1858) and the Augustine vineyards, a 20th century planting, but there are many other properties.

Muffa nobile **Italian** term, associated with wines that are *abbocato* or *amabile*. It implies that the **grapes** are allowed to develop *Botrytis cinerea*, but only after they have been picked, not while they are on the vine.

Mülheim **Mosel** vineyard.

Mull Both a noun and verb, this word first appears in the 17th century. It implies a hot drink, normally of wine or beer, with spices and similar flavourings, usually including lemon, and sometimes a beaten egg. By tradition a mull is heated by putting a red-hot poker into it, but it is quite acceptable if simply warmed up, though it must never be allowed to boil.

Müller-Thurgau (Pronounced 'Moo-ler Ter-gow') This is an important white **grape**, a cross of the **Riesling** and **Sylvaner**, or possibly Riesling and Riesling. Evolved in the 1880s, by a Herr Müller from the Canton of Thurgau in **Switzerland**. It was not, however, until the 1920s that **German** winegrowers began to try the grape in their vineyards. It is now well established, as the **variety** can make acceptable wine in an otherwise very bad year.

Müller-Thurgau wines have a fruity style, with a **bouquet** that is obvious, reminding some people of **Muscatel** or **Muscat**. It is now the grape most grown in Germany. Its presence can easily be noted because the vines, when seen from a distance, have a tufty, fluffy appearance, quite unlike the trimmer **Riesling**.

Muratie   Estate at **Stellenbosch, South Africa** that has been farmed since the earliest settlements. The original homestead appears to have been destroyed by fire and the present name comes from *murasie*, meaning ruin. It is run by the present owner, the daughter of Paul Canitz, who bought it in 1925. Current production stresses red wines, particularly the **Pinot Noir**, cultivated here when few other growers even thought of planting it. Miss Canitz has a great reputation for making quality wines.

Murray River   This river valley in **Australia** is of great importance because enormous quantities of wine are made there, also **distilleries** produce **brandy**. But the area is irrigated and, until comparatively recently, it was generally considered that this made it possible only to produce table **grapes** (and other fruit) and make wines intended for distillation. However modern knowledge of **vine** culture and the skilled management of **irrigation** – which is not a mere matter of pouring water over a vineyard so as to increase the size of the grapes, with consequent deterioration of ultimate wine quality – has resulted in great changes.

The knowledgeable Len Evans thinks that the table wines made in vineyards subject to controlled irrigation today can provide pleasant drinks at a low price. The main centre is **Renmark** (the name means red mud): **Berri, Loxton** and **Waikerie** are all names that may be found on wine **labels**.

Murrumbidgee   Huge **irrigated** area in **Australia**, and a region where other vineyards of great importance are sited. Many large concerns have properties there. See **McWilliams, Penfold, Wynn**.

Mus   See **crème de banane**.

Muscadelle   This white **grape** is grown extensively in parts of the **Bordeaux** region, where it contributes a marked perfume and some fatness to the white wines, especially the sweet ones. It is a different grape from the various **Muscats**, but in fact it is not certain if it is related in any way. There are plantations of this grape in **California** and other regions.

Muscadet   A white wine from around Nantes, along the southern banks of the **Loire**. Named after the **grape** from which it is made (originally the Melon de Bourgogne), it is very dry, excellent with shellfish, and at its best when drunk young and fresh. The Muscadet region is subdivided: that called Muscadet de Sèvre et Maine is possibly the best, the other areas are Muscadet du Coteaux de la Loire, and Muscadet. Some estates now bottle their wines in the Muscadet region and sometimes Muscadet is bottled *sur lie*.

Muscadine   Type of **vine** native to the **U.S.**, of which the **Scuppernong variety** is possibly the best known.

Muscat   One of the great white wine **grapes** of the world. It may have come originally from **Greece** and have been brought to **France** by the ancient

Romans. The name for the type most grown in France is Muscat Blanc à Petits Grains, or Muscat de Frontignan. The 'Muscat d'Alexandrie' is a **variety** that makes many wines and can also sometimes be a good table grape. The Muscat is grown fairly extensively to make a single grape wine in **Alsace**; and in some of the New World vineyards it makes pleasant white wines.

The Muscat is one of the very few wine grapes that makes wines that smell definitely 'grapey' – people either like the **bouquet** and flavour very much or cannot enjoy it: 'Muscat – Musk-rat' say many in the latter category! But Muscat wines are very varied: some that smell very opulent and indicate sweetness can actually be dry or even very dry in flavour.

Muscat de Beaumes de Venise   A sweetish wine, made from the **Muscat grape** at Beaumes de Venise in the **Rhône** Valley. It is slightly **fortified** to arrest the **fermentation**, pinkish-gold in colour and not cloying.

Must   Grape juice before **fermentation** turns it into wine.

Mustille   See *vins tranquilles*.

Mycoderma vini   The Latin name for the fungus which forms on the surface of certain wines and which is known in the Jerez region as '**flor**' and in the **Jura** as '*le voile*'. Its formation and action produces a particular taste and style of wine; the best-known example of which is a true *fino* **sherry**.

Myrtille   See *alcool blanc*.

N

Nacional (Pronounced 'Nath-i-o-nal') Term used referring to ungrafted vinestocks in the Douro region of **Portugal**. See **Noval**, *Phylloxera,* **port, vine**.

Nackenheim Vineyard in the Rheinhessen. See **Rhine**.

Nahe (Pronounced 'Naah') This tributary of the **Rhine** joins the greater river at **Bingen**, and the vineyards in the region are situated on porphyry rock. This gives the wines an individual, light but full character, which some people find reminiscent of the delicate **Mosels**, while others liken Nahe wines to certain of the Rheingaus. In general, Nahe wines come to their peak quite quickly, and can have a gentle crispness, often with a very sweet fragrance. The main centres are: Bingen, **Kreuznach** (the Narrenkappe is possibly the most famous site), Schloss Böckelheim (the Kupfergrube, Felsenberg, Mühlberg and Königsberg being well-known sites), **Niederhausen**, Norheim, Roxheim and Rüdesheim – this last being a completely different place from Rüdesheim on the Rhine. Rather as with the **Palatinate** wines, the years that are particularly good on the Nahe do not always coincide with those that are equally so on the Rhine and Mosel.

Napa Valley This district, in **California**, is the most northerly part of what is certainly the most important region for **U.S.** winemaking. Some of the finest wines come from the Napa Valley: many of them are the equal of any that Europe can show, although of course supplies of top wines are inevitably limited and local demand for the best wines makes it difficult for winelovers in other countries to sample the outstanding California wines. The countryside is varied. **Micro-climates** mean that, within a comparatively small area, one **winery** can make a great range of different wines – **dessert** and **apéritif** as well as table wines. This also means that some **vines**, which require a cool climate, can be cultivated on the slopes of the mountains; others, needing more heat, can thrive in warmer, flatter areas. The achievements of the wineries, large and small, is remarkable when it is remembered that, by Old World notions, they are recently established.

Among the best-known producers is **Schramsberg**, famous for its **sparkling wines**, which can be called 'Champagne' in the U.S. They are, in fact, made by

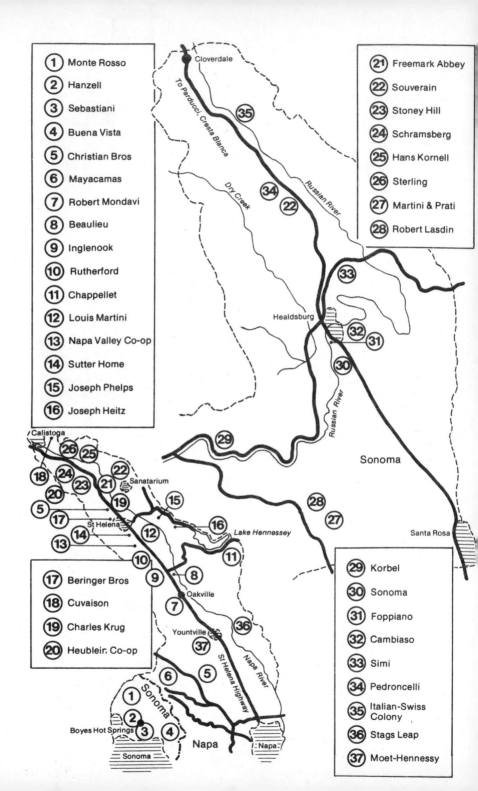

Cloverdale

To Parducci; Cresta Blanca

Russian River

Dry Creek

Healdsburg

Russian River

Sonoma

Santa Rosa

Calistoga

Sanatarium

St Helena

Lake Hennessey

Oakville

Yountville

St Helena Highway

Napa River

Boyes Hot Springs

Sonoma

Napa

Napa

① Monte Rosso
② Hanzell
③ Sebastiani
④ Buena Vista
⑤ Christian Bros
⑥ Mayacamas
⑦ Robert Mondavi
⑧ Beaulieu
⑨ Inglenook
⑩ Rutherford
⑪ Chappellet
⑫ Louis Martini
⑬ Napa Valley Co-op
⑭ Sutter Home
⑮ Joseph Phelps
⑯ Joseph Heitz

㉑ Freemark Abbey
㉒ Souverain
㉓ Stoney Hill
㉔ Schramsberg
㉕ Hans Kornell
㉖ Sterling
㉗ Martini & Prati
㉘ Robert Lasdin

⑰ Beringer Bros
⑱ Cuvaison
⑲ Charles Krug
⑳ Heubleir. Co-op

㉙ Korbel
㉚ Sonoma
㉛ Foppiano
㉜ Cambiaso
㉝ Simi
㉞ Pedroncelli
㉟ Italian-Swiss Colony
㊱ Stags Leap
㊲ Moet-Hennessy

the **Champagne method**, being outstanding in quality. Hans Kornell make quality sparkling and table wines. **Stony Hill**, Cuvaison, **Freemark Abbey**, Spring Mountain, **Beringer**, **Sutter Home**, **Souverain**, **Chateau Montelena**, **Caymus**, La Perla, Yverdon, **Chateau Chevalier**, **Lyncrest**, Burgess, **Diamond Creek**, **Oakville**, **Sterling**, Stonegate, Stone Bridge, **Franciscan Vineyards**, Mayacamus, **Chappelet**, Conradi Vineyard, **Carneros Creek**, Silveroak and Clos du Val are only some of the many medium-sized and smallish wineries and vineyard organisations now attracting attention. Names likely to be known on export markets and belonging to highly important establishments, include: **Beaulieu**, **Christian Brothers** (who own five wineries, three in the Napa Valley), Charles **Krug** (nothing to do with the Champagne firm), Robert **Mondavi**, Louis M. **Martini**, **Inglenook** and **Heitz**.

Nathan & Wyeth   Firm who are developing a vineyard and **winery** at Avoca, in the **Great Western** region of **Australia**. The winery makes quantities of **sparkling wine** by the **Champagne method**.

Navarre   Region in the north of **Spain**, making large amounts of wine, most of which is drunk locally. Some red and white is, however, exported and deserves attention by those who like fairly robust table wines.

Néac   Region north of **St Émilion** in the **Bordeaux** region, producing red wines. Now officially merged with Lalande de **Pomerol**.

Nebbiolo   **Italian** wine **grape** making red wines, which also gives its name to medium range wines in some Italian wine regions. Some of the finest Italian red wines, such as **Barolo** and **Gattinara**, are made from this grape. See **Tuscany**.

Nebuchadnezzar   See **bottles**.

Neckar   See **Württemberg**.

Nederburg   (Pronounced 'Nee-der-berg' stressing 'Nee') One of the most famous **wineries** at **Paarl** in **South Africa**. It was established in the late 18th century by a German: then, in 1936, another German named Johann Graue arrived to make the name world-famous. He developed both the vineyards and the winery, making red and white wines of high quality. Today the property belongs to Stellenbosch Farmers' Wineries and, since 1974, has attracted enormous publicity because of its annual wine auction. This is held in front of the beautiful house, and is attended by buyers from all over the world, who bid for the wines of a number of estates as well as those of Nederburg itself.

Neethlingshof   Estate in the **Stellenbosch** region of **South Africa**, making mostly white wines.

Négociant   (Pronounced 'Nay-go-see-on' stressing 'go') This **French** term is, in full, *un négociant eleveur* and is translated as '**shipper**': that is, someone who buys the wines and subsequently handles or is in charge of them. The precise significance as far as the U.K. wine trade is concerned is difficult to define, because a shipper may also be a retailer or wine merchant, or simply a wholesaler, selling to the retail trade. But the word *négociant* on a **label** of a French wine usually means that the person named is a shipper, because the term *marchand de vin* (literally wine merchant) means, in French, a small-scale distributor – not a wine merchant in the sense that anyone in the U.K. understands the word. Even a small-scale *négociant* is usually someone of substance and it is the shippers of certain of the great wine centres, such as **Bordeaux**, who are sometimes collectively referred to as *la noblesse du bouchon* (the bottle cork nobility).

Negus This drink of hot spiced wine gets its name from Colonel Francis Negus, who invented it in the 18th century. It is usually made with **port**, but any sweetish **fortified wine** may be substituted.

Nénin *Château* in the **Pomerol** region of **Bordeaux**, making fine red wines.

Nervo **Winery** in Sonoma, **California**.

Neuburger **Austrian** white wine **grape**, much used for *heurige* wines.

Neuchâtel **Swiss** wine region on the lake of the same name, making red as well as white wines, although the latter are the most famous. Some of the best should, according to tradition, form 'the star of Neuchâtel' – that is, spread out in a star-shaped slight effervescence – if poured into a tulip-shaped **glass**.

Neumagen **Mosel** vineyard which has been famous for its wines since Roman times, when it was an important shipping port. The stone carving of a ship carrying casks of wine dates from this period. The best-known site is Rosengärtchen.

Neusiedlersee (Pronounced 'Noy-seed-ler-zay' stressing 'seed') Large lake in the Burgenland region of **Austria**, hot and dry. Much wine, including red, is made around it.

New York State Large amounts of wine are produced in New York State: the **Finger Lakes**, **Hudson River Valley**, Niagara and Chatauqua are the most important regions. New England, New Jersey and Pennsylvania are also producers. Native **vines** abounded here when the first settlers arrived but, as these were – and are – *Vitis labrusca*, not *Vitis vinifera* (the wine vine), attempts to make wine from them met with scant success in early times. The wines have an odd smell and taste, sometimes described as 'musky', or 'foxy', that does not appeal to drinkers used to wines made from *Vitis vinifera*. The **Scuppernong**, **Concord** and **Catawba grapes** were developed by early winemakers but, in spite of the popularity of some of the **sparkling wines** made from them, it has been and is difficult for anyone who has some acquaintance with other wines from classic regions to understand and enjoy the assertive wines from this type of vine. There are also regulations affecting production that, while successful with these wines, are so different from those governing the better-known classic wines, that a major readjustment of the palate is necessary for appreciating wines made from the 'native' vines.

Because of this, many **wineries** have begun to experiment with **hybrids**, crossing *Vitis vinifera* and *Vitis labrusca* in various ways, as well as making other wines from classic wine vines. The N.Y. State wines are therefore of enormous interest, being quite unusual, and worth sampling even by those who find them difficult to enjoy. As yet, however, with the possible exception of the huge quantities of **kosher wine** (prepared according to strict Jewish dietary laws) and **sparkling wine** (which it is quite legal in the U.S. to call 'Champagne', even though it is not made by the **Champagne method**), few of the N.Y. State table wines have earned reputations outside their homeland. Visitors should certainly try them and form their own opinions.

New Zealand **Vines** were first planted here in 1819: James **Busby**, the first British Resident, made a **sparkling wine**. But the *Phylloxera* affected the vineyards at the end of the 19th century and not until World War II did the local wine-producers find it easy to market their wines. Today, classic vines are increasingly planted and the quality of the table wines is high enough to cause the major producers to try to launch them on export markets. The most important producers are **Montana**, **Corbans**, **McWilliams** and **Cooks**, but there are many other small firms.

All types of wine – still, **sparkling** (made by various methods), table wines and **fortified** – are made; **liqueurs** and **vermouths**, as well as wines, are made from a huge range of **grapes**, including, as might be expected, the better-known classic types. Some of the **Australian** wine companies have begun to take a serious interest in the New Zealand wine firms and vineyards; and it is likely that the New Zealand wines of the future will display both an individuality due to their special situation and a quality that should make them sought-after even across the world. The winemakers know that it is not possible to create a fine wine in a few years; they are content to improve the quality of what they produce and evolve their own style, with the assistance of all the technical resources on which they are now able to draw.

Niagara Falls Small, recently established **winery** in **New York State**.

Nicasio Small, recently established **California winery**, making a specialised, restricted amount of fine wines.

Nichelini **Winery** in the **Napa Valley, California**.

Niederemmel (Pronounced 'Nee-der-rem-mel') **Mosel** vineyard, of which the best-known site is probably Günterslay.

Niederhausen (Pronounced 'Nee-der-how-zen') Winegrowing region of the River **Nahe** in **Germany**.

Niedermennig (Pronounced 'Nee-der-may-nig') Wine parish in the **Saar** region of **Germany**, which in some years can make outstanding wines. The notable vineyards are Langenberg, Euchariusberg and Sonnenberg.

Niehaus, Dr Charles One of the great wine men of **South Africa**. He has been called 'the founder of the Cape **sherry** industry', but he is also one of the most respected authorities on table wines as well. His work at the **K.W.V.** at the most difficult period just prior to and during World War II cannot be overestimated and, even at what might be considered a great age, he maintains a remarkable judgment and palate for the wines of today. Officially retired, he remains the Mayor of **Paarl**, consulted and admired by all in the wine business both there and in many of the other wine regions of the world.

Nierstein (Pronounced 'Neer-stine') The most important wine district in the Rheinhessen (see **Rhine**). The name comes from the Latin for the spring (*Neri*) and the boundary stone (*stein*) as this region was between the **German** and

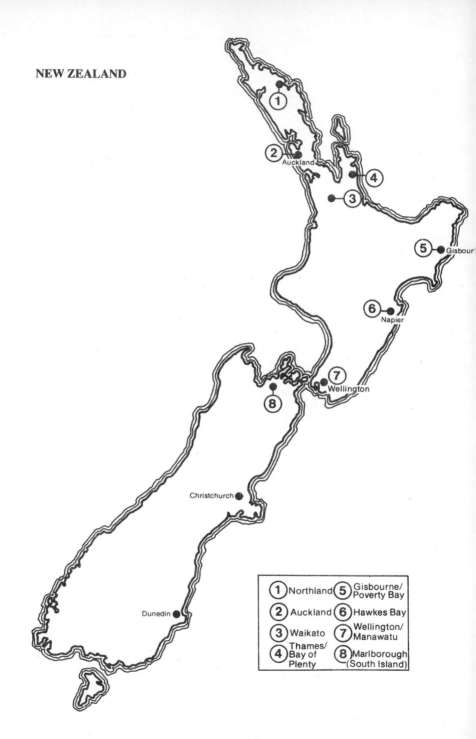

NEW ZEALAND

①Northland ⑤Gisbourne/
 Poverty Bay
②Auckland ⑥Hawkes Bay
③Waikato ⑦Wellington/
 Manawatu
④Thames/
 Bay of ⑧Marlborough
 Plenty (South Island)

Auckland

④

③

⑤ Gisbour

⑥ Napier

⑦ Wellington

⑧

Christchurch

Dunedin

Frankish areas. The **soil** is an unusual reddish sandstone. The finest wines are made entirely from the **Riesling**. There are numerous owners of Nierstein vineyards: Domthal is possibly the most famous site name.

Nietvoorbji The name of the farm north of **Stellenbosch, South Africa**, that houses the O.V.R.I., the Research Institute of the South African Wine & Spirit Board.

Nip A quarter **bottle**. Term usually employed with relation to mineral waters and spirits, but it can be used for wine as well, except that quarters of **Champagne** are usually referred to as 'splits'.

Nipozzano **Tuscan** subdivision of the **Chianti** area, where some *vin santo* is also made.

Noble rot See *Botrytis cinerea*.

Nog It has been said that the nog is the American version of a **wassail** bowl. It seems always to be based on eggs and may either be served from a large bowl, or as an individual mixture. It may also be hot or cold. The nog is invariably a filling drink.

Noilly Prat Louis Noilly founded the great French **vermouth** establishment at the beginning of the 19th century at Lyon, bringing his son-in-law, Claudius Prat into the business, which proved so successful that they moved to Marseilles. The firm is still a family concern, with huge installations at Sète as well as Marseilles and it is they who started the practice of maturing the **casks** of vermouth in the open air, exposed to the atmosphere of the sea and strong sun. Although Noilly Prat is most often associated with dry vermouth, they do make a sweet variety and also produce a *bianco* in their Italian installation.

Noir de Pressac The **Bordeaux** name for the **Malbec grape**.

Non-vintage See **vintage**.

North Para North Para Wines is on the river of the same name, in **Australia's Barossa Valley**. The establishment is not large but the **Hoffmans**, who have today concentrated on making **dessert** and red wines, are today the sixth generation to run the estate. This was first settled in 1848, by a man who had fought in the Prussian army at Waterloo in 1815.

North Port Brechin **whisky distillery**, established in 1820 in Forfar.

Nosing This term is used to refer to the appraisal by the nose of a wine or spirit – that is, sniffing, smelling. In the **sherry** *bodegas*, the wines from the different **casks** are mostly sampled only 'on the nose' and not put into the mouth. The same applies to the sampling of many spirits: Scotch, for example, is mainly 'nosed' by the **blender**, who, as with the **fortified wines**, would swiftly tire his or her palate if the liquid were taken into the mouth.

Noval, Quinta do (Stress second syllable) Probably the best-known single *quinta* or separate estate of the Douro Valley in north **Portugal**. Its wines are usually very fine and the property is additionally distinguished because part of it is still planted with the national vinestock (known as *nacional*), which is not grafted, in spite of the *Phylloxera*. The wine made from this ungrafted stock is kept separate and it is interesting to compare it with the other wine of the estate, a distinct difference usually being apparent, both for the **vintage** and

239

other types of **port**. There are other single *quintas* but Noval's reputation has stood high for a very long time. Noval's 1931 vintage is a particularly outstanding wine, and is considered by some to be one of the finest ports of the 20th century.

Novitiate of Los Gatos **California winery**, owned by the Sacred Heart Novitiate.

Noyau Pale pinkish-yellow **liqueur**, made from peach and apricot kernels, produced by several liqueur establishments. See **apricot** and **peach liqueurs**.

Nuits-St-Georges (Pronounced 'nwee') Parish in the **Côte de Nuits** in **Burgundy**, whose wines may be labelled simply 'Nuits' as well as 'Nuits-St-Georges'. The best-known growths include: Les St Georges, Les Vaucrains, Les Cailles, but there are a large number of sites. The best wines of Nuits tend to be more delicate than those of **Gevrey**, but they have a more assertive appeal than those of **Chambolle-Musigny**. The enormous variation in styles and qualities, however, combined with the appeal of the parish name among English-speaking people, has resulted in both confusion and abuse of a great wine name. The experience of having a genuine (and fairly priced) Nuits-St-Georges, of a particular site, would be a surprise and revelation to many people (although they might consider it expensive). The person who, pronouncing on Burgundy, asserts 'I like Nuits-St-Georges' is admitting great ignorance – the Nuits-St-Georges of Shipper X may be totally dissimilar from the wine of the same name of Shipper Y – and double or half the price! See **Côte d'Or**.

Numbered bottles Although at one time only a few of the greatest properties numbered their **bottles** (by a figure on the **label**), the fashion for doing so is increasing. It does imply a certain limitation of supply and, therefore, should be an indication of quality. It also shows whether the wine was bottled early or late, something which can be of interest in, for example, a great **claret**, because bottles with low numbers can be bottled – when this is done by hand – as much as weeks or even months apart from those with high numbers. The character of the wine may likewise be different. Otherwise it seems to be rather exaggerated as a piece of information about the wine in the bottle.

Nuragus **Sardinian** wine made from the **grape** of the same name. It is white and light in character, and is often used for making **vermouths** and **blending** purposes. The name comes from *nuraghe*, which means a curious type of building, circular in shape, dating from 2000-1000 B.C.

Nuriootpa Large **winery** in the **Barossa Valley**, **Australia**, owned by **Penfolds**.

Nussberger See **Austria**.

Nut liqueurs There are a number of these but, as nuts form a useful food or can be utilised for making sweets, nut **liqueurs** tend to be the specialities of the regions where nuts are abundant. *Eau-de-noix*, made from walnuts, is a Dordogne specialty, crème de noix is a sweeter version of this; crème de noisette is a liqueur made from hazelnuts. Crème mit Nuss is a German liqueur, including hazelnuts and chocolate; Crème de Noyau, a De Kuyper brand, is also known as 'Persico' and is well known in Holland.

O

O.I.M.L. See **proof**.

Oakvale **See Elliott.**

Oakville Founded in 1967 in the **Napa Valley, California, U.S.**, making a range of table wines.

Oban This Argyll **distillery** was built in 1794 by the Stephenson family. In the 19th century it suffered from the collapse of the previously highly successful **whisky** firm run by the Pattison brothers, who were sentenced to imprisonment in 1898. The distillery is now owned by the **D.C.L.** The single malt is said to be of great individuality.

Oberemmel **Saar** vineyard, of which the **Scharzberg** is the best-known site.

Obstbranntwein German term for fruit brandies. Also called *obstwasser*. The **brandy** must be produced without the addition of sweetening agents, **alcohol** or colour. Fruits used are: cherries, plums, mirabelles, sloes, apricots, peaches, bilberries, raspberries, blackberries, blackcurrants, strawberries and rowanberries. See *alcool blanc*, *eau-de-vie* and *wasser*.

Ockfen **Saar** vineyard of which the best-known sites are Bockstein, Geisberg and Herrenberg.

Octave See **casks**. An 'octave of **sherry**' is a range of 8 different sherries. It used to be possible to order such a thing (in 8 **glasses**) in old-fashioned British public houses and the equally old-fashioned (and probably now obsolete) sherry bar. There was the refreshment of a biscuit (see *tapas*) between the sherries. But I doubt that this is now to be found.

Oechsle (Pronounced 'Erk-sler') **German** system for measuring the amount of sugar in the **must**. A degree Oechsle represents the number of grams (0.04 oz) by which 1·75 pints (1 litre) of must is heavier than 1·75 pints (1 litre) of water (the sugar content is about 25% of this calibration). As far as the great sweet German wines are concerned, the higher the degree Oechsle the better, but fine wines in the dry ranges can be made with comparatively low degrees Oechsle. See **proof**, **strength**, **Balling**, **Baumé**, **Gay Lussac**.

Oeil de perdrix Literally 'partridge eye' though who, as has been pertinently commented, really knows the colour of this from personal acquaintance? In fact it implies a pinkness in colour. The term is sometimes applied to **rosé** wines or even to white wines in which a tinge of pink may be seen. It is also a term incorporated in certain branded names.

Oenology The study or knowledge of wine. An oenologist, in a wine firm, is usually the person responsible for the detailed care involved with the making and keeping of the wine – hence he (or she) is usually a scientist.

Ohio Up to the middle of the 19th century, this state was the greatest producer of wine in the **U.S.** Nicholas **Longworth**, at Cincinnati, was famous for the **sparkling wine** he made from the **Catawba grape**. The vineyards unfortunately were virtually destroyed by several **vine** plagues. Recently, however, attempts at a serious vineyard revival have been started in several regions.

Oïdium Tuckerii Powdery **mildew** is one of the great diseases of the **vine** and one which had affected many classic vineyards just before the great *Phylloxera* plague in the 19th century.

Okolehao A Hawaiian spirit, **distilled** from rice and molasses, which can be flavoured with taro root and matured in oak **casks**. A white type is flavoured with coconut juice instead of taro.

Olaschriesling, Olaszriesling See **Rheinriesling**.

Old Fettercairn A centre for illicit **whisky** distilling for centuries, this is now a **distillery** built in 1824.

Old landed See **Cognac**.

Old London landed See **Cognac**.

Old Pulteney The most northerly of mainland malts, this is an old-established **whisky distillery**, now owned by Hiram Walker.

Old Tom See **gin**.

Old Vienna Coffee Liqueur Branded liqueur made in Vienna by Meinl using French **brandy**.

Oldest wine At Speyer in the Palatinate, the Wine Museum has a glass phial containing a liquid. It looks cloudy, but is still definitely wine according to scientists, and is 1,600 years old.

Oliena Dark red **Sardinian** wine, made from the **Cannonau** grape, which apparently tends to be at the limit of **table wine strength** or even a little above – therefore not to be treated casually.

Olivier This property in the parish of Léognan, in the **Graves** south of **Bordeaux**, makes both red and white wines, but far more of the latter. They are sound wines, and are the monopoly of the firm owning the vineyard, Louis Eschenauer. The red was classed in the 1953 **Graves classification**.

Oloroso See **sherry**.

Oltrepò Pavese This **Italian** region is, according to Phillip Dallas, 'an extension into **Lombardy** of the famous **Piedmont** wineproducing hills'. A number of wines are made, the **Barbera** being possibly the best-known; but others, called after classic **grapes**, such as **Moscato** and **Pinot**, also appear. This is the region that produces **Frecciarossa**.

Opening bottles of sparkling wine See **service of wines**.

Opimian In 121 B.C., under the consulship of Opimius, wines of outstanding quality were made in Italy, especially in and around Rome. It is possible that this was the high point of a climatic change: perhaps the region became warmer subsequently. Many classical Latin writers refer to 'Opimian' wine: the poet Martial satirically anticipates our contemporary **wine snobs** by boasting about an Opimium wine 'personally trodden by the consul himself'. **Falernian** wine is particularly associated with the Opimian **vintage**, which was reportedly long-lived: the author Petronius' gourmet Trimalchio in *The Satyricon* was moved to think that his Opimian Falernian was a century old. Such special wines were put into smallish glass phials and sealed with gypsum.

Oporto A grape. See **Blauer Portugieser**.

Oppenheim Vineyard in the Rheinhessen (see **Rhine**) making very large-scale assertive wines which usually enjoy much popularity in export markets.

Opthalmo A grape. See **Cyprus**.

Optic Form of measure used in many British public-houses.

Orange bitters At one time widely used in **gin**, these **bitters** are both tonic and **digestive**. They are rather less popular today, possibly because of the increased use of **tonic** water with gin.

Orange Curaçao See **Curaçao**.

Orange gin See **gin**.

Orange liqueurs There are a number of **liqueurs** based on oranges. There is Aurum, of oranges and herbs, produced at Pescara in Italy; Van der Hum from South Africa, based on the bitter orange-type fruit Naartjie; the best-known brand of this in the U.K. is Bertram's. From **Australia** comes Marnique, a type of orange **brandy**; and the German **Pomeranzen** liqueurs are based on Pomeranzen oranges, both green and orange. There are also many types of Mandarine, made from the peel of tangerines. 'Half and Half' is a blend of Curaçao and **orange bitters**. Filfar is an excellent **Cyprus** bitter orange liqueur. The French firm of **Grand Marnier** makes two famous types: for the Cordon Rouge the orange peel is steeped in **Cognac**, not just **brandy**: the Cordon Jaune is slightly lower in strength; they were first made in 1880. See **Curaçao**.

Oregon Hill Crest Vineyard, in the Umpqua Valley, was founded in 1963 and there are now other **wineries** in production. The coolish climate has meant that their white wines have been the most successful to date.

Ortenau See **Baden-Württemberg**.

Orvieto Possibly the most famous wine of **Umbria** in Italy. There are red wines made, but the best-known are white, and it is the *abboccato* or *amabile* Orvieto that is most highly esteemed. These wines, predominantly from the **Trebbiano grape**, are made by allowing the grapes to develop a type of rot after they have been picked – this, in Italian, is termed *muffa nobile*. There is also a wholly dry white Orvieto. The wines have a curious full, but not wholly sweet, flavour; the dry whites are almost sharply bitter. They are bottled in a wicker-covered **flask**, called a *pulcianello*; the larger is called a *toscanello*.

Östrich (Pronounced 'Er-strich') One of the great Rheingau vineyards (see **Rhine**), producing wines of quality, often distinguished by a full-bodied character. The best-known site is possibly Doosberg.

Oude Meester   Large group of companies operating in **South Africa**, which includes those producing the Fleur du Cap and Bergkeller ranges, many table wines and spirits. It is also responsible for the small but excellent wine museum at **Stellenbosch**. More recently, in the same town, they have opened a very fine **brandy** museum which, to the best of my knowledge, is the only one of its kind in the world.

Ouillage   See **ullage**.

Ouzo   An **apéritif** or **liqueur**, flavoured with **aniseed**. The better types are made by adding aniseed and other herbs to a spirit that has been **distilled** twice. It is drunk chilled and, when water is added, it becomes milky. Made all over the Middle East, it is drunk all the year round but in the Greek Islands, **Cyprus** and Crete, it tends to be drunk mainly in summer. Some Greek ouzo is flavoured with mastic, which has a taste reminiscent of liquorice. Ouzo is never offered without something accompanying it to eat. It should not be kept under refrigeration, as it tends to turn cloudy. Ideally it should be served plain, with a glass of ice-cold water (and ice if wished) to add according to preference.

Overgaauw   (Pronounced – if the non-Afrikaans speaker ventures to try! – 'Ohfer-ch-ah-oh' with the 'ch' as in 'loch'). This is one of the **Stellenbosch** wine estates, under **vines** for at least two centuries and possibly more. It gets its present name from the maiden name of the grandmother of Abraham Julius van Velden, who bought it in 1907. Van Veldens run it still and both their red and white wines are highly respected, although their **Cabernet Sauvignon** is especially outstanding. See **South Africa**.

Oxidise   Term which, for wine, means that the beverage has changed as the result of exposure to the atmosphere, either in a **cask** that has not been topped up (see **rack**) or in an opened **bottle**. Some wines also change **colour** as a result of this. See **maderisation**.

Oxygénée   See **anisette**.

P

P.X.   See **Pedro Ximenez**.

pH   This term is one that is creeping into the vocabulary of many who wish thereby to assert their expertise in matters of wine. My friend Julian Jeffs Q.C., who is qualified to speak on such technicalities, has defined pH for me as 'The term pH stands for hydrogen power and is the measure of the acidity or alkalinity of a solution. . . . Water, or a completely neutral solution, has a pH of 7. If the pH is below 7, it indicates acidity and if it is above 7, alkalinity.' He goes on to cite the work of **U.S.** authorities, Amerine and Creuss, relating to **musts**, and then says 'The measurement of pH will indicate either volatile or fixed **acidity**, or both – and of course both are always present in any wine, since the volatile acids include not only **acetic** (which is produced to a limited extent even in a healthy **fermentation**) but also lactic and others . . . but I urge you not to simplify the matter by suggesting that the pH is determined solely by the amount of acids present. There is always a substantial buffering effect in wine, that is to say a mechanism caused by the presence of salts and the like which helps to keep the pH steady, so that the actual pH is brought about by the balance of a number of factors. The pH of wines varies in the course of the fermentation, for instance when the **malo-lactic fermentation** takes place, when **lees** fall, and so on.' Mr Jeffs further states in his letter to me that, in an average of 47 red **Bordeaux**, the pH figure was 3.4.

The scientist will be able to understand and appraise such information but, as another distinguished scientist friend warns, 'pH doesn't say much about taste . . . Two wines of the same pH can taste quite different, with one having a recognisably bitter and sharp acidic taste which is absent from the other.' This authority explains that pH 'is a scale from 1 to 14. Something which is a very strong acid has a low pH (say, 2 or 3) and a strong alkali has a high pH (10 or 12). Water is exactly neutral, at pH 7. The important thing is that, in the middle of the scale, a slight change of acidity makes a lot of difference to the pH reading, so it is very sensitive in that "delicate" region. So if water is pH 7, an alkaline juice would be around 7.5 or 8: an acidic drink would rate less than pH 7. A drink of pH 6 is going to be more acidic than a drink of pH 6.5.'

So those people who equate the pH figure with the acidity they suppose they note in a wine, are not only oversimplifying the significance of this matter, they are being as silly as those who generalise to the effect that *auslese* wines are sweeter than *spätlese* wines, or who think they can exactly assess alcoholic **strength** merely by **tasting**. It is interesting to know the details of a wine, if such knowledge enhances one's appreciation, understanding and enjoyment. Otherwise, such matters should be put aside while the drinker concentrates on tasting. Sometimes people ask whether a wine's acidity is 'good' or 'bad'? The answer to this must be 'Do you like the wine?' If the acidity balances the fruit in a healthy and well-made wine (however humble), then usually the acidity must be 'right'; if the wine is sour and halfway to being **vinegar**, then of course the acidity is 'wrong', the wine won't taste agreeable. If you really prefer sweetish wines, then you may not personally like a wine with natural high acidity: but there need not be anything amiss with the acidity of that wine.

Paarl Headquarters of the **K.W.V.**, the South African Wine Growers' Association, on the Berg River, and an important centre of production. See **South Africa**.

Pacherenc du Vic Bilh Region in the Pyrenees from which **Madiran** and Portet, a white wine made only after the **grapes** have shrivelled on the vine, come.

Pajarilla White wine from Aragon, in **Spain**.

Palatinate This is a large region of wine production along the slopes of the Haardt Mountains, south of the Rhinehessen. The name comes from the Latin *palatium* or palace (German *palast* or *pfalz*). The title of the province was borne at one time by the Elector Carl, who married the English Princess Elizabeth, daughter of James I. The **soil**, sandy and silicate, with clay, is completely different from that of most of the **Rhine** and **Mosel** vineyards. In addition to the **Riesling**, the **Sylvaner**, **Traminer** and some other **grapes** are cultivated. These two things, plus the more southerly situation, result in Palatinate wines being very assertively fragrant and, in good years which do not always coincide with the successful Rhine and Mosel **vintages**, the flavour of the Palatinate wines is full and rather rich. These wines are not yet well known in the U.K., but they can be extremely pleasing.

The Middle Haardt is the region where most of the vineyards producing the best wines are situated. They include those of Kallstadt, Dürkheim, Wachenheim, Deidesheim, Ruppertsberg and **Forst**; the last is famous for its Jesuitengarten site. One of the most respected owners in the Palatine was Dr Bürklin-Wolf at Wachenheim, and other important owners are Bassermann-Jordan, and Reichsrat von Buhl of Deidesheim. Carl Jos. Hoch is the big firm at Neustadt, and the famous Annaberg estate is where the **Scheurebe** grape, among others, makes very fine wines.

Palette Vineyard area in **Provence**, near Aix-en-Provence, producing white, pink and red wines from a number of **grape varieties**.

Palmela Red wine made in the **Setúbal** area of **Portugal**, near the town of the same name.

Palmer   Classed 3rd growth of **Cantenac-Margaux** which is well known and much respected, often ranking with the finest **Médocs**. Part of the property is owned by the firm of Sichel (**Bordeaux**), hence the Palmer wines are widely known in the U.K. and the **U.S.** The other owners are Mahler-Besse (Dutch) and Mialhe (French). See **classification**. They possess considerable fruit plus finesse, and all the owners are strict about never allowing the property **labels** to be put on a wine that they consider has failed to reach the highest standards. The 'off' years of Palmer, as well as the great ones, have notable charm.

The estate gets its name from Sir Charles Palmer, who bought it after the Napoleonic wars. He was never able to make a commercial success of it unfortunately, and the estate passed into the hands of the Pereire banking family who built the house. The *château* itself, badly damaged inside during World War II, has served as a place where many students of the wine trade have learned the practicalities of vintaging and vineyard work. The produce of the classed vineyard **Desmirail** is now incorporated in Palmer.

Palo Cortado   See **sherry**.

Palomino   One of the world's great wine **grapes**, it is the white grape that gives especial quality to *fino* **sherry**.

Palus   (Pronounced 'Pal-oose') This term, meaning 'marshy', refers to the river bank vineyards in the **Bordeaux** region, and these, in former times, produced the wines considered to be the best. Today they make only fairly ordinary wines although, thanks to improved knowledge and technology, *palus* wines can be pleasant drinks. With the one exception of the Île Margaux, which can be **A.O.C. Margaux**, wines made on the islands in the **Gironde** are also all categorised with the *palus wines*.

Pamid   Bulgarian red wine.

Pantellaria   Small island off the west coast of **Sicily**, especially known for its **Moscato** wines.

Pape Clément   Estate in the parish of **Pessac**, in the **Graves** region south of **Bordeaux**. It got its name because it was presented to the estate of the Archbishops of Bordeaux in 1305 by Bertrand de Goth, Archbishop of Bordeaux before he became Pope Clement V. It has always been reputed for the fine, delicate quality of its wines. For various reasons the estate was in a poor condition after the last war and consequently the wines were not classified when the Graves **classification** was carried out in 1953; but today they enjoy a great reputation and possess unusual charm. It was subsequently classified at the confirmation of this classification in 1959.

Parducci Wine Cellars   These are a family concern in Mendocino County, Sonoma, **California**, producing a range of table wines.

Parfait Amour   This is a **liqueur** based on citrus oils, scented and spiced, and usually made in varying hues of lilac or violet. Many European liqueur establishments still make it, but it seems to have had its main vogue at the turn of the century.

La Parrina   **Tuscan** region in **Italy**, making what are described as **Etruscan wines**, because the area was known to be an Etruscan settlement. The red is a full, supple, agreeable wine; the white, fairly full and somewhat aromatic, is equally so.

Parsac-St-Émilion   See **St Émilion**.

Partinico   **Sicilian** white wine of **apéritif** strength, made near Palermo.

Passe-Tout-Grains   Red **Burgundy** which is made from a mixture of **Pinot Noir** and **Gamay grapes**, 33% must be Pinot Noir. The fruity freshness of the wine can be delightful when it is well made. It does not usually have a very long life.

Passion Fruit   Sweetish **Australian liqueur**, based on citrus fruits.

Passito   Term applied to **Italian grapes** that have been lightly dried in the sun after being picked and before being pressed. This gives them a certain type of sweetness and concentration. The odd name means 'process all the grapes', and dates from the time when small growers were unable to vinify the different **grape varieties** separarely.

Pasteurisation   This process is named after Louis Pasteur (1822-95) whose work on **yeasts** in his native **Jura** established the existence of bacteria: it is a means of sterilising by heat which kills potentially or actually harmful bacteria. However, as with many other things, it is the variability, change and even the chances involved with wine that provide much of the fascination, especially as far as the fine wines are concerned. In killing the bacteria, the maker of the wine risks killing or, as it were, fossilising the wine itself.

There are different methods of pasteurising wine and some authorities consider that certain methods are acceptable, especially for wines in bulk and of a robust, not too fine character, which may otherwise be adversely affected by climatic variations, rough handling in transit and uninformed reception and service on arrival. Certain sweetish table wines can also withstand pasteurisation without harm. But for very fine wines, already in **bottle**, subjection to pasteurisation may mummify what was formerly something alive (those who deny the 'living' character of wine are denying the existence of life in the **yeasts** that make it and the **enzymes** in it).

People who insist on the 'purity' and, therefore, characterless inertia of their wines to the extent of not wanting them to be subject to change – either to improve or deteriorate – would do better to mix themselves something of a chemical nature or restrict their drinking to spirits. The work of the wine chemist and the wine technician are essential; but they should enhance the wines of the world, not degrade them to a uniform insipidity. See **wine snob**.

Pastis   The generic south of **France** name for the local **aniseed liqueurs**. Probably the best known is **Ricard**, with Berger another. The drink is virtually the same as **Pernod**.

Patent still   The patent or continuous still was invented at the beginning of the 19th century, when the commercial potential of various types of spirits began to be recognised. As the operation of the **pot still** requires time and skill, several versions of a still that simply went on producing, making spirits quickly and on a large scale were evolved. The most famous name in the history of this type of distillation is that of Aeneas **Coffey**, whose name is often used for the still that he patented in 1831. Although pot stills are often used for part of the

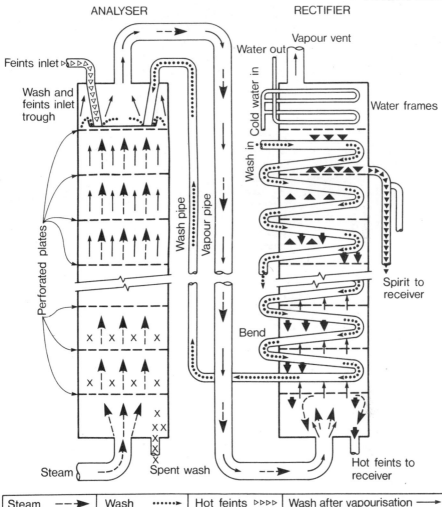

ANALYSER

RECTIFIER

Feints inlet ▷▷▷▷

Wash and feints inlet trough

Vapour vent

Water out

Water in Cold water in

Water frames

Perforated plates

Wash pipe

Vapour pipe

Spirit to receiver

Bend

Steam

Spent wash

Hot feints to receiver

Steam — —▶	Wash ••••••▶	Hot feints ▷▷▷▷	Wash after vapourisation — — ▶
Spent wash xx	Hot feints vapour ➡	Spirit vapour ▶	Spirit ▶▶▶▶

The column on the left is that of the analyser, into which the wash is taken and heated. It will be noted that it is spread in different layers over a surface heated by steam. As the heated wash trickles over the top of the still it passes over perforated plates, made of copper. At the same time, the steam rises through these plates so as to heat the wash which eventually vaporises. The vaporised alcohol (together with its various volatile impurities) rises again to the top of the still, while the residue of the wash is discharged at the bottom. The vapour becomes richer in alcohol as more and more steam is condensed, while the temperature falls.

The vapours that come up to the top of the analyser then pass into the base of the rectifying still, which is on the right. It too consists of a copper column. Within this is a set of horizontal perforated copper plates, in between these a zig-zagging pipe goes from top to bottom of the rectifying columns. This condenses the vapour passing through the rectifier and, as this vapour rises to the top of the column, it can then be directed away into the receiver. At the bottom of the rectifying still various elements remain which will be returned to the analyser for re-processing — continuously.

production of certain spirits, it is the patent or continuous still that makes possible the large-scale manufacture of **gin**, **whiskey** (not Irish) and **vodka**.

In very general terms, the liquid to be **distilled** is trickled down from the top of a tall column – made of copper, like the pot still – through various sections. During this process it is vaporised by the heat of steam pushed into the still. These vapours then rise to the top of this part of the still and subsequently pass into the rectifier, another column of perforated copper plates alongside the analyser or first still. Once again the vapour are forced to the top of the column and are directed off at the top, while any impurities remain at the bottom. The process, which varies according to the type of spirit being made, is complex but not difficult to understand if one can visit a distillery, see the columns, and realise what is going on inside which. These columns can be very large, like huge copper chimneys, or of modest size.

Pauillac *Commune* of the **Médoc** in which, among others, the great properties of **Lafite**, **Latour** and **Mouton Rothschild** are situated. Pauillac wines are usually of definite, some would say 'masculine' character, capable of achieving great magnificence if allowed to develop. They are not wines to choose casually for the beginner in **claret**, unless they are really matured or come from a fairly light year. They can be so big, profound and even hard that they can be difficult to understand. Because of their quality (and price) they deserve skilled handling. However at their peak they are possibly the greatest clarets of all. See **Bordeaux, classification**.

Pavie **St Émilion** classed vineyard, usually making very good wines. See **Bordeaux, classification**.

Pavillon Blanc de Château Margaux This is made in part of the **Château Margaux** vineyard in the parish of **Margaux**, in the **Médoc** in **France**. It is a rare thing to find a white wine in the Médoc, but in this portion of the estate there is a section of chalk where white wine vines are planted. The wine is pleasant rather than fine, and sold only with the **A.O.C.** Bordeaux Blanc as, according to the laws of *appellation*, it cannot have the A.O.C. Margaux.

Pazo Spanish word meaning 'a seignorial residence' according to Jan Read, and used in **Galicia, Spain**, where it signifies quality wines, red, white and pink. Mr Read reports the red is very dry and definitely *pétillant*.

Peach bitters The most famous of these is the recipe evolved about a century ago in Britain by a Mr Law, and these bitters still bear his name. They are prepared from an extract of peach kernel and other flavouring and used at one time to be much used in **gin**-based drinks.

Peach liqueurs See **apricot liqueurs**, for the essential manufacturing procedure is the same. See also **Southern Comfort, Noyau**.

Pearl wines **Australian sparkling wines**, made by the *cuve close* method, usually rather low in **alcohol** and inclined to be sweet. They are popular with young people and have been the introductory wine of many – the stoppers are supposed to be 'popped' or opened with an explosion, to signify gaiety, unlike the correct method of opening fine sparkling wine.

Pécharmant See **Bergerac**.

Pécs (Pronounced 'Petch') Town in Transdanubia in **Hungary** at the centre of important vineyards, dating from pre-Roman times.

Pédesclaux Classed 5th growth of **Pauillac**, which is sold chiefly to the **U.S.**, **Switzerland** and Belgium. See **Bordeaux, classification**.

Pedioncelli, J. **Winery** in the Alexander Valley, **California**, making well-reputed table wines.

Pedro Ximenez (Pronounced 'Him-may-neth' stressing 'may') One of the world's great wine **grapes** and important in the making of **sherry**. Often abbreviated to P.X.

Peg In former times many drinking vessels, especially tankards, would have small pegs, like studs, on the inside marking the measures. Hence the expression 'to drink a peg'.

Pelure d'oignon The term means 'onion skin' and is sometimes used for certain pinkish-orange **rosé** wines, though it can refer to the tinge taken on by some very old wines as a description.

Penedès Region in the hinterland of Barcelona, in the Catalan part of north-eastern **Spain**. Its wines are of high quality and well-known outside Spain these days. Huge quantities of **sparkling wines**, made by the **Champagne method**, are produced, also red, white and pink table wines. Those made by the TORRES establishment enjoy world-wide respect. The area vies with that of **Rioja** for generally producing the finest wines of Spain.

Penfold One of the great names in the **Australian** wine scene, the founder having arrived in the country in 1844. He was a doctor, trained at St Bartholomew's Hospital in London, and brought out **vine** cuttings with him. Later he dosed anaemic patients with the wine he made. His wife and servant worked in the vineyard with him, and his son-in-law eventually came into the business. From the first holding at Magill, the Penfolds – the descendants of the first Dr Penfold added his name to theirs – extended their holdings to other regions, including New South Wales, the **Barossa Valley**, Griffith, the **Hunter River**, **Murrumbidgee** and, most recently **New Zealand**. The **Auldana**, Modbury and Kalimna vineyards are the source of highly respected wines and The Grange, the original cottage of Dr Penfold, is the name put on the most sought-after Penfold wines. **Sparkling**, **fortified** and a huge range of table wines are marketed under the Penfold name.

Penn-Shore **Winery** in Erie County, Pennsylvania, **U.S.**, making a range of wines, of which the **sparkling wine** seems to have been successful and the table wines of interest. **Hybrids**, as well as *Vitis vinifera*, are apparently used.

Perda Rubia **Sardinian** wine, made from the **Cannonau grape**, in red and pink versions. The red is very dark in tone and tends to be slightly above the alcoholic **strength** of **table wine**. The **rosé** is apparently of good quality.

Perelada **Sparkling wine** made by the **Champagne method** in north-east **Spain**. Enormous quantities are produced and the quality is generally good. The name of this brand, made by the Costa Brava Wine Co., is included here, contrary to my usual practice, because it was the subject of the 'Spanish Champagne' case, heard in London in 1960. Twelve **Champagne** houses took legal action against Costa Brava at what the French newspapers excitedly called 'the second Battle of the Marne'. The decision established that the Spaniards could not **label** or sell their wine making any use of the word 'Champagne' and, in 1973, an agreement between France and Spain laid down that no use of the term 'Champagne' or *Champaña* can be made except for wines produced in the Champagne region of **France**. For all that, travellers in Spain will certainly be offered *Champaña* instead of the correct *Espumoso*. [This entry is also included because an otherwise good reference book is, in my opinion, quite wrongly biased about Perelada: the wines are not in any way 'infamous', as the author states in an excess of snobbism.]

Periquita   Red wine made in the **Setúbal** region of **Portugal**. It is also the name of a **grape** and it is perhaps of interest to know that the popularity of the brand name, Periquita, caused the main grape making it to receive the same name.

Perla   **Romanian** white wine made in Transylvania from a blend of the **Muscat**, **Wälschriesling** and **Feteasca grapes**.

Perlant   See *crèmant*.

Perlwein   German term meaning *pétillant*.

Pernand Vergelesses   Region in the **Côte de Beaune** of **Burgundy**, where both red and white wines are made. They lack fame – for which those who wish still to be able to afford fine Burgundy may be thankful – but they are of great delicacy and finesse and, in general, tend to possess a greater subtlety than many Côte de Beaune wines. I cannot begin to agree with one writer who describes the white wines as 'soft and heavy, without the breed of the great wines of Aloxe'. This is the sort of judgment pronounced by those who 'drink the label'. Pernand Vergelesses wines are certainly not like those of **Aloxe**: their close-knit, light, elegant style (when they come from reputable firms) makes them a pleasure to those who appreciate fine Burgundy. See **Côte d'Or**.

Pernod   This drink, based on wormwood with herbs, was evolved in the 18th century by Dr Ordinaire, a Swiss. He sold the formula to a Monsieur Pernod, whose establishment at Pontarlier has produced it ever since. As the original formula contain **absinthe** (subsequently banned by law), the recipe was later changed and Pernod is now flavoured with **aniseed**. It is yellow and is served with iced water, which turns it cloudy. If dripped through a lump of sugar on a special perforated spoon, the drink is made sweeter.

Perry   Alcoholic beverage made from pears, which can be either still or sparkling and is usually slightly sweet. It slightly resembles **cider**. Its best-known U.K. commercial version is Babycham.

Persico   See **nut liqueurs**.

Personal taste   As every experience of tasting is ultimately subjective, it is obvious that uniformity of preferences for drink can never be established – thank goodness! But what many people fail to realise is that, in appraising a wine or spirit, the experienced should be able to stand apart from their personal likes and dislikes and establish some idea of the well-made, good and adequate. No wise winelover will judge a wine (or spirit) as the result of a single tasting experience: they, as well as the beverage, may have been in a better or less good condition than is ideal on the one occasion. Those who consult writings about drinks, should attempt to see whether an author tends to say 'This is good' when what is really meant is 'I like it'. The same applies when one listens to anyone selling wine: do they find good qualities in it that they truly believe are there; or are they inclined to praise it simply because it is made or bought by them, and they have to sell it? The problem is never to be resolved, but its existence should be borne in mind.

Peru   Wine has been made in Peru since the 17th century, when the country was first discovered, but production is limited and exports virtually nil. Peruvian wines are something for the traveller to try on the spot. See **Pisco**.

Pessac   *Commune* just outside the city of **Bordeaux**, within the **Graves** region. The great estates are **Haut Brion** and **Pape Clément**.

Pétillant   French for slightly fizzy. *Pétillant* wines have a little more vivacity than those that are merely *spritzig*, but the amount of bubble in the wine is not legally defined. It is assumed in **France**, however, that a *pétillant* wine will have less than 4 atmospheres behind its **cork**. Many excellent wines, such as the *vinhos verdes* of **Portugal**, have a slight effervescent character but, in a wine of quality, this should never be so pronounced that it takes away from the character of the basic wine. See **pressure**.

Petit Meslier   One of the **Champagne** permitted **grapes**, not much cultivated today.

Petit Verdot   One of the **grapes** used in the making of fine red **Bordeaux**, which gives a certain freshness and beneficial astringency. Not much used nowadays.

Petit Village   **Pomerol** estate making good red wines that, in fine **vintages**, have nothing *petit* about them. See **Bordeaux**.

Petite Champagne   See **Cognac**.

Petite Sirah   Black **grape** which is cultivated in **California**. It does not seem, according to recent studies, to be related to the **Syrah** proper, but to be a type of **Durif** grape. It is cultivated in other vineyards throughout the world and should be appraised in its own right. However the wines I have myself been able to sample do not seem to have attained more than agreeable drinkability.

Pétrus   The best-known and, in the opinion of many, the finest of all the wines of **Pomerol** in the **Gironde** region of **France**. It was developed and established as remarkable throughout the world by a **woman**, Madame Loubat, who had married into the Libourne restaurant family who owned part of the property. The great years of Pétrus are remarkable for finesse and grandeur; the gravel of the Pomerol **soil** lightens the character of the wine so that it can compare with many of the fine wines of the **Médoc**. It possesses great charm and is easy to like, even by beginners.

Pewsey Vale   Vineyard in South **Australia** established in 1847. It was later allowed to decay, but has recently been rehabilitated by **Yalumba** for wine production.

Pez, Château de   Pez is a **bourgeois growth** from **St Estèphe**, in the **Médoc** region of **Bordeaux**, and is owned by a particularly dedicated man, M. Robert Doussans. Not only does he make very good wine as such, but his interest in viticulture and viniculture has resulted in his making a small amount of wine each year from separate **vine varieties** of the area, which students and enthusiasts are allowed to sample. The experience invariably establishes that, although the various **grapes** involved in the making of **claret** each make a distinct and important contribution, the result that the **blend** produces is far more satisfactory as far as the ultimate wine is concerned. This demonstrates how claret is, and must be, made from a mixture of grapes, each of which contributes to the final reputation and quality.

Pfalz   See **Palatinate**.

Phylloxera vastatrix   An aphid which, when brought from America to Europe in the later part of the 19th century, attacked roots of all **vines** and devastated the world's vineyards. As American vinestocks are resistant to it, most vines today are grafted on to American stocks, although some *nacional* ungrafted vines do exist. 'Pre-*Phylloxera* wines' (those from ungrafted stock) tended to be bigger, softer and longer-lived than from today's grafted vines. Experiments with ungrafted stock still continue.

Piat   See **pot**.

Piceno   Red wine from the **Marche** region of **Italy**, reported as light and agreeable.

Pichet   French word for a little jug which may be of wood, earthenware or china, used for wine and, sometimes, **cider**. It seems to have no standard size, but is usually of the capacity of a smallish **carafe**.

Pichon-Longueville   Classed 2nd growth of **Pauillac**. There are in fact two properties now, although originally all were one. That **labelled** without additions, with the suffix 'Baron', or more correctly 'Baron de Pichon', is the elegantly towered *château* on the left of the road as one drives north up the **Médoc**. That labelled 'Comtesse de Lalande' comes from the flat-topped *château* opposite. The Pichon wines are invariably fine; but although the Baron formerly seemed usually to be superior, it is possible that the Comtesse is proving more of a challenge nowadays. See **Bordeaux, classification**.

Picolit   White wine which is considered among the greatest made in **Italy** – when it is well made by a dedicated winemaker and not just a commercial production. It comes from **Friuli-Venezia Giulia** and, because the **vines** were affected by a disease, it became a great and costly rarity, although some is now produced again. It is never cheap. Light to medium gold, it is essentially a **dessert wine**, but has great delicacy and finesse. Anyone given the chance of tasting it at any time should not miss the opportunity.

Picoutener   See **Donnaz**.

Picpoul   See **Folle Blanche**.

Piedmont   **Italian** wine region, around **Turin** in north Italy. It is here that the great Italian reds, including **Barolo**, are produced; also the white **sparkling wines** of **Asti** and the majority of the famous Italian **vermouths**.

Piesport   **Mosel** vineyard of which the Goldtröpchen (little drop of gold), Günterslay and Falkenberg are the best-known sites. The Piesport wines, by virtue of a certain softness, have great popular appeal.

Pimm's   James Pimm evolved his 'original gin sling' in an oyster bar, in Poultry in the City of London, in 1841. It was marketed commercially by his successors in the 1870s. Employees of Pimm's sign an undertaking not to divulge what they may learn of the still secret formula for the recipe; the exact details are known only by the 'Secret Six' of the top men in the company.

The bases of Pimm's Cups were, according to numbers: 1-gin; 2-whisky; 3-brandy; 4-rum; 5-rye; 6-vodka. At the time of writing, only Number 1 is being made. The bottle is marked according to portions, but the drink may be served as a 'short', 'medium' or 'long' according to the desired dilution with fizzy lemonade. Ginger ale is an agreeable variation, and for the opulent; the 'King Pimm's' means dilution with **Champagne** or a quality **sparkling wine**. The trimmings – slices of cucumber, orange, plus a sprig of borage or mint – enhance but are essentially optional. Pimm's must be diluted, both because it is definitely 'strong drink' and because the flavour is not shown off unless minimum dilution is made.

Pinard   French army slang for the wine ration. Not to be confused with **Pinot** or **Pineau des Charentes**.

Pineapple   See **crème d'ananas**.

Pineau des Charentes   An **apéritif** of the Charente region of **France** which is grape juice and **Cognac**. It has its own **A.O.C.** and has a fruity flavour.

Pineau de la Loire   See **Chenin Blanc**.

Pinot   The name, or part of a name, given to one of the great families of wine **grapes** of the world. The Pinot Noir is the grape that makes the finest red **Burgundies**, and is also used to give fruit and body in the **blends of Champagne**. The Pinot Blanc is extensively cultivated in **Alsace**. The Pinot **Meunier** is a white grape of Champagne, so called because the whiteness of the powdery surface of its leaves is reminiscent of a miller's (*meunier*) coat. The Pinot Gris is used in Alsace, where it is sometimes referred to as the **Tokay d'Alsace**, and also elsewhere as Auxerrois, and, in **Germany**, as **Ruländer**.

Other names for the various Pinots include: Klevner and Weissburgunder for the Pinot Blanc in Germany; Malvoisie for Pinot Gris in **France**; **Cortaillod** for the Pinot Noir in **Switzerland**, **Spätburgunder** in Germany, **Savagnin** in France. Different varieties of Pinot are grown throughout the world, some of which may have local or national names. The **Chardonnay** has now been proved to be unrelated to the Pinots.

Pinotage   Black grape evolved in the 1920s at the Cape, **South Africa**, from a cross of the **Pinot Noir** and **Cinsaut** (known there as **Hermitage**). It is a most useful **variety** and its wines, unique to the Cape as far as I know, are sturdy, full-bodied and capable of attaining considerable quality among Cape reds.

Pipe   Type of **cask**.

Pipette   See *velenche*.

Pippermint   See **crème de menthe**.

Piquette   Neither a card game nor a military term, this is a word that in French means the apology for wine that results from adding water to the final pressings of the debris of grapeskins, stems and stalks left in the press. It is the sort of drink that ekes out the wine drunk by the poor and the word, when used in a wine context, means something very feeble and dreary.

Pisco   A type of **brandy** distilled from **Muscat** wine in several South American countries, but most notably in **Peru**. The 'Pisco Sour' is based on Pisco, plus **angostura** and eggwhite.

Pisse-vin   See **Aramon**.

Pitigliano   Southern **Tuscan** region of **Italy** making a light white wine, described as 'smooth but rather bitter'.

Pittyvaich-Glenlivet   Dufftown whisky distillery bought by Arthur Bell, who have built a modern distillery there.

Plavac   The Mali Plavac is apparently a black **grape** used for red wines in central Europe; the white Plavac is used for whites.

Pleasant Valley (1)   Installations in Henderson, **New Zealand**, started in 1902.

Pleasant Valley (2)   An important **winery** in the **U.S.** for historic reasons as well as its wines. It was founded in 1860 and was the first U.S. bonded winery. In 1865 it made the first 'Champagne' produced in **New York State**. This became so popular that, when an enthusiast called it 'the great Champagne of the west', the firm decided to market this wine as '**Great Western**'. This **sparkling wine**, which cannot use the name Champagne in the EEC, was produced even during **Prohibition**, because the company had a monopoly of supplying its wine to the clergy! A wide range of table wines is also made today. In 1962 the company became a subsidiary of **Taylor's** of Hammondsport.

Plonk   A wine of ordinary, everyday quality. Probably originated either in Australia or as the Australian version of *vin blanc*, in World War I.

Plovdina   Serbian red or light red wine, made apparently solely for local drinking. See **Yugoslavia**.

Plymouth gin   See **gin**.

Poire Williams   See *alcool blanc*.

Pokal   This is a type of German ceremonial **glass** or large goblet, elaborately decorated and often engraved and coloured, on a stem and frequently having a cover or lid. *Pokals* are large and require two hands to lift them, certainly when full. They were used for the official drink with which important personages were welcomed, rather like a **loving cup**. The glassworks of Bohemia and Silesia made a number of *pokals* and most museums will have one.

Pokolbin   Hunter Valley region in **Australia**. Pokolbin Winemakers, established in 1970, are the successors to **Drayton's** 'Happy Valley'.

Poland   Wine is not made in Poland, but the country is famous for **vodka**. Many different kinds and flavours are made.

Pomace   The crushed fruit – not necessarily **grapes** – after pressing. Term often used in connection with **cider** or **country wines**.

Pomeranzen   See **orange liqueurs**.

Pomerol   This **Bordeaux** wine region is situated slightly north-west of St **Émilion**. It produces red wines which generally possess a certain delicacy, due to a vein of gravel in the **soil**. Those who like the Pomerols find in them a finesse reminiscent of the great **Médocs**, distinct from the slightly more earthy roundness of the St Émilions. The greatest Pomerol is Château **Pétrus**: other fine estates are Gazin, **Petit Village**, **Nénin**, Lapointe, **L'Évangile**, La Conseillante, Lafleur, Lafleur-Pétrus, Trotanoy and Vieux-Château Certan. A good Pomerol would be an excellent choice to offer someone who wanted a wine with the immediate appeal of the St Émilions, plus the length, depth and finesse of some of the Médoc classed growths. See **classification**.

Pommard Well-known parish in the **Côte de Beaune** in **Burgundy**, making good red wines of firm character. Some of the better-known site names are: Les Rugiens, Les Épenots, Clos de la Commeraine, Les Argillières. See **Côte d'Or**.

Pomponne The type of **glass** associated with the Ordre des Coteaux, the **Champagne wine fraternity**. It is an elongated isosceles triangle, with a knob instead of a foot, so that it cannot be set down but must be drunk off, like a **stirrup cup**. The traditional adjuration to do this is '*Haut le pomponne!*' or 'Empty the *pomponne!*' It is supposed to have got its name because, when Madame de Pompadour passed through Champagne, it was in a glass of this type that she was offered refreshment as she leaned from the window of her carriage, without alighting.

Ponche Soto Dark brown **Spanish liqueur**, put up in a silver bottle.

Pontac (1) Pontac's Coffee House was established in London in the 17th century by Monsieur de Pontac, son of the Mayor of **Bordeaux**, in an attempt to popularise the wines of Blanquefort. Diarist John Evelyn records meeting Pontac there.

Pontac (2) A rather outdated white wine **grape**, a little of which is still grown at the **Allesverloren** estate at the Cape, **South Africa**.

Pontet-Canet Classed 5th growth of **Pauillac**, a very large property belonging to the Cruse family, and unusual in that it is one of the few **Médoc** *châteaux* to have actual personal cellars below ground. (**Lafite**, **Mouton Rothschild**, **Ducru-Beaucaillou** and **Beychevelle** are others.) The wines are never **château-bottled**; unless of course one is invited to a meal at the property, when the personal reserves will have been bottled on the estate. See **Bordeaux**, **classification**.

Pony A measure of spirit of 1 fl. oz (28 g). A pony **glass** is usually rather like a small tumbler, and may be used for **brandy**, **whisky** and other spirits.

Porrón A curiously-shaped container for wine, used in **Spain**. It is rather like a triangular **flask**, with a spout sticking out from the side. It evolved from the wineskin or bag in which wine was carried, from which drinkers would pour wine into their mouths without touching any part of the bag with their lips. Users of the *porrón* do the same, by holding the vessel above their heads, tilting it so that the wine pours in a thin stream from the pointed spout, and catching this in their mouths. It enables several drinkers to share wine from the same vessel without actually touching it – an early example of hygiene.

The use of the *porrón* has become elaborated so that an expert will hold the container a long way away, elongating the stream of wine: some will direct it to flow from their forehead down their noses into their mouth; others will toss the

257

vessel about, varying the stream of wine, swallowing meanwhile. Practice is necessary to be able to do it without getting wine all over oneself!

Port   One of the great **fortified wines** of the world, very much a wine created for the British taste and, in certain instances, seen at the peak of its perfection in the U.K. It is made in a defined area of the upper Douro, in northern **Portugal**, from a variety of **grapes**, both red and white. The grapes, traditionally pressed by foot in a stone trough called a *lagar*, are now often mechanically pressed; or an 'autovinificator' is used, which achieves the same end. At a certain point in the **fermentation** the process is arrested by the addition of **brandy**. The wine, once made, then goes down the River Douro to Oporto or, more correctly, to **Vila Nova de Gaia**, where the port **shippers** have their **lodges** or establishments. Here it is sorted out, differentiated according to quality and the style of wine for which it is destined.

Although the majority of ports are destined to spend their life in **wood** or **cask** (the pipe) the youngish wines can be bottled early and sold as Ruby Port, the colour being as the name implies. A fine ruby, left to mature in wood, will lighten in **colour** and increase in delicacy and may become a fine old Tawny Port. The best of the tawnies are as fine as any fortified wine – and the sort of wine the shippers drink themselves for sheer pleasure. Inexpensive tawnies may be made by blending ruby and white port. White port is used as an **apéritif**; it is made from white grapes only and is a pleasant warm weather drink. The finer white ports are completely dry, the fermentation process being allowed to finish using the grape sugar before the brandy is added. Cheaper white ports can be sweet or slightly sweet.

(People are often confused about the sort of wine that port is – but all port is a fortified wine and therefore of higher **strength** than table wine. All port, because its fermentation has been arrested by the addition of brandy, is possessed of a certain sweetness – but this should be a subtle thing, never cloying, and the wine should be balanced. The ports of each port house will differ in style; vintage ports differ in both according to the style of the house that declares them and their vintage.)

VINTAGE PORT: Some consider this to be the greatest **dessert wine** in the world. It is the wine made from the ports of one single year – which has been 'declared' as a **vintage** by the shipper whose wine it is. It is up to the shipper to decide whether to declare a vintage or not, and although certain years are declared by many port houses, by no means every one declares the same years. Each vintage year, naturally, has its own individuality. The wine selected as a vintage is bottled after spending only 2 or 3 years in wood. In former times it was invariably shipped to the U.K. and bottled there, but vintage ports must nowadays be bottled in Portugal. In former times it might be handled and bottled by a number of merchants buying it, as well as the **shipper** in his premises in the U.K.

The port in bottle is then laid down to mature, a splash on the side of the bottle indicating where its first recumbent position has been. This is important because the formation of the **crust** must be allowed to develop gradually for

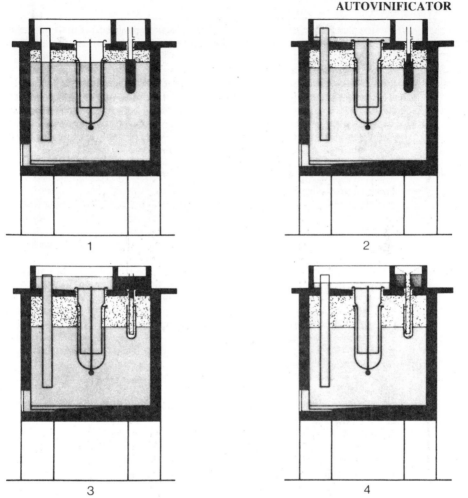

1. *The grapes are crushed mechanically and the juice is pumped into the fermentation tank. The autovinificator is fitted in the centre of the tank: on the right is the water valve; on the left the tube for the must to escape through.*

2. *As the must ferments, it gives off carbon dioxide. This gas fills the space above the must and forces it down as the pressure builds up. The must escapes through the tube on the left and spills — foaming furiously — into the subsidiary tank above.*

3. *At a certain point, the pressure is released and the must spills back into the autovinificator. This forces the water in the water valve up into its tank, thus opening the valve.*

4. *As the must pours through the autovinificator into the main tank, the carbon dioxide is vented through the water valve. As pressure drops and the main tank fills, the water valve closes. Then the whole cycle begins again.*

The natural sugar in the grapes becomes alcohol. At a certain point, the must is drawn off and grape brandy is added. If the fermentation is arrested by this addition at an early stage, the resultant wine is sweeter: the later the arrest of the fermentation, the dryer the wine.

the first 5 or 6 years of the port's life. If the bottle is disturbed at this point, the crust never seems to form satisfactorily and the **deposit** may remain in suspension in the wine, making it unpleasant to drink and spoiling the beautiful **colour**. Vintage port, even in a light year, is not really ready to drink before it is 8 to 10 years old, and ideally not before it is 15 years from its vintage. It can live very much longer than that – ports a century old are still sometimes shown to privileged guests of the port trade. If vintage port has to be moved, it will reform its crust quite satisfactorily, after a certain number of weeks or months, if this has originally formed properly. However it lives on this crust and should always be carefully **decanted** off before it is served.

As the port **bottle** is specially designed to enable the wine to be laid down for a long while – with a long, slightly bulging neck, into which a long, high quality **cork** is inserted – it should be handled with especial care. Because the extraction of a cork can present difficulty after many years, and it may crumble, the neck of the bottle is sometimes taken off. This is done either with heated bottle tongs, or by inserting the **corkscrew** gently into the cork, and then giving the bottle one or more sharp blows upwards under the flange of the lip with the back of a carving knife or similar heavy instrument. The bottle neck will then break neatly off and the wine can be poured – through a filter if there is any danger of glass or bits of cork. (Ideally practise with an empty, recorked bottle beforehand!) The bottle should, of course, have been standing up for at least some days before it is to be drunk. Vintage port should be drunk within 24 hours of being **decanted** as it will fade with exposure to the atmosphere. But ruby, tawny and white port (the last should be chilled) may be served for up to a week after the bottle is opened, or after they have been decanted to show off their colour: there is no deposit.

VINTAGE CHARACTER PORT: A wine of particular quality, blended, and ready for drinking once it has been bottled. It has great appeal, especially in circumstances where people want to drink a fine port but cannot consume a whole bottle – or cannot afford a vintage.

LATE BOTTLED VINTAGE PORT: Port of a single year which has been matured in wood for 3 to 6 years – unlike the 2 to 3 of vintage port – and which therefore is ready for drinking sooner, in fact as soon as it is bottled. It may bear a vintage date and the date when it was bottled. This also is a fine wine, made so that it can be easily drunk without having to be decanted, for the handling and serving of vintage port are not always everyday processes.

CRUSTED PORT: A **blend** of quality ports kept in cask for, possibly, 5 or 6 years before bottling and which therefore may throw a crust. This too is a fine type of port.

SERVICE: Apart from vintage port, which should be decanted at least an hour before serving, ruby and tawny and the others are served at the temperature of the room in which they will be drunk. White port is served chilled. **Glasses** should be of moderate to generous size: those used in many catering establishments are far too small for the port lover to be able to swing the wine around in the glass and enjoy its beautiful **bouquet**. The glorious

colour of fine tawny or vintage port should be appreciated by serving such wines in clear glass or **crystal**, though port decanters, for which Britain is famous, are usually elaborately cut to show off the wine inside the facets of the receptacle. It is traditional always to serve port from a decanter that is passed clockwise around the table – whether or not the tablecloth has previously been removed. This custom is variously attributed to the passage of the sun and certain legends, but in fact it is the most practical way of serving, because a right-handed person can easily pass the possibly heavy decanter over to his left. People help themselves to port, but the host is allowed a 'backhander', which means that he can help the chief guest on his right, who would otherwise have to wait until the decanter had passed right round the table before getting any wine. It is also considered correct always to take some, if only a few drops, of the port as it comes round and not to refuse. If anyone forgets that the decanter is in front of him, traditionalists remark, 'Do you know the Bishop of Norwich (or Winchester)?' This is supposedly because the original bearer of the title was a mean or unconvivial person, who would not pass on the port.

Port is traditionally the wine in which the loyal toast to the Sovereign is drunk at the end of special meals. But, although port is very much the 'Englishman's wine', it must be admitted that the French have drunk far more than the British in recent years, preferring it as an apéritif. They seldom drink it with dessert and indeed seldom drink vintage port. One other curious thing about a fascinating wine is that the great vintages in port in the past seldom coincide with the notable vintage years for table wines. Some of the greatest port years are those of 'off' or even non-existent years for other wines (but improved scientific vinification may change this in the future). Port, according to law, can only be sold as such if it is shipped over the 'bar' or past the spit of land outside Oporto, where the ships pass from the port.

Wines made in similar style are produced in other countries, and can achieve quality, even though they are not in any way the same thing. Some even bear vintage dates, and this can be of interest even to the most dedicated port lover. Although the wines of the Douro are now mostly produced from grafted vines as protection against the *Phylloxera*, there are some regions in the winelands of the world, such as the **Hunter River** in **Australia**, where the vines are still ungrafted and a type of port is made. Wines of port style are also made in **South Africa**, often making use of some of the port grapes. These can be extremely good, as are those of **California**.

Wines which are still, in very small quantities, made from ungrafted vines in the Douro region, will have the description *nacional* on their labels. Wines, also in small quantities, which come from a single property, or *quinta*, will have this denoted on the **label** also. One of the most famous of these is Quinta do **Noval**, where a proportion of the vineyard remains planted with the old, ungrafted *nacional* stock. Other well-known *quintas* are Roeda, **Vargellas**, Bôa Vista, and **Bomfin** to name only a few.

Port is traditionally the wine to lay down at the birth of a child (or the conception if this is a better vintage) for drinking at the twenty-first birthday. It

261

is safe to assume that a vintage wine will be very good, even if not yet at its peak, after this time: it will also be a sound investment.

Port Ellen Whisky distillery on the Isle of Islay, opened in 1825. Now owned by the **D.C.L.**

Portugal A large proportion of this country is under **vines** and, although the wines they produce are not all known on export markets, the wine trade between England and Portugal has been important for eight centuries which is why Portugal is the 'oldest ally'. The most famous Portuguese wine is **port**, which in fact is not drunk as much in its homeland as might be expected, having been virtually created for the British market. **Madeira** is the other great Portuguese **fortified wine**, produced on the island of the same name.

Table wines, red, white and rosé, are produced throughout most of Portugal. In very general terms, it is probably true that Portuguese white wines tend to be superior in quality to many of the reds. Usually, they may be better than most of the white wines of **Spain** of comparable price. But plenty of good red wines are made as well and quality improves year by year. It is interesting that Portuguese table wines have always been marketed for export under their own names as a rule, so that, even when these names are difficult to pronounce for strangers, the wines have earned their popularity in their own right, and have not been even vaguely associated with other classic names.

The *vinhos verdes* of the north are white and red *pétillant* wines, never rosé. In and around the Douro region, good red and some good white table wines, *consumo*, are made as well as port. The **Dão** region, just south of this, is very well known for its table wines. The wines of **Bucelas**, just north of Lisbon, are mainly white and are popular in Portugal, although seldom seen in the U.K. Those of **Colares**, on the coast west of Lisbon, are unusual because the sandy nature of the **soil** is resistant to *Phylloxera* and the vines are therefore not grafted. The wines are curious: the reds are rather earthy in flavour and rather big, though with a distinctive flavour not always easy to like. The sweet wines of Portugal, notably Grandjo, used to be very popular in Edwardian England but nowadays are rarely seen. The Moscato grape (also known as **Muscatel**) can make a pleasant **dessert wine** in many areas. The very local wines of the popular holiday regions, such as the Algarve, have not as yet succeeded in attaining more than pleasantish but ordinary quality. Some **sparkling wine** is also made in Portugal – the dry white wines being a good base. **Brandy** and some local **liqueurs** are also produced.

Posip (1) A white **grape**, which R.E.H. Gunyon supposes to be the **Furmint**.

Posip (2) A white wine made in **Yugoslavia** and enjoying some reputation for quality.

Posset This is a very old word, possibly of Middle English origin, implying a drink of hot milk curdled with ale or wine, flavoured with spices, sugar or honey, and taken as a remedy for a cold or fever. Drinks of this kind, with supposedly restorative properties, are often associated with the **loving cups** served to bride and groom on the wedding night (or restorative refreshments in houses of ill fame) from very early times.

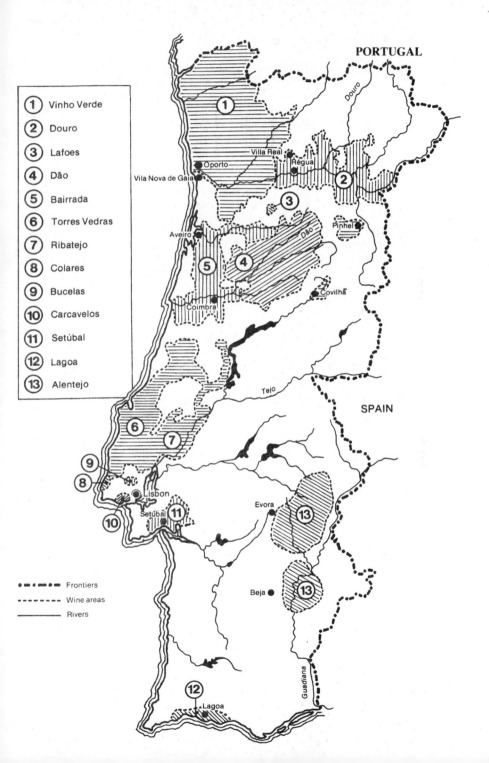

PORTUGAL

1	Vinho Verde
2	Douro
3	Lafoes
4	Dão
5	Bairrada
6	Torres Vedras
7	Ribatejo
8	Colares
9	Bucelas
10	Carcavelos
11	Setúbal
12	Lagoa
13	Alentejo

Villa Real
Oporto
Régua
Vila Nova de Gaia
Douro
Pinhel
Aveiro
Dão
5
4
Covilhã
Coimbra

Tejo

SPAIN

6
7
9
8
Lisbon
Evora
13
Setúbal
11
10
Beja
13

Guadiana

12
Lagoa

•—•—• Frontiers
- - - - Wine areas
——— Rivers

Postgate, Raymond (1896-1971)   One of the most important figures in mid-20th century wine writing. A classical scholar – his professor father made him speak Greek and Latin at meals and he always made his tasting notes in Greek – he was a man of vigorous and practical socialist views; he went to prison in World War I as a conscientious objector, in very much the same spirit as an ancestor of his, the Blessed John Postgate, had gone to the stake for his beliefs. He wrote a number of biographies, books on history, detective stories, founded and edited *The Good Food Guide*, and is much respected for *The Plain Man's Guide to Wine* (1951) and *An Alphabet of Choosing and Serving Wine* (1958). These provided well-written information for the thousands of people who had no background knowledge of wine but wished to learn something about it without encountering the pomposity and snobbishness of certain wine writers.

Raymond was a delightful, hospitable man, whose erudition never clogged his admirable writing style. He was an important witness in the 'Champagne Case' (1960) when certain French **Champagne** houses challenged the Spanish right to use the word 'Champagne' (see **Perelada**). Raymond's cross-examination was interrupted by the break for lunch; so he walked up from the Law Courts to attend a **wine tasting**, looked at the wines, had his own lunch and then returned for the end of the cross-examination. The French won their case and Raymond, asked if he hadn't felt nervous about the break while he was giving evidence, was surprised – he was going to tell the truth, he said, so why should he have been worried? And he wanted to see the wines that were being showed nearby.

Postup   **Yugoslav** red wine of a quality that has made it worth protecting by controls on production.

Pot   (Pronounced 'po') This measure of wine, formerly used in several parts of France, is now associated only with the **Beaujolais** (though it is by no means widely used even there). The bottle resembles an Indian club in shape, and holds about 17·5 fl.oz (50cl). A type of *pot* was recently adopted by the establishment of **Piat** for their Beaujolais wines, and is therefore referred to by them and their agents as a 'Piat de Beaujolais'. They also produce larger bottles of this type.

Pot still   The original device whereby liquids were distilled. It usually consists of a vessel – the pot – in which wine or another fermented liquid is put. The pot is heated and the vapour given off is conveyed from the pot through a long pipe, the 'swan neck', into another receptacle, where it is cooled and becomes a liquid once again. Depending on the type of spirit required, a second or even a third **distillation** may be undertaken. It requires great skill to control the heat of the fire and, once the still starts to run, the process cannot be stopped, so that stillmen often sleep alongside their stills when distilling is taking place. Another decision depending largely on the experience and skill of the operator – even in these days when instruments provide much information and mechanical devices control what were previously rather haphazard operations – is the decision when to cut the 'heads' and 'tails' of the distillate.

These are respectively the liquid that first comes over into the cooling vessel; this may be much too harsh and contain too many impurities to form a harmonious element in the ultimate distillate: the final 'tail' may be weak and insipid. So the stillman directs the distillate to be 'cut' at a certain moment: that is, he directs the first and last parts of the distillate away from the heart or main portion, and these are usually redistilled subsequently. The pot still produces a distillate of individuality; two neighbouring stills of apparently identical design and size, making use of the same water supply and controlled in apparently the same way, will yield different distillates, as has been found in the production of malt **whisky**.

All straight malt Scotch, Irish whiskey and **Cognac** are made by pot stills, also some special **rums**. The pot still is also used for part of the spirit required in many blends of the world's spirits. Originally evolved by the Arabs, for making perfumes, the use of the pot still seems to have been first known in Europe in the 13th century, being probably introduced by the Moors during their occupation of **Spain**. Pot stills are all made of copper. The word 'alembic' means a pot still. See **Coffey still**, **patent still**, Arnaud de **Villanova**.

Poteen, potheen   (Pronounced 'Pot-cheen') This word, which signifies 'little pot', was first used at the beginning of the 19th century and comes from the term **pot still**. In a portable or small form, it could be used to make Irish **whiskey** illegally, without paying the duty to the revenue officers. Some good spirit might be made, some very raw spirit also. Sometimes those **distilling** poteen would take their still out to sea on a boat, so as to ensure that the sea breeze would dissipate the odour of distilling, which might otherwise betray what was going on to the authorities. There are recurrent bursts of interest in poteen but it seems that its chief attraction is that it is illegal – the juvenile thrill of the midnight feast! No one able to drink a decent Irish whiskey could seriously prefer this haphazardly concocted, usually immature spirit. See **Excise**.

Potts   One of the **Australian** wine families. Frank Potts, born in England, established the property **Bleasdale** in 1850 in the Langhorne Creek area. The firm is still run by the Potts family.

Pouget   Classed 4th growth of **Cantenac-Margaux** owned by the proprietor of **Boyd-Cantenac**. See **Bordeaux, classification**.

Pouilly Fuissé   (Pronounced 'Poo-ee Fwee-say') One of the best-known white wines of the **Mâconnais**. The wines, made from the **Chardonnay**, are light, fresh and slightly firm. They used to be considered medium priced or inexpensive, but unfortunately for Europeans they suddenly became popular and smart in the **U.S.** The result was that prices soared and today they tend to be expensive. Areas of the vineyard sometimes named on labels are: Pouilly Vinzelles, Pouilly Loché, Pouilly Chaintré.

Pouilly-sur-Loire   Vineyard region near **Sancerre** in the upper **Loire**. See **Blanc Fumé**.

Poulsard   One of the black **grapes** mainly cultivated in the **Jura** and blended there with the **Trousseau**.

Pouring It may seem simple to pour the contents of a **bottle** into a **glass**, but there is a way to do it that is not only correct, but easy. Hold the bottle round the middle ('A woman by the neck, a bottle by the waist' says the wine trade) and, if it is swathed in a napkin so as to absorb any drips from a bottle taken out of the ice bucket, make sure that your grip is firm. Pour gently, if possible without splashing. Never fill any glass – the level of the wine poured should be one-third or, at most, halfway up the side of the glass. If it is filled in excess of this, the drinker will find it impossible to swirl the wine round and enjoy the **bouquet**, which is one of the pleasures of wine and one that has been paid for.

Do not rest the bottle (or **decanter**) on the side of the glass. If you do, sooner or later you will lean on the glass and upset it. When you have finished pouring, give the bottle or decanter a slight turn (clockwise if you are righthanded) as you begin to lift it away from the glass. This will prevent any drips falling on the tablecloth or table. Practise with a bottle of water if you are not certain how to do this – simply give the bottle a little turn as you lift it. If someone has hardly touched their glass of wine or makes a motion of putting their hand over the glass, this indicates that they do not want any more – do not insist on topping up the glass.

If, on a hot day, the wine has not had time to cool down to a refreshing temperature, pour a small quantity into each glass – people may be longing for a drink – and replace it in the ice bucket until it has cooled adequately. People who keep on topping up glasses can be a nuisance, sometimes they will do so with tepid wine, so that nobody ever gets a properly cool helping; sometimes, too, the drinker wants to concentrate on the wine and finds the 'refreshing' of the glass an interruption. In general, pour an adequate helping from time to time, don't fidget with frequent toppings-up. As the wine in the bottle or decanter is used, make sure that, if you go on pouring right to the last, the wine coming through the neck of the bottle is still bright. Any **deposit** will spoil the look of the wine in the glass and it is better to leave a mouthful in the bottle, that can later be used in the kitchen, than to ruin someone's final drink.

If anyone who is the host orders a second bottle in a restaurant, the **wine waiter** must be requested to allow this to be tasted out of a fresh glass before the glasses of other diners are topped up; should the second bottle be in any way defective, the wine remaining in all the glasses will be spoiled if this is simply poured on top of the contents of the first bottle. See **service of wine**.

Pourriture noble See *Botrytis cinerea*.

Pousse-café This curious drink, seldom made nowadays, consists of different **liqueurs** being poured carefully in layers into a tall **glass**. The heaviest go in first, the lighter liqueurs on the top, and so stay in their layers.

Pousse rapière See **Armagnac**.

Prädikatssekt See *schaumwein*.

Pramaggiore Region in the **Veneto** area of **Italy** where the red wines are reputedly good. The town Pramaggiore is the scene of an annual wine fair.

Preiselbeerlikoer German cranberry **liqueur**.

Premières Côtes de Bordeaux Region within the **Gironde** area, along the north bank of the River Garonne, producing both red and white wines; the latter are possibly the better known. Today these are becoming known on export lists.

Presque Ile These Wine Cellars, in Erie County, Pennsylvania, **U.S.**, are fairly recently established. They make a range of wines from French **hybrids** as well as *Vitis vinifera*.

Pressure The pressure inside a **Champagne bottle** – or that of any quality **sparkling wine** – is measured in 'atmospheres', one atmosphere equalling 15 lb. per in^2 (psi) (1.05 kg per cm^2). The term is easy to understand if one realises that, when air is compressed, it exerts force as when one blows up a balloon. The pressure inside many Champagne bottles is the equivalent of the pressure inside the tyre of a London bus – about 5.5 atmospheres. When the wine goes first into the bottle, the atmospheric pressure inside is slightly higher.

Preuve The **Cognac** version of the *velenche* or *pipette*. A narrow metal cup which can be lowered on a string or cord into a **cask** to take a sample.

Le Prieuré Classed 4th growth of **Cantenac-Margaux** which, because it now belongs to Alexis Lichine and some of his associates (who give it the name 'Prieuré-Lichine'), is well known in the **U.S.** See **Bordeaux, classification**.

Priorato Catalan wine region in **Spain**, getting its name from the 15th century Carthusian monastery called Scala Dei on the Sierra de Montsant. Priorato is actually a district within that of **Tarragona**, but the wines it makes are individual, both dry and sweet, and can achieve very good quality, deserving to be better known.

Prohibition In a drinks context, this means the period when the **U.S.** 'went dry' and alcoholic beverages could not be offered for sale. It began in 1919 (although some States had been dry long before then) and continued until 1933. The rise of gangsterdom as a means of supplying 'bootleg' liquor to the market was immediate, and appalling drinks were put on the market. The necessity for masking the frightful versions of basic spirits, that were often made in the bathtub, caused the great popularity of the **cocktail** and mixes.

Prokupac (Pronounced 'Pro-ku-patch') **Grape** used widely for red wines – to which it sometimes gives its name – in central Europe, including **Yugoslavia**.

Proof A measure of the **strength** of an alcoholic beverage. Proof spirit is a standard solution of pure spirit defined by U.K. **Customs**. Originally the scheme was evolved by a man named Clark in the 18th century, but his **hydrometer** (the instrument whereby the density of liquors – and, hence, their strength – could be calculated) was superseded by that of Sikes (or Sykes) in the early 19th century.

The Sikes system is used today to describe proof, but rather confusingly the U.K. and **U.S.** standards differ. 100% proof means approximately 57% pure **alcohol** by volume. The explanation of strength in terms of alcohol by volume is more easily understood according to the system evolved by the Frenchman, **Gay Lussac**. Thus, in the U.K., proof is about 52% of alcohol by volume, and each 0.5% over or under proof is stated as a degree under or over proof (O.P. or U.P.). But the U.S. proof is 50% of alcohol by volume.

It is a system which, for obvious reasons, will probably be simplified and internationally standardised in the future, but at the present time it is spirits that tend always to be quoted in terms of proof. Wines, both **table** and **fortified**, are more frequently expressed in terms of alcohol by volume (or Gay Lussac) by those familiar with this system and who find proof a complicated way of indicating a fairly simple fact. From 1980, the O.I.M.L. system of determining strength is mandatory in the EEC. This is similar to that of Gay Lussac but, whereas in that the liquid is weighed at 59°F (15°C), the new system weighs it at 68°F (20°C), so there is a minute difference.

Prosecco **Italian** wine region north of **Treviso**, in the **Veneto**, where white wines, still and **sparkling**, dry and sweet, are made. They enjoy good reputations, although they seldom feature on export lists.

Prosek Dalmatian **dessert wine**, which is said not to be **fortified**. See **Yugoslavia**.

Provence The wine region of Provence extends east, north and slightly north-west of Marseilles in the south of **France**. Red, white and rosé wines are made, most of them of no more than everyday quality, although some of the better known **V.D.Q.S.** and now the *vins de pays* are beginning to be popular outside the region. The rosés are robust and suitable for drinking with fish or meat; the reds are easy drinking, usually at their best when quite young; the whites are often rather tough and not as attractive when drunk in a cold, dampish climate as in the sun. A variety of **grapes** are used. Some well-known names seen on labels include: **Cassis** (nothing to do with crème de cassis **liqueur**), **Bandol**, Bellet, **Palette** and **Côtes de Provence**. Frequently unusually shaped **bottles**, decorated attractively with tags and with elaborate **labels** are used; but recent legislation, which has done much to improve the quality of the wines, also controls the manner of presentation.

Prunelle sauvage See *alcool blanc*.

Pruning As with other plants, the method of pruning **vines** is of great importance. The aim is to allow sufficient shoots to develop to bear **grapes** for the forthcoming **vintage**, with the shoots that will develop in the next year being given maximum protection and encouragement. Pruning must be done to keep up the quality yield of a vine, as well as enabling sufficient quantity of **grapes** to grow. In addition, vines in cold vineyards must be pruned so that they are kept aerated and risk as little frost damage as possible; in hot vineyards the pruning must enable the foliage to provide shelter for the fruit against the sun. Different regions use different methods of pruning, according to the vines planted, the type of vineyard (flat, sloping, steeply sloping and so on) and according to the methods of training or propping up the vines. See **trellising**.

Puglia Region in southern **Italy**, where enormous quantities of wine are made; most of it is intended for **blending** or for sending up to the north to make **vermouth**. Although there seems no reason why these wines should not be pleasant drinks on their own, so far those that have come my way on export lists have been nondescript and dull, but there are supposed to be some of reasonable quality.

Puisseguin-St-Émilion See **St Émilion**.

Pulcianello   The 17.5 fl.oz (50cl) straw-covered **flask** in which much of the wine of **Orvieto** is bottled.

Puligny-Montrachet   Parish in the **Côte de Beaune** in **Burgundy**, making some of the very finest white Burgundies. Because of the location, some parts of the great sites are in the parish of **Chassagne-Montrachet** as well. There are several **A.O.C.**s, of which certainly the most famous is **Le Montrachet**, which some would rank as the most outstanding white Burgundy of all. The vineyard's most famous owners are the Marquis de Laguiche, and Baron Thénard. It is very small, and consequently Le Montrachet is always expensive. The autoroute was diverted at enormous cost especially to preserve the integrity of Le Montrachet. Bâtard-Montrachet is possibly the best known of the other **A.O.C.**s from this area.

Pulque   Not to be confused with **mezcal** or **tequila**, this is a Mexican drink, made from the Maguey plant. It is made by piercing the heart of the plant and extracting the sap, which may already be **fermenting**. It may be further fermented or have flavouring added. It is low in **alcohol**. Pulque has not yet been commercially bottled or canned, but it is drunk in large quantities in special pulque bars in Mexico.

Punch   A mixed drink which, although it is nowadays usually assumed will be hot, can in fact be hot or cold. Punches which include milk are more nourishing and can even be non-alcoholic. Punch is usually served from a large bowl ladled out into individual glasses or cups. In the 18th and 19th centuries punch was drunk with meals, rather as mineral water might be today, hence the huge, ornate punch bowls which could stand on the table as centrepieces.

Puncheon   See **casks**.

Punt   The hollow at the base of many wine **bottles**. It serves, in wines that may throw a **deposit**, to retain this in the base of the bottle.

Punt e Mes   Registered name of a type of **vermouth** made by **Carpano** of **Turin**. Its origin, however, is interesting enough to be included. The Carpano establishment – a type of wine bar as well as a shop – was near the Turin Stock Exchange and therefore frequented by dealers. At this time, anyone ordering a drink would specify the particular flavourings, amount of bitterness or sweetness, and so on required. Each was mixed individually from the herbs and spices behind the bar.

One day in 1876, certain stocks had fallen by a point and a half on the Borsa. One businessman, who wanted to order his usual slightly bitter-sweet vermouth, said in Piedmontese dialect, '*Ca'm dag'n Punt e Mes*', signifying 'Give me one and a half "points" of bitterness in my vermouth.' Everyone roared with laughter – but the use of the expression caught on. Eventually Carpano (who had been the first firm to sell vermouth commercially) put the drink up in a bottle.

Purbrick   Well-known name in **Australian** winemaking. Eric Purbrick established the reputation for quality of Chateau **Tahbilk** (*sic*) in the Goulburn Valley north of Melbourne. Red and white table wines, some of them attaining considerable quality, are produced on this estate and by its **winery**.

Putt, puttonyos   Term used to indicate the amount of sweetness and quality in **Hungarian Tokay**. The **putt** is a container holding 6.6–7.7 gallons (30–35 litres) of grapes. Affected by ***Botrytis cinerea***, these (when crushed to a paste) are added to the fermenting **must**, which they make sweet. The number of **putts** indicates the amount of sweetness.

Q

QbA See *Qualitätswein bestimmer Anbaugebiete*.

QmP See *Qualitätswein mit Prädikat*.

Quaich This word comes from the Gaelic *cuach*, meaning a cup which is of Highland origin. It is like a small bowl with lugs or handles, sometimes two, three or four at the sides. Quaichs seem originally to have been made of wood, the more luxurious ones having silver or metal mounts; later they were made mostly of metal. **Whisky** or **brandy** was drunk from a quaich until comparatively recent times: it still is on certain ceremonial occasions in Scotland or among Scots throughout the world such as on New Year's Eve.

Qualitätsschaumwein See *schaumwein*.

Qualitätswein bestimmer Anbaugebiete Term recently introduced by the **German Wine Law** for labelling certain **German** wines. It signifies that the wine so labelled is a quality wine, coming from defined areas of production. Abbreviated to QbA.

Qualitätswein mit Prädikat Term recently introduced by the **German Wine Law** for labelling certain **German** wines. It means that the wine is a quality wine with a title, such as *kabinett*, *spätlese*, *auslese*. A *Prädikatswein* cannot be sugared, but the use of *natur* as a description has ceased. Abbreviated to QmP.

Quart de Chaume A sweetish white wine, from the vineyards around Chaume, in the **Coteaux du Layon** in **Anjou**. It gets its name from the vineyard having at one time belonged wholly to one proprietor, who reserved the personal right to take a quarter (*quart*) of each **vintage**. It can, with maturity, achieve very great quality in certain years.

Quarter See **casks**.

Queensland Wine is made – with some difficulty – in this region of **Australia**. The centre of the industry is the town of Roma.

Quelltaler See **Buring**.

Quetsch A plum **distillate**. See *alcool blanc*.

Quincy A dry white wine from the upper **Loire** which, as it is made from the

Blanc Fumé grape (or **Sauvignon Blanc**), slightly resembles **Pouilly** Blanc Fumé.

Quinta   Portuguese for 'estate'. The word is most used, in wine, to differentiate the various single estates of the Douro region of **Portugal**. See **Noval**.

R

Rabaud-Promis, Rabaud-Sigalas   Originally one vineyard, these are two estates classed as 1st growth **Sauternes**, in the *commune* of **Bommes**. At the present time, Rabaud-Sigalas is generally considered superior. See **Bordeaux, classification**.

Raboso   Red wine from the **Veneto** region of **Italy**. It appears to be well reported, but seems to be little known outside the area.

Rack   Procedure of transferring the wine, after it has been made, from one **cask** to another. According to the type of wine, this is done several times. It serves to take the wine off any initial heavy **deposit** which is left in the cask, allows the casks to be topped up after any evaporation, and lets the supervisers check that all is well with each cask. For a little while after a wine has been racked, it is not usually at its best for tasting.

Radgonda Ranina   **Yugoslav** sweetish white wine, known on U.K. lists as 'Tiger Milk'.

Rainwater   One of the most famous **blends** of **Madeira**, the origin of the term being subject to many interpretations. The firm of Cossart Gordon first marketed it.

Raki   See **arrack**.

Ramandolo (1)   **Veneto** wine from **Italy**, of which little appears to be known. Visitors to the area should attempt to sample it.

Ramandolo (2)   See **Verduzzo**.

Rancio   A term which is applied to certain wines – often **fortified** types – as they age and develop an attractive, special smell. It is a term of commendation.

Raspail   Yellow herby **digestive liqueur**, invented by François Raspail, whom some consider as the forerunner of Pasteur in the history of wine. No longer produced.

Rasteau   Region at the south of the **Rhône** which produces a curious sweetish wine, slightly **fortified**. It can be an agreeable **apéritif** or between-times drink in the region but is seldom seen elsewhere.

Ratafia   An alcoholic drink, usually slightly sweet, formerly served as a between-times refreshment. It is supposed to have received its name from being the drink taken at the signing of any agreement (the Latin words are *Ut rata fiat*). It is rarely seen today, but occasionally a ratafia may be made in a wine region, such as Ratafia de Champagne.

Rauenthal The word means 'rough valley'. This region on the Rheingau (see **Rhine**) is famous for wines which achieve an aristocratic character as well as the delicacy of the finest wines of the area. The Rauenthalerberg site has been under **vines** for seven centuries. The **State Domain**, Graf Eltz and Freiherr Langwerth von Simmern own substantial properties there.

Rausan-Ségla, Rauzan-Gassies Two estates in the **Margaux** region of the **Médoc**, both of them classed as 2nd growths. The vineyard was originally united. At present, the wine of Rausan-Ségla usually tends to be of superior quality. See **Bordeaux, classification**.

Ray, Martin Vineyards in **Santa Clara, California**, making quality table wines and specialising in fine **sparkling wines**. The name comes from the head of the firm.

Raya See **sherry**.

Rayne-Vigneau A classed 1st growth of **Sauternes**, in the *commune* of **Bommes**. See **Bordeaux, classification**.

Recioto Red wine from the **Veneto** region of **Italy**, although wines with this word as a prefix are found in the **Trentino-Alto Adige** also. The word is a shortened form of *orecchi* (meaning 'ears') and implies that only the outer points or ears of the bunches of **grapes** are gathered – that is, the ripest ones.

Rectify Process used in spirit production, whereby the spirit is adjusted, purified or refined. A rectifier may be fitted to a **pot still**. In the **patent still**, the second column is known as the rectifier. See **distillation**.

Red Traminer See **Gewürztraminer**.

Redding, Cyrus A 19th century writer of books on wine whose work remains more original and factually accurate than many.

Redman One of the **Australian** wine families, established by William Redman at **Coonawarra** in 1901. Interestingly the Redman family – at least this branch of it – were abstainers, because Mrs William Redman was a firm Presbyterian! The family expanded their business after World War II and, in 1954, began to market their first wine bearing their own label of Rouge Homme – a literal translation of their name. Bill Redman's son-in-law, Eric Brand, is also an important figure in Australian wine. Both the Redmans and Eric Brand own vineyards as well as making wines which are praised for their quality.

Refosco Dark red wine from **Friuli-Venezia Giulia**, which should be sampled by anyone able to get it in its homeland.

Regaleali Under this **label** some of the best **Sicilian** wines are marketed. This estate of Conte Tasca d'Almerità makes both red and white wines of character and interest.

Rehoboam see **bottles**.

Reil Middle **Mosel** parish, with several well-known sites, including Falklay, Goldlay and Staaden.

Remuage   The process of riddling or shaking and turning whereby the **deposit** in a **bottle** of **Champagne** is progressively directed into the neck of the bottle, so as to settle on the wine's first **cork**. The bottles subjected to this process are put neck down in slotted *pupitres*. They do, in fact, look quite like easels or desks: the first *pupitre* was supposed to have been made at Madame Clicquot's suggestion from one of her upturned kitchen tables. *Remuage* involves both shaking the bottle from side to side and turning it, with a special twist, so that the two types of deposit in the wine – the fine and the sticky – are both moved. The wine must be swung right round inside the bottle. When the *remueur* has finished – each handles two bottles at a time – he both turns the bottle slightly and inclines it at a sharper angle so that, eventually, it is virtually upside down.

The work is highly skilled; so *remueurs* are highly paid. However, in some **wineries** making use of the **Champagne method**, hand labour has been replaced by the use of huge metal frames, into which several dozen bottles can be stacked. These frames have bases with several facets, so that two men can swing the frame to and fro, turning it on the faceted base, and the deposit apparently comes down on to the first cork as required. The use of some mechanical device to achieve satisfactory results is sure to come, but it is yet to be seen whether the frames used in, for example, the **Penedès** region of **Spain** might be equally satisfactory if used in Champagne – the deposit in the wine may be of a different consistency.

Remuage in Champagne lasts from 6 weeks to 3 months, according to the wine. Patrick Forbes, in his great book, states the astonishing fact that a skilled *remueur* can rotate up to 100,000 bottles in a day and oscillate up to 40,000! Most Champagne houses only subject bottles up to the size of a magnum to *remuage* – for obvious reasons; but some stars of the cellars manage to handle jeroboams and at least one man can manage an even larger size. The noise made when the *remueurs* are at work is like that of giants clicking castanets.

Renmark   Town and vineyard region in the **Murray River** Valley, **Australia**, which was first named by George **Chaffey** in 1887: the aboriginal word means 'red mud'. Enormous amounts of wine are made and the area is also significant because many **vine varieties** are cultivated under **irrigation**. It appears that the region supplies many wines of everyday quality. See **Angove, Berri, Loxton, Waikerie, Hardy**.

Retour des Indes   This term, very seldom seen today but once conveying extra quality, was originally used to describe wines (especially **Madeira**) which had been used as ballast in ships making the round trip to India and back. The movement of the vessel and the circumstances of its passing through different climatic conditions produced a certain character in the wine, considered a great asset. These conditions are now imitated by the *estufa* process in the maturing of Madeira. See **East India**.

Retsina   Wine of **Greece** and the Greek islands, **rosé** or white, flavoured with resin. It should be served chilled. The flavour is strong and you either like it very much or you cannot stand it.

Reuilly (Pronounced 'Roy-ee') A dry white wine from the upper **Loire**, rather like **Quincy**, made from the **Sauvignon**.

Reynella This is one of the most famous names in **Australian** wine history. The original John Reynell, from Ilfracombe, Devon, arrived in South Australia in the early 19th century and soon married a fellow-passenger from the ship that had taken him there. Originally a general farmer, he began to concentrate on wine after John **MacArthur** sent him some cuttings. In 1845, when he became most seriously interested in planting vines and making wine, he dug out the Cave Cellar, oldest of its kind in Australia. Later he was obliged to sell some of his land, which went to what became the town of Reynella. Because of the deaths of Reynell menfolk in the two World Wars, the Reynella installations joined the Hungerford Hill Vineyards concern in 1970.

The estate now handles vast quantities of wine, a range of **grapes** being planted, although the stress appears to be on red wines, some **fortified wines** and **brandy**. The original cellar is now a store for special wines and a museum.

Rheims See **Champagne**.

Rheingau See **Rhine**.

Rheinhessen See **Rhine**.

Rheinpfalz See **Palatinate**.

Rheinriesling, Rhineriesling A white wine **grape**, producing some of the finest as well as many of the everyday white wines from rather northern vineyards and also making wine in many parts of the world. Many wines bear the name 'Riesling', although they are made from the **Wälschriesling** or Olaszriesling – a different and less noble grape – which appears all over the world under different names.

Rhine Germany's most famous river, which flows south to north and then east to west, is the centre of its most famous vineyards – or of all of them, if those of the tributary **Mosel** are also included. The region has a long and proud wine history, which is remarkable because these vineyards are situated so far north. The vineyards are comparatively small and production is carried on under difficulties, because of the climatic risks; but modern vinification enables at least moderately good wine to be made in years which before might have proved disastrous. The great **grape** of the region is, as might be expected, the **Riesling**. At the famous estates, it can produce wines of remarkable **bouquet**, fruit, subtlety and delicacy in certain years. But other grape **varieties**, including the **Sylvaner** and **Müller-Thurgau**, are now used. Rhine wines can also be among some of the most expensive wines in the world when wines of specific qualities (see **Germany**) are concerned. Many pleasant regional wines are also made, for immediate or short-term drinking. All are bottled in elongated **bottles** of brown glass.

RHEINGAU: The greatest region is the Rheingau, on the north bank between Lorch and **Hochheim**. The latter, incidentally, is supposed to have given the name **hock** to the English language. The Rheingau wines are very aristocratic, delicate (sometimes difficult for beginners to appreciate) and often endowed with a gentleness that makes them easily overwhelmed if they are served with food. At their finest, they should only be served with very simple foodstuffs. As far as the sweeter wines are concerned, they should be served quite alone, or possibly with fine fruit. The important names are: **Eltville, Erbach, Geisenheim, Hallgarten** (nothing to do with the well-known U.K. **shipper**), **Hattenheim, Hochheim, Johannisberg, Kiedrich, Kloster Eberbach, Östrich, Rauenthal, Rüdesheim** and **Winkel**. Some of the most famous estate-owners are: **Schloss Rheinhartshausen**, Graf von Schönborn (who owns part of the **Marcobrunn** site), Graf Eltz, and Freiherr Langwerth von Simmern (at Eltville), Prince von Löwenstein and Karl Franz Engelmann (at Hallgarten), Fürst Metternich (**Schloss Johannisberg**), and Graf Matuschka-Greiffenclau (**Schloss Vollrads**), but there are many others. The important viticultural school at Geisenheim is also an influential owner and the **State Domain**, which is the most important single proprietor in Germany, owns properties in the vineyards of Rüdesheim, Hattenheim, **Assmann-shausen** (where some red wine is made) Eltville, Erbach, Hochheim, Kiedrich, Rauenthal and **Steinberg**.

RHEINHESSEN: The vineyards of the Rheinhessen, one of the largest wine regions of the Rhine, are on the west bank of the river and behind it, before it turns westwards near Mainz. Both red and white wine is made here, but it is the whites that are most widely known. The most important parishes are: Bodenheim, Guntersblum, Laubenheim, **Nackenheim, Nierstein** and **Oppenheim**. There are few great estates like those on the Rheingau, and in general the wines, though they can be very good, seldom attain quite the quality of the finest of the Rheingaus. The red earth of the Nierstein vineyards in particular makes wines that come to maturity comparatively quickly, possessing a fullness, and slight softness that makes them usually immediately appealing, if perhaps a little lacking in finesse (see **soil**). The most famous vineyard of the Rheinhessen is at **Worms** in the south of the region, where the wines of the Church of Our Lady, the Liebfrauenstift, enjoyed a great vogue at one time – although in fact they are not usually as fine as some of the other wines. This church gave the name **Liebfraumilch** to the well-known **blended** wines widely sold for export today.

There are numerous other vineyards around the Rhine, many making wines that are pleasant to drink when one is on the spot and quantities that are used for **blending**. The whole subject of Rhine wines is complex, on account of their delicacy and individuality; and anyone wishing to know more should consult one of the specialised reference books listed in the Bibliography.

Rhône   The wine region that extends from just south of Lyon, in the east of **France**, southwards down almost to Avignon, along the banks of the River Rhône. Red, white and **rosé** wines are made, although possibly the reds and rosés are the best known. The most northerly region is the **Côte Rotie**, which is divided into the Côte Brune and Côte Blonde; then there are the vineyards of **Condrieu** and Château **Grillet**. Next, around the twin towns of Tain-Tournon, there are the vineyards of **Hermitage**, Crozes-Hermitage, St Josèph, St Péray, Cornas, with **Clairette de Die** produced nearby. Finally, spread out towards

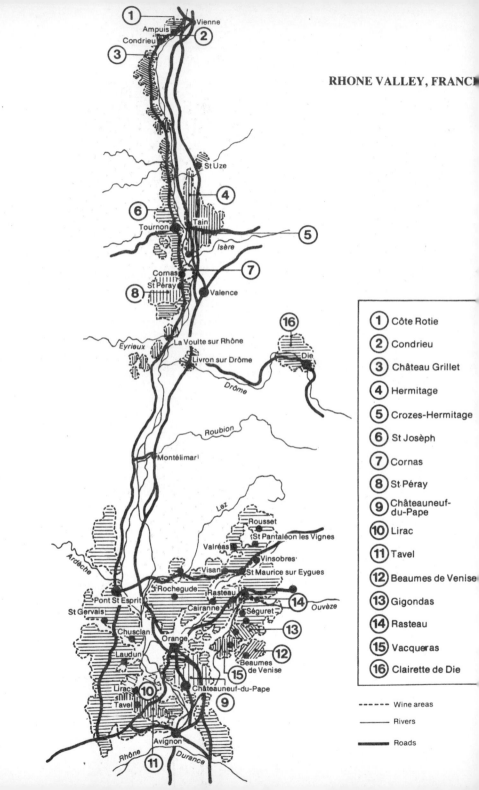

RHONE VALLEY, FRANCE

1. Côte Rotie
2. Condrieu
3. Château Grillet
4. Hermitage
5. Crozes-Hermitage
6. St Josèph
7. Cornas
8. St Péray
9. Châteauneuf-du-Pape
10. Lirac
11. Tavel
12. Beaumes de Venise
13. Gigondas
14. Rasteau
15. Vacqueras
16. Clairette de Die

- - - - - Wine areas
———— Rivers
━━━━ Roads

the mouth of the Rhône, lie the vineyards of **Beaumes de Venise, Châteauneuf du Pape**, Chusclan, **Gigondas, Lirac, Vacqueyras, Tavel** and others. Many produce both white and red wines. A variety of **grapes** is used, the most important being: **Syrah, Grenache, Viognier,** Roussanne, Marsanne, **Clairette, Picpoul, Mourvèdre,** Terret Noir and **Ugni Blanc**. Legislation permits the use of a number of these, plus others, in many of the wines.

Rhône wines were very popular in the 19th century in Britain and, before legislation restricted the abuse of nomenclature, many **Burgundies** were said to have gained their reputation because of being laced with the more robust red wines of the south. But fine red Rhône is quite different from Burgundy. Even allowing for the difference in the grape **varieties**, the sun-baked vineyards make full-bodied, assertive wines, some capable of attaining nobility with age, and most giving great pleasure even if they seldom prove very subtle. The whites are full, dry and very 'baked' in flavour; the rosés (of which Tavel is possibly the most famous in the world) are also large-scale in character, with pronounced **bouquet** and a rounded, dry, but full taste. All these wines are becoming of increasing importance to the winedrinker, because their prices have not yet risen as sharply as those of Burgundy, although they are more expensive than they were.

Vintages in this sunny region are seldom very varied, and the wines – except for the finest reds – tend to be ready for drinking and at their best fairly soon after they are made, although all will soften with time. Many, such as those simply sold as **Côtes du Rhône**, may be listed without a vintage date. In general, the reds are good accompaniments to any dish requiring something full-bodied and fairly assertive, such as big roasts, grills, spiced casseroles of meat, and game. The whites will partner most meat dishes, but can be rather overwhelming for delicate fish dishes, though they go well with piquant fish stews, or anything strongly flavoured with herbs. The rosés are robust enough to go with many meat dishes, even of a strongly flavoured sort, or cold or picnic food, and also with fish dishes, even with mayonnaise. Most of the Rhône wines will also partner pasta and, of course, any regional recipes, such as Provençal or Niçoise dishes. See **enemies to wine**.

Ribatejo **Portuguese** region near the Tagus River, where a large amount of wine is made, most of it of decidedly ordinary quality.

Ribeiro Region of **Galicia** in northern **Spain**, producing a quantity of wine. The authority Jan Read says the white is the better and better known.

Ricard Not to be confused with Richard (a well-known Chambéry **vermouth** establishment), this is a house making **pastis** in the south of **France**.

Ricasoli The 'Iron Baron', Bettino Ricasoli, is the most famous name in a family that have been known for **Chianti** at least since the 18th century. It was Bettino who, in the 19th century, worked out the way in which Chianti **vines** and wines might be enabled to produce fine quality wines. The Baron was a man of considerable achievements in many spheres as well as wine. The great castle of **Brolio**, the family estate, is one of the landmarks of the Chianti region and the wines that are made by the family firm are usually of marked quality.

The firm withdrew from the Chianti Classico *consorzio* with some of the other important producers of the Classico region, because they felt their wines were able to stand by themselves, without the specific label of the *consorzio*.

Riccadonna   Important producer of **Italian vermouth**, with its headquarters at Canelli in **Piedmont**. Founded by Ottavio Riccadonna in 1921, it is still a family concern.

Rice wine   As it is possible to make a form of 'wine' for anything that can be induced to undergo **fermentation**, rice has been used in the Far East to make a 'wine'. There appear to be several sorts of this, the best-known being **saké**. This is recorded as having been made at least since the 8th century. Presentation is usually in a little **bottle**, shaped like a **flask**, often of porcelain. The advantage of this is that the flask can be heated, as it is usual to drink the rice wine hot; although in many places where it is available, it is also used in **cocktails** and similar mixes. The alcoholic **strength** of rice wine is apparently about 17°, so it should not be quaffed casually like a **table wine**.

Riceys, Rosé de   A still pink wine made in the **Champagne** region; a pleasant drink but seldom found.

Rickey   A long mixed drink, like the **Buck**, but using the juice of a fresh lime instead of lemon.

Riddoch   Name of great importance in **Australian** wine history. John Riddoch was one of the pioneer agriculturalists of South Australia in the middle of the 19th century. He built a **winery** at **Coonawarra**, himself planting a large number of various types of **vines**, in addition to his fruit farming. Unfortunately, he seems to have been in advance of his time: when he died, in 1901, his winery was facing problems because the demand for its products was low and the wines were not suitable for **distilling**. A man who was to change the history of the Coonawarra region radically, Bill **Redman**, arrived in the year of John Riddoch's death.

Riesling   ('Ries' rhymes with 'geese') One of the great wine **grapes** of the world, capable of producing white wines of pronounced **bouquet**, elegance, with wonderful flavour and finesse. Its status as a noble grape means that it is often separately named on the wine **label**, wherever it is used. See **Rheinriesling**.

Rieussec   (Pronounced 'Ree-oo-sek') A classed 1st growth of the **Sauternes**, touching the vineyard of Château **Yquem**. See **Bordeaux, classification**.

Rio Negro   Wine region in **Argentina**.

Rioja   (Pronounced 'Ree-ock-ha' stressing 'ock') This region is in the north-west of **Spain** and takes its name from the Rio Oja, a tributary of the Ebro. Its wines have been recorded as providing quality since the 12th century and it is possible that they crossed the Atlantic with Columbus in 1492, because one of his colleagues was a Rioja man. Controls on the making and keeping of the wines have a long tradition: in 1635 wheeled traffic was prohibited in Haro (one of the main centres), for fear of disturbing the wine lying in the cellars below the streets. Logroño is the other. In the 19th century, many Rioja red wines were sent into **France**, to add **colour** and body to such wines as might be lacking in these attributes, and also to fulfil the demand for wines non-existent since the devastation of the *Phylloxera* plague.

There are three main regions: Rioja Alta, Rioja Alavesa and Rioja Baja. A variety of **grapes** are cultivated, the main black grapes being **Garnacho**, Tempranillo, Graciano and Mazuelo; the white grapes are mainly **Malvasia**, white Garnacho, Calagrano and Viura. Each grape contributes a different attribute to the wine and each of the three main regions will make a style of wine individual to its area. The wines vary enormously, according to the regions in which they are made, the proportion of grapes used (there are a huge range of possible combinations) and the style of winemaking. This last has been subjected to many changes and alterations in recent times, because it is the aim of the Rioja firms – many of whom belong to other huge Spanish wine establishments – to popularise their wines on export markets.

In former times, Rioja wines (the whites as well as the reds) were kept in wooden **casks** for several years, sometimes for as long as 6 years, before being bottled. A few **wineries** still make some of their wines like this, but others, influenced by the taste of export markets and the effect of modern technicians brought in to achieve wines of wide appeal, may only allow the wines to remain in **wood** a couple of years. As will be appreciated, the time a wine has spent in wood radically affects its flavour. The 'woodiness', resulting from long maturation in casks, is something – as far as the red wines are concerned – that some people find attractive and others do not: it is certainly quite different from the flavour of other red wines. The white wines may also be in wood for longer than many made today, when crispness is high in the list of qualities for white wines. The pink or rosé wines are, generally, rather full and 'warm' in style.

It is fair to say that, as made nowadays with the utilisation of many of the most modern methods, some Riojas appear to have lost much of their individuality and provide merely adequate drinking; others retain their definite style, whether this is liked or not. It is therefore very difficult to generalise, as the numerous *bodegas* all follow procedures thought advisable, either to retain characteristics liked in markets already established or to adapt the wines made to the tastes which skilful marketing may have created. There are certainly some Rioja wines that do possess individuality and quality to a marked extent, although others have often seemed to me to be insipid and hardly worth drinking.

The produce of the different *bodegas* must be sampled in order for the drinker to decide, but it should be stressed that the very cheap versions of Rioja wines are unlikely to be more than adequate. Quality, as with other wines, inevitably costs more in terms of selection, skill in handling and time in maturation. In view of the attempts made by many *bodegas* to modify traditional styles so as to appeal to a wide public, it should be emphasised that good Rioja simply cannot be likened to any other classic wine and certainly not **claret** or red **Burgundy**. The best Riojas, both white and red, are wholly individual and definite in character and merit appraisal in their own right.

Ripeau *Château* Ripeau is one of the *grand crus classés* of **St Émilion**, in the **Bordeaux** region. It is one of the larger vineyards and usually produces wine of serious quality. See **classification**.

Riscal One of the best-known names as regards **Rioja** wines. The *bodegas* were established in 1860 and the founder had as his aim the idea of making red wines like those of **Bordeaux**. Today the red wines (a little rosé is apparently also made) enjoy enormous popularity and are easy to like, as well as achieving fair to good quality.

Riserva Term applied to certain **Italian** wines of quality and especially to **Chianti**, when it signifies that the wine has been matured for at least 5 years in cask.

Rivesaltes One of the regions in the **Roussillon** district in the south-west of **France**. The wines are entitled to the **A.O.C.** Grand Roussillon. The wines are *vins doux naturels* and can achieve true quality.

Riviera del Garda From **Lombardy** in Italy, these light red and rosé wines can be very pleasant. The most famous is probably **Chiaretto**.

Roberts Rothbury **Hunter Valley** installation in **Australia** where, in the 1960s, the Roberts family planted a range of **vines**. Table wines have been made at the Belbourie property since 1970.

Robertson Wine region at the Cape, **South Africa**, where several estates produce quality wines.

Rock and Rye This curious American **liqueur** gets its name from the original recipe, which consisted of rye **whiskey**, with rock sugar (sugar candy) on the sides of the bottle. The range produced under the name includes liqueurs flavoured with various fruits.

Romania Both red and white wines are made in Romania and, nowadays, these are being exported in substantial quantities. The most esteemed Romanian wine is possibly **Cotnari**, a white **dessert wine** made from a blend of certain native **grapes**. There are a number of these and the wines may be named either according to the **vines** that make them – which include certain classic grape **varieties** as well as the native ones – or according to district. There are a variety of wines of everyday to medium quality which will probably become increasingly better known on export markets.

Römer, **Rummer** The most important type of traditional German **glass**, anglicised as 'rummer' but nothing to do with **rum**. It may have been introduced to **Germany** from Flanders and most of the German wine regions seem to have made versions of it. In general it is a shallow bowl with a ridged foot; this foot can be an extension of the bowl below the glass, or may be elongated into a stem. This is often decorated with several rings in the glass, also with 'prunts' or small decorative additions of glass stuck on the stem, or a knob in the middle. Green and yellowish-green glass were often used to make *romers*. Most museums show some examples.

Rondinella Red **grape** used in the **Veneto** region of **Italy**.

Roodeberg Brand name associated since before World War II with the **K.W.V.** for whom the great Dr **Niehaus** (better known possibly for his work with **South African sherry**) created a blend of wines to make this fullish, appealing red table wine. Today Roodeberg is probably the best-known and most popular South African wine in export markets: it demonstrates the Cape's character as well as showing the clear-cut style of a well-made wine. It benefits enormously by some **bottle age**, so anyone buying a youngish version would be well advised to keep it for some months before drinking.

Rooty Hill Important **Australian** wine area, where the plot now called Minchinbury, known for its **sparkling wine**, was awarded to a Captain Minchin in 1819. **Penfolds** own it today and the stress of the production at Minchinbury appears to be on white wines from a variety of classic **grapes**, including the **Traminer**.

Rosé (Italian *rosato*: Spanish *rosado*) The French word, most commonly used throughout the wine world for pink wine. It is made in many wine regions. Although formerly the best rosés were made only by allowing the skins of the black **grapes** to remain long enough in the fermenting **must** to tinge it with colour; nowadays it is often also permitted in many regions to make rosé by **blending** red and white wine. Rosés made in northern vineyards are apt to be paler in tone than those coming from the south, because the pigments in the skins of the black grapes are not sufficiently reacted on by the sun to tint the must to a deep colour. Mediterranean rosés, on the other hand, are almost like red wines in colour. Good rosé is a pleasant drink, but it is usually at its best when young and fresh and there are very few that benefit by being kept – a few of the single estate wines of **Tavel** and certain wines from very fine makers are exceptions. This is why a rosé seldom bears a **vintage** date.

Because of its light character and, often, its delicacy, rosé is not really an all-purpose or 'when in doubt' wine. It is often, erroneously, supposed to be less alcoholic also. It will, for example, tend to be overwhelmed by most hot meat dishes, such as roasts or stews; fat fish with sauces, such as turbot, salmon or sea bass, will also swamp it. It is therefore rather a silly choice if, at a restaurant meal a gathering of people choose fish and meat dishes; it is better to offer a robust white wine, or have both red and white. However rosé can be delicious with lightly-flavoured cold food, and will certainly go with rather delicately flavoured fish, as well as meat and plain poultry dishes. It should always be served chilled, but not iced to the extent that it tastes of nothing.

Rosebank This Falkirk **distillery**, built in 1824 on a site where **whisky** was being made in the 18th century, is praised as a typical Lowland malt and a good introduction to this type of Scotch.

Roseworthy This is the world-famous agricultural and **oenological** college to the north of Adelaide in South **Australia**. The winemaking course was established as recently as 1936, but the fame of those who are trained there has spread to every wine region. 'A Roseworthy man can make a contribution to any winemaker in the world' is a fair claim. For example, during the extremely hot summer of 1959 in Europe, one of the great **Graves** estates was entertaining an Australian (Roseworthy-trained) guest. Thanks to his advice, the wine, which risked **pasteurising** itself as temperatures mounted and the

must bubbled uncontrollably, was in fact kept under control and a good wine with correct equilibrium was made that year. Today controlling the temperature of the **fermentation vat** is routine, but it was a Roseworthy graduate, familiar with the problems of great heat at **vintage** time, who convinced the conservative French proprietor to follow certain procedures to slow up the fermentation and keep the must within bounds.

Rosolio   This appears to be a type of **liqueur** made in **Italy** by numerous religious houses. Philip Dallas says that a shop in Rome stocks about 60 different ones, based on herbs. The traveller should certainly try to sample them as they are seldom seen outside the area of production; some of them appear to be of a **digestive** character.

Rosso   **Italian** term, meaning 'red'.

Rotgipfler   **Grape** used for some **Austrian** wines.

Rouge Homme   See **Redman**.

Roussette   One of the white **grapes** used for **Seyssel**.

Roussillon   District in the south-east of **France**, along the Mediterranean coast and bordering on the Pyrenees, where a variety of wines are made. These include **Blanquette de Limoux**, **Corbières**, **Fitou**, and the *vins doux naturels* of **Rivesaltes**, as well as wines bearing the names of *Côtes* d'Agly and Roussillon dels Aspres. Until very recently these were not known outside their region, much less in export markets; but with new and improved methods of vinification and transport, some are beginning to attract wide attention because of their pleasant character and reasonable price. See *vin de pays*.

Rovalley   See **Liebich**.

Royal Brackla   Captain William Fraser established this Nairn **whisky distillery** in 1812, and King William IV gave it his Royal Warrant in 1835.

Royal Lochnagar   **Distillery** at Balmoral, Aberdeenshire, established in the early 19th century. It is now owned by the **D.C.L.** In 1848, Queen Victoria, Prince Albert and their children visited the establishment, after which the **whisky** it made was renamed 'Royal' Lochnagar.

Royal Mint-Chocolate   See **chocolate liqueurs**.

Rubesco   The red wine of the Lungarotti establishment at **Torgiano** in **Umbria**, **Italy**. It has achieved considerable success on export markets and is a robust, assertive wine which benefits by **bottle age**.

Rubino   Red Piave wine from **Italy**, which Philip Dallas says is worth attention.

Ruby Cabernet   **Grape** evolved in 1946 by Harold Paul Olmo, in **California**, by crossing the **Cabernet Sauvignon** and **Carignan**. Olmo also evolved the popular **Emerald Riesling**.

Rüdesheim   Not to be confused with Rüdesheim on the **Nahe**, this is situated on the north bank of the **Rhine** as the river turns from west to north, and it is both picturesque as a town as well as famous for its wines. These tend usually to have pronounced fullness of character and to be immediately appealing.

Ruedo   A wine from the **Montilla-Moriles** region of **Spain**, which Jan Read says is pale and light and has no experience of the *solera*. It is obviously something that the traveller should try to sample on the spot.

Ruffino   Large winemaking concern mainly associated with **Chianti** production in **Italy**.

Rufinà   One of the defined regions in which **Chianti** can be made.

Rülander   This is actually the **Pinot Gris grape**. It gets its German name because a merchant called Ruhland introduced it there in 1711. Also known as Grauburgunder.

Rully   (Pronounced 'Roo-yee') A region in the **Côte Chalonnaise** in southern **Burgundy**, producing red, white and **sparkling wines**.

Rum   Spirit **distilled** from sugar cane, although this does not mean that it is sugary or even sweet – for it has been distilled. It is made from fermented molasses, which is what is left after sugar has been made from sugar cane. Both **patent stills** and **pot stills** may be used in its production and, as British law defines rum as a spirit distilled from cane in cane-producing countries, this means that rum cannot be legally made in the U.K. Most rum consumed in the U.K. comes from Jamaica and Guyana in the West Indies, also Barbados and Trinidad. Cuba is another famous source of rum and, especially for the French markets, Martinique. For the **U.S.** market, Puerto Rico and the Virgin Islands are (or were) the main suppliers. In very general terms, Jamaica is associated with dark, definitely flavoured rums; Guyana for demerara, which is often also dark and almost aromatic; Barbados and Trinidad for lightish and rather dry rums; and Martinique and Guadeloupe for delicate, very fragrant rums. But nowadays many different types will be made in each rum region. Rum was connected with the slave trade and the British Navy for many years for obvious reasons – the trade between Europe and the West Indies – and the regular issue of rum to the Royal Navy was only discontinued in 1970; it served as both a stimulant and disinfectant.

The name's origin is much debated: some consider that it derives from the Latin *saccharum* (sugar), others that it comes from the 17th century words 'rumbustion' or 'rumbullion', which appear always to have been associated with the spirit. Rum can be light or dark in colour; the flavour and smell vary from pungent and rich to almost neutral. At one time the rich dark rums were in vogue; but currently the light rums, especially the white rums, are very popular, as they blend well with certain fruit juices in mixed drinks. The **strength** of the rum cannot be judged at all by its colour.

Although rum is, as might be expected, drunk by all sorts of the inhabitants of rum-producing countries, in the U.K. it is unusual that the white rums are very much classless drinks. In producing countries, rum is often drunk straight but, except as a purely warming, medicinal or between-times drink, it tends, especially with the white rums, to be served in mixes. Its popularity soared in the 1970s. As a hot drink, it has been famous for at least a century (see **grog**). Rum is matured in **wood** and that available in the U.K. will be at least 3 years old; the superior qualities will be older, although it tends to mature faster than other spirits. Occasionally a rum establishment will produce a very fine old rum which will, in delicacy and charm, be in the nature of a **liqueur**, and should be drunk like fine liqueur **brandy**. See **Bacardi, Daiquiri**.

Rumasa The enormous company that owns many of the firms making the wines and **sherries** of **Spain**. As their holdings may have extended and altered even by the time this appears in print, it is useless to list them.

Ruppertsberg See **Palatinate**.

Russia See **U.S.S.R.**

Rust **Austrian** wine region in the **Burgenland** district, making some good wines, especially those described as *ausbruch*, which signifies extreme ripeness as a result of late picking.

Rustenberg More correctly Schoongezicht-Rustenberg, this is one of the famous estates in the **Stellenbosch** region of the Cape, **South Africa**. It was in fact the first farm to be granted to a private owner in north Stellenbosch; the original Schoongezicht house was built in 1814 by the Hendrik Cloete whose father made the fine wines of **Constantia**. The property has survived many vicissitudes: today the white wines bear the name of Schoongezicht, the reds that of Rustenberg. They have won a name for quality and a following among customers.

Rutherglen See **Australia**.

Ruwer (Pronounced 'Roo-ver') Tributary of the **Mosel**, which it joins at the village of Ruwer. The wines from its principal parishes – **Waldrach**, **Kasel**, **Mertesdorf**, with the estates of **Grünhaus**, the **Karthäuser Hof**, **Eitelsbach** and **Avelsbach** – are capable of outstanding quality. They are usually immediately appealing: fresh, crisp and with a delicate but fascinating **bouquet**.

Ruzica Pink **Yugoslav** wine, made from the **Prokupac grape**.

Rye See **whiskey**.

Ryecroft Vineyard in the **McLaren** Vale region of **Australia**, first planted in 1886. The prime achievement of the director of the concern after World War II was to buy the wines of smaller concerns, **label**, and sell each as an individual product, along with information about the way in which the wine was made. The firm was called McLaren Vale Wines. It was taken over by Reed Industries in 1970.

S

Saar Tributary of the **Mosel** in **Germany**, the region includes many vineyards making particularly fine wines, possessing elegance and charm, some of them attaining outstanding quality in certain years and capable of much improvement with maturity. The most notable vineyards are: **Ayl, Falkenstein, Kanzem, Oberemmel, Ockfen, Saarburg, Serrig**, and **Wiltingen**. There are many site names within these, and there are also certain very important owners, such as the **Bischöfliches Konvikt**, and **Bischöfliches Priesterseminar, Hohe Domkirche** and **Vereinigte Hospitien**, all in Trier; Egon Müller, Von Hövel, Otto van Volxem, and Adolf Rheinhart. All the fine wines are made exclusively from the **Riesling grape**, the **soil** in this area being particularly favourable to it.

Saarburg Wine village on the **Saar**.

Sables St Émilion See **St Émilion**.

Sabra Israeli **liqueur**, made from bitter oranges and bitter chocolate. The name is supposed by some to relate to the sabra cactus of the desert, by others to refer to the name used (from the same derivation as the cactus name certainly) to denote inhabitants of **Israel** actually born in the country, as opposed to Jewish immigrants from other nations. See **orange liqueurs, chocolate liqueurs**.

Saccharometer Instrument used to measure the weights of **musts**. It looks like a fat thermometer with a larger than usual bulb at the end, and is put into a calibrated glass cylinder of must. Depending on the depth to which it sinks or how high it rides above the surface of the liquid, the degrees **Baumé** (or density) can be read. This, because it derives from the sugar content of the must, will then give an indication as to the possible alcoholic content of the finished wine. The importance of this is that the reading will show if it is necessary to **chaptalise** it, so as to bring the alcoholic content up to the degree required in the finished wine.

Saccharomyces ceriviseae What Lichine aptly describes as 'the workhorse of the winemaker', these are the wine **yeasts** that act upon the grape juice to transform it into wine.

Sack   This word is particularly associated with **sherry**, but although Falstaff's famous eulogy specifies 'sherris sack', the word itself did not necessarily mean sherry. There are several theories as to its origin, including that implying it was dry (*seco*), but the most likely would seem that it came from the verb *sacar*, which means to take out. This consequently came to be used in general for the wines of **Spain** that were exported. See *sekt*.

St Amour   Parish in the **Beaujolais** region of **France**, making charming, easy-to-drink, red wines.

St Clare   **Winery** in the **Clare-Watervale** region of **Australia**.

St Émilion (1)   One of the best-known regions within the **Bordeaux** wine region, taking its name from the picturesque little town, dominated by its church spire and containing many historic monuments. These include the monolithic church, excavated around the cell of the hermit, St Émilian. The wines are world-famous, pleasing by their generous, fruity nature and characteristic taste of the **soil** which nourishes the **vines**. There are a number of *communes* which have the right to call their wines 'St Émilion' and there are five which can, according to the **A.O.C.** regulations, add the suffix 'St Émilion' to their names: St Georges, Lussac, Montagne, Parsac, and Puisseguin. Sables St Émilion is an A.O.C. given to the wines produced on slightly sandy soil adjacent to St Émilion. On **labels** the word 'Saint' is usually given in full, on lists it is generally abbreviated. See **classification**.

Saint Émilion (2)   See **grapes**, **Ugni Blanc**.

St Estèphe   One of the most famous regions within the **Bordeaux** wine region, and the most northerly of the great *communes* of the **Médoc**. Its wines, which are all red, tend to have a certain toughness to them and they may take longer to mature to peak enjoyment than some of the other Médocs, but they can have long and impressive lives. The most famous properties are probably the classed growths **Cos d'Estournel**, **Cos Labory**, **Lafon-Rochet**, **Montrose**, and the very large estate of **Calon-Ségur**. Where the 'St Stephen' name came from, I cannot discover, but it is a very old form of the name. See **classification**, **saints**.

St George Rosé   The pink wine of Giorgio Odero, a well-reputed maker of **Frecciarossa** in **Lombardy**, **Italy**. The name is included so that there may be no risk of its being confused with **Nuits St Georges**.

St Georges-St Émilion   See **St Émilion**.

St Hallett's Wines   **Winery** founded by the Lindner family in the **Barossa Valley** region of **Australia** in 1918.

St Hallvard   Norwegian herb-flavoured **liqueur**.

St Josèph   See **Hermitage**, **Rhône**.

St Julien   One of the great wine *communes* in the **Médoc** within the **Bordeaux** region. Its wines are usually outstanding for their almost scented, intense **bouquet** and velvety flavour. The classed growths are: **Léoville-Lascases**, **Léoville-Poyferre**, **Léoville-Barton**, **Gruaud-Larose**, **Ducru-Beaucaillou** (all 2nd growths); **Lagrange**, **Langoa-Barton** (3rd growths); **Beychevelle**, **Branaire-Ducru**, **Talbot**, **Saint-Pierre-Bontemps** and Saint-Pierre-Sevaistre

(4th growths). There are many saints called Julian, but the one known as 'The Hospitaler' may be the origin of this parish: he has no known dates. See **classification, saints**.

St Laurent   See **Belgrave, Bordeaux**.

St Magdalene   This **whisky distillery** at Linlithgow, now owned by the **D.C.L.**, takes its name from St Magdalene's Cross, the lands of which were leased in the 18th century from the Countess of Dalhousie. Linlithgow is the birthplace of Mary Stuart, Queen of Scots.

St Nicolas de Bourgueil   (Pronounced 'Bor-guy') Region in **Touraine** in **France**, where fine red and some **rosé** wines are produced from the **Cabernet Franc**. The wines of St Nicolas de Bourgueil are generally considered to surpass those of **Bourgueil** and they remind some people of raspberries, others of violets. They are crisp and fairly light, but can, in certain years, achieve great delicacy and finesse if allowed to mature for some time, should they have been made in the traditional way. See **Loire**.

St Péray   See **Hermitage, Rhône**.

St Pierre Bontemps, St Pierre Sevaistre   These two classed 4th growths of **St Julien** in the **Médoc** were at one time separated, but are now united. The property belongs to the Antwerp wine merchants, Van den Bussche, and therefore the wines, usually fine, tend to be comparatively little known in the U.K. See **Bordeaux, classification**.

Saint Raphaël   French **apéritif** with quinine as one of the ingredients. There are three types: the red, full and sweetish; the white which is dryer; and an extra dry. There is a tradition associated with this drink that anyone who takes a lot will never go blind because, at the beginning of the 19th century, a Frenchman called Jupet prayed successfully to St Raphaël to restore his sight (but evidence is not conclusive on the subject).

St Romain   Vineyard in the **Côte de Beaune** region of **Burgundy**, producing both red and white wines which can attain true quality. They have not yet run the risk of being distorted through commercial exploitation.

St Véran   A comparatively new **A.O.C.** applying to white wines made from the **Chardonnay grape** made in the St Véran district of south **Burgundy**. Formerly sold as **Mâcon** Blanc, these wines are gaining greatly in popularity. See **Beaujolais Blanc**.

St Vincent   An early martyr of Spain, St Vincent of Saragossa (d. 304) is the patron saint of French winegrowers. His feast day (22 January) is particularly celebrated in **Burgundy**. He was a deacon and his martyrdom included being toasted on a grid-iron which he is often portrayed as holding. In legend, he asked to go back to earth from Heaven so as to taste French wine again and, when eventually discovered lingering in the cellars of **La Mission Haut Brion**, he was banished from Paradise! See **saints**.

Sainte Croix du Mont   Region on the north bank of the River Garonne in the **Gironde** region, making sweetish white wines which are sometimes likened to small-scale versions of **Sauternes**.

Sainte Foy Bordeaux   (Pronounced 'Fwah') Region to the east of the

Entre-Deux-Mers in the **Gironde**, producing sweetish white wines and a little red wine. St Faith may have been a martyr at Agen, in Aquitane, in early times.

Saints   A number of saints are associated with the making of wines and spirits, some of them being general patrons, others with local associations. **St Vincent** is the usual patron of French winegrowers, and his feast day, 22 January, is usually celebrated. St Martin of Tours (11 November), who lived in the 4th century, was the soldier who divided his cloak with a beggar. He is supposed to have rediscovered the advantages of **pruning** when his monastery's asses got into the vineyard and nibbled the vine shoots. To everyone's amazement, the damaged vines bore better than any later on. St Urbain, Bishop of Autun (25 May), is patron of German winegrowers, and St Kilian is patron of **Franconian vintners**. St Cyriak is a patron of the **Palatinate**. The associations between church and wine have been close for many centuries, and travellers in wine regions are likely to find many other saints commemorated for something to do with wine.

The Ice Saints, sometimes referred to by growers, are Sts Pancratius, Servatius, Boniface and Sophid, whose feast days occur in mid-May – the time when a late frost can seriously damage the **vines**.

Saintsbury, George (1845-1933)   A don (Regius Professor of Rhetoric at Oxford), journalist, political writer, and author of books of criticism and of what are now little-read works on English literature. He became famous in the wine world for his *Notes on a Cellar-Book*, (1920). This was an account of the wines he bought and what he thought when he drank them, from 1884 to 1915. (The original manuscript was sold for the second time at Christie's in 1977.) It certainly started a fashion for wine writing of a particular sort. He includes useful historical references and anecdotes, and the writer shows definite charm and enthusiasm for the company he entertains, as well as for the fare he provides. Many people have begun their wine reading with Saintsbury and no winelover can ignore him. He writes, however, in a style that seems somewhat mannered today. Some highly respected members of the wine trade share my own inability to find him other than irritatingly pompous and oddly ignorant of the background to the wines he drank, as well as being both ultra-conservative (perhaps he could hardly have been otherwise) and opinionated.

Saintsbury does not appear to have been one who easily shared his enjoyment of wine outside his personal friends. In his last years, when some very eminent winelovers – members of the trade and laymen – formed the Saintsbury Club, which is an organisation possessing a fine cellar and with a great tradition for its dinners and the speeches or 'orations' made thereat, the Professor would have nothing to do with them and their celebrations. However winelovers must read the reprint of the *Cellar-Book* and make up their own minds. (Personally, I am sure that I should have found him a 'Dear lady' condescending type of man and he does not seem as if he would have been responsive to questions at all.) Whereas even the scholar might have to be desperate to get anything from his other prose today, the *Cellar-Book* is a landmark in wine writing which no one can ignore.

Saké   Japanese **rice wine** which, according to taste, may be drunk either warm (when it is flavoured with spices) or cold. It is served in small porcelain cups without handles. The most reputed type comes from Nada.

Salamino di Santa Croce   **Lambrusco** as made in a region of **Emilia-Romagna**. The **grape** is called 'Salamino' after its shape, which is supposedly like a small salami – that is, a little sausage!

Salento   Wine region of **Puglia, Italy**, where the Matino wines appear to be well spoken of, although writers do not report on them.

Salter   One of the famous family names in **Australian** wine history. William Salter of Exeter, Devon, arrived in the country in 1839 but did not go into the wine business for some time. The Saltram vineyard has become closely associated with that of **Stonyfell** in recent years.

Saltram   See **Salter**.

Sambucca   Italian **liqueur**, with a taste of elderberry and liquorice. Sometimes it is drunk by pouring a film of it on the top of a cup of black coffee, setting light to this and drinking the coffee after the flame has gone out.

Samos   **Greek** island famous for its **Muscat** wine. It appears to have continued making wine even under Turkish occupation. The ancient Romans enjoyed 'Samian' wine.

San Joaquin   See **California**.

San Marino   Tiny republic near the Adriatic, inside **Italy**, making some red and sweet white wine, also a local **liqueur**.

San Michele   Danish tangerine **liqueur**, first made in 1930. Named for Dr Axel Munthe, author of the popular book *The Story of San Michele*, whose **Capri** house is shown on the back label.

San Severo   Red, white and pink wines are made in this region of **Puglia** in **Italy**, also some **sparkling wine**. Although many of them are used for **blending** purposes, some of the reds are reported as achieving individual quality.

San Silvestro   See **Mentuccia**.

Sancerre   Region in the upper **Loire** valley, in **France**, producing very fine dry white wines, which have become known and deservedly celebrated in comparatively recent times. The **grape** is the **Sauvignon** and much of the quality of the wines derives from the limestone on which the vineyards are situated (see **soil**). The dryness and elegance of good Sancerre is complemented by a floweriness and full flavour which is very attractive; sometimes the freshness is described as 'green'. Wines from specified properties can achieve great distinction.

Sandalford   Reputedly the oldest vineyard in Western **Australia**, this is 12 miles (19 km) outside Perth, and was planted in 1840 by Captain John Septimus Roe, who named it for an estate his family owned in England. The Roes still hold the property.

Sandeman   One of the great names in the **port** and **sherry** worlds, being established in **Portugal** in 1790 and a little later in **Spain**. The Sandeman family are still active in both concerns.

Sandweine   The term means 'sand wines' and is used for the wines made in the

Seewinkel region, east of Lake Neusiedl, in the Burgenland district of **Austria**. Because the vineyard **soil** is sandy, the ***Phylloxera*** has never invaded the area and to this day the vines are ungrafted.

Sangaree   This is a chilled and sweetened drink, based on wine, beer or a **liqueur**, served in a tall **glass** sprinkled with nutmeg.

Sangiovese   Black **grape** used in many **Italian** red wines; it is the backbone of **Chianti**. Locally the name is sometimes abbreviated to Sangioveltru or 'Sangiu'.

Sangría   Spanish mixed drink, usually of **wine**, fruit and aerated water. It can be white, or, more usually, red.

Sanguedetoro   See **Toro**.

Sanlúcar de Barrameda   See **sherry**.

Santa Clara Valley   **California** region where some of the most renowned **U.S. wineries** are situated. These include **Almadén** and those belonging to Paul **Masson**.

Santa Maddalena   Red wine of the **Trentino-Alto Adige** region of **Italy**, made from the **Schiava vine**.

Santenay   Region in the **Côte de Beaune** in **Burgundy**, producing both red and white wines. The former are possibly the most interesting and capable of achieving the greatest quality. They have a special fruitiness and light charm which is very attractive. See **Côte d'Or**.

Sapindor   French herb **liqueur**, made at Pontarlier in the **Jura** since 1825, and put up in **bottles** looking like pieces of tree trunk.

Sardinia   Although, until comparatively recently, Sardinian wines were merely wines known to the traveller in **Italy**, the development of the island as a holiday resort and the improvement in quality of the wines make it likely that many will be featured on export lists in the near future. The best-known so far are **Cannonau**, **Nuragus** and **Vernaccia**, as well as wines called after the classic wine **grapes** from which they are made.

Sassella   **Valtelline** red wine, made in **Lombardy** in **Italy**. It must have at least 95% **Nebbiolo** in it.

Saumur   This town on the River **Loire** in **France** is the headquarters of a famous French cavalry school, as well as the wine production of the region. Sparkling white wines are made in the suburb of St Hilaire-St Florent, the best-known probably being that of Ackerman Laurence, founder of the Saumur **sparkling wine** business. Many firms have their headquarters in or near Saumur for handling the white, **rosé** and sparkling or *pétillant* wines of the region. The rosé is made from the **Cabernet Franc grape** and is slightly more pearl-like in hue than that of **Anjou**. The sparkling wines are mostly made by the **Champagne method**. They are becoming widely appreciated thanks to modern methods of production and conservation. The still white Saumurs tend also to be rather too dry for many tastes, but both red and white can be very good.

Saumur-Champigny   Made from the **Cabernet Franc**, this red wine is somewhat high in **acidity**, but is capable of achieving quality.

Sauternes The name as applied to the French wines is always spelt with a final 's'. The region is to the south of **Bordeaux**, within the area of **Graves**. The wines are white and, today, must be sweet to get the **A.O.C.** Sauternes; but this was not always so. As recently as the early part of the 19th century, they were dry or dryish – though fairly full in character. The story has it that in the 19th century the owner of **Yquem** insisted on the vintagers waiting for his express instructions before picking. These were then delayed, arriving so late that the **grapes** shrivelled on the **vines**. When, in desperation, these grapes were pressed, the wine they made was superlative.

In fact the unique quality of Sauternes comes from the action of *Botrytis cinerea*. This settles on the grapes in certain years (humidity and a certain amount of warmth late in the **vintage** is necessary) and shrivels them, concentrating the juice inside. Its action is such that when, after successive passages by the vintagers through the vineyard (the grapes are picked one by one, using special scissors, rarely bunches), the wine can be made, the result is a luscious golden liquid. Records indicate that sweet Sauternes of this kind was first made in the early part of the 19th century; although the great sweet **German** wines were being made long before this. Unlike the German sweet wines, the Sauternes are fairly high in **alcohol** – this is why they are taxing to drink.

Within the Sauternes boundaries are the regions of **Bommes**, Fargues, Preignac, and that of **Barsac** adjoins it. Sauternes begin, continue and end sweet; they have a beautiful deep golden colour and great fragrance. Our ancestors drank them copiously, even at the beginning of a meal, but recently they have tended to go out of fashion. Menus showing that they were served with oysters exist, including one of a dinner given by President Roosevelt at the White House in 1937 for the visit of King George VI and Queen Elizabeth. They should always be served well chilled. The best-known property is Château **Yquem**. See *Trockenbeerenauslese*.

Sauvignon Blanc One of the great white wine **grapes** of the world, used in the **Bordeaux** region, the upper **Loire** (where the local name is **Blanc Fumé**), and in many other wine regions. It gives firmness and a steely dry style to the wines it makes.

Savagnin The **grape** used in the **Jura** for the wine of **Château-Chalon**. See **Pinot, Traminer**.

Savennières See **Loire**.

Savigny Region around the town of the same name in the **Côte de Beaune** in **Burgundy**. It produces red and white wines, some of considerable quality. See **Côte d'Or**.

Savoie, Savoy Region in the east of **France**, producing dry white still and **sparkling wines**. See **Crépy, Seyssel**.

Scapa **Whisky distillery** at Kirkwall, Orkney. It first operated in 1885, and is now owned by Hiram Walker.

Scharlachberg Literally 'the scarlet mountain', in the Rheinhessen (see **Rhine**). It probably got its name from being planted with **vines** yielding black

grapes in former times – not only would they make red wines, the leaves turn crimson in the autumn.

Scharzberg Not to be confused with **Scharzhofberg**, this is another notable site in the parish of **Wiltingen** in the **Saar** region of **Germany**. As with Scharzhofberg, the wines may be labelled simply with the vineyard name, without that of the parish.

Scharzhofberg See **Saar**.

Schaumwein German term for **sparkling wines**. The grades in ascending order are: *qualitätsschaumwein*, *sekt* and *prädikatssekt*.

Scheurebe George Scheu, of the Regional Institute for Viticulture at Alzey, evolved this white wine **grape** by crossing **Sylvaner** with **Riesling**. It was first grown in **Germany** in 1916. It makes very perfumed fruity wines, useful in some **blends**, but rather obvious and lacking subtlety for many people. Much used in the **Palatinate**. See **hybrids**, **varieties**.

Schiava Red wine **grape** used in north **Italy**, especially for the wines of the **Trentino-Alto Adige** region.

Schiedam See **gin**.

Schillerwein Wine made from both black and white **grapes** producing a type of **rosé**, and a specialty of the **Baden-Württemberg** region of **Germany**. It is nothing to do with the poet Schiller, although, rather confusingly, his statue in Stuttgart inclines many visitors to think so. The word comes from the verb 'to shimmer'.

Schiras, Schiraz Some think that the name came from a **grape variety** originally cultivated in the town of that name in Iran. See **Syrah**.

Schloss Böckelheim See **Nahe**.

Schloss Johannisberg One of the great estates of the Rheingau (see **Rhine**) at **Johan..isberg**, originally a Benedictine monastery. It was secularised in 1803 and given by Napoleon to General Kellerman. After Napoleon's defeat the estate was given to Prince Metternich, on condition that a yearly tithe was paid to the Imperial Court at Vienna, and it is still in the Metternich family.

The different qualities of the wines made were traditionally marked by differently coloured **labels** and seals: red seal was the ordinary **estate-bottling**; green includes *spätlese*; pink includes *auslese*, *beerenauslese*, *trockenbeerenauslese* (see **Germany**). Wine not considered of quality meriting any of these labels is made into *sekt* and also sold under the estate's name. The *kabinett* wines get a different scale of quality rating: orange, white, blue and gold, as from 1953; before that the ascending scale was: yellow, orange, violet, white, lilac, sky-blue, gold and blue, gold.

Schloss Rheinhartshausen Estate on the Rheingau, just outside **Eltville**, where the impressive house once belonged to the late Prince William of Prussia; this is now an hotel. There is an island in the **Rhine** immediately opposite, known as the Au or Aue which is mentioned in Wagner's opera *Parsifal*. **Vines** have been planted on the island, mostly **Pinot Blanc**.

Schloss Vollrads One of the great estates of the Rheingau (see **Rhine**) in **Germany**, which has been in the hands of a single family for longer than any other – since the beginning of the 14th century. It is the property of Graf Matuschka-Greiffenclau. The wines are made solely from the **Riesling grape** and a range of quality wines, all **estate-bottled** and some **sparkling wine** are produced. The wines tend to have a fullness and nobility of character which is very marked.

Schnapps This word is the German and the Dutch form of what, in Denmark, is 'schnaps', in Sweden 'snaps'. It means 'a snatch' or 'a gasp'. See **aquavit**.

Schooner Larger version of an **Elgin** – and therefore a doubly unattractive and unsuitable glass for any wine.

Schoongezicht One of the most beautiful estates in the region of **Stellenbosch**, **South Africa**, now bearing both this name and that of **Rustenberg**. Although white wines are made, the present policy is concentrated on the reds.

Schorle German name for a mixture of wine and fizzy mineral water – refreshing and light in **alcohol**. It can be ordered in most German wine bars.

Schramsberg This **winery**, in **California**'s **Napa Valley**, was first put under **vines** in 1862 by Jacob Schram. The wine made was praised by Robert Louis Stevenson. The winery underwent several serious crises and was actually closed in 1960. However, five years later, Jack L. Davies bought the house and estate and began to make wines that are now respected throughout the world – by those who can get them, for production is limited. The former Schramsberg wines were of various types, but today only **sparkling wines**, made by the **Champagne method**, are produced. The vineyards supply some of the **grapes**, others are bought in. There are several styles of wine made, but the quality of those produced seems to be of a very high standard.

The style of a Schramsberg wine is such that many easily confuse it with all but the finest **Champagne**, but there is a definite and subtle individuality. This is one of the great achievements of **U.S.** winemaking and it seems a pity that the term 'Champagne' should be applied to a wine that is superb in its own right because Schramsberg is great sparkling wine.

Sciacchetrà Sweet white wine from the **Cinqueterre** region of **Liguria** in **Italy**, made from the **Vernaccia grape**.

Scotch See **whisky**.

Scuppernong One of the best-known native **U.S. grapes**, of the *Vitis rotundifolia* species, from which wines with a pronounced, accentuated muskiness appear to be produced. In the past such wines enjoyed much popularity, but today tastes have changed.

Seagram This organisation is probably the biggest spirit establishment in the world, and it has enormous holdings in wine as well. It started in **Canada** in 1857, when Joseph E. Seagram began distilling at Waterloo, Ontario. Seagram produce 'Seven Crown', the best-selling **U.S. whiskey** at the time of writing. Their other brands include various **U.S.** and Canadian top-selling brands; they also bought Chivas Brothers of Aberdeen, makers of Chivas Regal and, more recently, The **Glenlivet**.

Seaview Old-established **Australian winery** near **McLaren** Vale. It makes a variety of table and **fortified wines**.

Sebastiani   Large **winery** near Sonoma in **California**, established at the beginning of the 20th century (though some of the vineyards are older than that). It makes a wide range of table wines, some of them from classic wine **grapes**.

Sec   This **French** word means 'dry'. However there are different notions of what this means: a **Champagne** that is *sec* is one that, because of its **dosage,** will be not entirely bone-dry; a *demi-sec* Champagne will be definitely sweet. But with other wines, the term is relative. The same applies to the **Italian** term *secco* or, indeed, the word 'dry' on any wine list or description of a wine – you have to know the context in which the word is used and the user.

Seewinkel   See **Austria**, *sandweine*.

Sekt   The name used for German **sparkling wine**, whether made by the **Champagne method** or the **Charmat method**, when made from at least 60% German **grapes**. The origin of the word is rather obscure but it is associated with the German Shakespearean actor, Ludwig Devrient, at the beginning of the 19th century, who would call for 'a cup of sack' after playing Falstaff, when he wanted his favourite drink – **Champagne**. *Sekt* is made in all the wine regions of **Germany** and can be a pleasant, fresh drink of quality. See **sack**.

Sémillon   White wine **grape** which is cultivated in many parts of the world. It is perhaps most famous in the **Bordeaux** region, where it is one of those used for the great sweet wines. It has a lightly perfumed **bouquet**.

Sénancole   Yellow herby **liqueur**, made by the monks of the Abbey of Sénanque, which was founded by the Cistercians in 1148. It is named after the river that flows at the foot of the valley below the Abbey, and is a play on the words *sana aqua* (health-giving water). Since 1930 the production has been commercially entrusted to a distillery at Salon-de-Provence, but the Prior of the Abbey still holds the secret formula and supervises the production, including the herbs which are gathered by the monks.

Seppelt   A great name in **Australian** wine history, with the Seppelt family still active in the business. Joseph Ernest Seppelt arrived in Australia in 1849 and settled near Tanunda, in the **Barossa Valley**, in 1852. Today, Seppeltsfield is a huge, town-like establishment, where table and **fortified wines** and **brandy**, also vast quantities of **vinegar** are produced. Chateau Tanunda (*sic*) is another Seppelt property in the Barossa, and there is also one at Dorrien. The company went public in 1970, but many Seppelts are still prominent within it and the wines enjoy a reputation for quality and individuality.

Sercial   (Pronounced 'Sair-see-al') Driest and lightest in **colour** of the four main types of **Madeira**. Usually served as an **apéritif** or by itself, though it can also be served with clear soup.

Serine   See **Syrah**.

Serprina   **Italian** white wine **grape**, which Philip Dallas cites as being used in the wines of the Colli Euganei, near Padua in the **Veneto**.

Serra, Junipero   This Franciscan friar is credited with being the first person to bring **vines** from the lower regions of **California**. He planted them at the San Diego Mission around 1769, in order to make wine for church purposes. The

grape that he used was the Criolla. This was possibly from Mexico but, as it is cultivated today in **Argentina**, it could have come from even further south, having been introduced by the Spaniards in the 16th century. Known in California as the **Mission** grape, it does not appear to have been successful in making wine of more than adequate quality.

Serradayres   Brand name of white and red table wines of **Portugal**, which possess style and refinement. The name means 'mountain of air'.

Serrig   (Pronounced 'Say-rig') **Saar** vineyard, of which Antoniusberg, Schloss Saarfelser Vogelsang, and Vogelsang are possibly the best-known sites.

Service of wine   There are few rules about this, but those that should be observed are intended to give maximum enjoyment of wine to drinkers – they are not just chi-chi.

For table wines that are not to be **decanted**, the **bottle** should be standing upright – ideally some time in advance in the dining-room for red wines – and the **capsule**, or part of it, should be removed so as to expose the **cork**. If you do not wish to take this off completely, be sure to cut around it below the lip of the bottle so that, when you remove the top of the capsule, the bottle's lip is quite clear of any fragment of capsule. This ensures that when the wine is poured there is no risk of any contact with the metal or plastic capsule which could affect its taste. (Some people find this unbelievable – but is it worth risking an expensive bottle if somebody who really may be sensitive to wine finds it metallic or 'off' in some way? A metal capsule can taint the wine poured over it – even if you can't tell, one of your guests may be able to do so.) The exposed top of the cork and lip of the bottle should be wiped clean of any dust or **deposit**; if the cork seems moist or sticky there is no need to be concerned, but it should be cleaned. The **corkscrew** should then be inserted and the cork extracted, gently and without jerking or haste, in a long slow pull. When the cork is out, the inside of the bottle neck should also be wiped, to make sure that no pieces of cork fall into the wine (though if they do, it is no great matter, as the first sample should be poured into the host's **glass**, precisely for this reason). Then the wine should be **poured**, in a steady stream, without splashing if possible as this may aerate an old wine too much.

If people are particularly interested in wine, the cork should be available for inspection – with older wines it can be fascinating to see how much or how far up the staining from the wine will have soaked. Sometimes people secure the cork to the bottle with a rubber band or, if a wine is decanted, they affix this to the neck of the **decanter**; there are even cork holders, which consist of a pair of pins or prongs on a short chain, which can be used to fasten the cork to the decanter. The cork is sometimes put into the **cradle** where it can wedge the bottle more securely than is usually possible, but my opinion that the wine cradle has no more place on a civilised dining-table than the chamber-pot has underneath it, will convince the reader who has studied the correct use of the cradle that the cork need not add to the presence of this object among the tableware.

The skilled person can, with a little practise, so cut the capsule that it forms a

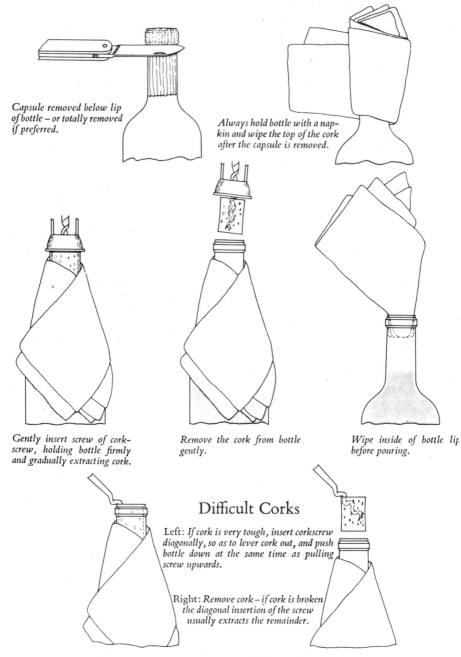

Capsule removed below lip of bottle – or totally removed if preferred.

Always hold bottle with a napkin and wipe the top of the cork after the capsule is removed.

Gently insert screw of corkscrew, holding bottle firmly and gradually extracting cork.

Remove the cork from bottle gently.

Wipe inside of bottle lip before pouring.

Difficult Corks

Left: *If cork is very tough, insert corkscrew diagonally, so as to lever cork out, and push bottle down at the same time as pulling screw upwards.*

Right: *Remove cork – if cork is broken the diagonal insertion of the screw usually extracts the remainder.*

holder for the cork: to do this, cut off the top part or 'lid', then cut nearly all the way round just below the bottle's lip, peel back the band that is thus made and stick the cork into this – it looks pleasant and is not difficult to do with a metal capsule, but a plastic capsule (which has to be cut off or wrenched off) and a bottle sealed by dipping the cork in wax (which has to be tapped off with a knife) cannot be cut in this way.

Always serve even a cheap bottle of wine correctly – you may find it surprisingly good simply because you have taken a little extra trouble.

IN THE RESTAURANT the educated **wine waiter** should have been instructed in the service of wine. Essentially, he follows the procedure as outlined above, but with a few additions: he should present the bottle to whoever has ordered it before drawing the cork. Not only may the **vintage** or supplier of the wine be different from that on the wine list, but the actual wine may have got into a different wine **bin**. So it is necessary for the person ordering the wine to approve that a particular bottle is the one he has ordered. With a white wine, he may also put his hand on the bottle to see whether it is cold or merely cool so that he can decide as to whether it requires a further period in the ice bucket or whether some may be poured at once.

The cork should be drawn while the person who has ordered the wine is looking on. For reasons of space, this must sometimes take place at the table, but ideally it should be on a side table or trolley brought up specifically for the purpose. But the person paying for the wine must see the cork drawn, unless, of course, he has ordered it to be opened and possibly decanted some time ahead of drinking – in such instances he has confidence that the wine waiter will handle the bottle correctly. The bad old days when any cheap wine might be put into a bottle bearing a famous **label** – its cork shown separately and ostentatiously to the customer – are in the past but . . . . It is as well to watch the handling of something for which you have paid a fair sum. This naturally applies to any decanting. If the eating-place insists on the use of the wine cradle, it is up to the diner as to whether he asks for this to be removed and the bottle stood up on the table; some advocate this, but there is obviously no point in making matters difficult for a harassed wine waiter who has the management's instructions which he must follow. Better, perhaps, to write later, deploring the use of the cradle and address your comment to the managing director of the establishment.

The host has a small sample of the wine poured into his glass to approve before it is served to other diners. This is so that he may get any 'bits' that come out with the first pouring, also so that he may judge whether the wine is in good condition, as well as whether it is at the temperature he prefers. Some people like their red wines served virtually luke-warm and if they insist on this (instead of gently bringing up the temperature by cuddling the wine in their glass or even putting their hands round the bottle), then the wine waiter may be told to 'do something about it'. This may well mean that he disappears and, by the time people have almost finished eating, returns with a bottle that has been plunged into hot water or virtually scorched over a stove. Anyone who behaves in this way is unlikely to be a real lover of wine and deserves all that comes to him, and so my sympathy is with the waiter.

But, as regards the wine's condition, it is fair to say that very often the '**bottle stink**' of the little bit of stale air in the bottle under the cork may create an unfavourable impression when the wine is first poured – so swing it about vigourously in the glass and do not be in a hurry to accept or reject. This, of course, is not easy in a busy restaurant, but since on several occasions a truly **corked** wine has not been immediately noticed by even the experienced, the only thing to do is taste in as leisurely a way as practicable. Unless a wine really stinks from the first sniff or, possibly more sinisterly, has no smell at all (this, to me, is often the indication of corkiness), then it is fair to request the wine to be poured and see what other people say. Faults may be evident by the time the bottle has gone round.

THE ORDER OF POURING in the home or around a restaurant table is for the guest on the host's right to be served first. After that, in a mixed company, it rather depends on the wine waiter as to whether all the women are served first, or whether he simply goes round the table. I have known scrupulous and traditional wine waiters ask me whether I should be served before or after my guests – when these might all be men! Personally, I think that it is simplest to serve people round the table. If you are enjoying the hospitality of a rather grand private house, where there may be several people dipensing the wine, then it is easy for the women to be served before the men. But the host – male or female – always gets the first sample to approve.

The timing of the service of wines is important but it is fair to say that in a restaurant you must watch this. If, when people have ordered food and wines prior to going to the table, they find that no wine is available when they eventually sit down, it is sense to ask for it and not to start eating until you get it. Otherwise, if staff see you eating away, they may think all is well – and this is when people get their **Mosel** with the roast and their **claret** with their ice-cream; the order may simply have got delayed. I do not necessarily recommend following the example of one wine trade friend who, if the wine were not ready to serve when he sat down in a restaurant, would insist on the entire table (not just the food) being cleared away and only permit it to be re-laid when the wine was presented! But he had the right idea. If, of course, the wine waiter takes your order in the bar, then he may present the bottle of the first wine to you there. But it is up to you to say what you want and be definite as to when you want it.

THE SECOND BOTTLE – if the host orders a second bottle of a wine previously approved by him, then he should be given a clean glass and taste the second bottle just as he did the first one. Until he has done this, the second bottle should not be poured. If it is faulty, and is poured, then the contents of the glasses around the table may be spoiled. I have seen two corked bottles be presented in succession, so it is worth while avoiding this. For each bottle, another glass and another sampling.

Of course if a bottle seems to be defective, the wine waiter should also try

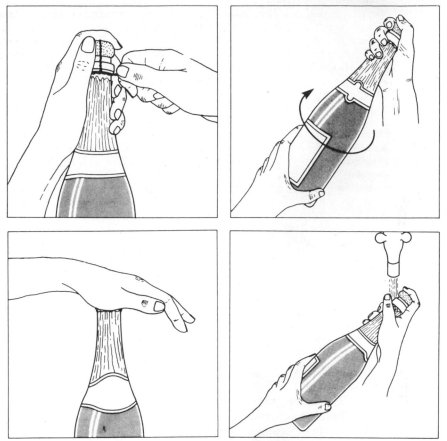

A napkin should always be used to cover the bottle, providing a good grip and protecting the hand in case the bottle splits. Here, however, for clarity, the process is shown without the napkin.

1.   Untwine the wire loop securing the muzzle underneath the capsule – this is usually to be done anti-clockwise. From this instant on, never leave go of the cork.

2.   Holding the bottle firmly, turn the bottle (if you turn the cork, you risk breaking off the top of the 'mushroom') while holding the bottle at a slight angle and not pointing it at anyone or anything breakable. When the cork begins to move, continue to hold it until it emerges with a discreet, fat sound and is received into your hand, not flying.

3.   Have a glass ready to take the first rush of bubbles but, if the wine is extra lively and threatens to foam down the side of the bottle, give the top of the bottle a brief pat with the palm of your hand, which will prevent any loss of the wine.

4.   If the cork refuses to budge, run hot water on to the neck of the bottle just below the cork for a few seconds. Hang on to the cork so that it does not fly out.

it – an experienced waiter will know if a query is justified but, in a good restaurant, 'the customer is always right' and the bottle should be replaced without a charge being made. A faulty bottle can be returned to the supplier, so no one loses. The incidence of really faulty bottles is so small that anyone finding something unpleasant about a wine should ask themselves if it is really the wine – or themselves. Anyone who has been drinking spirits, eating piquant or very acid food or snacks may be disappointed in even a fine and impeccable wine, so be careful before you reject a bottle. It is also worth smelling an empty glass before you do so: glasses wiped with a greasy or detergent-redolent cloth or insufficiently rinsed clear of any detergent, will make the finest wine in the world stink unpleasantly. Many wines are rejected because of smelly glasses or simply because the drinker does not like the contents.

Setúbal   **Portuguese** wine region near Lisbon, the wines of which were famous in history. The sweet whites were enjoyed especially by Edwardian Londoners; perhaps because the then Portuguese Ambassador was a friend of King Edward VII. The **Moscatel de Setúbal** is made in a delimited area nowadays. Red wines, notably **Periquita** and **Palmela** *clarete* are also made here. Jan Read mentions that a red **Moscatel** and Setúbal Roxo 'from the grape of the same name' are also made. Visitors should try to sample these.

Sève   Orangey, herb-flavoured **liqueur**, made by several establishments in **France**. It can be based on **Cognac**.

Sevenhill   **Winery** run by the Jesuits in the **Barossa Valley**, **Australia**, so called because of Rome being founded on seven hills. The fathers originally settled in the **Clare** region in the mid-19th century and started to make wine so as to have supplies for sacramental purposes. More recently, the utilisation of modern techniques has greatly increased the business and, in addition to **communion wine**, the winery now makes red and white table wines.

Seyssel   The best-known wines of 'Savoie, in the east of **France**, all white and either still or **sparkling**.

Seyve-Villard   French **hybridiser** who has evolved several successful **vines**, some of which bear his name.

Sforzato di Spina   **Italian** sweet wine made from partly dried **grapes** in the **Valtelline** region of **Lombardy**.

Shand, P. Morton (1888-1960)   Educated in England (Eton and Cambridge), also at the Sorbonne in Paris and in Germany, he lived at Lyon for some years. He was a considerable authority on architecture; but his wine books are some of the most interesting and worthwhile of his period: *A Book of Wines* (1926), *A Book of Food* (1927), *A Book of French Wines* (1928), and *A Book of Other Wines than French* (1929). Although naturally dated, these are important works, containing much valuable history, plus excellent eyewitness and factual reports of what was being grown in Shand's day. They show the importance of noting down impressions and reinforcing them with adequate background material.

Shaw, T. G.   A 19th century customs officer, who wrote *Wine, the Vine and the*

Cellar, published in 1862. He travelled in many wine regions. His observations and comments are of great interest but some of them incline the reader to the opinion that he did not really know a great deal about his subject and sometimes incorporated the views of other contemporary writers. However, if possible, his writings must be looked at.

Sherry Sherry is the wine that comes from the defined region around Jerez de la Frontera, in the south of **Spain**. According to U.K. law, it can be nothing else. Today in Britain wines which, by long usage, have been associated with sherry because of the way they are made but come from other vineyards, must, if they use the word 'sherry' on their labels, prefix it with the source of origin: i.e. British sherry, English sherry, **Cyprus** sherry, **South African** sherry, **Australian** sherry and Empire sherry. This does not imply that such wines are in any way inferior – but they are not and never can be 'sherry' in the sense of the word laid down by recent court proceedings.

The sherry vineyards are notable for the white soil, called *albariza*. The most important of the sherry **grapes** is the **Palomino Blanco** or Listan; the **Pedro Ximenez** grape is especially used for the great **dessert wines**. Sherry is made as all wine is made – by crushing the grapes so that the juice runs out. This was formerly done by men treading the grapes in special boots, with nails in the soles to prevent the pips being crushed into the juice; but now most of the traditional procedure has been superseded by mechanical methods. The juice then **ferments** tumultuously, and the wine goes into the *bodegas* of the various **shippers** engaged in the trade. Here it matures and, eventually, two types of wine are seen to have been produced. One, on which a veil of fungus-like substance eventually grows (which is called **flor**,) will develop into a *fino*. The other, which will not grow flor, will eventually become an *oloroso*. This is a greatly simplified explanation of the process, but these are the only two types of wine. It is also worth stressing that all sherry ferments right out, consuming all the sugar in the wine, so that it is completely dry in its first state. Any sweetening it later possesses will have been added or **blended** in.

THE SOLERA SYSTEM: The process whereby sherry is matured and a great **mark** continued. The term is used both for the actual process and for the collection of **casks** which make up the *solera*. In essence, the selected wines pass into the *solera* – a special winestore – chosen for them. When it is required to make up a consignment of sherry for shipping, wines are drawn off from the casks according to age and character and then blended. It is sometimes erroneously thought that the young wines go into the top or bottom rows of the *solera* casks, but this is not so: the arrangement and proportions in which the wines are drawn off and the cask refreshed from other wines is both complex and individual to the particular sherry house concerned. All the wines from a single *solera* have been selected originally to continue the traditional quality of that particular *solera*, which may date from many years back, and they will always remain in the same *solera*.

AGE: Sherry cannot be dated by vintage, due to the way it is made. Sometimes, however, a wine or a cask may bear the date on which the *solera* was established. Of course, all fine *amontillados*, *olorosos* and the great sweet sherries will have a high proportion of an old matured wine in them. But whereas the finest dry wines, such as the *finos* and *amontillados*, do not benefit at all by even a little ageing in **bottle**, the sweeter, softer wines can last a long while. Many of the trade would prefer always to drink sherry direct from the cask if possible. 'Old bottled sherry' possesses a changed charm, although it is a comparative rarity and is never cheap.

STYLES: *Fino* is the very dry crisp young wine.

Amontillado (which gets its name because some think it resembles the wines of **Montilla**) is a matured *fino* and can be a beautiful, mellow, nutty wine.

Oloroso – a rather fragrant, darkish-coloured wine – is not, essentially, a sweet wine at all, although it is a fullish one; any sweetening is provided by blending.

Manzanilla is a *fino* of particular delicacy; it can only be matured at the coast, at Sanlúcar de Barrameda, from which its slightly salty tinge is supposed to derive. If a *manzanilla* is moved to Jerez, it becomes an ordinary *fino*.

Palo Cortado is a curious and rather rare sherry, very fragrant, growing little or no flor, and very dry, though darkish in **colour**.

BLENDING AND SWEETENING: The sweet sherries – milks, creams and other sweet-sounding names – are unknown in Spain. They are made up for export markets, particularly for cold climates. The finer examples are based on top-quality matured wines; the cheaper wines are merely blended up. At their best they are produced from the finest old *olorosos*, sometimes darkened with a colouring agent and sometimes additionally sweetened with sweet wine of the region. As has been stated, all sherry starts by being completely dry, the sugar in the wine having been fermented out. But to suit various markets, many sherries receive slight or substantial sweetening. Some of the well-known styles are sold in both Spain and the U.K.; but this 'export' sweetening therefore accounts for the difference in taste that is occasionally noticed by travellers. It is considered a pity to sweeten a great *fino* – but it is also true that many people, especially when they are starting to drink wine, do not like anything completely dry. 'For the British market, call it dry, but make it sweet,' said a respected (and highly successful) sherry shipper, and about 85% of sherry drunk in the U.K. is in fact truly sweet. The delicacy of a bone dry wine also puts it at some risk as it will deteriorate more rapidly, once the **bottle** is opened, than a sweeter wine.

Sherry is blended to preserve the quality of **marks** which have become traditional and successful. A great sherry house can, if requested, blend a sherry to the demands of an individual wine merchant. However the greatest names of the finest sherries are, at least among the *finos*, borne by the wines that come from single *soleras*, without additional blending in of other wines from outside. It is confusion about this that leads some people to suspect sherry 'because it is blended' (whereas it obviously must be, in view of the fact that there is no **vintage** sherry), and others to misunderstand the *solera* system in which the finer wines are kept to themselves.

FORTIFICATION: All sherry is **fortified wine**. This is sometimes denied, because people misunderstand the term *vino de pasto*, but this merely means a wine to go with food. Indeed in Jerez people will drink sherry all through a meal. Sherry receives its first fortification (with added **alcohol**) when it is about 6 months old. For the very delicate wines, to make them resistant to infection, they may receive a slight additional fortification before they are shipped. Although there is nothing harmful involved, wines of low **strength**, even though slightly fortified, can throw a slight **deposit** or go cloudy: then the public suspects the wine as 'bad'. Wines bottled in Spain are sold liable to such hazards, but people who have the knowledge to buy these usually know that a slight trace of **deposit** means no harm, but possibly indicates quality. In Spain, sherry does tend to be very slightly lower in alcoholic strength than when shipped – another reason why visitors to Jerez are surprised to find they can drink so much of it.

SPANISH BOTTLING AND BOTTLING IN COUNTRY OF SALE: Although some fine Spanish-bottled sherries are available in the U.K. and more sherry is being bottled in Spain, it is a matter of taste whether these are preferred to the wines bottled in Britain or any other country where sherry is sold. The bottle used is traditionally the square-shouldered type, but this is merely a convention. What is important for the prospective purchaser of a bottle of sherry to consider is that, if he or she is about to buy a very delicate dry wine, this should not have been on the shelves of a merchant for several months or years – when the wine may have become flabby and dull. However this is a counsel of perfection, because obviously the turnover of stocks depends on demand and how can the customer know the shelf age of a bottle? So, in general, buy sherry as and when it is needed – and drink it soon after buying.

SERVICE: Sherry is a wine – even though its **colour** may vary from pale gold to velvety brown – and it should be served like any wine: chilled if it is a very dry **apéritif** wine; at room temperature (especially in cool weather) for the rounder and sweeter wines. However a recent vogue for pouring these 'on the rocks' appeals to some people. The chilling brings out the freshness and quality in any good *fino*: and a great *amontillado* or *palo cortado* should be at least cool, when its subtleties can be appreciated.

Once the bottle is open, the wine will deteriorate and it often astonishes people to learn that, ideally, no *fino* should be open, even in a cool place, for more than 4 to 5 days. Authorities on sherry will detect a deterioration in hours! An *amontillado* may last for a week, a sweet sherry for a fortnight – but all will change. If they cannot be drunk within this period, it is better to use them up in cooking rather than expect them to be drunk with any kind of enjoyment by people who may know something about wine. If you chill sherry in the refrigerator, it is better to put it back, once opened, into the least cool part and keep it there, rather than take it out and then put it back again on a future occasion.

GLASSES: The *copita* is ideal for sherry, as is the smallish goblet (but not too small) of bulbous shape. The types of glass which are utterly wrong – because they cheat the drinker of the wine's fragrance – are the incurving **Elgin** (which gives a mean measure), the **schooner** and the hideous 'thistle' glass. Portions should be about 10 to 12 out of a bottle, filling the glasses only by two-thirds or half.

SHERRY-STYLE WINES MADE IN OTHER COUNTRIES: Although a type of sherry is made in the U.K. from imported **must** and reconstituted dried grapes, this can seldom be more than a beverage of acceptable quality, varying from indifferent to fairly good. This is the kind of thing with which many people begin their wine drinking and it should be carefully chosen – but it must not be considered as a substitute for sherry, except when people are obliged to choose it for price considerations. The wines made in wineproducing regions according to the general procedure described above, however, are individual productions, meriting consideration in their own right. Again, they are not in any way substitutes for sherry. A fine wine of sherry style can compare interestingly with all but the very finest products of Spain. Indeed, just as it is possible to find exquisite Spanish wines, it is also possible to come across those of indifferent quality. The unsnobbish drinker might well prefer something really good from, say, Cyprus or South Africa to anything indifferent from Spain. What is essential to remember is that all these wines – whether they have the name 'sherry' on their labels, or are sold under a non-committal name or brand making no use of the word 'sherry' – will be quite different from anything else, and different from each other. Some are by no means cheap. In very general terms, quality must relate to price but vineyards, grapes and details of vinification and maturation will produce different wines. These are worthy of appraisal as wines, while many of them are of a quality which will surprise and please the palate. See **Montilla**.

Shipper   Literally one who ships the wine: the term can have several meanings, because a wine merchant may ship certain wines himself, yet a shipper (whether with headquarters in an export market or in a wineproducing region) may or may not be a merchant. But, in very general wine talk, the shipper is, by implication, someone from whom wine is bought for subsequent retail sale, and who buys it himself at source. The fact that a shipper may also own vineyards and actually make wine further complicates the issue; but there is nothing to prevent a firm or, indeed, an individual, fulfilling all three functions successfully.

Shrub   The word seems to have come into the English language in the mid-18th century. It comes from the Arabic *shurb*, meaning a drink or draught. Although its significance is not precise, it usually means a drink made with orange, lemon or a similarly acid fruit, plus a spirit, often **rum**. In the **U.S.**, it was often used in the 19th century to signify a type of syrup made with raspberry juice.

Sicily   The most famous Sicilian wine is **Marsala**, but a number of red, white and rosé table wines are made. Due to the progress of vinification and the need for cultivating a crop that can be exported, the wine industry is of great importance in an otherwise poor country. The Sicilians are proud of their wines and some will assert that, before controls became strict, it was these full-bodied southern wines that made the reputation of many of the more famous wines of the north. Most of the wines are made in **co-operatives**, but there are a few individual estates. The most important wine provinces are Catania and Trapani, but Palermo, Agrigento and Gela also produce wine. The main white **grapes** are: **Caterrato**, **Grecanico**, Inzolia; the main reds are Frappato, Nerello Mascalese and Pignatello. The wines tend to be high in **strength**. See **Corvo**, **Faro**, **Florez**, **Regaleali**.

Sieveringer   See **Austria**.

Sigalas-Rabaud   Estate at **Bommes** in **Sauternes**.

Sigerrebe   **German** white wine **grape**, evolved between the two World Wars by George Scheu. It makes very flowery scented wines, and is useful because it ripens very much earlier than most **varieties**. See **hybrids**.

Sikes, Sykes   See **proof**.

Simi   **Winery** in the Sonoma area of **California**, built by Italians in 1876.

Simon, André L. C.B.E. (1877-1970)   A Frenchman who, from before the World War I period, lived in England. He married an Englishwoman. He was probably the most important influence on wine writing in the middle of the 20th century. Having started in the **Champagne** trade as a salesman, he was always especially devoted to this wine, but he wrote extensively about all the wines of the world, about gastronomy and compiled an important work, *A History of the Wine Trade in England* as early as 1906. In 1933 he founded what is now The International Wine & Food Society and in the following year started the *Journal* of the Society, often travelling to establish branches of the Society in the **U.S.**, **Australia** and **South Africa**, as well as all over the U.K. and in other countries of Europe.

His books are numerous and, whereas his contribution to wine and gastronomic literature prior to 1939 is very great indeed, in his later years he tended to publish a lot of rather superficial work, often without adding to the research that had made his earlier writings so original and influential. The constant re-issuing (without always updating) of his books seems an exploitation of a great name today; and those who appreciate André's work should consider much of it as period writing, by now dated as to facts. His two volumes of autobiography are very charming.

André's kindness to those who wished to learn about both wine and food is certainly legendary and his personality – in appearance he was what everyone imagines a delightful Frenchman, loving the good things of life, to look like – was outstanding. Even when, nearly blind, he attended dinners and other public functions, his benevolence and gentleness were obvious and irresistible.

Simonsig   Estate in the **Stellenbosch** region of **South Africa**, making red and white wines that have won considerable reputations. The present owner, Frans **Malan**, is enthusiastically experimenting with different **grape varieties** and has even started to make a **Champagne method sparkling wine**.

Sirah   See **Syrah**, **Petite Sirah**.

Siran Estate at Labarde in the **Médoc** region of **Bordeaux**, making red wines of moderate to high quality.

Sissano Region in **Piedmont, Italy**, formerly well known for its red wine, because Count Cavour, the Prime Minister, used it to supply foreign embassies. Today the locality produces only a small amount, made chiefly from the **Nebbiolo**.

Sitges Catalonian wine region in **Spain**, making a variety of wines. Well known for its sweetish wines, made from the **Muscatel grape**. See **Penedès**.

Sling The origin of the word is possibly *schlingen*, to swallow. The most famous sling is **Pimm's**, but it will surprise many to know that a sling can, at least in theory, be either a cold or a hot drink. It usually contains lemon and some kind of fizzy mineral water.

Slivovitz See *alcool blanc*.

Sloe gin Fruit-flavoured **gins** are made in many northern countries, but this one is traditionally English. Such gins are made by steeping the fruit in the **alcohol** and possibly flavouring the result as well. Many housewives make their own, but there are several commercial brands, the best-known being that of Hawkers of Plymouth, who have made their 'Pedlar' for 3 centuries. Sloe gin is often associated in the British Isles with the **stirrup cup** or drink served to members of the hunt before they moved off, or simply to speed any parting guest.

Smith **Australian** wine family, now established in the **Barossa Valley**. Samuel Smith of Dorset arrived in Australia in the mid-19th century and began to plant **Yalumba** in 1849, working by night because he was engaged by someone else to labour during the day. The reputation of the wine from this vineyard grew steadily and the property expanded, while the **winery** grew in importance. Today it is very well known for its **port** and **sherry** type wines, but also makes a wide range of table wines.

Smith Haut Lafitte Estate in the parish of Martillac, in the **Graves** region south of **Bordeaux**, producing red and, since 1968, white wines. The property belongs to the firm of Louis Eschenauer. See **classification**.

Soave (Pronounced 'So-ah-vay') White Italian wine from the **Veneto**, made from **Garganega** and **Trebbiano grapes** around one of the most picturesque wine towns of north **Italy** of the same name. It is dry and rather delicately flowery, and should not be drunk with dishes of too strong a flavour.

Soft wines Term recently introduced in the **U.S.** for wines that may also be described as 'extra light'. Previously certain regulations stipulated that table wines had to attain an alcoholic **strength** of 10% of alcohol by volume. The soft wines may be as low as 7% as, of course, are certain other classic wines. See **fortified wine**.

SOGRAPE One of the huge **Portuguese** wine concerns, established in the 1860s. Its correct name is Sociedade Comercial dos Vinhos de Mesa de Portugal, and the controllers are the Guedes family, who make **Mateus** Rosé, Aveleda, and **Dão** Grão Vasco. See *vinho verde*.

Soil It is obvious that the soil in which any plant is grown will affect the yield of that plant. So with the **vine**, which shares with the olive the ability to grow and even thrive, in regions that are too barren and extreme in climate for other crops. But it should not be forgotten that the soil that is visible to the eye may be only a shallow layer over something quite different: the subsoil, or layers of this, are therefore another and possibly even more important influence on a plant whose tap root will be at least 12ft (3·7 m) in length. Then there is the **aspect** of the vineyard, also the various sources of water. Different springs underground may water patches of ground that are close together but, because the soil through which those springs flow may be different, the effect on the roots of the vines will be different too. See **irrigation**.

In general, very rich soil is not suitable for vines, or not for those that are going to make fine wine. There are exceptions, such as in **Madeira**, where the soil is rich but the vines are trained high, so that market garden crops can be grown under their shelter. But sometimes, as in the **port** vineyards or many of the **German** vineyards, the vines are grown on what look like patches of broken stones, with no earth to be seen. Light-coloured soil tends to be favourable to the cultivation of vines that will yield white wines of elegance and finesse – as in the **Champagne** and **sherry** vineyards; the reflection of the sunlight from the pale soil also has an effect, as it reflects the light up on to the vines and **grapes**. Stones are also liked in the soil of a vineyard, because they can reflect the sun's heat upwards, as in the **Rhône** Valley, and because they hold the soil beneath firmly and provide good drainage. Gravel is likewise conducive to the cultivation of vines for good wines – as witness the **Graves** region of **Bordeaux**.

Sand is good in many vineyards, because it provides a light-textured soil and vineyards wholly based on sand are protected against the *Phylloxera* aphid, which cannot live there. Clay by itself tends to make wines that are heavy and lacking in elegance, with a lot of body but seldom that nervous, inner **acidity** that is associated with breed. Chalk and limestone, which are not quite the same thing, are the light, pale soils; granite and schist are the very stony ones. Sandstone and any iron in the soil can make most interesting wines – there is a type of red sandstone called *alios* that is under nearly all the **Pauillac** region. The undulations of the subsoils in many regions, plus the very different topsoils in extensive vineyards, such as some of those in the New World, make generalisations difficult. Of course, a vine will be conditioned by the soil in which it is planted, also by the stock on to which it is **grafted**. But it is always valuable to see the soil of a vineyard – even feeling it can give an impression of what the vines grown there may yield.

Solbaerrum **Danish** blackcurrant **rum**, very fruity. It is often used with ice-cream poured over pancakes in its homeland.

Soledad Dry See **Torgiano**.

Solera See **sherry**.

Somló See **Hungary**.

Sommelier See **wine waiter, service**.

Sonoma See **California, Napa Valley**.

Sopron   See **Hungary**.

Sorbara   A **Lambrusco** wine from **Modena, Italy**, reputedly good.

Sorni   This region is in the **Trentino-Alto Adige** district of **Italy**. Red and white wines are made and apparently they deserve the attention of visitors.

Souche   French word for the vinestock or root. To buy *sur souche* is an expression used for 'buying on spec' — that is, before the **vintage** has taken place. The purchaser relies on his knowledge of climatic conditions and the past reputation of the wine concerned.

South Africa   The South African vineyards have a long tradition and their wines became popular at the beginning of the 19th century in Britain and, indeed, in many European countries. Competition from countries able to get wines quickly to the main consumers, however, presented the winemakers with serious problems in more recent times, and it has been due to the conscientious maintenance of quality and the efficiency of the way in which they have organised themselves that production is able to expand. The wine growers' **co-operative**, the **K.W.V.** (from the Afrikaans words), have five huge **wineries** and are able to conduct experiments of world interest with both **vines** and winemaking.

The vineyards are, roughly, in two main regions: the coastal region near the Cape, and that beyond the mountains of the Little Karoo, to the east. All types of table and **fortified wines** are made, and some **sparkling wine**, many of them from classic wine **grapes** specially imported. There is also a curious grape called **Steen**: at one time thought to have originated with the first plantings of vines 3 centuries ago, and now virtually a native of South Africa. This is now known to be the **Chenin Blanc**, which makes white wine, both dry and slightly additionally sweet especially when late **vintaged**. The wines made like **sherry**, sometimes using the Steen grape and also the Frandsdruift (the South African name for the **Palomino**) for the drier wines, are probably the most famous. They first became popular in the U.K. because of their low prices, due to a lower rate of **Customs** duty on Commonwealth wines in earlier times.

In the U.K., South African wines are mainly supervised by S.A.W.F.A. (the South African Wine Farmers' Association). For many years, this body put up a **blind** tasting of South African sherries with some from **Spain**, so that visitors might see if they could detect any difference. It is possibly fair to say that this was extremely difficult with the medium and sweet wines — especially if the Spanish wines were not of the first quality! But even the *finos*, made with imported and even some native 'flor', are wines that deserve appreciation in their own right. Good fortified **dessert wines** are also made.

The white table wines are possibly better known than the red, and those made from the Steen grape, Chenin Blanc, or the **Riesling** can be excellent drinks. The **Cabernet Sauvignon**, **Cinsaut** and other classic grapes make good red wines and there are plantings of other classic wine grapes, also the native **Pinotage** evolved at the Cape. There is also a considerable amount of **brandy** made, although this last is not often seen in export markets. The most famous **liqueur** made in South Africa is the orange flavoured Van der Hum.

310

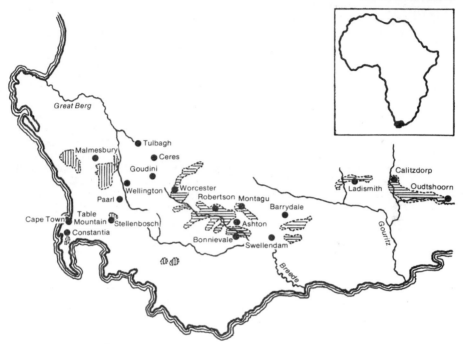

There are many big estates, making a range of wines, including **Twee Jongegezellen** at Tulbagh; **Nederberg**, **Bellingham**, and **Schoongezicht**, the first just outside **Paarl**, the great centre and K.W.V. headquarters, and the two latter between Paarl and **Stellenbosch**. Other estates making first-rate wines, red and white, include **Overgaauw**, **Uitkyk**, **Meerlust**, **Fairview**, **Backsberg** and many more. **Port** type wines are also made, those of the **Allesverloren** estate being very good.

Southern Comfort   American **whisky liqueur** flavoured with peaches and oranges. It is not based on **Bourbon**, although many reference books say this.

Southern Vales   **Australian** wine region, south of Adelaide. It should not be confused with the name of the Southern Vales Co-Operative Winery. The first **vines** were planted in the region in 1838 by John **Reynell**.

Souverain   The big concern of Pillsbury own the Souverain Cellars in **California's** Napa Valley and **Chateau Souverain** (*sic*) in the Sonoma region.

Spain   Enormous amounts of wine of all kinds are made in Spain, although it is only comparatively recently that the numerous table wines have featured among the quality wines on export lists. **Sherry** is of course well known, although the previously popular **Málaga** and **Tarragona** are now not often seen outside their homeland; however, wines of quality, some of them dry, can still be found in these regions. **Montilla** has recently received much encouragement from export buyers. **Rioja** is certainly the best-known wine region, and both red and white wines are made, the estate names and the names of some of the *bodega* owners becoming familiar, as well as the more ordinary qualities of wines. The **Penedés** region, in the hinterland of Barcelona, produces some first-rate red and white table wines, also huge quantities of **sparkling wines**. The better ones are made by the **Champagne method**; the largest establishments making more wine of this type than the big **Champagne** houses! **Priorato**, **Alicante**, **Alella**, **La Mancha**, **Valdepeñas**, **Galicia** and **Navarre** are some of the other wine regions where wines of individuality and some quality are beginning to be noticed today.

In the past, many bulk wines shipped to the U.K. used to be labelled 'Spanish Chablis', Spanish claret' and similar names, in an attempt to attract buyers with little knowledge of all but the most famous names and styles of classic wines. Today, however, the wines bear the names of their regions, or their estates, or are sold as branded wines. It is important to appraise them in their own right and not attempt to compare them with, say, French or other wines. Although some of them are still within the medium price range in the U.K., the finer Riojas, outstanding **vintages** of Penedés and such rarities as **Vega Sicilia** are now in the high ranges.

There are a number of **liqueurs** produced in Spain, the most famous being the yellow and green **Chartreuse** at Tarragona; *aguardiente*, flavoured with various things, such as **anis** and quinine bark, is made somewhat as *marc* is made. **Vermouth** is made, as well as large amounts of **brandy**; some of the latter being produced by the great firms engaged in the sherry trade and also some of the more respected table wine producers. Visitors to Spain should

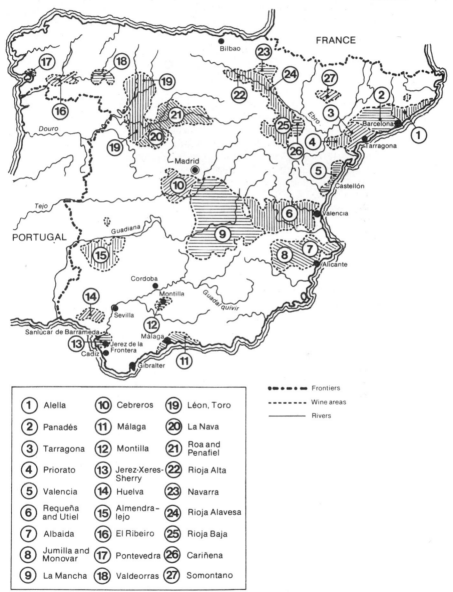

SPAIN

FRANCE

Bilbao

PORTUGAL

Douro

Tejo

Guadiana

Madrid

Ebro

Barcelona

Tarragona

Castellón

Valencia

Alicante

Cordoba

Montilla

Guadalquivir

Sevilla

Sanlúcar de Barrameda

Málaga

Jerez de la Frontera

Cadiz

Gibralter

① Alella	⑩ Cebreros	⑲ Léon, Toro	
② Panadés	⑪ Málaga	⑳ La Nava	
③ Tarragona	⑫ Montilla	㉑ Roa and Penafiel	
④ Priorato	⑬ Jerez-Xeres-Sherry	㉒ Rioja Alta	
⑤ Valencia	⑭ Huelva	㉓ Navarra	
⑥ Requeña and Utiel	⑮ Almendralejo	㉔ Rioja Alavesa	
⑦ Albaida	⑯ El Ribeiro	㉕ Rioja Baja	
⑧ Jumilla and Monovar	⑰ Pontevedra	㉖ Cariñena	
⑨ La Mancha	⑱ Valdeorras	㉗ Somontano	

●■ ● ■ ● ■ Frontiers
- - - - - Wine areas
———— Rivers

313

always try the local wines and spirits, although for the conservative traveller, a large number of the internationally known brands of the latter are made in Spain under licence.

Spanna See **Boca**.

Sparkling wine The bulk of this is white, but some is pink and there is some red. It can be made wherever wine is made, but the most satisfying wines for subjecting to the sparkling processes are usually white, of a fairly high **acidity**, otherwise the result will taste flabby. This means that most of the better sparkling wines come from fairly northern vineyards. Sparkling wines are made by the **Champagne method**, the **Charmat method**, or else **carbon dioxide** gas is simply pumped into them; wines made by the last method are not often seen in the U.K. A good sparkling wine, however it is made, will smell and taste wholesome and pleasant, the bubbles will be small, rise fast and go on rising for some time. If you wish to appraise the base wine from which a sparkling wine is made, leave the **stopper** out before finishing the **bottle** and try the wine 24 hours later, when it will have gone flat – this will show you what it is really like. See **transfer method**, *cuve close*.

Spätburgunder Black **grape** related to the **Pinot Noir**, used in some parts of **Germany**.

Spätlese See **Germany**. The term is sometimes used on other wine **labels** to indicate that the grapes have been late gathered: i.e. when they are extra-ripe.

Spier Estate near **Stellenbosch, South Africa**, owned by the Joubert family and making white and red wines. The gable, shown on the **label**, dates from the 18th century, when the cellar was first founded.

Spitting It often astonishes people that those whose business is wine spit out more than they swallow when they are sampling. But it must be so: to taste 100 or more wines – my own master would **taste** up to 300 in a day – would be quite impossible unless the samples were spat out. Some of the wines may not be attractive anyway: many – as far as fine wines are concerned – are certainly not enjoyable to drink if tasted while they are young. Also any wine undergoing the process of **fermentation** will go on fermenting in the stomach if it is swallowed. No human being can swallow even minute quantities of several dozen wines without being affected by their alcoholic content. Those whose business it is to 'taste' **fortified wines**, also those who are occupied with the selection and blending of fine **brandies** and Scotch and Irish **whiskies**, do this mostly 'on the nose', without necessarily putting the liquid into their mouths at all; indeed, there was one famed **blender** of Scotch who was a lifelong total abstainer – he worked entirely by his highly-cultivated sense of smell.

Spitting is routine in the world of wine and no one should therefore be squeamish about it. Either a spittoon of some kind is provided for those tasting or, as in a cellar, one spits on the floor: should this be concrete, when the splash-back can spatter shoes and clothes, the aim should be for any space between the casks, where the floor is more likely to be gravel. There are times when everyone else spits and therefore no one should be shy about doing so, there are also times – around the table – when it is pertinent to drink, and everyone does so. If in doubt, see what the more experienced are doing. It is fair to say that, in many instances in Germany, people will 'taste' sitting around a table with no sort of spittoon in sight: they do swallow the wines. It should also be possible for the serious – and careful – taster to ask for a spittoon on such occasions, even if this is only an extra glass. The same applies to tastings where the spittoons are few and difficult to reach – spit into a spare glass. I have known people shudder at such an idea. It is better than risking an upset stomach or getting drunk!

When I was beginning to learn about wine, I was told that the way to learn to spit was to lie in the bath and try to hit one's feet. It is possible to spit tidily: take only a little wine into the mouth and, when you want to eject this, push it out, making a sort of funnel with the tongue and sending the breath behind it. Don't just open the mouth – if you do, you must lean over the spittoon to avoid splashing. Keep your head up because, if you bend your neck, you will almost certainly miss the spittoon and possibly spit onto your own feet.

Although many modern tasting rooms provide individual spittoons into which the taster can silently eject the wine, it is impressive to see someone who really can spit do so. On some occasions I have known people spit over the shoulders of those who were blocking the spittoon. The **port** trade possibly spit better than any other branch of the wine business, though I do not know why. Can it be because the additional viscosity of the port makes a long trajectory easier to achieve? One establishment in **Gaia** has a spittoon running underneath the tasting bench, so that it is necessary to stand back and project the wine into this from afar (unless you cower down and bend your head). It was the chief taster of this establishment who is supposed to have established the record – 11ft 6in (3.5m) – that still stands for spitting, and there is a photograph to prove his feat.

However it is reasonable to say that anyone attempting to learn seriously about wine must be neither shy about spitting nor messy about doing so. It is not necessary to be self-conscious. In all the years during which I have been tasting I cannot remember ever having been affronted by seeing anybody spit. Indeed I cannot remember noting anything about anybody spitting, unless they clumsily splashed me. It is a normal procedure and in no way remarkable.

Split See **nip**.

Spring Mountain **Winery** in **California**'s **Napa Valley**.

Springbank This is a family-owned **distillery** in the centre of Campbeltown 'the **whisky** city'. First established in 1828, it makes a highly regarded malt Scotch.

Spritzer Term used for a mixture of one-third dry white wine and two-thirds carbonated water – Byron's 'hock and seltzer' hangover remedy.

Spritzig A German expression denoting the slight 'prickle' or *pétillance* in a young wine. This can be a great charm and also can indicate the youth of the wine, which may be a fine wine capable of achieving additional quality if further matured.

Spumante **Italian** term implying a fully **sparkling wine**, not necessarily made according to any specific method. See **Asti Spumante**.

Staadt   Wine village on the **Saar**.

Staatliche Weinbaudomäne   See **State Domain**.

Stabilise   See **pasteurise**.

Stains, Removal of wine   Manuals of household practice have all sorts of suggestions for the removal of stains, but I do not think that I have ever noticed them suggest the most obvious way of 'lifting' the stain of red wine. It is simply to drench the area stained with dryish white wine. The one wine will cancel out the other. I have demonstrated this so often, on the sleeves of dresses in front of an audience, that I am able to be definite that, if you can tackle the stain while it is still damp, there will be no need to have the material cleaned – I have done it with cream tweed and a friend did it with a red wine stain on white crêpe. Do not use a sweet or **fortified wine**.

If the stain has set and dried, then soaking in cold water will usually shift any mark of the wine – as it will shift a bloodstain. The use of salt and other things has never seemed really efficaceous to me, but I may have been unlucky. Soap and water can also lift many wine stains, even if these are on fabrics that otherwise have to be dry-cleaned.

Gin or **Vodka**, being colourless, are the spirits with which grease stains, such as lipstick or milk, can be removed from most fabrics.

Stanley   Winery founded at the end of the 19th century in the **Clare** region of **Australia**'s **Barossa Valley**. A wide range of table wines is now made and those sold under the name 'Leasingham' deserve serious appraisal throughout the entire world of wine, on account of their great quality.

Stanton & Killeen   Winery in north-west Victoria, **Australia**, under **vines** since the latter part of the 19th century, now making table and **fortified wines**.

State Domain   In **Germany**, the State Domain possesses important holdings in many of the most famous vineyards and is the largest single owner of these properties. The German name on their **label** is Staatliche Weinbaudomäne. The headquarters are at **Eltville**.

Steen   (Pronounced 'Stee-ern') This **grape** was at one time thought native to the Cape wine regions of **South Africa**, but fairly recently it has been established that it is in fact the **Chenin Blanc**. Cape wines are sometimes labelled as 'Steen', sometimes 'Chenin Blanc', and indeed, with time, a difference does seem to exist between the two as they are now. However, a late-**vintaged** Steen can demonstrate something of the character, fragrance and allure of a good Chenin Blanc from the **Loire** or elsewhere, although it has its own individuality and deserves independent appraisal.

Stein-am-Rhein   A vineyard in Schaffhausen in northern **Switzerland**, known for its white wines, although these are seldom seen outside the region.

Steinberg   One of the greatest Rheingau (see **Rhine**) vineyards, at **Hattenheim** in **Germany**. The wine is **vintaged** and matured at **Kloster Eberbach**. It is large-scale, distinctive in flavour and, although rather austere for some tastes, has undisputed nobility.

Steinhaeger   See **gin**.

Steinwein   Term used to denote the wines of **Franconia**, which are white, dry and slightly 'steely' in flavour. The term means 'stone'. See *bocksbeutel*.

Stellenbosch   See **South Africa**. The **Oenological** Institute is there and the beauty of the place itself is outstanding, as regards architecture as well as scenery.

Sterling   **Winery** and vineyards in the **Napa Valley, California**, set up in quite recent times by an Englishman, with his associates. It appears to enjoy an impressive site and the layout is in keeping, but the significant thing about this winery is that it aims to make wines only from the **grapes** of its own vineyards, not buying in any others.

Still   See **Coffey still, distillation, patent still, pot still**.

Stirrup cup   A drink traditionally served to members of the hunt before moving off, or to travellers taking hasty refreshment – hence often associated with the 'one for the road' farewell drink. When handed to the traveller too pressed for time to alight from his horse or carriage, a special type of **glass** was often used, with a longish stem and a knob at the end instead of a foot. A servant would fill this from jug or **bottle** but, as the drinker could not set it down, the contents would have to be emptied rapidly or even at a draught before the glass could be turned upside-down and set back on the tray. See *pomponne*.

Stomsdorfer   German **digestive** herb **liqueur**.

Stony Hill   **Napa Valley** vineyard and **winery** in **California**, established after World War II and concentrating on the production of quality white wines.

Stonyfell   These vineyards, in what is virtually a suburb of Adelaide in **Australia**, were first planted in 1858 by Henry Clark, at that time only aged 15. At the beginning of the business, he and his associates used to tread the **grapes** themselves in their spare hours in the cool of the evenings at **vintage** time. Stonyfell's history is one of ups and downs, but the wines steadily increased in reputation and, in recent times, the vineyard was run in conjunction with that of **Saltram**. Stonyfell today is under a variety of **vines** and the property is apparently steeply terraced. The **winery** is now used mainly for bottling and maturation.

Stoppers   A 'stopper cork' is one slightly trimmed or tapered so that it is easily inserted, which possesses a firm, usually plastic, top. Many **fortified wines** have this type of **cork** to facilitate service. A plainer type of stopper cork without a top is also used at **wine tastings**, when large numbers of bottles must be temporarily recorked, without the bother of having to drive back the original and probably tight corks; this type of stopper cork can, if thoroughly washed, can be used on many occasions.

Glass stoppers, such as are used for **decanters**, are sometimes forgotten once the process of decanting has got the wine into the decanter. But it really does make a difference, with an old wine, as to whether or not the stopper is then put back or left out. Once the decanter is in the warmish atmosphere of the dining-room, this brings the wine on and aerates it somewhat in advance of drinking time. So, if it seems delicate and you wish to be sure of keeping its charm within the decanter until it is poured, put the stopper back; but leave the stopper out with a wine that is still young, possibly even hard.

If the stopper of a decanter is put in when the decanter is put away, there is a risk – if it is not often in use – of it getting stuck. Should this happen, pour a little olive oil around the stopper where it joins the decanter, leave it for some hours and then try and ease it out. Should it appear to be stuck fast, try soaking the neck of the decanter in hot water, when the expansion due to the heat and also the oil may loosen it. If all else fails, you must take it to a chemist or laboratory equipment shop, where there are instruments for undoing glassware that is stuck in this way. Ideally, do not put stoppers into stored decanters; keep the dust out of a decanter by inserting a screw of paper.

STOPPERS FOR SPARKLING WINES There are various stoppers which, when inserted into a bottle of **sparkling wine**, will seal it and retain the sparkle in the wine for some time. They are of particular use when wine is served by the **glass**. If it is desired to seal the bottle and no stopper of this kind is available, it is possible to do so if a wedge-shaped piece is cut out of the original cork, enabling it to be re-inserted in the bottle, and then tied down with string. A special device is used as a **Champagne** stopper; this either clips over the the lip of the **bottle**, or fits on to it by means of a small lever. Both stoppers will keep the fizz in any **sparkling wine**.

Strathisla-Glenlivet This **distillery** at Keith, Banffshire, is one of the oldest in Scotland and was set up in 1786. At one time the **whisky** itself was sold under the name Strathisla, although the distillery itself was referred to as Milton. In 1950 the House of **Seagram** bought the premises and changed the name. Some of this whisky goes into their blends, 100 Pipers and Chivas Regal. The malt itself is described as 'full and fragrant, somewhere between **Glenlivet** and **Mortlach**'.

Strawberry vermouth Chambéry **vermouth** flavoured with Alpine strawberries. The brand name in the U.K. is Chambéryzette.

Strega Bright yellow Italian **liqueur**, flavoured with herbs and barks. There is a traditional saying that those who share Strega will always remain fond of each other.

Strength Alcoholic strength is something that is not of direct concern to anyone who drinks for enjoyment. It is rather like the skeleton of a human being – it has to be there for health and efficiency but only the specialist needs to bother much about that. Nor can it be exactly determined by **tasting** – this is a matter for the laboratory to work out. Some wines which people describe as 'heady' or 'heavy' may in fact be rather light in **alcohol**; the impression they give and the demands they make can be because of their **bouquet** and the fascination and complexity of their character. A 'little' wine, however, can be what the French rightly term 'treacherous' (*traître*) and be right up to the limits laid down for **table wine**. The only way this will be recognised by the drinker is by its effect on his system. The **Customs** and **Excise** levy duty on wines and spirits according to their strength, so that all fall into certain main categories; within these they can vary.

Approximate Strength of Principal Drinks

Wine or Spirit	Gay Lussac degrees	Sikes degrees
TABLE WINES		
Red, white, rosé, sparkling and still	7-14	12·3-24·5
FORTIFIED WINES		
Sherry, port, Madeira, etc.	18-21	31·5-36·8
Vermouth and many wine-based apéritifs	16-20	28·0-35·1
SPIRITS		
Brandy	40	70·1
Whisky, gin, rum, vodka	40-45	70·1-78·9
LIQUEURS		
These vary enormously, both according to type and brand. They can be only just about the strength of vermouth and the wine-based apéritifs, or as high as 55° Gay Lussac, 96° Sikes. But the strength is usually stated on the label, as the law in many countries requires. The majority are about	34	60

There is a belief – often held by peasant producers – that table wines which are right up to the limit of permitted strength are 'better' than others. This is not necessarily so. It depends on the wine. Some of the finer **Mosels**, for example, are comparatively low in strength. Because it directly affects the constitution of a wine, strength does tend to mean that a wine a degree or two higher in alcohol than a similar wine, will stand up to the hazards of travel better. As strength is limited by regulations governing the wines where they are made and by the British Customs and Excise, there is no likelihood of somebody having an extra-strong wine without knowing it. The strength of spirits, however, can vary more, although the strength of each can be checked by the **label**, where it must be given. See **soft wines**.

Something that occasionally gives problems is that, in very hot vineyards or in exceptionally hot years, the strength of a table wine can rise up to or even beyond the permitted limits of its class. It is thus brought into the category of **heavy** or **fortified wines**, as compared with **light** or table wines. Apart from the problems with the Customs and local regulations, this kind of thing can throw the wine out of balance, so that it is not necessarily a good thing at all.

Another source of confusion is the argument about 'Spanish strength' **sherry**, which some people take to mean that sherry in Spain is not a **fortified wine**. But all sherry *is* fortified, within greater or lesser degrees. What is often done is to increase the fortification slightly before a wine is shipped, so that its delicate constitution is not adversely affected. For example, a delicate *fino* may become slightly cloudy or throw a **deposit**, which the ignorant dislike, thinking there is something wrong with the wine. The strength of the principal drinks are shown in the table. At the time of writing, U.K. duty is levied at 3 strengths of wine: up to 15%, from 15 to 18%, and from 18 to 22%. Some spirits intended for export, such as **vodka** and **Scotch**, are of a higher strength.

Stück   See *halbstück*, **casks**.

Styria   See **Austria**.

Suau   **Barsac** estate in **Sauternes**, making good sweet white wines.

Suduiraut   Estate adjoining **Yquem**, in the *commune* of Preignac in the **Sauternes**, making good sweet white wines.

Sulphur   More accurately sulphur dioxide (abbreviated to SO_2) which is possibly the most used form of disinfectant for wine. It is employed to clean containers and anything with which wine will come into contact. Of course it is used in a diluted form, so that the sulphur can do its work without imparting any flavour to the wine. Candles of sulphur are often burned inside a **cask** to fumigate it; and the prudent use of the chemical dissolved in water can destroy potentially harmful bacteria in utensils and equipment. Indeed, it is difficult to know how winemaking would manage without sulphur. A wine that smells of sulphur, however, has received too high a dose for some reason: possibly to keep it clean, but maybe to conceal some flaw. The use of sulphur in a cellar can immediately be perceived by visitors, as the slight fumes tend to make one cough, until some degree of acclimatisation is achieved; a violent inhalation of sulphur fumes is extremely dangerous and should never be risked. The minute squirt of a sulphur solution into empty **bottles** before they are filled, which is routine in some bottling lines, ensures the cleanliness of the bottle and the probable satisfactory condition of the wine. So does the use of sulphur to disinfect **corks**.

Some people are under the impression that sulphur is only used for white wines, but in fact it is used for red wines as well; although, in my experience, it is seldom as obvious in a red wine as a white one. Ideally one should not be aware that it has been used at all.

Suomuurain   Finnish **liqueur** made from cloudberries.

Sur lie   Literally 'on the lees', the phrase is applied to wine bottled directly from the **casks**, which have not been **racked**, so that the wine is lying on the **lees**. The wine bottled *sur lie* will possess great freshness and sometimes a slight 'prickle' or *pétillance*, as if they are still 'working'. Bottling *sur lie* is particularly popular in the **Muscadet** region.

Sutter Home   This **winery**, established in the 19th century in **California**'s **Napa Valley**, makes a range of table wines, but those that appear to have attracted the most favourable comments are the **Zinfandels**.

Suze   See **gentian**.

Swan   Recently-established **winery** in the Sonoma region of California. It is owned by a former pilot who began making wine as a hobby and who has concentrated on an individual style of **Zinfandel** wines.

Swan Hill   A wine region in Victoria, **Australia**.

Swan, Joseph   Recently established **winery** near Santa Rosa in **California**.

Swan Valley   Region around Perth in Western **Australia**, where a number of **wineries** and vineyards are in production.

Swedish punsch   Not a mixed drink as some people suppose, but one made from **arrack**. In this context, it is a type of Batavian **rum** from the island of Java. It is dry, pungent and is sometimes diluted with hot water.

Switzerland   A considerable amount of wine is made in Switzerland, mostly around the Lake of Geneva and the **Rhône** Valley. The main regions are the **Chablais, La Côte, Lavaux, Valais, Vaud** and around Geneva itself. Nearly all the wines are white and many of the classic white wine **grapes** are used to make them, though sometimes these have Swiss names. The **Sylvaner** is here called the **Johannisberg**, Marsanne is known as the **Ermitage**. Of red wines, the best known is **Dôle** from the Valais (nothing to do with the French town of the same name). For the best reds the **Gamay** and **Pinot Noir** grapes are used; the outstanding white grape of Switzerland is the **Fendant** (a type of white **Chasselas**), which is often named on **labels**.

Good Swiss white wines are crisp, moderately fruity and often lively; those of **Dézaley** near Lausanne, deserve their good reputation. The 'star' of tiny bubbles, formed as wine is poured into the **glass**, is especially associated with **Neuchâtel**. The red wines can possess a rather scented **bouquet** and tend to be smooth in character, and also rather fruity.

Sykes, Sikes   See **proof**.

Sylvaner, Silvaner   One of the best-known white wine **grapes**, used in **Alsace** to make the wines bearing its name. It originated in **Austria** and is now cultivated in **Germany**, central Europe, **California** and elsewhere.

Syrah   (Pronounced 'See-rah') This black **grape** is also known as the **Schiras**, Sirah in **France**, and **Petite Sirah** in **California**. It has been grown in the **Rhône** Valley since Roman times and is the foundation of the finest wines of **Hermitage** and Crozes-Hermitage, also making a significant contribution to **Châteauneuf-du-Pape**. It has a marked velvety fragrance, makes wines with depth, length and can give great importance and charm with maturation.

Szamarodni   This word, used in reference to certain **Hungarian** wines, means 'as it is grown'. It comes from a Polish root, not a Hungarian word. Dry and sweet versions are to be found. See **Tokay**.

Szlankemenkå   See **Hungary**.

T

Table wine This term tends to be somewhat loose in significance and some foreign versions of the phrase – e.g. the French *vin de table* – have definite legal meaning today. However, essentially a table wine is a wine that is of a **strength** low enough to make it an accompaniment to a meal: although in Jerez **sherry** is drunk with meals. See **light wines**, *tafelwein*, **German Wine Law**.

Tabor Hill **Winery** in Michigan, **U.S.**

Tafelwein This term, recently introduced in the **labelling** of **German** wines is the lowest grade of the types of wine now being produced in accordance with the new **German Wine Law**. The full expression is *Deutscher Tafelwein*, by which is meant German **table wine**, without any additional qualification of site name or quality. *Tafelwein* on its own indicates that non-German wines may have been blended in it.

Tahbilk This **winery** and cellar is very well known; it is in the Goulburn Valley of Victoria, **Australia** and gets its name from an aboriginal word meaning 'place of many waterholes'. It had been under **vines** since 1845, but when Eric **Purbrick**, son of an English M.P., took over the estate in 1932, it was somewhat run down. Although he had no previous experience of wine, he made the estate world-famous: its wines – only table wines are produced – are individual and much esteemed.

Talbot Classed 4th growth of **St Julien** and a very popular **claret**. It belongs to the firm of Cordier. See **Bordeaux, classification**.

Talisker This famous **whisky** is made at Carbost in the Isle of Skye and has been in production since 1830, in spite of having been denounced from a local pulpit as 'one of the greatest curses'. In 1916 it was taken over by the **D.C.L.** The stills were moved twice before being sited at Carbost; in 1960, they suffered almost total destruction by fire. Its malt is described as light and peaty, but there appears to be some variation, due to the vagaries of the weather on Skye.

Tamdhu Most of the **whisky** made at this Knockando **distillery** goes for export. It was established in 1897 and belongs to Highland Distilleries.

Tamnavulin-Glenlivet The first word means 'the mill on the hill'. This **whisky**

distillery, built in the 1960s, was named for a watermill which was once on the site at Ballindalloch, Banffshire. It is owned by Invergordon Distillers.

Tangerine See **orange liqueurs**.

Tannat **Grape** used in the Pyrenees for red wines, such as **Madiran**.

Tannin Tannin comes from the stalks, pips and skins of the **grapes** and is the element that can give certain red wines a very long life. It is instrumental in making the wine throw a **deposit** on which it will live. While such a wine is young, however, the presence of the tannin will be pronounced and give it an almost astringent, bitterish flavour and draw the mouth of the wine **taster** slightly. This does not make for pleasant drinking, but a wine with the right proportion of tannin and the potential for maturing to produce great quality can be a wonderful drink when its time has come. Unfortunately, because people do not like the tannin in young, big, red wines and because producers cannot always afford to leave wines to mature slowly and naturally, the vinification is often carried out to make a wine that will be agreeable drinking at a much earlier date than would have been possible some decades ago. The great **clarets** of the past could wait 50 or more years, if the **vintage** had so made them so that they required long maturing. Nowadays few members of the wine trade find it possible to tie up capital long-term and, even in a year when very long-lived wines could be made, the tendency in even the finer wine regions is to make wines that will 'come round' much sooner.

There are various means by which this is done: the simplest is to take the **hat** off the **must** in the **vat** after a short time, so that comparatively little tannin is absorbed. Formerly, with the greatest clarets, this source of tannin might remain in contact with the wine for weeks, but now it is usually only left for a matter of days. There are still, however, makers of great red wines throughout the wine regions of the world who, in exceptional years, will make wines as far as possible in accordance with their traditional potentialities. White wines usually do not contain much tannin – a reason why they tend to have shorter lives than red wines, and also why they are inclined to be more delicate as regards the hazards to which wine is subjected: changes in climate, travel and so on.

When appraising wine, the presence of tannin should be recognised. If the wine seems capable of living with it and on its deposit for some time, it should be admitted as a good thing. This, however, cannot be an asset if the wine concerned is intended to be drunk while young and if the wine could not possibly achieve more quality by ageing. With wines in the medium and inexpensive ranges, the presence of tannin to a too marked extent is therefore obviously not a good thing. With the potentially great wines, in certain years, the tannin that can make them displeasing drinking at the outset will be the basis of their character as they develop.

Tapas This Spanish word means 'covers' and signifies the snacks served with **apéritifs**. Traditionally, in some British bars, a glass of **sherry** used to be served with a plain biscuit as a cover over the top of the **glass**, because it is inadvisable to drink without eating something.

Tapio Herb- and **juniper**-flavoured Finnish **liqueur**.

Tappit hen Large pewter drinking measure holding three English quarts (6pts or 4·1 litres), used in Scotland in former times. There is a reference to it in *Waverley* by Sir Walter Scott. See **glasses**.

Tarn Region in the southern part of **France** where the local wines now present a pleasant style in the numerous *vins de pays* being made.

Tarragona This wine from the Catalonia region of **Spain** was very widely exported before 1914, but today is hardly known outside its homeland. This is unfortunate, because the wines can achieve quality. The **dessert wines**, which are not usually as rich as **Málaga**, are generally much liked by the unprejudiced drinker who enjoys the occasional glass of something sweetish. In Edwardian times, Tarragona of the sweet type was often referred to as 'poor man's **port**'; and the description 'Tarragona port' was often seen before legislation enforced the protection of the word 'port'. Tarragona, however, is not necessarily a **fortified wine**, even when it is sweet. See **Priorato**.

Tartrates These are sometimes found in **bottles** of either red or white wine and cause some agitation to uninformed drinkers, who suppose that the apparent 'grit' at the bottom of the **bottle** or the splinters of **crystal**-like substance shining on the **cork** are harmful. In fact, although a bottle that has thrown heavy tartrates can always be returned to the supplier and exchanged (it can be rebottled), the presence of tartrates usually indicates that the wine is very fine – often, a bottle returned will, therefore, be passed to the directors' luncheon room! See **deposit**.

Tasmania Wine has been made in Tasmania, an island off the south-eastern corner of **Australia**, since the first part of the 19th century, but by the end of the century the vineyards appear to have been given up. This was possibly because of the depredations of various **vine** diseases, combined with a lack of knowledge as to how appropriate **grapes** might be grown in the area. It suffers from lack of heat and sun in many years. In the 1950s, however, vine planting was revived by a Frenchman, whose example has been followed by several other pioneers, some of them Italian. In some ways it is as interesting a revival as that of winegrowing in **England**. Up to the present, production has inevitably been on too small a scale for the wines to have made any impression on export markets.

Taste Volumes have been written about the sense of taste, as understood in relation to drinks. Taste is at least 75% smell, and many people would rate the percentage higher (you have difficulty in tasting when you have a cold). Actual tastes are divided into very few categories and physiologically most taste buds are only in the tip of the tongue. But in fact there are those who taste well who have not an acutely developed sense of smell (though they are in the minority in the drink trade), and everyone who tastes professionally would admit to tasting with different parts of their mouth – the feel of the wine on the top palate, the way it touches the sides of the mouth, the sensation it gives along the gums, are all different and all contribute to forming a general opinion of what something tastes like. There is the taste of the wine in the mouth (usually taken in with a little air, which sharpens it up); the taste as it goes down the throat; and the aftertaste, as one breathes when it has been swallowed.

Professionals in the drink business seldom drink or swallow the liquids they are tasting, for obvious reasons. If they did, they would be incapable of getting through more than a few at a time. Spirits and, sometimes, the **fortified wines**, are tasted primarily 'on the **nose**' (by smelling) for the same reason. Those who taste **brandies** or **Scotch** sometimes also rub a little of the spirit on their hands and then sniff their palms – of course without having used scented soap or lotion. This can reveal many things about the spirit – for example, it shows clearly when a brandy has been over-caramelised, because one's hands smell of vanilla. Wines being tasted seriously are spat out. In any event, to drink young wines can be definitely unpleasant; if they are still **fermenting**, they will upset the stomach. With practice, those whose business it is will be able to judge what they taste like without necessarily swallowing them.

Because of the importance of the smell of a drink, tasting **glasses** are usually tulip-shaped, elongated tulips or goblets, so as to concentrate the smell as it released to the nose of the taster. Anyone trying to taste seriously will pour only a little of the drink into a suitable glass. The liquid is swirled around while the **colour**, both at the centre and at the edge, is observed for brilliance, limpidity and actual tone. The liquid is then sniffed or 'nosed'. Next a little is taken into the mouth, plus a little air, and this is run over the whole of the mouth. Throughout, and when the liquid has been ejaculated, the impressions made are precisely noted, so that past experience can be a guide as to what the liquid may do in the future, as well as what it is like now.

It is useless for anyone to try to taste seriously if they have been told 'what they ought to think or say'. An uninformed but sincere opinion, precisely expressed, is more valuable – both to the drinker and those with whom he exchanges opinions – than any glib pronouncement repeated from the pages of a textbook or quoted from the speech of even a great authority. Only experience can give one authority in tasting, but only honesty and clarity of mind can gather the experience first. Those who taste – as those who drink – 'on the label' are wasting their own time and that of anyone who tries to teach them. See **personal taste**, **spitting**, **tasting terms**.

Tastevin The shallow cup used nowadays for tasting in **Burgundy**, when wines must be tasted in cellars, where a light is often lacking. There is a convex bulge in the centre and an irregular pattern of indentations: the **colour** of the wine, as it runs over these, may be perceived more clearly than in a **glass**. The vessel may be made of pottery, glass, silver or plate. Its handle is sometimes flat (which is why it can be mistaken for an ashtray) or else a loop, which in any case will be under the flat thumb-piece, so that the *tastevin* may be carried on a ribbon worn around the neck. The *tastevin*, or *tas* as it is sometimes abbreviated in conversation, is useful for tasting in special circumstances, and some people also find that to taste wine from it enables them to form a more precise impression of the wine's character, because the vessel presents the wine to the mouth differently from a tasting glass.

The Bordeaux *tas-de-vin*, now obsolete, but sometimes seen in museums, is like a saucer with a convex bulge, its interior is smooth and there is no handle. See **Chevaliers du Tastevin**.

Tasting matches A great deal of publicity has been given in recent years to contests arranged between teams who tackle a series of wines in a **blind** tasting. There is nothing wrong with this – if it is remembered that the ability to identify a wine, blind, although a creditable achievement, is not in itself the hallmark of anyone whose knowledge of wine is profound and whose ability to convey their impressions and enthusiasms (and criticisms) makes their opinions of value and interest. People who live in a wine region and within a wine country may have limited experience of tasting the wines of other regions and countries – but they may still know a great deal about the wines of their own region. The extensive ranges of wines listed in the U.K., however, has made it possible for many British tasters – who train seriously for such contests and work hard to alert themselves to the shades of smell and taste that may enable them to pick out wines, **grape varieties**, **vintages** and even estates and growers – to do their 'homework' selecting wines from all over the world. The added perspective that this can give to the right people can make what they say about all wines of great interest and value; they will not find wines 'better' or 'inferior' simply because they are more or less familiar with them, nor will they be inclined to comment adversely on a wine that they have never encountered previously.

Where tasting matches can, unfortunately, have the wrong kind of result, is when the findings of particular tasting panels mark certain wines higher than certain others – and it is then found that, perhaps, a wine of great repute has come second to something little-known . . . the makers or salesmen of the second wine therefore make great publicity out of this. Wines have their 'off' days like human beings and, in some circumstances, the presentation of some wines may not be truly fair. Indeed it is difficult to think how a big blind tasting might ever be 100% fair either to the wines or to the people.

Is the atmosphere dry or damp (humidity makes it very difficult for many people to taste and I, personally, invariably feel less than truly well when it is wet, so this should be taken into account)? Is the place where the tasting takes place lit by daylight or artificial light – and what sort of the latter? Do the tasters stand up or sit down — or are they free to do as they wish? Has whoever is presenting the wines attempted to do this so that those requiring several hours aeration or **decanting** are handled correctly, while those requiring chilling are neither frozen nor tepid – unless the sterner sort of taster wants to try such wines at room temperature, subjecting them to all the hazards this may involve? And, indeed, how has the selection of wines been made – are they of the same grape, from the same region, vintage, price range, grower and so on? Someone who might well be a highly respected taster and who could identify hundreds of wines of a certain type, might be absolutely lost if presented with wines previously only sampled when drinking them at someone's dinner-table!

This is why I think that a little cool reflection must establish that, even if a wine of one region is marked higher than a great **vintage** and famous estate from another *on just one occasion*, all sorts of qualifying conditions should be taken into account or, at least, accepted as being possibly influential. Exactly the same should be said about anyone tasting: the procedure involves a personal test, something that may be a challenge issued on a day when the taster is feeling slightly less than in perfect health, a little worried about some trivial matter, or too concerned about the issues involved if a good performance is not given.

So, tasting matches can be and, in my opinion, should be fun. Those who like training their palates and enlarging their experience will take great pleasure in competing. Those who do not want to compete are not to be criticised, as long as they continue to enjoy wine intelligently. Those people and those wines who do not 'show' to advantage on one occasion, should not be forgotten or marked down for ever. Their mistakes or, as far as a wine is concerned, the possible 'dumbness' or temporary lack of revealed quality should never be accepted as being typical and permanent.

The one thing that no tasting match should favour is a solemn approach to wine. Serious, yes, but the instant the impressed spectator begins to feel that the activity is exclusive, then the whole purpose of why wine is made and why its lovers find it so fascinating is brought to nothing. Everyone should attempt to taste. The good tasters should encourage and teach others. If they are wise as well as humane, they will know that everyone is fallible, that every wine of quality is variable; and that, if a tasting match is lost, it does not mean that every person and every wine in the contest is bad – only that, at a single contest, some people and some wines were even better than those that did not win.

Tasting parties   These are a comparatively new form of entertaining. At them there will be a selection of wines, possibly plus some form of food, for people to appraise. It is a variation on the wine and cheese party and, as a lighthearted social event when people drink rather than taste seriously, it can be both enjoyable and educational. Wines of holiday regions can be compared, different areas of classic wines, different **vintages**, different styles of the same wine – all are of interest.

More serious, but no less enjoyable tasting parties can be given by friends who get together to study wines. For such purposes, the stress is definitely on the wines, spittoons are included and the food – at least until the tasting is completely finished – is minimal and only to clean the palate (bread or plain biscuits). The tasting party can be an excellent and, if need be, inexpensive way of learning about wines, because only a very small amount of wine is poured for a tasting sample. An experienced pourer will get 20 to 24 samples out of each **bottle**. So, if people club together, they can afford a selection of bottles.

Any wine merchant is usually glad to help to organise a tasting: trade help is advisable, unless the person in charge of the occasion is fairly experienced, because procedure should be controlled, so that supplies go round fairly. Also it is useful to have somebody on hand to answer questions, even if no formal talk is to be given. Increasing numbers of tasting parties, both serious and primarily social are given, and they can certainly be a way of finding out about wines without the risk of spending money on a bottle that may not be liked. The palate can also be thus trained to appraise drinks so that future purchases can be assisted and greater enjoyment gained from even cheap bottles.

Tasting terms   As with other specialised activities, tasting has acquired a fairly extensive vocabulary of its own. In an attempt to translate what is a personal and sensory experience into words, lists of terms and phrases often appear in wine guides, some of them more likely to confuse than to enlighten the beginner – which leads to the jokes about wine 'in talk' and James Thurber's 'naïve little domestic Burgundy – but I think you'll be amused by its pretensions'. I do not know whether devotees of golf, bridge, music, ballet are similarly mocked – it is accepted that these worlds have their languages. But, because everyone drinks, everybody thinks that they have a right to try and describe various tastes. Of course this is so, but it usually takes a great deal of effort and concentration to find the exact word or phrase to express certain taste reactions – which is why serious tasters do not react well to those who rush up and engage in social chat when they are endeavouring to formulate an exact phrase in their notes while the wine is in their mouth!

There are certain terms that are easily understood and that have become part of a common language of wine: full-bodied, clean, finishing short, unbalanced, possessing depth, weighty, fresh, crisp, fleshy, elegant, dumb, reserved, trailing away (long finish), scented. Most people would be able to relate these to certain wines. Then there are the technical terms – it is imprudent to make use of these unless you know exactly what they mean or imply: volatile **acidity**, dirty, **maderised**, **oxidised**, **yeasty**. All these are terms that convey something is not right. The chemist or scientist will use highly specialised terms – good and bad – to express his experiences, if he is talking to fellow-technicians.

The member of the wine trade may make use of some foreign terms, especially French ones, in exchanging views with those on the same level of understanding: a *vin fin* (which is not really the same thing as a 'fine wine'), *bien equilibré* (well balanced – usually referring to the balance of fruit acidity and **alcohol**), *net* or *nette* (perfectly finished, clean, as it should be), *mou* (flabby) and so on. The exact meaning of some terms cannot be easily and shortly translated; and even those who don't speak the language will understand their significance.

Remember that tasting young wines is not in any way the same as drinking them when they are ready to be enjoyed. Great wines rarely taste enjoyable while they are young but the onlooker will detect hidden qualities, promise of character, something undeveloped, something mysterious. It is also important to remember that some words may have a special significance in relation to wine: for example '**light**' means a **table**, and '**heavy**' a **fortified wine**.

The whole point of trying to say or write what a wine 'says' when it is tasted, is essentially communication with even one other person. You may receive a clear impression of what a wine is like – but if you can't translate this so that somebody else understands what you have found in the wine, then both shared enjoyment and good business are barred. For example, if someone who has never tasted wines with any seriousness before, says to the buyer of a big firm 'That wine was nice'; the lack of precision is infuriating – all the man is doing is saying that he liked the wine. But why did he like it? If, however, he says 'I loved that wine – it smelt like spring flowers and had a fruity flavour – a bit like grapes but not really grapey, more like a ripe pear – and it freshened up my mouth, I'd like to drink more!' then this can be translated into the sort of impressions one might relate to, for example, a good **Alsace Gewürztraminer**.

People often do not realise that a description which may not seem to indicate praise, can be very much in a wine's favour: 'haystack' is my own shorthand for the sort of Gewürztraminer that I like; 'midden' was that of my own teacher. Communication is what is important – most people know what you mean if you say 'Smells of nice clean tiles', even though the wine really doesn't smell of tiles, it merely associates its smell with something that evokes 'clean tiles' in the taster.

In compiling a personal list of tasting terms, the winelover should be definite, using concrete rather than abstract words, and everyday analogies, being aware that something may seem unpleasant because it is unfamiliar, therefore should try to register it without simply saying 'horrid': then any reference to these terms can be a valuable guide, personally and generally. To cite from my own experience: why does the **Sauvignon grape** invariably say 'old steel carving knife' to me? I don't really know – but I have identified it, when I could not have known the grape was present, in a wine I was tasting for the first time.

If you are trying to register tastes and find that the terms you have heard or read – some of the books listed at the back have excellent vocabularies – don't help you, make up your own without hesitation. Try, when you have formed your own set of tasting terms, to relate them to the terms used by those who are involved in wine as business. Say 'continental lavatories', 'Cherry-ade', 'cough mixture', 'cold steel', 'this wine hasn't shed its puppy-fat', 'this wine is the sort of woman who always shows her underwear – and has dirty shoulder-straps', 'a military man of a wine', 'a gigolo', 'a pretty soubrette', 'a great aristocrat' . . . . all these phrases mean something to anyone of sensitivity. Never hesitate to say what you think of wines to the most important authorities, if you can do so in a way that shows you have thought out what the wine has 'said' to you.

Taurasi Red wines from a region in **Irpinia**, in **Campania**, **Italy**.

Tavel Region at the bottom of the **Rhône** Valley in **France**, where what is possibly the best-known *vin rosé* in the world is made. There are some large estates, selling their wine under their own **labels**, but in general the wine comes from small properties. Tavel is a clear, bright pink, with more body and fragrance than many **rosés**. Several **grapes**, black and white, are used to produce it; the predominating one being the **Grenache**. The skins of the black grapes are left in contact with the **must** in the **vats** just long enough to impart some colour. Good Tavel is a fine, robust wine, and never really cheap. Certain estate Tavels can develop well with maturation, but the majority are best when drunk fairly young.

Taylor   One of the main wine establishments in the **Finger Lakes** region of **New York State**. It was started in 1880 and, during **Prohibition**, kept in business by producing grape juice. Today the firm makes a wide range of everyday table wines, **sparkling wines** and mixes of various kinds. It now is associated with the **Pleasant Valley** company, well-known for their '**Great Western**' sparkling wine.

Taylor, Fladgate & Yeatman   **Port** firm, founded in 1692, known for its wines. Taylor's ports are usually very fine. Some term them 'feminine' ports, which I would not do; to me they have great delicacy but expert construction and longevity.

Tchoung-Tchoung   See **Choum**.

Tea liqueur   A Japanese **liqueur**, made from two types of tea. Formerly, tea liqueurs were produced by some European firms, but now seem to have been discontinued.

Teaninich   Built in 1800 at Alness, Ross-shire, this **whisky distillery** was originally famous for its 'modern' equipment in the 1890s. This included electric light and the telephone which linked the owner's office to that of the **Excise**.

Tears   See **legs**.

Teinturier   French general name for a black or red **grape** that, because of the strong pigments in its flesh, will impart plenty of **colour** to the **must**.

Tent   This word, sometimes seen on antique wine **labels**, was a corruption of *tinto*, meaning red. It should not be confused with certain grape **varieties** which have the prefix **tinta**, signifying that the grape is black.

Tequila   (Pronounced 'Tay-kee-yah', stressing 'kee') Not to be confused with **pulque** or **mezcal**, this is a Mexican drink, made by fermenting the cooked hearts or 'pines' of the Maguey, or *Agave tequilano*. It is matured, after which it may be light gold in colour. The traditional way to take it is first to lick a dab of salt off the back of your hand, then sprinkle a drop or two of lime or lemon juice on your tongue, and finally knock back the spirit, which should be chilled. Its effect, once in the stomach, is rather like that of **schnapps**, but the actual taste and smell do not appeal to many people, hence the chilling. It is also used in mixed drinks and is the base of the Marguerita **cocktail**.

Terlano, Terlaner   White wine region in **Italy** in the **Trentino-Alto Adige** area. The wines are traditionally made from a blend of white **grapes**.

Terra Calda Scorza Amara   A bright red **Lambrusco** which is reputed to have a pronounced **tannin** content. It comes from **Emilia-Romagna** in **Italy**.

Terrace   This word, indicating to many simply a paved elevated walk or outside extension of a room above the garden, has a different significance in the world of wine. The terracing of vineyards is done for several reasons: the walls that hold the terraces in place prevent the topsoil and, in some regions most or all the **soil** being swept away down hillsides in winds or heavy rains. The **vines** can be planted so as to follow the contours of steep slopes, sometimes only a few vinestocks or one row of them being planted on a terrace which, otherwise, might simply remain an uncultivated escarpment. The exposure of the wines to the air and the sun – their **aspect** – can be arranged by terracing so that they are adequately aerated, avoid the risk of frost from the ground, and enjoy the maximum advantages of the angle at which the sun strikes them. In river valleys, too, they also profit by the reflection of the sun on the water, which they would miss if planted thickly or in the flatter areas near the water. The vine, as grown on steep or at least sloping plots, also enjoys good drainage: it will be sheltered from the worst of the weather, if it is not too exposed (as at the top of a slope), but water draining from the top of the slope and going on down will not make the roots soggy. 'The vine likes to see the river but not to get its feet wet' is a **Bordeaux** saying, and the composition of the subsoil is of enormous importance.

In the past, terraces were much used, to hold the vinestocks in place as well as for the reasons previously given. In the vineyards near **St Émilion**, remains of Roman plantations can be seen, somewhat like stone troughs on the hillside. There are numerous and noticeable traces of terracing, like ghosts of vineyards, in many wine regions including England. The cultivation of some fruits in this way, to achieve maximum light and sun, is also traditional. However the use of mechanical cultivators has changed much in the terraced vineyards: it is necessary for a very small **tractor** to be used in many, so that it can be manoeuvred along a terrace on which one or two rows of vines are planted. Even so, the hand of man is necessary for the cultivation of the sort of vineyards seen on the **Mosel**, where the steepness is such that an ordinary visitor finds it difficult to keep a footing. Visitors will notice a few vines on tiny outcrops that one would think it impossible even for a goat to reach!

The '**high cultivation**' method, as worked out by Lenz **Moser** in **Austria** has made it possible for vines to be tended without the time-consuming and expensive laying-out of terraces. In **Sicily**, the Barone de Villagrande has abandoned some of his terraced vineyards in favour of slopes, because machines (labour is in short supply) can work these. The future use of mechanical pickers will certainly encourage the abandonment of terracing in many vineyards that want to produce wine of everyday or medium quality. At the same time, when space is limited, terracing must continue in some areas. In **Madeira** for example, where **trellises** of vines are cultivated fairly high with room for a second crop of market produce underneath them, the fertile soil and limitations of ground make this imperative.

Le Tertre, Château du Tertre   Classed 5th growth of Arsac in the **Médoc**, which, because this parish has no **A.O.C.**, bears the A.O.C. Haut-Médoc. See **Bordeaux, classification**.

Tête de cuvée   The term implies that it is the best wine of what is made under the particular name – but it should be borne in mind that the expression is not a fixed one as regards quality. It is chiefly used in relation to **Burgundies** and it will be appreciated that the various growths and the wines of various growers and **shippers** can vary so much that a *téte de cuvée* of one village and one grower, shipped by one firm, can be totally different in style and quality from that of the next village, even of the same year.

Theuniskraal   Estate making quality table wines in the **Tulbagh** region of **South Africa**.

Three star   The 'star' system is much used for **brandy**, not merely for **Cognac**. However, not even in Cognac does it have any legal significance. The various establishments make different qualities of brandy, to which they allot the numbers of stars. The Martell establishment makes possibly the best-known starred Cognac. Usually the more stars, the finer the brandy. But you need to know the 'star talk' of where you are: a three star **Greek** brandy, unlike the superior qualities of a three star Cognac, is a very tough, coarse spirit. The ordinary drinker there, wanting a brandy and water, should ask for five star. **Armagnac**, however, has tried to regularise the use of stars: a 'three star' or XXX Armagnac will be three years of age. See **V.O.**, **V.S.O.P.**

Tia Maria   See **coffee liqueurs**.

Tiger Milk   See **Radgonda Ranina**.

Tinaja   This is a huge, full-bellied, earthenware jar, used in the **Montilla** district for maturing wines, also in the **La Mancha** and **Valdepeñas** regions of **Spain**. The *tinajas* are made from a special type of clay, may be 10ft (3·1m) in height and are said to be large enough to contain from 660 to 2,640 gallons (3,000 to 12,000 litres). They would seem to be a relic of the gigantic *dolium* of classical Greek and Roman times, ancestor of the **vat**, examples of which can be seen in some museums.

The advantage of the earthenware is that it would obviously keep the wine cool in a hot atmosphere, and storage jars for wine in Roman times were often sunk in the earth, either wholly or partially. Excavations often show vat or jar openings in a floor, similar to some types of modern installations for keeping the wine under control during **fermentation**. *Tinajas* could also, of course, be regularly dampened with water. To this day, peasants in the Troodos Mountains of **Cyprus** make **Commandaria** in a huge jar of this kind, the culture or 'mother' remaining in the bottom.

Tinta   There are a number of different Tintas, black **grapes** used for **port**. The most important is the Tinta Francesca (originally the **Pinot Noir** of **Burgundy**, brought to Portugal in the 11th century). Other important ones are the Tinta Amarela, Tinto Cão, Tinta Roriz, and **Tintas das Baroccas**.

La Tintaine   A French herby **liqueur**, with **aniseed** the predominating flavour. The bottle has a sprig of fennel inside it. The invention of a **Languedoc** family, the name refers to the shield on a pivot, used for jousting practice in medieval times.

Tintas das Baroccas   One of the **port grapes** which is grown in other wine regions, notably at the **Allesverloren** estate at the Cape, **South Africa**, where it makes a quality **fortified wine**.

Toast   The origin of this expression is rather curious. In the 17th century, it became fashionable for gentlemen at drinking parties to allot a name – of a lady or a cause – to the wine in their **glasses** by associating the name with a spiced piece of toasted bread floated on the surface. The practice seems slightly reminiscent of onion soup but it was, as it were, the garnish or trim of a glass of wine to have it linked with a particular name or person. The ultimate tribute was to break the glass after drinking to the health of the person named, so that no less worthy toast should ever be drunk out of that glass. This lead to the making of toasting glasses, with very thin stems that could be snapped between the fingers after the glass was emptied. In those that survive, it is noticeable that the contents of the glass would have been small. Successive toasts were usual at gatherings of the time when the custom originated. The grinding of glasses underfoot or hurling them into the grate seems to have been a later development – and a rather theatrical or drunken excess.

   After 1688 and the Glorious Revolution, Jacobites would drink a toast to 'The King' – 'over the water' – while passing their glasses over a wine fountain or bowl of water, to indicate their treasonable sympathies, while preserving the letter of the law by drinking the loyal toast (the true King – a Stuart in their eyes – was across the Channel at the time). Another Jacobite toast was to 'the little gentleman in velvet' because King William (Dutch Billy) died from an injury sustained when his horse stumbled in a mole hole.

Tocai   **Italian** form of the name of the **Tokay d'Alsace** or **Pinot Gris grape**. Its name will often preface the place name on **labels**. It signifies a light, slightly aromatic white wine and should in no way be confused with the sweet wines of **Tokay** in **Hungary**.

Toddy (1)   This word first appears in the English language in the 17th century, and derives from a Hindu word implying an association with the palm tree. It has come to mean a spirit-based drink, often of **whisky**, topped up with hot water and flavoured if liked with spices or sugar. It need not, however, be a hot drink.

Toddy (2)   The name for the fermented palm sap which is used to make **arrack**.

Tokay   There are several types of Tokay made in **Hungary**: Tokay Eszencia, Tokay Aszú, Tokay **Szamorodni** (both sweet and dry), and Tokay **Furmint**. The first two – Eszencia and Aszú – are the wines that have made the great reputation of Tokay. Tokay 'essence' is reputed to have remarkable properties, including reviving people who were previously about to expire. This may be because of its high glucose content: actually it smells like toasted brown bread and treacle.

   Tokay Aszú is made by allowing the action of *Botrytis cinerea* to work on the ripe **grapes**. These are collected in wooden containers called *puttonyos*: the juice oozing from them is collected and put into **casks** where it ferments slowly over many years; this is actually a form of Tokay essence. The grapes for Aszú are crushed (formerly by the foot, nowadays by machine) to make a type of paste, the richness of the wine being expressed according to the number of *puttonyos* of Aszú paste added to the special cask containing the **must**. This is not topped up and a **flor** similar to that of **sherry** forms on the surface. This special cask is called a *gönc* and holds 26·4-30·8 gallons (120-140 litres). This type of Tokay is sweet – the higher the number of *puttonyos* the sweeter it will be – but the character of the wine is aristocratic, delicate yet definite, intensely sweet without being at all cloying, with a wonderful 'bloom' on the mouth. It is certainly one of the great wines of the world.

Wines are usually listed as 1-5 *puttonyos*, but one of 6 is also made. Tokay is bottled in 17 fl. oz (50 cl) **bottles** of a squattish shape with thin necks. The ordinary and dry Tokays are pleasant, usually fairly full-bodied white wines lighter in colour than the golden Aszú, and good partners for many rich, spicy Hungarian dishes.

Tokay d'Alsace   This is a **grape** used in **Alsace**, which is thought to be the **Pinot Gris variety**. It is also supposed to have been brought back from **Hungary** by the Alsace mercenary, Schwendi, whose statue in Colmar portrays him holding up a vinestock. However an authoritative Alsace grower told me that once, when he was going round the State Cellars in Budapest, the guide told the party that the Hungarians considered that the Tokay grape had been brought to their country by Schwendi! It is obviously one of the things that will never be known for sure.

Tobermory   This **distillery**, on the Isle of Mull, was built in 1823 and was known as Ledaig. Various problems resulted in its closure in 1924. It opened again – and closed – in 1972. In 1978 a businessman interested in reviving the establishment, renamed it Tobermory but, at the time of writing, the **whisky** (formerly known in its straight malt form as Old Mull) has not yet appeared on the market.

Tom Collins   See **Collins**.

Tomatin   This **distillery** at Tomatin in Inverness was built in 1897. It is the largest of all malt distilleries, is owned by an independent company and quoted on the London Stock Exchange – a unique thing among malt distilleries. Much of its **whisky** goes to Japan for **blending**.

Tomintoul-Glenlivet   This **whisky distillery** went into production in 1965. It is the highest distillery in Scotland and is situated at Ballindalloch, Banffshire.

Toni Kola   This **bitters**, evolved by a M. Gaboriau in Conakry, Africa, makes use of the kola nut, which has a more rapid action than quinine. The inventor gave his knowledge to a M. Sécrestat Aîné, who perfected and commercialised the drink, which is tonic and very slightly sweet.

Tonic water   This diluting fizzy drink became popular in hot countries before the advent of refrigeration. Its full name – Indian Quinine Tonic Water – implies its usefulness and advantages, where tap water could be dangerous. Schweppes' is the best-known tonic water; but the word 'tonic' may not legally be used to describe the product in the **U.S.**

Tonneau   **French** word used generally to signify **cask**. It has a specific meaning of measure in the **Bordeaux** region, where it signifies 198 gallons (900 litres). There is, however, no such cask as a *tonneau* in existence today: it is equal to about 4 *barriques*. See **tun**.

Torgiano   Red and white table wines from south of Perugia in **Umbria**, **Italy**. The **winery** of Dr Lungarotti has made them popular and well known, although their quality means that they cannot be cheap. A little pink wine, *vin santo*, and what seems to be a specially created **apéritif** called Soledad Dry are also made.

Tormore   This **whisky distillery** at Advie, Grantown-on-Spey, was the first new malt distillery to be built in the 20th century in the Highlands. Architect designed, it belongs to Long John International.

Toro   Town in the centre of a red wine region in north-west **Spain**, in the valley of the River Duero. The wines are apparently very dark in colour and are locally called Bull's Blood, though they should not be confused with either the **Hungarian** Bull's Blood, nor the branded wine 'Sanguedetoro' made by the firm of TORRES in Vilafranca del **Penedès**, Catalonia. Jan Read says that they are much drunk by the dons at the University of Salamanca.

Torres Vedras   Better known in British history for the famous 'lines' where Wellington's army encamped during the Peninsular Campaign, this region near Lisbon, in **Portugal**, supplies large quantities of everyday wine.

Toscanello   3·5 pt (2 litre) wicker-covered **flask**, used for the white wines of **Orvieto** in **Italy**.

Toul   The *vin gris* of Toul in **Lorraine**, in **France**, is a type of **rosé** enjoyable to try when in the region, but rarely seen otherwise.

La Tour Blanche   A vineyard belonging to the French Government, at **Bommes** in the **Sauternes** district, making fine sweet white wines.

La Tour-Carnet   Classed 4th growth of St Laurent in the **Médoc** which, as this is not an **A.O.C.**, bears the A.O.C. Haut-Médoc. It is a picturesque property. The wines are seldom seen nowadays, as the vineyard has been reduced in size. See **Bordeaux, classification**.

La Tour Haut Brion   Neighbouring estate to **La Mission Haut Brion**, in Talence, in the **Graves** area of **Bordeaux**. It makes a small quantity of red wine, well reputed, although I have never tasted it. See **classification**.

La Tour de Mons   A property of Soussans-**Margaux**, this vineyard belongs to the same owners as **Cantemerle**. Although not a classed growth, it makes wine usually considered very good. See **Bordeaux, classification**.

La Tour Martillac   Estate in the parish of Martillac in the **Graves** region, south of **Bordeaux**. It produces both red and white wines of quality and the vineyards are known for containing some of the oldest **vines** still producing in the Bordeaux region. The property belongs to the firm of Kressmann, who bottles the wines in their Bordeaux cellars. See **classification**.

Touraine   The wine region around Tours, along the River **Loire** in **France**. Red, white, rosé and white **sparkling wines** are made and are becoming of increasing importance in the export trade. The best-known quality wines are mostly white and include still, *pétillant* and sparkling wines. The best-known Touraine wine is probably **Vouvray** in all its styles, but the wines of **Bourgueil**, **Chinon**, **St Nicolas de Bourgueil** (all red), **Montlouis** and any with the prefix Touraine are all worth increasing consideration.

Touriga   There are several types of this red **grape** cultivated for **port**.

Tours-sur-Marne   See **Champagne**.

Traben-Trarbach   Important wine town on the Middle **Mosel**. The best-known sites are probably Geierslay and Würzgarten.

Tractor   The use of the tractor for spraying as well as for turning the soil, has radically affected the layout of vineyards because vines are now planted in rows wide enough apart to allow the tractor to pass between them. In the first stages of this big change, owners were reluctant to sacrifice even a single row of vines, but it was found that the tractor could effect huge savings in time and labour. Today there are many regions where the local people simply will not engage in the hard physical activity inevitable in a vineyard. The tractor can also be used in steep vineyards where **terracing** was previously necessary; people who only think of a tractor as a fairly large, cumbersome vehicle, will be surprised to find a huge range of different types and sizes, able to negotiate narrow terraces, steep slopes and awkward corners. Although much manual labour is still required in the finest vineyards, it is fair to say that it would not have been possible for so many wines to have been produced for everyday consumption without using the tractor, unless slave labour had been re-introduced.

Trakya   See **Turkey**.

Traminer   Well-known **grape** making white wines all over the world.

Transfer method   This is one of the methods used for making **sparkling wine**. In general terms, the wine is made and then bottled, as in the **Champagne method**, after which it is handled in a similar fashion. But when the time comes for the second **cork** to be inserted, the first corks are removed and the wine is decanted into a **vat** or tank, being kept under pressure so that the sparkle is not lost. Then, the **deposit** having been left in the large receptacle, the wine is rebottled and the second cork put in. The method is successful when used for the production of wines that will not benefit by the detailed care followed in the making of a **Champagne method** wine. It seems to have certain advantages over the **Charmat method** because the **fermentation** does take place in **bottle** – the small receptacle – rather than a vat or tank. It is inevitable, however, that the transference of the wine from tank to second bottle must involve both bulk handling and a certain exposure (even under pressure), so that authorities appear to consider that some of the intense vivacity and possibly some of the delicate attributes of the wine may thereby be lost.

Many good wines, however, are made in this way, including some of the **German** sparkling wines, and it is a process much followed in the **U.S.** In the latter country, where the regulations governing the use of the term 'Champagne' are not in force as they are in Europe, the wines made by the transfer method can usually be identified by their bearing on their labels the phrase 'fermented in bottle'. A Champagne method wine will have the description 'fermented in *this* bottle'. In wine regions where labour is cheap and the technical equipment of a **winery** considerable, its use has many obvious economic advantages. See **carbonated wines**, *cuve close*.

Trappistine   A French herb **liqueur** with an **Armagnac** base, yellow-green in colour, and rather herby in flavour.

Trebbiano   One of the best-known **Italian** white wine **grapes**, also grown in other parts of the world. See **Ugni Blanc**.

Trellising   In a few regions, vines are trained fairly high and made into veritable arbours, to ensure that the **grapes** get maximum exposure to the sun and minimum risk of frost from the ground. In the **Minho** region of northern **Portugal**, the vines are trained high so as to accentuate the **acidity** that makes the *vinhos verdes* of particular charm. Trellised **vines** can also be seen in parts of Italy. In general, if the traveller sees trellised vines, these may be for the production of table grapes, as may be noted in vines trained over walls, up the sides of houses, or to make an arbour in a garden. The **Moser** method of **high cultivation** involves a type of trellising and often two level rows of branches on a vine. See **Madeira**.

Trentadue   **Winery** recently established near Geyserville in **California, U.S.**

Trentino-Alto Adige   Region in the north of **Italy**, where vast quantities of wine are made of all types. It has been under **vines** for many centuries, as the **Etruscans** grew vines there, the Romans cultivated the vineyards to supply the wine ration for the Spanish troops quartered in the area and, in the Middle Ages, many German bishops and clergy became vineyard owners. Trentino – the area around the town of Trento – produces the dry red **Marzemino** referred to in Mozart's opera *Don Giovanni*. Trentino wines mentioned by Philip Dallas include many made from classic **grape varieties**, such as **Cabernet, Merlot, Riesling, Traminer** and **Moscato**; and the region's *vin santo* is very highly praised. The **Lagrein** grape makes an unusual pink wine: the white and red wines of **Sorni**, the red of Teroldego Rotaliano and the dry white **sparkling wines** seem of special interest.

In the **Alto Adige**, the red **Caldaro**, Meranese di Collina and Santa Maddalena wines are all made using the **Schiava** grape; the last two use nothing else. The **Terlano** white wines, of varying styles, use grapes such as the **Pinot** Bianco, Riesling Italico, **Sauvignon** and **Sylvaner**. There is also a red wine called Grauvernatsch which sound wells worth trying. Because of the proximity of **Austria** (the Alto Adige is sometimes referred to as the South Tyrol), **German** lettering and terminology are often used on wine **labels**.

Tres Castilles   See **anisette**.

Treviris glass   See **Mosel**.

Treviso   One of the regions of the **Veneto** area of **Italy**, where red, white and **sparkling wines** are made. Some of them are named for the **grapes** that make them, others for their regions. Philip Dallas notes that those of **Pramaggiore** are supposed to be the best, he also mentions the **Prosecco** area as excellent for dry wines. Most interesting of all are the red and white wines called **Venegazzù** which, he says, are outstanding among all Italian wines.

Trier   See **Mosel**.

Triple sec   See **Curaçao, orange liqueurs**.

Trittenheim   Mosel vineyard, making good wines. The best-known sites are probably Altärchen, Apotheke and Laurentiusberg.

Trockenbeerenauslese Term usually only associated with **German** wines, but sometimes now applied to other types of white wines of special quality. It means that the **grapes** have been left on the **vine** until they have become dried and like raisins, shrivelled up by the action of *Botrytis cinerea* or *edelfäule*, which leaves only a little concentrated juice in each. They have to be picked literally grape by grape, the pickers passing through the vineyard several times. The wine made from them will be luscious and sweet though, in wines of such quality, it should not be overpowering or cloying. See **German Wine Law**.

Troia **Grape** much cultivated in **Puglia**, **Italy**.

Trollinger See **Baden-Württemberg**.

Trottevieille (Pronounced 'Trot-veeay') This estate is one of the *Premiers Grand Crus* of **St Émilion** and is situated in the *Côtes* region of that wine area. According to the reference books, its vineyard enjoys sunshine all day long – and the wines possess an intensity and warmth that is doubtless partly due to this. Trottevieille is very well known in Belgium, but some does reach other export markets. See **Bordeaux, classification**.

Trotosky See **cherry brandy**.

Trou Normand This is the brand name of a **Calvados** but it is also an expression for the **digestive** helping of Calvados taken in the middle of one of the gigantic Normany feasts, especially at a wedding, (which might last for days) – a rustic equivalent of a sorbet. The drink helped the diners to revive their appetites and also served to cut the vast quantities of cream customarily served in this type of regional cooking. The traditional way of taking it was to toss it back in a gulp, like **schnapps**.

Trousseau Black grape used in the **Jura**, where it is blended with the **Poulsard**.

Tuica Romanian liqueur, made from plums. It sounds like a type of **slivovitz**.

Tulbagh See **South Africa**.

Tullibardine The local wells at Blackford, Perthshire, have been famous since the 15th century and this **distillery** was opened in 1949 on the site of a former brewery. Much of it goes into Findlater's vatted malt, Mar Lodge, and their **blended whisky**, 'Finest'.

Tun This curious word is of interest because the original – the French *tonne*, no longer used – was the measure whereby the capacity of the **Bordeaux** wine fleet, fetching the wines of the **Garonne** to the English court in the Middle Ages, was calculated. The giant **casks** were rolled from the quaysides directly into the holds – hence 'tonnage' is a vessel's capacity.

Tunisia Tunisia has made wine at least since Roman times: but the present wine business was established at the beginning of the 20th century, when the country was under French control. Both French and Italian settlers developed vineyards and built **wineries** around the Gulf of Tunis and the Cap Bon peninsula. Recently, however, with independence, it has been proving difficult to maintain the wineries so that their products can compete, in quality and technology, with those of European countries in which export markets could be found. All types of wine are made, notably a **Muscat**; but the red wines, slightly softer and suppler than the majority of those made in **Algeria** and **Morocco**, are possibly the most successful. Some are available in the U.K.

Turin   Centre of **vermouth** production in **Italy**.

Turkey   Red, white, and rosé wines are made in Turkey, although few are as yet known outside the Mediterranean. Red Buzbag and white Trakya are usually of pleasing quality.

Tuscan   Both red and white Tuscan wines of good quality are made in **Italy** from the region of **Tuscany** near to that which is now defined as only for **Chianti**. As Chianti is a term only permitted to be applied to a red wine coming from the delimited area, some good wine from nearby must now be labelled 'Red Tuscan'; and white wine that was formerly often called 'White Chianti', must be labelled 'White Tuscan'.

Tuscany   One of the great wine regions of **Italy**, within which are produced red and white **Tuscan** wines; **Chianti**, **Brunello**, red **Montepulciano** from near Siena, and many more. Together with Tuscany, **Elba** red and white wines must be included, the **Vernaccia** di San Gimigniano, the white Lacrima d'Arno, white **Montecarlo** and red **Montalcino**.

Tutti frutti   See *alcool blanc*.

Twee Jongezellen   One of the most famous **Tulbagh** estates in **South Africa**, this was originally called La Rhône, and was founded by a French Huguenot around 1700. Two farmers subsequently began to cultivate a portion of the land – these were the original 'two friends' of the estate's name today. It is possible that one of these was a Theron, a famous name of Huguenot origin at the Cape. Although some of the subsequent owners only had daughters, the estate passed directly from heir to heir until early in the present century, when N.C. Krone I married the then Theron heiress to Twee Jongezellen.

The present N.C. Krone is one of the most respected of winemakers, not only at the Cape but elsewhere, for it was he who designed the latest *chai* built at Château Loudenne, the Gilbey property in the **Médoc**. His son Nicky is now in charge of the **winery**. Twee Jongezellen makes only white wines, but there are a variety of these. 'N.C.' as he is known, experiments with wine **varieties** as with wines, making some of the outstanding wines of the Cape. Recently he evolved a new cross of **vines**, which he named after his own professor in **oenology**, Chandal.

U

U.S.A.   See **United States of America**.

U.S.S.R.   A vast range and huge quantity of wine is made in the south of the Soviet Union. This country actually ranks fifth in the statistics of world wine production. These wines are seldom seen outside their homeland and, as many are produced from **hybrid vines**, it is difficult to be very enthusiastic about their possible quality or their prospects as competitors with other classic wines. The Russian taste tends towards sweet wines, but a number of dry whites are also made and have been praised by tourists. They are all, as might be expected, produced by large concerns and there seem to be no specific estates. **Labels** naturally present problems to those who cannot make out the script, but often wines are simply given the name of their type and, possibly, a number to differentiate them from others in the same range. **Sparkling wines**, referred to as 'Champagne', are very popular in the Soviet Union and are being produced in increasing amounts.

Uerzig, Ürzig   (Pronounced 'Ert-zig') Middle **Mosel** parish producing fine wines.

Ugni Blanc   White **grape**,which is also known as the Saint Émilion in the Charente, where it is used for **Cognac**. It is cultivated quite extensively in parts of southern **France** and is the **Trebbiano Toscano** of **Italy**.

Ugni Noir   See **Aramon**.

Uiterwyk   (Pronounced 'Outer-veek') **Stellenbosch** estate in **South Africa**, under **vines** since the 17th century. It makes a range of wines, of which the red appear to have been the most successful as regards quality.

Uitkyk   (Pronounced 'Oat-cake') Estate at the Cape, **South Africa**, on the edge of both the **Stellenbosch** and **Paarl** regions. The name means 'Outlook' because of the wonderful views from the property. The particularly elegant house, built in 1788, is thought to have been originally designed as a Cape Town mansion – the plans possibly were purloined – by the French architect, Thibault. The estate does not seem to have concentrated on wine production until the late 19th century, but since then the reputation of its wines has increased. The present winemaker, son-in-law of the owner, has extended the range making both red and white wines, many of them of noted quality.

Ullage   The space in either a **bottle** or **cask** of wine between the level of the wine and the closure of the container – i.e. that occupied by air. A wine described as 'much ullaged' will show, in bottle, a big gap between the level of the wine and the **cork**. A wine 'on ullage' in cask may simply be resting on its **lees**. The ullage in the bottled wine may give pause to some prospective **tasters**, but it need not mean that the wine is bad or in any way inferior, although it could indicate that the wine will show signs of age. A wine in **wood** 'on ullage' may simply be waiting to be **racked** or bottled; the expression indicates its current state.

Umbria   Wine region of **Italy**, of which the most famous wines are those of **Orvieto**. Others are those of **Torgiano** and the Colli del Trasimene (the Trasimene Hills).

Underberg   These tonic **bitters**, used also as an **apéritif** and **digestive**, have been made in **Germany** for over a century. They are put up in single **nip** portions.

United States of America (U.S.)   To attempt to describe the wines of what is virtually a large continent in a small space risks making dangerous generalisations. Separate entries deal with the main regions and the more important **wineries**. The earliest explorers named the country 'Vinland' because of the quantities of wild **vines** they found when Norseman Leif Erikson arrived from Greenland around the year A.D. 1000. These vines, however, were native **varieties** and not *Vitis vinifera*. The later settlers both made wine from these and attempted to plant vineyards with European vines, some even bringing over workers from French vineyards. William Penn imported French and Spanish rootstocks in 1683, and Thomas Jefferson had a vineyard of European vines at his Monticello estate in 1773. All these plantings failed, however, because the vines did not adjust to the differences in climate in the east; so the local vines continued to be used for winemaking (see **Scuppernong**). It should be remembered that the use of wine for disinfectant, dietary and medicinal purposes as well as for its social properties was of great importance, so many attempts were made to increase vineyard plantings and winemaking.

The first *Vitis vinifera* plantings were made in **California** around 1769, when the Franciscan friar, Junipero **Serra**, brought cuttings from Mexico; the chain of Franciscan missions gave the name of **Mission** to this **grape** variety and wine was made for the use of the religious establishments from this time. But the authorities were well aware of the need to make ordinary wine if possible and extensive plantations in Pennsylvania, **Ohio** and Indiana were established with a type of native grape, so as to form the original commercial vineyards in the early 1800s. Although there were considerable ups and downs, the vineyards increased in size and extent. By 1880 a special report, which is cited by the authoritative Leon M. Adams, named Georgia, Illinois, Iowa, Kansas, Michigan, Mississippi, New Jersey, New Mexico, **New York**, Tennessee, Virginia and West Virginia as making wine in fair quantities. Meanwhile the

UNITED STATES OF AMERICA

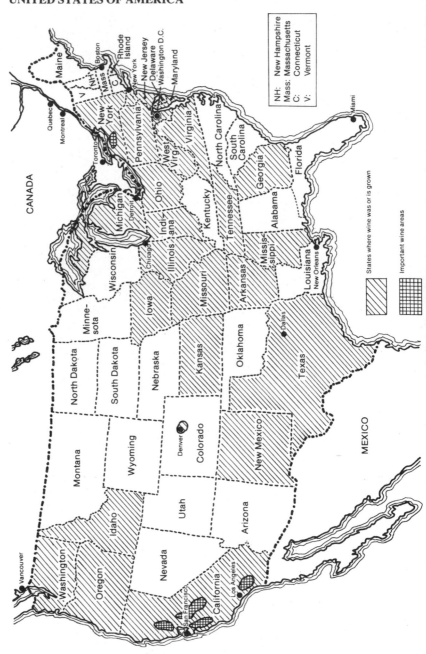

NH: New Hampshire
Mass: Massachusetts
C: Connecticut
V: Vermont

States where wine was or is grown

Important wine areas

CANADA

MEXICO

Maine
Boston
NH
Mass
C
Rhode Island
New York
New Jersey
Delaware
Washington D.C.
Maryland
Quebec
Montreal
V
Pennsylvania
Virginia
North Carolina
South Carolina
Florida
Miami
Toronto
West Virg.
Ohio
Kentucky
Tennessee
Georgia
Alabama
Detroit
Michigan
Indi-ana
Illinois
Chicago
Missouri
Arkansas
Missis-sippi
Louisiana
New Orleans
Wisconsin
Iowa
Minne-sota
North Dakota
South Dakota
Nebraska
Kansas
Oklahoma
Dallas
Texas
New Mexico
Wyoming
Colorado
Denver
Montana
Idaho
Utah
Arizona
Washington
Oregon
Nevada
California
San Francisco
Los Angeles
Vancouver

California vineyards were increasing: by the middle of the 19th century, at least one producer there was exporting to **Russia**, **China**, **Germany**, **Australia** and Britain. U.S. wines won many awards at the Paris *Exposition* of 1900.

The devastation of the vineyards caused by the ***Phylloxera*** affected all *Vitis vinifera* plantings in the U.S. as well as elsewhere, although the native varieties of wine vine continued to produce. The advent of **Prohibition**, however, was a more serious blow. Vineyards everywhere went out of production or at best were seriously neglected, because only a very small amount of wine for sacramental and medical purposes could be made (see **Communion wines**). The advocates of Prohibition even got references to 'wine' in the Bible altered to 'cakes of raisins', in a version of the Scriptures specially brought out at this time! Some growers of grapes, however, were able to remain in production for table grapes and fruit juices. The skills of the winemaker were forgotten during the 13 wholly 'dry' years while abuses of strong drink, appalling mixtures and gangsterdom dominated the U.S. liquor scene. It was apparently only as recently as 1968 that north Americans were beginning to accept table wines as part of civilised living. Immediately after Repeal, they tended to concentrate on drinking wines of a higher alcoholic content, such as the **fortified wines**. The wealthier bought imported wines.

Fortunately the skills of scientists, such as those in the wine department of **Davis**, at the University of California, were able to supply advanced knowledge when vineyards did return to production and gradually winemaking became big business. Today wine consumption is rising steadily, along with production, and the quality of the top wines made in California is equal to any in the world. **Tastings** are often misleading when they take place (often unwisely referred to as 'Olympics' or using similar names) between U.S. and European wines. Where the tasting is held will certainly affect the way in which the tasters – whoever they are – taste, because usually a wine tastes at its best in its own region. The sometimes claimed 'victories' for U.S. wines over those of the classic regions are not fair verdicts. What is certain, however, is that good U.S. wines are as good as any anywhere, if quality is compared with like quality. National and regional tastes differ and, as wine is something that has to be sold, it is the bulk wines that make up most U.S. production. Only a very small percentage of the total comes into the fine wine range and these are not easy to find, even on their home ground, because they are inevitably in short supply.

There are still many eastern wineries making use of the native vinestocks. However the flavour of the wines made, often described as 'foxy' as far as those made from *Vitis labrusca* are concerned, would seem to be definite and likely to appeal only to a few outsiders. European travellers often deplore the way in which north American hosts may pay large sums for European wines to entertain visitors, yet seldom offer U.S. wines; it is not only the quality but the individuality of these that fascinate any wine lover.

Although the cost of U.S. wines of the higher qualities to Europeans and indeed many export markets must put them at a price disadvantage, the

343

enormous interest in wine that is continually growing in the U.S. is a stimulant to both their quality and variety. In addition to the **blends**, and '**varietals**' as the Americans call the single grape wines, there is the odd **Zinfandel**, possibly a native grape but still of debatable origin. It is also to be remembered that the classic grapes – such as **Chardonnay**, **Sauvignon**, **Cabernet Sauvignon**, **Pinot Noir**, **Syrah** and others – inevitably undergo changes in some way when grown and treated in vineyards so very different from those in Europe, in which the wines they make have been known for centuries.

U.S. regulations are unfortunately complicated as far as wine is concerned and do not coincide with those of the EEC, so that interpretation of U.S. **labels** may be occasionally difficult – as witness the use of the term '**Champagne**' for certain sparkling wines. Although top quality wines from the best wineries usually only bear the name of a single grape variety, if the wine is truly 100% made from that grape, the proportion – although it is being increased from as little as 51 to 85% – need not legally be wholly that of the grape named on the label at the time of writing. This is all the more reason why European and other winelovers should acquaint themselves as thoroughly as possible with U.S. wines and the authoritative opinions of those qualified to pronounce on them.

THE REGIONS: Most important is **California**, because it makes the highest proportion of wine of any U.S. region. Huge amounts of **jug** or everyday bulk wines and also the finest wines of all are made there. The commercial fortunes of California's wines were founded by a Bordelais, with the appropriate name of Jean-Louis Vignes, who planted cuttings of *Vitis vinifera* at El Aliso (today part of Los Angeles) in the 1830s. Europeans thinking about California wines (the word is preferred in this form rather than with a final 'n') must bear in mind that the area is both extensive and extremely varied as to climate and **soils**; one large winery may make a huge range of table, **fortified** and **sparkling wines**. There are only a few that make wines solely from the grapes grown on the winery's own estate. The comment of one American visitor to **Bordeaux** – 'And where do you make the **sherry** wines?' – is therefore quite comprehensible. The important areas of California as far as wine is concerned are: the **Napa Valley**, Sonoma, the San Joaquin, **Santa Clara**, and **Livermore Valleys**, **Monterey**, Mendocino, Alameda, **Lodi**, Sacramento and southern California.

New York State is the second most productive wine region, with the **Finger Lakes** district the most important. The work of many experienced winemakers in recent years has resulted in interesting developments as regards vines as well as actual wine production. Experiments have been carried out with grapes to encourage the growth of *Botrytis cinerea*, for example.

Other states becoming increasingly concerned in winemaking include Michigan, Washington, Maryland, Oregon, Virginia, Missouri, Indiana, Illinois, Ohio, Texas and Arkansas. There are also small plantations in Idaho and Denver, Colorado and doubtless, by the time this appears in print, these will have increased in size and others have been established.

United Vintners The wine section of the huge Heublein organisation. They own numerous **wineries**, including 8 in **California**. The largest, in the San Joaquin Valley at Madera, handles the wines from most of the wineries in the organisation, except for those made by **Beaulieu** and **Inglenook**. Their main winery is that of the **Italian-Swiss Colony**. The majority of the wines appear to be those intended for everyday drinking.

Uruguay   All types of wines and spirits are made in this country but they are seldom exported, even to nearby countries, so that travellers should take the opportunity of trying them on the spot.

Usquebaugh   In Gaelic 'the water of life' or **whisky**.

Utiel-Requena   This **Spanish** region, in the west of Valencia, produces an enormous quantity of wine, red and white, with some sweet or dry '*licoroso*' also made.

V

V.D.Q.S. The initials stand for *Vin Délimité de Qualité Supérieure*. These wines are subject to regulations governing production and quality control which are slightly less demanding than those for the **A.O.C.** In **France**, where the description is in force, the initials must be used on the main **label** or else on a separate stick-on label. The V.D.Q.S. regulations were started in 1949 and many V.D.Q.S. wines have since become popular, notably those from regions in the south, where previously mainly only bulk wines for **blending** were made. The category encourages drinkers to discover new small-scale wines, some of them well made and of individual style, providing good drinks. See *Vin de pays*.

V.O. The term suggests 'very old', but in fact has no legal significance for either **Cognac** or most **brandies**. It usually simply implies that the spirit is in the superior category of the range produced by the establishment. Firms use their own symbols to categorise their brandies. V.O. **Armagnacs**, however, are between 5 and 10 years of age.

V.Q.P.R.D. The initials stand for *Vins de qualité produits dans les regions determinées*, and apply to EEC wines. For these, the **A.O.C.**s, which are all officially listed, are defined by the individual countries. Some confusion has arisen because it is not always realised that a **French** wine can also be a V.Q.P.R.D. wine: France is a member of the EEC.

V.S.O.P. A term usually applied to a **brandy**, implying it is of good quality, which is often interpreted as 'very special old pale'. The **colour** of the spirit is no indication of its age: some firms know that customers think that fine old brandy is dark and treacly, as if it had been long in **wood** – so they add a little caramel, either to colour the spirit, or simply to maintain the consistency of colour of a popular brand. A truly 'pale' brandy is one that has not been allowed to take on too much colour from the **cask** and is naturally a delicate bronze-gold.

As used in **Cognac**, where 'V.S.O.P.' is the big brand of Rémy Martin, the term has no legal significance, only the implication of age and quality. In **Armagnac**, however, a V.S.O.P. will be from 10 to 15 years of age. In other parts of the world, the term is used without legal restrictions and according to the decision of the producer of the brandy.

346

Vacqueyras (Pronounced 'Vac-kay-rass' equal stresses). A **Côtes du Rhône** Villages vineyard, making good, slightly soft and fluid red wines (plus a little pink and white) that are now becoming known on export lists.

Valais One of the most famous of **Swiss** wine regions, just north of Italy. A number of quite well-known wines are made here including **Dôle**, **Fendant**, **Johannisberg** and other red and white wines.

Valbuena See **Vega Sicilia**.

Valdeorras Region in Galicia, **Spain**, making red wines of adequate quality.

Valdepeñas (Pronounced 'Val-dy-pen-yass' stressing 'pen') A **Spanish** vineyard area around **La Mancha**, the country of Don Quixote. The name means 'valley of stones'. Large quantities of rather ordinary red and white wine are made, also some intended for **distillation** and **brandy** making. The wines are traditionally **fermented** in *tinajas*. Most of the wines are drunk while young, drawn straight from the *tinaja*, but some are nowadays aged a little in **wood** or sold for **blending**. Although some Valdepeñas wines do nowadays feature on occasional export lists, most of them are drunk as **carafe** or open wines, especially in cities such as Madrid.

Valdichiana White wine from the Chiana Valley in **Tuscany**, **Italy**.

Valencia See **Spain**.

Valgella Red wine from the **Valtelline** region of **Lombardy** in **Italy**. It must be made from at least 95% of the **Nebbiolo grape**.

Valley of the Moon Winery near Sonoma in **California**.

Valpantena Wine from the **Veneto** region of **Italy**, red and lightish in character, and dry.

Valpolicella Wine from the **Veneto** region of **Italy**, dryish and red, with a slight softness and fragrance that can be very appealing. The Corvina **vine** predominates in its composition.

Valréas Old-established vineyard in the **Côtes du Rhône** Villages region, nowadays making mostly red wine, plus a little pink.

Valtelline Region in **Lombardy**, **Italy** with a long and proud tradition for making good red wines that are capable of great improvement with maturation. The **Nebbiolo grape** is the foundation of most of them. Well-known names include **Grumello**, **Inferno**, **Sassella**, **Valgella**, **Castel Chiuro**, Villa Perla, Fracia, and the sweet **Sforzato di Spina**. These wines are not often seen on export lists, except perhaps in some Italian restaurants whose owners have family connections in the Valtelline; but visitors to the area should certainly try them.

Van der Hum See **orange liqueurs**.

Vandermint See **chocolate liqueurs**.

Var Département in the south of **France**, making pleasant red, white and pink wines, which occasionally feature on export lists.

Vargelas Douro Valley *quinta*, belonging to the **port** house of **Taylor**.

Varietal, **Variety** The American expression for 'grape variety'. A wine named according to its varietal is that named after the grape from which it is made. The nomenclature of wines is often according to grape variety in the **U.S.**

However the wines do not have to contain 100% of the grape named. At the time of writing the permitted proportion is being increased to 85%, but the **wineries** making the finest wines often make their wines only from 100% of the single variety. It is probably this that has caused some U.S writers on wine and, presumably, some American drinkers to believe that 'straight varietal' wines must be, somehow 'better' than those made from several grape varieties.

I have read an account of how one traveller in **St Émilion** understood a peasant proprietor to say that 'This region's wines are superior to those of **Médoc** – being made solely from the Bouschet'! (Local name in the St Émilionnais for the **Merlot**.) Of course this is not so: for lovers of **claret**, it is the skilful adaptation of the proportions of the vines planted according to the terrain that makes the individuality of the wines of the different estates. Indeed, I see no reason why this should be something limited to claret, especially as I find many straight **Cabernet Sauvignon** wines somewhat unyielding and up-and-down in style. These straight-backed wines might, as my notes often read, 'be so much better with even a small percentage of Merlot'.

What does seem important is that, when a wine is labelled with a single grape variety – varietal, *cultivar* or whatever the local name for this may be – then the wine should be made only from that one grape. Even a very small percentage of another grape can completely alter the **bouquet**, flavour and overall proportions of the wine, so that it is impossible to compare wines so as to note differences due to climate, **soil** or anything else, if the grape variety is not wholly the same. On the other hand, that small proportion of another grape can be the factor that makes a good wine out of rather an ordinary one. This is especially so with wines that, up to now, have been made from local grapes which can only make wines with predominantly local appeal. The matter is complex and worth thinking about by any serious lover of wine.

Vat   A large container for wine, which may be used to hold wine while it **ferments**, matures, or else for **blending**, according to the place and type of wine involved. Vats of ancient times were in fact huge jars; later they were made of wood, like giant upended **casks**. Nowadays they may be **wood**, cement, stainless steel, or be glass-lined. The French word is '*cuve*'.

Vaud   The biggest area under vines of the **Swiss** cantons, this comprises the regions of **Lavaux** and **La Côte**. It extends north of Lake Geneva.

Vayres   Region to the west of **St Émilion** in the **Gironde**, on the River Dordogne, producing both red and white wines. The whites, such as **Graves** de Vayres, are probably the best known. See **Bordeaux**.

Vega Sicilia   Red wine from Castile in **Spain**, which the authority Jan Read considers to be the finest wine of the country. Only a small quantity is made, produced by the one single company there, the vineyards being planted in several **varieties**, both black and white. The wine is slowly matured in **wood** for a minimum of 10 years. **Vintages** are individual and the wine is full of interest. Such wine as cannot be subjected to this maturation, from late of space, is **bottled** after 3 or 5 years, and sold under the name Valbuena.

Velenche   The *pipette* or *sonde* are alternative terms for the device used for drawing wine from the **cask**. It can be metal or glass and looks rather like a big syringe. It is plunged into the bunghole of the cask and filled. Having applied a finger to the top, the *velenche* is lifted out with the wine held within it. A fine stream of wine is then directed into the **glasses** of the tasters by slightly releasing the pressure of the finger on the top of the *velenche*. It is not very difficult to learn how to do this, but it looks difficult. In the **Cognac** region, an instrument known as '*une preuve*' is used instead, for drawing off brandy; this is rather like the cup of a *venencia* on a cord or wire.

Vendemia   Spanish term for the gathering of the **grapes**: i.e. the **vintage**.

Venegazzù   Red and white wines from the **Treviso**-Piave region of the **Veneto** in **Italy**, which Philip Dallas reports as being outstanding, especially the reds.

Venencia   The deep silver cup, on a long pliant whalebone handle, which is used in Jerez de la Frontera to draw samples from the **cask** without stirring up any '**flor**' on the surface of the wine. See **sherry**. It is very difficult to govern the instrument so as to pour wine from it into a **glass**, yet an expert will manage this. Some will pour into as many as 13 glasses held in the left hand, and swing the full *venencia* round the head without spilling a drop. The *venencia* used in **Sanlúcar de Barrameda** is slightly different, being made wholly of bamboo, the cup at the end being formed from the whole cane. Tourists often try to buy a *venencia* but the real thing is hard to find, because of the scarcity of whalebone. Sometimes a *venencia* is presented to very honoured visitors.

Veneto   Region of **Italy**, well known for both red and white wines, of which the most famous are probably **Bardolino** and **Valpolicella**, both red, and the white **Soave**.

Veraison   French term used to signify the turning of the **colour** of the ripening **grapes**. The black grapes acquire a blue-purple tinge; the whites have either a clear, pale celadon green tone, or else a rosy-gold. In the **port** vineyards, they say 'the painter has been round' when the bunches of grapes change colour.

Verde   See **Portugal**.

Verdelho   (Pronounced 'Vair-del-yo') One of the types of **Madeira**, also the **grape** from which the wine is made. The wine is a rather deep gold in colour and not quite as dry as **Sercial**, with a distinctive charm and sleek texture that can be very pleasing. Some describe the flavour as 'nutty', like hazelnuts. Verdelho is possibly the least-known of the Madeiras but it is a wine to please the discriminating. It can be served as an **apéritif** or with certain first courses, including fish.

Verdicchio (1)   A **vine** of ancient lineage – Pliny the Younger and Juvenal knew and praised it in the time of the Roman Empire.

Verdicchio (2)   The name of several wines of the Marches (**Marche**) region of **Italy**. When Hannibal's troops were about to advance and take Rome, they are supposed to have got so drunk on Verdicchio that they had to withdraw. The most famous Verdicchio is that 'dei Castelli di Iesi', meaning 'of the Iesi castle', which comes from near Ancona. This must be made from at least 80% of Verdicchio **grapes**, the remainder can be made up of **Trebbiano** or **Malvasia**

(see **Pinot**). Verdicchio is white, rather light in style and definitely dry. The Castelli di Iesi wines are usually bottled in elongated amphora-shaped curved **bottles**.

Verdun   Wine estate at **Stellenbosch**, **South Africa**, making a range of quality table wines, red and white, especially reputed for its **Gamay**.

Verduzzo   This **Italian** white wine comes from **Friuli-Venezia Giulia** and is made in two styles. There is a full but dry type; and that called **Ramandolo**, which is sweetish and described as *amabile*.

Vereinigte Hospitien   (Pronounced 'Ver-een-ig-ter Hors-pit-yen' stressing 'pit') German, meaning 'United Hospitals'. One of the important establishments at Trier in **Germany**, living on the sale of the wines from the vineyards with which they are endowed.

Vergenoegd   (Pronounced 'Fair-ch-noorchd', gutteral 'ch') Estate in the **Stellenbosch** region of **South Africa**. Under **vines** since at least 1700, and currently much reputed for its red wines.

Vermentino (1)   **Italian** white **grape**, used in various areas, including **Tuscany** and **Liguria**.

Vermentino (2)   A dry white wine, Vermentino di Gallura, from **Sardinia**, where it appears to be made at two **strengths**. The higher strength is just above that of table wine, therefore providing a pleasant **apéritif**.

Vermouth   A wine, flavoured with herbs, spices, barks and flowers by various methods: **infusion**, **maceration** and **distillation**. It is possibly the oldest form of wine in the world, because Hippocrates, Father of Medicine, made an aromatised wine in the 5th century B.C. Forms of vermouth have been made, for medicinal and **digestive** purposes, since the earliest records of wine, wherever wine was made. The name comes from that of the wormwood plant, *Artemisia absinthium* (see **absinthe**), called *vermut* in German, which was an ingredient of most vermouth recipes.

Vermouth began to be made commercially in **Turin** in the 18th century, and at the end of this century vermouth establishments were started in Marseilles and later in Chambéry. These three places are the centres of major vermouth production today, although vermouth can be made anywhere that wine is made. Different methods of production are used and different formulae used by the various vermouth houses, and each of the great vermouth establishments now makes a range of vermouth. It is incorrect to assume that 'French' is dry and 'Italian' sweet; although the methods of production in **Italy** do differ from those of **France**. White *bianco* vermouth, however, is particularly an Italian product – it is slightly sweet in general – and Chambéry, a very light, delicate vermouth, possesses a character of its own. Recently several firms have produced pink or rosé vermouth.

All vermouth was originally intended to be drunk neat, or in a combination of dry and sweet mixed, and it is interesting nowadays that the trend for straight vermouth is very definite. The **Americano** is perhaps the best-known mixed drink, apart from the **dry martini**. The usefulness of vermouth in the context of drinking fine wine is that, being 'grape' and not 'grain', it makes a good **apéritif**. Although vermouth is only very slightly stronger than **table wine**, it is a wine and it is important to remember that, once the **bottle** is opened, the wine will deteriorate after two or three weeks.

Cinzano, **Martini & Rossi**, **Noilly Prat** are the big names in vermouth manufacture, although there are many other firms making vermouth. Especially in Italy, these are the concerns that have often achieved great improvements by their benevolent encouragement of good table wine production.

Vernaccia (1)   (Pronounced 'Vair-natch-yah' stress 'natch') A white wine **grape**, cultivated in many regions of **Italy**.

Vernaccia (2)   The name of several wines. The most famous are possibly those of **Sardinia**, where Vernaccia seems to be a **dessert** or at least semi-sweet white wine; and the Vernaccia di San Gimigniano in **Tuscany**, where it appears to be a dryish table wine. From limited experience, I would associate such wines with an aromatic, full style. The authority on Italian wines, Philip Dallas, says that Vernaccia wines are among the few Italian white wines capable of considerable improvement with age.

Verona   Wine region around the picturesque town of the same name in the **Veneto** in **Italy**. **Valpolicella**, **Soave** and **Bardolino** are made there.

Véronique   The elongated **bottle**, usually clear in colour, with a triple ring of ridges around its neck, used for certain **French** white wines.

Verveine du Vélay   French **digestive** herby **liqueur**, made in both green and yellow.

Vespaiolo   **Vine** that makes the wine of the same name in the **Breganze** region of the **Veneto** in **Italy**. It is reported to be deep gold in colour, rather aromatic and full in flavour.

Vesuvio   White and red wines are produced in the **Campania** region of **Italy** on the volcanic slopes, and they are now beginning to be known on export markets, although they usually achieve no more than pleasant drinkability.

Vesuvio, Quinta do   This is one of the single **port** wine estates up the Douro Valley, belonging to **Ferreira**.

La Vieille Cure   French herb **liqueur**, made at Cenon in the **Gironde**, with a base of **Armagnac** and **Cognac**.

Vigneron   French, meaning someone who works in a vineyard. It can, of course, be collectively used and sometimes in its plural form – '*Les Vignerons*' – will imply a company or group of those who are concerned with growing **vines** and making wine. When spoken or written as a separate and single word, however, it simply means the individual vineyard worker. Some writers, affecting more knowledge of the French language than they usually possess, will use it to imply 'winemaker', but this is pretentious. As the word is not in *The Oxford English Dictionary*, people who do not speak French may, fairly, not understand the meaning. It is about as silly as the use of *vignoble* instead of the English word 'vineyard'. However, as *vigneron* does mean someone who works specifically in a vineyard, as compared with any other agricultural worker, one can understand the attempt to differentiate the two.

In most instances, however, the context will make it perfectly clear that a vineyard employee is referred to, rather than anyone concerned with potatoes or sugar beet.

Vila Nova de Gaia   Across the River Douro from Oporto in **Portugal**, Gaia is where, according to regulations, the **port lodges** are situated. Some are on the river banks; others perch on the steepish slopes above the Douro, wedged in among winding cobbled streets. The hillside must be completely undermined with cellars and the names of the firms on the roofs of the lodges are clearly visible even from far up the opposite banks in Oporto. To call Gaia a 'village', as one reference book does, is indicative that the writer has never been there – it is a town and of a fair size.

Villa Aanando   **Winery** in South Alameda, **California**, which has become known for its range of inexpensive wines.

de Villanova, Arnaud   Catalan of the early 14th century, who studied medicine and, about 1310, wrote The *Liber de Vinis*. His most important rôle was the introduction of the use of the **pot still** to a wider public than the Arabs (who first evolved it), and various savants and scientists who had begun to experiment with **distillates**.

Villány   See **Hungary**.

Vin blanc cassis   (Pronounced 'Van blon cas-eese') White wine, with the addition of **cassis**. This drink originated in **Burgundy**, where it was made with **Aligoté** plus the cassis for which the region is famous. It became known as *un Kir*, after Canon Félix **Kir**, Mayor of Dijon. Today the expression is known and used all over **France**, as well as the more ordinary term.

There are endless arguments about the ideal Kir: one essential is that the white wine should be really dry and fairly full – even hard. **Muscadet**, **Gros Plant**, a tough white **Saumur** or even a white **Rhône** will do, but nothing delicate. The proportions vary greatly, the Burgundians sometimes giving recipes involving one part cassis to three or four parts wines, but I think most people would find this far too strong: the drink should be blush-pink, not colonel's nose purple. For me, a good teaspoonful of cassis in a 5½ oz (155ml) **glass** is best.

Then there is the cassis – and about this I have crossed swords in print with several dear colleagues, for I maintain that the better the cassis the better the drink. Once, offering a series of guests a tasting of Kirs made with three different qualities of cassis, I found that all opted for a **vintage** cassis. This is made by Trénel who say, with truth, that as the spirit eats the fruit of the liqueur after some time, the younger vintage is the better. I also maintain that, if you use a fairly generous glass, then the cassis should be 'supercassis' or *double crème* – the terms do not mean that the cassis is sweeter, only a bit stronger. The ample measure merits the extra 'push'. I also think that the drink – which can be an excellent way of using up an otherwise undistinguished tough white wine – always needs the kick of the spirit, not just as flavouring. However there are those who like ordinary cassis and even those who say that blackcurrant syrup will do as well. With this last I cannot begin to agree, as one simply gets the very sweet blackcurrant flavour, minus any underlying lift of the spirit. But individuals should experiment and make up their own minds.

In the **Beaujolais**, the locals make this drink with cassis spiking their newly made red wine and call the result a *Rince Cochon* (pigswill, in the sense of swilling out the pig). However, when President Kruschev visited the region, it was felt they could hardly cope with explaining this familiar term to him even via the most adroit interpreter, so they renamed what is a really bright red drink *Un Nikita* for the occasion.

Recently, several other fruit spirits have begun to be used to make a variation of *vin blanc cassis*. Of course, the cassis can be used for **vermouth** cassis (use dry vermouth or Chambéry), or with a **sparkling** or *pétillant* dry wine. I have found the really dry *vinhos verdes* make a delicious base for this drink and there are those who put cassis in **Champagne**. The strawberry **liqueurs** can be used with sparkling wines: in **Alsace** they offer a version with framboise (raspberry) and the newest type of drink has been evolved with crème de myrtilles (bilberries), plus **Montlouis**. The inventor, Yapp of Mere, imaginatively terms this a *Mere*, because of the pronunciation of the first syllable of myrtille. However the strength of the liqueur must be noted, because some are far higher in **alcohol** than cassis. If used in the same proportions, they would merely stun the drinker, who may not have been prepared to accept anything equivalent to a 'double' of spirit in a glass of wine.

Vin clair   This term means the young wine of **Champagne**, at the stage when it is four to five months old and has not yet gone into **bottle**. It is, of course, a still wine at this stage.

Vin de consommation courante   This phrase means 'for everyday drinking' and is often used to refer to the *ordinaires* or non-vintage inexpensive wines.

Vin de curé   French expression for a sharp, virtually undrinkable wine – the local minister may actually enjoy the finest wines as gifts from his congregation, but the wine associated with him is that which a very hard-up or mean person might just manage to buy.

Vin de garde   French term implying a wine that is worth keeping, so that it develops and improves in quality.

Vin de la région   People often want a 'regional wine' but mistakenly ask the waiter for a *vin de pays*.

Vin de liqueur   There was a great row in the EEC in the late 1970s as to whether or not wines such as **port** and **sherry** should – as the French wished – be henceforth categorised as *vins de liqueur*, which would have totally confused all English-speaking markets. The term **fortified wine**, however, means nothing to the French: to refer to *un vin fortifié* implies that it was *viné* or hotted up (illegally) with **alcohol**. As far as I can now make out, *vins de liqueur* must now be made within the EEC; they cannot be alcoholically stronger than 22°; they have to be made from grape **musts** or wines of predetermined **varieties**, which would anyway reach a strength of not less than 12°; and they can receive the addition of neutral **alcohol**, or concentrated **grape** musts, or

distilled wine of a specified **strength**. All very complicated and not likely to affect the ordinary drinker much. But it is worth noting that certain specified wines can also be made from musts of fresh grapes that have not been fermented and that are not up to 12° of alcohol – this is what has happened with **Pineau des Charentes**.

Vin de marque Wine bearing a brand name, usually a standard type put out by an establishment for everyday drinking.

Vin de paille Literally, 'straw wine'. At one time reference books would say that it was a speciality of the **Jura**, but regulations now permit it to come from other areas, although most of it is made in the Jura. The **grapes** which, in the Jura, are usually **Poulsard** and **Trousseau**, are either laid out on straw mats after picking or else hung up on wire frames, so that they dry and shrink before they go to be pressed. The **fermentation** of straw wines apparently takes a long time. The regulations governing their production are apparently being considered at the time of writing. Straw wines, because of the concentration of the juice in the grapes by drying, tend to be **dessert wines**. They should certainly be tried by anyone visiting the beautiful area in which they are made.

Vin de pays This term, subjected to final legal definition in 1979, establishes a category of French wine below that of **V.D.Q.S.** but above that of *vin de table*: although the phrase *vin de table* may also feature on the label. *Vins de pays* are subject to strict controls, including that of a tasting panel, and the amount allowed to be produced from the defined vineyards is limited, so as to maintain quality. There are 77 at the time of writing and they are apparently the only EEC wines to bear the name of the specific region from which they come. The best known are those from the **Aude**, **Gard**, **Hérault** and **Tarn** regions, but there are plenty more beginning to be seen on export lists. They usually offer individuality of style, and in many instances give more interest than many V.D.Q.S. wines. These sometimes seem to be trying rather too hard to achieve **A.O.C.** status, and therefore are made to please, becoming somewhat bland and lacking in definition.

Sometimes people use the term *vin de pays* loosely, when what they really mean is *vin de la région* – that is, a local wine. Of course, the *vins de pays* are local wines too, but the term is now defined and the category must be respected. What one should not ask for is a *vin ordinaire*, as that indicates a 'very ordinary' wine – in other words, something of mediocre quality.

Vin de presse Literally 'wine from the press', by which is signified a wine made after the initial pressings have been drawn off. It is, therefore, not as good as a wine as that made from the first pressings. At the great estates, it is often reserved for local and domestic consumption.

Vin de table Meaning 'table wine', but strictly a category of French wines, subject to controls, below that of *vin de pays*.

Vin de tête The implication of this expression is that the wine was made from the first pressing of the **grapes** – the first two or three pressings are usually the best. Fine quality is to be expected.

Vin d'honneur The words signify a drink on a moderately formal occasion such

354

as the reception of an important visitor. **Champagne** is possibly the most usual drink, but in fact anything can be offered to greet the person or group it is wished to honour.

Vin doux naturel Literally 'natural sweet wine'. If produced in **France**, it will be made in one of the southern regions from the **Grenache**, **Muscat**, Maccabéo or **Malvoisie** grapes, **fortified** – although the French don't like the use of this term! (see *vin de liqueur*) – with from 5 to 10% alcohol, according to the decision of the maker. Some of the best-known of these wines are the **Muscats** of the south, especially Muscat de Frontignan, **Muscat de Beaumes de Venise** and the Grands **Roussillons**, Maury, **Rivesaltes**, **Banyuls** and Côtes d'Agly.

For the ordinary drinker, they are usually only a few degrees above table wine **strength**, making them alcoholically the strength of most **sherries**. They make excellent between-times drinks and, as the result of recent promotions, they can be found in many bars in France even far away from their homelands. In the U.K. unfortunately, they are penalised by the higher duty levied on them as wines being above 14° **Gay Lussac**. Travellers should try them as **apéritifs**.

Vin fou The **sparkling wine** of the **Jura** in **France**, which may be either white or **rosé**. The furious 'crazy' sparkle is made by bottling the wine at the peak of its first **fermentation**.

Vin gris A very pale pink wine, a speciality of **Toul** in **Lorraine** in the east of **France**. It is really a type of *vin rosé*.

Vin jaune Literally 'yellow wine', now subject to controls. It may only be made in the **Jura** region of **France**, solely from the **Savagnin** white **grape**, from demarcated vineyards. It is made according to a special method, whereby the wines are left in wooden **casks** for at least 6 years, during which time they are not topped up and when they are subject to the action of *Mycoderma vini*, which forms the veil (*voile*) on the surface of the wine. This curious phenomenon was important in the work of Pasteur, a native of the region, in his work on the discovery of the action of bacteria.

These yellow wines are strange; they have a yellowish-amber tone, are very assertive in **bouquet** and flavour, and slightly spicey. They are definitely 'important' and, although it is possible to drink them with food, they are perhaps best savoured by themselves as **apéritifs**. Travellers in the region should not miss trying them.

Vin ordinaire French expression for, literally, an 'ordinary wine' – in other words something for everyday drinking, without further qualification. It can be a good 'little' wine, but in general the term has come to imply something that is not particularly interesting and may even be common. See *vin de pays*.

Vin rosé Pink wine. See **rosé**.

Vin santo This term – the final 'o' of the first word is dropped – is a type of

Italian wine, made in a number of regions. It is white and therefore usually made only from white **grapes**. Sometimes it is actually dry, but most *vin santo* is sweetish or definitely sweet. The grapes are often put out to dry on mats before being pressed. Because this drying process, which concentrates the juice, sometimes lasts from the **vintage** in the autumn until just before Easter of the following year, it has been asserted that this is the origin of the name. But for various good reasons authoritative writers consider this unlikely: nor has the term anything to do with **communion wine**. *Vin santo* appears to be allowed to continue its life in **cask** for a number of years before being bottled and is supposed to improve with maturation in **bottle**. Philip Dallas finds that **Tuscan** *vin santo* has a 'bitter after-taste', although being sweet. I have not noticed this, but my experience is very limited.

Vin sauvage **Sparkling** white wine of the Gers region of south-east **France**. It is rather **acid** and foams violently at the outset when poured, rather like a *vin fou*. It is seldom drunk by itself, but is used to make a drink called *Pousse rapière*.

Vine All the fine wines of the world and most of the good ones are made from *Vitis vinifera* although others, such as *Vitis rupestris* and *Vitis labrusca*, especially the latter, are also sometimes used. It is the *labrusca* that has predominated in the eastern vineyards of the **U.S.**, although wines made from it have a curious character, that some describe as 'foxy'. There are a huge number of different types of vine (see **grapes**) and often the use of local as well as national names for them makes the subject a complex and often confusing one. The subdivisions of the main types of vine – **Rheinriesling**, **Wälschriesling**, etc – similarly complicate the issue; and the use of a single name, such as **Riesling**, **Muscat**, or **Pinot**, on a wine **label** need not always indicate the style of wine in the bottle. This is simply because of the **variety** of the different types of vine all bearing the same family name.

Vines will grow where no other crop can, with the possible exception, in hot countries, of the olive. They can withstand great heat and cold, but in general do not thrive in climates that are either tropically warm or humidly cold, as they prefer a fairly dry atmosphere at least for part of the year. The finest wines of all tend to be made just at the extreme limits of where it is possible to grow certain vines and where the vine has literally to struggle to live, combating either bouts of violent heat or bitter cold. Rich **soil** seldom seems good for vines if they are to make fine **table wines**. Slopes are favourable to vine cultivation, as they enable water to drain away and afford a certain protection; in addition, the direction in which they face is of great importance, so that the vines get the sun at the most advantageous angle. The way in which vines are planted in rows or on **terraces** is not merely for ease of cultivation, but so that the plants get the right amount of both exposure and shelter. Generally, the vines grown halfway or two-thirds from the bottom of a slope will make finer wine than those at the top, which risk over-exposure to the elements, or those at the bottom, which may suffer from bad drainage or too rich **soil**. Something that often surprises visitors to vineyards is that, unlike gardeners, vinegrowers prefer the sort of stony, gravelly, schistous soil that holds and reflects heat upwards, ensures good drainage, and contributes to the water flowing through the vineyard by the various minerals it contains.

The vine requires tending all the year round, but the two most important times in its annual cycle are the flowering of the vine in the spring and the **vintage** in the autumn. Otherwise it is **pruned**, trained, sometimes **trellised**, weeded, sprayed against pests and disease and, when it grows too old to bear economically, it is pulled up, and the vineyard left to rest for a period. The life of a vine varies; before the ***Phylloxera*** and before the time when vast amounts of inexpensive wine were required, vines tended to be left for longer before the vineyard was replanted. Vines of 50 to 100 years old were usual in some vineyards, yielding little but contributing quality. They are rarities today. Usually a vine will bear **grapes** that can be made into wine when it is from 3 to 5 years old; but young vines do not always yield grapes of sufficient quality for them to contribute to the making of the finest wines. In many of the great vineyards, vines will not be used for the *grand vin* of the property until they are 7 to 12 years of age. Their life will then vary, but most vines yield until they are 25 to 35 years old.

According to the type of vine, the situation of the vineyard and the sort of wine it is wished to make, the vines are made to grow high or low; some in single plants, others trained so that they form types of hedges. The amount of wine that each section of a vineyard can yield is controlled, as is the method of cultivation (see ***Appellation d'Origine Contrôlee***). In **Germany**, for example, it is estimated that each vinestock will yield 1.76 pts (1 litre) of wine as far as fine wines are concerned. In a vineyard making cheap wine the yield might be much higher; and so indeed might the yield in an exceptionally good **vintage**. It is considered that it 'takes two years to make a vintage', because the vine can benefit enormously by what has happened in the vineyard in the preceding year. That is why, in many classic vineyard areas, vintages of special interest often go in pairs: the second vintage is often finer than the first.

Vinegar   The vinegar bacteria, *Acetobacter*, acts upon the **alcohol** left in a newly made wine if this is not run off the mass of débris left in it, including the dead **yeasts**. See **fermentation**. The alcohol is then converted to **acetic acid**, which turns to vinegar. This is why cleanliness is essential in making wine and why the presence of a forgotten open **bottle** or undrained **cask** of wine in a cellar can infect the new wine. Therefore, in firms when wine vinegar is made, the vinegar is kept strictly apart from the wine.

It is also why the finest vinegar is wine vinegar. Anyone who wonders how this can vary, should compare a salad dressing made with very old wine vinegar, especially **sherry** vinegar (sherry yeasts are very vigorous), with the same dressing made with something inexpensive – or even with malt vinegar. This last, possibly adequate in the making of pickles, was described as 'only fit for stripping varnish off furniture' by the late Raymond **Postgate**.

Vinho verde   (Pronounced 'Veen-yo vaird') This is the 'green wine' of the **Minho** of north **Portugal**. The vines here are trained to grow high, along trellises and up high poles, so that the **acidity** in the **must** is high. The type of secondary **fermentation** which takes place after the wines are bottled, produces the slight 'prickle' or faint sparkle which is typical and refreshing. Strictly controlled, the wines are labelled with the stamp of their Association. The shape of **bottles** used varies, but two important points should be noted: *vinho verde* is meant to be drunk young, so that it never bears a **vintage** date; and although there is red and white (the bulk of *vinho verde* sold outside Portugal is white), there is no such thing as a pink (**rosé**) green wine. *Vinhos verdes* are usually very dry, although some intended for the British market are made slightly sweeter than they might be on their home ground. The sparkle or *pétillance* varies too, sometimes it is (quite permissably) increased a little.

Vino cotto   See **Marsala**.

Vino de pasto   Spanish **table wine**, literally 'wine with a repast'. The term could be taken to mean a table wine in the British sense (see **wine**) but in fact some **sherry** is sold as a *vino de pasto*. This type of sherry, however, may not be **fortified** up to the 'shipping **strength**' of a wine intended for export, so that it will not be so 'strong', although it may be stronger than an ordinary **light wine**. Also called *vino de mesa*.

Vino verde   Wine from Galicia in northern **Spain**; both red and white are made. They somewhat resemble their neighbours, the *vinhos verdes* of **Portugal**. The authority Jan Read states that some of them may also be *vinhos de aguja*, possessing a natural sparkle in the form of a quite definite *pétillance*, whereas some of the 'green' wines may only have the sort of 'prickle' that one can feel on the palate. He also says that red *vinos verdes* are traditionally drunk from white cups, so as to display their dark purple **colour** better.

Vino Vista   **Winery** in Sonoma, **California**.

Vins effervescents   There are several types of wine in this category, classified by the EEC in 1970. There is the *vin mousseux*, a **sparkling wine** produced solely through **fermentation**, with a sparkle of a certain degree (3 atmospheres according to the Decree, but this would not be very fully sparkling in my view). There is *vin mousseux gazéifié*, which has been made partly or entirely by the addition of **carbon dioxide**. There is *vin pétillant*, which is semi-sparkling (and not less than 1 and not more than 2.5 atmospheres); and *vin pétillant gazéifié*, which is the same type of wine that may have been made wholly or partly by the addition of carbon dioxide. There are also wines that can be made by the method *rurale*, a non-fermented **must** being used as a 'starter', as with **Blanquette de Limoux**, or a half-fermented must, as with **Clairette de Die**. See **carbonated wines**.

Vins tranquilles   These are wines which, according to both French and EEC legal regulations, are not **sparkling** but which may be very slightly fizzy: this fizz is known as *mustille*. Ordinary **bottles** and **corks** are used for them.

Vinsobres   Vineyard around village of the same name in the **Côtes du Rhône** Villages region, making mostly red wine, although a little pink and white is also produced.

Vintage   The word, much abused, implies that the wine bears the date of the year in which it was made – and therefore when it was vintaged, or harvested. There are two reasons why this can be important. With wines that are at their best when they are drunk young and fresh, when their charm is at its peak, it is helpful to know how young they are; so that they are not kept beyond the time when they are at their most enjoyable – old wines of certain types decline and may be disappointing or downright unpleasant. With wines that are capable of achieving great quality if allowed to mature over a period of time, it is also important to know how old they are – and, therefore, how soon they may be ready for drinking.

In the 'young and fresh' category, one might put **Muscadet**, certain sorts of **Beaujolais**, and types of the finer **German** wines that do not possess additional qualifications suggesting that they may get much better with keeping. In the 'When will they be ready to drink?' category are the great red **Burgundies**, **clarets** and many other red wines, also the finest German wines, certain white Burgundies and vintage **port**.

With regard to wines capable of changing and improving in **bottle** over a period of time, the characteristics of their vintage years is of great interest to the drinker. A claret of one year, for example, may need 15 or more years even to be drinkable; although the wine of the preceding or succeeding year from the same property may be at its best within 5 or 7 years. This is the sort of thing where only experience and knowledge of the experience of others can guide. Also the taste of the drinker is personal. In many wine regions, the drinker who lives there will prefer to drink even the finer wines while they are young; in the U.K. the tradition tends to be for the finer wines to be allowed to reach their maturity slowly and not risk losing the additional enjoyment that they may give even at what may seem a great age.

A really silly use of the word 'vintage' is when people insist on 'a vintage wine'. The term in itself implies that the wine so described is initially of quality and has the potential to get better – it cannot, therefore, be applied to the majority of the good wines that give immediate pleasure to the majority of drinkers. The bulk of **Champagne** and nearly all quality **sparkling wines** are non-vintage; most of the good 'everyday' wines are non-vintage. The sort of branded wines that can be bought anywhere in the world and assure the purchaser of a certain type of quality – and enjoyment – are non-vintage. **Sherry**, **port** (except for vintage port) and **Madeira** cannot be 'vintage wines' because of the way they are made; however high the proportion of old wines in them. Most *vin rosé*, all *vinho verde* and **Asti Spumante**, and many *commune* wines are non-vintage. No possible advantage is achieved by putting a date on them, as they are not inteded to be put down for long-term maturation. They will be ready to be enjoyed from the moment they are offered for sale in the bottle.

With certain of the finer wines, the 'off vintages' can be very interesting. These are the wines of years which are not generally considered as exceptional, but in which some good wine can be made. The owners of estates with great names are chary of putting their estate labels on to wines that may disappoint drinkers or that fall short of their owners' standards of quality. So, if an estate wine of a year not otherwise highly reputed is sold under its own name bearing the label of its estate, it will be well worth trying, because it may be a small-scale or lighter version of the wine as made in more favourable conditions. These are the wines to drink at lunchtime or as the first wines at a wine dinner. But everyone buying the wine of an unknown property or an estate without a reputation for quality, bearing a vintage date indicating that the wine must have been made in adverse conditions, is risking a possibly unsatisfactory experience. In an otherwise bad year, the conscientious owners will often declassify their wines or, if something has gone wrong that cannot be put quite right, put the wine into a house blend.

The ordinary drinker, whose knowledge is not equal to discriminating between what could be interesting in the off-vintages and what might be disappointing among the pretentious bottles, would be wiser to choose a non-vintage wine if in doubt. It is non-vintage wines that have introduced most people to wine drinking and form the bulk of the wine of the world.

Vintage charts   Charts of assessment in terms of points or 'good', 'medium', 'poor' are frequently published by wine merchants and societies whose members are supposed to be interested in wine. The use of such charts, however, cannot be very helpful, simply because assessments in these terms have to be personal. Indeed, sometimes they are astonishingly chauvinistic, as when the winegrowers of one particular region mark every single year high. Even almost-disastrous vintages, or those yielding dreary unattractive wines, are given points indicating some quality, or the comment 'fair'. It obviously depends on whether or not the compiler of the chart is selling wine! Also, whereas there will not be any 'great' wines made in a medium type of vintage, there can be indifferent wines made even in a vintage reputed as 'great', depending on the winemaker. Conversely, in some indifferent years, certain wines of moderate to superior quality may be found. With the improvements in winemaking, it is possible to make pleasant drinkable wines in years that formerly would have been disastrous: the great wines, capable of long-term maturation, are the rarities and few people would need a vintage chart before ordering such wines, which should be for special occasions anyway. The interested drinker can easily make a little time to learn about vintages of such wines where the date is of supreme importance – **port**, fine **claret**, red and white **Burgundy** and the greater **German** wines.

Vintner   *The Concise Oxford Dictionary* defines this as 'wine merchant' but, in the British wine trade, this somewhat archaic term usually refers to someone who belongs to The Worshipful Company of Vintners in the City of London. This is one of the associations formed in medieval times to protect their trading practices, maintain standards of their goods, educate their apprentices and assist their members. The Vintners' Company is an active body in the wine trade of Britain to this day, influential in educational and training programmes. Their beautiful hall is near the site of the town house of Alderman Sir Henry Picard, Master of the Company, who held the 'Feast of the Five Kings' (of England, Scotland, France, Denmark and Cyprus) in 1363 – some indication of the wealth and importance of a City Company.

The Vintners' Company have also had the privilege of keeping swans on the River Thames since at least the beginning of the 16th century. The swan, a protected bird, was in former times considered a great delicacy (although the medieval Dr Andrew Boorde recorded 'Old swans be very difficult of digestion'): the Vintners still hold their annual 'Swan Feast' in the autumn. They, together with the Crown and The Dyers' Company, own all the swans on the Thames. Each year, they 'up' or mark them – by nicking their beaks: in former times, birds were 'taken up' or out of the river in hard weather, so as to look after and preserve them. The occasion of Swan Upping, as well as the Swan Feast, is organised by the Company's Swan Warden, descendant of the original swanherd, who is known as 'Mr Swan'. About a quarter of those belonging to the Company are active in the wine trade.

With such associations, it will be appreciated that the casual use of the term 'vintner' is both misleading and discourteous: members of The Vintners' Company would rightly resent a wine merchant not connected with them in any way, being dignified by the term 'vintner'. However I have found numerous instances of the word being used by foreigners who suppose it to imply 'winemaker' or even simply somebody engaged in the wine trade. Today it does not have that significance at all and its inaccurate use – because it is not current in speech or writing any more – is unnecessary when there is the perfectly explicit term 'wine merchant' extant. In the English language, there are growers, vineyard owners, **shippers** and merchants – and sometimes one person or one firm may be all four. To confuse the public with words such as *vigneron, propriétaire, vignoble, négociant,* **wine taster**, **wine expert** and vintner is silly if one is speaking or writing in English, unless all those concerned really know what the words mean. See **Distillers, D.C.L.**

Viognier White **grape** making somewhat individual wines, of marked aromatic **bouquet** and definite dryness. It is cultivated in the **Rhône** Valley where it is used with black grapes to make various wines. However its chief fame is that, although it is vinified as a separate **variety** and sold under its own name by various producers, it is the single grape that makes the white wine of Château **Grillet**.

Visan Red, white and rosé wines are made in this **Côtes du Rhône** Villages vineyard, although the red is reported as the best. See **Rhône**.

Vitis vinifera The type of **vine** from which most wine is made: literally 'the winemaking vine'. See **grapes**.

Vivarais This beautiful region in the département of the **Ardèche**, in the **Rhône** Valley, makes agreeable red, white and pink wines that give much pleasure to visitors and are occasionally exported.

Vizetelly, Henry (1820-94) A remarkable Englishman, whose books are as charming for their illustrations as they are valuable for their accounts of wines in his time. A journalist and publisher, he later became the Paris correspondent for *The Illustrated London News* and lived in the city throughout the siege. However he also spent much time in the vineyards and in 1873 was appointed juror for Great Britain at the Vienna Exhibition, when he wrote his first book on wine. In 1876 he wrote *Facts about Sherry*; and in 1882 *A History of Champagne*, a great achievement with exquisite illustrations. In 1880 came *Facts about Port and Madeira*; this, like his other books, was beautifully illustrated.

The latter part of his life was devoted to publishing and he was not only fined for one translation of Zola (described as 'bestial obscentity') but also, in 1887, he was sent to prison for 3 months for publishing an expurgated version of Zola's works. Finally he wrote his autobiography. His wine writing is characterised by scrupulous attention to detail and admirable reporting: he never says that something 'is' so if, in fact, somebody only 'informed him that'. The drawings of details in winemaking and vinegrowing are meticulous.

Vodka Traditionally this is supposed to have originated in the 12th century, in the **Russian** fort of Viatka. The name was originally 'zhiznennia voda' (water of life) and the word 'vodka' or 'wodka' means 'little water'. Vodka is pure spirit subjected, in the process of its manufacture, to filtration which removes certain oils and **congenerics**. As it is these last that can give other spirits, such as **brandy**, their charm but also their potentially undesirable after-effects if taken in excess, vodka has the reputation of being a 'safer' drink, in spite of its high alcoholic degree. There are various sorts of vodkas, some flavoured with herbs and peels, but although these are popular in Russia, vodka in other countries is usually flavourless. There are different qualities, as well as different strengths, the **Polish** type being highly esteemed.

Vodka should always be served iced and the spirit, when poured, should give a slightly oily look to the **glass**. It is a drink which enhances the eating of little appetisers, such as the traditional Russian 'zakuski' (hors d'oeuvres) and, by its very neutrality, cleanness and **strength**, stimulates the sense of taste and appetite without impinging on what is being eaten. It is also used in many widely drunk **cocktails**, notably the 'Bloody Mary' (vodka and tomato juice) and 'Moscow Mule' (vodka and ginger-ale).

Voile See **flor**, *Mycoderma vini*, **Jura**.

Volnay Parish in the **Côte de Beaune** in **Burgundy**, making very fine red wines indeed. They are elegant and delicate, and some consider them to be the equal of the great wines of the **Côte de Nuits**. Les Caillerets is the best-known site name, but there are others. Wines labelled Volnay Santenots come from the parish of **Meursault**. See **Côte d'Or**.

Vöslau Region in **Baden** making red wines.

Vosne-Romanée (Pronounced 'Vone') Parish in the **Côte de Nuits** in **Burgundy**. Possibly most famous for the great red wines which have the right to the **A.O.C.**s Romanée-Conti, Romanée, Richebourg, La Tâche, Romanée-Saint-Vivant, Grands Echézeaux and Echézeaux. The last two are not so well known among English-speakers, because of the supposed difficulty of pronouncing the name (try 'eh-che-zoh'). Prose poems have been written about these wines, which are large in scale, with pronounced **bouquet** and outstanding flavour. They are, obviously, extremely costly and are definitely for special-occasion drinking. Well-known site names of Vosne-Romanée include Les Suchots, Aux Malconsorts, Les Chaumes and Les Beaux-Monts.

Vougeot See **Côte d'Or**.

Vouvray **Touraine** white wine region on the banks of the river **Loire**. The **wines** must be made from the **Chenin Blanc**. The chalky nature of the **soil** and the caves cut out of the rock in which many of the wines mature contribute to their elegance and vivacity. A variety of types are made, from wholly still to *pétillant* and fully **sparkling**; they also range from completely dry to luscious. Many reference books describe Vouvray simply as 'sweet' but this is not true. The wines of certain producers and specific sites are capable of attaining superb quality and it is a pity that, so far, many export lists simply refer to 'Vouvray' without indicating the type of the wine. Vouvray wine was for a long while considered to be a 'bad traveller' and the wines were seldom found outside their own region. However modern methods of making and caring for wines of delicate charm have enabled producers to popularise Vouvray in many export markets.

One of the remarkable things about Vouvrays is that, in an outstanding year and traditionally made, they can last for a surprising time, especially for a white wine. Twenty years or more is not uncommon. Also, even with the wholly sweet wines, there is usually a touch of dryness in the finish. Personally, I consider Vouvray not only as one of the greatest white wines of the Loire but, at its best, one of the outstanding wines – in each of the dry, sweet and sparkling categories – of the world. But the great wines are both scarce and expensive. Still, if anyone wishes to see the Chenin Blanc at its most magnificent, Vouvray is the place to look. I have never known this **grape** make wines of such greatness anywhere else. But only a few growers make the great Vouvrays.

Vulture (Pronounced 'Vool-tour-ay, stressing 'tour') Extinct volcano in the **Basilicata** or Lucania region of **Italy**, where the only wine of note appears to be the **Aglianico** del Vulture – a full red wine.

W

Wachau Important wine region east of Vienna in **Austria**, making mostly white wines. That known as Schluck (meaning gulp) is possibly the one most featured on export markets.

Wachenheim See **Palatinate**.

Wacholderbranntweine German for 'juniper brandy', this is a general term for juniper **distillates**; Steinhaeger is possibly the best known.

Wahgunyah Important wine region in Rutherglen in Victoria, **Australia**. One of its pioneer winemakers was George Sutherland, who built the **All Saints winery**. He modelled this on the Scottish Castle of Mey, at present the property of Queen Elizabeth the Queen Mother.

Waikerie South **Australia** vineyard on the **Murray River**.

Waldmeisterlikoer German **liqueur**, pale green in colour, based on woodruff. This plant, whose leaves are often likened to a star or the rowels of a spur, features in many mixed drinks. It was also used, in bunches, to freshen churches. It features often in *bowle*, a type of wine cup in **Germany**

Waldrach One of the regions producing fine wines in the **Ruwer**, a tributary of the **Mosel**.

Walporzheim Well-known town at the centre of red wine production in the **Ahr** Valley of **Germany**.

Wälschriesling A white wine **grape**, which some authorities consider to be a 'cousin' of the **Rheinriesling**, and some do not. It is sometimes called 'Italian Riesling'. It is much used in Central Europe. See **grapes**.

Warner Vineyards Important **winery** near Lake Michigan, **U.S**.

Warre **Port** firm, founded in 1670.

Wash The liquid that is produced when the action of **yeast** acts on the sugar in the **wort** to produce **alcohol**, in the making of **whisky**.

Wassail From the Old English *Wes hal*, meaning 'Be of good health'; this expression was used when saluting a guest, whose reply was '*Drink hal*'. It came to imply particularly the healths drunk around the season of the winter solstice (mid-winter) when life was usually at a low point. Later it assumed the sense of 'carouse', and special wassail carols are still sung. The fruit trees and domestic animals used to be 'wassailed' or serenaded so that they might thrive. A wassail bowl usually means a bowl of wine or liquor, sometimes spiced or hot, from which healths are drunk. In Shakespeare's time, apples were roasted and added to the drink. See **mull**.

Wasser This term may be added to certain types of **German liqueurs**, made from fully fermented fruits or berries, such as kirsch. See *alcool blanc*, *eau-de-vie*, and *obstbranntwein*.

Watervale **Australian** wine region north of Adelaide.

Wawern Wine village on the **Saar, Germany**. The best-known site is Herrenberg.

Weeper Term used of a **bottle** that has some stickiness around its **capsule**, indicating a seepage of the contents. This may mean that the wine will become **oxidised** but, although it is wise to use a weeping bottle reasonably soon after the detection of the fault, there need be no assumption that the wine will be defective at all. **U.S.** reference books use the term 'leaker' for this condition but Americans would be unwise to employ the word in a British context, as it implies a person who is incontinent.

Wehlen This little town on the **Mosel** lies opposite – across the river – the great Sonnenuhr (sundial) site, which makes some of the finest Mosels of all. Some people even prefer them to those of the great Doktor site at **Bernkastel**. For subtlety plus large-scale nobility, they are usually outstanding. Other sites making noble wines include Lay, Nonnenberg, Rosenberg, Münzlay and Michelsberg.

Weibel Winery in Alameda County, **California, U.S.**, specialising in **sparkling wines**.

Weinberg, Das German for a vineyard.

Weinbrand Brandy, produced in **Germany** from **grapes** imported for **distilling**. Well-known firms are Eckes, Dujardin and Asbach.

Weingart, Der German for a single wine estate.

Weinpicke, Die German for **wine tasting**.

Weinviertel **Austrian** wine region, north-east of Vienna.

Weissburgunder See **Pinot**.

Weissherbst Speciality of **Baden** in **Germany**, where the name – literally 'white picked' – means that the wine has been made from a black **grape**, such as the **Spätburgunder**, which has been vinified like a white wine. The skins are not allowed to remain in and tint the **must**.

Weltevrede Estate at Bonnievale, near Robertson in **South Africa**, making table wines but especially well known for its **Muscadel**.

Wente Vineyard at **Livermore** in northern **California, U.S.**, founded by Carl Wente in 1880. The firm is still a family concern, and a wide range of quality table wines is produced, both red and white.

Whipkull A mixed drink of egg yolks, sugar, cream and **rum**, traditionally served in the Shetland Islands at Yuletide – which is celebrated, by the conservative-minded, on 6 January (which would have been 25 December before the reform of the Calendar) and not at the solstice. It is considered to be

SCOTCH WHISKY DISTILLERIES

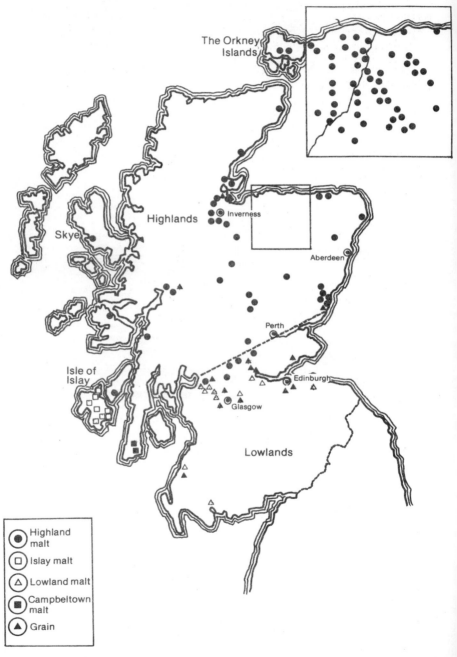

The Orkney Islands

Highlands

Skye

Inverness

Aberdeen

Isle of Islay

Perth

Edinburgh

Glasgow

Lowlands

⊙ Highland malt

□ Islay malt

△ Lowland malt

■ Campbeltown malt

▲ Grain

of Scandinavian origin because of its name. See **wassail**.

Whisky, Whiskey Used by itself, the single word 'whisky' (spelt without the 'e') usually implies that the spirit referred to is Scotch whisky, which can only be produced in Scotland, although other types of whiskey are made in different parts of the world. Whisky may be **distilled** from malted and unmalted barley, maize, rye, and mixtures of two or more of these. This is the original method by which whisky – and other distillates – were made. Scotch 'Malt' whisky is made only from malted barley and nothing else; Scotch 'Grain' whisky is usually made from unmalted barley plus maize or rye, mashed with malted barley. Straight malt is made in a **pot still**, and is distilled twice. It is then matured in **wood** (often American oak) and, ideally, **sherry casks**. It may be left for up to 15 years to mature and improve, but after about 20 years it may, like any other spirit, tend to take on too much 'woodiness' from the cask and can decline. Grain whisky is distilled in the **Coffey** or **patent still**, by a continuous process, and it does not require such long maturation as malt.

Before bottling, the blender will assemble the different types of whisky required to make up the various **blends**: there may be as many as 50 different whiskies in a world-famous blend. If, however, any reference to age is made on the **label** of a whisky, this must be the age of the youngest whisky in the blend, not just the average age of the whole blend. The **colour** of a whisky need be no definite indication of its age – although whisky takes colour from its cask, it can be coloured to some degree by the admixture of caramelised sugar. There are fashions about the colour of whisky – some markets prefer pale whiskies, others like a darker whisky – but the colour does not relate to strength or age.

The name comes from the Gaelic *uisge beatha*, or **usquebaugh**, meaning 'water of life'. The Scots have made it for centuries as a health-giving, stimulating drink and remedy against the hard climate of the Highlands. There is a record in 1494 to 'eight bolls of malt' required for making into *'aquavitae'*. See *eau-de-vie*.

STRAIGHT MALT WHISKY: At one time considered a drink only suitable for those leading an active out-of-door life, but recently it has become very popular with all kinds of people. Each distillery making malt will produce a completely individual whisky, and some malt goes into all good blends, indeed some is mostly destined for use in a blend. All malts have a more definite smell and flavour than grain whiskies.

There are four distinct types of malt: the Highland malts, made above a line from Dundee to Greenock, and themselves divided into Highlands and Glenlivets; Lowland malts, south of the line from Dundee to Greenock; Islay (pronounced 'Eye-la') from the Isle of Islay; and Campbeltowns, from Campbeltown in the Mull of Kintyre. Whisky is bottled normally at 40° **Gay Lussac** or 70° **proof** but there can be variations from this according to the type of whisky required and the demands of various markets. However it is not true that malt is 'stronger' than blended whisky.

DE LUXE WHISKIES: In addition to malts, which are always more expensive than blended whiskies, certain luxury whiskies are now made by many of the

POT STILL FOR MALT WHISKY

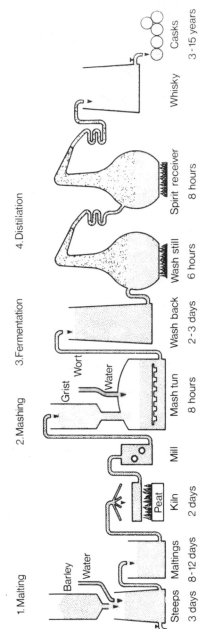

1. Malting | 2. Mashing | 3. Fermentation | 4. Distillation

				Grist	Wort				Whisky
Barley Water	Maltings	Kiln	Mill	Mash tun	Wash back	Wash still	Spirit receiver		Casks
Steeps	8-12 days	2 days		8 hours	2-3 days	6 hours	8 hours		3-15 years
3 days		Peat		Water					

1. *Malting. The first stages of the making of Scotch whisky require the barley to be first steeped, then spread out on the malting floor where it generates its own heat, prior to being dried in the kiln so that the process of germination is arrested. In many distilleries today, however, malt is mechanically processed, although the end result is the same. After the malt has been dried, it is allowed to cool and then, the rootlets of the barley being taken off (to be used for cattle feed), it is ground in the malt mill before passing to the mash tun.*

2. *Mashing. Here hot water is mixed into the malt which starts up the action of the diastase; this completes the conversion of the soluble starch into maltose. The resulting liquid, called wort, is drawn off (the husks that remain also go for cattle feed) and allowed to cool.*

3. *Fermentation. The wort then goes into the tun-room, where the huge 'wash backs' receive it. Yeast is added, so as to convert the sugar in the wort to alcohol over a period of a couple of days or more. As the temperature of the 'wash' rises, the yeast cells are killed off. The wash is now ready to be distilled.*

4. *Distillation. The wash is pumped into the wash still, or stills: these stills are huge bulbous copper vessels shaped like pots or cones — hence their name — and have a sideways-tilted top pipe, tapering into what is known as a 'swan neck' or 'lyne arm', which passes into the 'worm'. This worm is an ever-decreasing coil which winds through a tank kept cold by means of continuously-running water. The liquid that passes through the swan neck into the spirit receiver is called 'low wines'. This is again distilled. The beginnings and ends of the 'runs' of the first still are sent back to be redistilled, as they contain too high a proportion of impure spirit. The first part is known as 'foreshots', the second 'middle cut', and the third 'feints'. It is the middle cut that eventually passes over as whisky and this then goes into casks for subsequent maturation.*

great whisky firms. These are special because of the ages and qualities of the malts and grain whiskies used in them. A higher proportion of malt tends to be used and, sometimes, their alcoholic **strength** is higher.

SERVING: It may be served alone, with a carbonated drink or water, or form an ingredient in a mixture. Straight malt and luxury whiskies are usually drunk neat or with spring water (ideally, Loch Katrine water, but anyway the purest water available). Traditionally they are not drunk with ice; although this is naturally a matter of individual preference.

IRISH WHISKEY: Always whiskey with an 'e', its name implies the country of its origin. It is usually distilled three times, in huge pot stills, from cereals. The different brands of Irish are as individual as straight malt Scotch, and it is matured for at least 7 years. Some people find Irish whiskey gentler in character than straight malt. The Irish claim, with some reason, that their spirit was evolved before Scotch; the know-how of distilling was probably brought to Scotland by monks from Ireland. It is the base for **Irish coffee**, one of the most successful mixed drinks recently evolved. **Poteen** (or potheen) is an illegal version of the spirit. The **Irish Mist liqueur** is made from Irish whiskey.

OTHER WHISKIES: Whiskey – and quite good whiskey – is made in many parts of the world – there are even stories of a 'Scotch' from the Far East, bearing on its label the proud statement 'Prepared in Buckingham Palace under the personal supervision of His Majesty'! The best-known whiskies, apart from Scotch and Irish, are made in North America: in fact U.S. whiskies are the best-selling spirits in the world at the time of writing. (Although the U.S. is the most important customer for Scotch.)

RYE: This is made in both the U.S. and Canada. It must contain at least 51% rye grain. Most American rye is made in Pennsylvania and Maryland.

BOURBON: This is made only in the U.S. (it was originally made in Bourbon Country, Kentucky) and must contain at least 51% corn.

CORN WHISKEY: This may be made in a variety of regions in the U.S., and must contain at least 80% corn. It tends to be a rather raw, unmatured spirit.

CANADIAN WHISKEY: This must be made only from cereal grain and is generally a blend of grain spirits and rye distillate.

Other whiskies, such as are made in Japan, Germany and other countries, can be pleasant beverages. Many of the best are likely to contain a proportion of Scotch, usually malt. (Japan is the second most important export market for straight malt.) What are these whiskies like? Obviously each whisky is an individual product; but those other than Scotch mostly tend to be light in character, but not necessarily lighter in alcohol.

Widmer Large **winery** in Naples Valley, **New York State**, **U.S.**, founded in 1888 by John Jacob Widmer. It now belongs to the British firm, Reckitt & Colman. It has been most successful with its **dessert wines**.

Wiederkehr **Winery** at Altus, Arkansas, **U.S.**, the largest in the south-west. It makes a range of wines from *Vitis vinifera*, including some **sparkling wines**.

Wienerwald   Literally 'Vienna Woods'. the vineyards on the outskirts of Vienna in **Austria**. Famous for the *Heurigen* wines, but they also make other pleasant table wines.

Wiesbaden   Vineyard region around the elegant town of the same name, in the Rheingau. See **Rhine**.

Williamine   Pear **liqueur**. See *alcool blanc*.

Wiltingen   The greatest winegrowing parish in the **Saar**. Among a number of famous sites are Braune Kupp, Braunfels, Dohr, Hölle, Kupp, Rosenberg, Sandberg, **Scharzberg**, Scharzhofberg.

Wine   According to the Wine and Spirit Association of Great Britain, the definition is: 'The alcoholic beverage obtained from the juice of freshly gathered **grapes**, the **fermentation** of which has been carried through in the district of its origin and according to local tradition and practice.' This means that drinks made from fruits other than grapes, from imported dried grapes, or from imported **musts** are not, strictly, 'wine' in the U.K. Other countries have different regulations governing the definition, but generally it is the fact of the drink being made only from grapes, on the spot where they were grown, which is accepted.

Wine buff   Term which seems recently to have come into common usage: what it implies I do not quite know! The implication is that the 'wine buff' is somebody who is knowledgeable about wine; but the expression somehow seems to me to suggest that this knowledge has been briskly and superficially acquired, also that the possessor tends to show off about possessing it. I admit that I find the expression both inadequate and slick. If somebody loves wine, then they are a winelover; if they know something about it, then they are a student of wine. Those who find the term helpful should, of course, employ it. However, as it does not feature in any of my dictionaries, I do not use it.

Wine expert   The use of the word 'expert' is tricky in the context of wine. It has certainly been overused and abused. As those who really do know something about wine would admit, no human being can be an 'expert' in a subject that is constantly changing. Consequently, members of the wine trade and the more serious amateurs of wine are, rightly, humble enough to prefer that the term 'expert' should never be used about any of them. The would-be and so-described wine expert may, therefore, usually be regarded with some suspicion – he or she will be unlikely to have much knowledge if the title 'expert' is permitted to be used. However people do make use of the word, as when introducing a winelover either socially or, sometimes, in public appearances. The only thing to do then, it seems to me, is either to take the time to explain that nobody in wine will ever claim to be an expert and that therefore the word is somewhat in the nature of an insult or sarcastic comment – 'those experts who think they know . . . . .' – or else to ignore its use and, by whatever is subsequently said, to convince the audience that wine is not a subject where pomposity is inevitable. It is true, of course, that a certain amount of expertise in wine comes with experience – but the somewhat fine distinction should be stressed.

Wine fraternities, orders These are nowadays associations which, by picturesque ceremonies and the membership of influential persons, achieve publicity for the wines of many regions. As publicity attractions, they have definitely achieved success in many wine regions of Europe. Membership is usually bestowed as an honour (or it may sometimes be purchased); the officials are usually winegrowers, brokers, or persons of importance as regards the local wines. Membership of a wine order need not imply any specific knowledge of that wine though obviously a member may be an authority. See **Chevaliers du Tastevin**.

Wine lake Term recently brought into use in the EEC, which indicates that a surplus of wine in one country makes it impossible to sell it economically elsewhere. Overproduction of wine – in the light of technical advances – is a risk. If the surplus cannot be disposed of, a 'lake' is formed, like a 'butter mountain'.

Wine service See **Service of Wine**.

Wine snob A great deal of silliness is talked and written about the wine snob – who, of course, is merely a stupid person, likely to be motivated by price, rarity and pretty **labels** more than personal likes and dislikes. He can be extremely boring as well, if allowed to dominate a general conversation by pronouncing about wines at all. These days, many are so nervous about showing any serious enthusiasm for an interesting subject that the winelover risks being accused of being a wine snob even if, after being asked for an opinion, it is given. The company on such occasions probably only want a single sentence of facetious comment and are incapable of listening to any considered judgment on anything.

Such people often accuse the wine lover of being a wine snob simply because he or she wishes to enjoy sharing views and comparing experiences about something that happens to mean more and be more interesting to them than just a drink. It is possible, therefore, to divide the wine snobs into the snobs about wine – the label drinkers, boasters of prices paid and droppers of names – and the people who are simply boring about it. The person who really wants to learn something about wine, however, can usually learn from both – even if what not to do.

Wine taster The use of the *tastevin* appears to have brought this expression into use, so that people ask earnestly 'Are you a wine taster?' I invariably reply that it would be difficult to know anything about wine without tasting it! One might as well ask anyone concerned with food 'Are you a food eater?' Yet, as I did once have a request from an editor to instruct readers how to tell if a wine was 'off' without having to open the **bottle**, I can only suppose that the process of tasting is seen as some sort of mysterious occupation, into which only certain persons can ever be initiated. There is, as readers of this book will know, no mystery about **tasting**, but it is something that can be taxing and requires concentration; so perhaps what people who use the term 'wine taster' really mean is that drinkers drink, whereas tasters taste seriously.

Wine waiter The French term is *sommelier*. Both terms imply the person – man or woman – who takes the order for wine in a restaurant and either serves or supervises its **service**. Unfortunately, in many catering establishments nowadays, the wine waiter knows very little about wine in general and possibly less about the wines on the list of the house. He/she is merely directed by the managements to keep topping up the **glasses** as often as they can. This is a self-defeating practice if any customers know anything about wine, because, instead of drinking more, they will probably be infuriated into refusing to allow the unfortunate staff to fill glasses to the brim. In a thoroughly bad humour, they will not then order the second **bottle** that correct service and a relaxed atmosphere might have prompted.

Fortunately, there are at least some eating places where the wine waiter sees all the wines that are bought, sometimes even being involved with the choice as to which to buy, and can observe their progress, if these are able to be stored by the establishment. Some organisations do also attempt to teach wine waiters about wines in general and the correct service – so that the wines taste as enjoyable as possible. But, unless you are in a luxury or first-class retaurant, it is useless to expect the wine waiter to know very much. All the more reason, therefore, to give instructions clearly and simply (the *sommelier* may not speak your language) as to how your wine should be served.

In some of the classic wine regions, the wine waiter may certainly know a lot about these wines, though hardly admitting the existence of others. He may also sometimes be so much of a star turn, catering to the 'drinking the label' type of tourist, that he neglects the basics of service. I have known eminent Italian *sommeliers* pull corks through the **capsule** of the wine; one *sommelier* in a top Paris restaurant tipped all the **deposit** of a great **claret** into the **decanter** – explaining that the wine was 'past it' – and several others have argued with members of the wine trade as to whether a wine was or was not **corked**, including disputing this with the owner of the particular estate! So, although one can learn much from the wise and experienced wine waiter who truly loves his trade, it is wise to be careful and oversee the chi-chi indulged in by many of the ***tastevin***-bedecked *sommeliers* whose presence presumably justifies the exaggerated mark-ups on the bottles in many well-known eating-places.

As it is possible to teach anyone, male or female, the basics of wine service within a matter of hours – the experience that governs selection and handling of very fine bottles can come later – I personally favour the young *sommelier*, who shows both humility and interest, and may therefore have much to teach the diner. In order to encourage people like this, it is courteous to invite them to take a share of any interesting bottle – even if they know it, they may not have tasted it recently and this can be as rewarding to the serious as any tip.

Winery   This term is much used in the New World. It usually means a vineyard plus that place where the **grapes** from the vineyard are made into wine. Frequently a winery will handle grapes from other vineyards as well, if these belong to the owners or company owning the winery. There is much to be said for the word as a practical term. For a European, however, the term 'winery' suggests something slightly akin to 'factory' – i.e. where a wine is 'made' in the sense of being concocted. The term has a slightly derogatory significance, undeservedly. However, it would be extremely tactless to refer to a great French or German wine estate as a 'winery'.

Winkel   Rheingau region (see **Rhine**) producing many good wines, and also having within its boundary **Schloss Vollrads**, which is world-famous. The poet Goethe, who visited the Von Brentano estate at Winkel, praised the wines.

Wintrich   **Mosel** vineyard: the sites considered superior are Ohligsberg at **Lieser**, which belongs to Baron Schorlemer, and Geierslay, which belongs to Huesgen-Böcking.

Winzenheim   Wine parish in the **Nahe** region of **Germany**. Rosenhock, Berg, Honisberg and Rotmauer are all well-known sites.

Winzerverein   *Winzer* in German means winegrower, and this term, on a wine **label**, usually means that the wine has been sold through a **co-operative**. *Winzergenossenschaft* is a co-operative which makes the wine and sells it.

Women   Only a book in English would need to have such an entry – and it is to be hoped that future editions will not require its inclusion! In countries and regions where wine is made, there is nothing out of the way in a woman knowing about wine. Women have the same physiological equipment to taste and, if interested, can taste as well as any man. Indeed, because most women are concerned with smells of various kinds in their lives – household cleaning, cosmetics, flowers, the smells of health and sickness in themselves and their children – they often retain a good sense of smell (and taste) long after men have dulled and virtually lost theirs. The men who have been and are the great teachers in the world of wine make no difference between their men and women students.

There is, however, a regrettable tendency on the part of some women to adopt the attitude that they 'leave all that stuff about wine to my husband'. They deliberately choose not learn anything about wine, spoil **tastings** and serious discussions on wine by irrelevant chatter – and then say 'I'd love to learn about wine, but of course I haven't got the time!' I am also told that some women feel that dinners where fine wines are served don't show off their cooking as they might wish – because, of course, with the finest wines, the simplest, prime quality dishes are usually the best. But such ladies would appear to indulge in precisely the sort of pseudo-*cuisine* that is unfortunate, lacking in (aesthetic) taste and seldom very successful anyway; imitations of great chef cooking are not for the home.

So I retain my opinion that the marriage of food and wine is one of the most complex of domestic tasks, one of the most rewarding achievements when successful and that, as with marriage in general, it both deserves and should have the participation of both parties. Certainly there are very many women who are greatly respected as growers, makers of wine, buyers, controllers of quality, merchants and, even, writers on the subject. It is something of an impertinence for anybody to express surprise that this should be so.

Wood   Wines are spoken of as being 'in wood' when they are in either a wooden

cask or **vat**, prior to being bottled. The length of time they are kept in contact with wood in some form can influence them considerably, as is obvious when you think that wood is porous and the wine or spirit can both receive air and give itself out by evaporation when in a wooden vessel. The contribution of the cask can be great, as witness the use of **sherry** and other casks for the keeping of **whisky** and whiskey. A skilled **blender** can often detect what type of cask a sample has been drawn from simply by **nosing**.

Certain wood is unsuitable because it is too porous; other woods can impart too assertive a smell and flavour to the wine or spirit – chestnut, for example, can often affect the liquid disagreeably, although with care it can be used. Oak, of a particular type, is probably the ideal. Until recent times, the best casks were often of Baltic oak, but now supplies often have to come from the **U.S.** Experiments have been made in **Cognac** to try to see whether Limousin oak or Tronçais oak is most satisfactory. Some of the great **Bordeaux** estates put their new red wine into 'new wood'. This means new casks, previously seasoned, which will give immediately of their various attributes to the liquid kept in them. In the **Rioja** region, an enormous difference is made by the length of time a wine is kept in wood. Some stay in their casks for 4 years or even more, and this imparts a particular style that may or may not be liked by the individual drinker.

In the past, it was a hazard that a wine might be 'woody', smelling and tasting flat, soggy and altogether dreary; although this could sometimes be a transient stage through which a wine would pass during its normal maturation. A defect in a stave in a cask could convey this unpleasant woodiness, as compared with the pleasant style often associated with a matured wine which has been 'in wood' for the appropriate time.

The cost of casks, however, makes present-day supplies both expensive and difficult to get. The same applies to wooden **vats**, which are naturally difficult to keep in prime condition and to repair. Coopering is a declining trade; although some large firms do keep their own coopers to maintain and repair casks and vats.

For some time, the use of stainless steel, enamel and glass linings, or special concrete has been appreciated for the keeping of wines, especially white wines. The latter please by their fresh, crisp style if they are of the dry type and therefore exact control over their development is essential if they are to compete in international markets. The light 'star bright' dry wines of today frequently never go into a wooden container at all. This can also apply to many of the inexpensive or small-scale red and pink wines. These would gain nothing by maturation in wood and risk deteriorating or going out of condition unless kept in vessels that can be cleaned so that no possible danger of infection can lurk in them. The great red wines of the world, some of the sweeter whites and the **fortified wines** have an additional resistance to infection and the use of wood in making them can be an advantage. However the maintenance of the traditional vessels is costly and time-consuming.

Sometimes, a wine that has been kept in a vat made from stainless steel or concrete, may be given a few months' in a wooden vat prior to being bottled, just so that it can assimilate the contribution of the wood. There are even stories, that may be well-founded, of some very advanced **wineries** using special wooden chips in their vats, or even a type of 'essence of wood', so as to simulate the effect of a wooden cask or vat on the wine. There seems nothing amiss about such a procedure; although it is perhaps more interesting for the student to be able to compare a wine that has been in wood with a similar one that has not, and see which appears preferable.

There is a misunderstanding in the minds of many people about the supposed superiority of, say, a red wine that has been kept in wood for a long time. It is naturally up to the individual winemaker to select a vessel for the wine that will be satisfactory, not too expensive to use, and that can be maintained without too much trouble: different wines obviously need different treatment. But wine kept in wood will not necessarily go on improving, any more than a wine in **bottle**. Exposure to the air, which is inevitable as the contents of a cask evaporate and the level goes down, can have a bad effect on even the finest wine. This is why casks in a sherry *bodega*, a **port lodge** and in the great red wine cellars of Bordeaux and **Burgundy** are kept topped up, so as to leave only a very small space for the air to affect the wine before it is bottled. Of course, in the past, the great red table wines were often kept in wood for much longer than they are nowadays, but they had usually been made differently in the first place, probably had far more **tannin** (the **hat** being left in the **must** for weeks rather than days, as happens now) and they matured more slowly. Today's economic pressures do not permit this and it is important to bottle a wine before it gets tired and **oxidised**, while it is still full of vigour and is 'making itself'.

If you are in a wine region and visit a small farm where the owner makes wine, you may be offered a sample from a cask in which the wine has remained until it is required for domestic use, when some will be drawn off into a bottle, just as used to happen hundreds of years ago. It is unlikely that you will enjoy this type of wine as much as something that has been bottled according to today's expertise – although naturally such a wine is always interesting to try.

Woodside   Small **California winery** in San Mateo County.

Worcester   Picturesque town in **South Africa**, the centre of important production of dry white table wines, **dessert wines** and **brandy**.

Worms   Centre of the most southerly Rheinhessen vineyards (see **Rhine**), and famous for the Liebfrauenkirche (Church of Our Lady), which dominates the vineyards that surround it. The wines of the Liebfrauenstift are solely those of these vineyards around the Liebfrauenkirche, of which Langenbach is a very well-known proprietor. Nowadays they have nothing to do with **Lieb-fraumilch** even if they once had, which is a debatable point.

Wort   The liquid resulting from mixing hot water with the dried malt in the making of **whisky**. See **distillation**.

Württemberg   Region in South **Germany** which in fact produces very large quantities of red and white wine (the local consumption *per capita* is the highest in Germany), although these seldom achieve more than good everyday quality. They are worth trying when tourists visit the area. *Schillerwein*, a type of rosé, is also a speciality of the region. See **Baden**.

Würzburg See **Franconia**.

Wybong Park Vineyard in South **Australia**, belonging to the huge firm of **Penfolds**.

Wynn Distinguished name in **Australian** wine history. Samuel Weintraub (the latter name actually means 'grape') was born in Poland in 1892 and arrived in Australia in 1913. He soon changed his name to Wynn and, working hard and long, made a steady success in selling wine, in the catering trade and, eventually, in experiments in winemaking. He began to sell to the U.K. in the 1930s and at first concentrated on inexpensive wines. He bought what was subsequently known as the Modbury Estate near Adelaide in order to supply the demand for his various lines.

Samuel Wynn's operation expanded steadily, into the **Barossa Valley**, into New South Wales, into the **sparkling wine** business and, most importantly perhaps, into **Coonawarra**, where Wynn wines today have achieved a great reputation. The wines made here are still all from the **Cabernet** and **Hermitage grapes** or sometime a **blend** of both for the reds. A **Rheinriesling** has been made since 1962. Samuel Wynn's son David continues in charge of the firm, which was bought by a brewery in 1972.

X

X.O.   Categorisation of **Cognac**, which has no legal significeance or control but which, by implication, means that the **brandy** in the **bottle** is of superior quality, intended to be drunk as a **liqueur**. See **three star**.

Xynisteri   (Pronounced 'Zin-is-tair-y') A white **grape**, native to **Cyprus**.

Y

Yalumba This important **Australian winery**, near Angaston, was first planted by a Dorset settler, Samuel **Smith**, in 1849. Its name means 'all the country around'. Yalumba wines established a reputation for quality; today the stress appears to be on **fortified wines**, although a quantity of table wines are also made. The Smith family are still running the firm.

Yeast Yeast may be described as the power or driving force that makes wine. There are many kinds of yeast and, as the subject is complex, those who are both interested and able to understand a little chemistry are advised to consult specialist publications (see Bibliography). But in general terms, yeasts do not themselves cause **fermentation**, but excrete **enzymes** causing it to take place. Because, obviously, one cannot deal in detail with this aspect of the subject, the part yeast plays in winemaking is here described in general and lay terms.

WHAT ARE YEASTS? Yellowish substances produced by the propagation of a fungus (*Saccharomyces cerevisae*) which, in vineyards, is simply floating in the air. It is a part of the natural life of the district, and is spread by the action of insects. As far as wine is concerned, it is caught and retained in the bloom on the skin of the **grapes** (which is why, if it rains hard during the time when the grapes are to be gathered and wine to be made, fermentation can be difficult, because the bloom may have been at least partly washed off).

HOW YEASTS WORK: Wine yeasts are those that enable wine to be made (in regions where new vineyards are created, they are absent and may have to be imported from other wine regions). Wild yeasts of which the principal species is *Saccharomyces apiculatus*, may start up the fermentation in the **must**. But this is a primitive method of winemaking and these yeasts die at 4% of **alcohol** by volume. *Saccharomyces ellipsoideus* can ferment up to 12 or 14% of alcohol by volume, depending on the amount of sugar in the must. They can go a little higher, but usually cease to work completely at 16%.

This is why the alcoholic **strength** of table or natural wine is fixed at 14% of alcohol by volume. Wines from very hot vineyards, where the sunshine gives a high degree of sugar in the must, occasionally come into conflict with the **Customs**, because they may be higher in alcohol and, therefore, may be

378

charged 'heavy wine' duty. Yeasts of such wines are vigorous compared with others, which is why they can sometimes be used in vineyards where the original strain has become weak.

Yeast is affected by extremes of temperature and will not work if the atmosphere becomes too hot or too cold (or if the alcoholic level of the wine rises too high), exactly like baking. Also, if the dead yeasts are left in a made wine, the vinegar bacteria will feed on them – and the wine will turn to **acetic acid** or **vinegar**. This is why newly made wine is run off the **vat** or **cask** in which all the débris of pips, bits of skin and yeasts remain, so that it can pursue its life without being endangered. Some badly-made wines do, in fact, smell yeasty – this smell is easily recognised by anyone who has ever had yeast tablets as a type of tonic. The wines may not be harmful or even unpalatable, but the yeasty smell, if it remains noticeable, can indicate that they have not been properly supervised and cared for. But in general the presence of yeast in wine is something the taster and drinker need not be concerned with.

The specific action of certain yeasts of wine is exemplified by some of the **Jura** wines, with which Pasteur conducted his investigations and which resulted in his discovery of bacterial action. It is also seen in the way in which sherry is made (see **flor**) and also in wines made in a similar way to sherry. Sometimes these use native yeasts, sometimes a strain developed from imported yeasts. See **Australia, Cyprus, South Africa**.

Yeelbangera **McWilliam winery** in New South Wales, **Australia**.

Yellow Trebbiano See **Greco**.

Yenda **Brandy distillery** in New South Wales, **Australia**, belonging to the important **McWilliam** family. The **Wynn** family also make wines there.

Yering Vineyard region near Melbourne in Victoria, **Australia**, which produced wines earning much praise. However, due to various factors, mainly the expansion of Melbourne, it has no longer vineyards or winemakers.

Yquem, d'Yquem (Pronounced 'Ee-kem') Château d'Yquem is the most famous of the great **Sauternes** and invariably commands a high price, which often seems exaggerated. It was rated a *Premier Grand Cru* in the 1855 **classification**. Very luscious, it is always **estate-bottled**. In recent years, a dry version of the wine of the property has been made and sold under the name of 'Y' or Ygrec (the French name for the letter 'Y', pronounced 'ee-grek').

Yugoslavia Yugoslav wines were possibly responsible more than any others for the British becoming accustomed to drinking inexpensive table wines in the immediate post-war period of the 1950s. The country has old winemaking traditions and nearly all the vineyards are cultivated by peasant owners, although the selling of the wines is controlled by the State and **co-operatives**. Yugoslavia has been a model for many European countries in the way the wines have been made and marketed.

Of the different republics that make up the country, the most important for wine are Serbia and Croatia, in that order; but wine is also produced in Slovenia and Macedonia, and a little comes from Bosnia-Herzogovina. Many of the classic **grape varieties** are cultivated and some which are found in other eastern European countries in substantial quantities. There are also some native grapes: **Plavac**, a white grape; and Mali Plavac and **Prokupac** Crni for red being cultivated in many regions. In certain regions use is made of other native grapes, but here, as in many Balkan countries, the names are difficult for the outsider and sometimes are really only local names for a classic variety, so that too much attention need not be paid by the winedrinker who is not also a viticulturalist.

Possibly the best-known Yugoslav wines are the whites, notably those made from the **Riesling** grape, which bear a prefix indicating their origin. Sweetish white wines, such as **Radegonska Ranina** also known as Tiger Milk; and sweetish reds, such as **Dingac** and **Postup**, made from slightly dried grapes, are beginning to be known outside their homeland. Shippers are also beginning to include some **rosé** and dry red wines. It is probably fair to say that these wines, while usually of very good everyday quality and giving much pleasure for drinking, are, simply because of the uniform way in which they are produced and made, not as yet known for lasting properties or for any outstanding individuality such as may result from being made by a particular estate.

Z

ZD **Winery** founded in 1969 near Saroma, **U.S.**

Zahnacher **Alsace** vineyard near Ribeauvillé. Of great antiquity, it is planted with different **vines**, each being individually replaced when necessary. The wine is, as might be expected, highly individual and can attain great quality.

Zandvliet, Sandvliet Vineyard at Ashton, Robertson, **South Africa**. It is also known for the horses bred there.

Zebib **Egyptian** name for **ouzo**.

Zell **Mosel** vineyard known for Zeller Schwarze Katz (black cat), a name applied to the wines in general.

Zeltingen Middle **Mosel** parish producing fine wines. The best-known sites are probably Himmelreich, Schlossberg and Sonnenuhr.

Zierfandler **Austrian** white wine **grape**.

Zilavka White wine **grape** of **Yugoslavia**.

Zinfandel Red wine **grape**, used considerably in **California**. It makes wine that are highly rated by many, although the European palate can find it somewhat earthy, edgy and harsh, unless really well made and adequately matured. Its origin is the subject of debate: some suppose it to be a truly native grape, of *Vitis vinifera*; others that it was brought to California by the pioneer **Hungarian** winemaker **Harászthy**; others again that it may originally have come from **Italy**.

Zuti The yellow **variety** of the native **Yugoslav grape, Plavac**.

Zwicker Term used in the labelling of **Alsace** wines, signifying that both 'noble' and common **vine varieties** have been used.

Bibliography

The following is a list of books that I have found both useful and interesting. Because some of them are still in print and others may be found in libraries, I have included all those that I think merit attention from anybody seriously interested in wines and spirits. Inevitably, the list is virtually a catalogue of my own library because, to the professional writer, books are the tools of the trade and need to be available for consultation at any time.

Not all the books on my shelves, however, feature on this list. Some are, to a certain extent, reworked versions of other books; so I have cited the original if I think it more important. Some are not merely out of date (as this must be by the time it is published), but I have detected such errors in them as to make me wary of recommending them. In some instances, the latest edition or the edition that seems the best as regards reliable information is specified; there are some 'revised versions' of books that would bring down the fury of the original authors on those who have – no doubt with the best intentions – attempted to update, re-work, and generally 'edit' books that were of significance when they were first brought out.

While compiling this list of books, I have reread a number that I have not looked at for a long time. It is curious that those who truly care about wine – even though their ability to write, or their knowledge and experience was limited – do, if they loved their subject, still 'speak' even across centuries. Wine talk does not change much: and the authority of a thousand years ago is as interesting to the true wine lover as the latest 'controversial' writer who aims to shock the 'old fogies' of the wine trade – they are both equally stimulating!

WINE – General
Broadbent, Michael: *Wine Tasting* (Cassell & Co., and Christie's Wine Publications, latest edition 1979).
Burroughs, David & Norman Bezzant: *The New Wine Companion* (William Heinemann, 1980).
——: *Wine Regions of the World* (William Heinemann, 1979).
——: *The Wine Trade Student's Companion* (Collins, 1975).
Don, Robin, M. W.: *Wine* (Teach Yourself Books, 1977).
Embury, David: *The Fine Art of Mixing Drinks* (Faber & Faber, 1953).
Gold, Alec (Ed.): *Wines and Spirits of the World* (Virtue, 1968).
Hogg, A.: *Off the Shelf – Gilbey Vintners' Guide to Wines and Spirits* (Gilbey Vintners, 3rd ed., 1977).
Johnson, Hugh: *A World Atlas of Wine* (Mitchell Beazley, 2nd ed., 1977).
Lichine, Alexis: *Encyclopedia of Wines and Spirits* (Cassell & Co., 4th ed., 1979).
Marrison, L. W.: *Wines and Spirits* (Penguin, 1957).
Mendelsohn, Oscar A.: *The Earnest Drinker* (Allen & Unwin, 1950).
Penning-Rowsell, Edmund: *Red, White and Rosé* (Pan, 1967).
Postgate, Raymond: *An Alphabet of Choosing and Serving Wine* (Jenkins, 1955).
——: *The Home Wine Cellar* (Jenkins, 1960).
——: *The Plain Man's Guide to Wine* (Michael Joseph, revised ed., 1965).
Robinson, Jancis: *The Wine Book* (A. & C. Black, 1979).
Schoonmaker, Frank: *Encyclopedia of Wine* (Nelson, 1967 edition edited H. Johnson).
Sichel, Allan (Revised Peter Sichel): *The Penguin Book of Wines* (Penguin, 1971).
Vandyke Price, Pamela: *Entertaining with Wine* (Northwood Books, 1976).
——: *The Taste of Wine* (Macdonald & Jane's, 1975).
Wicks, Keith: *Wine and Wine-making* (Macdonald Educational, 1976).
Williams, H. i.: *Three Bottle Bar* (Faber & faber, 1952).
(various): *A Guide to Good Wine* (W. & R. Chambers, 1952).

Technical
Austin, Cedric: *The Science of Wine* (University of London, 1968).
Denman, James L.: *The Vine and its Fruit* (Longman, 1864).
Forbes, R. J.: *Short History of the Art of Distillation* (E. J. Bull, Leiden, 1948).
Frumkin, Lionel: *The Science and Technique of Wine* (H. C. Lea, 1965).
Galet, Pierre (Trans. Lucie T. Morton): *A Practical Ampelography* Cornell University Press, Ithaca, N. Y., 1979).

Massel, Anton: *Applied Wine Chemistry and Technology* (Heidelberg Publishers, Germany, 1969).

Moser, Lenz: *Un Nouveau Vignoble* (C.E.T.A., France, 1960).

Winkler, A. J.: *General Viticulture* (University of California, 6th impression).

Historical and Anecdotal

'A Practical Man': *The Butler, Wine-dealer and Private Brewer* (Biggs, 1853).

Allen, H. Warner: *A Contemplation of Wine* (Michael Joseph, 1951).

——: *A History of Wine* (Faber & Faber, 1961).

——: *Number 3, St James Street* (Chatto & Windus, 1950).

——: *Through the Wine Glass* (Michael Joseph, 1954).

Baker, Charles H.: *The Gentleman's Companion* (Crown Publishers, New York, 1946).

——: *The South American Gentleman's Companion* (Crown Publishers, New York, 1951).

Bell, B. & A. Dorozynshi: *Le Livre du Vin* (Deux Coqs d'Or, 1968).

Berry, C. W.: *In Search of Wine* (Constable & Co., 1935).

——: *Viniana* (Constable & Co., 1929).

Bespaloff, Alexis (Ed.): *The Fireside Book of Wine* (Simon & Shuster, New York, 1977).

Boulestin, X. M.: *What Shall We Have to Drink?* (William Heinemann, 1933).

Brett, Gerald: *Dinner is Served* (Hart-Davis, 1968).

Busby, James: *Journal of a Tour* (1833; facsimile, David Hill Press, Australia, 1979).

——: *Plain Directions for Planting and Cultivating Vineyards and for Making Wine* (1830; facsimile, David Hill Press, Australia, 1979).

——: *Treatise on the Culture of the Vine* (1825; facsimile, David Hill Press, Australia, 1979).

Butler, Frank Hedges: *Wine and the Wine Lands of the World* (Fisher Unwin, 1926).

Clair, Colin: *Kitchen and Table* (Abelard Schumann, 1964).

Coffey, Thomas M.: *The Long Thirst* (Hamish Hamilton, 1976).

Colchester-Wemyss, Sir Francis: *The Pleasures of the Table* (Nisbet, 1931).

Columella, Lucius Junius Moderatus: *De Re Rustica* (with trans., Loeb Classical Library, 1941).

Crawford, Anne: *A History of the Vintners' Company* (Constable & Co., 1977).

Druitt, Dr Robert: *Report on Cheap Wine* (Renshaw, 1865).

Dumay, Raymond: *Guide du Vin* (Stock, Paris, 1967).
Fisher, M. F. K.: *A Cordiall Water* (Faber & Faber, 1953).
Francis, A. D.: *The Wine Trade* (A. & C. Black, 1972).
Hardwick & Greenhalgh: *The Jolly Toper* (Jenkins, 1961).
Healy, Maurice: *Stay Me with Flagons* (Michael Joseph, 1940).
Hogg, Anthony: *Guide to Visiting Vineyards* (Michael Joseph, 1976).
—— (Ed.): *Wine Mine – a first anthology* (Souvenir Press, 1970).
Hyams, Edward: *Dionysos – a social history of the wine vine* (Thames & Hudson, 1965).
——: *Vin* (Newnes, 1959).
Juniper, William: *The True Drunkard's Delight* (Unicorn Press, 1933).
Latham, Jean: *The Pleasure of Your Company* (A. & C. Black, 1972).
Lucia, Salvatore P., M.D.: *A History of Wine as Therapy* (J. B. Lippincott, Philadelphia, Pa., 1963).
Macailey, Thurston: *The Festive Board* (Methuen & Co., 1931).
Maxwell Campbell, Ian: *Wayward Tendrils of the Vine* (Chapman & Hall, 1947).
Morny, Claude (Ed.): *A Wine and Food Bedside Book* (David & Charles, 1972).
Morris, Denis: *The French Vineyards* (Eyre & Spottiswoode, 1958).
Mortlock & Williams: *The Flowing Bowl* (Hutchinson & Co.).
Oliver, Raymond: *The French at Table* (Wine & Food Society, 1967).
Palmer, Arnold: *Movable Feasts* (Oxford University Press, 1952).
Penzer, N. M.: *The Book of the Wine Label* (Van Thal, 1947).
Ray, Cyril: *Ray on Wine* (J. M. Dent & Sons, 1979).
—— (Ed.): *The Complete Imbiber* (various volumes, various publishers).
Redding, Cyrus: *A History and Description of Modern Wines* (Bohn, 1860).
——: *Every Man his own Butler* (William Tegg, 1852).
R.F.G.S.: *Gleaning among the Vineyards* (Beeton, 1865).
Rhodes, Anthony: *Princes of the Grapes* (Weidenfeld & Nicholson, 1975).
Saintsbury, George: *Notes on a Cellar-Book* (1923; Macmillan reprint with preface by H. W. Yoxall, 1978).
Seltman, Charles: *Wine in the Ancient World* (Routledge & Kegan Paul, 1957).
Serjeant, Richard: *A Man May Drink* (Putnam & Co., 1964).
Shand, P. Morton: *A Book of Other Wines than French* (Knopf, 1929).
——: *A Book of Wines* (Guy Chapman, 1926).
Shaw, T. G.: *Wine, the Vine and the Cellar* (Spottiswoode, 1862).
Simon, André L.: *Bottlescrew Days* (Gerald Duckworth & Co., 1926).
——: *History of the Wine Trade in England* (1906; facsimile reprint, Holland Press, 1964).
——: *Wine and the Wine Trade* (Pitman Publishing, 1934).

Spencer, Edward: *The Flowing Bowl* (Stanley Paul, 1925).
Stendhal (Marie Henri Beyle): *Travels in the South of France* (Trans., Calder & Boyars, 1971).
Stern, G. B.: *Bouquet* (Chapman & Hall, 1927).
Stewart, Desmond: *Monks and Wine* (Mitchell Beazley, 1979).
Tannahill, Reay: *Food in History* (Eyre Methuen, 1973).
Tovey, Charles: *Wine and Wine Countries* (Hamilton Adams, 1862).
Watson, Rowland: *Merry Gentlemen* (Warner Laurie, 1951).
Waugh, Alec: *In Praise of Wine* (Cassell & Co., 1959).
Weinhold, Rudolf: *Vivat Bacchus* (Argus Books, 1978).
Wijk, Olof (Ed.): *Eat at Pleasure, Drink by Measure* (Constable & Co., 1970).
Williams, Neville: *Contraband Cargoes* (Longmans Green, 1959).
Wilson, C. Anne: *Food and Drink in Britain* (Constable & Co., 1973).
Wontaz, Fernand: *Le Grand Livre des Confréries des Vins de France* (Halévy, 1971).
Younger, William: *Gods, Men and Wine* (International Wine & Food Society, 1966).
Yoxall, H. W.: *The Enjoyment of Wine* (Michael Joseph, 1972).
Christie's Wine Reviews (Christie, Manson & Woods, various volumes).

FRANCE – General
Brunet, R. (Ed.): *Vignobles et Routes du Vin* (Librairie Larousse, Paris, 1977).
de Cassagnac, Paul: *French Wines* (Chatto & Windus, 1930).
Clos Jouve, Henri: *De la Romanée-Conti au Piccolo d'Argenteuil* (Jean Dullis, 1974).
Dion, Roger: *Histoire de la Vigne et du Vin en France, des Origines au XIXième Siècle* (Paris, 1959).
Dumay, Raymond: *Guide des Vins de Pays* (Stock, Paris, 1969).
Holland, Tim & Arthur Bone: *French Wines* (Macdonald Educational, 1978).
Jacquelin, Louis & René Poulain: *The Wines and Vineyards of France* (Paul Hamlyn, 1962).
de Kerdéland, Jean: *Histoire des Vins de France* (Hachette, Paris, 1964).
Kressman, Edouard: *Le Guide des Vins et des Vignobles de France* (Elsevier Sequoia, Lausanne, Switzerland, 1975).
——: *The Wonder of Wine* (Hastings House, N.Y., U.S.A., 1968).
Lichine, Alexis: *Wines of France* (Cassell, 7th ed., 1969).
——; (with Samuel Perkins): *Guide to the Wines and Vineyards of France* (Weidenfeld & Nicholson, 1979).
Montagueil, Georges: *Monseigneur le Vin* (Livre IV, Nicholas, 1927).
Morris, Denis: *The French Vineyards* (Eyre & Spottiswoode, 1958).
Quittanson, Charles: *Connaissance et Gloire du Vin* (Bres, 2nd ed., 1979).

Redding, Cyrus: *French Wines* (Houillston & Wright, 1860).
Scott, J. D.: *Vineyards of France* (Hodder & Stoughton, 1950).
Sepangueil: *Les Vins de Chez Nous* (Orléans).
Shand, P. Morton: *A Book of French Wines* (Cape, 1928; revised C. Ray, Penguin, 1964).
Simon, André L.: *The Noble Grapes and the Great Wines of France* (Rainbird, 1957).
Vandyke Price, Pamela: *Eating and Drinking in France Today* (Tom Stacey, 1972).
The Larmat Wine Maps of the major French wine regions.

Alsace
Dumay, Raymond (Ed.): *Le Vin d'Alsace* (Montalba, 1978).
Gyss, Jean-Louis: *Le Vin et l'Alsace* (Berger-Levrault, Paris, 1978).
Hallgarten, S. F.: *Alsace and its Wine Gardens* (Wine and Spirit Publications, 3rd ed., 1978).
Hugel, Jean: *Les Vins d'Alsace dans la Gastronomie* (Saisons d'Alsace).
Layton, T. A.: *Wines and People of Alsace* (Cassell & Co., 1970).
Riegert, Henri: *Où mûrit le vin d'Alsace* (C.O.P.R.U.R., 1969).
Sittler, Lucien: *L'Agriculture et la Viticulture en Alsace* (Editions S.A.E.P., Colmar, Ingersheim, 1974).
——: *La Viticulture et le Vin de Colmar* (Alsatia, 1956).
Wolff, Christian: *Riquewihr, son Vignoble et ses Vins à Travers les Ages* (Societé Archèologique de Riquewihr, 23rd Bulletin, 1967).
Wolff, Henri W.: *The Country of the Vosges* (Longmans Green, 1891).

Beaujolais
Foillard, Léon: *Le Vin de Nos Vignes* (Editions du Civier, 1950).
Moissy, Ribert: *Beaujolais* (Editions de la Baconnière, 1956).

Bordeaux
Andrieu, Pierre: *Petite Histoire de Bordeaux et de son Vignoble* (La Journée Vinicole, 1952).
Benson, Jeffrey & Alastair Mackenzie: *Sauternes* (Sotheby Parke Bernet, 1979).
Cocks, Charles & Edouard Feret: *Bordeaux et ses Vins* (1969 ed.).
Djuiker, Hubrecht (English Ed Pamela Vandyke Price): *The Great Wine Châteaux of Bordeaux* (Times Books, 1975).
Dormental, Charles: *Sauternes* (J. Biere, 1930).
Dumay, Raymond (Ed.): *Les Vins de Bordeaux et du Haut-Pays* (Montalba, 1977).

Farnoux-Reynard, Lucien: *Vins de Bordeaux, Vins de Châteaux* (I.A.C. Lyon, 1950).

Healy, Maurice: *Claret and the White Wines of Bordeaux* (Constable & Co., 1934).

Higounet, Charles (Dir.): *Histoire de Bordeaux* (6 vols, various authors, Historique du Sud-Ouest).

Lacoste, P. Joseph: *La Route du Vin en Gironde* (Delmas, 1948).

Penning-Rowsell, Edmund: *The Wines of Bordeaux* (Allen Lane & Penguin Books, 4th ed., 1979).

de Perceval, Emile: *Montesquieu et la Vigne* (Delmas, 1935).

Ray, Cyril: *Lafite* (Christie s Wine Publications, revised ed., 1978).

——: *Mouton-Rothschild* (Christie's Wine Publications, 1974).

Roger, J.-R.: *The Wines of Bordeaux* (Andre Deutsch, 1960).

Vandyke Price, Pamela: *Guide to the Wines of Bordeaux* (Pitman Publishing, 1977).

Les Grands Vins de Bordeaux (Société de l'Annuaire de la Gironde).

Vignobles et Vins d'Aquitaine (Bordeaux, 1970).

Burgundy

Allen, H. Warner: *Natural Red Wines* (Constable & Co., 1951).

Arlott, John & Christopher Fielden: *Burgundy, Vines and Wines* (Quartet Books, revised ed., 1978).

Bréjoux, Pierre: *Les Vins de Bourgogne* (Paris, 1967).

Bro, Louis: *Chablis* (Raymond Belleville, 1959).

Chidgey, Graham: *Guide to the Wines of Burgundy* (Pitman Publishing, 1977).

Dumay, Raymond (Ed.): *Le Vin de Bourgogne* (Montalba, 1976).

Gwynn, Stephen: *Burgundy* (Constable & Co., 1934).

Mazenot, René: *Le Tastevin à Travers les Siècles* (Editions des Quatres Seigneurs, Grenoble, 1977).

Poupon, Pierre & Pierre Forgeot: *The Wines of Burgundy* (Presses Universitaires de la France, Paris, 4th ed., 1974).

Rozet, Georges: *La Bourgogne Tastevin en Main* (Horizons de France, 1949).

Yoxall, H. W.: *The Wines of Burgundy* (Pitman Publishing, revised ed., 1978).

Champagne

Arlott, John & Christopher Fielden: *Krug, House of Champagne* (Davis-Poynter, 1976).

Dumay, Raymond (Ed.): *Le Vin de Champagne* (Montalba, 1977).

Forbes, Patrick: *Champagne, the wine, the land and the people* (Victor Gollancz, 1967).

Gault & Millau: *Guide Juillard de Champagne* (Juillard, Paris, 1968).

Kaufman, William I.: *Champagne* (Andre Deutsch, 1973).
Marc, G.: *La Route de Champagne* (Editions SAEP, Colmar-Ingersheim, 1971).
Ray, Cyril: *Bollinger* (Peter Davies, 1971).
Simon, André L.: *The History of Champagne* (Ebury Press, 1962).
Vandyke Price, Pamela: *Guide to the Wines of Champagne* (Pitman Publishing, 1979).
Vizetelly, Henry: *A History of Champagne* (Sotheran, 1862).
Publications of the C.I.V.C.

Loire
Badin, Jules: *Roussillon* (Peyre, 1938).
Bréjoux, Pierre: *Les Vins de Loire* (Paris, 1956).
Yapp, Robin & Judith: *Vineyards and Vignerons* (Blackmore Press, 1979).
Les Nobles Vins de la Touraine (Tours, 1937).

Rhône
Dumay, Raymond (Ed.): *Les Vins du Rhône et de la Méditerranée* (Montalba, 1978).
Hallgarten, Peter: *Côtes du Rhône* (S. F. & O. Hallgarten).
——: *Guide to the Wines of the Rhône* (Pitman Publishing, 1979).
Livingstone-Learmouth, John & Melvyn C. Master: *The Wines of the Rhône* (Faber & Faber, 1978).
Moison, Auguste: *Tavel* (Editions Henri Peladan, 1974).

GERMANY
Ambrosi, Hans: *Where the Great German Wines Grow* (Hastings House, N.Y., U.S.A., 1976).
Hallgarten, S. F.: *German Wines* (Faber & Faber, 1976).
——: *Rhineland – Wineland* (Arlington Books, 1965).
Langenbach, Alfred: *German Wines and Vines* (Vista Books, 1962).
Loeb, O. W. & Terence Prittie: *Moselle* (Faber & Faber, 1972).
Meinhard, Heinrich: *German Wines* (Oriel Press, 1971).
——: *The Wines of Germany* (David & Charles, 1976).
Ray, Cyril: *The Wines of Germany* (Allen Lane, 1977).
Rudd, Hugh R.: *Hocks and Moselles* (Constable & Co., 1935).
Schoonmaker, Frank: *German Wines* (Oldbourne, 1957).
Siegel Hans: *Guide to the Wines of Germany* (Pitman Publishing, 1978).
Simon, André L. & S. F. Hallgarten: *The Great Wines of Germany* (McGraw-Hill Book Co., New York, 1963).
German Wine Atlas and Vineyard Register (Davis-Poynter, 1977).

BIBLIOGRAPHY

ITALY
Bode, Charles: *The Wines of Italy* (Peter Owen, 1956).
Cinselo, Felice: *Dizionario del Gourmet* (Novedit, Milan, 1961).
Colutta, Flavio: *Guida alle Bottiglie d'Italia* (Longanesi, Milan, 1972).
Dallas, Philip: *Italian Wines* (Faber & Faber, 1974).
Deltori, Renato: *Italian Wines and Liqueurs* (Instituto Nazionale per il Commercio Estero, Rome, 1953).
Flower, Raymond: *Chianti – the Land, the People and the Wine* (Croom Helm, 1978).
Paronetti, Lamberto (Trans. Bruno Roncarati): *Chianti* (Wine & Spirit Publications, 1970).
Ray, Cyril: *Ruffino: the story of a Chianti* (Ruffino, 1978).
——: *The Wines of Italy* (McGraw-Hill Book Co., New York, 1966).
Roncarati, Bruno: *D.O.C.* (Harper Trade Journals, 1971).
——: *Viva Vino – D.O.C. Wines of Italy* (Wine & Spirit Publications, 1976).
Rossini, Alfredo: *La Bussola dei Vino* (Mondadori, Milan, 1972).
Veronelli, Luigi: *The Wines of Italy* (Canesi Editore, Rome, 1960).
Il Chianti Classico (Consorzio Vino Cinati Classico, Florence, 1974).
Sicilia Vitivinicola (1973)

SPAIN AND PORTUGAL
Barbedo Galhano, Amandio: *Le Vin 'Verde'* (Commissaõ de Viticultura do Regiaõ dos Vinhos Verdes, Portugal, 1951).
Postgate, Raymond: *Portuguese Wine* (J. M. Dent & Son, 1969).
Rainbird, George: *Sherry and the Wines of Spain* (Michael Joseph, 1966).
Read, Jan: *Guide to the Wines of Spain and Portugal* (Pitman Publishing, 1977).
——: *The Wines of Spain and Portugal* (Faber & Faber, 1973).
Reay-Smith, John: *Discovering Spanish Wine* (Robert Hale, 1976).

Madeira
Croft-Cooke, Rupert: *Madeira* (Putnam & Co., 1961).
Simon, André L. & Elizabeth Craig: *Madeira* (Sidgwick & Jackson, 1956).

Port
Bolitho, Hector: *The Wine of the Douro* (Sidgwick & Jackson, 1956).
Bradford, Sarah: *The Englishman's Wine* (Christie's Wine Publications, revised, 1978).
Cockburn, Ernest: *Port Wine and Oporto* (Wine & Spirit Publications).
Delaforce, John: *The Factory House at Oporto* (Christie's Wine Publications, 1979).
Fletcher, Wyndham: *Port* (Sotheby Parke Bernet, 1978).

390

Knox, Oliver: *Croft – a Journey of Confidence* (William Collins, Sons & Co., 1978).
Robertson, George: *Port* (Faber & Faber, 1978).
Todd, W. J.: *Port* (Jonathan Cape, 1926).
Velente-Perfeito: *Let's Talk about Port* (Instituto do Vinho do Porto, Portugal, 1948).
Vizetelly, Henry: *Facts about Port and Madeira* (Ward Lock, 1880).
Port and Sherry (George G. Sandeman, 1955).

Sherry
Allen, H. Warner: *Sherry and Port* (Constable & Co., 1952).
Croft-Cooke, Rupert: *Sherry* (Putnam & Co., 1955).
Fifield, William: *The Sherry Royalty* (Sexter, 1978).
Gonzalez Gordon, Manuel M.: *Sherry* (Cassell & Co., 1972).
de Isasi, Enrique: *A Jerez y por Jerez!*
——: *Con una Copa de Jerez* (Hauser y Menet, 1969).
Jeffs, Julian: *Sherry* (Faber & Faber, revised, 1970).
Rainbird, George: *Sherry and the Wines of Spain* (Michael Joseph, 1966).
Vizetelly, Henry: *Facts about Sherry* (Ward Lock & Tyler, 1876).
Jerez de la Frontera (Banco de Viscaya).
'Old Sherry' – the first hundred years of Gonzalez Byass (privately printed, 1935).

AUSTRALIA
Cox, Henry: *The Wines of Australia* (Hodder & Stoughton, 1967).
Evans, Len: *Complete Book of Australian Wine* (Paul Hamlyn, 3rd ed., 1978).
James, Walter: *Barrel and Book – a winemaker's diary* (Georgian House Pty, Victoria, Australia, reprinted 1951).
——: *Wine in Australia* (Georgian House Pty, Victoria, 1952).
Lake, Max: *Classic Wines of Australia* (Jacaranda Press, Queensland, 1966).
Simon, André L.: *The Wines, Vineyards and Vignerons of Australia* (Paul Hamlyn, 1967).
Wynn, Allan: *The Fortunes of Samuel Wynn* (Cassell Australia, N.S.W., 1968).
Wine – Australia (The Australian Wine Board, 1968).

NEW ZEALAND
Buck, John: *Take a Little Wine* (Whitcombe & Tombs, N.S.W., Australia, 1969).
Thorpy, Frank: *New Zealand Wine Guide* (Paul Hamlyn, 1976).

SOUTH AFRICA

Bolsmann, Eric H.: *Bertram's Guide to South African Wines of Origin* (privately printed).

de Bosdari, C.: *Wines of the Cape* (A. A. Balkema, Cape Town, 3rd ed., 1966).

Calpin, G. H.: *Sherry in South Africa* (Tafelberg Publishers, Cape Town, 1979).

Knox, David: *Estate Wines of South Africa* (David Philip, Claremont, Cape Province, 1976).

Leipoldt, C. Louis: *300 Years of Cape Wine* (Tafelberg Publishers, Cape Town, 1974).

Maxwell, Kenneth: *Fairest Vineyards* (Hugh Kartland, 1966).

Opperman, J. D. (Ed.): *Spirit of the Vine* (K.W.V., Paarl, 1968).

Scholtz, Merwe (Ed.): *Wine Country* (Buren, 1970).

Publications and reports issued by the K.W.V., Paarl.

UNITED KINGDOM

Barty-King, Hugh: *A Tradition of English Wine* (Oxford Illustrated Press, 1977).

Gayre, G. R.: *Wassail! In Mazers of Mead* (Phillimore & Co., 1958).

Gore-Browne, Margaret: *Let's Plant a Vineyard* (Mills & Boon, 1967).

Hyams, Edward: *The Grape Vine in England* (Bodley Head, 1949).

Ordish, George: *Wine Growing in England* (Hart Davis, 1953).

Pearkes, Gillian: *Growing Grapes in Britain* (The Amateur Winemaker, 2nd ed., 1973).

Rook, Alan: *The Diary of an English Vineyard* (Wine & Spirit Publications, 1971).

Smith, Joanna: *The New English Vineyard* (Sidgwick & Jackson, 1979).

Publications of the English Vineyards Association.

UNITED STATES

Adams, Leon I.: *The Wines of America* (Houghton Mifflin, Boston, 1973).

Benson, Robert: *Great Winemakers of California* (Capra Press, 1977).

Hall Brown, John: *Early American Beverages* (Bonanza Books, 1966).

Hannum, Hurst & Robert S. Blumberg: *The Fine Wines of California* (Dolphin Books, revised, 1973).

Massee, William E.: *Massee's Guide to Wines of America* (E. P. Dutton & Co., New York, 1974).

Melville, John: *California Wines* (Nourse, 1955).

Quimme, Peter: *The Signet Book of American Wine* (New American Library, New York, 1975).

Schoonmaker, Frank & Tom Marvell: *American Wines* (Duell, Sloane & Pearse, 1941).

Miscellaneous Wines

Gunyon, R. E. H.: *The Wines of Central and South Eastern Europe* (Gerald Duckworth & Co., 1971).

Halász, Zoltan: *Hungarian Wines through the Ages* (Corvina Verlag, Budapest, 1962).

Hallgarten, S. F. & F. L.: *The Wines and Wine Gardens of Austria* (Argus Books, 1979).

SPIRITS – General

de Barrios, Virginia B.: *A Guide to Tequila, Mescal and Pulque* (Minutiae Mexicanae, 1971).

Doxat, John: *Drinks and Drinking* (Ward Lock, 1971).

Fisher, M. I.: *Liqueurs* (Maurice Meyer, 1951).

Hallgarten, Peter: *Liqueurs* (Wine & Spirit Publications, 1967).

——: *Spirits and Liqueurs* (Faber & Faber, 1979).

Kirkeby, Henning: *Danish Akvavit* (Høst & Sons, Copenhagen, 1975).

Lichine, Alexis: *Encyclopedia of Wines and Spirits* (Cassell & Co., 4th ed., 1979).

Lord, Tony: *The World Guide to Spirits* (Macdonald & Jane's, 1979).

Ray, Cyril: *The Complete Book of Spirits and Liqueurs* (Cassell & Co., 1977).

Vandyke Price, Pamela: *The Penguin Book of Spirits and Liqueurs* (Penguin Books, 1980)

Williams, H. i.: *Three Bottle Bar* (Faber & Faber, 1952).

Le Livre de l'Amateur d'Alcools (Solar, Paris, 1970).

Brandy

Allen, H. Warner: *White Wines and Cognac* (Constable & Co., 1952).

Delamain, Robert: *Histoire du Cognac* (Stock, Paris, 1935).

Hannum, Hurst & Robert S. Blumberg: *Brandies and Liqueurs of the World* (Doubleday & Co., New York, 1976).

Lafon, R. & J., & P. Couillard: *Le Cognac* (J. B. Baillière, Paris, 1964).

Ray, Cyril: *Cognac* (Peter Davies, 1973).

Samalens, Jean & Georges: *Le Livre de l'Amateur de l'Armagnac* (Solar, 1975).

Gin

Doxat, John: *Stirred – Not Shaken* (Hutchinson Benham, 1976).

Lord Kinross: *The Kindred Spirit* (Newman Neame, 1959).

Watney, John: *Mother's Ruin* (Peter Owen, 1976).

Waugh, Alec: *Merchants of Wine* (Cassell & Co., 1957).

Whisky and Whiskey

Andrews, Allen: *The Whisky Barons* (Jupiter Books, 1977).

Bruce Lockhart, Sir Robert: *Scotch* (Putnam & Co., 1951).

Collinson, Frances: *The Life and Times of William Grant* (William Grant & Sons Ltd, Glasgow, 1979).

Cooper, Derek: *Guide to the Whiskies of Scotland* (Pitman Publishing, 1978).

Daiches, David: *Scotch Whisky* (Andre Deutsch, 1969).

Laver, James: *The House of Haig* (John Haig & Co. Ltd, Markinch, Fife, 1958).

Marshall Robb, J. C.: *Scotch Whisky* (W. & R. Chambers, 1950).

McDowall, R. S. J.: *The Whiskies of Scotland* (John Murray, 1967).

McGuire, E. B.: *Irish Whiskey* (Gill & Macmillan, 1973).

McNeill, F. Marion: *The Scots Cellar* (Richard Paterson, 1956).

Murphy, Brian: *The World Book of Whisky* (William Collins, Sons & Co., 1978).

Ross, James: *Whisky* (Routledge & Kegan Paul, 1970).

Sillett, S. W.: *Illicit Scotch* (Impulse Books, 1970).

Wilson, John: *Scotland's Malt Whiskies* (Famedram Publishers, 1973).

Wilson, Ross: *The House of Sanderson* (William Sanderson, South Queensferry, 1963).

——: *Scotch, its History and Romance* (David & Charles, 1973).

——: *Scotch Made Easy* (Hutchinson & Co., 1959).

——: *Scotch, the Formative Years* (Constable & Co., 1970).

Glenlivet (The Glenlivet Distillery, Grampian, 1959).

Scotch Whisky (Macmillan Publishers, 1974).

Scotch Whisky, questions and answers (The Scotch Whisky Association, 1969).

The Spirit of the White Horse (White Horse Distillery Ltd, London).

Publications of the Bourbon Institute.

Publications

Christie's Wine Review.

Cuisine et Vins de France.

Decanter.

The Journal of the International Wine & Food Society.

Marine & Air Catering (articles by the author, 1959-80).

Number 3, St James's Street (house magazine of Berry Bros & Rudd).

Revue de Vin de France.

The Times (articles by the author, 1969-80).

Wine & Spirit.